IOLO MORGANWG AND THE ROMANTIC TRADITION IN WALES

General Editor: Geraint H. Jenkins

A portrait of Iolo Morganwg by Colonel Taynton of Cowbridge

A Rattleskull Genius
The Many Faces of Iolo Morganwg

Edited by

GERAINT H. JENKINS

UNIVERSITY OF WALES PRESS
CARDIFF
2009

First published, 2005
Paperback edition, 2009

www.uwp.co.uk

British Library Cataloguing-in-Publication Data

A catalogue record for this book is available from the British Library.

ISBN 978-0-7083-2187-4

Printed in Great Britain by CPI Antony Rowe, Chippenham, Wiltshire

IN MEMORIAM
GRIFFITH JOHN WILLIAMS
(1892–1963)

Contents

IV. IOLO'S FRIENDS AND ENEMIES

Figures

Contributors

Mrs Glenda Carr, Academic Translator, Formerly Head of Translation Services and Tutor, University of Wales, Bangor

Dr Cathryn A. Charnell-White, Research Fellow, University of Wales Centre for Advanced Welsh and Celtic Studies

Dr Mary-Ann Constantine, Research Fellow, University of Wales Centre for Advanced Welsh and Celtic Studies

Dr Richard Crowe, Chief Legal Translator, National Assembly for Wales

Dr Andrew Davies, Research Fellow, University of Wales Centre for Advanced Welsh and Celtic Studies

Dr Damian Walford Davies, Senior Lecturer, Department of English, University of Wales, Aberystwyth

Dr Moira Dearnley, Independent Researcher, Llandogo, Monmouth

Dr Huw Meirion Edwards, Lecturer, Department of Welsh, University of Wales, Aberystwyth

Professor R. J. W. Evans, Professor of Modern History, University of Oxford

Dr Martin Fitzpatrick, Formerly Senior Lecturer, Department of History and Welsh History, University of Wales, Aberystwyth

Mr Daniel Huws, Formerly Keeper of Manuscripts, National Library of Wales

Professor Branwen Jarvis, Formerly of the Department of Welsh, University of Wales, Bangor

Professor Geraint H. Jenkins, Director, University of Wales Centre for Advanced Welsh and Celtic Studies

Dr David Ceri Jones, Research Fellow, University of Wales Centre for Advanced Welsh and Celtic Studies

Professor Ceri W. Lewis, Emeritus Professor of Welsh, Cardiff University

Dr Jon Mee, Margaret Candfield Fellow in English, University College, Oxford

Professor Prys Morgan, Emeritus Professor, Department of History, University of Wales Swansea

Mr Geraint Phillips, Manuscripts Librarian, National Library of Wales

Dr Brynley F. Roberts, Formerly Librarian, National Library of Wales

Mr Richard Suggett, Investigator, Royal Commission on the Ancient and Historical Monuments of Wales

Dr Huw Walters, Head of the Bibliography of Wales Unit, National Library of Wales

Preface

That colourful Edwardian, Sir T. Marchant Williams, whose searing tongue earned him the nickname 'the Acid Drop', once ventured to predict, with pardonable exaggeration, that the publication of the rich collection of manuscripts written and bequeathed by Iolo Morganwg would reveal 'that the like and equal of Iolo has rarely been seen in any country under the sun'. The aim of this series, entitled 'Iolo Morganwg and the Romantic Tradition in Wales', is less boldly expressed but just as ambitious. Firstly, we seek to rescue this remarkably many-sided man from those who have disregarded, misunderstood or ridiculed him in the past, and to rehabilitate him as a figure of singular importance in the history of Wales. Secondly, Iolo's archive in the National Library of Wales – a treasure trove of fascinating and diverse material – offers such a fertile field of enquiry for a wide range of disciplines that we plan to bring his entire correspondence and selections of his writings into the public domain. People living outside Wales know precious little about Iolo Morganwg and we hope to win the attention of a wide and appreciative audience. While it is not our aim (even if it were possible) to canonize Iolo, we take him very seriously and would like others to do likewise.

This particular volume, the first in the series, is designed to portray Iolo as a profoundly contradictory, multi-layered figure who passed through many phases, assumed a variety of identities, developed a wide range of interests, and made himself known to an extraordinary array of people within Wales and beyond. The bulk of the research on this project is being carried out by a team of research fellows working at the University of Wales Centre for Advanced Welsh and Celtic Studies, a dedicated research centre which is committed to tackling large-scale projects on a collaborative basis. I was especially glad to recruit Mary-Ann Constantine as project leader, not only because she shares my burning admiration for this challenging and exasperating figure but also because she brings to the project new and exciting perspectives on the Romantic period in Wales. Several members of the team – Cathryn A. Charnell-White, Andrew Davies and David Ceri Jones – have contributed to this volume, as have two honorary research fellows at the Centre – Daniel Huws and Richard Suggett – who are closely involved in the research effort. The project is monitored by a robust Advisory Committee, nine of whom have found Iolo so addictive that they eagerly responded to my invitation to contribute chapters. Five other scholars were also delighted to join this enterprise. I am glad to have this opportunity to tender my deepest thanks to all of them.

All scholars stand on the shoulders of their forebears and I should like to record my personal debt to the late Griffith John Williams, one of the five founders of the Centre for Advanced Welsh and Celtic Studies and one of the finest scholars in twentieth-century Wales. His writings on Iolo are a starting point for all of us. He was a genuinely inspiring figure, generous with his learning and utterly devoted to his subject. It is a privilege to dedicate this book to his memory.

On behalf of the project team, I should like to thank members of the staff of the National Library of Wales for recognizing the value of this scholarly enterprise and helping us with their customary courtesy and efficiency. Iolo often dreamed of seeing a National Library in his native land (not least because it would rescue his manuscripts from 'obscurity and oblivion') and some of us have come to believe that his benign ghost inhabits the Department of Manuscripts. Several other institutions and individuals deserve warm thanks for supporting this project. Without the generous five-year grant awarded to me by the Arts and Humanities Research Council, this undertaking would not have been possible, and I gladly record the Centre's debt to the Council. Likewise, I gratefully acknowledge the financial support of the British Academy, the Leverhulme Trust and the University of Wales. One of the great pleasures of directing a major collaborative project such as this is that so many scholars, colleagues and friends are willing to engage with the team in a lively and critical manner. Special thanks are owed to Brian Davies, J. Barry Davies, Meredydd Evans, Caroline Franklin, Ronald Hutton, Phyllis Kinney, Brian Ll. James, E. Wyn James, Bethan Jenkins, Andrew Prescott, Gethin Rhys and Hilary M. Thomas. The independent reader of the entire typescript made several valuable suggestions which have improved the structure and content of this volume.

The support staff at the Centre – Vera Bowen, Glenys Howells and Mary Olwen Owen – have given me unstinting assistance, and I owe an immeasurable debt to my personal assistant, Nia Davies, for processing the whole work with uncomplaining serenity. William Howells kindly compiled the index with his customary aplomb, while Leah Jenkins, Nia Peris and Nicola Roper at the University of Wales Press offered expert advice and guidance at every stage. It has been a pleasure to work on this volume and I very much hope that it will whet the appetite of readers for further studies devoted to the life and works of this endlessly fascinating 'rattleskull genius'.

July 2005   Geraint H. Jenkins

Acknowledgements

The British Library: Figs. 10, 22

Cardiff Central Library: Fig. 2b

The Czech Manuscripts Society: Fig. 5

The Institute of Geography and Earth Studies, University of Wales, Aberystwyth: Fig. 23

Meredydd Evans: Fig. 24a

The National Library of Wales: Frontispiece, Figs. 1, 2a, 3, 4, 6, 7, 8, 12, 14, 15, 16, 17, 18, 19, 20, 21, 24b, 25, 26, 27, 28, 29

The National Museum and Gallery, Cardiff: Fig. 30

The National Portrait Gallery: Fig. 9

Pontypridd Museum: Fig. 31

The Royal Commission on the Ancient and Historical Monuments of Wales (Crown Copyright): Figs. 11, 13a, 13b

Abbreviations

AC	*Archaeologia Cambrensis*
ANA	Maria Jane Williams, *Ancient National Airs of Gwent and Morganwg* (facsimile edn., Cymdeithas Alawon Gwerin Cymru / Welsh Folk Song Society, 1988)
BBCS	*Bulletin of the Board of Celtic Studies*
BL	British Library
CA	*The Carmarthen[shire] Antiquary*
Cardiff	Cardiff Central Library
CG	*Canu Gwerin*
CRhIM	P. J. Donovan (ed.), *Cerddi Rhydd Iolo Morganwg* (Caerdydd, 1980)
DWB	*Dictionary of Welsh Biography down to 1940* (London, 1959)
EA	*Efrydiau Athronyddol*
EHR	*English Historical Review*
GPC	*Geiriadur Prifysgol Cymru* (4 vols., Caerdydd, 1950–2002)
GRO	Glamorgan Record Office
IMChY	G. J. Williams, *Iolo Morganwg a Chywyddau'r Ychwanegiad* (Llundain, 1926)
JHSCW	*Journal of the Historical Society of the Church in Wales*
JMHRS	*Journal of the Merioneth Historical and Record Society*
JWBS	*Journal of the Welsh Bibliographical Society*
JWFSS	*Journal of the Welsh Folk-Song Society*
JWRH	*Journal of Welsh Religious History*
Lewis: *IM*	Ceri W. Lewis, *Iolo Morganwg* (Caernarfon, 1995)
LlC	*Llên Cymru*
LRO	Liverpool Record Office
MAW	Owen Jones, Iolo Morganwg and William Owen Pughe, *The Myvyrian Archaiology of Wales* (3 vols., London, 1801–7)
MC	*Montgomeryshire Collections*
MH	*Merthyr Historian*
Morgan: *IM*	Prys Morgan, *Iolo Morganwg* (Cardiff, 1975)
NLW	National Library of Wales
NLWJ	*National Library of Wales Journal*
ODNB	*Oxford Dictionary of National Biography* (60 vols., Oxford, 2004)
PBA	*Proceedings of the British Academy*

RAEW	Elijah Waring, *Recollections and Anecdotes of Edward Williams* (London, 1850)
RCAHMW	Royal Commission on the Ancient and Historical Monuments of Wales
TAAS	*Transactions of the Anglesey Antiquarian Society and Field Club*
TDHS	*Transactions of the Denbighshire Historical Society*
THSC	*Transactions of the Honourable Society of Cymmrodorion*
TLlM	G. J. Williams, *Traddodiad Llenyddol Morgannwg* (Caerdydd, 1948)
TRS	*Transactions of the Radnorshire Society*
UWB	University of Wales Bangor Archives
WHR	*Welsh History Review*
Williams: *IM*	G. J. Williams, *Iolo Morganwg – Y Gyfrol Gyntaf* (Caerdydd, 1956)
Williams: *PLP*	Edward Williams, *Poems, Lyric and Pastoral* (2 vols., London, 1794)
WMH	*Welsh Music History*

1

On the Trail of a 'Rattleskull Genius': Introduction

GERAINT H. JENKINS

The title of this volume, the first in a series devoted to the life and works of Edward Williams – a cultural phenomenon far better known by his bardic pseudonym Iolo Morganwg – is not a catch-penny attempt to attract attention and boost sales. With a combination of whimsy and egocentricity which was entirely characteristic of him, Iolo used to style himself a 'rattleskull genius'.[1] A convivial figure who loved to hear his own voice, he may have discovered the word 'rattleskull' in London-Welsh circles or possibly in Sheridan's English dictionary, where its meaning is given as 'a noisy empty fellow'.[2] His papers are laced with both English and Welsh equivalents – rattlebrain, rattlepate, rattlehead, babbler, prattler, chatterbox, *loliwr* and *rwdlyn*[3] – and during his lighter, self-deprecating moments he delighted in the description 'Whimsical Ned'.[4] As for genius, Romantics like Iolo believed that it was central to artistic and creative endeavour, and it was not uncommon for him to bracket himself with the likes of Milton, Newton, Hartley, Franklin and Priestley (who just happened to be among the finest exemplars of Rational Dissent) as people with special qualities of mind and the capacity for original thought.[5] Even in ripe old age, there were similar instances of serious frivolity. He summed up his achievements as follows: 'Iolo Morganwg, author of a book of English poetry priced one pound, Welsh psalms priced a shilling, a stonemason, builder, wall-shutter of Flemingston cemetery, Bard of the Society of Welsh Unitarians, Leader of the fools of the island of Britain' ('Iolo Morganwg, awdur llyfr prydyddiaeth Saesoneg Pris punt, Salmau cymraeg pris swllt, saer cerrig, adeiledydd, caeadfur monwent Trefflemin, Bardd cymdeithas Dwyfundodiaid Cymru, Blaenor ffyliaid ynys Prydain').[6]

---

[1]   NLW 21387E, no. 25.
[2]   Thomas Sheridan, *A Compleat Dictionary of the English Language* (3rd edn., 2 vols., London, 1790), s.v. 'rattleskull'. See also *OED* under 'rattle-brain'.
[3]   NLW 13117E, p. 114; NLW 21415E, no. 27.
[4]   NLW 21422E, no. 14.
[5]   NLW 21389E, no. 22.
[6]   NLW 21419E, no. 52.

Fig. 1 'Iolo Morganwg, a personal recollection.' An etching by Robert Cruikshank, from a sketch by Elijah Waring, in *RAEW*.

It is hard to think of a pre-twentieth century Welshman who has aroused so many mixed emotions as Iolo Morganwg. In his own day the antiquary Theophilus Jones dubbed him 'Mad Ned',[7] while English poets like Coleridge and Southey referred to him, normally with amused condescension, as 'poor Iolo' and 'wild Iolo'.[8] Visual representations reinforced this unflattering stereotype. When the caricaturist and illustrator, Robert Cruikshank, was invited by his first biographer, Elijah Waring, to depict Iolo on the basis of memoriter drawings of him in his dotage, he portrayed the Welsh bard as an eccentric geriatric, a curiosity separated from the real world by his idiosyncracies.[9] Throughout the Victorian period hardly anyone suspected that such an apparently innocuous creature could have tampered with historical records and created the most outlandish bardo-druidic fantasies. The sense of national pride which accompanied the establishment of a federal University of Wales in 1893, however, was tempered by a demand for academic rigour which placed the likes of Iolo and others associated with Gorsedd ceremonies under the microscope. Doubting Thomases were led by John Morris-Jones of the University College of North Wales, Bangor, a scholar and critic who was described as the 'chief of the academic cocks o' the walk'[10] in Wales and who wielded an enormous influence on scholarly practices. He did more than anyone to discredit Iolo in Edwardian Wales and subsequently. Discomfited by having been hoodwinked for so long by the forgeries of a humble stonemason, Morris-Jones depicted Iolo as a Mephistophelean figure who had contaminated the literary tradition of Wales. Only a few brave or foolhardy souls dared to protect Iolo's reputation against what T. Marchant Williams called 'the smirching touch of ungrateful and insolent pedants',[11] and it was left to another Professor of Welsh, Griffith John Williams of Cardiff, to subject Iolo's work to close forensic analysis over a period stretching from the Great War to his death in 1963.[12] Paradoxically, although Williams exposed Iolo's fabrications, as he cut through the mythology which surrounded his subject his admiration for him grew. Yet there remain still in Wales fastidious 'purists' who would rather sell their souls to Beelzebub than thumb the tarnished manuscripts of such a flawed figure.

---

[7] Cardiff 3.104, vol. 6, Letter nos. 92–3, Theophilus Jones to Edward Davies, 11 March 1804.

[8] See chapters 7 and 8 below.

[9] *RAEW*, frontispiece and facing p. 1. The two etchings are reproduced in this volume and may also be found, together with three other depictions of Iolo, in Tegwyn Jones (ed.), *Y Gwir Degwch: Detholiad o Gwyddau Serch Iolo Morganwg* (Bow Street, 1980).

[10] J. Gwynn Williams, *The University College of North Wales: Foundations 1884–1927* (Cardiff, 1985), p. 235. See also Allan James, *John Morris-Jones* (Cardiff, 1987), *passim*.

[11] T. Marchant Williams, 'The Conspiracy against the Gorsedd', *The Nationalist*, IV, no. 36 (1911), 4.

[12] See in particular *IMChY*; Williams: *IM*. For a warm appreciation of his work, see Ceri W. Lewis, *Griffith John Williams (1892–1963):Y Dyn a'i Waith* ([Caerdydd], 1994).

In an encyclical masquerading as an obituary to G. J. Williams, who died in 1963, Saunders Lewis observed that no one else would see the Iolo Morganwg that Williams had seen.[13] More than forty years later the time is surely ripe to re-evaluate our assumptions about Iolo, to rescue him from neglect and misrepresentation, and to bring his writings to the attention of a broader public. There are very good reasons why he should be accorded the import-ance his life and achievements so richly deserve. Firstly, over many years Iolo was ridiculed and demonized by a handful of critics as one who, 'like a great octopus squirting ink into the clearness of the waters' ('fel octopws mawr yn chwistrellu inc i eglurder y dyfroedd'),[14] preyed on the naivety of his countrymen. Nowadays, however, Iolo is no longer judged to be such an embarrassing figure. Indeed, he is in danger of becoming an unremarkable, marginal creature in his own land. As Hywel Teifi Edwards has recently argued: 'Everybody who knows anything about Welsh literature knows something about Iolo Morganwg. That's the problem: by taking him for granted we lose sight of his remarkableness' ('Y mae pawb sy'n gwybod rhywbeth am lên Cymru yn gwybod rhywbeth am Iolo Morganwg. Dyna'r drafferth: trwy ei gymryd yn ganiataol collwn olwg ar ei ryfeddod').[15] The *Welsh History Review*, the flagship of the Welsh historical armada, has published only one article which directly focuses on Iolo.[16] There are no statues of him or scholarships in his name, and in a recent poll of Welsh heroes organized by Culturenet Cymru Ltd the derisory number of votes (63) cast in his favour, which left him trailing far behind such luminaries as Cerys Matthews, Tommy Cooper and Tom Jones, suggests that his hold over the historical imagination is weaker than it has ever been.[17] In global terms, Iolo simply does not register. Contrast this with Robert Burns, a fellow 'labouring poet', who has over a thousand clubs and societies dedicated to him and whose works have been translated into fifty-one languages.[18] Since there is no major English-language biography of Iolo it is hardly surprising that scholars beyond Wales have either overlooked or misun-derstood him. In the late Roy Porter's book on the British Enlightenment Iolo is referred to as Edward Morgan (rather than Williams) and his bardic name is grotesquely misspelt.[19] A very recent work on eighteenth-century antiquaries

---

[13] Gwynn ap Gwilym (ed.), *Meistri a'u Crefft: Ysgrifau Llenyddol gan Saunders Lewis* (Caerdydd, 1981), p. 48.

[14] Gwyn Thomas, 'Llyncu Camel', *Taliesin*, 40 (1980), 85.

[15] Hywel Teifi Edwards in a review of Ceri W. Lewis, *Iolo Morganwg* (Caernarfon, 1995), in *LlC*, 19 (1996), 197.

[16] Geraint H. Jenkins, 'The Urban Experiences of Iolo Morganwg', *WHR*, 22, no. 3 (2005), 463–98.

[17] Culturenet Cymru 100 Welsh Heroes, *www.100welshheroes.com*. The winner of this largest ever online poll of Welsh heroes was Aneurin Bevan with 2,426 votes.

[18] Murray G. H. Pittock, 'Robert Burns and British Poetry', *PBA*, 121 (2003), 192.

[19] Roy Porter, *Enlightenment: Britain and the Creation of the Modern World* (London, 2000), pp. 240–1.

contrives to misspell his bardic name in two different ways,[20] and it has been known for him to be feminized as '*Iola* Morganwg'. When the National Portrait Gallery in London organized an exhibition designed to convey to the public a gallery of remarkable Regency faces, no place was found for Iolo among the so-called 'Romantics and Revolutionaries'.[21] Nor have his astonishingly original gifts as a forger been acknowledged. Even though eighteenth-century authenticity debates figure prominently in English scholarly circles, Iolo is conspicuous by his absence. He is omitted – with palpable disdain – from Nick Groom's *The Forger's Shadow*: 'He plays only a bit part in this book because he was so little read in his time; others will doubtless make a meal of him.'[22] For Iolo, to be snubbed or ignored was the most heinous of crimes.

Secondly, while all of us would pay homage to G. J. Williams for his truly heroic efforts in unmasking Iolo's forgeries and collecting a mass of data on his life and works, the days of the lone scholar are surely numbered. The sheer bulk and diversity of Iolo's writings cannot be adequately addressed and assimilated by one individual. Our knowledge and historical methods have expanded far beyond what G. J. Williams judged to be important although, as one of the founding fathers of the University of Wales Centre for Advanced Welsh and Celtic Studies, he would surely have approved of the different perspectives which collaborative scholarship can bring. Together, teams of scholars can achieve much more than by working separately and one suspects that Iolo would have appreciated the value of current multidisciplinary approaches and discourses in academic circles. With the above considerations in mind, a team of research fellows at the Centre for Advanced Welsh and Celtic Studies is currently unravelling the enigma of Iolo's character by exploring, analysing and bringing into the public arena selections of his extraordinary archive of papers in the National Library of Wales. In collaboration with external scholars, the team is engaged on (to paraphrase Elijah Waring) 'a long voyage of discovery' into a 'crowded archipelago of documents'[23] which forms one of the largest and richest archives in Wales. The most authentic visual image of Iolo (reproduced on the cover of this book) is the 1798 depiction by William Owen Pughe[24] of him in his prime, scribbling away at his desk. Those of us familiar with Iolo's archive have come to think of him as a man with pen in hand. He

---

[20] Rosemary Sweet, *Antiquaries: The Discovery of the Past in Eighteenth-Century Britain* (London, 2004), pp. 140, 467. Cf. John Barrell, *Imagining the King's Death: Figurative Treason, Fantasies of Regicide 1793–1796* (Oxford, 2000), pp. 403, 729.

[21] See *Romantics and Revolutionaries: Regency Portraits from the National Portrait Gallery London* (London, 2002).

[22] Nick Groom, *The Forger's Shadow* (London, 2002), p. 328.

[23] *RAEW*, p. 68.

[24] Although this idiosyncratic lexicographer was born William Owen, he later adoped the surname Pughe. In the interests of readability, William Owen Pughe has been used throughout this volume.

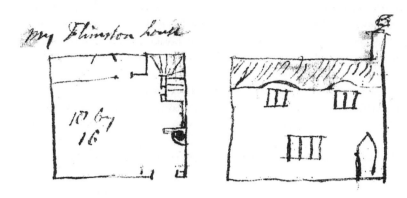

Fig. 2a 'My Flimston house' (NLW 21416E, no. 14). This is one of several sketches drawn by Iolo to illustrate his observations on houses in 'A General View of the Agriculture of Glamorgan' (1796). Iolo's vernacular cottage is shown with a pointed doorway in the lobby-entry position, mullioned windows, and is thatched with 'eyebrows' swept over the first-floor windows.

Fig. 2b This undated drawing (Cardiff 2.159) shows the cottage modernized with a central doorway and a parlour chimney. With Iolo's death in 1826, the lease of the cottage expired and no further rent was paid. The cottage became increasingly dilapidated, though it remained the home of Iolo's daughter, Margaret Williams, and contained a 'great quantity of books and papers'. Taliesin Williams belatedly offered to continue as tenant of the house, 'having a kind of veneration for it', but the steward of the Dunraven estate rebuffed him and allowed John Spencer of Gregory Farm to take possession of the cottage before lack of repairs led to its 'total destruction' (NLW, Dunraven Documents 428). The cottage is simply described as 'Ty a Gardd' in the tithe schedule (1841), but by 1850, according to Elijah Waring in *RAEW*, p. 153, not a vestige of the cottage remained.

fed on information as vampires feed on blood, and one suspects that he would sooner have parted with his wife than with the manuscripts which he used to call 'my own children'.[25] Furthermore, the books and periodicals which he bought and read bear witness to his broad range of intellectual and creative interests.

In his tiny home at Flemingston in the Vale of Glamorgan, a thatched cottage which was for most of the time in a lamentable state of disrepair, Iolo was surrounded by tottering piles of reading and written material. Letters, transcripts, books, magazines and what he described as 'a prodigeous heap of loose paper rubbish'[26] were crammed on every surface, many of them thickly clustered with cobwebs or distorted by damp. It is a minor miracle that this fascinating treasure-trove of data has survived, as far as we can tell, largely intact and now lies in the National Library of Wales.[27] Iolo was an incorrigible hoarder: every piece of information was grist to his mill and he could not bear to part with any scrap of paper. Although historians like to tidy the past, the recent impact of postmodernism, post-structuralism and critical theory has highlighted the diversity of the past, its lack of order and coherence. Iolo epitomizes all of this. In spite of the commendable attempts of his son Taliesin and, much later, cataloguers at the National Library of Wales, to impose some kind of order upon his collection, the sense of chaos still shines through. The whole collection has a lumpy, cluttered feel which reflects Iolo's own kaleidoscopic character. He worked in sustained bursts, sometimes demonically so, writing thousands upon thousands of words in an admirably clear and intelligible hand.

Iolo was a compulsive letter-writer, and the cornerstone of the archive is his marvellous correspondence, *c*.1,350 letters covering the period 1770 to 1826, which testifies to the speed of his intellect, his intimate knowledge of a wide range of subjects, and his fraught relationships with others.[28] These letters offer a human face, warts and all, to the man, as well as constituting an invaluable part of his literary and historical legacy. The rest of this rich, sprawling archive resembles a Chinese box of revelations. There is something to inform, surprise

[25] NLW 13221E, p. 119, Iolo Morganwg to William Owen Pughe, 20 July 1805. His cottage was described as follows *c*.1815: 'This Cottage consists of only one small room below, and divided above into two very small bedrooms, never finished, unceiled and only the bare thatched roof at each side about 4 feet above the floor so that it is only in or near the middle that a grown person can stand upright.' NLW 21310E, no. 53.

[26] BL Add. 15024, ff. 275–6, Iolo Morganwg to Owain Myfyr, 10 October 1798.

[27] The bulk of his manuscripts are in NLW 13061B–13178B; 21287B–21433E. Detailed descriptions of the contents are given in the Handlist of Manuscripts in the National Library of Wales.

[28] The overwhelming majority of his letters are in NLW 21280E–21286E. His letters to William Owen Pughe are in NLW 13221E, 13222C, 13224B, and to Owain Myfyr in BL Add. 15024, 15027, 15029–31. A critical edition of this correspondence will be published in this series in due course.

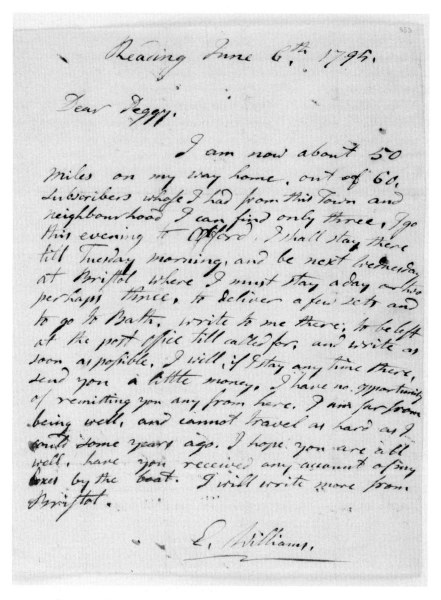

Fig. 3 A letter, dated 6 June 1795, from Iolo Morganwg to his wife Margaret (Peggy) Williams (NLW 21285E, Letter no. 853).

and savour on virtually every page. Thousands of poems, hymns, triads and proverbs jostle for attention with genealogical and historical notes, anecdotes and fables, etymological notes and idiomatic expressions, autobiographical drafts, transcripts of chronicles and memorial inscriptions, as well as sketches, maps and plans. There are richly textured, sophisticated essays on religion and politics cheek by jowl with intemperate rants and harebrained proposals. Contradictions cascade across the pages and some of the sections on bardic mythology are particularly mystifying. Alongside much repetition and banality there are tantalizing snippets of information dashed off in a hurry, shrewd aphorisms and, of course, brilliantly imaginative forgeries. Who else in late Georgian Wales could have spun wicked satires on George III or William Pitt, penned an essay on celibacy in Wales, listed untold instances of the longevity of Glamorgan nonagenarians and centenarians, provided detailed notes of species of apples and pears, lamented the 'literary barbarisms' of writers from north Wales, and coined an untranslatable Welsh word like *anghyflechtwyndedigaetholion* or a verbless Welsh sentence which ran to 116 words. Iolo was an avid annotator and his papers are laced with fascinating marginalia. Elijah Waring was right to describe his mind as 'an old curiosity shop'.[29]

Contributors to this volume have been invited to explore the multifaceted nature of Iolo's personality, career and writings, to reflect on the sheer diversity of his interests and the multiplicity of his experiences, and to celebrate (and, as far as possible, explain) the contradictions and ambiguities which clouded the life of this restless, wayward genius. Iolo lived through a period of change which, for a book-loving, radically minded craftsman, proved to be at once exhilarating and unsettling. Whilst acknowledging that Iolo changed the climate of opinion in Wales by reminding the wider scholarly world of the rich treasure of culture possessed by one of the forgotten peoples of Europe, Branwen Jarvis[30] reminds us of Iolo's debt (which he seldom acknowledged) to the work of his eighteenth-century predecessors in creating the so-called cultural renaissance of the times. His career unfolded against a backdrop of improvement, industrialization and modernization which reshaped society, while Romanticism, Evangelicalism and the Enlightenment offered opportunities for new ideologies and discourses to emerge. Small wonder, therefore, that a myriad Iolos emerged: the druidic bard, the labouring poet, the romantic myth-maker, the consummate forger, the political radical, the agricultural commentator, the dedicated transcriber of Welsh manuscripts, the apostle of anti-trinitarianism, and one of the fathers of modern Welsh nationalism. Iolo was able to remake or reinvent himself, to metamorphose seemingly at will, to delude himself as well as others, and to blend creativity, fantasy and practicality. Given his interest in soul migration and the manner in which his life was one of constant flux, mutation and change, it may not be too fanciful to consider him in the context of Marina Warner's recent exploration of how

---

[29] *RAEW*, p. 11. 'His memory was literally heaped up with materials both curious and multiform.'

[30] See chapter 2 below.

metamorphic processes can shape individual identities in strikingly unexpected ways.[31]

Although Iolo's individuality and idiosyncracy are undeniable, we must also locate him within his socio-economic and cultural context. Wales was changing in profound ways in this period. New patterns of ownership, the development of trade, urban growth, the influence of the printed word and literacy, and the success of revivalist movements had led by the end of the eighteenth-century to the emergence of a diverse group of middling sorts which included artisans, craftsmen and farmers, many of whom were gifted all-rounders and progressive thinkers.[32] The writings of Gwyn A. Williams offer an intriguing general model in which these new social groups are portrayed as highly influential animators in Welsh life. He underpinned his analysis of the artisans, tradesmen and journeymen who inhabited the transatlantic world of radical Dissent with the thought of Antonio Gramsci, notably the notion that 'organic intellectuals' provided the dynamic in society which led to a new populist identity based on democratic rights.[33] This intelligentsia, with its powerful cultural aspirations, constructed alternative models to conservative politics and predestination theology, and 'proclaimed the rebirth of a Welsh nation'.[34] Much more difficult is the challenge of incorporating Iolo's own malleable identities and interests within a convincing model. The interdisciplinary ethos of Romanticism meant that there was no strict distinction between the arts and the sciences, manuscript and printed material, creative and critical writing, and by the same token one of the principal features of Enlightenment discourse was its diversity of voices.[35] Iolo the Romantic poet and the Rational Dissenter was also attracted to Hinduism, Brahminism and the Jewish cabbala. Multiple interests of this kind were not viewed as a sign of

---

[31] Marina Warner, *Fantastic Metamorphoses, Other Worlds* (Oxford, 2002), p. 2. See also, for a different perspective on shape-shifting, Emyr Humphreys, *The Taliesin Tradition* (London, 1983), pp. 48–9.

[32] Geraint H. Jenkins, *The Foundations of Modern Wales: Wales 1642–1780* (Oxford, 1987), pp. 257–426; idem, 'Wales in the Eighteenth Century' in H. T. Dickinson (ed.), *A Companion to Eighteenth-Century Britain* (Oxford, 2002), chapter 30.

[33] Gwyn A. Williams, 'Gramsci's Concept of *Egemonia*', *Journal of the History of Ideas*, XXI, no. 4 (1960), 586–99; idem, *Proletarian Order, Antonio Gramsci, Factory Councils and the Origins of Italian Communism 1911–1921* (London, 1975); idem, 'Marcsydd a Sardiniwr ac Argyfwng Cymru', *EA*, XLVII (1984), 16–27.

[34] Gwyn A. Williams, *The Welsh in their History* (London, 1982), p. 38.

[35] See Ian Haywood, *The Revolution in Popular Literature: Print, Politics and the People, 1790–1860* (Cambridge, 2004) and the remarks of J. G. A. Pocock in 'Enthusiasm: The Antiself of Enlightenment' in Lawrence E. Klein and Anthony J. La Vopa (eds.), *Enthusiasm and Enlightenment in Europe, 1650–1850* (San Marino, CA, 1998), p. 7. The place of Wales in the historiography of Enlightenment is discussed by R. J. W. Evans, 'Was there a Welsh Enlightenment?' in R. R. Davies and Geraint H. Jenkins (eds.), *From Medieval to Modern Wales: Historical Essays in Honour of Kenneth O. Morgan and Ralph A. Griffiths* (Cardiff, 2004), chapter 9.

weakness in Iolo's day. On the contrary, versatility was encouraged and the manner in which many-sided people, including autodidacts, mastered a variety of crafts as well as range of literary genres commanded respect. There is considerable merit in the approach successfully deployed by Jon Mee in illuminating the radical rhetorical practices of William Blake through the Levi-Straussian concept of the 'bricoleur'. Iolo certainly fits the image of the protean craftsman who worked with his hands and his brains to draw on a wide range of disparate data, tools and repertoires to create a 'bricolage'.[36] His encyclopedic knowledge and energy enabled him to provide the Welsh with a new version of their history by exhuming usable elements from the past, concocting new theories, and asserting their rights as a distinct and distinctive people. Yet, as Martin Fitzpatrick's appraisal of the chaotic genius of David Samwell indicates,[37] figures like Iolo inhabited so many worlds and embraced so many contradictory and unpredictable views that they cannot easily be integrated into a single unifying entity. Iolo's unsystematic cast of mind was far too eclectic, far too susceptible to new or fashionable ideas, and far too prone to reconfigure the past by fair means and foul to be reducible to a comprehensive synthesis. Indeed, to impose a sense of coherence on such a dazzlingly chaotic figure might prove a disservice.

As the following chapters reveal, nothing about Iolo Morganwg is straightforward: he disregarded conventions and his life was peppered with apparent ironies, paradoxes and contradictions. Consider these riddles: the penurious craftsman who was obsessed by the lives of gentry families; the doting family man who was no stranger to misogyny; the champion of the Welsh language (and especially the Gwentian dialect) who wrote principally in English; the gifted literary and historical forger who adopted the motto 'The Truth against the World' ('Y Gwir yn erbyn y Byd'); the pastoral poet who praised the bucolic delights of rural Glamorgan and yet thrived on urban life; the Bard of Liberty who dedicated a volume of English poetry to the Prince of Wales; the unbending abolitionist who eventually (and reluctantly) profited from the ill-gotten gains of his Jamaican-based, slave-owning brothers; the promoter of justice, humanity and benevolence who turned against, abused and mistreated friends and benefactors; and the Unitarian radical who hobnobbed with literary parsons. Diversity, ambiguity and complexity lay at the heart of Iolo: therein lies much of his appeal. It is wholly fitting that he should have coined the Welsh word for 'unique' (*unigryw*).

In many ways Iolo's life can be seen as a restless quest to discover and define himself, and to express his individuality. The key factor which enabled him to

---

[36] Jon Mee, *Dangerous Enthusiasm: William Blake and the Culture of Radicalism in the 1790s* (Oxford, 1992).
[37] See chapter 17 below.

develop multiple identities was the independence afforded by his trade. Richard Suggett demonstrates that 'Ned the stonecutter' mastered and cherished his craft, and that his career as an itinerant mason offered opportunities for modest self-betterment and, more significantly, entry into a wide variety of social and intellectual domains.[38] Had he been the son of a tenant farmer he would probably have disappeared without trace, but being a *maensaer* (stonemason) – a craft above all others in his view – helped him to turn his mind and hand to most things.[39] He could fashion a *peithynen* (a four-sided wooden billet or writing-frame on which words or compositions in the bardic alphabet were inscribed) with a small pocket-knife, play the flute and set bones.[40] Even though it would be hard to find a more inept businessman, he was a builder, a lime-burner, a farmer and a sea trader. He sold tea, coffee and books, and applied for posts as a customs officer and a superintendent of ironworks.[41] He learned to read French and Latin, dabbled with Sanskrit and Greek, and turned himself into a self-styled authority on language and literature, history, theology, dialectology, agriculture, archaeology, architecture, horticulture, music, folk customs and any other subject which caught his fancy. As a nomadic craftsman, he cherished his independence – 'I am determined to remain inde[pen]dent of all the world'[42] – and prided himself on the fact that his 'celebrity', such as it was, owed nothing to rank or wealth.

Not even Iolo's most starry-eyed admirers, however, would claim that he could speak or write with authority on all the subjects which he claimed to have mastered. As we shall see, his great strengths were his knowledge of Welsh poetry and prose, history, folk culture and music. He was also well-versed in domestic architecture, agriculture and landscape gardening, and he deserves to be remembered as Glamorgan's first field archaeologist. Yet the breadth of his reading almost certainly surpassed its depth. He was not a full-time scholar who had reaped the benefits of a university education, and, like many autodidacts, he had an unfortunate tendency to venerate the writings of those whom he could not fully comprehend. His archive brims with unfinished drafts, half-grasped ideas, rambling lists and flights of fancy. Prone to accept things at face value and lacking the capacity for sustained critical exposition, he accumulated data, borrowed ideas and relied on hearsay, anecdotes and circumstantial evidence as well as his own fertile imagination. He confessed to William Owen Pughe that he was prone to throw out 'hints that are entirely

---

[38] See chapter 9 below.
[39] Iolo's 'Cân y Maensaer, neu'r Maensaer mwyn' is in NLW 13146A, pp. 424–5.
[40] NLW 13087E, pp. 21–36; NLW 13093E, pp. 185–6; Williams: *PLP*, I, pp. xv–xvi; NLW 21389E, no. 12; NLW 13222C, pp. 137–40, Iolo Morganwg to William Owen Pughe, 30 October 1800.
[41] NLW 21410E, no. 9, Iolo Morganwg to the Revd Gervase Powel, 28 February 1781; NLW 21285E, Letter no. 865, Iolo Morganwg to Richard Crawshay, 20 June 1800.
[42] NLW 21387E, no. 9. Cf. Williams: *PLP*, I, p. xix.

spontaneous and purely things of the present moment'.[43] Little wonder that he found it difficult, sometimes impossible, to sustain a consistent line of argument and to resolve the contradictions which bedevilled his life.

The fact that Elijah Waring invariably referred to Iolo as 'the Bard' bears witness to his status as a poet. Both Ceri W. Lewis and Huw Meirion Edwards, who offer different but complementary perspectives, agree that his reputation as a forger has obscured his great merits as a poet of extraordinary technical virtuosity.[44] He was genuinely fond of Welsh poetry and it became the ruling passion in his life. He composed remarkably fine *cywyddau* which he fathered on his hero Dafydd ap Gwilym, the greatest of Welsh poets, and he also penned exquisitely beautiful love lyrics. He played around with his poetic identity – styling himself 'Iorwerth Gwilim' and 'Iorwerth Morganwg' before settling upon his famous bardic pseudonym 'Iolo Morganwg' *c.*1790. Later, he acquired the suffix BBD – Bard by the Privilege and Rite of the Bards of the Isle of Britain (Bardd wrth Fraint a Defod Beirdd Ynys Prydain) – which he sported proudly. As the champion of the freer metrical system known as 'Mesurau Morgannwg' or 'Dosbarth Morgannwg' (Glamorgan Measures or Old Classification), an intimidating eisteddfod adjudicator, and (so he insisted) the last authentic survivor of the ancient bardo-druidic system, he exerted a powerful influence on the development of the Welsh poetic tradition in the Romantic age.

Another persona which Iolo scrupulously cultivated until at least the mid-1790s was as the loquacious, fun-loving Ned the lad. Masonic activity offered opportunities for lively discussion and debate, and his conviviality in Cowbridge taverns and in Gwyneddigion circles was legendary. Among the Cowbridge topers Iolo had a reputation as one 'that will drink, will guzzle late with any ten alive', and Walter Davies (Gwallter Mechain) marvelled at his capacity to keep tables 'in a roar by your effusions'.[45] An audience with Iolo in London was an occasion to savour and his loud, persistent and often querulous voice dominated conversations. Never drawn to the dull-witted or the ponderous, he enjoyed the company of unconventional or challenging men. He was especially friendly with the naval surgeon David Samwell, a combative, cosmopolitan figure whose tales of Tahitian beauties, cannibalism, the epic journeys of Captain James Cook and Maori songs became the stuff of legend among the Gwyneddigion. According to Edward Charles, Samwell was 'tall, stout, black-haired, pock-marked, fierce-looking, wondrous friendly in company, and very fond of the cup',[46] characteristics with which Iolo could

---

[43] NLW 13221E, pp. 115–18, Iolo Morganwg to William Owen Pughe, 5 December 1801.

[44] See chapters 4 and 5 below.

[45] NLW 21424E, no. 16a; NLW 21280E, Letter no. 86, Walter Davies to Iolo Morganwg, 24 July 1810.

[46] R. T. Jenkins and Helen M. Ramage, *A History of the Honourable Society of Cymmrodorion and of the Gwyneddigion and Cymreigyddion Societies (1751–1951)* (London, 1951), p. 107.

easily identify. In searching for the essence of this volatile, scholarly philanderer and opium-addict, Martin Fitzpatrick leaves us in no doubt that Samwell, like Iolo himself, can be viewed through many lenses.[47]

As Iolo immersed himself in the esoteric lore of the druidic bards and shared a glass with boisterous friends, his ego became quite disproportionate to his physical size. Having hoodwinked the gullible Gwyneddigion into believing that his forged *cywyddau*, published in the year of the French Revolution, were the authentic poems of Dafydd ap Gwilym, he reinvented himself in the early 1790s as 'Bard Williams', a labouring poet descended from the ancient British Druids. He went up to London to make himself known to a variety of social groups and to delight in what his despairing wife called 'bilding castels in the ayre'.[48] This chapter in his hectic life, and especially the vicissitudes and personal sacrifices caused by the publishing process, is told by Mary-Ann Constantine, who fills a notable gap in our knowledge by demonstrating how Iolo painstakingly prepared endless drafts of English poems in a vain bid to make his name in the wider literary world and to bring to him and his long-suffering family financial rewards.[49] Female admirers were happy to entertain this 'primitive genius' in their parlours. Smitten by his charm, his melodramatic version of his childhood and his passion for bardo-druidism, they readily subscribed to his two-volume collection *Poems, Lyric and Pastoral* (1794) and filled his head with notions of self-importance.

Living in great poverty and on the edge of self-destruction during his time in the capital, Iolo experienced what might nowadays be termed a mid-life crisis. His growing dependence on laudanum led to surges of energy and debilitating fits, to trances and somnambulism. Such was his torment that he turned to self-therapy and a spartan diet, neither of which seems to have dulled his reputation for creativity, his clever puns, quick-fire jokes and withering one-liners. He found himself in the grip of the Madoc mania (the fruitless quest for the so-called Welsh Indians in America), a legend which he assiduously promoted, and it is hard not to admire the chutzpah which prompted him to establish the first modern Welsh national institution – the Gorsedd of the Bards of the Isle of Britain (Gorsedd Beirdd Ynys Prydain) in 1792 – whose vision he conveyed with great intensity and passion. Increasingly, however, he drew on the hard-headed intellectualism of Enlightened thinkers and political theorists as well as on the imaginative well-springs of the Romantics, a conjunction which has puzzled many writers. As Martin Fitzpatrick has pointed out elsewhere:

---

[47] See chapter 17 below.

[48] NLW 21283E, Letter no. 608, Margaret (Peggy) Williams to Iolo Morganwg, 10 December 1794.

[49] See chapter 6 below.

Historians have struggled to understand the peculiar combinations of rationality and emotionalism which characterized such writers. Were theirs the dissociated sensibilities of intellectuals at the cusp of Enlightenment and Romantic culture? Or were they manifesting pre-existing creative tensions within the late Enlightenment, which may have been resolved differently had not the French Revolution provoked a destructive counter-Enlightenment?[50]

No longer was Iolo content simply to recreate the past imaginatively; he was determined to change the present, a desire which gave him a powerful sense of mission.

Bewitched by Tom Paine's *Rights of Man*, Iolo now adopted the persona of 'Bard of Liberty'. In spite of censorship, treason trials and 'gagging' acts, he composed a copious maze of politico-religious essays, squibs, satires, parodies and burlesques aimed against hereditary monarchies, aristocratic wealth, priestcraft, war and violence. Iolo could be found wherever minds and ideas flourished. He rubbed shoulders with middle-class radical intellectuals and plebeian agitators, 'Friends of Peace' and anti-slavery campaigners. Even though he was manhandled by 'Church and King' mobs, tossed out of Newgate prison by an irate gaoler, and twice brought before the Privy Council, he was not cowed into silence. Iolo's political radicalism has often been ignored or discounted by historians and this imbalance is at least partly redressed by several contributors to this volume.[51] Notwithstanding the unflattering contemporary references to Iolo as 'the poor Welsh Bard', Damian Walford Davies argues that during his sojourn in London Iolo's radical credentials were held in some esteem by Coleridge, Southey and others, and that his writings were invoked by Coleridge and Wordsworth in their attempts to refute the powerful philosophical arguments presented by William Godwin in *An Enquiry concerning Political Justice* (1793).[52] The fact that Iolo dined with Godwin shows that he was *persona grata* in the highest intellectual circles, a point reinforced by Jon Mee's observation that eclectism of thought reflected the openness of radical and millenarian discourses in the mid-1790s. Mee establishes stimulating circumstantial points of contact and parallels between Iolo and William Blake. The Unitarian publisher, Joseph Johnson, clearly exercised a strong influence over them and, although Iolo never mentions Blake in his letters or papers, he may have encountered him at Johnson's shop and stimulated his interest in the mysteries of 'British Antiquities'.[53] It is important also to emphasize that, unlike many of his illustrious acquaintances in London, Iolo Morganwg did not retreat from the political arena:

[50] Martin Fitzpatrick, 'Enlightenment' in Iain McCalman (ed.), *An Oxford Companion to the Romantic Age: British Culture 1776–1832* (Oxford, 1999), p. 303.
[51] See chapters 7, 8 and 12 below.
[52] See chapter 7 below.
[53] See chapter 8 below.

declarations such as 'there is very warm blood in my heart, and every drop of it solemnly dedicated to the cause of Truth' litter his manuscripts.[54] As Geraint H. Jenkins reveals,[55] the return of this Unitarian firebrand to Wales in 1795 did not signal his withdrawal from politics or a denial of his radical self. Far from it. He defied loyalists by actively promoting his Gorseddau as a vehicle for bardism, radical Dissent and the democratic cause, and, by becoming a forthright standard-bearer of anti-trinitarianism and the self-styled 'Bard of the South Wales Unitarian Society', he continued to stir things up. As late as 1818, at the age of seventy-two, he was still fulminating against magistrates for 'driving the Poor into madness' and was penning a pamphlet, entitled *Vox Populi Vox Dei!*, which reaffirmed his loathing for Old Corruption.[56] A year later he publicly reiterated his commitment to the Jacobin cause by stealing a march on leading members of the Anglican establishment at the famous Carmarthen eisteddfod. Democratic fires still burned in his soul up to his death in 1826.

Always hungry to learn and ready to question everything except his own dogma, Iolo assumed another persona from around 1796 onwards as an expert on agriculture and mineralogy. His experiences as a farmer and businessman had not dimmed his enthusiasm or his schoolboy sense of wonder. He still bubbled with improbable notions about growing tea, wild rice and sugar maple in his native Glamorgan,[57] but what is much more striking is the vast amount of perceptive and detailed information he amassed and assimilated on soils, rocks, minerals, fossils, mines, quarries, flowers, fruits, shrubs, hedges, crops and animals in south Wales.[58] He knew every species of bird and flower in his locality, and nothing gave him greater joy than growing apple trees in the most improbable locations. Although his impressive work for the Board of Agriculture was judged to be too subversive in its political comments, it nevertheless revealed his skills as a topographer, a statistician and a cartographer as well as his expertise in farming and industrial developments. David Ceri Jones suggests that his socio-economic ideas bear the imprint of physiocratic writings,[59] and printed sheets in his papers confirm that he kept an eagle eye on philosophical issues, commercial initiatives, government legislation and reports.[60] His detailed knowledge of scientific and technological change

---

[54] NLW 21396E, no. 12. See also NLW 21400C, nos. 27, 27a–b, 28a, 30, 32.
[55] See chapter 12 below.
[56] Cardiff 2.279, Iolo Morganwg to magistrates at Cowbridge, 13 March 1818; Edward Williams, *Vox Populi Vox Dei! or, Edwards for Ever!* (Swansea, 1818).
[57] NLW 21285E, Letter no. 857, Iolo Morganwg to members of the Bath Agricultural Society, 19 July 1796.
[58] NLW 21413E, no. 3; NLW 1808Eii, Letter no. 1526, Iolo Morganwg to Walter Davies, 12 August 1806.
[59] See chapter 10 below.
[60] NLW 13089E, pp. 120–4; NLW 21404F, nos. 1–17.

suggests that had he been born in the vicinity of Birmingham he would have wormed his way into the elite circle of artisans, tradesmen, scientists, inventors and thinkers who belonged to the famous Lunar Society and who delighted in exploring all aspects of human knowledge.[61]

Among the hats which Iolo increasingly wore with pride was that of the remembrancer. As the history of nineteenth-century Europe shows, the past was a source of inspiration for a nation's identity, and Iolo certainly became from the 1790s onwards a talismanic figure among a people who lacked self-esteem and who increasingly yearned for a place in the sun. Iolo had never been entirely at ease in the literary mainstream of the capital, partly because he loathed metropolitan condescension, partly because of his profound dislike of encroaching Britishness as expressed in 'Rule Britannia' and 'The Roast Beef of Old England', and partly because movers and shakers in England were so hostile to the notion of the cultural distinctiveness of Wales that they could not possibly represent its interests. He was acutely aware that, without a national university, a museum or a library, the Welsh would remain a neglected and marginalized people. Obsessed by what he called *yr hen ddywenydd* (the old happiness),[62] by which he meant the study of the language, literature and history of his native land, especially his beloved Glamorgan, he believed that history was important because it helped people to understand the present as well as the past, and because it could be summoned for use in the construction of nations. Prys Morgan claims that Iolo himself was 'a remarkable historical phenomenon' and shows how his mythical interpretation of the past was not only tailored to what he believed to be the needs and aspirations of Wales but was also a political statement in itself.[63] Iolo's mentor, John Walters, had invented the word *gwladgarwch* (patriotism) in 1776 and, by 1798 (a year of rebellion and reaction), the word *cenedligrwydd* (nationality) had also been coined and had entered Welsh-language discourse.[64] By this stage, as countless triads confirm, Iolo's Anglophobia had deepened and his preface to *The Myvyrian Archaiology of Wales*, a flawed *magnum opus* published in three volumes between 1801 and 1807, offered his people a coherent vision of their own history by bringing 'long hidden truths to light, long neglected remains of genius into a renewed celebrity'.[65] Vernacular words and phrases, and the classification of dialects, were central to this process of nation-building and, as

---

[61] Jenny Uglow, *The Lunar Men: The Friends who made the Future 1730–1810* (London, 2002).

[62] Lewis: *IM*, p. 158.

[63] See chapter 11 below.

[64] *GPC*, s.v. 'gwladgarwch', 'cenedligrwydd'. For an account of the enormous expansion of Welsh vocabulary in this period, see Prys Morgan, 'Dyro Olau ar dy Eiriau', *Taliesin*, 70 (1990), 38–45. See also Caryl Davies, *Adfeilion Babel: Agweddau ar Syniadaeth Ieithyddol y Ddeunawfed Ganrif* (Caerdydd, 2000).

[65] *MAW*, II, p. xi.

Richard Crowe demonstrates, over a period of three decades (1776–1806) Iolo's frequent visits to major libraries in Wales and England greatly enhanced his knowledge of prose and poetry, and his own personal collection of Welsh words swelled from *c.* 9,000 to 25,000.[66]

Iolo's writings fused vivid sweeping narratives of national history with microcosmic depictions of localities. By combining factual information, imagination, subjectivity and passion, he offered his countrymen a new and compelling sense of the relevance of the past. Iolo the historian was unquestionably an articulate and decisive agent of cultural change and by the last two decades of his life he had earned a reputation as 'the venerable Bard of Glamorgan' and the Grand Old Man of Welsh letters.[67] Young turks and experienced writers, antiquarians and travellers, bishops and literary parsons sought his advice and, as Malkin put it, here was 'an antiquarian, profound and sagacious in every thing curious relating to the customs, manners, and history, of his native principality'.[68] In so far as he was the first to collect Welsh folksongs in a systematic way, Iolo Morganwg is to the Welsh what Robert Burns is to the Scots, John Clare to the English and Gérard Nerval to the French. His mother had planted in him an abiding passion for music and, compared with the heavily fabricated literary texts he produced, Iolo's *penillion* and folk-songs (to quote Daniel Huws's arresting phrase) step out 'in rustic innocence'.[69] Six years before he died he called for the establishment of a Welsh 'Academy' to promote literature, history, antiquities, music and folklore in Wales.[70] By that stage he had successfully 'married' the Gorsedd of the Bards to the provincial eisteddfodau held from 1819 onwards, thereby reinforcing his commitment to liberty, druidism and Welsh culture in general.

This brings us to the vexed question of Iolo's persona and role as a literary and historical forger, a theme which inevitably casts its shadow over several chapters in this volume. Questions which postmodernist critics pose regarding the validity of objective knowledge, the nature of truth and the blurring of fact and fiction are highly relevant to Iolo.[71] It bears repeating here that he was a child of his age. Throughout Europe imaginative myth-makers were transcribing, annotating, mimicking and fabricating a mass of literary and historical material in order to fill or supplement what they believed to be

[66]   See chapter 14 below.
[67]   NLW 21280E, Letter no. 4, William Anthony to Iolo Morganwg, 19 February 1813; Letter no. 18, Lionel Thomas Berguer to Iolo Morganwg, 21 September 1813; NLW 21282E, Letter no. 418, W. J. Rees to Iolo Morganwg, 3 November 1821.
[68]   Benjamin H. Malkin, *The Scenery, Antiquities, and Biography, of South Wales* (2 vols., London, 1807), I, p. 195.
[69]   See p. 333 below.
[70]   NLW 1895Ei, Letter no. 82, Iolo Morganwg to David Richards (Ifor Ceri), 26 December 1820.
[71]   Richard J. Evans, *In Defence of History* (paperback edn., London, 2000), p. 9.

inexplicable gaps in the record.[72] The nostalgia for past glories, both real and imaginary, was coupled on the part of the public with a subliminal desire to be taken in as thoroughly as possible. Macpherson's *Ossian* captivated readers and writers far beyond Scotland and it was translated into every major European language.[73] On the Continent, too, there are significant comparative contexts for the kind of nation-building which Iolo advocated. As R. J. W. Evans demonstrates in his analysis of the culture and politics of forgeries in central Europe,[74] making the past a glorious, attractive and integral part of national ideologies and aspirations became de rigueur among marginalized ethnic groups. In Elias Lönnrot's imaginative Finnish epic, the *Kalevala*, in Théodore Hersart de La Villemarqué's creatively edited collection of Breton songs, the *Barzaz-Breiz*, and in Vác[es]lav Hanka's counterfeit early Czech manuscripts, *Rukopis zelenohorský* and *Rukopis králo[vé]dvorský*, we see (as did Iolo) how the growing power of nationality was based on a reinvented, usable past.[75] Thus, to describe Iolo merely as a confidence trickster, a charlatan and a rogue is to miss the point.

Thanks to the painstaking detective work of G. J. Williams and others, we know that Iolo fabricated enough material to fill scores of volumes. His principal feat, of course, was to compose brilliant *cywyddau* and pass them off in 1789 as the authentic work of Dafydd ap Gwilym. Emboldened by his success, he then began to spin fabulous tales, fabricate *brutiau* (chronicles), conjure up imaginary poets like Rhys Goch ap Rhicert, develop the ingenious metrical system called 'Glamorgan Measures' ('Mesurau Morgannwg'), and infuse hundreds of bogus triads and epigrams with memorable shafts of

---

[72] For the background, see Ian Haywood, *Faking It: Art and the Politics of Forgery* (Brighton, 1987); Roy Porter and Mikuláš Teich (eds.), *Romanticism in National Context* (Cambridge, 1988); Anthony Grafton, *Forgers and Critics: Creativity and Duplicity in Western Scholarship* (London, 1990); Gwyneth Lewis, 'Eighteenth-century Literary Forgeries, with special reference to the work of Iolo Morganwg' (unpublished University of Oxford D.Phil. thesis, 1991); Groom, *The Forger's Shadow*; Paul Baines, *The House of Forgery in Eighteenth-Century Britain* (Aldershot, 1999); Judith Ryan and Alfred Thomas (eds.), *Cultures of Forgery: Making Nations, Making Selves* (London, 2003). Issues of authenticity in Iolo's writings and his role as a forger of national identity are the focus of the researches of Dr Mary-Ann Constantine, leader of the Iolo Morganwg project at the Centre for Advanced Welsh and Celtic Studies. See Mary-Ann Constantine, 'Ossian in Wales and Brittany' in Gaskill (ed.), *The Reception of Ossian in Europe* (London, 2004), pp. 67–90; eadem, 'Pious Frauds and Perjurers: Iolo Morganwg's Truth against the World' in Peter Knight and Jonathan Long (eds.), *Fakes and Forgeries* (Amersham, 2004), pp. 119–34, 207–11.

[73] Gaskill (ed.), *The Reception of Ossian in Europe*, p. 15. See also Fiona Stafford, *The Sublime Savage: James Macpherson and the Poems of Ossian* (Edinburgh, 1988) and Howard Gaskill (ed.), *Ossian Revisited* (Edinburgh, 1991).

[74] See chapter 3 below.

[75] Gwyn A. Williams, 'Romanticism in Wales' in Porter and Teich (eds.), *Romanticism in National Context*, pp. 9–36. See also Prys Morgan, 'From a Death to a View: The Hunt for the Welsh Past in the Romantic Period' in Eric Hobsbawm and Terence Ranger (eds.), *The Invention of Tradition* (Cambridge, 1983), pp. 43–100. For a wider context, see Murray Pittock, *Inventing and Resisting Britain: Cultural Identities in Britain and Ireland 1685–1789* (Basingstoke, 1997) and idem, *Celtic Identity and the British Image* (Manchester, 1999).

wisdom. The dynamic which drove Iolo to fabricate the past continues to exercise scholars. The roots of his neuroses, obsessions and what G. J. Williams called his 'old itch' to favour the bogus and express himself in 'abnormal ways' clearly lie deep in his upbringing.[76] Although we should not take too literally Iolo's version of his relationship with his mother, he clearly adored her. Ann Matthew was an intelligent, well-read and socially pretentious woman who plied her eldest son with books and periodicals, and urged him to rise above the ordinary. Mollycoddling and manipulating him by turns, she exerted such a powerful influence on his young mind that he was overcome with grief when she died in 1770. Thereafter, he was determined to live up to her high expectations of him. As he strove to make a living as a stonemason and win approval as a writer, he became acutely conscious of the difficulties of recasting received opinion (as well as deep-seated prejudices) on literary matters. Ceri W. Lewis has rightly highlighted the significance of his sense of inferiority and his resentment over the neglect by *Deudneudwyr* (his pejorative appellation for the Welsh speakers of north Wales) of the cultural tradition of his native Glamorgan.[77] Iolo felt uncomfortable among those from north Wales because 'when ev[er] a Silurian expression dropt from me it was often carped at'.[78] One can readily understand why, in his obsessive desire to promote himself, he composed a breathtaking array of poems, histories and triads which reflected well on the literary history of south Wales. Untroubled by self-doubt or false modesty, he developed an inflated sense of the 'I', and 'Myfi, Iolo Morganwg' (I, Iolo Morganwg) became a familiar trope in his writings. His addiction to laudanum (which does not figure as prominently in this volume as might have been expected) also progressively played its part in opening up new avenues in his imagination. For over fifty years, Iolo took copious daily doses of laudanum to ease the pain caused by respiratory problems and other ailments. Easily available from apothecaries and grocers, laudanum was the paracetamol of the times;[79] it was cheap and effective, and during Iolo's suicidal years in London, when he doubted his own sanity, he claimed that its anaesthetizing properties saved him 'from the jaws of death'.[80] But opium also acted as a stimulant and, as Iolo fortified himself with generous helpings, his imagination was

---

[76] G. J. Williams, *Iolo Morganwg* (Cardiff, 1963), p. 16. See also Williams: *IM*, chapter 2.

[77] Lewis: *IM*, chapter 4. Cf. Morgan: *IM*, pp. 78–87.

[78] NLW 13221E, p. 13, Iolo Morganwg to William Owen Pughe, 12 March 1788. Elsewhere he wrote: 'Some Deudneudians [inhabitants of north Wales] arrogate to themselves the modern Literary dialect. I say arrogate, for it is arrogance.' NLW 13138A, p. 129. See also Cathryn Charnell-White, *Barbarism and Bardism: North Wales versus South Wales in the Bardic Vision of Iolo Morganwg* (Aberystwyth, 2004).

[79] Roy Porter and Dorothy Porter, *In Sickness and in Health: The British Experience 1650–1850* (London, 1988), pp. 217–25; Virginia Berridge and Griffith Edwards, *Opium and the People: Opiate Use in Nineteenth-Century England* (London, 1987), p. 24.

[80] NLW 21387E, p. 6.

sharpened, thereby allowing all kinds of improbable ideas, facts and fictions to collide or interconnect in his mind in unexpected ways. Alethea Hayter has noted how prone opium-eaters are to produce makeshift or disjointed drafts of their work.[81] Iolo was an obsessive writer and reviser of drafts, and he transcribed so much material over a long period of time that it eventually became utterly unmanageable. Obsessed by his own virtuosity, exorbitant ambitions and impractical projects, he overstretched himself: 'My multiplicity of engagements, too many irons in the fire, greatly perplex me, all my Irons burn ere I can work them.'[82] In February 1803 he admitted to William Owen Pughe that the prospect of 'turning over a vast heap of crude papers, of endeavouring to find out their connections, which I have now forgotten, is a thing that I cannot think of without a degree of dread'.[83] Bewildered and frustrated by the profusion of drafts in his cottage and unable to differentiate between genuine transcripts and forged documents, he simply lost his way and failed to bring many cherished projects to fruition.

Iolo's papers also offer other hints. In speculating on the way in which the transcriber Caradog of Llancarfan might have worked in the medieval past, he tells us more about how he himself handled sources:

> In different transcripts he might write from memory of what he had written before, and not from a copy before him, at least in part, and perhap[s] in great measure: this would be no violation of historical fidelity in one who from very frequent practice had almost the whole of his subject deeply impressed on his memory.[84]

Since medieval chroniclers were happy to omit material or amplify it from memory, Iolo felt fully justified in following suit by applying liberal doses of his own imagination. He simply could not resist tinkering with transcripts, intruding bogus data, rewriting unattractive or tedious passages and reconstructing narratives. Geraint Phillips makes the interesting suggestion that creating forgeries and making imaginative leaps came more easily to Iolo than writing original material and that by transferring the responsibility to other authors in the past he absolved himself of blame for any perceived defects or errors.[85] As Moira Dearnley[86] and several other contributors to this volume reveal, some of his contemporaries were convinced that he was an untrustworthy egomaniac and a peddler of frauds, but since few of them could rival Iolo's knowledge and intellect he was free to perpetrate his deceptions and

[81]   Alethea Hayter, *Opium and the Romantic Imagination* (rev. edn., Wellingborough, 1988), p. 52. For its effects on Iolo, see Geraint H. Jenkins, *Facts, Fantasy and Fiction: The Historical Vision of Iolo Morganwg* (Aberystwyth, 1997).
[82]   NLW 13222C, pp. 131–4, Iolo Morganwg to William Owen Pughe, 7 March 1797.
[83]   Ibid., pp. 161–4, Iolo Morganwg to William Owen Pughe, 15 February 1803.
[84]   BL Add. 15030, ff. 16–17, Iolo Morganwg to Owain Myfyr, 6 October 1800.
[85]   See p. 408 below.
[86]   See chapter 19 below.

illusions without fear of scholarly refutation. Richard Suggett identifies some of the elements – disingenuousness, the use of artful circumstantial detail, and wicked humour – which disarmed colleagues and readers of his forgeries.[87] As a result, whereas Ossian's poems were exposed as fakes in the early nineteenth century, Iolo's fabrications embedded themselves in the Welsh literary canon for the best part of a century, following his death in December 1826. The way in which he succeeded in recreating and reinventing what he reckoned to be a more relevant, meaningful and heroic version of the past is one of the most extraordinary achievements in the entire cultural history of Wales.

What of Iolo himself and his relationships with the many different kinds of people who figure in this volume? His circle of acquaintances, friends and enemies was as wide as that of any Welshman of his day, and this companionship clearly played a vital role in strengthening and cross-fertilizing his intellectual and creative development. Yet, as his autobiographical writings and letters (as well as the following chapters) abundantly show, his dealings with others was a tale of soaring hopes and profound disappointments. At no stage during his career was he able to place his finances on a secure footing and, at times, only his considerable gifts as a mason saved him from the workhouse. Although he never prized wealth, his own poverty deeply affected what he was able to achieve as well as his own mood swings. To his dying day, he remained edgy, dissatisfied and unappeased. Ill health took a visible toll on his mind and body. Over the years he suffered from fevers, quinsy, migraines, asthma, gout, rheumatism and a myriad other ailments. On rainy days he gasped for breath, and when frosts came his joints throbbed unbearably. When the effects of laudanum bit deeply, he would cross a terrifying boundary into the world of hallucinations, illusions and madness. Mounting discomfort and pain meant that from c.1805 he was unable to lie down to sleep. Characteristically, he refused to bear his ailments with stoical resignation. On the contrary, he raged against the pain and the inconveniences they imposed upon him and, as he became increasingly infirm and immobile during his twilight years, he became even more cantankerous and impossible to live with.

But Iolo's flaws of character, especially his compulsive need to fall out with just about everyone he met, cannot simply be attributed to his penury and infirmity. The plain fact is that he was by nature a prickly individualist who could not resist provoking people or stumbling into controversies. Life so often became a matter of Iolo *contra mundum*, and his 'alliance to the *genus irritabile*',[88] as Waring delicately put it, meant that he could neither be silent nor be shocked into silence. He once confessed to a clerk at the Royal Literary Fund Society that all poets were prone to be fractious: 'Poets are said to be in general

---

[87] See pp. 222–6 below.
[88] *RAEW*, p. 14.

unreasonably irritable, and Welshmen are so to a proverb and in me much of the last, and something of the first, character has very much prevailed.'[89] Scorning 'that infernal Goddess Prudence',[90] Iolo wrote scathingly about others and conducted ferocious feuds over long periods. Never one to forget a slight, he preferred to allow grudges to fester and to brood over the 'betrayals' of others. This trait is laid bare in the chapters by Geraint Phillips and Glenda Carr which focus on the stubborn battle of wills between Iolo, William Owen Pughe and Owain Myfyr, and on how all efforts to repair relations from 1806 onwards proved fruitless.[91] Even in his final, much enfeebled year, he was still launching splenetic attacks on the 'massive corruptions' (*llygredigaethau anferthfawr*) which sullied the writings of William Owen Pughe.[92] To cross Iolo was to run the risk of making an enemy for life. As he sought to outwit or wrongfoot his rivals, a wild streak of mischief would appear. He dubbed David Thomas (Dafydd Ddu Eryri) 'Bleddyn Fin Pladur, alias Deio'r Cwrw' ('Bleddyn Scythe-edge, alias Dai the Beer') and Evan Williams, the Cardiganshire-born London bookseller, 'Skin-devil-Williams'.[93] He railed against 'Smatter-dashers' like Edward 'Celtic' Davies for mounting literary hobby-horses and galloping off into 'the most entangled wilderness',[94] and claimed that John Hughes, a Wesleyan minister and antiquary who served as an adjudicator at eisteddfodau, knew 'no more of the ancient Welsh versification, than he knows of the Art of spinning monthly new moons out of a clap of thunder'.[95] A coruscating reviewer, he did not spare even those who had served him well in the past. One of his victims was Theophilus Jones, author of *A History of the County of Brecknock*, a work which Iolo mauled viciously:

> In this incongruous jumble may be found a few shrivel'd grains of historical truth: the very few grains of an immense field over which a pestilential blast has passed, leaving hardly any thing behind but a superlatively smutty crop; amongst which the rankest weeds have sprung up in loathsome abundance.[96]

Even the dead were maligned: Lewis Morris was variously dubbed a scoundrel, a pigmy and a 'coxcombical pretender',[97] while the odes of Goronwy Owen

---

[89] BL, Royal Literary Fund M1077, file no. 27, no. 8, Iolo Morganwg to Edmund Baker, 7 November 1805.

[90] NLW 21387E, no. 9.

[91] See chapters 18 and 20 below.

[92] NLW 21286E, Letter no. 1005, Iolo Morganwg to Taliesin Williams, 17 January 1826.

[93] NLW 13222C, pp. 185–6, Iolo Morganwg to William Owen Pughe, 15 August 1805; BL Add. 15030, ff. 1–2, Iolo Morganwg to Owain Myfyr, 15 November 1798.

[94] See chapter 20 below; *Cambrian Register*, 3 (1818), 381–5, Iolo Morganwg to Evan Williams, 31 March 1811.

[95] NLW 21286E, Letter no. 994, Iolo Morganwg to Taliesin Williams, 23 September 1823.

[96] NLW 13136A, p. 96.

[97] NLW 13222C, p. 170, Iolo Morganwg to William Owen Pughe, 23 June 1803. Cf. NLW 13138A, p. 68.

(no friend to Glamorgan men) were deemed 'ridiculous, and utterly void of sense'.[98] Iolo regularly annotated printed prospectuses of forthcoming eisteddfodau organized by the Gwyneddigion Society with comments like 'Damned Stuff', 'verbose jabber' and 'hah!!!', and ridiculed friends whose literary efforts did not meet his exacting or quirky standards.[99] Misspellings, solecisms and misprints were exposed with gleeful relish, and it is not the least bit surprising that his London-based benefactors, notably Owain Myfyr and William Owen Pughe, tired of his importunities, ingratitude and abusive manners. Footslogging was his favourite mode of travel and, as he tramped from place to place 'with all my ears open',[100] he used to remonstrate with impudent children or curse thieving millers, drunken bumbailiffs, pettifogging lawyers, idle parsons, caterwauling Methodists, swindling landlords and, most of all, the governors of the land:

> I am now and then a little irritated at what I observe passing in the world. Rascal, Scoundrel, Villain, Devil, are [words] that I am often under a severe necessity of using. By these names I have thousands and thousands and Tens of thousands of times called those that held the highest offices, and thus as often or oftener have I termed their diadem'd masters. I cannot help it. Truth imposes the task upon me.[101]

Wherever he went he courted controversy, acrimony and even fisticuffs. One April night, as he walked to St Mellons, he was accosted by two rascals who took exception to his acerbic comments, struck him with a whip and dragged him by his hair along the road.[102] At Gelli-gaer an innkeeper assaulted him, crying: 'Damn you, you follow or attend, the Backsides of Parsons (or Clergymen). You shall have no bed here nor Tea either nor any thing else' ('Dammo chwi, dilyn tinau'r offeiriaid yr ydych chwi. Ni chewch chwi un gwely yma na the na dim arall').[103] When he angrily confronted thieves stealing produce from his garden, one of them challenged him: 'Put your nose in my Arse, I will do as often as I please' ('Dodwch eich trwyn yn y nhin i, mi wna hynn sawl gwaith ag y mynno i').[104] Iolo's unconventional demeanour and provocative behaviour often brought out the worst in others.

Yet, even this tetchy rebel with a cause had an affectionate and tender side to his character. This hitherto neglected theme is explored in Cathryn A. Charnell-White's study of women and gender in his private and social

---

[98] G. M. Ashton, 'Some Annotations by Iolo Morganwg', *JWBS*, VII, no. 1 (1950), 24–5. See also Iolo's derisive annotations to his copy of Thomas Evans, *Traethawd Byr ar yr Athrawiaeth o Ryddid ac Angenrheidrwydd Philosophyddawl* (Caerfyrddin, 1809), in Cardiff 2.1020.

[99] NLW 21403E, nos. 1–4.

[100] NLW 13224B, p. 32, Iolo Morganwg to William Owen Pughe, 15 August 1805.

[101] NLW 13174A, p. 25.

[102] NLW 21392F, no. 26[v].

[103] NLW 21410E, no. 39. The Welsh and English versions are quoted verbatim.

[104] NLW 21410E, nos. 56–64. The Welsh and English versions are quoted verbatim.

relationships, and the way in which he sought, with varying degrees of success, to reconcile the difficulties of dealing with a doting mother, a feisty wife, dutiful children, simpering or reluctant patrons, and wilful paupers and prostitutes.[105] In his locality he was alive to the needs of others. His medicinal skills made him 'a ready courier for the sick or afflicted among his neighbours'[106] and he could be counted on to write letters and wills on behalf of the illiterate poor. His commitment to benevolence, justice and freedom, together with his willingness to champion the underdog (including piteously poor young women like Alice John and Catherine Thomas[107]), greatly endeared him to the lower orders of society. His Quaker sympathies and Romantic sensibilities, as well as his Paineite radicalism, alerted him to the iniquities perpetrated by the 'Cowskin heroes, alias negro drivers, alias Bloodhounds at Bristol'[108] against enslaved blacks in the Caribbean and elsewhere, and, as Andrew Davies indicates,[109] his avowed determination never to accept a penny from his slave-trading brothers wavered only when worries over the future security of his children plagued him during his latter years. He was brave enough to berate William Pitt not only for waging a war of terror against dissidents but also for imposing swingeing taxes which either drove the poor to the New World or dispatched them to an early grave.[110] Peel away the spiky layer which Iolo presented to the public and one encounters a much more humane and sensitive figure who had a very clear idea about social obligations and who fretted about the lot of deprived people. 'No idea can be more grievous to me', he wrote, 'than that of quitting this life without having been in some degree the benefactor of mankind.'[111]

This brings us finally to Iolo's literary and historical legacy, a theme taken up by Brynley F. Roberts and Huw Walters.[112] Taliesin ab Iolo's affection for his father and pride in his work were so deeply rooted that it never entered his head that some of the material he had inherited might be false. No one at the time could have convinced him that he had been handed a poisoned chalice. Although his long-awaited biography of his father never materialized, he

---

[105] See chapter 16 below.

[106] *RAEW*, p. 128.

[107] For Alice John, see Cardiff 2.279, Iolo Morganwg to magistrates at Cowbridge, 13 March 1818; for Catherine Thomas, see pp. 374–6 below.

[108] NLW 21400C, no. 23. For the background, see C. M. MacInnes, 'Bristol and the Slave Trade' in Patrick McGrath (ed.), *Bristol in the Eighteenth Century* (Bristol, 1975); Madge Dresser, *Slavery Obscured: The Social History of the Slave Trade in an English Provincial Port* (London, 2001). Iolo's connections with Bristol are discussed in Mary-Ann Constantine, *'Combustible Matter': Iolo Morganwg and the Bristol Volcano* (Aberystwyth, 2003).

[109] See chapter 13 below.

[110] The National Archives, PRO 30/8/190/83 LH, Iolo Morganwg to William Pitt, 16 December 1796.

[111] NLW 21387E, no. 23.

[112] See chapters 21 and 22 below.

brought a substantial amount of Iolo's writings, especially on bardism and druidism, into the public domain. In so doing, he ensured that Iolo's posthumous reputation attained mythological proportions. By the mid-Victorian period neo-druidism was flourishing mightily and had become a thing of great wonder and puzzlement to innocent observers at venues such as the Rocking-stone (*Y Maen Chwŷf*) at Pontypridd. When Evan Davies (Myfyr Morganwg), who claimed to be the authentic successor of Iolo as archdruid of Wales, collaborated with John Williams (Ab Ithel) in engineering the spectacular Gorsedd ceremony held at the famous Llangollen eisteddfod in September 1858, the bardo-druidic vision of Iolo reached its apogee. Many of our stock perceptions of Iolo date from this time and, even as the bitter-sweet cocktail of bizarre pageantry and mumbo-jumbo entertained the masses, a new generation of university-trained Welsh academics was beginning to bring greater scholarly rigour to bear on the historical provenance of the Gorsedd of the Bards and the voluminous writings of Iolo Morganwg.

However churlish it would be to criticize such a productive figure as Iolo Morganwg for failing to complete or publish his promised autobiography, it is still a matter of regret that we have no printed memoirs entitled (what else?) 'The Confessions of a Welsh Opium Eater',[113] a work which might have been a valuable counterweight to Elijah Waring's oft-quoted but misleading portrait. Yet Iolo lives on through his unpublished papers, which remain a source of delight as well as a storehouse of information. His strong belief, which lies at the heart of modernity, that he was duty-bound to outlive his mortal existence by leaving behind him a body of influential ideas and writings, looms large in all his work and, even though he had a low opinion of the academic institutions of his own day, he is one of those genuinely original figures whose ideas and ambitions continue to resonate, disconcert and provoke. He knew that no nation can flourish without a strong institutional base and, in so far as he dreamed of, and campaigned for, a national library, a Welsh 'academy' and a Welsh college, Iolo Morganwg ranks among the makers of modern Wales. Emblazoned on that extraordinary new building, the Wales Millennium Centre in Cardiff – a cultural hive located within walking distance of Iolo's haunts in the Vale – are words composed by the poet Gwyneth Lewis, who has to her name a highly regarded Oxford doctoral thesis on Iolo Morganwg as a literary forger. Iolo, above all others, would have appreciated this irony and, in particular, the significance of her words: 'Creating truth like glass from the furnace of inspiration' ('Creu gwir fel gwydr o ffwrnais awen').

---

[113] The notorious opium addict, Thomas De Quincey, published his famous *Confessions of an English Opium Eater* in 1822, four years before Iolo's death. Five editions had been published by 1845.

I. Contexts

2

Iolo Morganwg and the Welsh Cultural Background

BRANWEN JARVIS

Iolo Morganwg's manifold endeavours, intended as a whole to create for Wales, and especially Glamorgan, a tradition and a proud identity, were shaped and directed by the cultural context in which he found himself. However, the cultural influences upon him were not simply Welsh. His itinerant way of life, in particular his sojourns in London, Kent and Bristol, and the influence of political and religious radicalism in England, France and America played a profound part in shaping his outlook. Any study of his cultural background must, therefore, be wide-ranging.

One recent comment upon the world of scholarship in eighteenth-century Britain has drawn attention to its basic nature: 'In the logocentric world of the eighteenth century that [scholarship] meant manuscripts.'[1] The comment was made in the light of Samuel Johnson's visit to Scotland to search for evidence which would corroborate the claims made in the Ossianic poems which James Macpherson, in 1761, claimed to have discovered. Johnson and others made the journey north to search for manuscript evidence which was not, of course, available. In this single example of eighteenth-century scholarly activity we can discern several correspondences with the activities of Iolo Morganwg, though Iolo, of course, combined within himself the roles of both Macpherson and Johnson. He created, Macpherson-like, a bardic tradition, but he also provided the manuscript evidence, albeit false, to support his creation. In this, he was an example of the duality which a recent historian has discerned in Welsh cultural life. On the one hand, we have the Romantic thrust of a largely imagined past, 'forming a kind of anti-Enlightenment' and, on the other, a scientific, evidence-based approach which formed part of the Enlightenment attitude to learning.[2]

The 'creativity' of Macpherson and Iolo Morganwg forms part of an important and well-documented cultural movement, that of establishing and

[1] Rosemary Sweet, *Antiquaries: The Discovery of the Past in Eighteenth-century Britain* (London, 2004), p. 137.
[2] R. J. W. Evans, 'Was there a Welsh Enlightenment?' in R. R. Davies and Geraint H. Jenkins (eds.), *From Medieval to Modern Wales: Historical Essays in Honour of Kenneth O. Morgan and Ralph A. Griffiths* (Cardiff, 2004), p. 156.

promoting Celticism in general and a theory of Celtic origins in particular. The Celtic movement was allied to a deep interest in druidism. English scholars, searching for a history of national origins, had for the most part no difficulty in absorbing a Celtic, or Ancient British, strand into their make–up. For instance, Daniel Defoe's *The True-Born Englishman*, first published in 1701, claimed that his compatriots were a mixture of Briton, Roman, Saxon, Dane and Norman.[3] The study of Celtic origins had been placed on a sound scholarly footing by Edward Lhuyd's comparative etymological studies. English antiquarians, who lacked Lhuyd's linguistic skills, concentrated on the study of stones and earthworks as a means of uncovering the past. Ancient stone circles were interpreted by many as sites of druidic worship; thus, in 1740, the antiquary William Stukeley gave the title *Stonehenge, a temple restor'd to the Druids* to his study of the site.

The study of Celtic origins, so widespread in England during the eighteenth century, existed on at least three levels. The first was the genuinely scholarly level earlier referred to, which was based largely on observation and fieldwork. Side-by-side with this, however, there was an attempt to provide a theory of origins based largely on tradition and conjecture. This was by no means a new subject; it had received particularly lively attention in the sixteenth century following the publication of what would nowadays be termed 'revisionist' histories criticizing the origin myth of Brutus and the escape from Troy. The ideas of William Camden and others were vigorously disputed at that time and, in the eighteenth century, by Welsh scholars.[4] Thirdly, overlying the debate on these two levels, there was a Romantic primitivism derived from ideas of druidism and bardism.

By the fourth quarter of the eighteenth century in England, interest in Celticism had reached its peak and began to decline in the 1790s. The elaborate bardic edifice built by Iolo Morganwg, however, proved long-lasting. Indeed, it still survives in the activities of the Gorsedd of the Bards of the Isle of Britain, whose 'druidical' ceremonies at the National Eisteddfod remain a major attraction. The ceremonial has long since lost historical credence, but the myth created by Iolo remains powerful and is a testament to the success of his

---

[3]   Sweet, *Antiquaries*, p. 121.

[4]   One such critic was Rowland Vaughan, in his preface to *Yr Ymarfer o Dduwioldeb* (a translation of *The Practice of Piety*) in 1630: 'Yr ydym ni yn meddiannu yr ynys hon ou blaen hwy, er bod Camden ai gau athrawiaeth ddyscedig a llawer o ddiscyblion iddo yn gwadu Brutus ac yn haeru mai Ieffrey o fynyw o scrifennodd o honaw gyntaf' ('We were in possession of this island before them, although Camden and his false learned doctrine and many of his followers deny Brutus and assert that it was Geoffrey of Monmouth who first wrote of him'). See Garfield H. Hughes (ed.), *Rhagymadroddion 1547–1659* (Caerdydd, 1951), p. 119. In the eighteenth century, Theophilus Evans's popular *Drych y Prif Oesoedd* (Mirror of the First Ages), published in 1716 but best known in its 1740 second edition, vigorously expounded the same view of early history.

underlying mission: to create a glorious past for Wales. His creative Romanticism produced a movement strong enough to have its own momentum, powerful enough to allow it to coexist with contradictory historical truths.

Even in more objective eighteenth-century historical activities, emotional attachments and local loyalties played their part. The aggrandizement of localities, counties in particular, was a marked cultural feature of the eighteenth century. In part, the movement was inherited from sixteenth-century county historians; in part also, it arose from the detailed observation of particular areas inherent in eighteenth-century travel literature and in explorations for the purposes of fact-gathering. This gathering of factual material relating to certain counties or localities covered diverse fields, ranging from the study of dialects, archaeological remains and agricultural practices to the recording of social customs. Iolo's incessant travels on foot throughout Wales were part of this localized fact-finding mission. Lewis Morris, that other towering polymath of eighteenth-century Wales, had also undertaken such journeys for his projected great work, 'Celtic Remains', which remained unpublished until 1878.

Praise of Anglesey was a deep-seated feature in the letters of the Morris brothers and, above all, in the poetry of their exiled protégé, Goronwy Owen. It was seen, too, in Henry Rowlands's *Mona Antiqua Restaurata* (1723; 2nd edn., 1766), in which love of a county was tied to the wider interest in druidism. In England, too, there was a strong tradition of using the county as an appropriate unit for the study of history. Among the best-known county histories were William Borlase, *Observations on the Antiquities Historical and Monumental, of the County of Cornwall* (1754; 2nd edn., 1769), in which the study of druidical remains was an important component; John Hutchins, *History and Antiquities of the County of Dorset* (1773); and John Nichols, *The History and Antiquities of the County of Leicester* (8 vols., 1795–1815). In Rosemary Sweet's view, the profusion of county histories was rooted particularly in the self-interest of the landed gentry: 'there was . . . a strong sense of county feeling amongst the landed elite; this manifested itself in the county history . . . the illustration of their seats'.[5] County histories in Wales were published somewhat later: Theophilus Jones, *A History of the County of Brecknock* (2 vols., 1805–9), Samuel Rush Meyrick, *The History and Antiquities of the County of Cardigan* (1808), and Richard Fenton, *A Historical Tour through Pembrokeshire* (1810), though John Thomas, headmaster of Beaumaris school, had published *A History of the Island of Anglesey* much earlier, in 1775. Philip Jenkins views these Welsh histories in a slightly different light as the aspirational product of a 'new gentry' seeking to incorporate ancient traditions and antiquarian activity into their own lives.[6]

---

5   Sweet, *Antiquaries*, p. 37.
6   Philip Jenkins, *The Making of a Ruling Class: The Glamorgan Gentry, 1640–1790* (Cambridge, 1983), p. 272.

The provenance of these writings was typical of eighteenth-century culture. History, in the main, was neither philosophical nor interpretative in nature: it was based on the close observation of artefacts, customs, manuscripts and language. While some indulged in flights of fancy, particularly with regard to origins, the overwhelming emphasis was placed on recording what could be observed in the field and in libraries. It was a way of describing the past which embodied much of the spirit of the Enlightenment. Much of Iolo's legitimate work embodied this spirit, and so, in a twisted way, did his forgeries. They sought to create a manuscript corpus which would be scientifically observable by others, false data which arose not from the imagination only but also from the knowledge of true scholarship. Much of Iolo's own scholarly work falls, therefore, into the mainstream of eighteenth-century activity. The nature of these activities was such that the lack of Welsh academic and public institutions was not as serious a disadvantage as might appear at first sight.[7] Manuscripts were largely housed in the libraries of gentry houses, or had come into the possession of other scholars. One of these was David Thomas (Dafydd Ddu Eryri), well known as a bardic master, who was visited by Iolo while he was collecting material for *The Myvyrian Archaiology of Wales* on behalf of Owen Jones (Owain Myfyr):

> E fu Edward Williams neu Iolo Morganwg yn y wlad yn hir o amser, dim llai na chwarter blwyddyn, rhwng Mon ac Arfon, efe a ysgrifennodd lawer allan o'm ysgrif-lyfrau i, etc., dros Mr O. Jones neu O. Myfyr o Lundain yr oedd ef ar waith, oblegid y mae O. Jones wedi dechrau argraffu ar ei draul ei hun.[8]

> (Edward Williams or Iolo Morganwg has been in the area for a long time, not less than a quarter of a year, between Anglesey and Arfon. He wrote much out of my notebooks etc. He was at work on behalf of Mr O. Jones or O. Myfyr of London, for O. Jones has started printing at his own cost.)

In 1802 Iolo himself described this visit in a letter to Walter Davies (Gwallter Mechain). He went to Beaumaris, where he stayed from August until October, reading manuscripts, visiting other scholars and pursuing his Gorsedd activities:

> yn darllen ac yn copio llawysgrifau Paul Panton, ac yn ymweled a llenorion y cylchoedd, Dafydd Ddu Eryri a Peter Bayley Williams o Lanrug, ac yn cynnal 'Gorsedd' i urddo beirdd Gwynedd ar Ben y Bryn yn Ninorwig.[9]

> (reading and copying Paul Panton's manuscripts, and visiting the literary men of the surrounding areas, Dafydd Ddu Eryri and Peter Bayley Williams of Llanrug, and holding a 'Gorsedd' to ordain the poets of Gwynedd at Pen-y-bryn in Dinorwig.)

---

[7]   Lewis: *IM*, p. 28.
[8]   Quoted in Meirion Ll. Williams, 'Hanes yr Eisteddfod ym Môn 1800–1850' (unpublished University of Wales Ph.D. thesis, 2004), p. 57.
[9]   Ibid.

Another letter describes Iolo, unsparing of himself, writing at a tavern in Beaumaris from four in the morning until midnight.[10]

The practicalities of Iolo's life as a scholar mirror those of his predecessor Evan Evans, or Ieuan Fardd, who is generally considered to be the greatest scholar of Welsh literature in the eighteenth century. A Cardiganshire man, Evans was educated at Edward Richard's school at Ystradmeurig and at Merton College, Oxford. He became acquainted with Lewis Morris, who took him under his wing and, in all probability, introduced him to William Vaughan of Corsygedol, who gave him support and encouragement over a long period. Later, he was supported by Paul Panton of Plas-gwyn, Anglesey, who provided him with a small annuity. Evans lived his life as a lowly curate, in parishes in England as well as in Wales, often filling posts for no longer than a few months. He lived an unhappy, peripatetic life and was frequently in debt; his life oscillated between periods in gentry houses (from 1771 to 1778 he was employed in the library of Sir Watkin Williams Wynn at Llanforda and later at Wynnstay), brief curacies, and periods spent at home with his mother in Lledrod. He was mentally troubled and prone to drink.[11]

Iolo Morganwg's way of life, then, was not unique: despite periods spent at his craft, and periods spent in data-gathering pursuits in the employment of Owain Myfyr, his financial position was always precarious. There is a wider cultural parallel, too, between Iolo Morganwg and Evan Evans. The lineage of the leading Welsh scholars of the eighteenth century is usually drawn from Edward Lhuyd at the end of the seventeenth century, through his pupil Moses Williams, to Lewis Morris to Evan Evans and Iolo Morganwg. These men, in varying degrees, straddled more than one culture. Wales was undoubtedly the centre of their world: 'now as I am come to England, I have not so much to say', said Lewis Morris in February 1743, during one of his journeys.[12] They were passionately devoted to the study of the language: 'yr Iaith odidoccaf dan y ffurfafen' ('the most magnificent language under heaven'), according to Richard Morris.[13] Woe betide those who sought to do her harm; in a letter to his brother Richard, William Morris recounted what occurred when the poet William Wynn had occasion to listen to Robert Hay Drummond, Bishop of St Asaph, a Scotsman, fulminating against the Welsh language:

[10] G. J. Williams, 'Llythyrau Llenorion', *Y Llenor*, VI (1927), 42.
[11] Aneirin Lewis has an excellent account of his life and literary connections in 'Ieuan Fardd a'r Gwaith o Gyhoeddi Hen Lenyddiaeth Cymru' and 'Ieuan Fardd a'r Llenorion Saesneg, in W. Alun Mathias and E. Wyn James (eds.), *Dysg a Dawn: Cyfrol Goffa Aneirin Lewis* (Caerdydd, 1992), pp. 121–45, 146–69.
[12] Hugh Owen (ed.), *Additional Letters of the Morrises of Anglesey (1735–1786)* (2 vols., London, 1947–9), I, p. 118.
[13] Ibid., I, p. 264. This was in a letter to William Vaughan, dated 14 June 1755.

Yr Esgob ar ei giniaw efo'g offeiriada' a goreuwyr y wlad, oi fawr ddoethineb a
ddywedodd ei fod yn tybiaw mai gwell a fyddai ped fai'r iaith Gymraeg wedi ei
thynnu o'r gwraidd, etc., a speech worthy of a Welch bishop! O na ba'sai Risiart
Davies neu ryw rai eraill or Hen Esgobion Cymreig yn medru cyfodi o farw'n fyw
i grafu llygaid yr Alban allan o'r tyllau, – ond beth bynnag, fe ddechreuodd y bardd
gynhyrfu, ac a roes i'r Scottyn wers y persli. Ni sonnia fo mwyach am ddifa yr hen
iaith o flaen y cadarn fardd.[14]

(The Bishop, dining with the clergy and the important men of the locality, in his
great wisdom declared that in his opinion it would be better if the Welsh language
were pulled up from the root etc., a speech worthy of a Welsh bishop! Oh that
Richard Davies or some others of the Old Welsh Bishops could not rise up from the
dead to claw the Scot's eyes from their sockets – but anyway, the poet started to
become agitated, and gave the Scotsman a dressing down to remember. He dared no
longer talk of destroying the old language in front of the determined poet.)

But they were also deeply connected, through their professions, their travels
and their reading, to a wider world. From Dafydd ap Gwilym through William
Salesbury to William Williams, Pantycelyn and Saunders Lewis, the pinnacles
of Welsh literature have often, though not always, been reached via a juxtaposition with outside movements and other cultures. Eighteenth-century Welsh
scholarship is an important example of this phenomenon.

It is significant that Iolo Morganwg's own linguistic background was
thoroughly bilingual. The Vale of Glamorgan, like Edward Lhuyd's Shropshire
and Denbighshire borderland, was a shifting area in terms of linguistic
geography. In both cases, too, binary linguistic patterns were deepened by
family backgrounds which were more complex than usual. Among the
Oxford-based scholar Moses Williams's friends and correspondents were the
English scholars Thomas Hearne, John Hudson, William Wotton and
Humphrey Wanley; Evan Evans was closely connected with Daines
Barrington, Thomas Gray and Bishop Thomas Percy. Like Evan Evans, Moses
Williams, as we have seen, had held curacies in England.

The non-institutional pursuit of Welsh learning, then, displayed certain
informal patterns: the primacy of observation in the field, constant travelling,
the use of gentry libraries, the careful copying of manuscripts, sporadic
patronage, the enrichment of the whole by external influences. But informal
networks can in themselves provide 'institutions' of a kind. Welsh scholars had
the support of others in the field. The voluminous correspondence of the
Morris circle of poets and scholars, among themselves and others, provides
abundant instances of powerful scholarly networking. Lewis Morris in

---

[14]   J. H. Davies (ed.), *The Letters of Lewis, Richard, William and John Morris of Anglesey, (Morrisiaid
       Môn) 1728–1765* (2 vols., Aberystwyth, 1907), I, p. 237.

particular used correspondence as the medium of scholarly and critical leadership. Here he writes to the young Evan Evans:

> Let me have a short *Cywydd* from you now & then, and I'll send you my observations upon them which may be of no disservice to you. That sent in your last, I here return you, with a few corrections. It doth not want many, use them or throw y^m into ye fire, which you please. Dont swallow y^m without examination, the authority of good poets must determine all.[15]

Letters, too, could be supplemented by visits. William Wynn wrote as follows to Lewis Morris from Llanbryn-mair in February 1746:

> To renew our Correspondence is what I wanted of all things . . . I am highly delighted with your Scheme of publishing some Queries (I suppose in the Magazines) concerning our Language, Poetry & History . . . I shou'd be glad of the Favour of seeing those things before you made them public, that, if I shou'd happen to stumble upon any thing to the purpose, I might communicate it in time . . . As I am a Housekeeper, I wish you wou'd come and spend a week with me, when you are most at Leisure, or longer if your Business will admit of it, then we might conn over these and other things with much more satisfaction than by Letters.[16]

We should not, therefore, suppose that life in rural Wales meant cultural isolation; nor should we suppose that the only centres of cultural activity important to Wales were in English towns and cities such as London or Bristol. The letters of the Morris circle, some of whose members had far-flung seafaring and business interests, reveal a remarkably wide range of geographical and cultural links, stretching from remote country villages to America. When the Cymmrodorion Society was founded in London, Lewis Morris's 'Constitutions' (1755) cast a wide net:

> And the Society do heartily invite their Brethren of the *Welsh* Colony in *Pensylvania* to correspond with them; being very desirous of perpetuating the antient *British* Language in that Province . . . They are also desirous of Correspondence with all Historians and Antiquarians, of what Nation soever . . .[17]

William Morris, who remained in Anglesey and showered his attention on his family and his beloved garden, wrote letters which are remarkably lively and well informed. To him, Dublin was an important centre in all ways, supplying him with goods from 'best wheaten bread' to unusual seeds, but a source also of news and information. Irish newspapers supplemented those sent from London by his brother Richard:

[15] Owen (ed.), *Additional Letters*, I, p. 207.
[16] Ibid., I, pp. 178–80.
[17] R. T. Jenkins and Helen Ramage, *A History of the Honourable Society of Cymmrodorion and of the Gwyneddigion and Cymreigyddion Societies (1751–1951)* (London, 1951), pp. 236–7.

As to newspapers we have the *Gazzeteer* and *London Evening Post* regularly in this place, likewise yᵉ *Com. Senate.* We have also by each pacquet boat from Dublin the Irish newspapers, which take in all the English news, both from the printed and written letters, with yᵉ abstracts of the votes of the British House of Commons when sitting, etc.[18]

Even though William confessed that he 'don't take any of these papers', he obviously had access to them.

Individual effort and interpersonal contact predominated in eighteenth-century scholarly life. However, there was also a strong movement aimed at founding learned societies in order to promote learning among scientists, antiquarians and men of letters. Several Welsh societies were founded which were less specialized and sought to promote Welsh matters in general. The Welsh society, in whichever form, has been described as 'the new Welsh organisation of the century'.[19] The most influential of these was the Cymmrodorion Society, founded in 1751. Its gatherings, highly convivial in nature, provided a meeting-place for exiled Welshmen and for those corresponding members who happened to be visiting the metropolis. For all the drinking and jolly fraternizing, however, the declared aim of the society was serious and scholarly: to promote the Welsh language, to discover the manuscript tradition, and to undertake a programme of publication. This developing and nurturing of a learned tradition places the Cymmrodorion Society squarely within a European pattern, for the founding of such societies was widespread. For instance, in a letter to Edward Richard, Lewis Morris maintained that members of the society were consciously seeking to emulate a French pattern: '[they] talk of publishing some Memoirs in the nature of those of the Royal Academy of Sciences at Paris'.[20] Many years later, in 1820, Iolo Morganwg still longed to see an institution based on French models set up in Wales:

I have conceived that something more must be done towards instituting a Literary Welsh Society, for the cultivation of the Welsh Language and Literature . . . The Academy that I would humbly propose should proceed as much as possible on the Plan of the French Academies of Inscriptions, of Belles Lettres etc. I mean as far as circumstances would admit, for it would be madness at present, and I fear for a long time to come, to think of such nobly supported and endowed Colleges as those of the French Academies are. What I would humbly suggest in the incipient state of such an Institution would be to establish a Welsh Corresponding Academy . . . The annual meetings would bring together many persons of learning in the Language, its Poetry, its History, Antiquities etc., and obtain information of others sufficiently

---

[18]   Davies (ed.), *Morris Letters*, I, p. 52.
[19]   Prys Morgan, *The Eighteenth Century Renaissance* (Llandybïe, 1981), p. 66. See also Emrys Jones (ed.), *The Welsh in London 1500–2000* (Cardiff, 2001).
[20]   Owen (ed.), *Additional Letters*, II, p. 457.

qualified to become members, and those members to correspond with each other and with the Chairman or more properly President.[21]

Iolo Morganwg's own involvement with the London societies lay mainly with the Gwyneddigion Society, though he also had links with the Caradogion and the Cymreigyddion Societies.[22] The Gwyneddigion Society had been founded in 1770, partly as a result of what was perceived by some to be the increasing Anglicization of the Cymmrodorion Society as it recruited more and more gentry members. The two main planks of the Gwyneddigion's activities were its ambitious publishing programme, largely underwritten by Owain Myfyr, and the rejuvenation of the eisteddfod movement. Iolo Morganwg was, of course, highly important in the development of both spheres of activity. As we have seen, he travelled the length and breadth of Wales, avidly collecting material for *The Myvyrian Archaiology of Wales*. Indeed, Owain Myfyr's support of Iolo was of inestimable importance. As G. J. Williams claimed, it was his support which enabled Iolo to develop into a national figure.[23] The modern eisteddfod, whose beginnings are usually seen in the eisteddfodau held under the auspices of the Gwyneddigion from 1789, was moulded in Iolo's own image when he succeeded, in 1819, in introducing to the proceedings neo-druidical Gorsedd activities, which were largely the fruit of his own imagination.[24]

Not for nothing, then, are the words 'renaissance' or 'remaking' frequently used to describe the cultural activities of eighteenth-century Wales, particularly from the 1740s onwards. But antiquarianism, manuscript collecting, learned societies and eisteddfodic activities aside, no 'renaissance' would have been possible without the large expansion of book publishing which occurred in the eighteenth century. There occurred a marked rise in the literacy of the labouring and agricultural classes, the result largely of the work of the Welsh Trust, the SPCK and especially Griffith Jones's remarkable circulating schools, of which 3,325 had been founded in nearly 1,600 places by the time of his death in 1761.[25] His vision was practical: to teach the uneducated to read – in Welsh if that was their mother tongue – so that they might be able to read the Bible and simple religious texts. He was instrumental in creating a restricted, but widespread, level of literacy among the poorer people.

---

[21] NLW 1895Ei, Letter no. 82, Iolo Morganwg to David Richards, 26 December 1820. Quoted in Williams: *IM*, p. 70.

[22] Lewis: *IM*, p.15.

[23] Williams: *IM*, p. 202.

[24] See Hywel Teifi Edwards, *Yr Eisteddfod* (Llandysul, 1976), pp. 39–42.

[25] Geraint H. Jenkins, 'The Eighteenth Century' in Philip Henry Jones and Eiluned Rees (eds.), *A Nation and its Books: A History of the Book in Wales* (Aberystwyth, 1998), p. 112.

Iolo Morganwg himself was the product of a somewhat higher class of craftsmen and small businessmen. The rise of this class, and the contribution made by some of its members to the furtherance of scholarship and literature and to the formulation and dissemination of religious, political and philo-sophical ideas is one of the most noteworthy features of the century. As Rosemary Sweet has pointed out, 'there was a long and honourable tradition of antiquaries who came from relatively humble backgrounds . . . [which] continued throughout the eighteenth century, and if anything became more marked as the opportunities for autodidactism and the acquisition of printed literature became greater'.[26] This class, side-by-side with members of the gentry, participated in the expansion of book learning. For most of the eighteenth century, the appetite for reading was met privately. Books were sometimes passed from hand to hand from the collections of those members of the gentry, the clergy, schoolmasters, lawyers and businessmen who bought them. At other times, permission was granted to read in private homes. By the beginning of the nineteenth century, book-reading and book-lending had become more formalized following the founding of book clubs, which acted as lending libraries. Other clubs had been founded earlier. It is notable that, of the early book clubs in Wales, one was established at Cowbridge, near Iolo Morganwg's home, in 1736. Another was founded at Pembroke sometime before 1741; others were founded slightly later at Carmarthen, Holyhead and Denbigh.[27] The book club at Cowbridge may well have helped to feed Iolo's voracious appetite for books.[28] During Iolo's lifetime, printing and publishing in Wales expanded rapidly. Much of the printing of Welsh material initially occurred in Shrewsbury, Bristol and Chester, but Welsh towns such as Carmarthen, Brecon, Bala, Denbigh and Swansea later became important centres. Printing became a thriving trade, so much so that Iolo advocated it as a venture to his son Taliesin in 1817: 'The fair and legal profits of printing are very great . . . if you could set up an honest Printing office, you would soon have all the business of Wales; at least of South Wales.'[29]

The movement to promote literacy, particularly among young people, continued largely through the Sunday school movement which produced, in 1807, a guide to reading entitled *Sillydd Cymraeg*.[30] It quickly went into several

---

[26] Sweet, *Antiquaries*, pp. 57–8. Cf. Geraint H. Jenkins, 'Historical Writing in the Eighteenth Century' in Branwen Jarvis (ed.), *A Guide to Welsh Literature c.1700–1800* (Cardiff, 2000), pp. 23–44.

[27] Eiluned Rees, 'The Welsh Book Trade from 1718 to 1820' in Jones and Rees (eds.), *A Nation and its Books*, p. 130.

[28] Lewis: *IM*, p. 29.

[29] NLW 21286E, Letter no. 956, Iolo Morganwg to Taliesin Williams, 28 July 1817. Quoted in Rees, 'The Welsh Book Trade', p. 126.

[30] The analysis of Welsh books which follows is based on the data in Eiluned Rees, *Libri Walliae: A Catalogue of Welsh Books and Books printed in Wales 1546–1820* (2 vols., Aberystwyth, 1987).

editions, as did the later *Cyflwyniad i blentyn i ddysgu darllen Cymraeg* (*c*.1820). There are also examples of practical guides in Welsh in other spheres, too, from an early period. The first edition of *Cyfarwyddiad i fesur-wyr*, a guide to mensuration, appeared from Thomas Durston's press in Shrewsbury in 1715, and was republished several times up until 1784. *Llyfr Meddyginaeth ir anafys ar chlwfus*, a medicinal guide which also included a section on cookery, ran to five editions between 1733 and 1774. By the time of Iolo's death, nineteenth-century models of Dissenting culture were taking root, and in 1818 a guide to the principles of singing, *Egwyddorion Canu*, was published in Merthyr Tydfil (where Iolo by this period was spending much time). Religious literature abounded with works in the practical and didactic mode, the most famous of which was William Williams, Pantycelyn's *Ductor Nuptiarum: Neu, Gyfarwyddwr Priodas* (1777), a guide to marriage for those who professed Methodism.

As might be expected, books published in Wales during the eighteenth and early nineteenth centuries were overwhelmingly religious in nature. Devotional, explanatory, hortatory and polemical works poured from the presses. Some were of general appeal, particularly those of a devotional and practical nature, while others, reflecting the turbulence of eighteenth-century religious life, were disputational in tone. Particularly popular were *Pattrwm y gwir-Gristion* (Thomas à Kempis's *De Imitatione Christi*), which ran to sixteen editions (including reissues) between 1684 and 1775, and the works of John Bunyan. *The Pilgrim's Progress* had been translated into Welsh by Stephen Hughes in 1688 and ran to twenty-one editions (in whole or in part) between then and 1819. The work's central image, that of Christian life as a pilgrimage and preparation, exerted a deep influence on the hymns of William Williams, Pantycelyn. Other works by Bunyan, including published sermons, were also widely read.

The outstanding figures among authors who wrote originally in Welsh, again from the point of view of the numbers of issues, were Morgan Llwyd, Thomas Charles and William Williams. The works of Morgan Llwyd which were most frequently published were *Gwaedd Ynghymru* and *Dirgelwch i rai iw ddeall ac i eraill iw watwar, sef tri aderyn yn ymddiddan*, both of which had originally appeared in 1653. They provided vivid calls, in a lofty prose style, for the people of Wales to prepare themselves spiritually for the second coming of Christ, though it must be said that the complex and somewhat recondite nature of Llwyd's work must have limited its influence.

One of the founders of the Bible Society, Thomas Charles, who was the great practical educator of the Methodist movement, was a prolific writer. His *Geiriadur Ysgrythyrol*, a huge scriptural dictionary or concordance in four volumes, which he began publishing in 1805, became a byword among nineteenth-century readers, but other, lesser, works were also highly popular. His *Hyfforddwr yn Egwyddorion y Grefydd Gristionogol*, a guide to the principles of Christianity, was republished or reissued on twelve occasions between 1807 and 1820.

Practical though most of Thomas Charles's work was, in temper and subject-matter it formed part of that great flowering of literature (written originally in Welsh rather than translated) which flowed from Calvinistic Methodism. As Derec Llwyd Morgan has pointed out, this flowering was marked by a clarity and underlying unity of theme and purpose which made its influence all the more profound.[31] And not profound only, but also pervasive and long-lasting, as the images, themes and modes of expression of Methodist literature, its hymns in particular, became part of the cultural fabric of Nonconformity as a whole in the nineteenth century and in the first part of the twentieth century. Greatest among the Methodist writers was William Williams, Pantycelyn. In purely numerical terms he was the most prolific of eighteenth-century published authors: between 1744 and 1791, close to a hundred issues and reissues of his works appeared, with several important reissues in the early years of the nineteenth century. In terms of the intellectual and imaginative quality of his work, he was a towering figure. His greatness lay not only in hymns, of which there are about a thousand, with two hundred in English, but also in his other, more sustained, writings. He was a master of the religious elegy, a new Methodist literary vehicle, of the long religious poem, and of prose works intended to deepen and enhance the spiritual growth of adherents.

In the Vale of Glamorgan, Iolo's own region, Calvinistic Methodism became an increasingly powerful force during his lifetime. Several *seiadau*, or 'societies', were formed, some of which went on to build their own meeting-houses. Early societies were founded at Aberthaw, Aberthin, Cowbridge, Dinas Powys, Newton Nottage, Fonmon, Llanbleddian, Llysworney, Moulton, Porthceri, St Andrews, St Nicholas, Sully and Tre-os, all within a fairly small radius of Iolo's home.[32] The movement was well under way in the Vale when he was a young man, influenced in no small measure by the powerful presence of David Jones (1736–1810), the incumbent of Llan-gan. People came to his church in their hundreds to listen to him preach and to take communion. By 1771 he had built a meeting-house, Salem, Pen-coed, to accommodate his followers. By means of lyrical preaching, he appealed directly to the hearts of his listeners. Williams Pantycelyn claimed that he could 'make the stoutest oak bend as easily as rushes' ('[gwneuthur] i'r derw mwyaf caled/ Blygu'n ystwyth fel y brwyn').[33]

---

[31] Derec Llwyd Morgan, 'Llenyddiaeth y Methodistiaid, 1763–1814' in Gomer M. Roberts (ed.), *Hanes Methodistiaeth Galfinaidd Cymru* (2 vols., Caernarfon, 1973–8), II, p. 457.

[32] See the list of early societies in ibid., I, pp. 445–8.

[33] The description is drawn from his elegy to Daniel Rowland in N. Cynhafal Jones (ed.), *Gweithiau Williams Pant-y-celyn* (2 vols., Treffynnon, 1887–91), I, p. 588.

Two leading figures who came under his influence were Thomas William (1761–1844) and John Williams (1728–1806), both of whom were accomplished hymn-writers. Thomas William in particular was a fine poet; his hymns and religious elegies display careful craftsmanship and a moving, albeit rather melancholy, lyricism. For some years, he lived in Iolo's village of Flemingston. John Williams, who lived close by at St Athan, was a friend of Iolo. Both poets became embroiled in religious controversy and left the Methodist association at Aberthin following the expulsion of Peter Williams, one of the leaders of the Calvinistic Methodist movement and the author of many works, in particular commentaries on each chapter of the Bible found in his famed 'Beibl Peter Williams'. He was accused of Sabellian heresy by the *Sasiwn*, or 'Association', of Methodists which met at Llandeilo in 1791. Following his expulsion, several stormy events occurred at Aberthin.[34] Iolo Morganwg was present at one particularly difficult meeting when Sabellian members of the congregation were turned away; he had attended as a result of his friendship with John Williams, and probably also because he viewed the Sabellians as potential allies in the Unitarian movement. Eventually, members of the Aberthin meeting formed a new congregation which, in 1814, allied itself to the Independents.

The story has been briefly recounted here because it illustrates the changing and often volatile nature of religious life in the Vale of Glamorgan. Calvinistic Methodism, which Iolo professed to despise as 'maddened Church-and-Kingism', permeated both Anglican and Dissenting congregations, and was frequently a controversial force. It was also, as we have seen, an energizing movement which propelled some adherents towards more radical denominations; in other cases, however, traditionalism prevailed. At the time of his death in 1810, it appears that David Jones was still opposed to the ordination of Methodists outside the framework of the established church. It is believed that Richard Bassett (1777–1852), who held incumbencies in the Vale of Glamorgan, and who was also a leading Methodist and a trustee of several of their chapels in Glamorgan, was the last Anglican clergyman in Wales to profess Methodism.[35]

Iolo Morganwg's Unitarianism was, of course, part of his radical stance in matters religious and political. The Wales into which he was born, halfway through the eighteenth century, was a country marked by quietude and traditionalism on the one hand and by reform, new awakenings and even revolution on the other. Iolo became part of the movements for radical reform

---

[34] The events are recounted in Gomer M. Roberts, *Emynwyr Bethesda'r Fro* (Llandysul, 1967), pp. 25–9. See also E. Wyn James, 'Thomas William: Bardd ac Emynydd Bethesda'r Fro', *LlC*, 27 (2004), 113–39.

[35] E. Wyn James, 'Iolo Morganwg, Thomas William a Gwladgarwch y Methodistiaid', *LlC*, 27 (2004), 172–6.

and new beginnings, many of which were well under way at the time of his birth. His declaration that there is 'Nothing [going on] in South Wales'[36] might have been true in the context of the activities of the London societies, but in general it was an exaggeration. South Wales was in fact a notable cradle of radical political and religious thought, though the development of that thought was usually London-centric.

The highly influential Richard Price (1723–91), mathematician and philosopher, was born in the village of Llangeinor into a well-known Dissenting family. Both his father, Rees, and his father's brother, Samuel, were ministers who had been educated at the Dissenting academy at Brynllywarch, in Llangynwyd. Samuel Price was a friend of Isaac Watts and his co-minister for a long period; he played an important part in his nephew's upbringing. Richard Price, like his father and his uncle, received a Dissenting education, at Pentwyn, Chancefield and Moorfields. Dissenting academies were thus an important strand in the cultural make-up of Wales during the later seventeenth and the eighteenth centuries. They were usually led by individual scholars in their own homes, and the best of them provided intending ministers with a fine, and surprisingly liberal, education. In England, academies turned to English as a medium of instruction, but their counterparts in Wales clung to Latin, thus depriving the Welsh language of what might have proved to be a significant widening of its domain. Barred from the universities, Dissenters were nonetheless able to benefit from a wide-ranging education which combined the religious and the secular. As R. Tudur Jones has argued, this combination of diverse intellectual elements had far-reaching effects: 'One striking effect of this was that the academies became pioneers in the provision of scientific education and produced scholars whose cultural background combined elements of the humanities and the sciences as well as theology' ('Un o ganlyniadau trawiadol y ffaith hon oedd i'r academïau droi'n arloeswyr mewn cyfrannu addysg wyddonol a chynhyrchu ysgolheigion a gyfunai yn eu diwylliant elfennau dyneiddiol a gwyddonol yn ogystal ag elfennau diwinyddol').[37]

Richard Price, then, was a product of this remarkable tradition. He is considered the father of modern actuarial science, and was elected a Fellow of the Royal Society in 1765 for his mathematical work. His work on ethics, *A Review of the Principal Questions and Difficulties in Morals* (1758), foreshadowed later work by Kant. His thinking on economics led William Pitt the Younger to seek, and accept, his advice on economic policy in 1786. Two years later, he was invited to establish the financial policies of the American states. His advisory pamphlet, *Observations on the Importance of the American Revolution*

---

[36] Quoted in Williams, 'Llythyrau Llenorion', 37.

[37] R. Tudur Jones, *Hanes Annibynwyr Cymru* (Abertawe, 1966), p. 126. The English translation is taken from the English version, edited by Robert Pope, *Congregationalism in Wales* (Cardiff, 2004), p. 96.

(1784), is considered to have had an influence on the American constitution. He supported the French Revolution in his celebrated sermon, *A Discourse on the Love of our Country* (1789), a work which was a seminal influence on Iolo Morganwg.[38]

Other products of the Dissenting tradition also point to a Wales which could begin to nurture, if not bring to full fruition, an influential, radical mindset. The political pamphleteer David Williams (1738–1816) was fairly close to Iolo Morganwg in age. He was born in the parish of Eglwysilan; his home, Waunwaelod, was close to the famous chapel at Watford, one of the most important centres of Calvinistic Methodism. He himself became a Dissenting minister, having been educated at the Carmarthen academy, which had acquired a reputation for theological unorthodoxy. He later left the ministry and earned his living as a schoolmaster, tutor and writer in London. His work in the deist tradition, *A Liturgy on the Universal Principles of Religion and Morality* (1776), was praised by Frederick II, Voltaire and Rousseau. In 1782 Williams published his *Letters on Political Liberty*, a defence of American colonists, which advocated a highly radical programme of political reform. The letters, translated into French, became extremely influential in France. Williams was subsequently awarded honorary French citizenship and became an adviser to the Girondins. He was also instrumental in founding, in 1790, the Royal Literary Fund, a fund intended to assist impoverished authors (including Iolo). His *History of Monmouthshire*, one of the county histories already discussed, was published in 1796.[39]

The religious and political activist Morgan John Rhys (1760–1804) was a younger contemporary of Iolo Morganwg. Again, the pattern of his upbringing and outlook was similar. Born at Llanbradach, he was educated at the Carmarthen academy and at Bristol before entering the Baptist ministry. In all that he did, he was fired by a missionary zeal for liberty in religion and politics. Forced to flee to America because of his Jacobin sympathies, he delighted in its freedoms. In a letter to a friend, he wrote:

> Oh! that I could stretch forth a brother's hand and draw my oppressed countrymen from their ecclesiastical and royal prisons to this hospitable shore that they might sacrifice a free-will offering in the temple of freedom which rises in the new world magnificently fair; that they may behold its collossal pillars, and with transports of joy, adore the universal parent within its dome. Under the shade of the tree of Liberty, we may traverse this continent, and notwithstanding the blast of tyrants its branches will soon cover the globe . . . in America there are no dissenters; the curse of religious establishments has been banished from the land; the inhabitants have

---

[38] For Price's career, see D. O. Thomas, *The Honest Mind: The Thought and Work of Richard Price* (Oxford, 1977).

[39] For Williams's career, see Whitney R. D. Jones, *David Williams: The Anvil and the Hammer* (Cardiff, 1986).

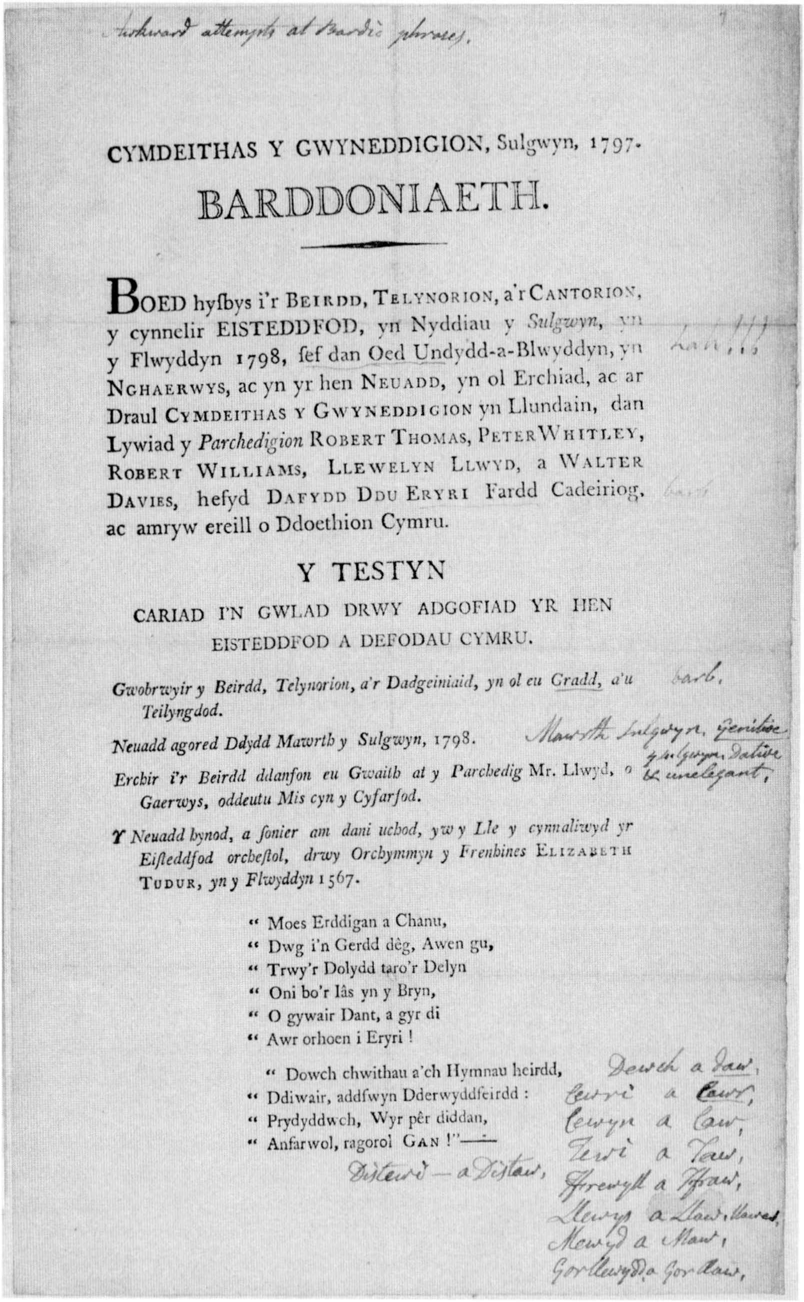

Awkward attempts at Bardic phrases.

CYMDEITHAS Y GWYNEDDIGION, Sulgwyn, 1797.

BARDDONIAETH.

BOED hyſbys i'r BEIRDD, TELYNORION, a'r CANTORION, y cynnelir EISTEDDFOD, yn Nyddiau y *Sulgwyn*, yn y Flwyddyn 1798, ſef dan Oed Undydd-a-Blwyddyn, yn NGHAERWYS, ac yn yr hen NEUADD, yn ol Erchiad, ac ar Draul CYMDEITHAS Y GWYNEDDIGION yn Llundain, dan Lywiad y *Parchedigion* ROBERT THOMAS, PETER WHITLEY, ROBERT WILLIAMS, LLEWELYN LLWYD, a WALTER DAVIES, hefyd DAFYDD DDU ERYRI Fardd Cadeiriog, ac amryw ereill o Ddoethion Cymru.

Y TESTYN

CARIAD I'N GWLAD DRWY ADGOFIAD YR HEN EISTEDDFOD A DEFODAU CYMRU.

Gwobrwyir y Beirdd, Telynorion, a'r Dadgeiniaid, yn ol eu Gradd, a'u Teilyngdod.

Neuadd agored Ddydd Mawrth y Sulgwyn, 1798.

Erchir i'r Beirdd ddanfon eu Gwaith at y Parchedig Mr. Llwyd, o *Gaerwys, oddeutu Mis cyn y Cyfarſod.*

Y Neuadd hynod, a ſonier am dani uchod, yw y Lle y cynnaliwyd yr Eiſteddfod orcheſtol, drwy Orchymmyn y Frenhines ELIZABETH TUDUR, *yn y Flwyddyn* 1567.

"Moes Erddigan a Chanu,
"Dwg i'n Gerdd dêg, Awen gu,
"Trwy'r Dolydd taro'r Delyn
"Oni bo'r Iâs yn y Bryn,
"O gywair Dant, a gyr di
"Awr orhoen i Eryri!

"Dowch chwithau a'ch Hymnau heirdd,
"Ddiwair, addfwyn Dderwyddfeirdd:
"Prydyddwch, Wyr pêr diddan,
"Anfarwol, ragorol GAN!"——

Fig. 4 A printed poster, advertising the 1798 eisteddfod at Caerwys, sponsored by the Gwyneddigion Society. The unflattering marginal comments are by Iolo Morganwg (NLW 21403E, no. 7).

made a noble barter; they enjoy in its stead all the blessings which are forever flowing from the Fountain of Freedom. Free enquiry after truth and a candid investigation of every subject, is a natural consequence in the system of equality, here a man may do both without suffering in his person or property.[40]

His love of political freedom and religious toleration coexisted with his patriotism. He had served his country well before his emigration to America, in particular in his work for the Sunday school movement and by his Welsh-language publications. He published some twenty pamphlets in Welsh and around ten in English, as well as several journals, notably *Y Cylchgrawn Cymraeg* (1793). His patriotic dreams reached their apogee in America, where he bought land to establish a colony called Cambria.[41] In the colony's chief town, named Beulah, he set up a free school, a library, a printing press and a church which was open to all denominations. He died in the town of Somerset, Pennsylvania, in 1804, having been appointed a judge a few years previously.

Iolo Morganwg knew Price and Williams personally, as indeed he knew other leaders of rational, freedom-loving thought. When he went up to London in 1791 he joined an intellectual milieu which centred on political societies in this tradition, some of which had been formed specifically to further the principles of the French Revolution. The Gwyneddigion Society had within its membership men such as Owain Myfyr, William Owen Pughe and John Jones (Jac Glan-y-gors) who supported the new politics in France. In 1790 the Gwyneddigion Society had set *Rhyddid* ('Liberty') as the subject of both the *awdl* and the essay competition for its eisteddfod at St Asaph. For Iolo Morganwg, as for others of his persuasion, the years immediately following 1789 were sweet, untainted as yet by later developments. He expressed his optimism memorably in 'Gwawr Dydd Rhyddhad' ('The Dawning of the Day of Freedom'):

> Mae gwawr
> Dydd ein rhyddhad yn deffro'n awr,
> Disgleirdeb y gwirionedd mawr;
> O! gwêl y bore'n deg ei dardd,
> Mae'n gwenu ar hyd y bryniau draw,
> Mae'r haul gerllaw a'i dywyn hardd.[42]

> (The dawn
> Of our day of liberation now awakes,
> The brilliance of the great truth;

---

[40] See John T. Griffith, *Rev. Morgan John Rhys* (Carmarthen, 1910), pp. 126–7.
[41] The prospectus of the 'Beulah Settlement' is reproduced in ibid., pp. 244–7. For Rhys, see Gwyn A. Williams, *The Search for Beulah Land: The Welsh and the Atlantic Revolution* (London, 1980).
[42] *CRhIM*, p. 39.

O! see the morning bright at its awakening;
It smiles along the distant hills,
The sun is at hand with its beauteous shine.)

Other important poems which he composed in the radical mould include 'Breiniau Dyn' ('The Rights of Man'), titled in honour of Tom Paine, and the 'Newgate Stanzas', which recorded his experiences on visiting his friend William Winterbotham, who was serving a two-year sentence for preaching a sermon criticizing George III and the government.[43]

Iolo Morganwg's regard for freedom in political and religious thought led him to that most liberty-loving of Dissenting movements, Unitarianism. He figured among those who professed the ideas of Joseph Priestley, who had also deeply influenced that leading figure of Welsh Unitarianism, Thomas Evans, better known as Tomos Glyn Cothi, and nicknamed 'Priestley Bach' ('Little Priestley'). Tomos Glyn Cothi had embraced early the principles of Unitarianism, and he possibly became acquainted with Iolo as he visited fairs in Glamorgan to sell his woollen wares.[44] He was the most influential figure of the period among Welsh Unitarians. His famous sermon 'Datganiad Ffydd' ('Declaration of Faith'), delivered near Gwernogau in Carmarthenshire in 1794 and published by John Ross at Carmarthen in 1795, voiced the beliefs of the small group of radical religious thinkers to which he and Iolo belonged:

yr wyf yn credu . . . fod UN ac nad oes ond UN bywiol a gwir Dduw . . . Y Tad Cyffredinol . . . Mewn perthynas i Iesu Grist yr wyf yn credu mai efe yw yr hwn a ordeiniwyd neu a neilltuwyd gan Dduw ei Dad i fod yn Ddatguddiwr o'i ewyllys a chennad ei ras at ddynolryw . . . yr wyf yn credu ar dystiolaeth yr Ysgrythyrau mai *dyn* oedd Iesu Grist megis ninnau, yn feddiannol ar yr un nattur a'r lleill o ddynolryw . . . Nid oes hawl gan neb awdurdodau gwladol ar wyneb y ddaear i daro i mewn neu ymyrryd mewn matterion crefyddol.[45]

(I believe that there is ONE, and that there is only ONE living and true God . . . the Father of all . . . In relation to Jesus Christ I believe that he is the one ordained or chosen by God his Father to be the Revealer of his will and the messenger of his grace to mankind . . . I believe on the testimony of the Scriptures that Jesus Christ was a *man* like us, possessed of the same nature as the rest of mankind . . . No civil authorities on earth have the right to bear upon or interfere in religious matters.)

---

[43] E. G. Millward (ed.), *Blodeugerdd Barddas o Gerddi Rhydd y Ddeunawfed Ganrif* (Llandybïe, 1991), pp. 242–5; NLW 21334B, pp. 21–8.

[44] T. Oswald Williams, *Undodiaeth a Rhyddid Meddwl* (Llandysul, 1962), p. 236. For the relationship between Tomos Glyn Cothi and Iolo Morganwg, see Geraint H. Jenkins, '"A Very Horrid Affair": Sedition and Unitarianism in the Age of Revolutions' in Davies and Jenkins (eds.), *From Medieval to Modern Wales*, pp. 178–86.

[45] Quoted in Williams, *Undodiaeth a Rhyddid Meddwl*, p. 237.

Adherents of the ideas outlined by Tomos Glyn Cothi formed the Unitarian Society of South Wales at a meeting at Gellionnen in west Glamorgan in October 1802. Iolo Morganwg himself was a leading member of the group, and it was he who wrote the rules and regulations of the Society, *Rheolau a Threfniadau Cymdeithas Dwyfundodiaid Deheubarth Cymru*, which were published in 1803. This orderly and constructive contribution to the most rationalist of denominations coexisted, however, with Iolo's Romantic fanta-sizing. He claimed that there existed in the Uplands of Glamorgan a secret group of druidic Unitarians called 'Gwŷr Cwm y Felin' (The Men of Cwm y Felin), and that Unitarianism was therefore the ancient and pure religion of the Early Church, transmitted through the centuries by druidic lore and practice.[46] Such complexities and dualities abound in the admixture of regular religious and political beliefs and imagined histories which we see in Iolo.

The complexity is revealed, too, in the enormous diversity of his interests, which derived partly from individual genius and partly from the multifaceted richness of his cultural background. The main religious and philosophical ideas and movements which surrounded Iolo, in his native Glamorgan and in his forays further afield, have already been mentioned, but he was equally the product of a less exalted cultural milieu, that of the ordinary people of Glamorgan. He was often moved to criticize this traditional way of life, its roughness and its lack of care for higher things. He informed William Owen Pughe in 1802 that his daughter Peggy was accompanying him to London, where she would 'see some things of which she can never know any thing in this obscure and low village'.[47] During a journey over Pumlumon in the summer of 1799 his thoughts were decidedly at variance with Rousseauesque ideas of the elevated nature of simple country people: 'Ignorance and brutality are always hand in hand. That imaginary amiable simplicity so much talked of by no great philosophers that they suppose attends ignorance I have never had the good fortune to meet with.'[48]

Such derogatory remarks are in tune with an important strand in eighteenth-century thought. So common were such criticisms that Thomas Gray had been moved to defend simple people in a poem destined to become one of the best-known literary works of the period, his 'Elegy in a Country Churchyard'. Welsh writers, too, had been part of the critical chorus. Poor though his own material circumstances were, Goronwy Owen was an intellectual snob of the first order and declared proudly that folk poetry was the province of 'y llangciau tywod a'r merched nyddu' ('the sand boys and the

---

[46] Williams: *IM*, pp. 73–4.
[47] Ibid., p. 65.
[48] Ibid.

spinning girls') and that he had no regard for such worthless products of rustic culture.[49]

However, Iolo was a creature whose enthusiasms led him in many directions, some of which were apparently contradictory. One of the great driving forces in his life was his love for *mwynder Morgannwg* ('the gentleness of Glamorgan'). The life of Glamorgan, both the Vale and Uplands, in the eighteenth and early nineteenth centuries, was rich in folk-poetry, tales and customs, and much of its tradition was expressed in its lively dialect, which Iolo described as 'Silurian' and which he lovingly recorded. Griffith John Williams, our principal authority on Iolo, summed up this aspect of Glamorgan life in a passage whose lyrical enthusiasm conveys the infectious nature of Iolo's passion for a Glamorgan story partly created, or at least embellished, by him, but rooted in a reality which later scholars have thoroughly documented:[50]

> hwn yw'r bywyd y meddyliai Iolo amdano wrth sôn am yr hen Forgannwg lawen gynt, gwlad lle y cedwid yr hen arferion, gwlad y taplasau haf, a'r gwylbmabsantau, a'r fedwen haf, a'r pebyll, a'r ddawns forisgaidd, gwlad o bobl lawen, haelionus, gerddgar, lle yr oedd y beirdd yn canu am lawenydd bywyd ym mhentrefydd y Fro ac yn hendrefydd y Blaenau.[51]

> (this is the life that Iolo had in mind when he talked of the old joyful Glamorgan of olden days, a country which preserved the old customs, the country of summer fairs, and parish wakes, and the maypole, and the tents, and the morris dance, a country of merry, generous, music-loving people where the poets sang of the joy of life in the villages of the Vale and the homesteads of the Uplands.)

Iolo described in his manuscripts the dialect, tunes, folk poetry, pastimes and customs of his native territory and bequeathed to later generations an account of a rich aspect of eighteenth-century life which, even in his own time, was swiftly disappearing. It would be simplistic to claim that the inherent seriousness of Calvinistic Methodism and other forms of religious Dissent brought about the demise of this life, but there is no doubt that changing moral and religious habits of mind hastened the end of a culture which was the product of long centuries of a simpler and more primitive way of shaping reactions to life's basic rhythms and experiences.

It is one of the more remarkable aspects of Iolo's vision that he sought to preserve and record the details of this culture in a structured and scholarly way. Others before him had interested themselves in recording diverse aspects of everyday life in Wales, among them John Jones of Gellilyfdy, Edward Lhuyd

---

[49] J. H. Davies (ed.), *The Letters of Goronwy Owen* (Cardiff, 1924), p. 140.
[50] For a scholarly, but lively, account, see Allan James, *Diwylliant Gwerin Morgannwg* (Llandysul, 2002).
[51] Williams: *IM*, p. 65.

and Lewis Morris, but Iolo was the first to propose an orderly programme of research.[52] His desire to establish a learned academy included the furtherance of such folk studies, but his ideas remained unheeded in his own lifetime.

Although the appeal to this cultural past was undoubtedly nostalgic and Romantic in nature, it must also be remembered that Iolo brought to bear upon it a rational and scholarly approach. The scholarly and learned part of Iolo's nature, like the Romantic part, also had Glamorgan roots. Early in his career he came into contact with a circle of scholar-poets in the more northerly parts of Glamorgan, men like Lewis Hopkin, John Bradford, Rhys Morgan, Dafydd Nicolas and Edward Evan. It was in the company of craftsmen and farmers such as these that Iolo encountered the eighteenth-century literary renaissance, for these were men who devoted themselves to the study and rediscovery of classical Welsh poetry and who sought to emulate past masters. They also devoted themselves to the study of the Welsh language, antiquities and local history. Close to his home lived two pioneering lexicographers, Thomas Richards of Coychurch and John Walters of Llandough, near Cowbridge, who not only encouraged Iolo's passion for Welsh words but also his serious study of Latin and French.[53]

The culture of Glamorgan, then, offered Iolo an intellectual present and a future as well as a romanticized past; a remarkable window on Wales, certainly, but also pathways which led him to the tumultuous world of eighteenth-century European culture. It may well be that in the coming together, and the occasional clashing, of these various strands, in the fusion of the age-old and the new, the imaginative and the rational, fertile ground was created for the development of Iolo's enormously complex and diverse ideas and activities.

[52] Lewis: *IM*, pp. 146–7.
[53] Richard M. Crowe, 'Thomas Richards a John Walters: Athrawon Geiriadurol Iolo Morganwg' in Hywel Teifi Edwards (ed.), *Llynfi ac Afan, Garw ac Ogwr* (Llandysul, 1998), pp. 227–51.

3

'The Manuscripts': The Culture and Politics of Forgery in Central Europe

R. J. W. EVANS

Since this chapter is not directly about Iolo Morganwg at all, we must begin by identifying relevant aspects of Iolo's work to be borne in mind for the comparative purposes which the following case-study seeks to serve. Iolo made up or doctored, for literary and historical effect, texts that were roughly 'medieval' in date. His fabrications were plausible: Wales possessed authentic ancient lyrics and epics, even if Iolo thought she needed more. They were topical, satisfying to Romantic notions of the decades around 1800 and the contemporary vogue for values of pristine civility. They were emulative: following other models, and called forth by other kinds of – more or less – venerable source which they challenged. In particular, they responded to English dominance (or to a perception of it), though Iolo belonged to a largely bilingual culture. They were clever and successful, attracting little contemporary suspicion; full exposure came much later, only from the 1890s onwards, and left lasting confusion over how much had been faked. Even now it is hard to tell truth from fiction, as at times it must have been for Iolo himself; historically, the two became conflated in genesis and impact. Not least, Iolo's inventions were formative: they created channels and themes for national self-expression.[1]

We shall find central-European parallels for all these features. The reason for that lies in shared patterns of European intellectual development beginning in the period when Iolo was a youth. Two sources of it – to set the scene in utmost brevity – stand out for the years around 1760: the one British in origin and the other Continental. The first is the Ossianic corpus, that supposed rendering, by its editor James Macpherson, of an antique oral tradition, in an exotic vernacular, which had come under pressure from the dominant English language and culture. The society of Fingal, Ossian and the rest, primitive but noble, quickly made a huge impact, not only in Britain, but also abroad.[2] It

---

[1] IMChY; Williams: IM, passim; Lewis: IM, pp. 39–73.

[2] See Howard Gaskill (ed.), Ossian Revisited (Edinburgh, 1991), Fiona Stafford and Howard Gaskill (eds.), From Gaelic to Romantic: Ossianic Translations (Amsterdam, 1998), and Howard Gaskill (ed.), The Reception of Ossian in Europe (London, 2004).

encouraged a search for, or invention of, other folk-songs, ballads and the like, whose most famous immediate product were the verses attributed to one 'Thomas Rowley' by the young Thomas Chatterton. The authenticity of the Ossian poems was impugned from the start by significant critics; not least, the Welsh reaction remained distinctly guarded. Gradually, and hastened by the exposure of the ill-fated Chatterton, the probity of Macpherson fell under a cloud. His defenders could point to the undoubted literary qualities of the texts – and use that as an assurance that Macpherson could hardly be responsible (a trope we shall encounter again). Moreover, they could adduce the complex processes of transmission of such writings to fend off hostile conclusions, even if no persuasive original materials in Gaelic could be presented. Still, by the 1800s, in the light of a forensic investigation of Macpherson's posthumous papers, faith in Britain that the poems were at least partially genuine ebbed away fast. Yet, elsewhere, the cult was just reaching its height.[3]

Throughout these years there was an enormous German enthusiasm for Ossian, stretching via the likes of Goethe as far as Vienna, where the Catholic priest Michael Denis issued a multi-volume translation.[4] But Germany had her own equivalents, the most important of which was the *Nibelungenlied*. First published almost simultaneously with Ossian, these dramatic fables with their shadowy (pre-)historic associations helped feed a fashion for folk-songs and ballads, and contributed to a search for the roots of popular culture which was most eloquently espoused at the philosophical level by Johann Gottfried Herder (a close contemporary of Iolo). The vogue for the *Nibelungenlied*, too, reached a climax after 1800, when it assumed the guise of a proto-national text, with numerous editions (one of them actually designed for the pockets of German soldiers fighting the French). At that time it was established, following similar claims for the authorship of the Homeric corpus, that the stories of the Nibelungen represented the work of several hands, fashioned by generations of ballad singers.[5] The *Nibelungenlied* is, of course, genuine: over the years, some

---

[3]   For example, Octave J. Delepierre, *Supercheries littéraires, pastiches, suppositions d'auteur, dans les lettres et dans les arts* (London, 1872), pp. 116–22. Cf. James A. Farrer, *Literary Forgeries* (London, 1907), pp. 145–60.

[4]   Rudolf Tombo, *Ossian in Germany* (New York, 1901), lists several translations for most years through into the 1830s. Uwe Böker, 'The Marketing of Macpherson: The International Book Trade and the First Phase of German Ossian Reception' in Gaskill (ed.), *Ossian Revisited*, pp. 73–93; F. J. Lamport, 'Goethe, Ossian and Werther' and H. Gaskill, '"Blast, rief Cuchullin. . . !": J. M. R. Lenz and Ossian' in Stafford and Gaskill (eds.), *From Gaelic to Romantic*, pp. 97–118.

[5]   Josef Körner, *Nibelungenforschungen der deutschen Romantik* (Leipzig, 1911), (p. 192 for the 'Feld- und Zeltausgabe'); Otfrid Ehrismann, *Das Nibelungenlied in Deutschland: Studien zur Rezeption des Nibelungenlieds von der Mitte des 18. Jahrhunderts bis zum Ersten Weltkrieg* (München, 1975). Cf., more generally, John E. Härd, *Das Nibelungenepos: Wertung und Wirkung von der Romantik bis zur Gegenwart* (Tübingen, 1996); Joachim Heinzle et al., *Die Nibelungen: Sage – Epos – Mythos* (Wiesbaden, 2003).

thirty medieval manuscripts have been found. But that was less evident at the time, and discrepancies abounded. The *Lied* could, so it appeared, be dated back roughly to the year 1300. But what did such authenticity mean, in the age of Ossian and other transcribed oral records? And if it was important to be authentic, could that not be contrived?

Indeed, much genuine uncertainty existed as to the yardstick for validity and truth within this heady world of dubious texts in the fledgeling nineteenth century. Many viewed 'translation', across languages or within different forms of the same one, as an original and creative activity. As yet, palaeographical skills were at best limited, and views of ancient history distinctly shaky. But one thing had already become apparent from the example of Ossian (and it was stressed by Herder too): all nations were equal in this quest, and small obscure ones might in due course even have an advantage. The classic case is Finland, where Elias Lönnrot's adaptation of folk legends from Karelia into the *Kalevala* by 1835 – over 20,000 lines in 50 cantos, though few could read it in Finnish yet – involved both the discovery and the invention of a national treasure.[6] The concurrent efforts of Théodore Hersart de La Villemarqué in Brittany, and the nature of their authenticity, will be discussed in another volume in this series.[7]

However, as Breton and Finnish patriots knew, it was large neighbouring nations which usually led the way. Let us consider for a moment the French and Russian examples. French enthusiasm for Ossian, and for the bardic tradition generally, distracted during the 1790s, soon revived in a post-revolutionary antiquarian fervour and yielded some curious fruits. Most puzzling were the elegant compositions attributed to a late medieval poetess, Clotilde de Surville, first published in 1803. Suspect from the outset, they nevertheless retained their place in the canon for eighty years. Meanwhile they were further embroidered by Charles Nodier, himself not only a literary inventor and tale-teller, but the founder of the modern professional study of plagiarism.[8]

More significantly for us, from the same part of France as the supposititious Clotilde, and on the same press in the same year as her verses, Antoine Fabre d'Olivet introduced samples of the work of thirteenth-century troubadours, with his own translation, allegedly from a manuscript posted to him by one of

[6] Elias Lönnrot, *The Kalevala: An Epic Poem after Oral Tradition*, trans. and intro. Keith Bosley (Oxford, 1989).

[7] H. de La Villemarqué, *Barzaz-Breiz: Chants populaires de la Bretagne*, with an introduction by Y.-F. Kemener (Paris, 1999). Mary-Ann Constantine is preparing a volume, entitled '*The Truth against the World*', in this series.

[8] Charles Nodier, *Questions de littérature légale: Du plagiat, de la supposition d'auteurs, des supercheries qui ont rapport aux livres*, ed. J.-F. Jeandillou (Genève, 2003), esp. pp. 75 ff. on Clotilde. The work had two editions, anonymously in 1812, and in 1828. Delepierre, *Supercheries littéraires*, pp. 98–108 (still thinking Clotilde genuine). Farrer, *Literary Forgeries*, pp. 250–82. Jean-François Jeandillou, *Supercheries littéraires: La vie et l'oeuvre des auteurs supposés* (Paris, 1989), pp. 45–77.

their descendants. Fabre takes us into his confidence: he wishes to 'laisser à la sagacité du lecteur à juger quel degré de confiance méritent les manuscrits que je me suis occupé de traduire' ('leave it to the wisdom of the reader to judge the reliability of the manuscripts I have taken upon myself to translate'); but is confident that they can 'devenir pour les Troubadours du midi ce que le livre des poésies d'Ossian a été pour les Bardes du nord' ('do for the Troubadours of the Midi what the poems of Ossian did for the Bards of the north'). He proclaims them as the remains of a culture overwhelmed by the intolerance and feudality of the French state; and, however spurious his texts, they announced the revival of what became the 'Occitan' movement (a word which Fabre invented) of the Felibrige.[9]

Then there came the Parisian literary hoaxes of the 1820s, especially those perpetrated by the youthful Prosper Mérimée. He first astonished the public with the sparkling *oeuvre* of a hitherto unknown Spanish dramatist called Clara Gazul; then, almost immediately, he trumped this with the outlandish doings of an eminent guzla-virtuoso and folk-singer from the Balkans, Hyacinthe Maglanovich.[10] Both Iberia and the east of Europe afforded fertile soil for the Romantic imagination, and the latter is important in the present context. Nodier, too, had connections to the Slavs and a penchant for their lore and myth. As such, both he and Mérimée were part of a much larger phenomenon, spurred on by the writings of Herder and promoting the image of the primitive, simple, but vibrant and guileless traditions of the Slavs. The legacy was ambiguous enough: were the ancestors whom it celebrated peaceable or warlike? Yet it helped stimulate a massive local output, which raised its own questions about authenticity: the Serbian ballads 'collected' by Vuk Karadžić and others are the most celebrated examples.[11]

Behind this vogue for Slavdom stood the enhanced role of Russia in the Europe of Napoleon and after. Here, too, there were new legends to cultivate, about the people and their leaders, about heroes and villains in a more and more explicitly national pantheon. Most acclaimed was the early epic called the 'Lay of Igor's Campaign', which recounted, with poetic fire and sensitivity, the exploits of a late twelfth-century warlord, in a redaction apparently written down sometime around 1400. Discovered in 1792, the text was published eight years later. But then the key manuscript perished in the great fire of Moscow after Borodino. Thus, doubts about the text's genuineness persisted (and its first editors had, at the very least, furnished it with a generous dose of Ossianic

---

[9] A. Fabre d'Olivet, *Le Troubadour: Poésies occitaniques du XIIIe siècle*, ed. M. Barral (Nîmes, 1997), esp. intro. (quoted pp. ii, vii). Cf. Jeandillou, *Supercheries littéraires*, pp. 17–33.

[10] Jeandillou, *Supercheries littéraires*, pp. 140–82.

[11] Vuk Karadžić (ed.), *Narodne srpske pjesme* (4 vols., Lipsci, 1823–33). The first, smaller, editions appeared in Vienna in 1814–15. Cf. Duncan Wilson, *The Life and Times of Vuk Stefanović Karadžić, 1787–1864: Literacy, Literature, and National Independence in Serbia* (Oxford, 1970).

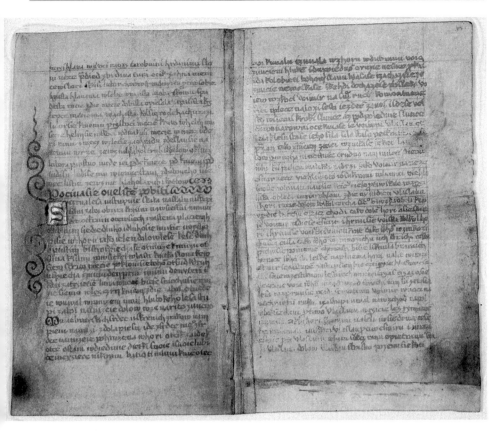

Fig. 5 The 'Manuscript of Dvůr Králové' was discovered by Vác[es]lav Hanka in September 1817 in a tower of the decanal church of St John the Baptist in Dvůr Králové (Königinhof, in north-east Bohemia).

sentimentality). Yet stories about Prince Igor and his kind now supplied a remarkable boost to confidence and interest in Slavonic antiquities as a whole.[12]

The Czechs' past belonged here too: they had been a leading sector in the wider Slav heritage ever since the pioneering mission of St Cyril and St Methodius to the Bohemian lands. Already by the early twelfth century they had a chronicler in Latin: Kosmas, who recorded tales about the country's first ruler Krok, his daughter Princess Libuše, her ploughman husband Přemysl, and

[12] For the background, see D. Likhachev (ed.), *A History of Russian Literature, 11th–17th Centuries* (Moscow, 1989), pp. 134–61; Yu. A. Andreyev (ed.), *Slovo o polku Igoreve* (Leningrad, 1990). Cf. Roman Jakobson, 'The Puzzles of the Igor Tale on the 150th Anniversary of its First Edition', *Speculum*, XXVII (1952), 43–66. In a further twist, Edward L. Keenan, in *Josef Dobrovský and the Origins of the Igor Tale* (Cambridge, MA, 2003), has now made a circumstantial but outré case for Dobrovský – shortly to be introduced – as the creator of this MS.

the rest. Then, from the fourteenth century there were annals in Czech, notably the one attributed (wrongly) to a certain 'Dalimil', which embroidered these stories in a national direction, with fierce censure of the growing German presence in Bohemia. Later fabulous accretions reached their peak in the more sophisticated but highly credulous narration of Václav Hájek (the Theophilus Evans of his people), whose *Kronika česká* of 1543 constituted a favourite repository of Czech folk legends. Meanwhile the Hussite wars had confirmed Bohemia as a state dominated by her own Slavonic culture and language.

Yet the Czechs were also always, in relation to other Slavs, in some sense 'westernized': for all the censure of a Dalimil, Bohemia formed part of the Holy Roman Empire and Teutonic influences were strong. They intensified further when, firstly, the Reformation tended to assimilate the Hussite legacy within a larger body of predominantly Lutheran Protestantism; and then, secondly, a failed revolt brought Bohemia's more wholesale incorporation within an international Catholic state ruled by the Habsburg emperors. Subsumed within the Austrian political system and German culture, those Czechs who preserved some form of national consciousness – a small and disparate grouping – clung to the glories of their earlier history.

Only in the age of Enlightenment did the pendulum begin to swing back. In the context of a general movement for reform in Austria, which was largely led from Bohemia, patriotic intellectuals and nobles in the country set up fresh cultural institutions. These culminated by the second decade of the nineteenth century in plans for a new National Museum in Prague, whose collections would embody the heritage of both ethnicities, German and Czech. At the same time the fortunes of the latter started to revive. That involved – so typically for smaller nations of Europe at that time – a modest re(dis)covery of the Czech language: it benefited from a chair at the Charles University, even from legislation for its employment in some secondary schools. The pivotal figure in this process was Josef Dobrovský, the doyen of international Slavonic studies. From the turn of the century Dobrovský found himself imparting his skills to a circle of pupils, mostly from simple rural backgrounds, members of a first generation of patriots who would be not just Bohemians, but avowedly Czechs. They included Josef Jungmann, subsequently a great grammarian, and a painter and art-restorer, František Horčička, as well as a trio all born in 1789–91: Josef Linda, Václav Svoboda, and Vác[es]lav Hanka. This last, in particular, the son of a peasant who doubled as innkeeper, early began to stake a claim for himself as poet and critic.

Dobrovský remained critical, cool, and cosmopolitan, sceptical about the longer-term survival of the Czech tongue (he himself wrote and mostly spoke in German). But his disciples were captivated by the new Romantic mood. Hájek's fantasies about Bohemia's past had been exploded in the 1760s by a learned cleric; yet his charm lived on in amended form: even Herder had reworked his story of Libuše. Alongside editions of old Czech verse, Hanka translated Serb ballads and the lay of Igor; Linda was absorbed by Ossian. All this comprised a parochial and obscure Slavonic enterprise as yet; but it could perhaps be the means to a larger end: a challenge to the resurgent hegemonic culture of a state fortified by its military encounter with the French Revolution and Napoleon. The agenda was thus a little akin to that of a certain radical Welsh stonemason. The dreamers in Prague set themselves against a Germandom in full romantic flood and buoyed, in an era where priority of civilization had come to mean so much, by masterpieces like the *Nibelungenlied*. The stage was set for the most spectacular, protracted and lastingly significant literary forgery in modern European history.

On 16 September 1817 Hanka was visiting friends, two of them clerics, at the country town of Dvůr Králové, north-east of the capital and not far from his birthplace. The conversation turned to some curios, arrows from the Hussite wars with feathers cut from old parchment, stored in a strongroom under the church tower, and Hanka was invited to examine them. Accounts – some later given under oath, as we shall see in due course – differ in their details, but they agree that he emerged from the vault with a different parchment, a manuscript which, on closer inspection, proved to contain medieval Czech poems, apparently fragments of a much larger corpus. Some told epic tales of eleventh- to thirteenth-century military heroes, mostly victorious over Germans, while others were lyrical, brief and affecting. The following day Hanka reported excitedly on his find to Dobrovský. It 'exuded the spirit of Homer', he said. The master shared his student's enthusiasm, and promptly incorporated a glowing reference in his forthcoming history of Czech literature. This 'Manuscript of Dvůr Králové' (*Rukopis králo[vé]dvorský* (hereafter *RK*)), was bestowed upon Hanka by a grateful municipality, and rushed into print by the beginning of 1819.[13]

Meanwhile, by curious chance, another early Czech manuscript had emerged. Sent anonymously late in 1818 to a sympathetic aristocrat associated with the founding of the new museum, it was accompanied by an anonymous letter (in German), which claimed that the text had been discovered in some (unidentified) castle where it was in danger from its owner, one of numerous landowners who despised all things Czech. This text was more sensational still: much shorter (only 120 lines in all), written in green ink, in a strange jumble of minuscule and majuscule without division into words, it told of a far earlier, more shadowy age. It related the judgment of Libuše (whence its original designation, *Libušin soud*), a fresh instalment in the life of this first matriarch of

---

[13] The circumstances, and all those who may have been involved, are reconstructed from all available evidence (including sworn testimony later assembled for court proceedings: cf. below) in Miroslav Ivanov, *Tajemství RKZ* (Praha, 1969), pp. 16–92.

Bohemia, when she held court on the rock of Vyšehrad in an inheritance
dispute. The work cast much light on the primal practices of Czech justice,
political counsel and communal organization; it confirmed the wisdom and
peaceableness of early Slavonic social organization. This manuscript, which
subsequently – as again we shall see in due course – came to be known as the
'Manuscript of Zelená Hora' (*Rukopis zelenohorský* (hereafter *RZ*)), was quite
simply the oldest written record of any Slav nation, and older than anything
equivalent in German.

RKZ[14] aroused vast interest at home and abroad. They were not just historic
documents, but almost universally acknowledged as masterpieces of medieval
creative literature, with their intense depictions of nature and sophisticated play
of emotion. Immediately translated into Russian, they made a particular
impact in other Slav lands. The *arriviste* Hanka was decorated by the tsar, and
efforts were made to secure chairs there for him and Czech colleagues; he
received a further prize of 3,000 roubles in 1839.[15] But the West was hardly
less impressed, thanks to Svoboda's German version – praised by Goethe – and
then renderings, indirectly, into English by John Bowring (who had connections, though only industrial ones, with Iolo's Glamorgan).[16] At home *RKZ*
helped to consolidate the beginnings of a new Czech establishment in Prague,
with Hanka as librarian of the museum where the manuscripts were now prize
possessions. One of its leading members was the young and recently arrived
František Palacký, who became secretary and editor of the museum journal
(issued in two languages at first, but only the Czech one prospered).

<hr>

[14] In what follows I shall use the standard Czech abbreviations of the two Manuscripts: '*RK*'
and '*RZ*', plus '*RKZ*' for both together. There is a huge literature on them, but mostly in
Czech and (during the nineteenth century) in German (where *RK* is known as the
Königinhofer Handschrift and *RZ* as the *Grünberger Handschrift*). However, English and French
compendia on literary forgery, hoax etc., hardly mention them, so I make no apology for the
narrative thread in what follows. The two best introductions, by coincidence (though not
wholly so: cf. below) appeared in Prague in the same year, 1969. They could not be more
different. M. Otruba (ed.), *Rukopisy Královédvorský a Zelenohorský: dnešní stav poznání* (hereafter
Dnešní stav), is matter-of-fact and bloodless; it includes texts, facsimiles and an excellent bibliography. Ivanov, *Tajemství*, is cast as a gripping detective story, even with an exciting and not
implausible denouement; though unannotated, it is steeped in the known sources, and even
uncovers new ones.

[15] V. A. Frantsev, *Ocherki po istorii cheshkago vozrozhdeniya. Russko-cheshkiya svyazi kontsa XVIII.
i pervoi poloviny XIX. st.* (Varshava, 1902), pp. 72 ff, 129–92 on chairs, 255 ff., on roubles; idem,
Pis'ma k V. Gankě iz slavjanskich zemel' (Varshava, 1905).

[16] Goethe: *Sämmtliche Werke* (40 vols., Stuttgart/Tübingen, 1840), xxxii: 406 ff., xxxiii: 321;
Cheskian Anthology: Being a History of the Poetical Literature of Bohemia with Translated Specimens
(London, 1832). Bowring founded the Llynvi ironworks at 'Bowrington' (Maesteg): George
F. Bartle, *An Old Radical and his Brood: A Portrait of Sir John Bowring* (London, 1994), pp. 60 ff.
Cf. also James Naughton, 'The Reception in Nineteenth-century England of Czech
Literature and of the Czech National Revival' (unpublished University of Cambridge Ph.D.
thesis, 1977); abstracted in E. Schmidt-Hartmann and S. B. Winters (eds.), *Grossbritannien, die
USA und die böhmischen Länder, 1848–1938* (München, 1991), pp. 107–17.

Nominated historiographer of the Bohemian estates, the protégé of noble sponsors of the burgeoning national movement, Palacký began his life's work on a history whose conceptual foundations were deeply penetrated by *RKZ*. 'With the discovery of *RK*', he wrote, 'a new unimagined world opened before us, as the bewitching power of sounds unusual, yet familiar to our spirit, throbbed in our hearts.'[17] Palacký would soon be joined by the Slovak Šafařik, whose pioneering work on Slav antiquities likewise owed much to the Manuscripts, as did the linguistics and lexicography of Jungmann, who was convinced that *RKZ* afforded proof of a native bardic tradition.[18]

There was one fly, or rodent, in the ointment. Dobrovský had immediately smelt a rat with *RZ*. He was suspicious of its peculiar palaeography, but even more of its philology; in fact, he thought it a crude fake – and a piece of treachery – by one or more of his disciples, based on the (genuine) *RK*. At first he kept his doubts private, though he did communicate them to his colleague Bartolomej Kopitar, the court librarian in Vienna. Then, when his advice to delay the publication of *RZ* was overridden, he expostulated openly with all the force of a savant scorned about this 'flagrant fraud by a rascal'. A painful altercation ensued, with Svoboda defending *RKZ* as sublime creations of the Czech spirit almost irrespective of their date: even if *RZ* were a fake, its creator would deserve admiration as a 'second Chatterton'.[19] Dobrovský, embittered at the imputation that he was less patriotic than his critics, was bullied into silence and isolation. This brief preliminary phase of the controversy concluded with his death in 1829. But its themes would return.

The second phase of the story of the Manuscripts, from the 1840s to the 1870s, saw *RKZ* as much integral parts of the national culture of the Czechs as eisteddfodau and the Gorsedd became in Wales. Palacký and Šafařik produced a critical edition in 1840 of the 'oldest monuments of the Bohemian tongue', while Hanka issued numerous versions in Czech and other languages.[20] Importantly the Manuscripts, as historical documents, were not subject to censorship; hence they could feature in school textbooks. They 'decided our national consciousness', as one future leader recalled: 'once we read [*RK*] we felt deep in our hearts that we were Czechs'.[21] Thus they added powerful stimulus to the revolutionary political movement, led by Palacký, which swept Bohemia in 1848–9; and they provided solace in subsequent adversity.

[17] Jiří Kořalka, *František Palacký, 1798–1876: životopis* (Praha, 1999), supersedes all previous accounts of Palacký's life. Quoted: F. M. Bartoš, *Rukopisy královédvorský a zelenohorský* (Praha, 1946), p. 46.

[18] Josef Jungmann, *Historie literatury české* (2nd edn., Praha, 1849), p. 8.

[19] Bartoš, *Rukopisy*, pp. 39 ff.

[20] *Die ältesten Denkmäler der böhmischen Sprache* (Prag, 1840), comprises *RZ* and fragments; *RK* was due to appear in a parallel edition, but (suspiciously?) never did so. The *Polyglotta Králodvorského rukopisu*, issued by Hanka in 1852, with reprints in 1872 and 1876, contained full or partial translations into twelve foreign languages, as well as into modern Czech.

[21] Hermenegild Jireček, cited in Otruba (ed.), *Dnešní stav*, pp. 176 ff.

Correspondingly deeper mistrust of *RKZ* now spread among opponents of Czech national aspirations. It found a handle in some further newly unearthed codices, intrinsically linked to the Manuscripts, whose credentials seemed much more fragile. Two single-leaf texts shared material with them: the 'Song of Vyšehrad' (*Píseň vyšehradská*), allegedly found by Linda just before the discoveries of 1817–18; and the 'Love Song of King Wenceslas' (*Milostná píseň krále Václava*), which turned up in a Prague library just afterwards and actually contained a copy of one of the *RK* poems on the back. Then there were glosses to a medieval vocabulary book, 'Mater Verborum'; Czech interlinear translations of part of St John's gospel and a psalter; weird attributions in an early illuminated manuscript; and, finally, another Libuše text, unearthed as late as 1849. All these were problematical, to say the least, and widely recognized as such (when tested chemically, some showed paint instead of ink); and almost all could be linked to Hanka, especially the 'Prophecy of Libuše' (*Libušino proroctví*), the crudest of all.

From these it was a shorter step to call *RZ*, and even *RK*, into question. Kopitar, from a safe distance, had already pointed the finger at Hanka. German scholars abroad began to do so in the 1840s. During the following decade, elements in the embattled local germanophone regime sought to subvert the message of the Manuscripts, though the Prague chief of police was hard pressed to convince Vienna. Then, anonymous accusations in a journal edited by David Kuh led to libel proceedings in the name of the ageing Hanka. Thus the circumstances of his discovery came under a spotlight, with testimony from those who had (or claimed to have) been present, including depositions that *RK* had been seen in the church at Dvůr Králové before 1817. The court found for the prosecution; but Kuh avoided prison, apparently through the intervention of the minister of justice.[22] This bizarre and rather tasteless affair (for Kuh's Jewishness also came into play) raised the temperature considerably. It was by no means a straight ethnic contest: most of the German press in Bohemia supported the antiquity of the Manuscripts, while many Czechs thought the sentence on Kuh severe. And what of the droll spectacle of Palacký, who despised Hanka personally, regarding him as a slovenly, sly and unscrupulous guardian of the nation's literary treasures, arguing that the librarian, although much given to petty forgery, was quite incapable of achievements like *RKZ*![23] He could not, it appeared, even *transcribe* them properly.

In the aftermath, German Slavists moved to a more targeted offensive. In the

---

[22] František Roubík, 'Účast policie v útoku na Rukopisy roku 1858' in J. Klik (ed.), *Od pravěku k dnešku: sborník prací z dějin československých k šedesátým narozeninám Josefa Pekaře* (2 vols., Praha, 1930), pp. 435–49. Cf. A. N. Pypin, *Moi zametki* (Moskva, 1910), pp. 219 ff.

[23] Bartoš, *Rukopisy*, pp. 78 ff.; Ivanov, *Tajemství*, pp. 101 ff. Hanka's own (acknowledged) poetic *oeuvre* is hardly sparkling: *Hankowy pjsně* (4th edn., 1841), an expansion to 83 from the original (1815) 12 'songs'.

very first issue of the *Historische Zeitschrift*, launched at Munich in 1859, a rising young classicist, Max Büdinger, repudiated *RKZ* in no uncertain terms.[24] Then there was Julius Fejfalik, a Czech-speaking German from Moravia, a kind of Thomas Stephens (of *The Literature of the Kymry* fame). Fejfalik divined that the whole mood of the Manuscripts, especially their nationalism and their depiction of pagan Slavdom, rang false for their supposed period of composition; and he added, on philological grounds, a more palpable claim – worrying for those who prided themselves on *RKZ*'s equivalence to Homer or the *Nibelungenlied* – that they must be predominantly the work of a single author. Moreover, Bohemia's best-known historian after Palacký, Tomek, now at last, through a series of accidents, established the provenance of *Libušin soud*, including its putative connection with the castle of Zelená Hora in western Bohemia: another finding which – despite Tomek's absolute commitment to the cause – would weaken defence of both the Manuscripts, since if *RZ* had already been removed from its store-room in 1817, as Tomek seemed to show,[25] it could not have plagiarized *RK*, and what then of the striking similarities between the two texts?

Thus doubts about *RZ* became inseparable from those about *RK*. Even Šafařík began to have some: they contributed to his depression, attempted suicide and death in 1861. Hanka, who died the same year, kept silent until the end. Yet Palacký reasserted the validity of (almost) the whole corpus of manuscripts, with an asperity whetted by the crude national hubris of some of his German antagonists.[26] Besides, whereas Büdinger emigrated from Austria and Fejfalik went to an early grave, a new vintage of vigorous defenders, including Šafařík's son-in-law Josef Jireček and his brother, presented *RKZ* as central to the whole Slavonic tradition in the country.[27] Now, with the arrival of constitutional government (before long Jireček would be a minister in Vienna), Czech culture flourished as never since the Middle Ages, with *RKZ* central to its self-confidence. Throughout the greatly expanded school system, capped in 1882 with a separate university when the ancient Carolinum was divided on ethnic lines, children and students were taught that the Manuscripts

---

[24] Max Büdinger, 'Die Königinhofer Handschrift und ihre Schwestern', *Historische Zeitschrift*, 1 (1859), 127–52, building on a briefer denunciation by the noted palaeographer Wattenbach.

[25] W. W. Tomek, 'Svědectví o nalezení Libušina soudu', *Časopis Musea Království Českého*, 33 (1859), 28–57, 102–6. Cf. Ivanov, *Tajemství*, pp. 222 ff. This part of the story is too tangled even to introduce here.

[26] Kořalka, *Palacký*, pp. 383–8 (Büdinger wrote, for example, of 'das Unding einer čechischen Nationalität') ('the absurdity of a Czech nationality').

[27] Josef and Hermenegild Jireček, *Die Echtheit der Königinhofer Handschrift kritisch nachgewiesen* (Prag, 1862), a detailed and intemperate reply to Fejfalik. Eidem, *Die altböhmischen Gedichte der Grünberger und Königinhofer Handschrift* (Prag, 1879): 'In Wesenheit Fragen über das slawische Kulturwesen sind, von deren Lösung das Endurtheil abhängt' ('In essence it is questions of the nature of Slavonic culture on whose solution the final judgement depends') (p. ii).

were finer than Homer.[28] The most salient institutional focus for Czech pride was the new National Theatre, financed (like the nascent University of Wales at just the same time) by popular subscription. In 1881 it opened (and after a fire in 1883 it reopened) with Bedřich Smetana's opera *Libuše*, a kind of paraphrase of *RZ*.[29] The composer had written it in readiness a decade earlier (before his *Má vlast*, which also draws on the Vyšehrad motif). Simultaneously, Richard Wagner was completing his *Ring of the Nibelungen* cycle and Aleksandr Borodin was beginning his *Prince Igor*.

The third phase of the controversy was the most intense and decisive: in fact, it witnessed a remarkable transformation within a few years. The death of Palacký in 1876 released a pent-up flood of misgivings from within the Slav and Czech camp. Influential critics from outside, like Jagić and Petrushevich, built on the earlier forthright condemnation of *RKZ* by the Slovene Kopitar. But the real shift took place at home, among those who had until that point been true believers. Firstly, Antonín Vašek delivered a full-frontal philological assault on Hanka. Then Alois Vojtěch Šembera experienced a similar conversion. The scales fell from his eyes, he tells us, when he read that first letter from Hanka to Dobrovský: for how could the man have deciphered and grasped such recalcitrant texts so soon, unless he possessed prior knowledge?[30] These men were incontestable patriots: Vašek was father to one of the greatest Czech poets; Šembera spent decades fighting for Slav culture in Vienna. Yet both were hounded by the press in a vicious polemical campaign; and both died, probably prematurely, in the course of the next three years.

One of the defenders was a rising star of the reconstituted university, the philologist Gebauer (author of a vindication of the codex from St John). Within a few years, however, he, too, had changed his mind. The catalyst was the arrival in Prague of Tomáš G. Masaryk as professor of philosophy and editor of a new university journal entitled *Athenaeum*. Still an outsider trained in Vienna (where he had experienced the persecution of his friend Šembera), Masaryk directed a three-pronged assault in 1886. While Gebauer minutely reviewed the circumstances of *RK* in the light of Hanka's known proclivity to forgery of other documents, Masaryk himself made the wider case for the probability that the Manuscripts were a romantic hoax. Then Jaroslav Goll, at the head of a positivist-influenced new phalanx of professional historians,

---

[28] Bartoš, *Rukopisy*, pp. 10 ff.

[29] Mirko Očadlík, *Libuše: vznik Smetanovy zpěvohry* (Praha, 1939). Smetana could have had part of the Libuše story from Kosmas, Hájek etc.; but there is no doubt that *RZ* gave the subject its full national aura.

[30] A. Vašek, *Filologický důkaz, že Rukopis královédvorský a zelenohorský, též zlomek Evangelia Sv. Jana, jsou podvržená díla Václava Hanky* (Brno, 1879); Alois V. Šembera, *Libušin soud, domnělá nejstarší památka řeči české jest podvržen, též zlomek Evangelium Sv. Jana* (Vídeň, 1879); idem, *Die Königinhofer Handschrift als eine Fälschung nachgewiesen* (Wien, 1882), esp. pp. 1–8 on Hanka's letter.

weighed in decisively by tackling those sections of *RKZ* most vulnerable to source criticism: the anachronistic and unsupported evidence in *Libušin soud*; the lays known as 'Oldřich' (about the recapture of Prague from the Poles *c.*1204), 'Beneš Heřmanův' (on the defeat of Saxons *c.*1204) and 'Jaroslav' (on defence against the Tatars in 1241).[31]

Now the very uniqueness of the Manuscripts appeared to be their undoing. Still no links had been ascertained to authentic medieval evidence (that had always puzzled even Palacký). Yet they contained many hints or reminiscences of later texts, especially Hájek, who it now seemed had even supplied the names for Beneš Heřmanův and Jaroslav. All sorts of circumstantial reasons were advanced as to why the texts might have been fabricated around 1817.[32] Angry rebuttals followed, orchestrated by Julius Grégr, leader of the Young Czechs, the fast-growing mass party (a more effective version of Cymru Fydd) which would soon take control of Bohemia. 'It's the duty of every single one of us', announced a prominent newspaper editor, 'to act decisively and to contribute ardently and courageously as far as we can to the defence of our most rare national treasure.'[33] Gebauer (not helped by his German name) and others suffered a campaign of intimidation. Moreover, the first full chemical tests, conducted simultaneously and notably thorough (one of the scientists involved was Šafárik's son), seemed – paradoxically? – to confirm the antiquity of *RKZ*, though they did sound one caution: an initial in *RK* had proved to contain Prussian blue, a pigment allegedly discovered only in 1704. But if their form was vindicated, the content of the manuscripts appeared deeply compromised. Soon the texts were removed from school use. In 1899, one disputed jumble of characters in *RZ* was even exposed as reading 'V Hanka fecit' (V Hanka made it).[34]

By the first years of the twentieth century the Manuscripts controversy was largely over internationally. Foreign commentators more or less quietly abandoned *RKZ*, with greater or lesser degrees of nostalgia. In France, Ernest Denis, building on earlier scepticism of the palaeographer Gaston Paris, seems in his influential work of 1903 to have regarded the matter as settled. In Britain, Czechophiles like Morfill and Maurice laid the Manuscripts to rest.[35]

---

[31] Jaroslav Goll, *Historický rozbor básní Rukopisu králodvorského: Oldřicha, Beneše Heřmanova a Jaroslava* (Praha, 1886); summarized in Bartoš, *Rukopisy*, pp. 51 ff., and by J. Meznik in Otruba (ed.), *Dnešní stav*, pp. 147–77.

[32] A highly skilled analysis of the stages whereby philologists and historians undermined the 'citadel' of *RKZ* , with the final assault in 1886, is given by Václav Flajšhans, *Jak to vlastně bylo? Naše rukopisy a vídeňská vláda* (Praha, 1932), though ironically Flajšhans had himself opposed the demolition in the 1890s.

[33] Bartoš, *Rukopisy*, p. 9.

[34] L. Dolenský in *Listy Filologické*, 26 (1899), 460–8.

[35] Ernest Denis, *La Bohême depuis la Montagne-Blanche* (Paris, 1903). I have used the Czech version, *Čechy po Bílé Hoře* (3rd edn., 2 vols., Praha, 1921), II, part 1, pp. 153 ff., 205–7; part

At home the struggle was by no means over; but the grounds of disagreement shifted and their political dimension became more apparent. Masaryk, together with most professional opinion in the humanities, took a demonstratively progressive view. They were not necessarily political liberals (among them, for example, was the great conservative historian Pekař); but they wanted to draw a line under such spurious markers of nationhood. Czech culture could stand on its own feet − indeed, it emerged strengthened by its exercise of critical judgment on sensitive issues.

Defenders regrouped. They stressed the dangers of conceding to enemies of the nation on such a grave issue of self-respect, especially of selling short the glories of the Slavonic past, and the absence of proof that Hanka et al. could have created or did create such convincing and potent documents.[36] The material proofs, such as they were, still favoured their side. The Prussian blue was now explained as a piece of later refurbishment − and Hanka's purported self-revelation soon stood revealed as a kind of 'anti-hoax'. One of the defenders, Jozef Píč, curator of archaeology at the National Museum, took some leaves of *RKZ* to palaeographical experts in France and Italy. Somewhat bewildered and pressed for time, the latter pronounced them probably genuine. Píč returned to Prague in triumph. But detractors of his hasty and superficial way of proceeding poured scorn on him. A few days later he shot himself.

The First World War heightened national tensions. There were even signs by 1918 that the authorities wanted to use the *genuineness* of *RKZ* (what a contrast with sixty years before!) against Masaryk, by now the chief opponent of the Monarchy in emigration. In the aftermath of the war, just one hundred years after the first publication of *RKZ*, the Czechs gained their own state, and local Germans were forced into subordination. Ironically, there was, henceforth, scope for Czechs to practise those traditions of political wisdom and military independence to which the Manuscripts (if authentic) had borne such eloquent early witness. Yet, more importantly, Masaryk became President, and most of the leading guard in the humanities at least agreed with him that Czech identity was closer to critical modernism than medievalizing mythopoeia. By the same token, support for *RKZ* now went with anti-Masarykian attitudes and with expertise in other fields, especially natural science. It was led by František Mareš, a physiologist of no small repute, a vitalist philosopher and ex-rector of the Charles University, and included the

3, pp. 216–18, which is actually dedicated to the three 'iconoclasts' of 1886 by the translator and editor, Jindřich Vančura. For Britain, cf. Naughton, 'Reception', and the various editions of Francis Lützow's *Bohemia: An Historical Sketch* (London, 1896 etc.) and idem, *A History of Bohemian Literature* (London, 1899 etc.).

[36] For example, Martin Žunkovič (ed.), *Rukopisové zelenohorský, Píseň pod Vyšehradem a královédvorský* (Olomouc, 1912), Preface.

likes of Karel Andrlík, professor of chemistry, and Viktorin Vojtěch, professor of photography.

The defenders formed a 'Czechoslovak Manuscripts Society' (*Československá* (later *Česká*) *společnost rukopisná*) and conducted various further tests on the documents themselves, which confirmed, at least to their own satisfaction – and no one succeeded in faulting them on technical grounds – that *RKZ* were of medieval origin. They devoted much energy to parrying palaeographical, philological and historical objections, elaborating for instance the minutiae of the Tatar raid of 1241 described in 'Jaroslav', one of the cruxes of *RK*, and refuting some of the manifold charges of anachronism.[37] By the later 1930s upholders of the Manuscripts constituted a distinctly nationalist pressure group on the conservative flank. One of their leaders, Jan Vrzalik, a pupil of Pekař, became president of the quasi-fascist Vlajka movement. When the left-wing musicologist Zdeněk Nejedlý repudiated *RKZ* in 1937 (he had long been an active sceptic about their more improbable musical allusions), his lecture ended in a riot. Their views placed the defenders in a curious posture when Nazi Germany took over the country, given the anti-Teutonic sentiments expressed in *RKZ*; the more so once the front opened up against Russia.[38]

As a consequence, the Manuscripts fell totally under a cloud with the Communist takeover of Czechoslovakia after 1945. Nejedlý became minister of culture. For twenty years *RKZ* were a non-subject (at a time when the Soviet regime at home limited debate about the lay of Igor precisely to protect its authenticity), despite the fact that Masaryk counted for the new regime as the ultimate bourgeois-nationalist *persona non grata*. Then the approaching 150th anniversary of Hanka's find brought renewed activity: especially two initiatives, in strange counterpoint with the liberalization of the Communist system which would shortly culminate in the Prague Spring. The National Museum and the Academy Institute of Literature combined to produce a full account of *RKZ* and the controversy which had surrounded them. It is a sober and rather solemn analysis, issued in 1969, after the Warsaw Pact invasion, leaving no loopholes for authenticity, and still rather censorious about the whole affair. The report could incorporate some telling fresh research on Romantic sources for *RKZ* from other Slavonic lands, especially a Russian translation of Ossian.[39] However, it was not very inquisitive about the actual

---

[37] Mareš wrote 8 books on *RKZ* between 1927 and 1938, the most important of which are *Pravda o Rukopisech zelenohorském a králové dvorském* (Praha, 1931) and *Marnost bojů proti Rukopisům* (Praha, 1933). Cf. the reproachful but charitable judgment on him by one of his chief opponents, Bartoš, *Rukopisy*, pp. 92 ff. Another was Flajšhans, *Jak to vlastně bylo?*, a veteran from several decades of the controversy.

[38] J. Kočí in Otruba (ed.), *Dnešní stav*, pp. 41ff.; Petr Čornej, 'Vystoupení Zdeňka Nejedlého proti RKZ v roce 1937 a jeho ohlas', *Česká literatura*, 25 (1977), 46–53.

[39] Julius Dolanský, *Neznámý jihoslovanský pramen Rukopisů královédvorského a zelenohorského* (Praha, 1968), on the influence of the Croatian poet Kačić-Miošić; idem, *Ohlas dvou ruských*

circumstances of the forgery, the tangled web of evidence surrounding Hanka himself, and it left a new autopsy of the manuscripts themselves to a companion volume – a volume which failed to appear.

Simultaneously, a freelance writer, Miroslav Ivanov, immersed himself in the mystery with extraordinary thoroughness. Convinced by the end of his investigation that *RKZ* could not be genuine, he also sought to establish how they could have been fabricated, introducing as the *éminence grise* behind the whole enterprise that painter friend of Hanka's whom we met earlier, František Horčička, an expert restorer and experimenter in artistic materials, a man even employed at the castle of Zelená Hora and somehow implicated in the discovery of *RZ*.[40] Ivanov it was who assembled a team to establish for good and all whether the Manuscripts, as physical objects, were in any sense genuine.

Now the plot becomes surreal (worthy of a Hrabal or Kundera, whose prose was just then exploring the absurdities of the system). *RKZ* were removed to the Criminological Institute of the notorious state police, where an examination by miscellaneous experts, including Ivanov, was begun in the early months of 1968, just as Dubček came to power. By the autumn of that year, with Russian tanks in the streets around, they reached a provisional verdict that *RZ* was a palimpsest, using real parchment and adapting some real medieval lettering. Similar conclusions would follow for *RK*.[41] But by then the participants were caught up in the 'normalization' process which reversed the Prague Spring. In the end, their adverse judgment on the Manuscripts, delivered in 1975, was promptly contested by another raft of specialists and withheld from publicity as a state secret.[42]

Eventually the 'Ivanov protocols' were issued after the velvet revolution. In the heady atmosphere of the early 1990s, however, these conclusions only gave rise to fresh altercation.[43] Amid a resurgence of national feeling, *RKZ* gained new legitimacy precisely because they had been repugned by the Communists. The Manuscripts Society was refounded, with an associated publishing house and an extraordinarily comprehensive website.[44] Defenders of authenticity now make the running. Historians and literary critics still tend wearily to insist that the case is closed, without taking up the full implications of regarding

---

básníků v Rukopisech královédvorském a zelenohorském (Praha, 1969), on the influence of Kheraskov and Karamzin; idem, *Záhada Ossiana v Rukopisech královédvorském a zelenohorském* (Praha, 1975 (but completed in 1968)), on the 1792 translation by Jermil Kostrov.

[40] Ivanov, *Tajemství*, pp. 499–565.

[41] Ibid., pp. 566–631; Miroslav Ivanov, *Záhada Rukopisu královédvorského* (Praha, 1970).

[42] Miroslav Ivanov, *Utajené protokoly, aneb, Geniální podvod* (Praha, 1994), relates the events of 1968–75. Eventually *RKZ* did spawn their fictional comedy of the absurd: Josef Urban, *Poslední tecka za Rukopisy* (Praha, 1998).

[43] *Sborník Národního Muzea*, řada C, 36 (1991), nos. 1–4, for the protocols. Jiří Urban and K. Nesměrák, *Fakta o protokolech RKZ* (Praha, 1996), contests their claims.

[44] *<http://kix.fsv.cvut.cz/rkz>*, making available much material by opponents as well as defenders. There is a short English summary.

RKZ as factitious.[45] Yet those implications – besides being beguilingly postmodern – would surely offer us further valuable insight into the mentality and inspiration of national revival.

What lessons can we bring back to Wales from this extraordinary controversy? Manifestly the Manuscripts represent a much more open case than Iolo's fakes. Outsiders (including other Slavs) could test more of the evidence, including *RKZ* themselves, at least vicariously, whereas Iolo (re)wrote rather than actually forged documents and his manuscripts long remained in private hands. Again, the Czech affair was far more vehement, and the stakes much higher, not least politically: in that respect *RKZ* brought together, as it were, Dafydd ap Gwilym with Owain Glyndŵr. Little in Wales could match the bitterness of the long-running saga of *RKZ*, which proved impossible to terminate once positions were truly entrenched. On the other hand, Iolo's fabrications actually created institutions, whereas the Czech Manuscripts merely adorned existing ones. Little in Bohemia recalls Iolo's Glamorgan localism, or his assertion of bardic continuity. Religion was not at issue there – at least until Masaryk and the Hussite revival, which promoted a patriotic ideal *counter* to the legacy of *RKZ*; nor was radicalism at issue – this again came only later, when *RKZ* had been dethroned.

There do, however, seem to be important parallels. Both Wales and Bohemia witnessed the defensive backlash of a subordinate nationality against the ascendancy of a Germanic culture. The resultant forgeries were masterly: they were extremely hard to detect and at first eminently suited to the perceived needs of the nation. But later refutation of them, or at least scepticism, likewise became a national interest. In Wales, the reaction was less clear-cut than the Masarykian campaign, which grounded an ethnic mission for the pursuit of truth – 'Veritas vincit' ('Truth conquers', *Pravda zvítězí*) – precisely in the exposure of ethnic myth. Is that not, however, essentially the story of the modern Gorsedd, based on an attractive, colourful and agreed fiction, which nevertheless links to the true values of a pristine cultural tradition? Certainly Masaryk's stance impressed Saunders Lewis – who, in 1930, also noticed the similarities between the Manuscripts and Iolo's fakes.[46]

Let us return at the end to Václav Hanka, our putative chief forger, as Iolo Morganwg is chief subject of this volume. Also a country lad and autodidact (or at least pleased to be thought so), Hanka, too, came to move in more elevated circles without ever quite feeling comfortable or satisfied there. On the other hand, he was not known as a drug addict, and seems to have been a Russophile conservative in politics. Hanka enjoyed greater international fame

---

[45] Miroslav Hroch's excellent *Na prahu národní existence: touha a skutečnost* (Praha, 1999), does not discuss *RKZ*. Vladimír Macura, *Znamení zrodu: České národní obrození jako kulturní typ* (2nd edn., Jinočany, 1995), hardly does so either, but is alive to their ambiguities.

[46] Saunders Lewis, *Canlyn Arthur: Ysgrifau Gwleidyddol* (2nd edn., Llandysul, 1985), pp. 125–44.

than Iolo, but he shared the same rootedness in place (he never left Bohemia, except for one visit to Dresden) and was infused with a similarly intense nationalism, bound in with love of language in its historical and dialectal development. Even more than Iolo, Hanka has been grievously neglected by posterity. Only one short biography of him exists, written in his lifetime – and by a German.[47] Incongruously, he was contemned and ignored by those who thought him a forger; whereas for those who did not, Hanka likewise remained ultimately a nobody: just a patriot who happened to be in the right place (Dvůr Králové!) at the right time, and whose talents it was in any case necessary to depreciate – as Palacký did with such gusto – in order to weaken any supposition that he could have created *RKZ*. Besides, how could the vain and ambitious Hanka have remained mute about his achievements? (It is one of the striking features of his behaviour that he kept *very* silent until his death – even the trial proceedings were arranged on his behalf and conducted in his absence.) Was he privately relieved or outraged when people defended his honour by claiming that *RKZ* stood far beyond his creative powers?

Thus much mystery remains in Hanka's case too: indeed, perhaps more of it than with Iolo. Was Hanka really educated, clever or creative enough, and did he have time, to counterfeit on such a heroic, Ioloesque scale? Or if he operated collectively – using Linda, and/or Svoboda, and/or Horčička and others – how could that have remained concealed to this day?[48] After all, the more conspirators, the harder to keep such a fiercely contentious plot secret for so long. No one has ever yet explained how bogus manuscripts, against the testimony of many witnesses, could have been introduced into the church at Dvůr Králové, or passed off as a find from Zelená Hora, unless the plot were remarkably widely ramified. Sincere believers in *RKZ* have no doubt been fired over the years, alongside all substantive arguments, with a touch of romantic yearning for medieval originals. Yet, as Iolo's example also shows us, fakes can be at least as exciting and puzzling as true articles.

---

[47] A. A. [Legis-]Glückselig, 'Venceslav Hanka, ein Beitrag zur Geschichte der Cultur und National-Literatur Böhmens und der Slaven überhaupt', *Almanach Libussa*, XI (Prag, 1852), 285–369. This was the basis for the account by his Russian admirer, Aleksandr Pypin, *Moi zametki*, pp. 269–312.

[48] Only Linda's *Jaroslav Sternberg v boji proti tatarům* (1823; repr. Praha, 1930) offers a possible clue.

II. The Bard

4

Iolo Morganwg and Strict-Metre Welsh Poetry

CERI W. LEWIS

It would be extremely unfortunate if the well-attested accomplishments of Iolo Morganwg as an ingenious, impressively erudite and remarkably prolific literary forger were allowed completely to overshadow his prowess as a poet, for some of his best compositions, in both the strict and free metres, deservedly rank among the most splendid creations of the Welsh muse in the eighteenth century. That notable achievement may have had an inherited genetic component, for there is some basis for Iolo's claim that his mother Ann William (née Matthew), who exercised an abnormally powerful influence on him in his early, formative years, was a descendant of some of the great master-poets (*penceirddiaid*) of Tir Iarll.[1] With that percipience which characterized so much of his work, Iolo fully realized that this district was the most important nursery of the bardic culture and literary life of Glamorgan from a comparatively early period and that the talented master-poets from whom his mother may have been descended constituted the most important bardic family ever to arise in his native Glamorgan, one whose works conferred great distinction on the literary history of the region.[2] Naturally, his keen awareness of this important connection was a source of great pride for Iolo, and it inspired some of his actions and important pronouncements. And it is surely significant that, of all the many subjects that aroused his intelligent interest at various stages in his long and extraordinarily industrious life, none appealed to him to a greater extent, or for a longer period, than Welsh bardism in all its manifold aspects. At a comparatively early period in his life, he began making strenuous efforts to master the detailed rules governing the Welsh strict metres and the general art of versification, including stanzaic forms, rhyme, the forbidden faults which

---

[1] NLW 13144A, pp. 181–6; NLW 13141A, pp. 363–4; W. Watkins, 'Merched y Tŷ Talwyn', *Y Cymmrodor*, IV, part 1 (1881), 101–5; Williams: *IM*, pp. 86–94, 101–3, 165–6; Lewis: *IM*, pp. 19–21, 28–9.

[2] On Tir Iarll ('The Earl's Land'), the district which included the parishes of Llangynwyd, Betws, Cynffig and Margam, see J. S. Corbett, *Glamorgan: Papers and Notes on the Lordship and its Members*, ed. D. R. Paterson (Cardiff, 1925), p. 70; *TLlM*, pp. 22, 32–6; Williams: *IM*, pp. 7–9; T. B. Pugh (ed.), *Glamorgan County History, Volume III: The Middle Ages* (Cardiff, 1971), pp. 31–2, 501–9.

every bard was strictly enjoined to eschew, the quantity and stress of syllables, and the intricate system of consonantal alliteration, internal rhyme and balanced stresses known as *cynghanedd* in Welsh. Nor could any dedicated novice who aspired to reproduce in his own verses some of the distinctive stylistic features of the great master-poets afford to disregard the frequent use made by the latter of *sangiadau*, that is, words or phrases (often of an emotive, descriptive or exclamatory nature) interpolated in parenthesis, which are subject to the strict demands of *cynghanedd* and rhyme and which, though cutting across the normal grammatical order of words, can nevertheless, when employed by a skilled bard, frequently fulfil a vital aesthetic function and make a significant contribution to his overall meaning. Clearly, the mastery of his medium which Iolo Morganwg triumphantly displays in his best strict-metre compositions was the product of great innate ability combined with unremitting diligence and meticulous attention to artistic detail.[3]

This is not to imply, however, that his early efforts to master the intricacies of the bardic craft were entirely unaided. Iolo himself maintained in one of his autobiographical essays that he was under ten when he first began studying the rules of the bardic craft as set out in Siôn Dafydd Rhys's grammar and that his tutor was his namesake, Edward Williams, of Middle Hill in the parish of Llancarfan.[4] The latter, he maintained, permitted him to borrow the aforesaid grammar and also gave him detailed oral instruction. When he eventually returned this work, Edward Williams, deeply impressed by the progress of his pupil, gave him

> another small vol. entitled Flores Poetarum Britan[n]icorum one part of it contained a Treatise on verse metres by Captain Middleton who printed it in 1594, and about the same time a Welsh version . . . of the whole book of Salms in those ancient and intricate metres this also Mr E. Wms. lent me. in these books I studied the welsh prosody & versification.[5]

This is both interesting and revealing, for when Iolo asserted elsewhere that he and his friend Edward Evan, of Aberdare, had been instructed in the intricacies of the bardic craft in the manner in which all the old master-poets and their disciples had been trained – that is, orally, and hence in a manner fundamentally different from that adopted by the contemporary bards of the other major regions, whose training consisted solely of perusing various bardic manuals – he completely forgot (or he conveniently chose to overlook) this assertion that he, too, began mastering the rules of Welsh poetic art by studying the works mentioned above. Furthermore, he stated elsewhere that he first began

---

[3] For an authoritative account of all the major aspects of the art of strict-metre Welsh poetry, see John Morris-Jones, *Cerdd Dafod: Sef Celfyddyd Barddoniaeth Gymraeg* (Rhydychen, 1925).
[4] NLW 13141A, p. 133.
[5] NLW 21387E, no. 13.

composing Welsh verse when he was around fifteen and that soon afterwards he 'became a[c]quainted with . . . Edward William[s]'.[6] And although Iolo, as was his wont when discussing his early teachers, heaped unstinting praise on the learning and poetic accomplishments of Edward Williams, the few compositions by the latter that have survived in manuscript sources are undeniably mediocre.[7]

Of greater importance in the development of Iolo Morganwg as a strict-metre bard was his prolonged contact, from a comparatively early period in his life, with the close-knit fraternity of bards and 'grammarians' who dwelt in the Uplands (*Blaenau*) in the northern part of Glamorgan. These included Lewis Hopkin, of Hendre Ifan Goch in the parish of Llandyfodwg;[8] John (or Siôn) Bradford, of Betws Tir Iarll, whose name probably occurs more frequently than any other in Iolo's numerous fabrications;[9] Rhys Morgan, of Pencraig-nedd;[10] Dafydd Nicolas, of Aberpergwm;[11] and Edward Evan, of Aberdare.[12] All of these had devoted some attention to the contents of the early bardic grammars and had succeeded in acquiring the basic elements of the old bardic learning and skills. One notable feature of this small group was that the early Welsh literary traditions had become closely linked with Dissent, an important consideration for Iolo when, later in his life, he began expatiating on the beliefs and dogmas of the ancient druidic bards and on their steadfast adherence to the pristine purity and simplicity of the early Christian faith. Undoubtedly, it was his early and sustained contact with this small group, together with his close association with many of the local historians, littérateurs and lexicographers who had been inspired by the scholastic and antiquarian revival whose initial impetus had been provided by the brilliant career of Edward Lhuyd, that accounts, to a large degree, for Iolo's impressive learning, his firm grasp of the literary traditions of Wales and the evident mastery he ultimately acquired of the intricate rules of strict-metre Welsh verse.[13]

[6] Williams: *IM*, p. 114. This is yet one more example of the inconsistency frequently encountered in Iolo's writings, especially when he purported to recount in his autobiographical essays some salient features of his early life. See the different versions in NLW 21387E.

[7] Williams: *IM*, pp. 115–16; Lewis: *IM*, pp. 30–1.

[8] L. J. Hopkin-James, *Hopkiniaid Morganwg* (Bangor, 1909), pp. 70–148, 215–300, 342–3, 347–67; *TLlM*, pp. 231–6; *DWB*, pp. 365–6; Ceri W. Lewis, 'The Literary History of Glamorgan from 1550 to 1770' in Glanmor Williams (ed.), *Glamorgan County History, Volume IV: Early Modern Glamorgan from the Act of Union to the Industrial Revolution* (Cardiff, 1974), pp. 612–14.

[9] *IMChY*, pp. 163–6; *TLlM*, pp. 237–40; *DWB*, pp. 47–8; Lewis, 'Literary History of Glamorgan', pp. 614–16.

[10] D. R. Phillips, *The History of the Vale of Neath* (Swansea, 1925), pp. 541–6; *TLlM*, pp. 230–1; *DWB*, pp. 649–50; Lewis, 'Literary History of Glamorgan', pp. 611–12.

[11] T. C. Evans (Cadrawd), *History of the Parish of Llangynwyd* (Llanelly, 1887), pp. 186–8; Phillips, *History of the Vale of Neath*, pp. 546–53; *TLlM*, pp. 241–3, 290–300; *DWB*, p. 686; Lewis, 'Literary History of Glamorgan', pp. 616–17.

[12] NLW 13159A, pp. 142–5; R. T. Jenkins, 'Bardd a'i Gefndir (Edward Ifan o'r Ton Coch)', *THSC* (1946–7), 97–149; *TLlM*, pp. 245–51 (chiefly); *DWB*, p. 228; Lewis, 'Literary History of Glamorgan', pp. 618–19.

[13] Lewis, 'Literary History of Glamorgan', pp. 622–9.

Hardly less important in providing him with some of the basic elements of the bardic craft was the informal guidance he received in his youth from John Walters, a scholarly clergyman who was rector of Llandough, near Cowbridge, and vicar of the neighbouring parish of St Hilary. He remained one of Iolo's staunchest friends throughout his life and frequently passed constructive critical judgements on his compositions.[14] Another erudite clergyman, Thomas Richards, who was licensed in 1742 as perpetual curate of Coychurch and Peterston-super-montem in Glamorgan, was an equally important influence.[15] He was the compiler of *Antiquae Linguae Britannicae Thesaurus: being a British, or Welsh-English Dictionary.*[16] One important aspect of this work, which Richards endeavoured to update until his death in 1790, was that it provided young bardic novices like Iolo Morganwg with a convenient source for interpreting the more difficult elements in the vocabulary of the great strict-metre poets. Not surprisingly, therefore, it was a work they frequently consulted in the latter half of the eighteenth century when they composed their *awdlau* and *cywyddau.* This work undoubtedly instilled in Iolo a deep and abiding interest in Welsh lexicography, and Thomas Richards was one of the scholars who helped to arouse Iolo's interest in the literature of Wales, especially in the works of the strict-metre bards.[17]

By 1767, the year in which he celebrated his twentieth birthday, Iolo Morganwg had been rigorously trained in the craft of the old *penceirddiaid* and, as the contents of his manuscripts amply confirm, he had spent long periods transcribing the compositions of several of the most renowned strict-metre bards, including some of the Poets of the Princes, Dafydd ap Gwilym, and other famous figures who had sung in the popular *cywydd* metre. He had received ample opportunity, therefore, to acquaint himself with the exacting artistic standards of the strict metres. He frequented, from the period of his youth, the minor eisteddfodau that were held at various times in Glamorgan, and eventually he attracted the attention and admiration of some of the local bardic fraternity.[18] The verses he composed during this comparatively early period in his career include a short eulogistic ode addressed to Dafydd ap

---

[14] NLW 6515B; NLW 13157A, p. 158; T. C. Evans (Cadrawd), 'John Walters and the First Printing Press in Glamorganshire', *JWBS*, I, no. 3 (1911), 83–9; J. Ifano Jones, *A History of Printing and Printers in Wales and Monmouthshire to . . . 1923* (Cardiff, 1925), pp. 85–9; *TLIM*, pp. 308–18; Williams: *IM*, pp. xliv, xlvi, 135–50, 169–73, 391–411; *DWB*, pp. 1011–12; Lewis, 'Literary History of Glamorgan', pp. 633–5.

[15] *IMChY*, pp. 168–9; *TLIM*, pp. 300–9; Williams: *IM,* pp. 133–5; *DWB*, p. 854; Lewis, 'Literary History of Glamorgan', pp. 630–3.

[16] This was published in Bristol in 1753, and a second edition appeared in 1759.

[17] For the two lexicographers, see Richard M. Crowe, 'Thomas Richards a John Walters: Athrawon Geiriadurol Iolo Morganwg' in Hywel Teifi Edwards (ed.), *Llynfi ac Afan, Garw ac Ogwr* (Llandysul, 1998), pp. 227–51.

[18] Williams: *IM*, pp. 123–8; Lewis: *IM*, p. 74.

Rhisiart – Dafydd Ionawr, in all probability – and several *cywyddau* on love, and on religious and elegiac themes.[19] Composed before 1773, a year that was an important milestone in his bardic career, they contain no obvious indications of the inspiration or of the strong romantic emotions that characterize the magnificent verses he composed at a later date and which rightly won for him a secure place as one of his nation's ablest Welsh poets. These early compositions are replete with obsolete words, many of which had been taken from Thomas Richards's dictionary.[20] This undoubtedly reflects an element of vain exhibitionism. Later in his career, however, after he had acquired more maturity and flair, he consciously eschewed this annoying practice, and came to understand how obsolete words and phrases could be used in a more selective and artistically telling manner. Verbosity was another of his early weaknesses, a failing which he readily acknowledged.[21] Nor could he entirely resist the urge to imitate some of the compositions by other bards whose works he had read, one of the strongest impulses that prompted many of his literary fabrications. He also found it difficult at times to control his violent temper, and we occasionally find him mercilessly berating some of his hated enemies in the manner of the old satirists.[22] Although they do not possess any marked artistic merit, these verses clearly demonstrate that he was intimately acquainted with the different strands in the works of the great master-poets.

Love is the dominant theme of several of the early *cywyddau* preserved in his autograph. These had obviously been inspired by his reading of the works of Dafydd ap Gwilym (*fl.* 1320–70) and Dafydd ab Edmwnd (*fl.* 1450–97) and, in this connection, the period 1773–6 is one of fundamental importance in his development as a Romantic strict-metre bard. In 1773 he went to London and, later, to Kent, and it was not until 1777 that he returned to his native Glamorgan. One of the most important tasks he discharged during his sojourn in London was to transcribe the *awdlau* and *cywyddau* he had seen in the copy which Owen Jones (Owain Myfyr) had made of Lewis and William Morris's collections of the compositions of Dafydd ap Gwilym.[23] This proved to be one

---

[19] Williams: *IM*, pp. 128–9; Lewis: *IM*, pp. 74–5.

[20] One of the most notable examples of this proclivity is the elegy *Dagrau yr Awen neu Farwnad Lewis Hopcin Fardd, o Landyfodwg ym Morganwg* (Pont-y-Fon, 1772), which contained so many obsolete words that Iolo felt constrained to add at the end two pages of explanatory notes! A facsimile copy of the original was published in Hopkin-James, *Hopkiniaid Morganwg*, pp. 355–67.

[21] BL Add. 15024, Letter no. 1, ff. 183–4. In this letter addressed to Owen Jones (Owain Myfyr), on 25 January 1776, Iolo admitted that a poem he had composed in the *cywydd* metre was 'much too long' and that he was 'very apt to be superfluously prolix on every subject'.

[22] Williams: *IM*, pp. 131–2; Lewis: *IM*, p. 76.

[23] The copy made by Owen Jones is now Bangor 6 in the library of the University of Wales, Bangor. For the copy transcribed by Iolo Morganwg *c.*1775, see NLW 13090E, pp. 209–454. See also *IMChY*, pp. 3, 7; Williams: *IM*, p. 213; Thomas Parry (ed.), *Gwaith Dafydd ap Gwilym* (Caerdydd, 1952), pp. cl–clxix and the accompanying chart between p. clxviii and p. clxix.

of the most exciting discoveries of his life and it led to a new and outstand-
ingly fruitful period in his bardic career. Prior to his sojourn in London, he
had studied compositions by Dafydd ap Gwilym preserved in the manuscripts
of Tomas ab Ieuan, the late seventeenth-century copyist from Tre'r-bryn, in the
parish of Coychurch,[24] and in Llyfr Hir Llanharan, which had been transcribed
by Llywelyn Siôn (1540–1615?),[25] and he intended including a number of
these poems in a volume he hoped to publish. However, his acquaintance with
the compositions contained in those transcripts did not leave any significant
mark on the poetry he wrote before 1774. But from that year down to *c*.1790
the work of Dafydd ap Gwilym became unquestionably one of the most
important influences on his strict-metre verses, including not only those
compositions he openly acknowledged to be his own work but also those he
attributed to other bards. For many years he turned frequently to the copy he
had made of Owain Myfyr's manuscript, and he was drawn irresistibly to
imitate Dafydd's work, not with the intention – at least, at first – of deceiving
anyone, but simply because the serious mental disturbances that frequently
troubled him and prompted many of his actions and pronouncements would
not allow him to do otherwise. The influence of Dafydd ap Gwilym's work can
clearly be discerned not only in the various themes on which Iolo composed
his verses, but also in the vocabulary and pervasive mood of those poems.[26] No
less unmistakable are manifestations of certain features of the Romanticism
which powerfully influenced attitudes to art, music and literature in many of
the countries of western Europe in the late eighteenth and early nineteenth
centuries, with its emphasis on feeling and the sublime and the free expression
of the passions and individuality.[27] However, similar manifestations can also be
detected in the exemplifying lines and couplets which Iolo included in the
early lists he drew up of miscellaneous vocabularies – 'the little Welsh scholar'
(*y Cymreigyddyn*), as they are called in his manuscripts. These include the
earliest of his literary forgeries.[28]

It was after his return to Glamorgan in 1777 that Iolo composed most of his
best strict-metre verses, poems which have secured for him a place among the
leading Welsh poets. In those verses he refers to the man who had been

---

[24]   *TLIM*, pp. 167–73; Williams: *IM*, p. 154; Lewis, 'Literary History of Glamorgan', pp. 589–92;
       Lewis: *IM*, p. 81.
[25]   *TLIM*, pp. 79–80, 157–60, 177–8; Lewis, 'Literary History of Glamorgan', pp. 582–3; *DWB*,
       p. 602.
[26]   Lewis: *IM*, pp. 81–2.
[27]   On the general European background, see Meyer H. Abrams, *The Mirror and the Lamp:
       Romantic Theory and the Critical Tradition* (New York, 1953); Lilian R. Furst (ed.), *European
       Romanticism: Self Definitions* (London, 1980); Jerome J. McGann, *The Romantic Ideology: A
       Critical Investigation* (Chicago, 1983); Roy Porter and Mikuláš Teich (eds.), *Romanticism in
       National Context* (Cambridge, 1988).
[28]   Lewis: *IM*, p. 82.

wandering for some time in England and elsewhere and who, tiring at last of that aimless existence, decides to return to the beloved land of his infancy. This is the theme of the excellent *cywydd* which he attributed to Hywel Llwyd of Llancarfan, and which becomes a memorable paean of praise to Glamorgan. The author of this splendid *cywydd* was unquestionably one who had acquired a firm mastery of the strict metres.[29] Praise for his native region is the central theme of another *cywydd* by him, which he attributed to Edward Dafydd of Margam, the most distinguished of the seventeenth-century Glamorgan bards.[30]

Unsurprisingly, in view of the strong Romantic influences which can be detected in his work, love is the central theme of a number of the *cywyddau* he sang in his passionate youth, and the object of his intense affection was 'Euron', a maid 'with the ruddy glow of dawn on her cheek'.[31] She was not an idealized figment of his imagination, for Iolo stated that she was Margaret (Peggy) Roberts, whom he married in St Mary Church on 18 July 1781, a girl 'that, from a child, I dearly lov'd', he declared in an English sonnet, and before she had acquired any property, as he proudly proclaimed in a letter he sent to Owain Myfyr in 1781.[32] It was to her that the bard, who at that time called himself Iorwerth Gwilim, sang some of the most charming love-poems composed in strict metres in the eighteenth century, verses that are not marred by the meaningless 'filling-in' words and phrases and the stereotyped imagery which greatly detract from the works of many bards who sang in the sixteenth and seventeenth centuries. One of the earliest of these verses was a *cywydd* he sang to youthful love. A maid should love, the poet maintains, while she is still in the full bloom of youth, before she is afflicted by the ravages of old age, and he therefore earnestly implores Euron to make love with him while it is still spring in the land:

> I gaer llwyn, ar gwr llannerch,
> Lle tirion i sôn am serch;
> Lle tawel yw, ni'n gwelir,
> I'n llawen oed mewn llwyn ir.

(To the fortress of the bush, on the edge of the glade,/ A pleasant place to speak of love;/ It is a quiet spot, where we will not be observed,/ To our joyous tryst, in the verdant grove.)

---

[29] NLW 13127A, pp. 221–6; NLW 13141A, pp. 103–6; *IMChY*, pp. 72–6, 230–1; Williams: *IM*, pp. 241–2; Lewis: *IM*, pp. 82–3.

[30] NLW 13141A, pp. 161–5; *IMChY*, pp. 80–2, 232–4.

[31] 'A gwrid y wawr ar ei grudd'. See 'Cywydd y Serch' in Tegwyn Jones (ed.), *Y Gwir Degwch: Detholiad o Gywyddau Serch Iolo Morganwg* (Bow Street, 1980), p. 11.

[32] See G. J. Williams, 'Cywyddau Cynnar Iolo Morganwg', *Y Beirniad*, VIII, part 2 (1919), 79. For the sonnet called 'The Dream', from which the short quotation has been taken, see Williams: *PLP*, II, p. 176.

But it should never be forgotten that winter, with its bleak ravages, will come inexorably. Thus will old age overtake all mortal beings, and as the beauty of youth will assuredly vanish to a great extent, it behoves us all not to delay for one moment. Everything beautiful has its fleeting moment and then passes away. He neatly summarizes the burden of his poem in a memorably simple couplet:

> Cred, awen! cariad ieuanc
> Sy benna' lles bun a llanc.

(Believe, O Muse! that young love/ Is the chief good for a maid and a lad.)

With that in mind, we find the two still deeply in love with one another in their old age and deriving inestimable comfort and pleasure from the memories they share of the glorious springtime of their lives.[33]

Another theme which frequently inspired his muse was the tribulations that sometimes come in the wake of true love, and although these *cywyddau* are not, on the whole, as accomplished as some of his other love-poems, they contain lines which elevate them above many of the strict-metre verses composed by other bards on the same theme.[34] However, the love-poems which undeniably show the greatest originality are the two Iolo addressed to 'Y Gwir Degwch' ('The True Beauty'). It was not the striking physical beauty of the maid which had aroused his intense love for her, the poet avers, but the fact that she was endowed with great virtue and a pure, kind heart. These were the qualities that constituted the 'true beauty'.[35]

Equally commendable is his 'Cywydd yr Awen yn Lled Ddynwared Horas', which portrays its author in Kent in bleak midwinter. Not surprisingly, with the poet stranded in Hengist's terrain and the harsh winter roaring mercilessly around him, he experiences pangs of intense depression. Nevertheless, he succeeds in composing a love-poem to Euron and to the joys of summer in glorious Glamorgan and, as soon as he begins to sing of his beloved, he feels the warm inspiration of the true muse in his breast. He hears the sweet voice of his dear maid and experiences the incomparable enchantment that can be found in love's dreams and reveries. He quickly realizes that only by thinking of Euron and singing her praises would he restore a feeling of happiness and well-being to his mind and banish his melancholic spirit.[36]

Understandably, in view of the great influence that Dafydd ap Gwilym's work had upon him, his strict-metre verses include four compositions in the *cywydd* metre which dispatch birds as love-messengers.[37] The most beautiful of

---

[33] Williams, 'Cywyddau Cynnar Iolo Morganwg', 79–80.
[34] Jones (ed.), *Y Gwir Degwch*, pp. 28–35; Lewis: *IM*, pp. 84–6.
[35] Jones (ed.), *Y Gwir Degwch*, pp. 20–7.
[36] Ibid., pp. 67–70.
[37] Ibid., pp. 41–57.

these is the one addressed to the skylark. The poet bemoans the fact that he is unable to sing as freely or as sweetly as the bird, for the pangs of love are afflicting his breast and depriving his muse of its creative power. Were it not for those pangs, he could sing like the 'eloquent birds of the bush'. But, alas, his grievous fate is to experience unrequited love, and he proceeds to describe his emotional distress. He ends the poem by addressing the skylark, who is being dispatched as a love-messenger by one whose breast is shattered because of his deep love for Euron.[38]

Another splendid composition which reflects the influence of Dafydd ap Gwilym is the one in which the poet holds a discourse with summer, 'Cywydd Cynhadledd y Bardd a'r Haf', which is also sometimes known as the poem in which its author sends summer as a messenger to Glamorgan ('Cywydd Gyrru'r Haf i Forgannwg'). That Iolo made several copies of this *cywydd* suggests that he held it in high esteem – and rightly so, for it is one of the best poems to be composed in the *cywydd* metre during the eighteenth century, a poem which develops into an eloquent encomium to the great natural beauty and exquisite charm of Glamorgan in summertime.[39]

The poems selectively mentioned above provide incontestable proof that Iolo, while he was still comparatively young, had succeeded in acquiring an impressive mastery of the highly intricate art of strict-metre Welsh poetry. Sometime after 1781, however, the responsibilities and tribulations of life's daily routine and, possibly, some personal adversities of which we now have no certain knowledge, began seriously to impair his poetic inspiration and, ultimately, to obliterate it completely. Iolo himself openly acknowledged the loss of his great poetic talent in a letter he addressed to John Edwards (Siôn Ceiriog) in September 1784.[40] This marked another turning-point in his career. The poignantly moving poem on the death of the muse ('Cywydd Marwnad yr Awen'), which bids a sad farewell to his poetically productive youth, shows conclusively that he was firmly convinced that the creative muse had irretrievably deserted him.[41] This poem is unquestionably one of the saddest in Iolo's poetic canon. As we have seen, he married in July 1781 and, as he famously remarked on one occasion, 'The marriage bed is the muse's tomb'.[42] Is this, one wonders, the true explanation for the complete loss of the poetic inspiration which so sadly afflicted him soon afterwards?

Although the work of Dafydd ap Gwilym was undoubtedly the major

---

[38] Ibid., pp. 48–53.

[39] NLW 13087E, pp. 309–10; D. Gwenallt Jones (ed.), *Blodeugerdd o'r Ddeunawfed Ganrif* (4th edn., Caerdydd, 1947), pp. 84–8, 147–8; Williams, 'Cywyddau Cynnar Iolo Morganwg', 85–6; *IMChY*, pp. 80–2, 232–5; Lewis: *IM*, pp. 90–1.

[40] Part of this Welsh letter is quoted in *Y Beirniad*, VIII, part 2 (1919), 87.

[41] Jones (ed.), *Y Gwir Degwch*, pp. 71–3.

[42] BL Add. 15024, Letter no. 6, f. 196, Iolo Morganwg to Owain Myfyr, 20 September 1783.

influence on Iolo's strict-metre compositions, Dafydd ab Edmwnd also worked
his spell. Indeed, a variant version of one of that bard's most memorable
couplets occurs twice in Iolo's early *cywyddau*.[43] Throughout his long life he
had doted on the works of the great master-poets and he had striven to
reproduce in his own verses the outstanding features of their diction, phrase-
ology and style. But although parts of his work are undeniably imitative, Iolo's
early *cywyddau* must be accorded a prominent place in eighteenth-century
strict-metre Welsh poetry, partly because of their high artistic accomplishment,
and partly because their author was deeply conscious of the mysterious
enchantment of the solitary recesses and uninhabited glades, the sumptuous
splendour of summer, the beauty of birds and the beguiling charm of the green
underwood and trees in foliage. This mood is noticeably absent from the
compositions of other eighteenth-century strict-metre Welsh bards. Around a
hundred years elapsed before any other Welsh bard succeeded in capturing a
similar mood in his work. Unfortunately, the world of nature lost its great
charm and fascination for Iolo well before his fortieth birthday and, as a result,
one searches in vain in the verses he composed in his middle age for the mood
of enchantment that can so easily be detected in the best of his early *cywyddau*.

It is difficult to explain satisfactorily why these compositions were disregarded for so long. He showed them, shortly after they had been written, to
some of his London-based friends, who praised his work unreservedly. Indeed,
some of them were firmly convinced that Iolo was one of Wales's most gifted
bards. Robert Hughes (Robin Ddu yr Ail), of Anglesey, genuinely believed,
according to Owain Myfyr, that they were the best poems ever composed on
their particular themes in the Welsh language.[44] However, little attention was
devoted during the nineteenth century to the exceptional poetic talent that
had produced these works. Iolo never bothered to publish them, in spite of the
effusive reaction of his London-based friends and associates, and therefore most
nineteenth-century critics and literati were completely unaware of their
existence and value. Moreover, the forged *cywyddau* Iolo attributed, *inter alios*,
to Dafydd ap Gwilym – as well as the free-metre verses he claimed had been
composed by Rhys Goch ap Rhicert and other poets – were generally
accepted, without demur, as the genuine work of those talented individuals.
After Iolo had shown his early *cywyddau* to several of his London friends, he
put them to one side and apparently forgot about them. It has been suggested
that he ceased to place much value later in his life on what were called the
'vain exploits' of his youth, and that therefore he decided to hide these compositions completely from view. This is the reason, it was maintained, why such
little attention was devoted to these *cywyddau* until the early years of the

---

[43]   Lewis: *IM*, p. 94.
[44]   Williams: *IM*, p. 228.

twentieth century.[45] There may be some basis for this explanation. But it must also be remembered that nineteenth-century Welsh historians and critics concentrated heavily on other aspects of Iolo's multifaceted career: it was the erudite antiquarian, the prolific hymn-writer, the anticlerical Unitarian, the fervently democratic Druid, and the staunch defender of freedom and the inalienable rights of man who occupied their attention, not the Romantic poet who was liberally endowed with such great creative talents.

Those talents are manifested not only in the compositions which Iolo readily claimed to be his own work, but also in those poems by him, in both strict and free metres, which he attributed at various times to other poets, including some who were merely figments of his own imagination. He found it extremely difficult to resist the urge he frequently experienced either to forge a completely new composition, carefully and skilfully imitating, as he did so, the diction and style of a particular bard, or else to change and adapt parts of a genuine text and add new sections to it. On his return to Glamorgan in 1777, having spent some time in London and Kent, he devoted a great deal of attention to the *cywyddau*: he altered and 'improved' lines, or added an occasional couplet here and there. He did this, at first, not to enhance the glory and prestige of his beloved Glamorgan, nor to create in the body of the text some basis for his own whims and pet theories. It is hard to identify any specific purpose to these literary forgeries, which were probably prompted by that overpowering urge to change and 'polish' that had troubled him from an early age. Some of the earliest manifestations of this compulsion are to be found in the transcripts he made of parts of the work of Dafydd ap Gwilym.[46] On the other hand, the additions Iolo made to the compositions of other bards frequently reflect his own theories and reveries, for they belong to a later period in his life, when he had arrived at several firm conclusions regarding the history of the professional guild of bards and had incorporated in the picture he had formed of that organization many strange ideas that had struck him as he pored avidly over the works of the great master-poets.[47]

Another important development occurred shortly after his return to Glamorgan in 1777. He was no longer content merely to doctor – or add – lines and couplets in the transcripts he made of the poems which he encountered in various manuscript sources: he now began to forge entire compositions and to attribute their authorship to some of the renowned older bards. Among those skilfully executed forgeries were several strict-metre poems which he attributed to Dafydd ap Gwilym and which were included in the edition of his work published in London in 1789 under the auspices of the

[45]   Williams, 'Cywyddau Cynnar Iolo Morganwg', 91.
[46]   *IMChY*, pp. 42–55.
[47]   Ibid., pp. 137–59; Lewis: *IM*, pp. 96–7.

Gwyneddigion Society.[48] When Owain Myfyr and William Owen Pughe were actively engaged in preparing it for publication, they received at various times from Iolo a number of *cywyddau* which, he claimed, represented authentic work by Dafydd discovered by him in old manuscripts in Glamorgan. The editors included two of these compositions in the main body of the volume, while sixteen were published in an 'Appendix' at the end. It has been established beyond any reasonable doubt that Iolo himself had forged the two poems included in the main body of the book as well as twelve of those that appeared in the 'Appendix'.[49] It is difficult to detect any clear motive for these forgeries. Indeed, in all of the many lines of verse which Iolo composed and attributed to Dafydd ap Gwilym, only two examples occur of a clear, unambiguous reference to Glamorgan. The artistry Iolo displayed in these forgeries, some of which were probably written in the period 1777–81, when he was between thirty and thirty-four, was quite remarkable and, since the general standard of Welsh linguistic scholarship left much to be desired during that period, it is hardly surprising that these forgeries deceived a very large number of people for many years. Indeed, many critics seriously believed 'for a long time that those compositions ranked among the best examples of the work of Dafydd ap Gwilym, and during the nineteenth century they received as much attention and praise as any other products of that bard's muse, a fact which clearly testifies to Iolo's great poetic genius and to his powerful command of the Welsh strict metres.

Equally striking is the critical acumen Iolo Morganwg displayed when discussing various aspects of the work, history and organization of the professional poets who sang in the strict metres. In spite of the mental disturbances which often afflicted him and at times seriously impaired his judgement, he was, on the whole, an extraordinarily well-informed and percipient scholar who, before his death in 1826, had acquired a better understanding of the general development of Welsh literature, and especially of its strict-metre poetry, from the fourteenth century down to his own day than any of his contemporaries. As far as we can now tell, he made the first serious attempt to trace the history of the professional guild of bards, who formed the central part of his wide-ranging studies. His manuscripts contain many references to the purpose and significance of the bardic assemblies, to the so-called 'Statute of Gruffudd ap Cynan', the 'Chairs' of the various regions and their respective mottoes, the early bardic grammars and the men whose names were traditionally associated with them, the genealogies of some of the leading bardic families, the triads and the Welsh strict metres. His unpublished work, 'The

---

[48] Williams: *IM*, p. 252.
[49] For a discussion of the background and a detailed, incisive analysis of these poems, see *IMChY, passim*. An analysis of this particular edition of Dafydd's work may be found in Thomas Parry, '*Barddoniaeth Dafydd ab Gwilym*, 1789', *JWBS*, VIII, no. 4 (1957), 189–99.

History of the Bards', on which he worked intermittently for over thirty years, and which he considered to be one of his life's great achievements, contains some interesting examples of his critical acuity.[50] He suggested in this work that the measure known in Welsh as *englyn unodl union* had developed from the Latin elegiac couplet.[51] A similar suggestion was offered many years later by John Rhys[52] and by the celebrated English poet and Jesuit priest, Gerard Manley Hopkins,[53] who had learned Welsh, and it was generally accepted for some time until it was decisively rejected by John Morris-Jones in his authoritative volume on the art of strict-metre Welsh verse.[54] Again, it was generally believed for many years that E. B. Cowell, of Cambridge, was the first to suggest that there were some correspondences between the poetry of the Continental troubadours and trouvères and the work of Dafydd ap Gwilym.[55] It was certainly to Cowell that Dr Theodor Max Chotzen accorded this distinction.[56] However, these correspondences had been noted by Iolo in his manuscripts, and 'The History of the Bards' contains an interesting discussion on this theme. Unfortunately, however, Iolo's percipience never received the recognition it so richly deserved, for he never published what was a truly important discovery.

In another section of the same unpublished work he traced some of the main stages in the development of the intricate system of *cynghanedd*, one of the most distinctive features of strict-metre Welsh verse. This section was written almost a century-and-a-half before Thomas Parry published a valuable paper on this subject.[57] He also realized that the strategic site of Catraeth

---

[50] NLW 13108B. Iolo also called his work on Welsh bardism 'The History of the *British* Bards' (my italics). Parts of this manuscript were later published in the *Cambrian Journal* for the years 1858 (161–9), 1859 (10–29, 132–41, 241–55) and 1860 (7–21), and in *Archaeologia or Miscellaneous Tracts relating to Antiquity*, XIV (1803), 168–204. See also NLW 13097B and 13107B, *passim*.

[51] NLW 13108B, p. 32.

[52] John Rhys, 'The Origin of the Welsh Englyn and Kindred Metres', *Y Cymmrodor*, XVIII (1905), 1–185.

[53] William H. Gardner, *Gerard Manley Hopkins (1844–1889): A Study of Poetic Idiosyncracy in relation to Poetic Tradition* (new edn., 2 vols., London, 1958); Tom Dunne, *Gerard Manley Hopkins: A Comprehensive Bibliography* (Oxford, 1976).

[54] Morris-Jones, *Cerdd Dafod*, p. 318.

[55] E. B. Cowell, 'Dafydd ab Gwilym', *Y Cymmrodor*, II, part 2 (1878), 101–32. See also Ifor Williams and Thomas Roberts (eds.), *Cywyddau Dafydd ap Gwilym a'i Gyfoeswyr* (2nd edn., Caerdydd, 1935), pp. xxxvi ff.

[56] Theodor Max Chotzen, *Recherches sur la Poésie de Dafydd ab Gwilym, Barde Gallois du XIVe Siècle* (Amsterdam, 1927), pp. 14–15.

[57] Thomas Parry, 'Twf y Gynghanedd', *THSC* (1936), 143–60; idem, 'Pynciau Cynghanedd', *BBCS*, X, part 1 (1939), 1–5. Iolo attempted to establish general guidelines which scholars might profitably adopt with a view to determining whether or not certain poems could be attributed to the period of Aneirin and Taliesin, and he demonstrated how the system of *cynghanedd* had developed in the odes composed by the Poets of the Princes. See NLW 13108B, pp. 180 ff.

mentioned in 'Y Gododdin', the long poem which is attributed to the late sixth-century bard Aneirin, is to be identified with Catterick in Yorkshire.[58]

Iolo was probably the first to grasp the significance in the history of the bardic order of the important eisteddfod held at Carmarthen, probably in 1453, under the patronage of Gruffudd ap Nicolas of Dinefwr. He saw clearly the significance of the changes Dafydd ab Edmwnd had made at that eisteddfod in the canonical twenty-four metres.[59] However, he then fabricated some enchantingly colourful details about various bardic assemblies of a similar nature that had been held in Glamorgan, where the changes established in Carmarthen had been overthrown. He also grasped the general purpose and significance of the two eisteddfodau held at Caerwys, Flintshire, in 1523 and 1567, for he saw clearly that these gatherings, like the one in Carmarthen, had been convened in order to safeguard the status and privileges of the strict-metre bards, by preventing untrained poetasters and hucksters from infiltrating the professional guild and, with a view to achieving that end, by firmly fixing the rules that governed the craft of the poet and minstrel.[60] Having studied the history of these two bardic assemblies, he raised the following intriguing consideration: 'Enquire whether the Caerwys Bards, or Eisteddfod, were not the Bardic offspring of the Cheshire Minstrels, or an institution in imitation of, or copied from, theirs? Flintshire is to this day within what remains of the palatinate of Chester.'[61]

Only a well-informed scholar who had mastered all these details could have forged as successfully as did Iolo the documents which provided the basis for his remarkable volume, *Cyfrinach Beirdd Ynys Prydain* ('The Secret of the Bards of the Isle of Britain'),[62] a work which clearly reflects the great interest he had taken over the years in Welsh prosody. It was undoubtedly a highly perceptive scholar, endowed with a detailed knowledge of the works of the old chiefs-of-song, who devised the so-called 'Glamorgan Measures' or 'Old Classification' presented in that work. Iolo himself called this collection of poetic measures, a number of which were skilfully devised by him, 'The Twenty-four Qualities'. He claimed that this metrical system consisted of the measures used in bygone days by the bards of the Isle of Britain, and he ingeniously argued that this system, by virtue of its venerable antiquity, should be accorded a far more privileged place in the indigenous bardic tradition than that established by

[58]   Williams: *PLP*, II, p. 16 (see the note at the foot of the page).
[59]   G. J. Williams, 'Eisteddfod Caerfyrddin', *Y Llenor*, V (1926), 94–102; D. J. Bowen, 'Dafydd ab Edmwnt ac Eisteddfod Caerfyrddin', *Barn*, 142 (1974), 441–7; Morris-Jones, *Cerdd Dafod*, pp. 349–50; Williams: *IM*, pp. xli, 276–7.
[60]   Gwyn Thomas, *Eisteddfodau Caerwys/The Caerwys Eisteddfodau* (Caerdydd/Cardiff, 1968), and the works listed therein.
[61]   NLW 13138A, p. 41.
[62]   Edward Williams, *Cyfrinach Beirdd Ynys Prydain*, ed. Taliesin Williams (Abertawy, 1829). This work was published posthumously.

Fig. 6 Another etching by Robert Cruikshank of Iolo Morganwg, based on a 'memoriter drawing' by Elijah Waring, reproduced as a frontispiece in *RAEW*.

Dafydd ab Edmwnd at the Carmarthen eisteddfod. The principles established by the famous Swedish botanist, Carolus Linnaeus (or Carl von Linné, 1707–78), for the identification and classification of plants can be discerned in Iolo's description of the metres,[63] another indication of the astonishing breadth and variety of his interests and of his insatiable curiosity. Undoubtedly, the volume *Cyfrinach Beirdd Ynys Prydain* demonstrates that he had acquired a more detailed knowledge of the esoteric lore of the professional poets and of the contents of the old bardic grammars than any of his contemporaries. It is difficult to find a scholar who can seriously vie with him in this field prior to the advent of John Morris-Jones.

Significantly, one of 'The Twenty-four Qualities' listed in the aforementioned volume is the *Dyrif* or 'Carol', a composition in free metres having regular accentuation and occasional touches of *cynghanedd*.[64] The discussion in this section shows clearly that Iolo fully understood the fundamental difference between the syllabic strict-metre verse and the poetry composed in the accentual free metres that became increasingly popular in Wales from the sixteenth century onwards as the professional guild of bards began to decline.[65] With characteristic percipience, he emphasized that the distinguishing feature of the *dyrif* was regular accentuation of the lines and stanzas.[66] This was possibly the first intelligent attempt to note the fundamental difference between strict- and free-metre verse. And since he claimed that it was Glamorgan bards of the fifteenth and sixteenth centuries who had rediscovered the old classification of the indigenous Welsh metres, he correctly maintained that free-metre verse was not a new genre of poetry introduced to Wales from England at the beginning of the modern period but rather a style of verse that had been composed by Welsh bards from time immemorial.[67]

Iolo's manuscripts show that he had formed a clearer picture of the beginning of the *cywydd* period in the history of Welsh literature than any of his predecessors, and some important features noted by him had to be rediscovered by Welsh scholars in the twentieth century. He traced the development of the measure called *cywydd deuair hirion*,[68] and his attention was drawn to the

---

[63] Morris-Jones, *Cerdd Dafod*, pp. 372–9; J. L. Larson, *Reason and Experience: The Representation of Natural Order in the Work of Carl von Linné* (Berkeley, 1971); Wilfrid Blunt and William T. Stearn, *The Compleat Naturalist: A Life of Linnaeus* (rev. edn., London, 2001).

[64] Williams, *Cyfrinach Beirdd Ynys Prydain*, pp. 159–71.

[65] Ceri W. Lewis, 'The Decline of Professional Poetry' in R. Geraint Gruffydd (ed.), *A Guide to Welsh Literature c. 1530–1700* (Cardiff, 1997), pp. 29–74, and the references listed at the end of the chapter.

[66] Williams, *Cyfrinach Beirdd Ynys Prydain*, pp. 159–60.

[67] Cf. Thomas Parry, *A History of Welsh Literature*, trans. H. Idris Bell (Oxford, 1962), p. 164: 'a little examination of the free verse will suffice to prove that some kind of similar verse existed in Wales all through the centuries'.

[68] This is a strict metre consisting of rhyming couplets, with full consonance or *cynghanedd* throughout (except in its earliest form), each couplet consisting of lines of seven syllables

short example of this metre contained in the bardic grammar associated with Einion Offeiriad (*fl.* 1330) – or Eden Dafod Aur, as Iolo occasionally maintained. Since this short example does not contain regular *cynghanedd*, he reasoned that it must be attributed to a period earlier than that in which Dafydd ap Gwilym sang and therefore it must have been the latter who was pre-eminently responsible for popularizing the measure.[69] And when he forgot about the fictitious figures he sometimes attempted to associate with the earliest extant copies of the bardic grammar, figures who were the creations of his own overactive imagination, he came to the conclusion that it was Einion Offeiriad who was the author of this important treatise and that the ode the latter sang to Rhys ap Gruffudd (d. 1356) proves that he flourished in the first half of the fourteenth century.[70]

Since Iolo was unquestionably the outstanding authority in his day on the literary history of Glamorgan, it is hardly surprising that his work sheds much valuable light on the bardic life of the region. He saw that Tir Iarll was the most important nursery of the bardic culture and literary life of Glamorgan from the fifteenth century onwards, if not, indeed, from an appreciably earlier period.[71] This was an extremely important discovery for anyone interested in tracing the long bardic history of the region. He also realized that Llywelyn Siôn, who was born at Llangewydd, near Bridgend, was a professional scribe who had made important contributions to the literary life of Glamorgan by transcribing, at the behest of some of the local landed gentry, several important manuscripts.[72]

In 1780 Iolo began tracing the descent of the leading strict-metre bards of Glamorgan from the fourteenth century down to his own day, noting the chief-of-song in each period and identifying the relevant bardic disciples.[73] He succeeded in doing this with a remarkable degree of accuracy, an astonishing

---

rhyming a stressed syllable with an unstressed one, or vice versa. See Morris-Jones, *Cerdd Dafod*, pp. 328–9.

[69] See, for example, G. J. Williams and E. J. Jones (eds.), *Gramadegau'r Penceirddiaid* (Caerdydd, 1934), p. 31 (lines 20–5) and p. 52 (lines 16–21); Williams: *IM*, p. xliii; Thomas Parry, 'Datblygiad y Cywydd', *THSC* (1939), 209–31; D. J. Bowen, 'Dafydd ap Gwilym a Datblygiad y Cywydd', *LlC*, VIII, nos. 1–2 (1964), 1–32.

[70] This was another important fact which had to be rediscovered by Welsh scholars in the twentieth century. See Ifor Williams, 'Rhys ap Gruffudd', *THSC* (1913–14), 193–203; idem, 'Awdl i Rys ap Gruffudd gan Einion Offeiriad. Dosbarth Einion ar Ramadeg a'i Ddyled i Ddonatus', *Y Cymmrodor*, XXVI (1916), 115–46; Williams and Jones (eds.), *Gramadegau'r Penceirddiaid*, pp. xvii–xxix; Thomas Parry, 'The Welsh Metrical Treatise attributed to Einion Offeiriad', *PBA*, XLVII (1961), 177–95; J. Beverley Smith, 'Einion Offeiriad', *BBCS*, XX, part IV (1964), 339–47; Iestyn Daniel, 'Awduriaeth y Gramadeg a briodolir i Einion Offeiriad a Dafydd Ddu Hiraddug' in J. E. Caerwyn Williams (ed.), *Ysgrifau Beirniadol XIII* (Dinbych, 1985), pp. 178–208; Ceri W. Lewis, 'Einion Offeiriad and the Bardic Grammar' in A. O. H. Jarman and Gwilym Rees Hughes (eds.), *A Guide to Welsh Literature 1282– c.1550* (rev. edn., Cardiff, 1997), pp. 44–71.

[71] *TLlM*, pp. 22, 32–3; Williams: *IM*, pp. 7–9.

[72] NLW 13089E, p. 315. On Llywelyn Siôn, see the references cited in n. 25 above.

[73] NLW 13116B, pp. 373–4.

feat when it is borne in mind that he was apparently the first to attempt this task and that most of his contemporaries had only the vaguest notion of the development of the bardic tradition. Nor was his attention confined in this respect to his native county, for he traced, once again with a striking degree of accuracy, the lineage of the chief bardic teachers in north Wales from the period of Dafydd ab Edmwnd in the fifteenth century to the days of Rhys Cain, Gruffudd Hafren and various other bards in the seventeenth century, when, for a variety of reasons, the professional guild of bards came to a sad end in north Wales.[74] These feats were based not only on a very wide and detailed study of the substantial corpus of strict-metre verse composed by the prolific *cywyddwyr* but also on every scrap of vital information he had managed to glean in his youth from elderly acquaintances who had been familiar with the last of the wandering bards and minstrels. He naturally considered information obtained in this way to be extremely important, for he fully understood that the indigenous bardic tradition had been mainly an oral one prior to the fifteenth century, a fact he ingeniously used whenever he felt it necessary to account for apparent inconsistencies in some of his literary forgeries.

During the latter part of his life, from 1788–90 until his death in 1826, Iolo Morganwg became obsessed with the notion that the strict-metre Welsh bards were the descendants of the ancient Druids, the sages and, according to some authorities, the priests of the early Celtic and Brythonic world, to whom there are explicit references in the works of various Classical authors, both Greek and Roman.[75] That notion constituted an important part of the contemporary *Zeitgeist*.[76] The professional poets themselves, prompted by the bardic tradition and by Geoffrey of Monmouth's influential *Historia Regum Britanniae* (c.1139), considered their learning and art to be of an exceptionally high standard. Indeed, according to Gruffydd Robert, the sixteenth-century Renaissance scholar and Catholic exile, they were convinced that 'neither Greeks nor Romans could ever be compared with the old Welsh master-poets'.[77] Some scholars expressed the view that the bardic traditions extended back to those close descendants of Noah who had founded Celtic colonies in western Europe, and that therefore it could be assumed that the Druids had inherited the

---

[74]   NLW 13139A, p. 198.

[75]   T. D. Kendrick, *The Druids: A Study in Keltic Prehistory* (London, 1927); James L. T. C. Spence, *The History and Origins of Druidism* (London, [1949]); Françoise Le Roux, *Les Druides* (Rennes, 1986); Nora K. Chadwick, *The Druids* (Cardiff, 1966); Stuart Piggott, *The Druids* (London, 1968).

[76]   See Aidan L. Owen, *The Famous Druids: A Survey of Three Centuries of English Literature on the Druids* (Oxford, 1962); G. J. Williams, 'Leland a Bale a'r Traddodiad Derwyddol', *LlC*, IV, no. 1 (1956), 15–25; Lewis: *IM*, pp. 174 ff; Geraint H. Jenkins, 'Iolo Morganwg and the Gorsedd of the Bards of the Isle of Britain', *Studia Celtica Japonica*, 7 (1995), 45–60; idem, *Facts, Fantasy and Fiction: The Historical Vision of Iolo Morganwg* (Aberystwyth, 1997).

[77]   G. J. Williams (ed.), *Gramadeg Cymraeg gan Gruffydd Robert* (Caerdydd, 1939), pp. ix, [275].

illustrious traditions of the great biblical patriarchs.[78] 'Druidomania' coloured much of historical thinking from the sixteenth century onwards, and some antiquarians propounded the theory that the ancient circles of standing stones in Avebury and at Stonehenge were the remains of ancient druidic temples.[79]

No literary figure was more deeply affected by these ideas than Iolo Morganwg. In his romantic reveries, which may have been partly induced by his habit of taking regular doses of laudanum '[to] relieve a very troublesome cough',[80] he became convinced that many of the details he had read about the ancient Druids contained a fascinating portrayal of his own distinguished bardic ancestors. Following the death in 1789 of his friend and fellow-bard, Edward Evan, of Aberdare, he genuinely believed that he was the last living descendant of the *'Ancient British Bards'*[81] and that it was, therefore, his preordained responsibility to explain both to his contemporaries and to countless future generations the richness and glory of the indigenous Welsh tradition. He maintained that the ancient druidic traditions had been preserved in Glamorgan, especially in Tir Iarll in the more inaccessible Uplands where, he argued, they had found a secure retreat after those traditions had been destroyed in all the other major regions of Wales by the internecine warfare of the Middle Ages. He asserted that there were still bards in Glamorgan who, in marked contradistinction to 'the modern book-taught poets' who hailed from other parts of Wales, had inherited the 'Secret of the Bards of the Isle of Britain', which had been transmitted in the time-honoured manner by bardic teachers *orally* instructing their pupils, over many generations, from the period of the ancient Druids down to his own day, and that he, as a member of a distinguished bardic fraternity known as the 'Brotherhood of Glamorgan Bards', belonged to that resplendent tradition.[82] It was this fraternity that had safeguarded the 'Chair of Glamorgan', which had upheld standards among the strict-metre bards and faithfully adhered to the ancient practices and ceremonies. One significant indication of the way this ancient tradition had been preserved in Glamorgan was the fact that the bards there continued to hold Gorseddau, as they had done throughout the centuries, in the open air, according to the long-established druidic custom, between the stone circles that had inspired the imagination of so many antiquarians.[83] He derided the

---

[78] Williams, 'Leland a Bale a'r Traddodiad Derwyddol', 15 ff.; Lewis: *IM*, pp. 174 ff.

[79] Owen, *The Famous Druids*, pp. 101–37; Lewis: *IM*, p. 179; Cardiff 4.253, pp. 101, 109, and *passim*.

[80] Lewis: *IM*, pp. 55–7.

[81] *Gentleman's Magazine*, LIX, part 2 (1789), 976–7; *TLlM*, pp. 245–6; Williams: *IM*, pp. 464–5.

[82] See the letter Iolo addressed to Owain Myfyr on 10 July 1780, now preserved in BL Add. 15024, f. 188[r–v]. Iolo also refers in this letter to the establishment of 'a yearly association [of Glamorgan bards] at Llantrisaint'. In a note appended to the letter he gave an example of the work that had already been accomplished by this 'Brotherhood' in its annual eisteddfod at Llantrisaint.

[83] The word *gorsedd* < Brythonic *γor-essed-* < Indo-European *uper-en-sed-*, a formation from

view expressed by Henry Rowlands that the main seat of the Druids in Britain
had once been located in Anglesey,[84] and he concluded that the bardic 'Bryn
Gwyddon', which he believed was their original centre, was to be found in his
own native province, for he could not easily forget the cromlechs found in
Dyffryn Golych,[85] near St Nicholas, nor the stone circles located in various
places on the mountains and hills of south Wales. And, *more suo*, he claimed to
have in his possession *authentic* manuscripts which shed much valuable light on
early bardic teaching, doctrine and practices, which the strict-metre bards in
Glamorgan had fortunately inherited. He referred in his writings to the closely
guarded secrets of the Druids, including the 'mysterious symbol' /|\ of the
ineffable name of God, 'being the rays of the rising sun at the equinoxes and
solstices conveying into focus "the eye of light"'.[86] This symbol was devised by
Iolo to represent the divine attributes of Love, Justice and Truth in the
ceremonies and regalia of the Gorsedd of the Bards of the Isle of Britain
(Gorsedd Beirdd Ynys Prydain). He paid detailed attention to the vestments
that the druidic bards allegedly wore on ceremonial occasions and to their
beliefs, teachings, arcane lore and rituals. Included in the various elements
which, to the end of his life, he kept adding to his intricate druidic system were
ideas he had formulated after studying works on the Jewish cabbala, Hinduism,
Brahminism, mysticism and theosophy.[87] The Gorsedd also became firmly
attached to Unitarianism[88] and developed distinct political undertones.[89] Iolo's
ideas received some publicity in 1792 when his London-based friend, William
Owen Pughe, included in the introduction to a work he published that year a
substantial section on 'Bardism'.[90] This was based on material which Iolo had
given him, when he visited London in 1791, from 'The History of the Bards'.

---

    the primitive root **sed-* 'sit' (as in Latin *sedeo*), originally meant 'mound of earth, tump or
    knoll, hillock, tumulus', and it also occurs occasionally in the Laws of Hywel Dda to denote
    a court or tribunal or judicial assembly held in the open air. See Timothy Lewis, *A Glossary
    of Mediaeval Welsh Law based upon the Black Book of Chirk* (Manchester, 1913), p. 161, *s.v.*
    However, the word was invested with an entirely new meaning by Iolo; he used it to denote
    a special assembly of druidic bards who met 'in the face of the sun and in the eye of light'.

[84] Henry Rowlands, *Mona Antiqua Restaurata* (Dublin, 1723), pp. 34 ff., 70, 83; Owen, *The
    Famous Druids*, pp. 73–82; NLW 13089E, p. 460; NLW 13130A, p. 292; Williams: *IM*, pp.
    182–5.

[85] He connected *golych* with *goluch* 'praise, worship, reverence, prayer' (see *GPC*, p. 1453, s.v.)
    and with *golychu* 'to praise, worship, pray, implore' (ibid., p. 1454, s.v.).

[86] Dillwyn Miles, *The Secret of the Bards of the Isle of Britain* (Llandybïe, 1992), p. 63.

[87] The small cottage in Flemingston where he lived for the greater part of his life contained
    many works on these subjects and other kindred matters. See also Michael Franklin, 'Sir
    William Jones, the Celtic Revival and the Oriental Renaissance' in Gerard Caruthers and
    Alan Rawes (eds.), *English Romanticism and the Celtic World* (Cambridge, 2003), pp. 20–37.

[88] Lewis: *IM*, p. 185.

[89] Ibid., p. 186.

[90] William Owen Pughe, *The Heroic Elegies and other Pieces of Llywarç Hen* (London, 1792),
    pp. xxi–lxxx.

In order to provide some 'substance' for the remarkable druidic world he saw so clearly in his fertile imagination, he fabricated, with great skill and patience, scores of notes and documents, including a large number of triads on various themes which, he asserted, the professional bards had declaimed in the Gorsedd assemblies of bygone ages, for he saw that some of the old authentic Welsh triads had a mnemonic purpose. With dazzling ingenuity, he wrote triads on the art of poetry, triads of bardism, triads of wisdom, theological triads and law triads, which he associated with the name of Dyfnwal Moelmud and in which he endeavoured to depict various practices in the so-called 'Golden Age'.[91] Around 1791 he devised a peculiar alphabet, called *Coelbren y Beirdd*, which he claimed had been used by the Britons and the ancient Druids and which, once again, had been safeguarded throughout the centuries by the Glamorgan bards.[92]

Modern scholarship has shown conclusively that there is no historical foundation for Iolo's account of the development of the Gorsedd and for the alleged connection between the professional strict-metre bards and the ancient Druids.[93] Nevertheless, it is beyond question that this aspect of his work exercised a powerful influence on very many of his contemporaries, for it was Iolo who was pre-eminently responsible for transforming the old bardic assembly into a *national* institution, which became an important focus for many of the literary and cultural activities of Wales, while the warm romantic glow that so enchantingly suffused the essays in which he discussed the old bardic meetings, some of which probably never existed outside his own creative imagination, proved to be a factor of great importance in the remarkable development of the eisteddfod in the nineteenth century.[94] The romantic aura surrounding the rituals, dogmas and ceremonial vestments of the Gorsedd, as described by Iolo, succeeded in arousing the interest and firing the imagination of many scholars and literati. His influence can clearly be detected in the great

---

[91] See *MAW*, vols. II and III; *IMChY*, pp. 198, 214; G. J. Williams, 'Hanes Cyhoeddi'r *Myvyrian Archaiology*', *JWBS*, X, no. 1 (1966), 2–12.

[92] See, for example, NLW 13097B, pp. 49–76, 154–73, 177–80, 200–9, 212–14, *passim*; NLW 13107B, pp. 2–35, *passim*; NLW 13087E, pp. 15–25, 29; NLW 13089E, p. 315; NLW 13093E, pp. 155–74, 183–4, 187, 197, 203; Taliesin Williams (ed.), *Coelbren y Beirdd* (Llandovery, 1840); idem (ed.), *Iolo Manuscripts* (Llandovery, 1848), pp. 203–9, 617–23; John Williams (ab Ithel) (ed.), *Barddas* (2 vols., Llandovery, 1862; London, 1874), I, pp. 142–51; Miles, *The Secret of the Bards*, pp. 64–5; Lewis: *IM*, pp. 182–3.

[93] John Morris-Jones, 'Gorsedd Beirdd Ynys Prydain', *Cymru*, X (1896), 21–9, 133–40, 153–61, 197–204, 293–9; idem, 'Derwyddiaeth Gorsedd y Beirdd', *Y Beirniad*, I, no. 1 (1911), 66–72; G. J. Williams, 'Yr Eisteddfod a'r Orsedd', *Y Llenor*, I (1922), 131–8; idem, 'Gorsedd Beirdd Ynys Prydain', ibid., III (1924), 162–71; idem, 'Gorsedd y Beirdd a'r Seiri Rhyddion', *LlC*, VII, nos. 3–4 (1963), 213–16; idem, 'Hanes yr Eisteddfod a'r Orsedd' in Aneirin Lewis (ed.), *Agweddau ar Hanes Dysg Gymraeg: Detholiad o Ddarlithiau G. J. Williams* (Caerdydd, 1969), pp. 124–47.

[94] Lewis: *IM*, pp. 194–5.

eisteddfod held at Llangollen in 1858, an extremely important event in the history of that institution.[95] Nor can it be denied that the colourful Gorsedd ceremonies, on which Iolo obviously left an indelible stamp, have helped to attract thousands of visitors to the National Eisteddfod of Wales over the years.

No less noteworthy is the astonishing transformation which, as a result of Iolo's work and activities, occurred in the views held by many scholars and antiquarians of the literary and cultural status of Glamorgan. During the first half of the eighteenth century Glamorgan was not generally regarded as being of any great importance in the literary history of Wales. No bardic assembly of any significance, it was widely believed, had ever been held within its boundaries, and the references occasionally made to Glamorgan bards were, on the whole, decidedly disdainful.[96] Nor did the dialectal vocabulary of the province merit the attention of any serious lexicographer.[97] By approximately the end of that century, however, Glamorgan was increasingly being regarded as probably the most important, and undoubtedly the most interesting, province in the whole of Wales. By that stage, it was widely believed that, more than any other region, Glamorgan had preserved the time-honoured national literary traditions. Had not its bards retained and safeguarded the Gorsedd of the Bards of the Isle of Britain, that most distinctly Welsh of all literary institutions, with its colourful ritual ceremonies and practices? And had not the same bards succeeded in preserving the *peithynen*[98] and *Coelbren y Beirdd*, as well as transmitting from one generation to another all that was vitally important in the old esoteric bardic lore? Furthermore, many places in Glamorgan became indissolubly linked in the minds of thousands of Welsh people with the colourful literary pageant so skilfully depicted in the large body of spurious material which Iolo had produced.[99]

Nor was the great enthusiasm engendered by Iolo's work confined to Wales. One of his Glamorgan friends was informed by the French scholar, Charles Fauriel, that the account of the Gorsedd published in 1792 had made a deep impression on several scholars and intellectuals in Paris, while Iolo's London-based Welsh friends and acquaintances considered that work to be probably the most important contribution any individual had ever made to Welsh studies, for it had convincingly demonstrated, in their opinion, that Wales was one of the great nations of the world, with a glorious history that could be traced

---

[95] G. J. Williams, 'Eisteddfod Llangollen, 1858', *TDHS*, 7 (1958), 139–61.

[96] *Cambrian Register*, I (1795), 343.

[97] J. H. Davies (ed.), *The Letters of Goronwy Owen (1723–1769)* (Cardiff, 1924), p. 68.

[98] This word is the diminutive of *peithyn, peithin*, a borrowing from *pectin-*, the stem in the oblique cases of Latin *pecten* 'comb, rake' etc. Iolo Morganwg used this word to denote the wooden frame used in printing the bardic alphabet he had devised. This frame could hold 'a number of three- or four-sided staves which could be turned in order to read the letters carved on them'. See *GPC*, p. 2720, s.v.; Miles, *The Secret of the Bards*, p. 64.

[99] *TLIM*, pp. xii–xv.

back to the days of the early patriarchs.[100] The widespread enthusiasm with which Iolo's work was received convincingly demonstrates that he had succeeded in adding a fascinating new dimension to his nation's past and that he had, thereby, effectively invented a tradition. His inspired fabrications, especially those relating to the work, organization, arcane practices and colourful ceremonial vestments of the strict-metre Welsh bards, testify clearly to his brilliant virtuosity, while the huge impact those fabrications had on his contemporaries and, for some considerable time after his death, on successive generations of his literature-loving compatriots, is a striking example of the great creative power of an ingeniously embellished historico-literary myth.

[100] G. J. Williams, *Iolo Morganwg* (London, 1963), pp. 31–2.

5

A Multitude of Voices: The Free-Metre Poetry of Iolo Morganwg

HUW MEIRION EDWARDS

There can be little doubt that the many-sidedness of Iolo Morganwg has tended to obscure his precocious poetic talent. As the vast range of his literary and historical forgeries was exposed during the course of the twentieth century, scholars concentrated their attention on the forger and myth-maker whose opium-enhanced vision of a druidic past was generally regarded as one of the most remarkable creations of the Romantic imagination. From the 1780s especially, Iolo's poetic gift, indeed his own identity as a Welsh-language poet, became increasingly subservient to that all-embracing vision. The recognition he deserved was sacrificed in order to create a dazzling body of verse supposedly composed by a succession of Glamorgan poets over a period of six hundred years, a succession of which he, Iolo Morganwg, by the late 1780s claimed to be the sole survivor.

Although some of Iolo's early *cywyddau* were known to a few of his London acquaintances, on the whole his youthful poems, ascribed in his manuscripts to Iorwerth Gwilim (a Welsh version of Edward Williams) and Iorwerth Morganwg, were carefully concealed from prying eyes. With a few exceptions, such as an early elegy published in Cowbridge in 1772[1] and his two volumes of Unitarian hymns, *Salmau yr Eglwys yn yr Anialwch* (Psalms of the Church in the Wilderness) which appeared in 1812 and 1834, prior to the twentieth century his published Welsh poetry was attributed to others. Most famously, the forged *cywyddau* of Dafydd ap Gwilym – or as he was later styled by Iolo, Dafydd Morgannwg – published by the Gwyneddigion Society in 1789,[2] were generally believed to be genuine and were well received in the nineteenth century. The same is true of the enchantingly lyrical free-metre poems attributed to Dafydd's so-called Glamorgan precursor, the twelfth-century 'love-poet' Rhys Goch ap Rhicert, which were published with summaries in

---

[1]   Edward Williams, *Dagrau yr Awen neu Farwnad Lewis Hopcin fardd, o Landyfodwg ym Morganwg* (Pont-y-fon, 1772).

[2]   Owen Jones and William Owen Pughe (eds), *Barddoniaeth Dafydd ab Gwilym* (Llundain, 1789).

English and a few translations by Iolo's devoted son, Taliesin ab Iolo, in the *Iolo Manuscripts* in 1848.[3] It was ab Iolo, too, who, in 1829, three years after his father's death, published his highly influential – and highly misleading – bardic treatise *Cyfrinach Beirdd Ynys Prydain* (The Secret of the Bards of the Isle of Britain).[4] As will become apparent, its metrical exempla, attributed to a host of real and fictitious Glamorgan poets of the sixteenth and seventeenth centuries, figure among Iolo's most polished poetic creations. His extraordinary inventiveness and versatility were such that he was hardly regarded as a poet in his own right in nineteenth-century Wales.

Iolo's rehabilitation as a Romantic poet began with Griffith John Williams. In a series of articles from 1919 onwards[5] and in his groundbreaking work of literary detection, *Iolo Morganwg a Chywyddau'r Ychwanegiad* (1926), he revealed an accomplished poet in both the strict and free metres and drew attention for the first time to works which preceded his daring poetic forgeries. The extent of Iolo's deception is more graphically revealed in Williams's major biography of Iolo, the first volume of which covered the period up to 1788.[6] But so, too, are his subject's literary accomplishments, whether under his own name or in the guise of others. The unfinished second volume of the biography was supposed to contain a more detailed discussion of Iolo's poetry; it was also the author's intention to publish a collection of his strict- and free-metre verse, including poems attributed to others.[7] Iolo's reputation was enhanced slightly when Thomas Parry included two free-metre and two strict-metre poems in *The Oxford Book of Welsh Verse* (1962)[8] – three of these were originally ascribed to others – in which he described him as a 'very fine poet' whose 'reputation as an antiquary completely obscured his merits as a poet'.[9] (His earlier history of Welsh literature, *Hanes Llenyddiaeth Gymraeg* (1945), had made no mention of Iolo's free-metre poetry, apart from a reference to Rhys Goch ap Rhicert as an excellent poet.[10]) It is only since 1980 that a more balanced evaluation has been possible; that year saw the publication of two editions of Iolo's verse. Tegwyn Jones's selection, *Y Gwir Degwch: Detholiad o Gywyddau Serch Iolo Morganwg*,[11] left no doubt about Iolo's virtuosity in the *cywydd* metre. These early poems of love and wild nature, inspired mainly by Euron, Iolo's future

[3]   Taliesin Williams (ed.), *Iolo Manuscripts* (Llandovery, 1848), pp. 228–51, 645–51.
[4]   Idem (ed.), *Cyfrinach Beirdd Ynys Prydain* (Abertawy, 1829).
[5]   These are listed in Lewis: *IM*, pp. 236–7. The first of G. J. Williams's articles was 'Cywyddau Cynnar Iolo Morganwg', *Y Beirniad*, VIII (1919), 75–91.
[6]   Williams: *IM*. The projected second and third volumes were not completed.
[7]   See ibid., pp. 128, 242n.
[8]   Thomas Parry (ed.), *The Oxford Book of Welsh Verse* (Oxford, 1962), nos. 186–9.
[9]   Ibid., p. 557.
[10] Thomas Parry, *Hanes Llenyddiaeth Gymraeg hyd 1900* (Caerdydd, 1945), p. 236.
[11] Tegwyn Jones (ed.), *Y Gwir Degwch: Detholiad o Gywyddau Serch Iolo Morganwg* (Bow Street, 1980).

wife, Margaret (Peggy) Roberts, have a passion and sensitivity which set them apart from the mainstream of eighteenth-century strict-metre poetry. Since they have so much in common with the forgeries attributed to Dafydd ap Gwilym, who was a formative influence on the young Iolo, most readers would have been more surprised by the sheer scope and variety of P. J. Donovan's 1980 edition of the free-metre poems, *Cerddi Rhydd Iolo Morganwg*.[12] Donovan's excellent selection of close to a hundred poems forms the basis of most of the following discussion.

The poems are divided into three sections: those which Iolo claimed as his own; those which are left unascribed in his papers; and those which are ascribed to others. Not surprisingly, nearly two-thirds of the poems belong to the final section. The first section contains a meagre sixteen poems, which amount to nearly all the free-metre poems attributed to Iolo in the manuscripts (a small number have been omitted due to their poor quality, as have the long and rather tiresome series of aphoristic and proverbial verses composed in the simple four-line *triban* (triplet) metre).[13] Some of the poems from the early and mid-seventies are likely to have found their way to the second section of Donovan's edition; one of them, dated 1773,[14] typically describes the poet's hatred of London and his longing for the fields of the river Thaw in Iolo's own corner of the Vale of Glamorgan. Several of his early poems are likely to have been attributed to others as his vision of his county's glorious bardic past took shape. Such may be the case with 'Cwyn, Wenno, cwyn . . .', which is claimed to have been composed by Dafydd y Nant – a seventeenth-century cleric who was to loom large in Iolo's bardic vision – when he was just fifteen. The poem was published by G. J. Williams in 1923 as one of Iolo's early works.[15] But it is also probable that poems written under his own name were deleted from the record, as seems to have been the case with a group of twenty-five *cywyddau* of which only a couple remain, judging by the headings in one of Iolo's tantalizing lists.[16] Indeed, he may even have thought of publishing a collection of his verse at Cowbridge at the age of twenty-three if the following heading, written around the year of his mother's death in 1770, is to be believed: '*Blaendardd yr Awenŷdd neu Gasgliad o bryddestau ar amrŷw Achosion* gan Iorwerth Gwilim o Drefflemin y Morganwg'[17] ('The Shoots of

---

[12]   The fullest discussion of the free-metre poetry is Lewis: *IM*, chapter 7; for a chronological survey of the poetry published pre-1980, see Morgan: *IM*, pp. 24–56.

[13]   *CRhIM*, p. ix. Cf. the *tribannau* in E. G. Millward (ed.), *Blodeugerdd Barddas o Gerddi Rhydd y Ddeunawfed Ganrif* (Llandybïe, 1991), pp. 246–7.

[14]   *CRhIM*, no. 31. At the end of the poem, Iolo wrote 'Twickenham near London September 9th 1779' ('Twickenham gerllaw Llundain Medi'r 9fed 1779'), but then changed the year to 1773 (ibid., p. 154).

[15]   Ibid., no. 37; G. J. Williams, 'Caneuon Cynnar Iolo Morganwg', *Y Llenor*, II (1923), 52.

[16]   Williams, 'Cywyddau Cynnar Iolo Morganwg', 78.

[17]   Williams: *IM*, p. 133.

the Muse or a Collection of poems on various subjects by Iorwerth Gwilim of Flemingston in Glamorgan'). Did the mature Iolo feel embarrassed by some of his youthful efforts or was he perhaps wary of betraying to posterity his aptitude for imitation in his adoption of an array of styles and verse-forms from an early age?

Even in the handful of poems which bear his name, his versatility and mastery of Welsh versecraft are quite striking. Iolo's innate creativeness was matched by an insatiable thirst for knowledge and a search for perfection. By the age of twenty he had immersed himself in the difficult art of *cerdd dafod* through his close association with a community of poets, grammarians and antiquaries which thrived mainly in Upland Glamorgan. Lewis Hopkin, John Bradford, Dafydd Nicolas of Aberpergwm and others had themselves been inspired by the eighteenth-century literary awakening led by the Morris brothers of Anglesey, and although Iolo was to claim that they received their training (unlike their north Wales counterparts) through oral tradition in an unbroken line of Glamorgan bards, they, in fact, derived most of their knowledge from books. Such, too, was Iolo's experience: he studied bardic grammars, pored over manuscripts of medieval poetry, and by his early twenties, using the pseudonym Iorwerth Gwilim, he was competing in strict verse against his fellow poets in local eisteddfodau such as the one held in Llantrisant in 1767. There are also some scurrilous satires from this period and amusing pieces inspired by local incidents.[18] Not content to confine himself to the *cywydd* and *englyn* metres of classical tradition, he dabbled early in a variety of freer metrical forms. Having seen a manuscript collection of sixteenth-century *cwndidau*, a popular metre closely associated with Glamorgan, he promptly penned a poem in the same mould, closely imitating the language and style of the originals.[19] Likewise, the anthology *Blodeu-gerdd Cymry* (1759) inspired him to master the intricate metres made popular by Huw Morys and Edward Morris a century earlier, in which the form was determined by the accompanying melody and accentuated by the skilful use of *cynghanedd*. The following lines are from a poem claimed to have been written in 1768 on the melody 'Cainc Dyfnder y Nos' or 'Morfa Rhuddlan':

> Mi glywais o goedydd gân newydd gan eos,
> O dewlys unigwerdd y dolau sy'n agos,
> Yn ochr y maes ebrwydd yn nechrau mis Ebrill,
> Dair wythnos cyn Mai y chwibanai wych bennill . . .[20]

---

[18] Ibid., pp. 131–2. Iolo's papers contain several vicious satires aimed at Owen Jones (Owain Myfyr) once their relationship had turned sour in the early years of the nineteenth century, cf. NLW 13148A, p. 175.

[19] Williams: *IM*, p. 130.

[20] *CRhIM*, no. 6.

(I heard from the woodland a nightingale's new song/ From the secluded, green, sturdy court of the meadows nearby,/ By the edge of the burgeoning plain in early April,/ Three weeks before May it whistled a fine verse.)

As so often with Iolo's writings, the date cannot be taken at face value, especially since the poem is described as 'A song composed by Iolo Morganwg 1768' ('Cân a gant Iolo Morganwg 1768'),[21] a name only adopted by Iolo from around 1790 onwards. If it is indeed such an early poem, Iolo's mastery of form and *cynghanedd* are quite remarkable. As well as the *cynghanedd sain* (based on internal rhyme and alliteration) so typical of this genre of carol-style poetry, the poem is peppered with complex but seemingly effortless instances of consonantal correspondence (*cynghanedd groes*) sustained over twelve syllables, as seen in the second and third lines above. Iolo's acquaintance with the rigours of *cerdd dafod* from a young age instilled in him a discipline and a love of word-play which were to serve him well as he strived to master an array of metrical forms. His technical virtuosity was to reach its climax in the original fusions of strict and free metres contained in *Cyfrinach Beirdd Ynys Prydain*.

G. J. Williams has drawn attention to an unquestionably early poem[22] which echoes the religious and biblical carols composed in the popular *tri thrawiad* (three beat) metre throughout the seventeenth and eighteenth centuries. Here we can clearly glimpse the youthful imitator honing his craft, though his use of some archaic bardic vocabulary is rather incongruous. The young Iolo's love of medieval words and syntax gleaned from manuscripts and from the dictionary of Thomas Richards – described by Iolo as 'My greatly respected and highly honour'd friend and instructor'[23] – betrays a natural tendency towards imitation. It is regarded as a weakness in the *cywyddau* of the same period; he later became more selective in his use of Middle Welsh vocabulary, especially in his less formal free-metre verse. In another poem, ascribed to the young Iorwerth Gwilim, in which Iolo seems to be feeling his way as a free-metre poet, the metre is relatively uncomplicated: stanzas of four thirteen-syllable lines rhyming aabb with surprisingly little alliterative embel-lishment.[24] The poet's protestations, however, seem somewhat overcooked:

> Pan rodiwyf tros y werddol e fydd yr adar mwyn
> Yn seinio nâd alarus wrth glywed maint fy nghwyn;
> Mae atsain prudd f'uchenaid yn treiddio'r bryniau syth,
> Ond calon gwen lliw'r manod nid yw'n nawseiddio fyth . . .

[21] Ibid., p. 7. The poem was published by G. J. Williams as an example of Iolo's early verse, 'Caneuon Cynnar Iolo Morganwg', *Y Llenor*, I (1922), 266.

[22] Williams: *IM*, pp. 130–1.

[23] Lewis: *IM*, p. 75.

[24] *CRhIM*, no. 14.

Rhowch benthyg eich puroriaeth i mi sydd garwr clau,
Ymunaf hwn â'r awen er profi meddalhau
Ei chalon oer gallestrig a'i mynwes hardd a ffraw
Sy fel y rhew tragwyddol yn eitha'r gogledd draw . . .

(Whenever I cross the green meadow the gentle birds/ Chant a mournful dirge on hearing how great my lament;/ My sigh's sorrowful echo penetrates the steep hills,/ But the heart of the snow-coloured girl never softens.

Lend me your music, I who am a true lover,/ I shall join it to the muse to try and soften/ Her cold, flint-like heart and her fine, beautiful breast/ Which are like the eternal ice in the farthest reaches of the north.)

Such a self-consciously literary treatment of the theme of the unrequited lover has more in common with the poems of *Poems, Lyric and Pastoral* (1794) than with Iolo's Welsh verse. Generally speaking, while his Welsh output tended to echo the popular indigenous tradition of free-metre poetry which flourished from the sixteenth century onwards, Iolo's English poetry – published in 1794 but in many cases composed much earlier – was heavily influenced by the more learned and literary works of Shenstone, Collins and other pre-Romantics of the mid-eighteenth century. The two volumes of *Poems, Lyric and Pastoral*, with their curious mix of pastoral rusticity, political radicalism and Iolo's own brand of druidism, were meant to forge his literary reputation in fashionable London as the Welsh 'Bard of Liberty'. The Welsh-language poet, on the other hand, had different ambitions, and rarely strived for any great originality of theme or imagery. His free-metre love-poetry, in particular, is largely conventional. Two poems ascribed to Iorwerth Morganwg, the bardic name assumed by Iolo from 1773–4, skilfully imitate the intricate epithetical style of composition associated with Huw Morys and his emulators. The first, set to the English melody 'Go a Maying', draws on a stock of well-worn epithets such as 'siriol wiw seren' ('fine, merry star'), 'lliw'r ewyn' ('colour of foam'), 'lliw'r cwrel' ('colour of coral'), 'duwies' ('goddess') and 'ail Dido' ('Dido's equal'), though the ending with its desire for married bliss and its promise of eternal love calls to mind some of the *cywyddau* addressed to Iolo's future wife, Euron, around the same period.[25] The second, a lyrical description of the spring awakening, which develops into a dialogue between the pining poet and a cuckoo, draws on a long and popular tradition of bird-dialogues in Welsh.[26]

Of the sixteen poems in the first section of Donovan's edition, six – numbers 3, 4, 5, 8, 10 and 12 – belong to a group of poems labelled 'The scattered love-poems of Iolo Morganwg' ('Pennillion serch gwasgar Iolo Morganwg')[27] and

---

[25]   Ibid., no. 9.
[26]   Ibid., no. 15.
[27]   Ibid., p. 151.

all have the same basic four-line metre. They are composed in the manner of the traditional harp-stanzas (*penillion telyn*), one of the simplest of all Welsh metrical forms, far removed from the complexity and verbosity of the carol-style poems discussed above. 'Cwyn Merch ar ôl Ei Chariad' ('A Girl's Lament after Her Lover'),[28] for instance, echoes the verbal formulae of an essentially oral tradition:[29]

> Doco'r fynwent, doco'r ywen,
> Mi fûm ganwaith yno'n llawen,
> Gyda mab, ni cheisiwn gelu,
> Ag oedd fy nghalon yn ei garu.

> Doco'r fynwent, doco'r ywen,
> Doco ddarfod bod yn llawen,
> Doco'r lle mae'r mebyn hawddgar
> Yn fud yn gorwedd yn y ddaear . . .

(There's the graveyard, there's the yew-tree,/ A hundred times I've been joyful there,/ With a lad, I did not seek to hide it,/ Whom my heart loved.

There's the graveyard, there's the yew-tree,/ There's an end to being joyful,/ There's the place where the lovely lad/ Lies silent in the ground.)

The final stanza contains a characteristically simple but effective contrast between the positive and comparative forms of the adjective *trwm* (heavy):

> Trwm yw'r ddaear y sy'n gaead
> Rhyngo i fyth a'm annwyl gariad;
> Hiraeth trymach, fil o weithiau,
> Sy'n gorwedd ar fy nghalon innau.

(Heavy is the earth which is forever a cover/ Between me and my dear beloved;/ A thousand times heavier is the longing/ That lies upon my heart.)

A similar effect is achieved in the following verse:[30]

> Fe gŵyn yr haul pan ddêl boreddydd,
> Fe gŵyn y tarth oddi ar y meysydd,
> Fe gŵyn y gwlith oddi ar y meillion,
> Gwae fi! pwy bryd y cwyn fy nghalon?

(The sun rises when morning comes,/ The mist rises from the fields,/ The dew rises from the clover,/ Woe is me! When will my heart rise?)

[28] Ibid., no. 3.
[29] The first-line index of T. H. Parry-Williams's collection, *Hen Benillion* (Llandysul, 1940), p. 212, lists thirteen instances of the opening formula 'Dacw . . .'.
[30] *CRhIM*, no. 8.

With an engaging lack of sentimentality consistent with the genre, the poems
convey the distance between poet and beloved, either through separation,
rejection or death, and between the poet and his native land. That land is, of
course, Glamorgan. In one short but striking poem,[31] just as in the *cywyddau*
to Euron, the girl's beauty and moral virtues are implicitly identified with the
unparalleled qualities of 'Gwladforgan' itself. The opening verse is disarmingly
direct:

> Mae tŷ gwyn bach ym Mro Gwladforgan,
> Ac yn ei gylch mae gwlad a pherllan,
> Ac yno'n trigo gyda'i dynon
> Mae'r unig ferch a gâr fy nghalon.

(There is a little white house in the Vale of Glamorgan,/ With an orchard and
countryside all around it,/ And who lives there with her folk/ But the only girl my
heart loves.)

For Iolo, ever restless, ever driven by his work as a stonemason and by his
scholarly pursuits, the simple rustic cottage of his own upbringing becomes the
focal point of a yearning for stability and contentment:

> Gwae fi na chawn ryw fwthyn bychan
> Yng nghlais rhyw ddyffryn yng Ngwladforgan,
> I dreulio'm einioes a thrigfannu
> Gyda'r ferch ag wy'n ei garu . . .
>
> Ni ŵyr un dyn pa faint gofalon
> Y mab a fytho'n caru'n ffyddlon,
> Fo'n cael ei yrru gan ei alwad
> Ymhell oddi wrth ei annwyl gariad.[32]

(Alas that I could not have a little cottage/ On the side of some vale in Glamorgan,/
To spend my life and dwell/ With the girl I love.

No man knows how great are the cares/ Of a lad whose love is true,/ And who is
driven by his vocation/ Far away from his dear beloved.)

The carefree stability of country life, Wales itself and, above all, Glamorgan, are
all idealized in stark opposition to England, 'gwlad y Saeson' (the land of the
English):

> Doco'r môr sy'n rhannu'n greulon
> Rhyngof a Morgannwg dirion,
> Fy nghorff sydd yma'n dirfawr gwyno,
> A'm calon glaf yn aros yno.

---

[31]   Ibid., no. 10.
[32]   Ibid., no. 5.

'Wyf yma'n rhodio gwlad y Saeson,
Ymhell ar ôl mae'm holl gyfeillon,
'Wyf yma beunydd yn cwynfanu,
Gan hiraeth am lawenydd Cymru.

Doco'r tir a wela i'n amlwg,
Doco ran o Fro Morgannwg,
Doco'r bwthyn gwyn lle'm ganed,
Am hwn mae 'nghalon mewn caethiwed.

Gwyn fyd na bawn ym Mro Gwladforgan,
Mewn bwthyn bach o eiddo'm hunan,
Yn nawdd boddlondeb a thawelwch,
A lle aneddu mewn llonyddwch.[33]

(There's the sea which separates me cruelly/ From gentlest Glamorgan,/ My body is here lamenting deeply,/ And my ailing heart remains there.

Here I am on English soil,/ All my friends left far behind,/ Here I am each day complaining,/ Full of longing for the joys of Wales.

There's the land I clearly see,/ There's a part of the Vale of Glamorgan,/ There's the white cottage where I was born,/ Because of it my heart remains captive.

O to be in the land of Glamorgan/ In a little cottage of my own,/ In the sanctuary of contentment and tranquillity,/ With a place to dwell in peace.)

The theme recurs in the equally modest *triban* metre, a form more closely associated with Glamorgan:

Myfi sydd Gymro gwirion,
A galar yn ei galon,
Gwaith bod ymhell dan dynged ddrwg
O Fro Morgannwg dirion . . .

Dychwelyd wyf yr awron
I Fro Morgannwg dirion,
At un a'm câr, a'm bwthyn bach,
Lle byddaf iach fy nghalon . . .[34]

(I am an honest Welshman/ Whose heart is full of grief,/ Ill-fated to be far away/ From gentlest Glamorgan.

I am now returning/ To gentlest Glamorgan,/ To one who loves me and to my little cottage/ Where my heart will be restored to health.)

[33] Ibid., no. 4.
[34] Ibid., no. 13.

This poem, and a similar one, are apparently reworkings of popular *tribannau* of longing for Glamorgan,[35] examples of Iolo's fondness for adaptation and embellishment which, it will be seen, is an essential element in his manufactured 'tradition' of free-metre verse. The exile's heart is heavier still in a poem purportedly written in Kent in 1775 when Iolo was suffering one of his many bouts of ill health.[36] As spring awakens all around him, the housebound poet is overcome with self-pity:

> Gwae finnau'n brudd na fedrwn fyned
> I Fro Morgannwg, man lle'm ganed,
> Mewn daear yno i gael gorffwys:
> Aed Duw â'm enaid i baradwys.
>
> Yn hyn o fyd llawn twyll a dolur
> Ni chefais eto fawr o gysur,
> Pob peth yn ffoi fal gwynt o'm dwylo,
> Cyn profi dim ond golwg arno.
>
> Yn hyn o fyd, er maint fy ngobaith,
> Ni welais fawr ond twyll a gweniaith;
> Hawdd fyd i'r awr, o wreiddiau 'nghalon,
> A rydd im wared o'm trallodion.

(Woe is me in sorrow that I may not go/ To Glamorgan, the place I was born,/ To rest in its earth:/ Let God take my soul to paradise.

In this world of ours full of deceit and pain/ I am yet to find much comfort,/ Everything escapes my hands like the wind/ Before I've hardly set eyes on it.

In this world of ours, in spite of all my hopes,/ I've hardly seen anything but deceit and flattery;/ Blessed shall be the hour, from the very bottom of my heart,/ That delivers me from my woes.)

Despite the hyperbole, one senses here the very real frustrations experienced by Iolo as he reluctantly plied his trade in Kent during the mid-1770s.

---

[35] Compare *CRhIM*, nos. 11, 13 with Tegwyn Jones (ed.), *Tribannau Morgannwg* (Llandysul, 1976), nos. 26, 50 (a *triban* recorded by Iolo himself). The first verse of *CRhIM*, no. 11 was cited by Iolo in the diary he kept of a visit to England in 1802. Upon his return: 'Vale of Glamorgan opens to view. One of its songs and tunes occurs. There is som[e]thing Strange in the powerful effect of these provincial, or local things. The Swiss have their *mal de pays*. So have the Glamorganians. I mentally sung the following old popular Stanza to the ancient tune in two parts of Triban Morganwg and felt my eyes Streaming with tears: Mi wela'r mor yn amlwg/ Mi wela Fro Morganwg/ Pan fwyf yn hon am bwthyn bach/ Mi fydda'n iach fy ngolwg.' NLW 13174A, p. 90ᵛ. He then attempted a second stanza of his own (a close variant occurs in *CRhIM*, no. 13), before adding, with uncharacteristic modesty: 'But who can equal the old one? What would I not give to know the name and æra of its author? Any addition to this beautiful thing can never have a good effect, will never establish itself.' Ibid., p. 92ʳ.

[36] *CRhIM*, no. 7 and p. 151.

Although his movements during 1775 are uncertain, in the letters he wrote from Sandwich in 1774 to his father, his brother Thomas, and the lexicographer John Walters, he often bemoaned his ill health and talked of returning home to Flemingston. He told his father:

> my Master has many hands at work, but most of them are the most Ignorant set of Blockheads that ever were seen . . . the Englishmen are damn Mad (to use their own phrase) that a Taffy Should rule them, whilst on the other hand my master will lay all their errors to my charge. At night I have so much writing work, and sometimes drawing, for my Master, that I have no time to do any thing for my self.[37]

Iolo was not to return to Glamorgan until 1777, having spent more than four years away from home, mainly in London and various parts of Kent. In a poem he claimed to have written in May of that year, despondency turned to ecstasy. The poem, vibrant with the sweeping rhythms of the *tri thrawiad* metre, is a paean to Glamorgan – its unsurpassed natural beauty, fruitfulness, whitewashed cottages and the civility of the people:

> Bûm hir o flynyddoedd, ansiriol amseroedd,
> Yn aros yn nhiroedd a siroedd y Sais,
> Ond eilydd yn unman i siriol fro seirian
> Gwladforgan ne wiwlan ni welais.
>
> Cyfrifir hi beunydd yn frasaf o'r gwledydd,
> Yn llannerch llawenydd, a'i gweunydd yn gain,
> Gardd Gymru'n dra chymwys y'i gelwir, fro gulwys,
> Gwlad irlwys, paradwys tir Prydain . . .[38]

(For many years, unhappy times,/ I tarried in the lands and shires of the English,/ But nowhere have I seen the equal/ Of the bright, merry land of Glamorgan.

It is considered daily the most fertile of lands/ And the grove of joy whose meadows are fair,/ It is most aptly called the Garden of Wales, a region most dear,/ A lush land, Britain's paradise.)

It is also for Iolo a land of poets in which he is free to roam at one with wild nature, a Romantic self-image which is echoed in the *cywyddau* and the English poetry thought to belong to this period, as well as in his autobiographical writings:

> Caf dreiglaw'n y tawel mewn irgoed, man argel,
> Lle'm daw ar bob awel llais angel y serch,
> A rhiniau'r awenydd i'm bryd, a mi'n brydydd,
> Lle bydd y man llonydd mewn llannerch.

---

[37] NLW 21285E, Letter no. 773, Iolo Morganwg to Edward Williams, Senr., 13 September 1774.
[38] *CRhIM*, no. 1. The date of composition is uncertain since the earliest copy dates from the 1790s; see ibid., p. 151 and Williams: *IM*, p. 237.

Caf feddu pob hawddfyd, awr heddwch a rhyddid,
Caf wenferch, caf wynfyd, a bywyd heb wg,
Caf serch ac anerchion a pharch i 'mhenillion
Gan ddynion tai gwynion Morgannwg . . .

(I may wander in silence through the verdant woods, a secluded spot,/ Where the voice of the angel of love reaches me on every breeze,/ My mind filled with the charms of the muse, and I a poet,/ In that peaceful place in a grove.

I shall have the greatest contentment, a time of peace and freedom,/ A fair maid, and bliss, and a life free of frowns,/ I'll have love and fair greetings and respect for my verses/ From the men of Glamorgan's whitewashed houses.)

Whether or not the poem was in fact written in 1777, it is clear that his poetry was given a fresh impetus by his return to his homeland, excited by the encouragement of the Gwyneddigion Society in London and inspired above all, it seems, by having studied a copy made by Owen Jones (Owain Myfyr) of the Morrises' sumptuous collection of the poetry of Dafydd ap Gwilym. As he himself once wrote: 'In 1778 [sic] I came home and settled in Wales, where animated by something joyfully melancholy, on tracing again the scenes of youth I wrote many things in verse.'[39] Much of his best poetry, in both strict and free metres, belongs to this period. And as his vision of the glories of Glamorgan past and present became ever more obsessive – no doubt fuelled by the patronizing disdain of those from north Wales towards the supposed poverty of the region's literary heritage – he began to assume a host of different poetic identities. Just as some of the cywyddau were attributed to Dafydd ap Gwilym, most of Iolo's free-metre poetry was now composed in the name of poets, real and fictional, from Glamorgan's imagined past. He has been aptly described as a chameleon-like poet, a poet who was willing to sacrifice his own complex character in order to present a whole cast of other actors; who, as well as romanticizing Wales and Glamorgan and romanticizing poetry, was exceptionally fond of romanticizing himself.[40] From the early 1780s he became obsessed with the idea that he and Edward Evan, a Dissenting minister from Aberdare, were the last of the 'Ancient British Bards', the only remaining links of an unbroken chain that stretched back to the Middle Ages and ultimately to druidic times. The remarkable body of verse attributed to others

[39] NLW 21387E, no. 9.
[40] Bobi Jones, 'Bardd seciwlar mwyaf y 18fed ganrif', Barddas, 178 (1992), 10, 14. A contributing factor, he suggests, may have been the 'split' in his personality caused by the fact that English was his mother tongue. It has also been suggested that Iolo's creation of characters such as Rhys Goch ap Rhicert, Geraint Fardd Glas o'r Gadair and, interestingly, Sioni'r Maeswn Dimai may conceivably have been influenced by the freemasons' custom of assuming nicknames which were used in letters, prose and operas. See Geraint H. Jenkins, 'Cyffesion Bwytawr Opiwm: Iolo Morganwg a Gorsedd Beirdd Ynys Prydain', Taliesin, 81 (1993), 50–1.

was meant to prove the richness and quality of the county's literary tradition over several centuries. By the early 1780s Iolo claimed that his own muse was a spent force. Around the year of his marriage, 1781, he composed a *cywydd* lamenting the death of the muse,[41] and two years later, in a letter to Owain Myfyr, he wrote: 'The married life with all its advantages, has too many cares and anxieties, too much bustle and business, to allow a man, especially a man of narrow circumstances, to attend much to the Muses, to study, and litterary persuits or amusements.'[42] The 1780s were indeed troublesome years for Iolo, a decade of failed business ventures, legal wrangles, even imprisonment. But it would be wrong to assume, as Iolo would have us believe, that his creative powers were on the wane. Although little appears in his own name, throughout the 1780s he continued to expand his impressive collection of Glamorgan poetry, whilst at the same time perfecting his forgeries of Dafydd ap Gwilym. When he believed that all the world was against him, he sought comfort in his vision of the bardic past. During the year he spent in the debtors' prison in Cardiff in 1786–7 he probably composed a large part of his bardic treatise *Cyfrinach Beirdd Ynys Prydain*.

Cyfrinach Beirdd Ynys Prydain purports to be a copy of the bardic treatise compiled by the so-called Glamorgan *pencerdd* or master poet Edward Dafydd of Margam (in this case a real seventeenth-century poet) following a fictional eisteddfod of 1681. According to Iolo, its metrical system, labelled 'The Glamorgan Classification' ('Dosbarth Morgannwg') was older and more valid than the familiar twenty-four strict metres of *cerdd dafod* established by Dafydd ab Edmwnd in the Carmarthen eisteddfod of *c.*1453. The treatise displays, in equal measure, Iolo's unparalleled knowledge of Welsh metrics and his boundless creativity. His greatest departure from tradition is his introduction of a whole section on free-metre poetry, which he considered to have been an integral part of Glamorgan's bardic tradition from an early period. His 'twenty-fourth element of *cerdd dafod*' is the 'song' or 'carol' ('Dyrif, neu Garol, yw'r pedwerydd ansawdd ar hugain ar gerdd Dafod').[43] The metres which fall under this category are accentual rather than syllabic and are therefore able to be sung. The *dyrif* is said to correspond to the Latin *lyrica*; whereas the Roman poets performed to the accompaniment of a lyre, the Welsh were accustomed to the *crwth* (crowd) and the harp.[44] In fact, any of the other twenty-three metrical

---

[41] 'Cywydd Marwnad yr Awen', Jones (ed.), *Y Gwir Degwch*, pp. 71–3; A. Cynfael Lake (ed.), *Blodeugerdd Barddas o Ganu Caeth y Ddeunawfed Ganrif* (Llandybïe, 1993), no. 94. Cf. the unascribed *CRhIM*, no. 28, a dialogue poem recounting a dream in which the poet accused the hard-hearted muse of having deserted him in the midst of his troubles; the muse is 'worse than sorrow, worse than my wife' ('Gwaeth na'r gofid, gwaeth na'm gwraig').

[42] BL Add. 15024, Letter no. 6, f. 196, Iolo Morganwg to Owain Myfyr, 20 September 1783.

[43] Williams (ed.), *Cyfrinach Beirdd Ynys Prydain*, p. 159.

[44] Ibid., p. 170.

types described by Iolo may be classed as a *dyrif,* so long as they have regular stress patterns.[45] This, of course, tends to blur the distinction between free- and strict-metre poetry and, indeed, P. J. Donovan included several of these exempla in his edition of free-metre verse. Some are exquisitely intricate, such as the following lines from a poem attributed to Dafydd y Nant:

> Teg fore 'mis Ebrill yn ebrwydd y codais,
> I'r coedydd ar ofron tir hyfryd ymdeithiais;
> I'm dethol fyfyrdod oferdyb ni luniais
> Ar lennyrch y glasgoed, ond glwysgerdd a brydais . . .[46]

(One fair morning in April I rose hastily/ And made for the woods on the slope of a pleasant land;/ In my refined contemplation I harboured no frivolous thoughts/ In the glades of the greenwood, but composed a fine song.)

This is Iolo's own elaboration on the already tortuously difficult strict metre *tawddgyrch gadwynog.* There is *cynghanedd* in the middle of each line (e.g. *Ebrill/ ebrwydd*) and between the end of each line and the beginning of the next (e.g. *codais/coedydd*). The pattern is sustained over three eight-line stanzas, with the added complication that the end of each stanza rhymes with the beginning of the next, thereby ensuring that the metre may be retained unaltered.

Iolo's metrical inventiveness is one of the more striking features of the body of verse he attributed to others. His metrical innovations generally have a more lyrical quality than the 'genuine' metres of *cerdd dafod*, in keeping with his conviction that the poetry of his native Glamorgan had always been less formal and sober than that of the north, influenced as it was by the gentler traditions of Continental poetry in the wake of the Norman conquest. This is especially true of the freer metrical forms of the twenty-fourth section of *Cyfrinach Beirdd Ynys Prydain*. These, according to Iolo, had been banished from the official classification at Carmarthen in the mid-fifteenth century, having been devalued by artless rhymesters.[47] However, refined by touches of *cynghanedd*, they had remained popular in Glamorgan down to the eighteenth century in the verse of the *teuluwr* or *bardd teulu* (household poet) – a *dyrif* or *carol* may also be termed *cân deuluaidd*[48] (domestic verse), a term related by Iolo to the informal occasional verse of the so-called medieval 'household poet' of the bardic grammars. His vision was of a vibrant and popular tradition of love-song, seasonal verse and light-hearted balladry which reflected the joys and customs of a bygone age. His great procession of Glamorgan poets belongs

---

45 Ibid., p. 160.
46 *CRhIM*, no. 46. Cf. p. 60, Williams (ed.), *Cyfrinach Beirdd Ynys Prydain* and the slightly variant version on pp. 90–1.
47 Williams (ed.), *Cyfrinach Beirdd Ynys Prydain*, p. 170.
48 Ibid., p. 159.

mainly to the sixteenth and seventeenth centuries, and includes his own grand-father on his mother's side, Edward Matthew, who was in fact descended from the region's outstanding family of medieval bards. The great bulk of the poetry which Iolo composed in their names consists of lyrics of love in a natural setting, pastorals and May-songs, with bird-messengers and bird-dialogues a common feature (a summer carol and a love-poem attributed to Edward Matthew[49] are typical examples). The poems are all well crafted, though they tend to recycle a fairly limited set of themes and poetic conventions, which is hardly surprising since Iolo was intent on creating a convincing homogeneous verse tradition.

Some of these poems are very fine examples of their genre, including the well-known bird-messenger poem which begins:

> A minnau'n hwyr myfyrian yn unig wrtho i'm hunan,
> Yn ymyl coed yn rhodian gerllaw i lan Elái,
> Clywn rywiog lais yr eos yn hygar o lwyn agos,
> A chryno'i chân ddechreunos tra llon ym myrnos Mai.[50]

(As I was lost in thought one evening by myself,/ Strolling near the woods by the banks of the river Ely,/ I could hear the nightingale's soft voice calling pleasantly from a nearby grove,/ Its song so fine at nightfall, so joyous on that short May night.)

The poem ends with a closing formula typical of the popular free-metre tradition:

> Os gofyn neb yn unman pwy ganws hyn i'r geingan,
> Mab ifanc yn San Ffagan o brydydd diddan dwys;
> Mae gwaeledd yn ei galon am honno, deuliw'r hinon,
> Fe yrr ei chlod o gylchon mewn cerddi llon a llwys.

(If anyone should ever ask who sang this song to the fair maid,/ It was a young lad from Saint Fagans, a pleasant, earnest poet;/ His heart is filled with sickness on account of her of the colour of sunshine,/ He'll spread her praise abroad in fine merry poems.)

The love-messenger motif is given a humorous twist in a poem in which the fretful bird at first refuses to comply, for fear of being caught by the poet's beloved in the grove.[51] It asks how the girl might be recognized, to which the poet replies:

---

[49] *CRhIM*, nos. 47–8.
[50] Ibid., no. 35. The poem was anthologized by Thomas Parry in *The Oxford Book of Welsh Verse*, no. 186; cf. also Millward (ed.), *Blodeugerdd Barddas o Gerddi Rhydd y Ddeunawfed Ganrif*, no. 102.
[51] *CRhIM*, no. 88.

Haul y bore'n aur yn codi,
Canol dydd yn wyn oleuni,
Lliw'n ymachlud y rhos cochon,
A'r lliwiau i gyd ar wen lliw'r hinon.

Aur yw gwallt y ferch benfelen,
Gwen ei bron fal haul ar donnen,
Coch yr hinon ar ei gruddiau,
Lliw'r haul yn machlud heb gymylau . . .

(The gold of the rising sun,/ The white light of midday,/ The sunset-hue of red roses,/ All these are the colours of the fairest maid.

Gold are the locks of the blond-haired girl,/ White her breast like a wave in sunlight,/ Her cheeks the red of the blazing sun,/ The colour of a cloudless sunset.)

Iolo's flair for writing engaging love-lyrics is apparent in a little-noticed poem from the second section of Donovan's edition.[52] The poet pledges to devote his life to his love; his only wish is that they may make a home together in the Vale, untouched by pride and unknown to the world beyond. The poem is less static and also less conventional than many, and creates an impression of serenity reminiscent of the early *cywyddau* to Euron:

Ein serch yw'n unig gyfoeth, gwell rhan i'r doeth nid oes,
Nid gwledd ond cariad tyner, a chynnal mwynder moes,
A digon byth, o'm coeler, yw meddu'r fwynber ferch,
A chael ymborthi'n ddifeth, lwys eneth, ar ei serch . . .

Mi chwiliaf eitha'r coedydd a chlawr y meysydd mwyn
I gasglu blodau gwiwserch bob llannerch a phob llwyn,
Mi bletha'r rhain yn lwysber â gwead syber serch
I wneuthur coron iraidd i 'mheraidd fwynaidd ferch.

Pan ddelo gwres canolddydd a thwymder hirddydd haf,
Tŷ dail yn deg ei blethiant yn ymyl nant a wnaf,
Mi gronna'r dyfroedd claerwyn sy'n rhodio'r dyffryn dir,
Er disychedu 'nghariad dan len yr eiliad ir . . .

Wynebaf bob diffygion a chyrch blinderon dwys,
Â'n ddewr drwy dân gofidi er noddi'r lili lwys,
Y nos yn wyliwr arni, gofalu amdani'r dydd,
Mae'n oll yn oll i 'nghalon, liw blodau gwynion gwŷdd.

Ond os bydd hi'n anghywir, y fanwl feinir fach,
E ddarfu'r hedd i'm dwyfron, a nwyfiant calon iach,

[52] Ibid., no. 26.

I bellter byd enciliaf, ag enaid claf i'm clwy',
Ni roddaf serch cystuddloes ar ferch i'm einioes mwy.

(We have no wealth but love, for the wise the finest portion,/ No feast but sweet affection, and dwelling in gentle civility,/ And it is enough, believe me, to have the kind, sweet girl,/ And to feast unfailingly, fair maiden, on her love.

I'll search the deepest woodland and the face of the fair meadows/ To gather true love's flowers from every glade and grove,/ I'll knit them together finely with the weaving of noble love/ To make a green chaplet for my sweet, gentle girl.

In the midday heat and the warmth of the long summer days,/ I'll fashion a finely-woven house of leaves near a stream,/ I'll dam up the pure white waters that flow through the valley/ To quench my sweetheart's thirst under the cover of the green bower.

I'll face up to every hardship and the assault of every grim affliction,/ I'll brave vexations' fire to protect the fair lilly,/ By night I'll watch over her and care for her by day,/ To my heart she is everything, colour of white blossom.

But if ever she's unfaithful, my comely little maiden,/ There will be no more peace in my breast, nor the passion of a healthy heart,/ Then I'll retreat to the earth's end, aching from an ailing soul,/ And as long as I live my grief-stricken love will seek no other.)

Far better known, ever since they were published in 1848,[53] are the twenty love-poems attributed to Rhys Goch ap Rhicert. These are unlikely to have been composed before 1799,[54] when Iolo's bardic pronouncements were becoming increasingly bolder. The following passage reveals his motive for transforming an obscure twelfth-century nobleman into an outstanding medieval poet:

> About 1130 flourished *Rhŷs Goch ap Riccert ap Einion ap Collwyn*, in Glamorgan. he for the most part, if not wholly, retained the metres and manner of the older schools. But in his poems we find a cast of gallantry which had not before been to any considerable degree admitted into the Welsh Poetry . . . in this Poet's Sentiments and manner we find something of the manner of the *Provençal Troubadours*. the *Norman Barons* who had settled in Glamorgan were those who opened the way for this new cast in Poetry. their Castles or Courts were the Gates thro' which it entered into Wales . . . in the works of *Rhŷs Goch ap Riccert* the clear dawn of this new manner appears, which in a century and a half afterwards brightened into the bright summer's noon of *Dafydd ap Gwilym*. Thus founded by *Rhŷs Goch ap Riccert* and beautifully superstructed by *Dafydd ap Gwilym*, we see a new school established in

---

[53] Williams (ed.), *Iolo Manuscripts*, pp. 228–51. Fourteen of the poems are included in *CRhIM*, nos. 66–79.
[54] G. J. Williams, 'Rhys Goch ap Rhiccert', *Y Beirniad*, VIII (1919), 214–15.

the *Silurian district of Wales*, differing greatly from such as preceded it but much more congenial to human nature in its civilized state.[55]

Thus, under the civilizing influence of continental *amour courtois*, the poems are full of the joys and sufferings of unrequited love. Much of the content and imagery is cleverly drawn from the *cywyddau* of Dafydd ap Gwilym and his imitators, and there are echoes, too, of the genuine twelfth-century love-poetry of the prince-poet Hywel ab Owain Gwynedd and of the tales and romances of medieval Welsh prose. As well as the sleepless love-sick poet, the bird-messengers and the leafy bowers, there are a few humorous pieces which recall some of Dafydd ap Gwilym's narrative poems; for instance, in one poem the lovers' tryst is rudely interrupted by the jealous husband.[56] However, despite some archaic forms, the language is patently not twelfth-century and, stylistically, these poems are more akin to a type of early free-metre poetry which was popular in late sixteenth-century Wales. Five of the twenty poems have been identified as reworkings of known poems from that period which Iolo had seen, ironically, in a north Wales manuscript.[57] The others have the same delicately lyrical quality which is created largely by the crisp *carol deuair* (carol in a rhyming couplet) metre in which most of the poems are written. It was a metre that Iolo knew to have been popular in Glamorgan since the sixteenth century, but here was evidence of a vigorous tradition of free-metre love-poetry in the region at least four hundred years earlier. The following lines, part of a long, sensuous description of female beauty from head to foot, are a typical example:

Bun a welais,	man y rhodiais,
Ne'r alarch gwyn	ar glawr dyffryn;
Cerddai dyn wâr	wyneb daear,
Yn hardd beunes	drwy'r melyndes,
Ac ni phlygai	man y cerddai,
Dan wyndroed hon	un o'r meillion.
Harddach bun fain	na chyflen gain
Blawd o gylchon	ar ddrain gwynion . . .[58]

(I saw a maiden where I was strolling,/ Colour of the white swan on a valley lake;/ The refined maid walked the earth's surface/ Like a beautiful peacock through the

---

[55]   Ibid., 225–6.

[56]   *CRhIM*, no. 74.

[57]   See Williams, 'Rhys Goch ap Rhiccert', 211–26; Ifor Williams, 'Rhys Goch ap Rhiccert', *Y Beirniad*, III (1913), 230–44. The five poems – *Iolo Manuscripts*, pp. 228–51, nos. 1, 2, 3, 13 and 20 – have been omitted from *CRhIM*, as has no. 19, which was written in the *cywydd* metre. The lax use of *cynghanedd* in the *cywydd* was presumably an attempt to show the metre at an early stage in its development, providing further evidence of Rhys Goch's importance as a precursor to Dafydd ap Gwilym.

[58]   *CRhIM*, no. 66.

yellow haze,/ And where she walked there did not bend/ Under her fair foot a single clover./ Fairer is the slender maid than the splendid veil/ Of blossom that covers the hawthorn.)

As forgeries, the poems attributed to Rhys Goch ap Rhicert are, at least for modern readers, wholly unconvincing, a curious hybrid of Elizabethan and medieval lyric. Considered purely as love-lyrics, they include some of Iolo's finest creative works.

In attempting to create a later body of verse, Iolo was on more familiar ground. For the most part, originality was carefully avoided, and he was content to weave together the motifs and epithets of a genuine tradition of Welsh free-metre poetry which dated at least from the sixteenth century. His vision of a thriving Glamorgan-based tradition of love-lyric and seasonal song is not entirely fictional. As in the case of the well-known love-song 'Bugeila'r Gwenith Gwyn' (Watching the White Wheat), attributed by Iolo to Wil Hopcyn of Llangynwyd,[59] several of his poems seem to have been artistic reworkings of earlier material in the style of Burns,[60] though it is often notoriously difficult to come to any clear conclusions.[61] Indeed, Iolo claimed that many of the free-metre verses in *Cyfrinach Beirdd Ynys Prydain* were recorded from oral tradition.[62] One is a simple song about the maypole at Coity, near Bridgend, attributed to a certain Gruffydd Morys:

> Trigolion Bro Gwladforgan, cyfeillion diddan dewch
> Yn dyrfa lan,
> Y mawr a'r man,
> A newydd gan a gewch;
> I Fedwen hardd y Coetty 'ddwy'n meddwl clymmu clod;
> A ddaeth o'r Rhath,
> Mae'n ddeunaw llath,
> Nid oes ei bath yn bod;
> A'r chwech Mab ifanc glandeg a'i dygai'n deg ar daith,
> O'r Rhath lle'r oedd . . .[63]

59 Parry (ed.), *Oxford Book of Welsh Verse*, no. 190. See G. J. Williams, 'Wil Hopcyn a'r Ferch o Gefn Ydfa', *Y Llenor*, VI (1927), 218–29; VII (1928), 34–46.

60 Daniel Huws, *Caneuon Llafar Gwlad ac Iolo a'i Fath* (Cymdeithas Alawon Gwerin Cymru, 1993), compares Iolo's methods with those of Robert Burns and John Clare, suggesting (pp. 10–11) that Burns's example may have influenced Iolo from the 1790s onwards. He also discusses the folk-tunes recorded by Iolo, which include at least eight versions of a melody belonging to the popular *triban* metre (pp. 12–23). See also chapter 15 of this volume.

61 Possible examples are *CRhIM*, nos. 24, 32, 47 and 50. The bawdy songs 'Cân y Ferch a Gollwys ei Phais' (no. 45: Dafydd y Nant) and 'Canu'r Cryman' (no. 90: Wil Hopcyn) differ from most of Iolo's work in style and content.

62 'Y Pennillion Cynnrych a ddangoswyd, a gymmerais, lawer o henynt o benn gwlad a gwerin . . .', trans. Williams, *Cyfrinach Beirdd Ynys Prydain*, p. 169.

63 Ibid., p. 168.

(Good people of Glamorgan, my merry friends,/ Gather round,/ Great and small,/ And you shall hear a new song;/ It's to the fair birch of Coity that I wish to to sing my praise,/ Which came from Roath,/ It's eighteen yards long,/ The like you've never seen;/ And six handsome lads carried it well on its journey/ From Roath where it used to be . . .)

Iolo has a similar song in the name of Wil Tabwr, a colourful but entirely fictional figure who he claimed had flourished in the reign of Charles II:

> Dewch bawb yn awr o'r ienctid mwyn
> I ben y twyn i chwarae . . .
>
> Fe gwnnwyd bedwen ar y ton,
>   Un hardd yw hon i'r olwg,
> A llawer torch sydd arni'n wir
>   O'r brafa'n Sir Forgannwg;
> Y Sir Gaer coch a ganodd sen
>   I'n chware llawen diddrwg,
> Mae'n haeddu cael, y baglwr cam,
>   Y cebyst am ei wddwg . . .
>
> Bydd Siôn y gwëydd a Siani goch
>   Yn canu'n groch eu cynnwr;
> Cawn Wil y saer yn chwalu serch
>   Wrth Fagi, merch y ffermwr.
> Y crythwr cloff a chwâr yn glic,
>   Cawn chwedlau Dic y Dwndwr,
> Mi ddala' bunt bydd chwerthin glân
>   Pan glywer cân Wil Tabwr . . .[64]

(Come all you merry youngsters/ To the hilltop where we'll play . . . They've raised a birch-pole on the green,/ Most pleasing to the eye,/ With many a wreath upon it,/ The fairest in all of Glamorgan;/ That Carmarthenshire redhead who sang abuse/ To our jolly, harmless sport/ Deserves to have – the crooked oaf –/ A noose around his neck . . . Siôn the weaver and red-haired Siani/ Will sing with raucous riot;/ Wil the carpenter will prattle about love/ With Magi, the farmer's daughter./ The lame *crwth*-player will nimbly play,/ We'll hear the tales of Dic y Dwndwr,/ I'll wager a pound there'll be laughter aplenty/ On hearing Wil Tabwr's song.)

The poem evokes the merriment attached to seasonal customs which Iolo may have remembered from his youth and which he saw disappearing in the face of Methodism and increasing industrialization. It may be based on the type of seasonal songs composed by the likes of Wiliam Robert o'r Ydwal, a blind folk-poet from Iolo's own parish of Llancarfan who was active during the first

---

[64] *CRhIM*, no. 94.

half of the eighteenth century. Of particular interest are his song in praise of the morris dancers of Llancarfan – as in Wil Tabwr's song, the dancers and musicians are referred to by name – and another which is an invitation to dance around the maypole on Wenvoe's village green.[65] With their depiction of carefree village life, convenient formulae, dialectal features and carol-style touches of *cynghanedd* in harmony with the melody, these fairly crude songs offer a fascinating glimpse of the remnants of a genuine popular verse tradition which was expanded and embellished by Iolo.[66] He may have been exaggerating when he wrote, citing the examples of Wil Tabwr and Wil Hopcyn:

> Convivial songs of great merit are also pretty numerous in S[outh] W[ales]. Some of them perfect paterns of excellence . . . Summer songs or May songs, Harvest songs, &c. are to be found in S[outh] W[ales] but not as in N[orth] W[ales] prophanely devotionol. They are of a cheerful and inn[o]cently convivial cast.[67]

But, like so many of his grand claims, it contains at least an element of truth.

Woven into the largely traditional fabric of this body of verse are some of the salient themes of the poetry which Iolo wrote under his own name. There is again a strong emphasis on marriage and fidelity, consistent with his idyllic portrayal of Glamorgan and its civilized, morally irreproachable inhabitants. Most strikingly, several of his poets are portrayed as returning exiles overcome with longing for their homeland. In the poems attributed to others, the stability of the simple rural existence for which he claimed to yearn is an essential element of his vision of Glamorgan's harmonious past. According to Iolo, 'Cân y Porfelwr' ('The Shepherd's Song'), written *c.*1640 by Hywel Llwyd of Llancarfan, 'is one of the fines[t] pat[t]erns of British pastoral that was ever written in either of our Languages'.[68] It begins:

> Bûm yn aros amser hir
>   Yn estron dir y Saeson,
> Heb ystyriaeth yn fy mryd
>   Yn bydio'n ynfyd ddigon;
> Tra bu'r ientid yn ei rwysg,
>   Mi borthais frwysg feddylon,
> Pob difyrrwch gwlad a thre
>   A gelai le'n fy nghalon;
> Ond 'wy'n meddwl rhodio 'nawr,
>   Er gochel mawr ofalon,
> Llwybrau mwyn llonyddwch maith
>   Yn unrhyw daith â'r doethion.

65   See G. J. Williams, 'Wiliam Robert o'r Ydwal', *LlC*, III, no. 1 (1954), 47–52. On Iolo's interest in the folk-songs and folk-customs of Glamorgan, see Williams: *IM*, chapter 1.

66   On the Glamorgan tradition of free-metre poetry, see *TLlM*, chapters 4, 6.

67   Williams: *IM*, p. 58.

68   Ibid., pp. 300, 239.

Er mwyn hyn cymerais dro
  I waelod Bro Gwladforgan,
Ac yn awr aneddwr wyf
  Yn annwyl blwyf Llancarfan,
Lle bu gynt fy mam a'm tad
  Yn byw'n eu gwlad heb ogan,
Yn eu bwthyn calchwyn hardd,
  Ac wrtho gardd a pherllan;
Dyma'r man lle mae fy mryd
  Ar dreulo 'myd yn gyfan,
Trigo tra bo yno i chwyth
  Yn hyn o'm nyth i'm hunan.[69]

(For a long time I tarried/ In the foreign land of England,/ Without heed,/ Living a most foolish life;/ Whilst I was in the full flush of youth/ I entertained some drunken thoughts,/ All the delights of town and country/ Would find a place in my heart;/ But I now intend to walk −/ To avoid great cares −/ The gentle paths of lasting peace/ On the same journey as the wise.

That is why I made my way/ To the bottom of the Vale of Glamorgan,/ And now I dwell/ In the dear parish of Llancarfan,/ Where my mother and father once/ Lived in their own neighbourhood without reproach,/ In their fair whitewashed cottage/ With its garden and its orchard;/ This is where I'm now intent/ On spending the rest of my days,/ Living till my dying breath/ In my very own nest.)

In contrast to Iolo's own unsuccessful attempts at farming in the mid-1780s, the poet proceeds to extol the virtues of the shepherd's carefree life.[70] He is honest, modest, God-fearing, an organic part of his own community:

Mewn tawelwch y mae'n byw,
  Gan ofni Duw'n wastadol,
Dyn serchogaidd yn ei blwyf
  Ac ynddo nwyf rinweddol . . .
Einioes hir a gaiff o'i swydd
  Ac iechyd rhwydd naturiol,
A phan dderfydd yma'i fyw,
  Caiff nef gan Dduw'n dragwyddol.

(He lives in tranquillity,/ Always in fear of the Lord,/ In his parish a loving man/ Of virtuous disposition/ . . . His vocation will ensure him a long life/ And prosperous rude health,/ And when his life here comes to an end/ God shall grant him eternal paradise.)

[69] CRhIM, no. 54.
[70] Cf. ibid., nos. 20, 39 ('Cân y Ffermwr') and 93 ('Welsh Pastoral').

The theme reappears in a more politicized form in *Poems, Lyric and Pastoral*, in which Iolo declares that 'A Poet in the character of a Shepherd' was best placed to 'represent primeval simplicity and virtue . . . and the complex ideas derived from art'.[71] His constant championing of the common man, his opposition between rural and urban life,[72] nature and artifice — all distinctly Rousseauesque — are among those elements in his poetry which are in tune with late eighteenth-century Romanticism. It is fitting that Iolo should have composed a poem in praise of his own humble vocation, 'Cân y Maensaer'[73] ('The Stonemason's Song'), which he claimed to be a traditional Glamorgan song. The skilled craftsman is naturally just as honest, just as contented, just as indispensable as the farmer. However, Iolo's long-suffering wife, Margaret (Peggy), may have found a certain irony in the words, 'Gwyn fyd y ferch a fytho'n wraig/ I'r gŵr y sy'n gosod ei sail ar y graig' ('Blessed is she who is the wife/ Of a man who lays his foundation on a rock'), and in the reference to building castles, rather more substantial constructions than Iolo's notorious 'castles in the air'.

When Iolo, encouraged by the success of his Dafydd ap Gwilym forgeries two years earlier, took a copy of *Cyfrinach Beirdd Ynys Prydain* with him to London in 1791, part of his dazzling vision of Glamorgan's literary heritage was revealed to the Gwyneddigion Society. As a poet, he was now driven by a new ambition: to establish his reputation as the 'Bard of Liberty' in the wake of the French Revolution. The fiery radicalism of the 1790s which informed the heady mixture of pastoral lyricism, bardism, druidism and Jacobinism within *Poems, Lyric and Pastoral* — 'a talisman of political fellowship and token of ideological support' for many London radicals[74] — is to a lesser extent reflected in the Welsh poetry of the same period. In the grand, didactic odes which Iolo composed as part of the newly invented Gorsedd ceremonies,[75] he loudly proclaimed the virtues of democracy — freedom, equality, fraternity, and above all the bright light of truth which he believed to be the very essence of bardism. It has been seen that his poetry had always been concerned with values such as honesty, fidelity, personal freedom and moral decency in

---

[71] Williams: *PLP*, I , pp. 173–4.

[72] On his antipathy towards London in the early 1790s, see Geraint Phillips, 'Math o Wallgofrwydd: Iolo Morganwg, Opiwm a Thomas Chatterton', *NLWJ*, XXIX, no. 4 (1996), 391–410. His attitude towards mercantile Bristol and its association with the slave trade is discussed by Mary-Ann Constantine, *Combustible Matter: Iolo Morganwg and the Bristol Volcano* (Aberystwyth, 2003).

[73] *CRhIM*, no. 32.

[74] Damian Walford Davies, *Presences that Disturb: Models of Romantic Identity in the Literature and Culture of the 1790s* (Cardiff, 2002), p. 145.

[75] See, for instance, 'Can am ddaioni Duw o'r dechreuad i genedl y Cymry, yn rhoi iddynt ymhob oes wybodaeth am dano ei Hun a'i wirionedd, a ddatganwyd yng Ngorsedd Alban Hefin, ar fynydd y Garth, Llanilltyd Faerdref, ym Morganwg, 1797', in T. C. Evans (Cadrawd) (ed.), *Gwaith Iolo Morganwg* (Llanuwchllyn, 1913), pp. 13–20.

Fig. 7 'Cân y Maensaer, neu'r Maensaer mwyn' was a song of praise to the gentle stonemason by Iolo Morganwg (NLW 13146A, p. 424).

general, but the writings of the middle-aged Iolo are more explicitly political.[76] Two poems from this period are particularly noteworthy since they express his deeply held political convictions concisely and powerfully. The first is 'Breiniau Dyn' – named after Tom Paine's *Rights of Man* – which Iolo claimed to have sung at Gorsedd ceremonies held in Glamorgan in 1798:

> Rhyddid y sydd yn awr
> Fel llew rhuadwy mawr,
>   Pob tir a'i clyw;
> A'r gwir sydd ar ei daith,
> Dros yr holl ddaear faith,
> Yn seinio peraidd iaith
>   I ddynol ryw.[77]

(Freedom now/ Is like a great roaring lion,/ It is heard in every land;/ And truth is on the march/ Through the whole wide world,/ Uttering sweet words/ To humankind.)

As in France, the *ancien régime* would be wiped away and the twin evils of warmongering monarchs and corrupt priests brought to account:

> Clyw'r brenin balch di-ras,
> A thi'r offeiriad bras,
>   Dau ddiawl ynglŷn,
> Hir buoch fal dau gawr
> I'r byd yn felltith fawr,
> Yn sarnu'n llaid y llawr
>   Holl freiniau dyn . . .
>
> Mae'r gwledydd oll fel Ffrainc
> Yn rhoddi'r orsedd fainc
>   I freiniau dyn.
>
> Gorfoledd, cwyd dy lais,
> Cwymp holl deyrnasoedd trais,
>   Maent ar eu crŷn;
> Cawn deyrnas hardd ei gwedd
> Tan farn Tywysog Hedd,
> Yn hoenus cawn o'r bedd
>   Holl freiniau dyn.

(Listen, haughty, wicked king,/ And you, the well-fed priest,/ Two devils bound together,/ You have long been like two giants,/ The world's great curse,/ Trampling into the dirt/ All the rights of man . . .

---

[76] See Lewis: *IM*, pp. 129–40.
[77] Millward (ed.), *Blodeugerdd Barddas o Gerddi Rhydd y Ddeunawfed Ganrif*, no. 108; see also ibid., p. 331.

All countries, just like France,/ Are yielding the throne/ To the rights of man./ Jubilation, raise your voice,/ The kingdoms of tyranny are all falling,/ They're trembling now;/ We shall have a splendid kingdom/ Governed by the Prince of Peace,/ We shall retrieve from the grave, alive and well,/ All the rights of man.)

The poem 'Gwawr Dydd Rhyddhad' ('The Dawn of Freedom Day') heralds the providential dawning of a new 'Eden':

> Iôr nef,
> Bydd e'n waredwr, a'i law gref
> O dan ein llwyth, fe wrendy'n llef,
> Fe rwyma'r traws, fe dyr ei gledd,
> Mae'n geidwad nerthol i'n rhyddhau,
> Yn agosáu â neges hedd.[78]

(Lord of heaven,/ He shall be our redeemer, with his strong hand/ Beneath our burden, he shall hear our cry,/ He shall shackle the wicked, shatter their swords,/ He's a powerful saviour who shall set us free,/ Approaching with tidings of peace.)

In both poems the hymn-like clarity of style and metre adds much to the impression of dignity and unshakable conviction. Iolo's democratic and humanitarian convictions, especially his loathing of slavery, are apparent in his vast output of Unitarian hymns – well over three thousand in all – although, as poetry, these very rarely reach the same heights.[79]

Throughout his career Iolo seems to have had an obsessive need to prove that he, an untutored Glamorgan journeyman mason, could be a more prolific hymn-writer than Pantycelyn; become a more ardent radical than Tom Paine; devise a metrical system that excelled that of Dafydd ab Edmwnd; compose love-poems which were the equal of Dafydd ap Gwilym; and become a finer historian and antiquary than Lewis Morris. As a poet he closely resembled Lewis Morris. Both were heavily influenced by Dafydd ap Gwilym; both experimented with a range of strict and free metrical forms, including the humble *triban* and *pennill telyn*; both took a keen interest in folk-poetry; and both were polymaths whose poetry has to some extent been overlooked. It is a comparison that Iolo would have loathed. Despite his early admiration for Lewis Morris, he later came to regard him as a north Wales charlatan, and even had the audacity to accuse him of forgery.[80] It is precisely because, in his view, the cultural awakening inspired by the Morris brothers had not gone far enough that he developed an alternative, more beguiling vision of Wales's past. His forging of a stronger national identity and of a national institution in the

---

[78] *CRhIM*, no. 27.
[79] The hymns are discussed in Lewis: *IM*, chapters 8, 9. For examples of the many poems denouncing the slave trade, see Evans (ed.), *Gwaith Iolo Morganwg*, pp. 52–60.
[80] Williams: *IM*, p. 211.

form of Gorsedd Beirdd Ynys Prydain (Gorsedd of the Bards of the Isle of Britain) has been seen as one of many Romantic revivals among the smaller nations of late eighteenth- and nineteenth-century Europe.[81] His escape through poetry into an imagined past is itself deeply Romantic, and his pre-occupation with love and natural scenery, with rurality and the concerns of the common man, is a significant departure from the neoclassical values of the mid-century revival. A recent study has revealed his likely influence on Wordsworth and Coleridge,[82] but the kind of Romantic imagination and individualism that distinguishes the *Lyrical Ballads* is on the whole lacking in Iolo's work. As a free-metre poet he is most remarkable for his versatility, for his uncanny ability to adopt a multitude of styles and voices which all bear the hallmark of the same unique creative talent.

[81] Gwyn A. Williams, 'Iolo Morganwg: Bardd Rhamantaidd ar gyfer Cenedl nad oedd yn Cyfrif' in Geraint H. Jenkins (ed.), *Cof Cenedl V: Ysgrifau ar Hanes Cymru* (Llandysul, 1990), pp. 57–84; idem, 'Romanticism in Wales' in Roy Porter and Mikuláš Teich (eds.), *Romanticism in National Context* (Cambridge, 1988), pp. 9–36.

[82] Walford Davies, *Presences that Disturb*, pp. 155 ff. See also chapter 7 below.

6

'This Wildernessed Business of Publication': The Making of Poems, Lyric and Pastoral (1794)

MARY-ANN CONSTANTINE

I shall be very sorry to find that, occasion'd by what I have experienced of mental distress and confusion during the course of this wildernessed business of publication, I have omitted in my list the name of a subscriber. I hope I shall be pardoned for whatever may be discovered of this nature. Whether what I have said in the account of my life will be deemed a sufficient apology for the length of time that this work has been at press I know not. The sons of affluence can never be proper judges of what may or may not be done in a struggle with the gigantic difficulties that I have experienced.[1]

The publication of the two volumes of *Poems, Lyric and Pastoral* (1794) brought Iolo Morganwg to a state of nervous collapse and near financial ruin, and caused considerable hardship and distress to his family. Yet the painful 'length of time' of the book's production, roughly between 1790 and 1794, corresponds to one of the most intensely energetic periods of his life. During these years, in Glamorgan, Bath, Bristol and London, Iolo moved in an extraordinarily wide range of social circles. He was politically active, poetically creative, and became, in short, a character on the English literary scene.[2] As a result, this period is perhaps unparalleled in Iolo's life for the opportunities it offers to examine his sense of himself as an author, and his presentation of himself to others – questions of more than psychological interest, given the wider context of his activities as a forger.

The immediate aim of this chapter, however, is more specific and more concrete. It looks closely at the processes that took *Poems, Lyric and Pastoral* from its inception in the late 1770s to its final published form, and at the difficulties involved in getting a book into print. Iolo's experiences as a 'self-taught

---

[1] NLW 21387E, no. 11.

[2] For accounts of Iolo's activities during this period, see Damian Walford Davies, *Presences that Disturb: Models of Romantic Identity in the Literature and Culture of the 1790s* (Cardiff, 2002), pp. 135–92; Gwyneth Lewis, 'Eighteenth-century Literary Forgeries with special reference to the work of Iolo Morganwg' (unpublished University of Oxford D. Phil. thesis, 1991), chapter VI; Morgan: *IM*, pp. 31–9.

journeyman mason' bring some exceptionally well-documented primary material to a growing literature dealing with the practicalities of book production in the Romantic period;[3] they can also be related to recent stimulating work on other eighteenth- and nineteenth-century writers from the labouring classes.[4] The second part of this chapter shows how the shape of the collection changed over a period of twenty years, from the 1770s when Iolo first began to 'scribble English verse' up to the very end of 1793, when the last sheets went to press. It examines the fate of an early poem ('Winter Incidents') through several drafts to publication. What kinds of pressures, external or otherwise, shaped the final work? What was excluded, and why?

The sources for this chapter are first and foremost the letters, which provide an invaluable chronology in an otherwise chaotic archive. Writing home to his wife Margaret (Peggy) and to his mentor John Walters, Iolo gives a mass of detail about the process of collecting subscriptions towards the book and the seemingly endless setbacks in its printing. The rest of the Iolo manuscripts, especially those in the Iolo Aneurin Williams collection, contain numerous drafts, versions and lists of poems to be included in the volume, along with printed proposals, trial dedications and lists of subscribers. And there are many, often revealing, drafts of the extraordinary preface, Iolo's bitter introduction to his demurely titled book.

In his early twenties, following the death of his mother in 1770, Iolo began a period of travel and work from home. In 1773 he went to work as a mason in London, where, through John Walters, he was able to make contact with an active literary Welsh expatriate community: in the Welsh School there he saw the papers of Lewis Morris and manuscripts containing the poetry of Dafydd ap Gwilym which would have a profound effect on his own writing in Welsh. His work as a mason took him to Dover, Sandwich and Faversham, and over the next two or three years he moved between Kent and London.

---

[3]   See, for example, Clifford Siskin, *The Work of Writing: Literature and Social Change in Britain 1700–1830* (Baltimore, 1998); William Zachs, *The First John Murray and the Late Eighteenth-century London Book Trade* (Oxford, 1998); E. J. Clery, Caroline Franklin and Peter Garside (eds.), *Authorship, Commerce and the Public: Scenes of Writing, 1750–1850* (Basingstoke, 2002); Isabel Rivers (ed.), *Books and their Readers in Eighteenth-century England* (Leicester 1982; a further collection of 'New Essays' with the same editor and title appeared in 2001); William St Clair, *The Reading Nation in the Romantic Period* (Cambridge, 2004).

[4]   Although Iolo's manipulation of the 'peasant-poet' persona has long been acknowledged (Lewis, 'Eighteenth-century Forgeries'; Morgan: *IM*), his inclusion in a recent major anthology of labouring-class writers raises new questions about class, cultural identity and the authorial voice: see Tim Burke (ed.), *Eighteenth Century English Labouring-Class Poets: Volume III, 1780–1800* (London, 2003) and John Goodridge, 'Identity, Authenticity, Class: John Clare and the Mask of Chatterton', *Angelaki*, I, no. 2 (1993/4), 131–48. On the self-taught tradition, see William J. Christmas, *The Lab'ring Muses: Work, Writing and the Social Order in English Plebeian Poetry, 1730–1830* (London, 2001); Morag Shiach, *Discourse on Popular Culture: Class, Gender and History in Cultural Analysis, 1730 to the Present* (Oxford, 1989).

The dates ascribed to poems by Iolo himself cannot, for various reasons discussed below, always be trusted, but numerous pieces in the manuscripts must have been written during this period. Many of them, such as various satirical or convivial songs, would not be included in the published collection. Among those that were, a few can be dated by external factors: verses beginning 'When golden morn's reviving rays/gives lustre to the dewy vale' were written, for example, on the back of a 1776 advertisement for a cutler's business in Maidstone.[5] 'On first hearing the Cuckoo' was published in the *Town and Country Magazine* in August 1775, and subsequently reappeared in the first volume of *Poems*, inevitably altered ('but the sentiments are still the same'), and with a note darkly accusing an unnamed writer of having plagiarized it several years after its first appearance.[6] Writing to his father from Kent, Iolo mentioned another publication: 'I scribble english verses sometimes, the inclosed was printed last wednesday in the Canterbury Gazette.'[7] The same letter shows that he was already weighing up possibilities for publishing in London, not poetry, but on antiquarian matters:

> I have wrote some remarks on the antient History of Britain, and an eminent Bookseller at London promises to print it for me and take Books in payment. I have some thougts of a[cce]pting this offer, I might otherwise publish it by subscription, which way some tell is best.[8]

Although English poetry in various forms was already a significant part of his life, Iolo's real passion at this time was for things Welsh. His letters to John Walters are full of excited derivations and etymologies; in 1777 he wrote to Owen Jones (Owain Myfyr) with thoughts on the 'druid' stones at Avebury.[9] He composed and sent *englynion* and *cywyddau* to the London Welsh literati for comment and improvement, telling Jones in 1776: 'I always thought myself more successful in my British than my English Poetry, indeed a great part of my happiness consists in the little knowledge I have of the British Language and Poetry.'[10] Comparison of an early poem in Welsh of wintry exile in Kent with the grandly titled 'Soliloquy in a Cowhouse near Twickenham where the

---

[5] NLW 21392F, no. 45. The verses were incorporated into 'Rural Incidents', Williams: *PLP*, I, p. 8.
[6] Williams: *PLP*, I, p. 53. Cf. NLW 21392F, no. 3, where the plagiarizer appears to be named as Logan (the sentence has been crossed out).
[7] NLW 21285E, Letter no. 782, Iolo Morganwg to Edward Williams Senr., undated.
[8] Ibid.
[9] Jon Cannon and Mary-Ann Constantine, 'A Welsh Bard in Wiltshire: Iolo Morganwg, Silbury and the Sarsens', *Wiltshire Archaeological and Natural History Magazine*, 97 (2004), 78–88.
[10] NLW 21285E, Letter no. 783, Iolo Morganwg to Owain Myfyr, 25 January 1776. For his contacts with the London Welsh at this period, see Ffion Mair Jones, 'Gydwladwr Godi[d]og . . .': Gohebiaeth Gymraeg Gynnar Iolo Morganwg', *LlC*, 27 (2004), 140–71, and chapter 18 by Geraint Phillips in this volume.

author was oblidged to take up his lodgings in a very tempestuous night in the winter 1774', or of his Welsh love-poems to his future wife with the apostrophes to various Celias and Delias in *Poems*, suggests that his self-appraisal, in this instance, was not far wrong.[11]

Iolo's return to Wales in 1777 began the period of his greatest creativity as a Welsh poet, thanks mainly to his inspired connection with the medieval poetry of Dafydd ap Gwilym. Over the next decade he produced not only the forged Dafydd poems, but many lyrics and love-songs in his style; he became fluent in complex metres and acquired a rich medieval vocabulary. But he continued with his English poetry and, as a letter from the younger John Walters, then studying at Oxford, makes clear, as early as 1781 he was already collecting, recopying, and revising his work with an eye to publication:

> I have your manuscript Volume, which came in the Box: it is now before me. I frequently peruse some of the pieces it contains; and they give me additional pleasure in every new perusal . . . With your concurrence, I will continue to make corrections in it at intervals of leisure, and watch an opportunity of publication that may be attended with honour and profit to the author – if profit may be expected by an author in this iron (this golden age, indeed, of literary merit, but iron age of its rewards).[12]

Although Iolo complained to John's brother Daniel that his marriage (in 1781) had killed his muse, and although he went through a period of acute financial difficulty which led to several months in Cardiff gaol, he did not abandon his aim of becoming a published poet in English. His next appearance in print was more decisive. In November 1789 the *Gentleman's Magazine* carried his flamboyant 'Ode Imitated from the Gododdin of Aneurin' and the much-cited description of the worthy, sober, reclusive and 'absolutely self-taught' Edward Williams, one of the last people in Britain to be 'admitted a *Bard* in the ancient manner; a custom still retained in Glamorgan, but I believe, in no other part of Wales'.[13] And so the year which saw the publication in Welsh of his forged Dafydd ap Gwilym poems was also the year of his rather theatrical entrance into English letters, not as a Shenstonian poet of nature, but as a full-blown British bard. *Poems, Lyric and Pastoral* would offer a disconcerting mix of both of these voices, and more.

The description Iolo offers of his poetic development in the preface to *Poems* creates the impression of a quiet, introspective writer, inspired by his reading and by scenes of natural beauty, who was urged reluctantly into print around 1790 by the 'advice of Friends'. But he clearly had every intention of

---

[11] 'Cywydd yr Awen yn lled Dynwared Horas', partially cited in Lewis: *IM*, p. 88; the 'Cowhouse' poem is in NLW 21422E, no. 1.

[12] NLW 21283E, Letter no. 523, John Walters to Iolo Morganwg, 13 April 1781.

[13] *Gentleman's Magazine*, LIX, Part 2 (1789), 976–7, 1035–6.

publishing from very early on. The death in 1787 and 1789 of both Daniel and the young John Walters deprived him of encouragement and one possible entrée into the world of English letters, but there were others, and other kinds of impetus. The years 1785 to 1787, for example, saw successful re-editions or new volumes of poetry by Robert Burns and Ann Yearsley, both of whom had recently begun their careers by publishing through subscription, and both of whom were rapidly becoming types of a distinctively regional and labouring-class poetic tradition.[14]

In 1789 Thomas Wyndham, owner of the Dunraven estate, was elected to the county seat of Glamorgan against the favoured candidate of a powerful clique of aristocrats, including the duke of Beaufort and the earls of Bute and Plymouth. His election was perceived as a victory for local interests, and Iolo's verses for the campaign, some of which were printed, drew on a familiar combination of radical sloganeering and local patriotism to present Wyndham as an opponent of crass nobility and external interference:

> No *tyrant Lord* can thee subdue
> No Scottish *Thane* thy Sons enslave
> Rise, Glamorgan, sing with me
> WYNDHAM, PEACE, and LIBERTY.[15]

The account in the preface implies that verses such as these won him attention locally, and that he was persuaded to venture into print as a result: the names of pro-Wyndham Glamorgan gentry on an early subscription list bear this out to some extent.[16] But it seems equally likely that much of the impetus to publish came from the appearance of his ode in John Nichols's *Gentleman's Magazine* and the interest shown in him thereafter (by, for example, the Irish antiquarian Joseph Walker, who urged support for him in the subsequent issue).[17] Contact with the *Gentleman's Magazine* had presumably allowed Iolo to secure John Nichols as his printer: by May 1790 (and possibly well before then) Nichols was taking in subscriptions.[18] To build up his list Iolo had first

[14] Ann Yearsley's 1785 debut volume, *Poems, on Several Occasions*, was published by subscription under the patronage of Hannah More; her 1787 *Poems, on Various Subjects* was published by Robinsons of London, with the support of Frederick Hervey, earl of Bristol. Burns's *Poems, Chiefly in the Scottish Dialect* came out by subscription in 1786 and was into a successful third edition by 1787. For a comparison of Burns and Iolo as song collectors, see chapter 15 by Daniel Huws in this volume.

[15] NLW 21402F, no. 6; Philip Jenkins, 'Glamorgan Politics 1789–1868' in Prys Morgan (ed.), *Glamorgan County History, Volume VI, Glamorgan Society 1780–1980* (Cardiff, 1988), pp. 1–18.

[16] NLW 21392F, no. 66. Note, however, that the 'Earl of Bute' appears in capitals in the final subscription list to *PLP*, having ordered no fewer than six sets.

[17] *Gentleman's Magazine*, LX, Part 2 (1790), 801–2.

[18] NLW 21280E, Letter no. 311, William Owen Pughe to Iolo Morganwg, 13 May 1790. A manuscript draft of a 'Proposal to Publish', dated July 1789, has Nichols heading the list of those taking in subscriptions: NLW 21387E, no. 1.

to enter the Bath/Bristol literary circuit. After an initial disappointment involving an unhelpful 'Mr Matthews', he found champions for his project in John Curre of Itton Court and the Revd John Carne of Nash.[19] Some time afterwards, Iolo wrote of his success to John Walters:

Mrs Smith of Piercefield and Mrs Bowdler had by Mr Curre invited me to their Patronage, I waited on them, and was not disappointed, unless it was in being warmly befriended by them far beyond my most sanguine hopes, those very amiable Ladies (I should have sooner mentioned Mis[s] Bowdler) have laid me under obligations to them that the most refined language of gratitude, exerted with its utmost force can never express, – but still, tho' I knew it not then, there was a something wanting, something necessary for me to know. I fortunately became acquainted with Mr Anstey the celebrated Author of the New Bath Guide, he was an old experienced Author, and initiated me into many Mysteries of Authorship, without the knowlege of which I should never have succeeded. I might have had many Subscriptions, but not have been able to collect them in so short a time that the money received might not be to much expended – I, according to his advice, of Miss More's of Mr Melmoth's, the celebrated Translator of Pliny and of Mr Meyler's (a capital Bookseller) printed proposals with one of my pieces as a specimen, and acted in such a manner as I was advised to do.[20]

Iolo's specimen, *The Fair Pilgrim*, an expansive but not inelegant translation from Dafydd ap Gwilym, was printed at Bath and quickly earned him a flood of 'very respectable' names: 'Lady Aubrey, Lord Vernon, Lord Howard, Lord Fielding – Countess of Bute, Lady Harries. &c of Literary names – Miss Hannah More, Mr Melmoth, Mr Anstey, Miss Lee, Revd Dr Gabriel (the Antagonist of Dr White) Revd Mr Bowles (a successful Poet) Mrs Piozzi (who is a Welsh Woman and speaks Welsh), Revd Dr Peckard (master of Magdalen College Cambridge) and many others, so that I may be a little vain of my List.'[21] He also received considerable support from the Glamorgan gentry.

Christopher Anstey's role in all this is intriguing, as is the presence of

[19] Probably William Matthews, then Secretary of the Royal Bath and West Agricultural Society. Note Iolo's claim that he was 'noticed by' Curre in 1789: NLW 21387E, no. 1.
[20] NLW 21285E, Letter no. 798, Iolo Morganwg to John Walters, 24 February 1791.
[21] Ibid. Two printed copies of *The Fair Pilgrim* are preserved in NLW 21392F: no. 66 is the earliest, with an attached proposal and a subscription list of some sixty names; no. 64 is a deluxe 'third edition' of the poem only, with extensive notes. Both date from 1791. The final subscription list, which included over 600 names from an extraordinary range of social backgrounds and political persuasions, would repay further study: the lively account by James Harris, 'The Fringe of a Welshman's Book', *The Red Dragon*, VIII (1885), 582–98 contains fundamental errors, and J. Kyrle Fletcher's, 'Iolo Morganwg's List of Subscribers', *JWBS*, VI (1943), 39–41 does little more than comment on its breadth. For a discussion of publishing by subscription at this period, see Zachs, *The First John Murray*, pp. 68–70; James Raven, *Judging New Wealth: Popular Publishing and Responses to Commerce in England, 1750–1800* (Oxford, 1992), p. 56, and Paul Korshin, 'Types of Eighteenth-century Literary Patronage', *Eighteenth-Century Studies*, 7 (1974), 463–5.

Hannah More. Anstey, by then elderly, seems to have been most directly involved in shaping the content of the proposed volume, criticizing and even correcting verses, much as the young John Walters had done (if, one suspects, with rather more condescension). Although in 1791 Iolo was glad enough to be initiated into the 'Mysteries of Authorship', Anstey's 'interventions' would come to antagonize him deeply, as various comments in the manuscripts make clear.[22] The reasons for this are complex; chief among them was Iolo's proclaimed (and in retrospect, breathtakingly ironic) determination 'not to impose on the public by giving them any thing that was not absolutely my own'.[23] But another reason was the shadow of the very public dispute in 1786 between Hannah More and her protegée Ann Yearsley, the 'Bristol Milk-woman', part of which had centred on More's supposed alterations of Yearsley's texts.[24] More, though supportive of Iolo, was not as closely involved in his work and, unlike Anstey, did not fall from his grace, but remained with Mrs and Miss Bowdler among the 'brightest stars' in what would become a very overcast sky. In 1791, however, things looked promising enough, with the Bowdlers, Curre and Carne assiduously sending him names to swell the list. There were also many presents of books, and recommendations to gentry in London, Oxford, Gloucester and Cheltenham: 'I am upon the whole in good spirits, the prospect, for once in my Life, seems to open fair before me.'[25]

Part of the system for obtaining subscriptions involved leaving the specimen and proposal on view at various booksellers, who would take in names. One proposal printed late in 1791 by John Nichols lists booksellers in London, Bath, Oxford and Cambridge.[26] There are two notable absences here. The first is the radical publisher Joseph Johnson, who headed a list of London sellers on the title-page of 1794; the only London booksellers named at this stage in the proceedings are G. G. J. and J. Robinson, Paternoster Row (the publishers of Yearsley following her split with More). The second absence is Bristol, whose booksellers (though named in the earlier printed proposal) were presumably struck off after an incident over the summer, in which Iolo wrote an open letter expressing his 'fixed resolution not to disgrace my list with the names of any villainous abettors of the slave trade, who so exultingly rejoiced lately in

---

22 See, for example, several drafts of poems marked 'Anstey's interpolations' in NLW 21392F, nos. 52–4.

23 NLW 21387E, no. 9.

24 For the dispute, see Tim Burke's introduction to Ann Yearsley's *Selected Poems* (Cheltenham, 2003) and Anne Stott, *Hannah More: the First Victorian* (Oxford, 2003), pp. 70–8. I discuss Iolo's connections with both women at greater length in a forthcoming chapter in Damian Walford Davies and Lynda Pratt (eds.), *Romantic Wales*.

25 NLW 21285E, Letter no. 798, Iolo Morganwg to John Walters, 24 February 1791.

26 NLW 21400C, no. 5. For a helpful analysis of the overlapping functions of 'bookseller' and 'publisher' in this period, see James Raven, 'The Book Trades' in Rivers (ed.), *Books and their Readers*, pp. 14–15.

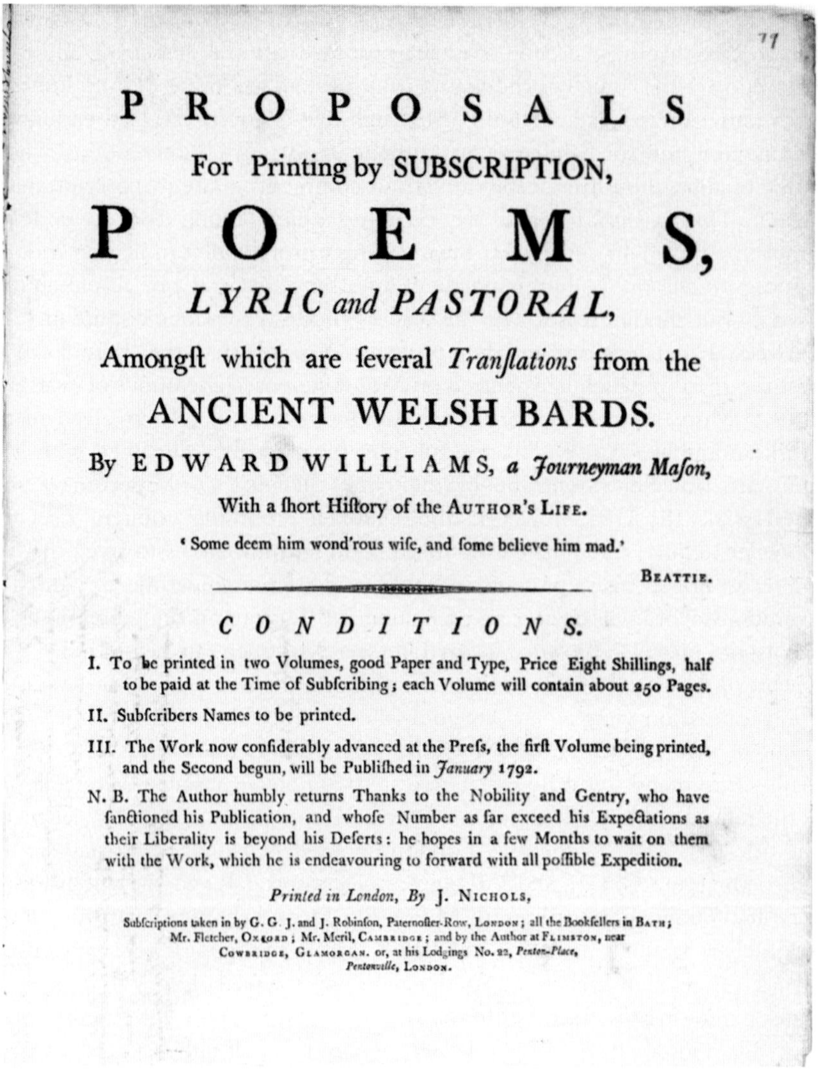

P R O P O S A L S

For Printing by SUBSCRIPTION,

P O E M S,

LYRIC and PASTORAL,

Amongſt which are ſeveral *Tranſlations* from the

ANCIENT WELSH BARDS.

By E D W A R D   W I L L I A M S, *a Journeyman Maſon*,

With a ſhort Hiſtory of the AUTHOR'S LIFE.

' Some deem him wond'rous wife, and ſome believe him mad.'

BEATTIE.

C O N D I T I O N S.

I. To be printed in two Volumes, good Paper and Type, Price **Eight Shillings**, half to be paid at the Time of Subſcribing ; each Volume will contain about **250** Pages.

II. Subſcribers Names to be printed.

III. The Work now conſiderably advanced at the Preſs, the firſt Volume being printed, and the Second begun, will be Publiſhed in *January* **1792**.

N. B. The Author humbly returns Thanks to the Nobility and Gentry, who have ſanctioned his Publication, and whoſe Number as far exceed his Expectations as their Liberality is beyond his Deſerts : he hopes in a few Months to wait on them with the Work, which he is endeavouring to forward with all poſſible Expedition.

Printed in London, By J. NICHOLS,

Subſcriptions taken in by G. G. J. and J. Robinſon, Paternoſter-Row, LONDON ; all the Bookſellers in BATH ; Mr. Fletcher, OXFORD ; Mr. Meril, CAMBRIDGE ; and by the Author at FLIMSTON, near COWBRIDGE, GLAMORGAN. or, at his Lodgings No. 22, *Penton-Place*, *Pentonville*, LONDON.

Fig. 8 Proposals for the printing, by subscription, of *Poems, Lyric and Pastoral* by Iolo Morganwg (NLW 21400C, no. 5).

your City, on the failure of the humane Mr Wilberforces Bill'.[27] The proposal of 1791 implies that the work was already well in hand (one and a half volumes printed) and was expected out in January 1792.

---

[27] This is discussed further in Mary-Ann Constantine, *Combustible Matter: Iolo Morganwg and the Bristol Volcano* (Aberystwyth, 2003).

In September, Curre wrote encouragingly, assuring Iolo that he would 'be recompensed by much more than barren fame, which could, personally, be no great object to You, as you must, without emoluments of a more lucrative kind, relapse into a life of labour and penury'.[28] Although Iolo was now based in London, staying at William Owen Pughe's house in Pentonville, the realities of that life of labour were never far away, as letters from Peggy would continue to remind him, painfully, over the next three years: 'Dear Ned, you promised to send soon to us I think it high time for me to reminde you of that promise haveing eaten the last bit of bread we had a Tuesday night.'[29] And Curre, despite his optimism, was nevertheless worried that Iolo was overstretching himself: 'I wish you had not bespoke a thousand copies. Is there no way of reducing that number to 500 or 600?'[30] That he was aiming high is suggested by jotted notes and calculations comparing length and layout and the quality of paper and type in the volumes of poetry produced by Yearsley and Burns: 'EW's collection will contain 400 pages fine Crown Octavo new type, 20 lines per page exclusive of the History of his Life.'[31]

As Iolo's focus shifted inevitably to London, the practicalities of boosting the subscription list were taken on by the 'Honourable Mrs Nicholl' of Remenham, near Henley.[32] Her short, efficient notes to Iolo are full of instructions, and much of his time in London must have been taken up with wearisome trajectories of soliciting, thanking and waiting on various gentry:

> I wish you to call on The Honble Miss Nevill No 6 Curzon Street May Fair the first opportunity, about eleven o Clock is the most likely hour to find her at home, or at five in the afternoon, she has promised me to subscribe and will pay you the above subscriptions.[33]

That the business was not entirely to his taste becomes increasingly evident from her tone:

> Miss Flower thinks that you shew rather a coolness with respect to the subscriptions, which she has been at some pains to procure for you, and as each suspicion would

---

[28] NLW 21280E, Letter no. 58, John Curre to Iolo Morganwg, 18 September 1791.

[29] NLW 21283E, Letter no. 603, Margaret (Peggy) Williams to Iolo Morganwg, 22 September 1791.

[30] NLW 21280, Letter no. 58, John Curre to Iolo Morganwg, 18 September 1791. A normal first print-run for this type of poetry would have been 500: see Zachs, *The First John Murray*, p. 68; St Clair, *The Reading Nation*, p. 582 (for Robert Bloomfield).

[31] NLW 21392F, nos. 81, 86. I am grateful to Tim Burke for drawing my attention to these. The volumes finally appeared as duodecimo, not octavo.

[32] She was married to the Revd John Nicholl of Remenham. I have not been able to establish why this family should have taken such an interest in Iolo.

[33] NLW 21281E, Letter no. 285, M. Nicholl to Iolo Morganwg, 6 February 1792. Cf. Letter nos. 286–7, in similar vein.

operate to your prejudice in diminishing the number of subscribers, I could wish
you to call soon.[34]

Mrs Nicholl also set about obtaining permission to dedicate the collection to
the Prince of Wales. After much toing and froing, this was confirmed in April.
It is possibly at this point that the paradox of Iolo's situation began to bite.
Writing to Peggy, he claimed to be ashamed of this 'bit of vanity', but assured
her that it would help sell the book.[35] An undated letter from John Aikin
(promising to obtain the names of Anna Laetitia Barbauld and Joseph Priestley
for the subscription list) advises him to accept: 'I am at present inclined to
think, that you will do right to avoid offending those friends who have
obtained permission for a dedication to the P. of Wales. This may be done in a
simple manner, so as to carry no appearance of adulation.'[36] To this period, no
doubt, can be dated various frustrated draft letters to London gentry, which
begin as polite solicitations and turn rapidly into defiant tirades; and to this
period, too, belong the increasingly desperate drafts of the dedication to the
prince,[37] some of which, in their attempts to avoid any 'appearance of
adulation', become tortuous and lengthy essays condemning flattery and
monarchy on the one hand, and extolling the revered connection of the Prince
of Wales with Ancient British Bardism on the other. The final published
version, a single sentence, smacks of exhaustion.

Iolo's resentment at his dependence on aristocratic patronage, compounded
by guilt at leaving his family and anxiety over the slowness of the publication,
seems to have paralysed him. By late April 1792 worried letters from Curre
and Carne were clearly not being answered, and at times even Peggy did not
know where he was.[38] A letter he wrote to her in June explains some of the
practical and technical difficulties he was facing, and his underlying unhap-
piness at his treatment in London:

> I had obtained a frank for this day, in hopes of being able to send you one or two
> of the sheet that is now at the press, for I had prepared paper for ten copies more
> than the usual number, with a view of sending them to different places, that my
> subscribers might see how I go on. As I never thought of this when the first sheets
> of the second volume were printed off, I can not send any of those without breaking
> sets, but the sheet for which I had prepared is not yet printed off, and the frank could

---

[34]   NLW 21281E, Letter no. 291, M. Nicholl to Iolo Morganwg, 8 March 1792.
[35]   NLW 21285E, Letter no. 808, Iolo Morganwg to Margaret Williams, 5 May 1792.
[36]   NLW 21280E, Letter no. 1, John Aikin to Iolo Morganwg, undated.
[37]   See, for example, NLW 21286, Letter no. 1024, Iolo Morganwg to an unnamed 'Sir', undated.
       For the draft dedications, see NLW 21392F, nos. 87–94. Mrs Nicholl furnished him with a
       ready-made version written by her husband, which he did not use: see NLW 21281E, Letter
       no. 294, M. Nicholl to Iolo Morganwg, 2 May 1792.
[38]   See NLW 21280E, Letter no. 47, John Carne to William Owen Pughe, 26 April 1792 and
       Letter no. 60, John Curre to John Nichols, 25 May 1792.

not be kept beyond its date, so that I am now disappointed. I wait for the printing of this sheet to send it to Mr Carne, Mr Curre, &c, but parliament being now prorogued, and all members in the Country, 'twill not be very easy to procure franks, and matters are now so with me that I can not possibly pay postage. I shall feel, before I have completed the work, some of the greatest hardships that I ever yet experienced. I could bear it well enough myself, but you and the little children must of course also suffer. I cannot possibly afford you any relief, till the whole is printed.[39]

A source of constant expense was the postal system, which involved the receiver paying the costs, with additional fees for enclosures and packages; this could be avoided if the writer had access to franks, the prerogative of members of parliament.[40] The practical difficulties were compounded by temperamental ones. In the metropolis, it seems, the complexities of class had a harder edge:

I was treated with so much superciliousness by one to whom I had Letters of Recommendation from Cowbridge that I resolved not to give any other person of an opportunity of behaving to me so again. I continued in this humour a good while – at last I thought otherwise, and waited on another with letters also of recommen- dation, and was by him treated in the same manner. I never after applied to any one. I have found London very different from Bath and Glamorganshire, I wish I had printed at Bath . . . there will be money wanted for what I never dream'd of. But it is now too late to repent.[41]

Although his letters to Peggy do not always admit as much, he was busy with other things, meeting friends, organizing the first Gorsedd of the Bards on Primrose Hill on 21 June and firing off contributions to the hunt for 'Welsh' Indians in America.[42] But by the end of the summer he seems to have suffered a complete breakdown, a paralysis of will which left him incapable of marking proofs or answering the necessary letters, and which, in a dramatic sequence of letters to Peggy, developed into a full-blown paranoid conviction that his children had died and that she was hiding the truth from him:

nobody knows where I am, because when I die I do not wish for any one to know who or what I am. you advise me to write to Mr Carne. Mr Curre &c, I shall never be able to write to any body. I wanted to write to so many that those wants overpowered me entirely, yet if my little ones were all living and well I could do something yet. I try every way to throw of my distressing ideas but I can not do it. I know 'tis foolish, – it is rather odd for a person to be mad and at the same time in

[39]   NLW 21285E, Letter no. 809, Iolo Morganwg to Margaret Williams, 20 June 1792.
[40]   See NLW 21285E, Letter no. 813, Iolo Morganwg to Margaret Williams, 6 November 1792, in which he complained that 'the three letters cost me three shillings'.
[41]   Letter 21285E, Letter no. 809, Iolo Morganwg to Margaret Williams, 20 June 1792.
[42]   See Gwyn A. Williams, *Madoc: The Making of a Myth* (London, 1979), pp. 118–53. Iolo had planned to go in search of the 'Welsh' Indians himself, but withdrew from the expedition at around this time.

full possession of all his senses, memory, and understanding, but something very much like this I experience at present.[43]

The thought of his waiting subscribers tortured him: 'it would now be a heaven to me if I could be sure of being able to send my books to my subscribers soon, and spend the remainder of my life, not only in a prison, but in the darkest dungeon – and spend eternity in Hell'.[44] In between the sleeping in fields, the wandering, the laudanum and the Chatterton-haunted thoughts of suicide there were, as in any depression, moments when things seemed less black and he could write: 'my work goes along middling'.[45] But London life was expensive. By November 1792 he had run out of money to pay for paper. He wrote to John Carne, seeking financial assistance, but Carne refused: 'I have been much hurt that you have so long disappointed your Subscribers.'[46] Enraged, Iolo turned to the Bowdlers. They sent him money immediately, and the printing continued.

Carne's refusal and the background to it, cloaked in dark hints, loom large in the published preface. Iolo clearly came to believe (and the facts are hard to ascertain) that at some point in the autumn of 1792 an article or announcement had appeared in one of the Bath newspapers, suggesting that he was planning to emigrate to America, the implication being that he would take the subscribers' money with him.[47] Discovering this story after Carne's refusal, Iolo immediately suspected the machinations of William Rees, a Glamorgan attorney-at-law with whom he had crossed swords over his debts in the 1780s. He sent at least one hysterical reply to Carne, warning that he would unmask Rees (who was related to John Curre), and threatening, for good measure, to kill himself and his family.[48] Into draft after draft of the preface to his poems he poured his bitterness against 'weathercock friends', 'inveterate enemies' and the 'malice which has every where pursued me with great indefatigability, lurking behind every bush by which I passed'.[49]

[43] NLW 21285E, Letter no. 810, Iolo Morganwg to Margaret Williams, 20 July 1792; see also Letter no. 812 in the same volume. For the effect of laudanum on his innate paranoia at this period, see Geraint Phillips, 'Math o Wallgofrwydd: Iolo Morganwg, Opiwm a Thomas Chatterton', *NLWJ*, XXIX, no. 4 (1996), 391–410.

[44] NLW 21285E, Letter no. 811, Iolo Morganwg to Margaret Williams, 9 August 1792. Iolo's experience contradicts Korshin's claim that the 'sense of obligation which pervades and often exacerbates the traditional patron-client relationship is usually diminished or wholly absent in the author-subscriber relationship', Korshin, 'Types of Eighteenth-century Literary Patronage', p. 464.

[45] NLW 21285E, Letter no. 820, Iolo Morganwg to Margaret Williams, 12 October 1792.

[46] NLW 21280E, Letter no. 48, John Carne to Iolo Morganwg, 5 December 1792.

[47] NLW 21387E, no. 9 (and see note 42 above).

[48] The episode is summarized in an admirably restrained reply from John Curre, written on 14 January 1793 (NLW 21280E, Letter no. 61). Iolo's state of mind during this period makes it likely that the 'machinations' were at best exaggerated.

[49] NLW 21387E, no. 9.

Early in 1793 he regained some energy, achieved a rapprochement with Curre (though not Carne) and at least the prospect of an additional boost to his income through the sale of Peggy's family farm.[50] On 6 April, back in London after a brief visit home, he was in buoyant mood, sending Peggy his newly composed 'Ode on Converting a Sword into a Pruning Hook'. But two days later, in a grim fulfilment of his own paranoid fears, came news of the death of his three-year-old daughter: he left London immediately, and did not return for over four months. He spent the entire summer at home, working on his collection of bardic triads: William Owen Pughe kept him informed of events in London, such as the rather desultory Gorsedd organized by Dr John Williams of Sydenham.[51] In September he set off on foot on a 250-mile journey back to London, where, after more delays, the printing resumed. It is likely, as Jon Mee points out elsewhere in this volume, that support from the radical Unitarian Joseph Johnson at this time helped him to see the 'wilder-nessed business' through to the end. Johnson took over as the main publisher/bookseller, encouraged him to include more bardic material, and by October was supporting Iolo's next projected work, a 'History of the Bards'.[52]

Even at this late stage the practical problems continued: all private printing, for example, ground to a halt 'for the last ten days of every month, as the Magazines, and other periodical publications employ the Presses'.[53] He was also obliged to buy an extra 'bundle' of printing paper at a cost of thirty-eight shillings, and there were many other unexpected costs, the detailed listing of which cannot have afforded much comfort to Peggy:

> I have my poems all printed the history of my life in the press. I have paid the compositor about fifteen shillings for altering somethings that were before composited. I could have this done without ready money, by mentioning the matter to Mr Nichols, but in that case the expence would have been Master's price, and not much less than three pounds. As soon as all but the list is printed off, I will go with the Work to some that have promised me subscribers, and perhaps come down to Glocester and Bath, and of Course to Wales. There is so much work at the press now that I was obliged to stuff the pressmen last week with more than four shillings worth of ale, porter, and Gin to get out the poems. And if I can not by some means

---

50 NLW 21283E, Letter no. 604, Margaret Williams to Iolo Morganwg, undated. There are also indications that he was receiving help from the Royal Literary Fund at this period: see NLW 21282E, Letter no. 448, William Royou to Iolo Morganwg, 26 October 1792, and British Library, Royal Literary Fund, M1077/reel 1, file no. 27, no. 2, Letter no. 1335, Iolo Morganwg to the Committee, 13 May 1794, thanking them for a grant of ten guineas.

51 NLW 21282E, Letter no. 320, William Owen Pughe to Iolo Morganwg, 11 July 1793.

52 NLW 21285E, Letter no. 822, Iolo Morganwg to Margaret Williams, 30 October 1793. Johnson was not prepared to take the financial risk of publishing it himself: a printed proposal for 'The History of the Bards', promising to start printing in January 1795, shows that funding was again to be 'by subscription' (NLW 21400C, no. 10). This 'History', like many other planned works, never appeared.

53 NLW 21285E, Letter no. 821, Iolo Morganwg to Thomas Williams, 26 October 1793.

or another stuff them with a little more, I shall not have the whole done in the course of next month. I was obliged to buy new shoes, new stockings, one new shirt, for old things are wearing out apace. I have so many literary friends that call on me to take an evening [c]up of tea and spend an hour or two in the morning or evening that more goes at one time on such occasions than would serve me for two or three days. I had the two guineas my Brother sent me, but sixteen pence was charged for carriage . . . in a place like this where many sixpences go out almost dayly, money flies away, I could have in some cases, spent less money, but if I had done so less, far less, of my work would have been done – If I could for the following twenty days before the n[ex]t magazine comes on, but afford to treat the Printers to the amount of five shillings I should do wonders.[54]

Another month or two went by, but the pressmen must, eventually, have been duly stuffed with gin, and *Poems, Lyric and Pastoral* came out early in January 1794. By now a familiar figure in Unitarian and radical circles associated with Johnson's bookshop, and with his next project well on the way, Iolo quashed Peggy's continued complaints with a confident assessment of his financial outlook as a published author:

I am pretty sure that I shall have more than a hundred pounds clear besides the copy right for which I have lately been offered twenty pounds a year as long as I live by a settled annuity, but I will not accept of it. I shall put a second edition soon to the press this will bring me a clear profit of three hundred pounds and in two or three years more I shall print a third edition, and so on. I have lately received letters from the greatest and most learned Critics of this age which you shall see soon, and all speak very highly of my poems . . . In short you will pretty soon be convinced that it is much better for every Author to write for the Public, who in consequence of that will buy his books for ages, than to write what will only gratify the vanities and abet the causes of great men . . . I have written for the nation at large, I may say for the world, and some will enjoy the profits of an edition of a thousand copies every three or four years for ever.[55]

Iolo was not alone in thinking he had joined the new republic of letters, nor in believing that it was now possible to make a living as an author, if not the 'ample fortunes' of 'Pope, Swift, Churchil and others who wrote for the public at large'.[56] Yet even at this stage there were further unexpected setbacks and costs: 'I have not yet had many books distributed the few that have been I am obliged to pay the money received for them to the Binder for making

---

[54] NLW 21285E, Letter no. 822, Iolo Morganwg to Margaret Williams, 30 October 1793.

[55] NLW 21285E, Letter no. 825, Iolo Morganwg to Margaret Williams, 18 January 1794. On copyright, see St Clair, *The Reading Nation*, pp. 43–65, and Mark Rose, *Authors and Owners: The Invention of Copyright* (Cambridge, MA, 1993).

[56] NLW 21285E, Letter no. 825, Iolo Morganwg to Margaret Williams, 18 January 1794. Although very few writers had the success of Pope, other contemporary models must also have offered hope: Yearsley made £500 on her first volume (*Selected Poems*, p. viii).

others up.'[57] The distribution of the volumes and the collection of outstanding payment would, in fact, prove the major weakness of Iolo's subscription system: money received, a few shillings at a time, on delivery of books to the names on his widely scattered list was almost immediately swallowed up by the cost of binding further copies, or of simply remaining in London waiting for subscribers to return; he was also obliged to catch the season in Bath and the terms in Oxford and Cambridge. In a defensive draft letter to an unnamed lady subscriber written around this time, he claimed 'what I have received never paid me sixpence a day for the time lost' and he again compared his experience, unfavourably this time, with those of Burns and Yearsley, 'whose business of procuring subscribers and collecting the money was done all by others'.[58]

A whole year after publication, in fact, and to the real despair of his wife, Iolo was still in London, and though he could tell her that every good review (and they were good, by and large)[59] added 'one hundred pounds at least' to his (purely theoretical) gains from the sale of copyright, he was beginning to realize that there was to be no immediate profit from his publication: 'I am now convinced that I shall never receive much of the money due to me – I should have p[er]ished by the subscription had it not been for a few that the Booksellers sold.'[60] Yet he stayed on, waiting, as he told her, for a potentially lucrative audience with the Prince of Wales, but also determined to make the most of his contacts to build on his new career as a writer: 'this business must be made a substitute for my trade'.[61] There were, presumably with Joseph Johnson's encouragement, plans for a second edition, and many proposals for all manner of radical pamphlets and essays. And there is no doubt that Iolo's determination to stay on in London was driven by more than a consideration of his future prospects as an author. By 1795 he had perfected his role as the 'Welch bard' to a lively network of radical and Unitarian friends and acquaintances, including George Dyer, John Thelwall, Thomas Holcroft and the Aikin-Barbauld circle; in January he met William Godwin, and now or shortly afterwards, Coleridge and Southey.[62] Such company brought the very real threat of imprisonment or harrassment (his papers were searched on more than

---

[57] NLW 21285E, Letter no. 825, Iolo Morganwg to Margaret Williams, 18 January 1794. On binding books after publication, see St Clair, *The Reading Nation*, pp. 192–3.

[58] NLW 21286E, Letter no. 1025, Iolo Morganwg to an unnamed subscriber, undated.

[59] *Poems, Lyric and Pastoral* was reviewed in the *Analytical Review*, XVIII (1794), 196–200; *Monthly Review*, XIII (1794) 405–14; *Critical Review*, XI (1794) 168–75, and briefly in the *Gentleman's Magazine*, LXIV, Part 2 (1794), 1113–14. The latter, which was critical of his politics, was the only one not to mention the author's humble origins.

[60] NLW 21285E, Letter no. 848, Iolo Morganwg to Margaret Williams, 12 February 1795.

[61] NLW 21285E, Letter no. 842, Iolo Morganwg to Margaret Williams, 13 September 1794; he used almost the same phrase in Letter no. 843.

[62] See chapters 7 and 8, by Damian Walford Davies and Jon Mee, in this volume.

one occasion), but the sense of engagement, of being part of the action, must have been a powerful attraction in itself.

At the end of April came a letter from Peggy, 'greatly distresed and wore out to death' with details of her long attendance on his father during his last illness. Angry and accusing ('you was composed enough to write and and had money to spare to print when you did not know whether your children had bread or not'), she was nonetheless surprisingly loyal to Iolo's authorial enterprise, listing people to whom she has delivered books in Glamorgan, and ending on a poignantly conciliatory note: 'do not minde disappointments but com home we will do somthing again'.[63] Still he did not come home. Not long afterwards came yet another 'disappointment', as his meeting with the prince produced, not the fifty guineas he had been expecting, but a mere two.[64] He remained in London another month, and then, finally cutting his considerable losses, he walked home in June via Bath and Bristol, delivering sets of his poems wherever he could.

As James Raven has noted, the distressed author was a familiar figure in prefaces to publications of the Romantic period, and could be deployed cynically enough.[65] But Iolo's complaints seem scarcely exaggerated: for him, the business of publication did prove a nightmarish tangle of practical, financial and emotional difficulties. Although one can assume that his letters to Peggy tended to make the worst of his situation, the sheer clumsiness and financial risk of the subscription process when not controlled by a single patron are only too evident. Despite the sale of the farm in 1793, the grants from the Royal Literary Fund and subventions from friends and supporters, it is far from clear at times how he and his family survived. Although it may well be the case, as Gwyneth Lewis has claimed, that his definitive return to Wales and Welsh literature in 1795 was the result of his precarious political situation, the immediate impulse seems to have been as much financially motivated as anything.[66] He did not, in any event, consider himself a poetic failure in English. He had plans for a second 'expanded' edition well into the next century, and he never sold the much-vaunted copyright.[67]

Poems, Lyric and Pastoral is an exceptionally contrary work, a wolf in sheep's clothing, its mild scenes of rural content prefaced in anger and shot through

---

[63] NLW 21283E, Letter no. 610, Margaret Williams to Iolo Morganwg, 28 April 1795.

[64] NLW 21285E, Letter no. 852, Iolo Morganwg to Margaret Williams, 2 May 1795. On the practice of writing elaborate dedications to the monarchy in this period, see Korshin, 'Types of Eighteenth-century Literary Patronage', p. 488.

[65] Raven, *Judging New Wealth*, p. 60.

[66] Lewis, 'Eighteenth-century Literary Forgeries', pp. 193–4; see also Walford Davies, *Presences that Disturb*, pp. 135–67.

[67] See NLW 21286E, Letter no. 971, Iolo Morganwg to Dr Dale, 17 April 1819. A written and a printed proposal for the second edition (both undated) name Longman and Rees, rather than Johnson, as the London booksellers (NLW 21400C, nos. 13, 13a).

with snarling footnotes. The conflicted nature of the work clearly owes much to the history of its publication discussed above. During its years at press, as its author changed, so did the shape and contents of the collection, and there is no doubt that the printed and manuscript specimens circulated among potential subscribers in 1790–1 can have given only a partial sense of the book which finally emerged. The radical-bardic note of big set-piece poems like 'Ode on Converting a Sword into a Pruning Hook' and 'Ode on the Bardic Mythology', the 'querulous' anger of the preface and the 'king-flogging' notes, all of which reach their fullest expression after 1792, must have surprised more than one subscriber to the rural songs of the humble mason.[68] Iolo was perfectly aware of this when he wrote somewhat nervously to Hannah More, hoping that she would not find the work to be that of 'a very bad man'.[69]

It should not be inferred, however, that the vociferous radical note running through *Poems* was some kind of late overlay. It is true that the London years, the contacts and new friends, not to mention the treatment he received on the doorsteps of 'supercilious' gentry, radicalized him, but it would be quite wrong to treat the conventional, not to say conservative, aspects of Iolo's pastoral verse as belonging somehow to an 'early' period, and to separate out the confusion of voices merely in terms of chronology. The fact is that both radical and conservative elements (and much depends, of course, on one's definition of those terms) inhabit Iolo's work from the beginning, and his 'development' as a writer defies straightforward trajectories in either direction. This defiance is to some extent deliberate: the organization of the poems in the two volumes makes no attempt to show a progression from youthful verses to a later style. Indeed, a manuscript note shows that Iolo resisted organization of any kind and chose to present his poems 'all jumbled together'.[70] But another reason for resisting the separation of an early and late Iolo is his obsessive habit of revision.

A scattering of poems in the two volumes are given dates: the rationale for noting these is not always clear, but it can be useful – the indication that the 'Ode on Converting a Sword into a Pruning Hook' was recited at a Gorsedd on Primrose Hill in September 1793 shows how late those sheets must have gone to press. Among the dated poems in the first volume is 'Winter Incidents: written in 1777'.[71] There are five manuscript drafts of the poem, and the

[68] The indefatigable Mrs Nicholl of Remenham was one of them: had she 'known Edward Williams's principles, she would not have subscribed to any of his writings; for she would not purchase poetry fine as Homer's, were it written by a Republican'. NLW 21280E, Letter no. 297, M. Nicholl to Iolo Morganwg, 19 May 1794.

[69] NLW 21286E, Letter no. 1023, Iolo Morganwg to Hannah More, undated.

[70] NLW 21387E, no. 39. Elsewhere he seems to have been planning a generic division into odes, lyric pastorals, songs and miscellanies: NLW 21392F, no. 18.

[71] Williams: *PLP*, I, pp. 121–8.

earliest is given here in full.[72] Signed 'Iorwerth Gwilym' (Iolo's earlier pen-
name), there is nothing in the style or handwriting to rule out its given date:

> Bleak winter comes the tempest roars
> and enters all the village doors
> Wild geese are clanking in the skie,
> And swans to flooded valleys flie,
> the sea Gull in the meadow screams,
> And woodcocks feed on woodland streams
> Now comes from northern hills the snow
> Strew'd on our [those, the] milder vales below
> The boys run out with Butter'd slice
> and often slide on chilling ice
> on with high glee conjuctive strain
> to roll the snowball o'er the plain,
> The sturdy farmer blows his nails
> and his unlucky lot bewails,
> not destined like the drunken squire
> To lounge before the parlour fire,
> The poet in some garret high [bard in hearthless]
> Thro shatter'd window views the sky,
> Prudential thought to number there
> his realms of [many] castles built in air,
> Then far above the groveling throng
> he for his dinner cooks a song,
> Mean while the sportsman seeks the plash
> where clamrous teal the waters dash,
> thro mud and water to the chin
> he trudges on thro thick and thin
> like Tom o bedlam, with his Gun
> Not for the profit but the fun
> let him [go Tom] if blood can thus delight
> go serve mad kings be paid [talk big] and fight
> with well-directed cannon Balls
> knock down a thousand harmless Gauls
> and shew [prove] that he can mock with skill
> the fool who said thou shalt not kill.
>
> Sweet [meek] robin from inclement skies
> now to some cot for shelter flies
> hopes here within protecting walls
> to pick the scanty crumb that falls,
> yet from some hole the watchful [sneaking] cat

---

[72] NLW 21392F, no. 83. The succeeding drafts, in order, are NLW 21388E, no. 2; 21328A,
pp. 239–43; 21329A, pp. 26–31 (an exact copy in 21331B, pp. 39–43); 21333B, pp. 113–18.

or mamy's boy the wicked brat
watch the poor bird with anxious care
to kill or catch him in a snare.
Ill-treated thus the mournful guest
May flutter long but find no rest,
his plaintive note for mercy calls
but all in vain, the warbler falls
falls a sad prey to ruthless minds
and from [in] vain hope destruction finds,
Poor Robin in this hostile cot
Well pictures out poor [the] mortal's lot
Small evils thus we strive to shun
And in th'attempt are oft undone.

The qualities of this are precisely those appreciated by modern readers of John Clare: the birds crowding noisily into those first lines, the credible cast of characters who shiver, run, stamp their feet, eat 'butter'd slice' and get muddy.[73] It displays some of that immediate, totalizing awareness of the world that is not merely description 'for its own sake'; as with Clare, there are some pointed messages here, too, in the wry picture of the idealistic (and hungry) poet looking down on the 'groveling throng' through his broken window, or in the neat juxtaposition of the chilly farmer and the lounging squire, or in the powerful declaration of pacifism ('And shew that he can mock with skill/ The fool who said thou shalt not kill'). The rather disconcerting identification of the muddy struggling figure of the wildfowler with *Lear*'s Tom o' Bedlam (not an obvious model for a killer) may perhaps have come about by association with the phrase 'go serve mad kings'. In any event, it shows that Iolo's feelings about war and the monarchy, expressed in some of the more wolfish notes to *Poems, Lyric and Pastoral*, were far from being a later development, as some have claimed.[74] The extended final episode of the doomed robin strikes a different note from the crowded couplets that precede it, and, in its rather gloomy moralizing, points the direction the poem will take; further stanzas squashed crosswise in the margins suggest that this is a poem wanting to grow. Additions to subsequent drafts include an opening list of absent spring and summer birds whose exaggerated silence, ironically enough, drowns out the noise of the others:

no feather'd songster chaunts a lay
To cheer the short, the joyless day

---

[73] Compare the activities of the birds in the first lines of Clare's 'The sinken sun is takin leave' in Eric Robinson, David Powell and Margaret Grainger (eds.), *The Early Poems of John Clare: 1804–1822* (2 vols., Oxford, 1989), I, p. 5.

[74] Williams: *IM*, p. 229.

the Blackbird in the copse alone
has quite forgot his mellow tone
we hear no linnet on the thorn
no joyous lark rouse up the morn[75]

Other additions include an expansion of the 'mad Tom' episode, which becomes a first-person contemplation of war and a declared commitment to a pacifist solidarity reaching across nations:

If chilld by cold it be my chance
To meet a brother born in France
a wandering stranger sore distressd
by want, by hopeless thoughts oppressd
He, tho ten thousand cannons roar
shall enter at my friendly door
forget his cares, no longer weep
and in my Cot in safety sleep.[76]

Ultimately, even though the entire robin episode is sliced off and used as a separate poem elsewhere, the piece doubles in length. The vocabulary goes upmarket and latinate: the swans 'seek shelter in Silurian vales', the breeze 'with gellid rigour teems' and lively verbs like 'clanking' disappear. So, too, does the figure of the wry poet, leaving in his place a pervasive narrating voice which controls the action with commands and gestures – 'observe', 'hark!', and so on – keeping the various scenes at a distance and presenting the characters as types. But the most far-reaching transformation of the published version (and this is far less evident in any of the drafts) is that every little incident is 'moraliz'd' to within an inch of its life, as the playing children (lines 9–12 in the first draft) find to their cost:

The village boys with morn awake
To trace the surface of the lake,
And, thoughtless, run at passion's call,
In slipp'ry paths, where many fall:
The just resemblance let me scan;
'Tis *rash desire*, unthinking man;
Though seeming joy thy wish attends,
The fell deceit in ruin ends.
Observe yon prattling lisper strain,
To roll the snow-ball o'er the plain
So misers heap, with sore turmoil,
What never can re-pay their toil.[77]

[75] NLW 21328A, p. 239.
[76] NLW 21388E, no. 2.
[77] Williams: *PLP*, I, p. 123 (lines 29–40).

It is precisely the *unjustness* of these resemblances that is most striking: the gleeful children are, even toned down (and deprived for good measure of their 'butter'd slice'), less than convincing models for the adult vices they supposedly represent. The moral has at best no organic connection with the original image, and at worst constitutes a kind of betrayal (the snowball-rolling was initially 'conju[n]ctive', the 'sportive toil' of a happy group: what peculiar effort of will was required on the part of the author to conjure up thoughts of misers?). In the end, the poem is weighed down by this sententious matter: dressed for the drawing room, it loses much of its energy. It is tempting, of course, to read into this a much deeper betrayal: writing for a polite audience, in a language they appreciate, the labouring-class poet has traded in his 'real' voice for a pastiche style which he never truly masters.

But does this not presuppose too much? Although the parallels between them are fascinating, Iolo was no John Clare, and there is no sign that he would have regarded his early 'Winter Incidents' as anything but immature. His aesthetic models were Shenstone, Collins, Thomson, and he worked hard (and with a good deal of pride) to achieve something like their literary style. Indeed, the *Analytical Review* praised this very poem for its 'pleasing lines', in which 'description and reflection are happily combined'.[78] It is nevertheless difficult, from a post-Clare perspective, to evaluate this kind of emulation sympathet-ically: the first draft sounds so much 'truer' to our sense of what a rural labourer *ought* to be doing in verse, and the revisions head so inexorably away from an unusual (and therefore radical) style towards familiarity and convention. And yet against this conformist tendency must be weighed the sustained devel-opment of the poem's political message. Although the punchy effect of the original is much diluted by the change in tone and style, the imagined scenario involving a wandering French exile sheltered in the poet's own home has, by the published version, taken over the second half of the poem altogether.

The gap between early and late versions is not always so striking or so instructive, as the *Town and Country* piece on the cuckoo confirms: a comparison of the 1777 and 1794 published versions reveals innumerable changes, but it is difficult to see them tending in any particular direction. 'Stanzas Written in London' and 'Castles in the Air' are similar cases. But the example of 'Winter Incidents' shows how difficult it can be to generalize about Iolo's development as an English poet: lines which appear to have been 'composed mechanically, without inspiration'[79] had in fact been worked over painstakingly in the course of a decade. A mere six lines remain completely unchanged from that early draft. In what sense is this a poem 'written in 1777'?

Iolo's obsessive revision of his work went well beyond the individual texts

---

[78] *Analytical Review*, XVIII (1794), 196.
[79] 'wedi eu cynhyrchu'n beiriannol ddiawen', Lewis: *IM*, p. 80.

to affect the shape of the volume until the very last minute ('I paid the compositor . . . for altering somethings that were before composited'):[80] as we have seen, the later insertions and alterations undoubtedly added variety to the book, pulling it away from conventional pastoral towards a more distinctive bardic style. The manuscripts, unsurprisingly, reveal an even greater versatility of style, subject and verse-form than the published volumes could contain; many poems must have been excluded as unsuitable, others for reasons of space.[81] Among the former are the songs written for different convivial groups, like the poem for the 'Drive Away Care Club', dated in one manuscript to his time in Faversham in 1773,[82] or a lively song about a stonecutter from Iolo's early London period, which is funny, bawdy and rich in technical vocabulary – a find which partly compensates for the dearth of detail about his trade in *Poems* itself.[83] Such pieces were not confined to his early years, and there are several interesting songs dealing with local Glamorgan characters and events, or written for his radical friends in London. The endlessly revised lists of titles for the projected volume show that a few of these lighter or more satirical pieces were at some stage intended for inclusion (and many reappear in lists for a projected second edition). Among them is a 'Hymn to Jumpers', an attack on the unseemly 'Enthusiasm' of various Methodist sects, set to the tune of 'A begging we will go'.[84] Another, admired by the young John Walters as early as 1781, is an amusing, if somewhat laboured, anti-classical 'Hymn to Pan' ('Prefer ye scriblers if ye can/ Your Phoebus to my frying Pan'); another, a straight piece of misogynist wit: ('When God made man he made old Adam first/ Had he stopped there this earth had ne'er been cursed').[85] Pieces composed in London show Iolo exercising his bardic functions of memorial and celebration on behalf of fellow radicals in poems like *Trial by Jury*, which was recited in the Crown and Anchor tavern on 5 February 1795 to mark the acquittals of Tooke, Hardy and Thelwall; or 'The Newgate Stanzas', a spirited account of his visit to William Winterbotham in Newgate prison:[86]

---

[80] Iolo's habit of last-minute revision, made possible by the moveable type used at the time, was not unusual: Wollstonecraft and Hazlitt were both 'last-minute' writers. See St Clair, *The Reading Nation*, p. 182.

[81] The main volumes of English poetry are NLW 21328A, 21329A, 21330E, 21331B, 21332B, 21333B, 21334B and 21335B (post-1795). Since most consist of lists of titles and copied/ revised texts, there is a great deal of overlap in terms of content; some may have been designed to be left with various patrons or potential subscribers. There are local songs in NLW 21424E and many other single texts throughout the archive. NLW 21392F is an important miscellaneous collection, containing mostly English poems on loose papers from a wide range of dates.

[82] NLW 21335B.

[83] NLW 21392F, no. 73. This poem will be discussed further in a forthcoming special issue of *The Eighteenth Century: Theory and Interpretation*.

[84] NLW 21329A (and many other copies).

[85] NLW 21328A, pp. 37–9, 85.

[86] NLW 21334B, nos. 6, 8. For an account of the Newgate episode, see *RAEW*, pp. 47–8, and

Of late, as at the close of day
To Newgates cell I bent my way
Where Truth is held in thrall
I wrote, that all might plainly see
My name, the Bard of Liberty
And Terror seized them all!

Iolo's unpublished English poems deserve more attention than can be given to them here: in many cases their local details or scathing wit give them a life, or a historical interest, lacking in the more conventional pastoral scenes that were included in the final collection. In particular, more needs to be said on the subject of Iolo's translations and adaptations from Welsh: there are versions of early Welsh *englynion*, for example, which push English versification further and in more interesting directions than any of the supposed translations 'from the Welsh' in *Poems* itself.[87]

The conflict of voices in *Poems, Lyric and Pastoral* can be partly explained in terms of its chronological development, the distinction between early and late voices being masked by the deliberately 'jumbled' structure and by endless revision. Separating them out, one can see a development from the young, though not apolitical, poet of pastoral to the radicalized bard of Nature. Certain themes, such as the vices of London set against the virtues of rural life, are revisited regularly. But the contradictions, surprises and changes of direction in the two volumes are also a valuable record of the book's difficult genesis, and a testament to their author's determination in guiding it through the press. His achievement is not lessened by the support he received from a broad social range of friends and advisors, and from his own long-suffering (if not always, as he would have had the world think, 'cheerfully submissive') family.[88]

Geraint H. Jenkins, 'The Bard of Liberty during William Pitt's Reign of Terror' in Joseph F. Nagy and Leslie E. Jones (eds.), *Heroic Poets and Poetic Heroes in Celtic Tradition: A Festschrift for Patrick K. Ford. CSANA Yearbook 3–4* (Dublin, 2005), pp. 196–7.

[87] See, for example, 'Hill of Snows', NLW 21392F, no. 33. The translation issue is discussed by Gwyneth Lewis, who argues that Iolo did try to introduce a Welsh element into the English of *Poems, Lyric and Pastoral* ('Eighteenth-century Literary Forgeries', pp. 173–4). Two of the reviews singled out the translations for especial praise.

[88] NLW 21387E, no. 21.

7

'At Defiance': Iolo, Godwin, Coleridge, Wordsworth

DAMIAN WALFORD DAVIES

A polarized view of the dynamics of political struggle in the 1790s – 'Jacobins' ranged against, and finally shut down by, the forces of reaction – clearly runs the risk of eliding the heterogeneity and fissures of radical Dissent. Metropolitan radicalism in particular was hardly a coherent body of thought or action; 'Patriot', 'Jacobin' and 'Friend of Freedom' were all highly contested identities. Coleridge's taxonomy of the 'professed Friends of Liberty' in 'A Moral and Political Lecture', delivered at Bristol in late January 1795, offers a lively digest of difference.[1] Energized by diverse intellectual traditions, radicalism was a broad church (or meeting house, or Temple of Reason): revolutionary activism contended with philosophical anarchism; interventionists with gradualists and 'armchair agitators';[2] the intellectual elite with the rank-and-file of popular societies; atheists with deists, Unitarians and Christians. Thus, although each would claim radical credentials, Godwin could argue with Thelwall, as the young Unitarian Coleridge could with both Godwin and Thelwall. This chapter traces some of those fault lines by exploring the ways in which Coleridge and Wordsworth enlisted Iolo Morganwg during the 1790s as an instructive exemplum in the case against what they saw as the false and facile 'theory' of Godwin's *An Enquiry concerning Political Justice* (1793) – 'a book popular among the professed Friends of civil Freedom',[3] as Coleridge scornfully put it in 1795. Kathleen Coburn's suggestion that 'Williams perhaps had more influence on the early Romantics, especially Coleridge and Southey, than has been recognised'[4] can be confirmed. Iolo was a conditioning presence in the poets' formative opposition to Godwin's 'atheistical' philosophy of reason

---

[1] Lewis Patton and Peter Mann (eds.), *Samuel Taylor Coleridge: Lectures 1795 on Politics and Religion* (London, 1971), pp. 8–15.

[2] Nicholas Roe, *Wordsworth and Coleridge: The Radical Years* (Oxford, 1988), p. 168.

[3] Patton and Mann (eds.), *Lectures 1795*, p. 164.

[4] Kathleen Coburn (ed.), *The Notebooks of Samuel Taylor Coleridge* (3 vols., London, 1957–73), I (Notes), #605. For Iolo's acquaintance with English men of letters, see Herbert G. Wright, 'The Relations of the Welsh Bard Iolo Morganwg with Dr Johnson, Cowper and Southey', *Review of English Studies*, VIII, no. 29 (1932), 129–38.

– an opposition which hinged on the key issues of gratitude, domestic affection and pride. The reaction of Coleridge and Wordsworth against 'a book which builds without a foundation'[5] shaped their own political trajectories and moral identities in the late 1790s in important ways. It is argued here that Iolo's confrontation with Godwin, together with the tenets of his bardic Jacobinism and his *Poems, Lyric and Pastoral* (1794), played a crucial role in that development.

Romanticists have become accustomed to discussing the reticular literary and political culture (metropolitan and provincial) of the 1790s and early nineteenth century in terms of 'conversations', 'coteries', 'exchanges', 'networks' and 'dialogic relations'. Metropolitan radicalism was sustained by the congregational, associational temper of the age, and radical identities were fashioned and inscribed in a variety of spaces and forms – as much by correspondence, dinner-party conversation, subscription lists and intertextual dialogue/allusion as by political lectures or mass meetings of the London Corresponding Society in Copenhagen Fields.[6] This chapter locates Iolo during the period 1791–5 at the very heart of these radical networks – circles in which Coleridge and Wordsworth were also turning in the mid-1790s – and seeks to reconstruct the conversations Coleridge, Iolo and Wordsworth (independently) had with Godwin, whom they met in London within three months of each other. Coleridge certainly knew Iolo by May 1796, by which time Iolo had presented him with a copy of *Poems, Lyric and Pastoral*;[7] an earlier acquaintance through their mutual friend John Prior Estlin, the Unitarian minister at Bristol, or through other Bristol Unitarians, is likely. There remains no firm evidence that Wordsworth actually met Iolo, but their 'conversation' can be heard as poetic allusion at the end of the decade.

★ ★ ★

Iolo arrived in London in 1791 with the aim of marketing himself as a poet in English literary circles and securing the patronage and subscriptions that would enable him to see *Poems, Lyric and Pastoral* through the press. He also positioned himself within London's radical networks, securing contacts such as the Unitarian Joseph Johnson (who offered advice on various projects)[8] and

---

5   Patton and Mann (eds.), *Lectures 1795*, p. 164.
6   See, for example, Gillian Russell and Clara Tuite (eds.), *Romantic Sociability: Social Networks and Literary Culture in Britain, 1770–1840* (Cambridge, 2002) and Damian Walford Davies, *Presences that Disturb: Models of Romantic Identity in the Literature and Culture of the 1790s* (Cardiff, 2002).
7   Coleridge's copy is now at the Victoria University Library, Toronto. On the fly-leaf preceding the title-pages of volumes I and II, Iolo has written 'From the Author'.
8   See Iolo's letter of 30 October 1793 to his wife Peggy: 'I shall first translate the Bardic Triades

making the acquaintance of Tom Paine, Joseph Priestley (whom he saw off to America[9]), John Oswald, John Thelwall, John Horne Tooke, David Williams, the political philosopher (with whom Iolo claimed kin), Anna Laetitia Barbauld, George Dyer, Gilbert Wakefield, Charles-Maurice de Talleyrand (whom he is said to have met at David Williams's house), William Winterbotham and, of course, the author of *Political Justice*. He also frequented meetings of the Society for Constitutional Information and the London Constitutional Society.[10] Such connections provided Iolo with a salutary awareness of a broad spectrum of radical opinion. As he made clear in a letter of 19 February 1795 to his wife Margaret (Peggy), he was present at the trial of Horne Tooke, 'an eye and an ear Witness to Pitt's Perjury'[11] (a reference to what Coleridge described in his 'Letter to Edward Long Fox' as Pitt's 'epileptic memory' during his examination as a witness). And to celebrate the acquittal in late 1794 of the high-profile defendants of the Treason Trials – Thomas Hardy, Horne Tooke and John Thelwall – Iolo was asked to compose a song – *Trial by Jury, The Grand Palladium of British Liberty* – which he sang at the Crown and Anchor tavern on 4 February 1795.[12] His radical conversations were truly international: he sent a copy of *Poems, Lyric and Pastoral* – a talisman of radical fellowship and a token of ideological support – to the 'Edinburgh martyrs', Thomas Muir and Thomas Fyshe Palmer, who had been recently transported to Botany Bay. Palmer acknowledged the gift in a moving letter of 25 September 1795, informing Iolo that 'Mr Muir took away the book last night and sat up till five this morning reading it'.[13]

Iolo's was, of course, a Jacobinism with cultural difference. His radical identity was expressed at this time in the form of an elaborate, pseudo-antiquarian bardic discourse – 'a made Dish, cooked up from obscure scraps ... spiced with an immoderate quantity of wild Invention', as John Walters put it[14] – which functioned as a subversive vehicle for his Jacobin sympathies. Ingenious expositions and poetic dramatizations of the 'leading articles' of bardism in such works as *Poems, Lyric and Pastoral* (with its 'King-flogging

---

... I was yesterd[ay] at Mr Johnson St Paul's Church yard and he told [me] that Dr Geddes, Dr Aikin, and others of the first literary abilities spoke well of it' (NLW 21285E, Letter no. 822). In a letter of 21 January 1794 to John Walters, Iolo stated that he knew Joseph Johnson well (NLW 21285E, Letter no. 826).

9   According to Elijah Waring, 'The Bard attended him to the place of embarkation, and was one of the last persons the Doctor conversed with upon British ground': *RAEW*, p. 134.

10   Preserved among Iolo's papers are the minutes of a meeting of the SCI held on 18 May 1792: NLW 21401E, no. 35.

11   NLW 21285E, Letter no. 850, Iolo Morganwg to Margaret Williams, 19 February 1795.

12   See NLW 21285E, Letter no. 848 and Walford Davies, *Presences that Disturb*, p. 144.

13   NLW 21282E, Letter no. 376, Thomas Fyshe Palmer to Iolo Morganwg, 12 September 1795.

14   Cardiff 3.104, vol. 6, Letter no. 3, John Walters to Edward Davies, 10 May 1793.

Notes'[15]) and in the Iolo-influenced prefatory dissertation to William Owen Pughe's *The Heroic Elegies and other Pieces of Llywarç Hen* (1792), together with the mummeries of the Gorsedd ceremonies on Primrose Hill (accounts of which found their way into the press), were a means of articulating radical opposition. His self-appointed status as the 'Bard of Liberty' was a persona that wed Jacobin ideology to august bardic duty. Iolo's Gorsedd and his accounts of the bardic 'system' amount to a model – indeed, a constitution – for a utopian republic established on the radical principles of liberty, social equality, peace, common property, public accountability and a bold, freethinking search after 'Truth'. Iolo's 'Ode on Converting a Sword into a Pruning Hook' in *Poems, Lyric and Pastoral* unmistakably provided Coleridge with a template for his own picture of imperialist oppression in 'Ode on the Departing Year', composed in December 1796 – around the time Iolo presented Coleridge with a copy.[16] It is clear that Iolo's profile was such that the forces of reaction took him seriously as a subversive presence whose activities had to be monitored. His letters regularly complained of his being watched and intimidated by (in Coleridge's phrase) the 'captain commandant of the spy-gang',[17] John Reeves (founder in 1792 of the Association for Preserving Liberty and Property against Republicans and Levellers), and his army of spies and informers – 'vermin working out of reach', as Wordsworth was to describe them in Book X of *The Prelude* ('very loyal sons of Bitches',[18] as Iolo phrased it more demo(cra)tically).

His letters at this time railed against what he called 'Church and Kingism' – systems of political and religious imposition anathema to his Christian-Unitarian radicalism. One of his projected pamphlets was entitled 'Kingcraft versus Christianity', another 'War incompatible with the Spirit of Christianity – an Essay By An Ancient British Bard'.[19] Exchanges with his radical contacts no doubt involved similar animated discussions of the way in which 'the man who would now preach up the scriptural doctrine of Government, would, notwithstanding our pretended tolleration be as infallibly consigned to the stake and faggot at this day as ever Cranmer, Hooper, and others were';[20] of how 'all Systems of Church and Kingism, are, as if with might and main, preaching Christianity out of the World';[21] and of how 'the evils that now deluge the nominally-Christian World are the unavoidable effects of Church-and-Kingical

[15] NLW 21285E, Letter no. 826, Iolo Morganwg to John Walters, 21 January 1794.
[16] See Walford Davies, *Presences that Disturb*, pp. 155–6.
[17] Patton and Mann (eds.), *Lectures 1795*, p. 303.
[18] NLW 21285E, Letter no. 841, Iolo Morganwg to Margaret Williams, 27 August 1794.
[19] NLW 21285E, Letter no. 822, Iolo Morganwg to Margaret Williams, 30 October [1793]; Letter no. 826, Iolo Morganwg to John Walters, 21 January 1794.
[20] NLW 21285E, Letter no. 826, Iolo Morganwg to John Walters, 21 January 1794.
[21] NLW 21285E, Letter no. 850, Iolo Morganwg to Margaret Williams, 19 February 1794.

hypocrisy, Priestcraft, and imposition – blasphemously called religion, but productive of all the bad effects of open, rank, and professed Atheism'.[22]

With the same vehemence Iolo could also condemn the deistical and atheistical tendencies of certain elements of the radical movement. For Iolo, who by 1798 was professing himself a 'Unitarian Christian',[23] as for the Unitarian Coleridge, Jesus was the model reformer and social activist. Although Iolo shared much common political ground with Paine, he objected violently, as did Iolo's acquaintance Gilbert Wakefield, to Paine's deist attack on Christianity in *The Age of Reason* (1794), and immediately set about preparing an answer to his 'Atheistical work'.[24] 'I am as much a republican as Tom Paine and more of a leveler', he proclaimed, 'because I am so on the principles of Jesus Christ, a Sanculotte indeed in whom there is no guile.'[25] The reply to Paine never appeared, but fragments of it have survived; they represent an attempt to meet the 'would-be-thought-of Philosophical' Paine 'on his own ground'.[26] Another of Iolo's fascinating religious and political manifestos shows him to be quite capable of calling Paine 'Iscariot' as readily as Coleridge could address William Pitt as 'O calumniated Judas Iscariot!' in *Conciones ad Populum* (1795):

> I find my old Friend Tom Paine, who has been labouring hard to destroy, in his attempted subversion of Christianity, to deprive a very great number of human beings of the best comforts, the most solid consolations that this life afforded them; he has thus acted a very malevolent part, and is no longer worthy to be called by the truly noble title of Citizen Paine. He has here acted the part of Judas. Look at his rights of Man, his Common Sense, &c. In those he Salutes the Christian Religion with Hail Master and a Kiss. We poor fools thought it the Kiss of Friendship, of Love, of Charity. How have we been mistaken? But to view the rank villainy of this second Iscariot . . . Whilst I thus endeavour to repulse Iscariot Paine let it not be insinuated that I am slyly veering about, that I am changing my political opinions, which have long been known, for which I have to my infinite Joy and satisfaction been abused and injured in person and property. I am still an honest Republican . . . Democrate, Leveler, Jacobin, Sanculotte . . . I glory in all these titles.[27]

As with Paine, so also with Godwin. Iolo would certainly have been a member of the intellectual circles in which Godwin's *Political Justice* was discussed. Although Iolo left no formal record of his response to Godwin's work, it is safe to assume that, while much of Godwin's philosophical anarchism would have found favour with him ('equality of rights and conditions, non-violence,

[22]   NLW 21285E, Letter no. 838, Iolo Morganwg to Hugh Jones, 4 June 1794.
[23]   NLW 21285E, Letter no. 862, Iolo Morganwg to Miss Barker, 26 March 1798.
[24]   NLW 21285E, Letter no. 837, Iolo Morganwg to Margaret Williams, 28 May 1794.
[25]   NLW 21396E, no. 35.
[26]   See NLW 21396E, nos. 21, 22, 33, 35.
[27]   NLW 21392F, no. 9.

Fig. 9 A portrait of the philosopher and novelist, William Godwin, by James Northcote. Oil on canvas, 1802.

the utterance of truth',[28] for example), his Christian principles would have made him deeply suspicious of certain aspects of Godwin's atheistic radicalism. One can also assume that Iolo would not have scrupled to inform Godwin of that fact. Moreover, the influence of *Political Justice* among metropolitan radical intellectuals and, indeed, 'among rank-and-file working-class members of the Corresponding Society' – due in part to John Thelwall's efforts – would also have troubled him.[29] For Iolo, as for Coleridge, aligning oneself as a radical necessarily involved orienting oneself vis-à-vis *Political Justice*. On this ground, Iolo, Wordsworth and Coleridge can be seen to constitute a fascinating anti-Godwin triumvirate in the 1790s.

★ ★ ★

Coleridge met William Godwin on 21 December 1794 at the invitation of Thomas Holcroft. Godwin was not meeting a devotee. On 11 September 1794, Coleridge had written to Robert Southey (who was to become a close acquaintance of Iolo): 'Godwin thinks himself inclined to Atheism . . . He is writing a book about it. I set him at Defiance.'[30] And in a letter of 17 December 1794 to Southey, Coleridge defined his own radical and metaphysical 'systems' against those of the atheistical Holcroft and expressed his desire to see Godwin comprehensively refuted over dinner in a few days' time by the Unitarian Christian and classical scholar, Richard Porson:

> Holcroft *opposes* [our system] violently – & thinks it not *virtuous*. His arguments were such as Nugent and twenty others have used to us before him – they were *nothing*. There is a fierceness and *dogmatism* of conversation in Holcroft, for which you receive little compensation either from the variety of his information, the closeness of his Reasoning, or the splendor of his Language. He talks incessantly of Metaphysics, of which he appears to me to *know nothing* – to have *read nothing* –/ He is ignorant as a Scholar – and neglectful of the smaller Humanities, as a Man –/ Compare him with Porson! My God! to hear Porson *crush* Godwin, Holcroft, &c – They absolutely tremble before him! I had the honor of *working* H[olcroft]. a little – and by my great *coolness* and command of impressive Language certainly *did him over* . . . He absolutely infests you with *Atheism*.[31]

After his meeting with Coleridge, Godwin noted in his diary: 'talk of self love & God', which suggests that Coleridge challenged Godwin's atheism – perhaps, as Nicholas Roe remarks, by 'invoking Priestley and Hartley, Frend

---

[28] Patton and Mann (eds.), *Lectures 1795*, p. lxxiii.
[29] Roe, *Radical Years*, p. 167.
[30] E. L. Griggs (ed.), *Collected Letters of Samuel Taylor Coleridge* (6 vols., Oxford, 1956–71), I, p. 102.
[31] Ibid., I, pp. 138–9.

and Dyer to confound Godwin's arguments from *Political Justice* and Holcroft's "incessant metaphysics" and "Atheism"'.[32] The lectures on politics and religion, which Coleridge delivered in 1795 at Bristol (there is evidence to suggest that Iolo was in the audience[33]), articulate 'a considered Christian alternative to Godwin's atheistic radicalism'[34] on several specific fronts. As Patton and Mann have suggested, there is 'much evidence for believing that Godwin was the real opponent in Coleridge's mind during the inception and preparation of the lectures'.[35]

Wordsworth met Godwin in the company of George Dyer at William Frend's house on 27 February 1795. This time Godwin was meeting a devotee and it was the first of many audiences. However, Wordsworth's admiration for Godwin and the faith he initially placed in the philosophy of *Political Justice* as a system of 'enquiry' that would lead to the enlightened reformation of both society and the individual would soon wane. Indeed, it would deepen into a mid-decade moral crisis – the product of Wordsworth's realization that the hubristic ethical and political road-map of *Political Justice* betrayed a lack of understanding of, and sympathy for, human nature. Citing Wordsworth's account in Book X of *The Prelude* of the moral 'despair' he experienced following his disenchantment with *Political Justice*, Nicholas Roe has charted 'Wordsworth's . . . development from Godwinian radical to poet' and his 'extinction as a Godwinian being'.[36] That disillusionment would be inscribed in the chilling portrait of Rivers in Wordsworth's play *The Borderers*, and, as we shall see, in poems in the *Lyrical Ballads* which, invoking Iolo, offer a critique of Godwinian pedantry and dogmatic intellectualism.

The 'near coincidence'[37] of Wordsworth, Coleridge and Iolo at this time is tantalizing. Iolo met Godwin in early January 1795; Godwin's diary for 2 January reads: 'Tea Dyers, w. Porson, Holcroft, Williams bard, Staley, Thelwal, Channels and Mrs Spence'; and for 3 January: 'Dine at Northmore's w Walker Manch.r, Wakefield, B Hollis, Disney, Dyer and Williams b; talk of God.'[38]

---

[32]   Roe, *Radical Years*, p. 116.
[33]   Among Iolo's papers is a printed flyer advertising Coleridge's lectures on the 'English Rebellion', which were due to begin on 23 June 1795. As Mary-Ann Constantine has argued, Iolo was in Bristol on 15 June 1795 on his way back to Glamorgan, and he may very well have been present at Coleridge's lecture on the slave-trade, delivered at the Coffee-house on the quay on 16 June, and have picked up a flyer for the series of lectures due to begin the following week. Mary-Ann Constantine, 'Iolo Morganwg, Coleridge, and the Bristol Lectures, 1795', *Notes and Queries*, new series, 52, no. 1 (2005), 42–4.
[34]   Patton and Mann (eds.), *Lectures 1795*, p. lxvii.
[35]   Ibid., p. lxvii. See also Nicola Trott, 'The Coleridge Circle and the "Answer to Godwin"', *Review of English Studies*, new series, XLI, no. 162 (1990), 212–29.
[36]   Roe, *Radical Years*, pp. 194, 220.
[37]   Ibid., p. 93.
[38]   Bodleian Library, Oxford, Abinger MSS, dep. e. 201 (No. VI). Quoted by kind permission of the Bodleian Library, Oxford.

Godwin's reference to 'Williams bard' distinguishes Iolo from the other Welsh Williams – David – with whom Godwin in 1792 had discussed the substance of *Political Justice* prior to publication.[39] The assembled company on each occasion consisted of some of the most famous radicals and intellectuals of the day. One is tempted to suppose that Godwin's brief reference to the topic of conversation on 3 January bespeaks an animated debate in which Iolo would surely have played an active and vocal part. Indeed, there are good grounds for believing that the gatherings of 2 and 3 January 1795 were the occasion of aggrieved exchanges between Godwin and Iolo which were to make a profound impression on Coleridge (and through him, on Wordsworth) and further galvanize Coleridge's opposition to Godwin at a time when he was contemplating an 'answer to Godwin' – a formal rebuttal of the 'absurdities and wickedness of [Godwin's] System'.[40]

★ ★ ★

A few weeks after first writing to John Thelwall with an overture of friendship ('Pursuing the same end by the same means we ought not to be strangers to each other'[41]), Coleridge wrote to him on 13 May 1796 to defend himself against Thelwall's charge that he had treated 'systems & opinions with the furious prejudices of the conventicle, & the illiberal dogmatism of the Cynic' and to take issue with the infidel 'New Philosophy' and its enactment in the social arena. Godwin's 'system' and conduct serve as stark examples:

> Godwin, whose very heart is cankered by the love of singularity & who feels no disinclination to wound by abrupt harshness, pleads for absolute Sincerity, because such a system gives him a frequent opportunity of indulging his misanthropy. – Poor Williams, the Welch bard – (a very meek man) brought the tear into my Eye by a simple narration of the manner in which Godwin insulted him, under the pretence of Reproof – & Thomas Walker of Manchester told me, that his Indignation & Contempt were never more powerfully excited than by an unfeeling and insolent Speech of the said Godwin to the poor Welch Bard.[42]

The reference here to Thomas Walker of Manchester (who founded the Manchester Constitutional Society in 1790 and who was prosecuted unsuccessfully in 1792 for treasonable conspiracy) suggests that Godwin's 'reproof' and 'insolent speech' occurred at the gatherings of 2 and 3 January 1795 which he logged in his diary. We know that the conversation on the latter occasion

---

[39] Bodleian Library, Oxford, Abinger MSS, dep. e. 202. See also C. Kegan Paul, *William Godwin: His Friends and Contemporaries* (2 vols., London, 1876), I, p. 71.

[40] See Griggs (ed.), *Collected Letters*, I, pp. 267–8.

[41] Ibid., I, p. 204.

[42] Ibid., I, p. 214.

partly turned on the subject of Christian belief, which would have provoked
Godwin's ire – and ignited Iolo's fire. But Coleridge's reference to 'Poor
Williams' and his emphasis on the tear-jerking nature of the tale suggest that
something closer to home was also at stake.

Discussing 'Gratitude and Ingratitude' in his *Lectures on Education* (1789),
David Williams had declared that gratitude

> is an effect of beneficence so natural, that the obligations of it in children, are
> generally acknowledged; and filial ingratitude deemed infamous . . . though the duty
> be natural, clear, and readily acknowledged: no vice is so much complained of in life;
> no misfortune so frequently lamented in families, as ingratitude.[43]

Illustrating the immutable dictates of reason and justice in the infamous 'fire
clause' of his *Political Justice*, Godwin took a contrary view. If Archbishop
Fénelon and his chambermaid – who might be one's wife, mother or
benefactor – were caught in a flaming building and only one of them could
be saved, one is under a moral obligation, Godwin argued, to save the author
of the 'immortal Telemachus' since 'The life of Fénelon would still be more
valuable than that of the chambermaid; and justice, pure, unadulterated justice,
would still have preferred that which was most valuable.' Filial gratitude
receives short shrift in *Political Justice*: Godwin admits that a mother endures for
her child 'the pains of child bearing', and nourishes it 'in the helplessness of
infancy', but claims that 'When she first subjected herself to the necessity of
these cares, she was probably influenced by no particular motives of benevolence to her future offspring.' 'What magic is there in the pronoun "my"', he
contends, 'to overturn the decisions of everlasting truth? My wife or my
mother may be a fool or a prostitute, malicious, lying, or dishonest. If they be,
of what consequence is it that they are mine?'[44] Godwin was later to soften his
stance on the domestic affections, but here a cold appraisal of utilitarian worth
outweighs natural human affection. Disseminating Godwin's philosophy in the
political lectures of *The Tribune*, Thelwall characterized gratitude in terms of a
heinous moral synecdoche that sabotaged political justice:

> I am not afraid, however, of popularising those ideas which I believe to be true,
> because the persons who first propagated them have encountered reproach . . . If
> gratitude . . . has a tendency to draw the human mind from the consideration of the
> whole, and to fix it, from a principle of self love, upon a few individuals, then I shall
> be obliged to conclude that gratitude is no virtue, but that, on the contrary, it is an
> enemy to that great fountain of all virtue – Justice! . . . It is mistaking a part for the
> whole, and confining our exertions to a few particular individuals, merely because

---

[43]   David Williams, *Lectures on Education* (3 vols., London, 1789), II, p. 166.
[44]   William Godwin, *An Enquiry concerning Political Justice* (2 vols., London, 1793), I, p. 83.

they have done more for us than we were entitled to, and thereby neglecting that great scale of justice . . .[45]

In the light of this, Kathleen Coburn has suggested that Godwin's humiliation of Iolo was related in some way to Iolo's strong attachment to his mother:

Williams's mother died when he was twenty-three, and the personal anecdotes given in his introduction to his poems reveal a particularly close relation to her. One may reasonably conjecture that Godwin's contempt for Williams may have had something to do with the strength of that filial affection of which Godwin at this time disapproved, which disapproval in turn met with sharp criticism from Coleridge.[46]

A gifted and cultured woman of noble south Wales stock, Ann Williams, née Matthew (1713–70) was a formative influence on Iolo. It was she who introduced him to English literature, arithmetic and music. 'Let the Reader pardon my filial partiality', Iolo remarks in an autobiographical fragment, before listing his mother's many accomplishments (which included knowledge of 'surgery and Physic').[47] In the preface to *Poems, Lyric and Pastoral*, Iolo made public his affection for, and gratitude to, his mother, suggesting that he owed her his 'original turn for poetry' and emphasizing the traumatic effect her death in 1770 had on him: 'I was very pensive, melancholy, and very *stupid*, as all but my mother thought . . . After my mother's death I could no longer be happy at home, where she was *never more to be seen*.'[48] Much of the self-portrait in the preface was a pose designed to appeal to potential patrons and literary editors, but, as G. J. Williams remarks, 'everything suggests that we can accept his portrait of this mother'.[49] *Poems, Lyric and Pastoral* also contains an emotional sonnet, 'To the Memory of my Mother' – 'Oh, my *lost mother*! – still I weep for thee'.[50] Paternal affection and grief also haunt the preface as Iolo, accounting for the delay in publication, recorded the death of 'one of my *dear children, a favourite little girl*' – his beloved Lilla – during his absence in London.[51]

Iolo could also eloquently formulate the *societal* significance of such filial and paternal devotion. A letter of 26 March 1798 stresses the importance of domestic affections in the moral make-up of those in authority:

I would have every Legislator as well as his elector a married man, a legislator [should] be acquainted with all the feelings of humanity before he can possibly Judge as he ou[ght] human actions, before he can make just allowances for human

---

[45] See *The Tribune* (3 vols., London, 1795–6), I, pp. 229–36.
[46] Coburn (ed.), *Notebooks*, I (Notes), #605.
[47] Quoted in Williams: *IM*, pp. 92–3.
[48] Williams: *PLP*, I, pp. xv–xvi.
[49] Williams: *IM*, p. 94; my translation.
[50] Williams: *PLP*, II, p. 97.
[51] Ibid., I, p. xiv.

frailties. [?] can be acquainted with these feelings unless he has passed thro' the
several stages of Husband, and Parent, wherein only the best and finest sensibilities
of huma[n] nature become known to us, and without these sensibilities man is little
better [than] a Devil (witness Billy Pitt).[52]

At a time (1794–7) when Coleridge was setting Godwin's atheism and the
philosophy of *Political Justice* 'at Defiance', the figure of the slighted Welsh bard
would have both dramatically confirmed and helped to galvanize his
opposition. In the third of his lectures on 'Revealed Religion', delivered at
Bristol in May 1795, Coleridge had squarely confronted *Political Justice* on the
issues of gratitude and the domestic affections in order to refute what he saw
as simplistic 'theory' divorced from any knowledge – either observed,
intuitively felt, or physiologically proven – of human nature. Jesus, and the
associationist philosophy of David Hartley ('see this *demonstrated* by Hartley',
as Coleridge put it in a typically forthright footnote to 'Religious Musings')
were Coleridge's authorities here. Love of God is nurtured by one's position in
'networks of living relationships':[53]

> The filial and paternal affections discipline the heart and prepare it for that blessed
> state of perfection in which all our Passions are to be absorbed in the Love of God.
> But if we love not our friends and Parents whom we have seen – how can we love
> our universal Friend and Almighty Parent whom we have not seen. Jesus was a son,
> and he cast the Eye of Tenderness and careful regard on his Mother . . . Jesus knew
> our Nature – and that expands like the circles of a Lake – the Love of our Friends,
> parents, and neighbours lead[s] us to the love of our Country and to the love of all
> Mankind. The intensity of private attachment encourages, not prevents, universal
> philanthropy . . .

Coleridge proceeded to condemn the 'anti-familial'[54] doctrines of *Political
Justice*:

> the Stoical Morality which disclaims all the duties of Gratitude and domestic
> Affection has been lately revived in a book popular among the professed Friends of
> civil Freedom – a book which builds without a foundation, proposes an end without
> establishing the means, and discovers a total ignorance of that obvious Fact in human
> nature that in virtue and in knowledge we must be infants and be nourished with
> milk in order that we may be men and eat strong meat. Of this work it may be truly
> said, that whatever is just in it, is more forcibly recommended in the Gospel and
> whatever is new is absurd. Severe Moralist! that teaches us that filial Love is a Folly,
> Gratitude criminal, Marriage Injustice, and a promiscuous Intercourse of the Sexes
> our wisdom and our duty.[55]

---

[52]   NLW 21285E, Letter no. 862, Iolo Morganwg to Miss Barker, 26 March 1798.
[53]   Patton and Mann (eds.), *Lectures 1795*, p. lxx.
[54]   Ibid., p. 162n.
[55]   Ibid., pp. 162–4.

Iolo's treatment by Godwin was a compelling exemplum of the moral effects of Godwin's refusal to countenance 'obvious Fact[s] in human nature'. Coleridge was to articulate these objections again in *The Watchman* of 17 March 1796 as part of an attack on the disseminator of Godwinian doctrine, John Thelwall:

> You have studied Mr Godwin's Essay on Political Justice; but to think filial affection folly, gratitude a crime . . . may class you among the despisers of vulgar prejudices, but cannot increase the probability that you are a PATRIOT. But you act up to your principles. – So much the worse! Your principles are villainous ones! I would not entrust my wife or sister to you – Think you, I would entrust my country?[56]

Coleridge's letter of 13 May 1796, in which he informed Thelwall of Godwin's shabby treatment of their mutual friend Iolo, was part of Coleridge's effort to educate his atheist friend out of his adherence to the pernicious categorical imperatives enjoined by Godwin. It is clear from Coleridge's *Notebooks* that Iolo figured in Coleridge's political, moral and poetic consciousness at this time as a poignant human focus of competing ethical and political ideologies. Adding, probably in late September 1802, to some notebook entries of 1798 on 'Infancy & Infants', Coleridge imagined Iolo's devotion in religious terms: 'Poor Williams seeking his Mother, in love with her Picture – & having that vision of Beauty & filial affection, that the Virgin Mary may be supposed to give'; and, as an entry of November/December 1799 makes clear, he planned to 'introduce poor Williams' into his projected 'poems on Infancy'.[57]

It is important to stress, however, that Coleridge's pitying references to Iolo as 'poor Williams' and 'the poor Welch Bard' obscure the profound respect in which Iolo was held as a radical thinker. Iolo inspired far more than pity, however formative in Coleridge's intellectual development 'poor Williams', the victim of Godwin's unconscionable 'Sincerity', may have proved. Indeed, it seems likely that Iolo's bardic writings played a significant role in Coleridge's thinking on the related issue of 'the Godwinian system of Pride' – another vice he saw as characterizing those 'Friends of civil Freedom' who, like Godwin, were inclined to atheism: 'We find in Jesus nothing of that Pride which affects to inculcate benevolence while it does away every home-born Feeling, by which it is produced and nurtured.'[58] Coburn has suggested that Coleridge's anti-Godwinian strictures on Pride in a 1795–6 notebook entry –

> Hymns to the Sun, the Moon, and the Elements – six hymns. – In one of them to introduce a dissection of Athesim – particularly the Godwinian System of Pride[.]

---

[56] Lewis Patton (ed.), *The Watchman* (London, 1970), pp. 98–9; see also pp. 194–8.
[57] Coburn (ed.), *Notebooks*, I (Text), #330 (15) and I (Text and Notes), #605.
[58] Patton and Mann (eds.), *Lectures 1795*, p. 162.

Proud of what? An outcast of blind Nature ruled by a fatal Necessity – Slave of an ideot [*sic*] Nature![59]

– may have been influenced by Iolo's discussion of pride in his 'outlines of Bardism, Druidism, or the Ancient British Philosophy' in *Poems, Lyric and Pastoral*:

> *Pride* is the utmost degree of human depravity; it supplies the motive for perpetrating every kind of wickedness, it aims at *Superiority* and *Power*, which none but GOD is, of *right*, entitled to ... PRIDE is the destroyer (CYTHRAUL [devil, adversary]) of the works of the CREATOR, the subverter of all order, forces itself obtrusively into a station that was never allotted to it. All men are equal in the CREATOR's paternality, as his children ... PRIDE casts down into the *lowest point of existence*.[60]

The poems and bardic triads in *Poems, Lyric and Pastoral* also railed repeatedly and vociferously against 'Pride's malignant ardour' and 'odious birth'. Coleridge may also have known the similar strictures on Pride in the 'Sketch of British Bardism' which prefaces the *Heroic Elegies and other Pieces of Llywarç Hen*, in which Iolo's bardism was invested with a levelling subtext.[61] If, as Patton and Mann suggest, 'Coleridge's response to Godwin's work was one of the most important single factors in his early political thinking', then Iolo should be seen as integral to that education; and if '*Political Justice* did not so much nourish [Coleridge's] radicalism as push it in another direction by force of reaction',[62] then Iolo was a catalyst of that trajectory away from the moral bankruptcy of Godwinian theory.

★ ★ ★

Poems, Lyric and Pastoral figures in Duncan Wu's list of Wordsworth's reading as one of the books Wordsworth may have read.[63] It is indeed likely that Coleridge should have introduced Wordsworth, probably around 1797–8, to the English poems of a man such as Iolo, many of whose acquaintances were also known to Wordsworth. Coleridge is also likely to have informed Wordsworth of their 'near coincidence' in London's radical circles, of Iolo's

---

[59] See Coburn, *Notebooks*, I (Text and Notes), #174 (16). See also Coleridge to Josiah Wade, 27 January 1796, on Erasmus Darwin's atheism: 'He bantered me on the subject of religion ... all at once he makes up his mind on such important subjects, as whether we be the outcasts of a blind idiot called Nature, or the children of an all-wise and infinitely good God'; Griggs (ed.), *Collected Letters*, I, p. 177.

[60] Williams: *PLP*, II, pp. 200–1.

[61] William Owen Pughe, *The Heroic Elegies and other Pieces of Llywarç Hen* (London, 1792), p. lvii.

[62] Patton and Mann (eds.), *Lectures 1795*, p. lxxvii.

[63] Duncan Wu, *Wordsworth's Reading, 1770–1799* (Cambridge, 1993), p. 161.

bardic radicalism and, one suspects, of his encounter with the author of *Political Justice*. It is certainly possible that Wordsworth and Iolo actually met in the early 1790s at that gravitational centre of metropolitan radicalism, the bookshop and home of Joseph Johnson (who, in 1793, had published Wordsworth's *An Evening Walk* and *Descriptive Sketches*).

It is possible to go further by positing the influence of one of Iolo's pieces from *Poems, Lyric and Pastoral* on Wordsworth's 'A Poet's Epitaph', written in late 1798 and published in 1800 in the second edition of the *Lyrical Ballads*. Wordsworth's poem can be seen to enlist Iolo's satirical pastoral as part of a response to Godwin, whose philosophy Wordsworth had welcomed earlier in the decade. In this respect, Iolo's poem represents a more pointed and politicized analogue of 'A Poet's Epitaph' than Theocritus' 'Epigram XIX' and Burns's 'A Bard's Epitaph', both of which have also been seen as models for Wordsworth's poem.

In a masterful piece of self-promotion published in the *Gentleman's Magazine* in November 1789, Iolo had contrasted bardic inspiration with the artificial art of 'modern book-taught poets'.[64] 'The Learned Ignorants, A Song, written in 1772', included in *Poems, Lyric and Pastoral*, elaborates on the distinction. It would certainly have caught the attention of the Wordsworth who, in 1795 and 1796, had realized that Godwin was not a sage with an emancipating blueprint for society but rather 'a nit-picking pedant':[65]

> Ye book-poring pedants, by learning made fools,
> Whose skulls are well-stuff'd with the rubbish of schools,
> Ye boast your old *ballads* that classics ye call,
> Your *Homers*, your *Virgils*, your devil and all;
> True, you know *Greek* enough to make any dog sick,
> Nor less are ye skill'd in the cant of *Old Nick*;
> But, how does it happen? ye constantly prove
> Mere dunces indeed in the language of *Love*.
>
> A tatter'd *Oxonian* I t'other day met,
> One of those that make books (I was quite in a pet),
> He was filching from *Horace* old thoughts for a song,
> Where through the green wood I walk'd pensive along;
> He look'd wild around him, and ask'd with surprize,
> If Duns or Bumbailiffs occasion'd my sighs,
> But I sought my dear Phillis, and flew from the grove,
> Alas! the poor *Soph* knows but little of *Love*.
>
> Once forc'd from my charmer abruptly to part,
> Grief harrow'd my soul, drew the blood from my heart;

---

[64] See *Gentleman's Magazine*, LIX, part 2 (1789), 976–7, 1035–6.
[65] Roe, *Radical Years*, p. 196.

In my way an absurd astronomical ass
Bo-peep'd at the sky through a queer-fashion'd glass;
He saw my sad looks, and the briny tears run,
And suppos'd 'twas by staring, like him, at the Sun;
At the Sun! yes, you block-head, but not that above,
'Twas a brighter by far, the bright eyes of my *Love*.

One morning in May, as I walk'd by the rill
That tinkles along near the foot of yon hill,
Gay Spring bloom'd around, how serene the sweet air,
And, weeping, I wish'd my dear *Phillis* was there;
When a booby old *Botanist*, haunting the place,
Through a pair of broad spectacles star'd in my face;
This *eye-seed*, quoth he, will your anguish remove: –
'Twas a *weed-monger's* tale, that knew nothing of *Love*.

As saunt'ring last night in the pine-shaded walk,
Where often I'm bless'd with my charmer's dear talk;
I long'd to behold her, look'd anxious around,
But my fair-one, alas! was no where to be found;
A *Philosopher* ask'd, if I wept, sigh'd, and whin'd,
Like *Heraclitus* once, for the whims of mankind?
A *Philosopher* you! that's amazing, by Jove!
And ignorant thus of the nature of *Love*.

In a glade far-sequester'd, as lately retir'd,
I wept the sad absence of her I admir'd;
When a son of old *Galen* came hobbling that way,
And, like other dull sots, wanted something to say;
He ask'd me, observing my tears and my sighs,
If a *lachrymal fistula* flooded my eyes?
Alas, the poor *Doctor*! 'twas easy to prove
His heart never felt the keen *lancet* of *Love*.

As, weeping, I pass'd by the church t'other day,
In search of my Phillis who rambled that way;
I was taken to task by a preaching old *prig*,
'Twas a *double-chinn'd Priest*, in a full-bottom'd wig;
He of fasting and pray'r made a wonderful din,
And hop'd, he pretended, I wept for my sin;
But how can *he* claim those bless'd mansions above,
That's not of the faith and religion of *Love*?

The billet from Phillis, her hand and her seal,
Drew me out of the parlour my tears to conceal;
When a grizzly old *Alchymist* meets me, and cries,
'You've been toiling in smoke, I perceive by your eyes;'

His *Philosopher's stone* turns a brick-bat to gold,
Yet *Love's* nobler essence he ne'er could unfold;
But I flew to my charmer, we met in the grove,
And join'd soul to soul in th'endearments of *Love*.

Hush, Pedants, be mute! you may think me quite rude,
Because I dare thus on your studies intrude;
But quit this dull farce, your poor college grimace,
And study the charms of a *pretty girl's* face;
The tender expressions of love-tutor'd eyes;
And construe the language of heart-speaking sighs;
Do this, and your learning to wisdom improve,
And you'll own that true knowledge is nothing but *Love*![66]

There are suggestive points of contact between Iolo's poem and Wordsworth's 'A Poet's Epitaph':

Art thou a Statesman, in the van
Of public business train'd and bred?
– First learn to love one living man;
Then may'st thou think upon the dead.

A Lawyer art thou? – draw not nigh;
Go, carry to some other place
The hardness of thy coward eye,
The falshood of thy sallow face.

Art thou a man of purple cheer?
A rosy man, right plump to see?
Approach; yet Doctor, not too near:
This grave no cushion is for thee.

Art thou a man of gallant pride,
A Soldier, and no man of chaff?
Welcome! – but lay thy sword aside,
And lean upon a Peasant's staff.

Physician art thou? One, all eyes,
Philosopher! a fingering slave,
One that would peep and botanize
Upon his mother's grave?

Wrapp'd closely in thy sensual fleece
O turn aside, and take, I pray,
That he below may rest in peace,
Thy pin-point of a soul away!

---

[66] Williams: *PLP*, I, pp. 85–90.

– A Moralist perchance appears;
Led, heaven knows how! to this poor sod,
And He has neither eyes nor ears;
Himself his world, and his own God;

One to whose smooth-rubb'd soul can cling
Nor form nor feeling great nor small,
A reasoning, self-sufficing thing,
An intellectual All in All!

Shut close the door! press down the latch:
Sleep in thy intellectual crust,
Nor lose ten tickings of thy watch,
Near this unprofitable dust.

But who is He, with modest looks,
And clad in homely russet brown?
He murmurs near the running brooks
A music sweeter than their own.

He is retired as noontide dew,
Or fountain in a noonday grove;
And you must love him, ere to you
He will seem worthy of your love.

The outward shews of sky and earth,
Of hill and valley he has view'd;
And impulses of deeper birth
Have come to him in solitude.

In common things that round us lie
Some random truths he can impart,
The harvest of a quiet eye
That broods and sleeps on his own heart.

But he is weak, both man and boy,
Hath been an idler in the land;
Contented if he might enjoy
The things which others understand.

– Come hither in thy hour of strength,
Come, weak as is a breaking wave!
Here stretch thy body at full length;
Or build thy house upon this grave. –[67]

---

[67] James Butler and Karen Green (eds.), *Lyrical Ballads, and Other Poems, 1797–1800* (London, 1992), pp. 235–7.

The general similarity between the two pieces is apparent in the roll-call of stock middle-class professionals whose characteristics and capacity for emotional, intuitive and imaginative response are measured (and found wanting) against those of a more feeling soul. Moreover, there are compelling details common to both. Iolo's astronomer who 'Bo-peep[s] at the sky' and his bespectacled botanist who recommends 'eye-seed' offer models for Wordsworth's curiously conflated physician–philosopher–field-biologist – 'all eyes' – who 'would peep and botanize/ Upon his mother's grave'.[68] Indeed, the focus in Iolo's poem on eyes, vision and the lack of vision of pedantic 'porers' – 'the bright eyes of my Love'; 'eye-seed'; 'a *lachrymal fistula* flooded my eyes'; '"You've been toiling in smoke, I perceive from your eyes"'; 'love-tutor'd eyes' – is also apparent in Wordsworth's – 'thy coward eye'; 'One all eyes'; 'And he has neither eyes nor ears'; 'The harvest of a quiet eye'. The astronomer of Iolo's poem, though without his exact double in Wordsworth's, finds one in the 1802 additions to the Preface to *Lyrical Ballads*, in which Wordsworth has his own 'A Poet's Epitaph' in mind:

> The Poet writes under one restriction only, namely, that of the necessity of giving immediate pleasure to a human Being possessed of that information which may be expected of him, not as a lawyer, a physician, a mariner, an astronomer, or a natural philosopher, but as a Man.[69]

Iolo's poetic persona who walks weeping 'by the rill/ That tinkles along near the foot of yon hill', in 'a glade far-sequester'd' and 'in the grove' is a prototype of Wordsworth's rustic wanderer who is 'retired as noontide dew/ Or fountain in a noonday grove' and who 'murmurs near the running brooks/ A music sweeter than their own'. The ideal in Iolo's piece is a simple being among the glades who can 'construe the language of heart-speaking sighs'; in Wordsworth's, it is a similarly artless, meditative being receptive to the language of Nature – and by implication, to such poems as 'A Poet's Epitaph'. In a discussion of Wordsworth's anxieties regarding readership and reception, Lucy Newlyn interprets the 'retired' rustic of 'A Poet's Epitaph' as 'unmistakably . . . a poet in the Wordsworthian mould' and as an ideal reader of the poem-epitaph onto whom Wordsworth projects 'both his own self-image, and (in a reflexive doubling of that image) his best hopes of being understood by his readers: "And you must love him, ere to you/ He will seem worthy of your love"'.[70] It is a 'self-image' which Wordsworth recognized in both Iolo's person

---

[68] Commenting on the strange conflation of professions in Wordsworth's stanza, James H. Averill has suggested that Wordsworth is thinking of a particular 'physician-philosopher' – Erasmus Darwin. See Averill, 'Wordsworth and "Natural Science": The Poetry of 1798', *Journal of English and Germanic Philology*, LXXVII, no. 2 (1978), 245–6.

[69] R. L. Brett and A. R. Jones (eds.), *Lyrical Ballads* (London, 1965), pp. 257–8.

[70] Lucy Newlyn, *Reading, Writing, and Romanticism: The Anxiety of Reception* (Oxford, 2000), p. 126.

and his poetic persona – an act of recognition that construes Wordsworth himself, in Newlyn's terms, as the ideal reader of Iolo's poem, and Iolo as the model reader of Wordsworth's.

'The Learned Ignorants' sets up a clear opposition between the cold formality of classical and Augustan poetry, written in a language unmotivated by Nature, and the simplicity of a 'plainer and more emphatic language' which acts as a window on Nature and allows the 'great and simple affections of our nature' to be 'more forcibly communicated', as Wordsworth put it in the preface to the *Lyrical Ballads*.[71] The linguistic programme of the *Lyrical Ballads*, as set out in the prefaces of 1800 and 1802, was perfectly in tune with Iolo's bardic formulations on poetic 'naturalness' in *Poems, Lyric and Pastoral*:

> A Poet in the character of a Shepherd, an occupation the most proper of all others to represent primeval simplicity and virtue, describes objects as they naturally present themselves to the senses, and affect the mind; or utters sentiments that spring from the simple notions and inborn feelings of those that are unacquainted with the abstractions of philosophy, and the complex ideas derived from art . . . It would, perhaps, not be amiss if our modern Critics and Poets would take into consideration the following maxim of the Welsh Bards, from their Poetic Triades . . . The three primary and indispensable requisites of poetic genius are, An eye that can see Nature; A heart that can feel Nature; And a resolution that dares follow Nature.[72]

The Welsh bards figure here as theorists of a doctrine of radical linguistic 'simplicity' of which the preface to the *Lyrical Ballads* was to become a celebrated expression. Iolo's statements obviously prefigure – and perhaps inform – Wordsworth's preface, which famously argues that 'low and rustic life' was chosen as a subject since 'in that situation the essential passions of the heart . . . are less under restraint, and speak . . . a more permanent and a far more philosophical language than that which is frequently substituted for it by Poets'.[73]

William Knight noted in 1896 that Wordsworth's portrait of an ideal, feeling soul in 'A Poet's Epitaph', 'clad in homely russet brown', is indebted to James Thomson's description of the Bard in *The Castle of Indolence* (1748):[74]

> He came, the Bard, a little Druid-Wight,
> Of wither'd Aspect; but his Eye was keen,
> With Sweetness mix'd. *In Russet brown bedight,*
> As is his Sister of the Copses green,
> He crept along, unpromising of Mien.[75]

---

[71] Brett and Jones (eds.), *Lyrical Ballads*, pp. 245, 247.
[72] Williams: *PLP*, I, pp. 173–4, 175–6.
[73] Brett and Jones (eds.), *Lyrical Ballads*, p. 245.
[74] William Knight (ed.), *The Poetical Works of William Wordsworth* (8 vols., London, 1896), II, p. 77.
[75] Canto II, ll. 289–93, my emphasis; James Sambrook (ed.), *Liberty, The Castle of Indolence and other Poems* (Oxford, 1986), p. 208.

The echo of Thomson is unmistakable, but the contemporary bard and 'Druid wight' Iolo (small, keen-eyed) was surely also a model for Wordsworth's responsive rustic. Moreover, Wordsworth would have recognized in Iolo a mirror of himself – an act of identification in which Edwin, the protagonist of James Beattie's poem *The Minstrel* (1771 and 1774 – a significant influence on both the young Wordsworth and the mature poet of *The Prelude*) plays an interesting role. In a letter of 1793 Dorothy Wordsworth described Wordsworth as Edwin's second self – 'Beattie's "Minstrel" always reminds me of [Wordsworth] and indeed the whole character of Edwin resembles much what William was when I first knew him'[76] – while Mary Moorman has emphasized that the solitary Edwin, alive to Nature's wonders, was 'a poetic creation after [Wordsworth's] own image'.[77] William Wordsworth would also have seen his own Edwinian image in the Edward Williams (the mirroring of names is provocative) of *Poems, Lyric and Pastoral*; intriguingly, an anonymous reviewer of the volume in the *Critical Review* declared that 'Those who have read Beatie's [*sic*] Minstrel, will be struck with the similarity between young Edwin' and Iolo the 'rustic poet'.[78]

The grounds of Wordsworth's identification with Iolo, however, were not merely biographical or stylistic. Their dialogue inscribed a political alignment which helped Wordsworth exorcise his former Godwinian self. 'The Learned Ignorants' is a piece to which Wordsworth could readily ascribe a specifically anti-Godwin agenda, and Iolo's poem was enlisted as part of a critique of Godwinian intellectualism in 'A Poet's Epitaph'. 'The Learned Ignorants' is levelled from the outset against all 'book-poring pedants, by learning made fools'; describing the atheistic Moralist (here, a moral philosopher) in 'A Poet's Epitaph' as 'A reasoning, self-sufficing thing,/ An intellectual All in All!', Wordsworth surely had in mind the Godwin of *Political Justice* – the 'Moralist' who had famously insulted Iolo and whose philosophy was predicated on reason and (in Wordsworth's phrase from *The Prelude*) the 'independent intellect'. Coleridge, of course, had characterized Godwin as a 'Severe Moralist' in his vindication of gratitude and filial affection at Bristol in 1795. Wordsworth had already written a powerful analysis of perverted Godwinian reason (and of pride, filial love and gratitude – 'a heavy burden to a proud soul') in *The Borderers*, and was to write devastatingly in *The Prelude* of the 'barren seas' of Godwinism which took him far from the 'arbours' of 'blessèd sentiment and fearless love' (significantly, 'blissful gratitude and fearless love' in the 1850 version). Employing metaphors of sight and blindness to emphasize the moral

---

[76] Ernest de Selincourt and Chester L. Shaver (eds.), *The Letters of William and Dorothy Wordsworth: The Early Years, 1787–1805* (Oxford, 1967), pp. 100–1.

[77] Mary Moorman, *William Wordsworth: A Biography: The Early Years – 1770–1803* (Oxford, 1957), pp. 60–1.

[78] *Critical Review*, XI (June 1794), 169.

and imaginative myopia of the Godwinians, Coleridge in the third of his Bristol lectures on 'Revealed Religion' called them the 'dim eyed Sons of Blasphemy',[79] and quoted Beattie's *Minstrel* to characterize Godwinian atheistical 'sensualists', blind to Nature as the language of God:

> The dark cold-hearted Sceptics creeping pore
> Through microscope of Metaphysic Lore;
> And much they grope for Truth but never hit[.]
> Their heavy powers, inadequate before[,]
> Their earthy Lusts make more and more unfit[,]
> Yet deem they Darkness Light, and their vain Blunders Wit.[80]

Likewise, Wordsworth in the fragment 'Not useless do I deem' – written for *The Ruined Cottage* and envisaged at this time (1798) as part of the redemptive project of *The Recluse* – asked:

>   For was it meant
> That we should pore, and dwindle as we pore
> Forever dimly pore on things minute,
> On solitary objects, still beheld
> In disconnection, dead and spiritless;
> And still dividing, and dividing still,
> Break down all grandeur, still unsatisfied
> With our unnatural toil while littleness
> May yet become more little, waging thus
> An impious warfare with the very life
> Of our own souls?[81]

In this context, Iolo's poem, which berates canting 'sophisters' who murder to dissect and 'porers' blind to 'the language', 'the nature' and 'the religion of Love', would have appealed to Wordsworth and Coleridge as a satirical intervention in the debate with Godwin. Moreover, Wordsworth's line 'One that would peep and botanize/ Upon his mother's grave' gains an added tragic *frisson* as it conjures up both the bereaved Iolo at his mother's grave – tellingly, Iolo was well known as an accomplished botanist and herbalist – and, troublingly, a prying, bespectacled Godwin, who, in the words of *The Prelude*,

>   sacrificed
> The exactness of a comprehensive mind
> To scrupulous and microscopic views
> That furnished out materials for a work
> Of false imagination.[82]

---

[79] Patton and Mann (eds.), *Lectures 1795*, p. 165.
[80] Ibid., p. 158–9.
[81] Jonathan Wordsworth, *The Music of Humanity* (London, 1969), pp. 270–1.
[82] *The Prelude* (1805), X, 843–7; Jonathan Wordsworth (ed.), *The Prelude: The Four Texts* (London, 1995), p. 448.

The conclusion to Iolo's poem, which scorns pedantry and enjoins a deepening of 'learning' into 'wisdom', anticipates other poems in the *Lyrical Ballads* such as 'Anecdote for Fathers' – 'a humorous deflation of the overworked Godwinian intellect, that would "think, and think, and think again"' – and 'Expostulation and Reply', which 'consigns Godwin and Wordsworth's former Godwinian self to one common intellectual grave'[83] by famously recommending a 'wise passiveness'.

Iolo aids Wordsworth's exorcism of Godwin's influence in another of the *Lyrical Ballads*, 'Simon Lee, the Old Huntsman' – a poem which is pitched towards a dramatization of gratitude. As Wordsworth explained in the Fenwick note, the poem narrates an actual encounter with an old servant of the Alfoxden estate in Somerset, Christopher Tricky.[84] The locus of the poem, however, is Wales: 'In the sweet shire of Cardigan,/ Not far from pleasant Ivor-Hall . . .' Time's toll on Simon Lee's body is mirrored in the abandoned state of Ivor Hall: 'His master's dead, and no one now/ Dwells in the hall of Ivor . . .' In 'Simon Lee and Ivor Hall: A Possible Source', Peter Bement suggests that Wordsworth's decision to change the setting from Somerset to Cardiganshire 'may have been motivated by a desire to avoid giving offence at Alfoxden', and that 'the abandoned "hall of Ivor" calls to mind the ruins, at Bassaleg, near Newport in Monmouthshire, of the palace of Ifor ap Llywelyn, known as *Ifor Hael* ("Ivor the Generous") . . . famous in Welsh literary and antiquarian circles as the supposed patron of the great medieval poet, Dafydd ap Gwilym'.[85] For Iolo, the relationship between Dafydd and Ifor Hael represented a model which he sought to resuscitate in the 1790s by cultivating the patronage of the Prince of Wales. Furthermore, Bement argues that Wordsworth might have known of this historical 'hall of Ivor' from the famous series of *englynion*, 'Llys Ifor Hael' ('The Palace of Ifor Hael') by Evan Evans – poet, antiquarian, scholar and friend of Thomas Gray and Thomas Percy. Wordsworth might have seen Evans's own translation of his *englynion* or heard it discussed during a visit in 1791 or 1793 to Downing, Flintshire, home of Thomas Pennant, one of Evans's patrons.

Iolo's poem 'To Ivor the Liberal, on being presented by him with a pair of gloves, from the Welsh of Dafydd ap Gwilym', from *Poems, Lyric and Pastoral*, informs 'Simon Lee' in significant ways.[86] This poem, a free rendering of Dafydd ap Gwilym's *cywydd* to Ifor Hael, 'Diolch am Fenig' ('Thanksgiving for

---

83   See Roe, *Radical Years*, pp. 197–8.
84   Jared Curtis (ed.), *The Fenwick Notes of William Wordsworth* (London, 1993), p. 37.
85   Peter Bement, 'Simon Lee and Ivor Hall: A Possible Source', *The Wordsworth Circle*, CXIII, no. 1 (1982), 35–6.
86   For a complementary discussion of 'To Ivor the Liberal' and 'Simon Lee', see David Simpson, *Wordsworth's Historical Imagination: The Poetry of Displacement* (London, 1987), pp. 151–5. Simpson's emphasis is very different from mine.

a pair of Gloves'), may have provided Wordsworth not only with the phrase 'Ivor Hall' but, more important, with anti-Godwin ammunition. The poem is prefaced by the following account of Ifor Hael (who from 1789 onwards became a household name for generosity owing to the publicity Iolo gave him):

> IVOR THE LIBERAL, *in Welsh* IFOR HAEL, *was Lord of* BASELEG, *in the County of* MONMOUTH. *He lived about the middle of the fourteenth century, and was celebrated by the Bards of his age, and of all succeeding ages, for his unexampled liberality. He was the warm patron of* DAFYDD AP GWILYM, *the most renowned Bard of his time, whose works are to this day held in the highest estimation.*[87]

The first lines of the poem celebrate Ivor's welcoming hall and expansive benevolence. Iolo patently modernizes and radicalizes him — this is a medieval Welsh lord with not a little of the George Dyer of the *Dissertation on the Theory and Practice of Benevolence* and the *Complaints of the Poor People of England* about him:

> THOU IVOR, darling of the Muse,
> Who through the world thy fame pursues;
> Proclaims thy worth in ev'ry clime,
> Whilst rapture fills her lay sublime;
> And feels her thrilling soul expand,
> Whilst foster'd by thy bounteous hand.
> Thy ample gate, thy ample hall,
> Are ever op'ning wide to all;
> And, warm'd in Heav'n, thy ampler mind
> Dilates in Love to all mankind.[88]

'Jesus knew our Nature — and that expands like the circles of a Lake — the Love of our Friends, parents, and neighbours lead[s] us to the love of our Country and to the love of all Mankind', Coleridge was to state a year after this poem appeared. The discourse of praise and gratitude at the heart of the Welsh poetic tradition then becomes the defining characteristic of Iolo's piece:

> As, lately, sitting at thy board,
> Where ev'ry guest thy worth ador'd,
> With grateful warmth I tun'd my lays,
> And felt high transport in thy praise . . .
> Thy Bard, esteem'd the nobler guest,
> Was with distinguish'd bounty bless'd;
> The gifts of NUDD could not excel
> The gloves that to my portion fell;

---

[87] Williams: *PLP*, I, p. 192.
[88] Ibid., pp. 192–3.

> Surpassing MORDAF's boon of old,
> For both my gloves were cramm'd with gold;
> And RHYDDERCH's hand could not reward
> With nobler meeds his tuneful Bard . . .
> Great IVOR's friendship shall inspire
> His Bard with ARTHUR's martial fire
> His grateful Bard, that dares advance,
> Unarm'd, against that warrior's lance . . .[89]

It seems highly likely that Wordsworth's 'Ivor Hall' is the result of an English ear's processing of the second element of 'Ifor Hael' (correct pronunciation, [haɪl]): an interesting act of 'translation' which allows 'generosity' ('Hael') and the feeling it inspires – gratitude – to exist in Wordsworth's poem as a suggestive cross-cultural echo from the outset ('In the sweet shire of Cardigan,/ Not far from pleasant *Ivor-Hall*'). The phrase brings with it from Iolo's poem an anti-Godwin charge which bolsters Wordsworth's critique of Godwin's position on gratitude in 'Simon Lee'.

It is worth quoting Godwin's strictures on gratitude again:

> My benefactor ought to be esteemed, not because he bestowed a benefit upon me, but because he bestowed it upon a human being. His desert will be in exact proportion to the degree, in which that human being was worthy of the distinction conferred. Thus every view of the subject brings us back to the consideration of my neighbour's moral worth and his importance to the general weal, as the only standard to determine the treatment to which he is entitled. Gratitude therefore, a principle which has so often been the theme of the moralist and the poet, is no part either of justice or virtue. By gratitude I understand a sentiment, which would lead me to prefer one man to another, from some other consideration than that of his superior usefulness or worth.[90]

'Simon Lee' is a highly self-conscious poem which asks us to negotiate the knowing (and at times infuriating) narrator carefully and sceptically. However, commentators such as Legouis, Hutchinson and Moorman have read 'Simon Lee' as a poem which sends 'Godwinian theories whistling down the wind'[91] by vindicating 'the instinctive character of the emotion of gratitude as against Godwin, who represented it as an unjust and degrading sentiment'.[92] Wordsworth's famous ending strikes at the root of Godwinian morality:

> I struck, and with a single blow
> The tangled root I sever'd,

---

[89] Ibid., pp. 193–5.
[90] Godwin, *An Enquiry concerning Political Justice*, I, p. 84.
[91] Moorman, *William Wordsworth*, p. 383.
[92] Thomas Hutchinson (ed.), *Lyrical Ballads, 1798* (3rd edn., London, 1920), p. 234. See also Émile Legouis, *The Early Life of William Wordsworth 1770–1798*, trans. J. W. Matthews (New York, 1965), pp. 309–10.

At which the poor old man so long
And vainly had endeavour'd.

The tears into his eyes were brought,
And thanks and praises seemed to run
So fast out of his heart, I thought
They never would have done.
– I've heard of hearts unkind, kind deeds
With coldness still returning.
Alas! the gratitude of men
Has oftener left me mourning.[93]

The status of Iolo's poem as an adaptation of a *cywydd* of gratitude is significant: Wordsworth's reference to 'Ivor Hall' in 'Simon Lee' and his relocation of the poem to Wales are part of a larger debt to Iolo's poem and the tradition of which it is part – one which invests 'Simon Lee' with a superadded, Welsh-inflected, critique of Godwin on gratitude. In addition, it might not be fanciful to hear an echo of Coleridge's letter to Thelwall – 'Poor Williams, the Welch bard – (a very meek man) brought the tear into my Eye by a simple narration of the manner in which Godwin had insulted him' – in Wordsworth's conclusion: 'The tears into his eyes were brought . . .'

'Near coincidence' in London in the winter of 1794–5, succeeded by fruitful convergence, formative exchange and enabling dialogue: the relationship between Iolo, Coleridge, and Wordsworth is a choice example of the role those 'networks of living relationships' played in defining and rearticulating radical identities in the 1790s. Rejecting Godwin's *Political Justice* was crucial to the development of Coleridge and Wordsworth as thinkers; it was also vital to their survival as poets. Both emerged from the ideological contests of the 1790s with their moral and imaginative sympathies intact. Iolo helped to validate Coleridge's distrust of Godwinism. In Book X of *The Prelude*, Wordsworth recalled how, after he had 'Yielded up moral questions in despair' during his Godwinian crisis, Coleridge and Dorothy had offered 'a living help/ To regulate [his] soul', maintaining for him 'a saving intercourse/ With [his] true self'.[94] Iolo Morganwg played a significant part in that redemption.

[93]   Ll. 93–104; Butler and Green (eds.), *Lyrical Ballads*, p. 67.
[94]   *The Prelude* (1805), X, 906–7 and 914–15; Jonathan Wordsworth (ed.), *The Prelude*, p. 454.

8

'Images of Truth New Born': Iolo, William Blake and the Literary Radicalism of the 1790s

JON MEE

'I well knew this honest, ingenious and worthy poetical stone mason, and received much pleasure, and instruction in his society': so wrote the antiquarian Francis Douce in his subscription copy of *Poems, Lyric and Pastoral*.[1] At around the time Iolo Morganwg's volume was published Douce was also following his literary curiosity in another direction. Richard Twiss had written to him in September 1794 to tell him: 'You will see several more of Blakes books at Johnsons in St. Ps Ch.Yd.' Douce has clearly been interested in the description by Twiss a fortnight earlier of William Blake's *The Gates of Paradise* and *Songs of Innocence*. Douce's antiquarian tastes were eclectic, but were at least partly fuelled by a search for what he perceived as the authentic spirit of British liberty.[2] Blake's *Songs of Innocence* (1789) contains the poem 'The Voice of the Ancient Bard':

> Youth of delight come hither:
> And see the opening morn,
> Image of truth new born.
> Doubt is fled & clouds of reason.
> Dark disputes & artful teasing.[3]

In 1789, the year in which Blake first published these lines, Iolo was presenting himself as a descendant of the 'Ancient British Bards' in the *Gentleman's Magazine*. The first joint collection of Blake's *Songs of Innocence and of Experience* (1794) took the bardic theme further with an 'Introduction' to its 'Experience' section defined as 'the voice of the Bard' in its opening line.[4] Both poets, by 1794, were self-consciously figuring themselves in terms of the ancient bard.[5]

---

[1] For Douce's copy, see Douce W. 118–19 in the Bodleian Library, Oxford.
[2] See Gerald E. Bentley Jr., *Blake Records* (2nd edn., London, 2004), p. 64.
[3] David V. Erdman (ed.), *The Complete Poetry and Prose of William Blake* (rev. edn., London, 1988), p. 31.
[4] Ibid., p. 18.
[5] On the sources of Blake's knowledge of Welsh antiquities, see Arthur Johnston, 'William Blake

This chapter examines these and other parallels between Iolo's *Poems, Lyric and Pastoral* and Blake's *Songs of Innocence and of Experience*, collections that were both, after various vicissitudes, first published whole in 1794. Before turning to discuss the content of the two collections, however, more needs to be said about their situation in the radical London of the 1790s, in particular in terms of a comparison between two 'self-taught' poets who were adventurers in what seemed initially at least to be a world of expanding opportunity.

At the beginning of the 1790s the London book trade was in a state of rapid development. Authors and publishers were experimenting with different forms of publishing in this time of flux. Mary-Ann Constantine has discussed the development of Iolo's project in her chapter in this volume. Blake tried to take control of his career for himself in so far as he printed and sold his own illuminated books. Yet, for all their hopes that they could be independent of middlemen, both enjoyed encouragement from the publisher Joseph Johnson. In fact, Johnson had often been involved with subscription projects, and, as we shall see, helped to sell and at least once co-published with Blake, whom he regularly employed as a copy engraver for his other books.[6] Johnson's motivations were probably personal and ideological rather than strictly commercial in both cases. Everything we know about 'Honest Joe' suggests he would have wanted to encourage two writers from beyond the educated elite.[7] On Iolo's printed list of subscribers his name appears in italics, indicating that he was among 'my most distinguished friends'.[8] Johnson was a committed Unitarian and he published a considerable amount of religious material broadly sympathetic to Rational Dissent from the 1770s through to his death in 1809, but he was interested in the reform of the establishment of church and state more generally. Involved in the publication of Thomas Paine's *Rights of Man* (1791–2), he also published many of the writers involved in the so-called 'Revolution controversy' sparked by Edmund Burke's *Reflections on the Revolution in France* (1790). In 1788 he had set up the *Analytical Review* to provide a broadly reformist commentary on books and current affairs. Although Iolo's *Poems* was, strictly speaking, published by subscription for the author, the anonymous

and "The Ancient Britons"', *NLWJ*, XXII, no. 3 (1982), 304–20 and G. E. Bentley Jr., '"The Triumph of Owen"', ibid., XXIV, no. 2 (1985), 248–61.

6   For Blake's employment history with Johnson, see Gerald E. Bentley Jr., *The Stranger from Paradise: A Biography of William Blake* (London, 2001), pp. 108–9. On Johnson and subscription, see the account of his role in the publication, with John Murray, of Lavater's *Essays on Physiognomy* in William Zachs, *John Murray and the Late Eighteenth-century London Book Trade* (Oxford, 1998), p. 83. Murray was a long-time collaborator with Johnson on several schemes. Blake worked as an engraver on the edition.

7   For details of Johnson, see Gerald P. Tyson, *Joseph Johnson: A Liberal Publisher* (Iowa City, 1979) and Helen Braithwaite, *Romanticism, Publishing and Dissent: Joseph Johnson and the Cause of Liberty* (Basingstoke, 2003).

8   Williams: *PLP*, I, p. xiv.

review in the *Analytical Review* gives Johnson's name as the publisher: his name also appears first among the booksellers listed on the title-page. Iolo's stay in London falls in the period when Blake did most work for Johnson as a commercial copy engraver.[9] Blake had engraved designs for Erasmus Darwin's *The Botanic Garden* (1791), for instance, as well as a portrait of the author for Johnson's reissue of David Hartley's *Observations on Man* (1791). Both books spoke directly to the progressive Unitarian sensibilities that provided the most supportive context for Iolo's time in London. William Godwin's diary records that on 3 January 1795 Iolo joined him in dining with Gilbert Wakefield, Thomas Brand Hollis, John Disney and George Dyer.[10] Their 'talk of God' was, one imagines, typical of the kind of free enquiry that stimulated the eager readers of Darwin and Hartley. On 9 January, Iolo wrote to Johnson himself and sent 'Compts. To Literary friends that frequent your Shop, Dyer, Disney, Aikin, Mr & Mrs Barbould, G. & W. Morgan, & all others, all in your family &c Shop'.[11] He had become friendly with the inner circles of progressive Unitarianism in the capital. Anecdotal evidence suggests that Blake, for his part, may sometimes have attended the publisher's dinner parties, but their relationship was probably structured around the poles of employer and employee rather than publisher and writer. Even so, by the autumn of 1794 at the latest, Johnson was at least displaying Blake's illuminated books in his shop, a major resort for both lounging men of letters as well as book buyers at the time (as Iolo's 1795 letter suggests). If Blake was not exactly part of the inner circle hailed by Iolo, at least he seems to have received the publisher's encouragement and support. Proofs for a poem entitled *The French Revolution* exist – dated 1790 – which bear Johnson's name as the prospective publisher, though there is no reason to believe that the poem was actually ever brought out. Johnson had also taken some part – we do not know the details – in the publication of Blake's *The Gates of Paradise* (1793), for his name appears as co-publisher alongside Blake's own.

Iolo claimed that he had got as far as printing half the second volume of *Poems* by November 1792. Then his 'little stock of cash failed'.[12] The death of his daughter on top of these woes drove him to the verge of breakdown. Johnson may well have resurrected the project in a characteristically charitable spirit. In a letter of 30 October 1793 to his wife Margaret (Peggy), Iolo reported to her that he had been showing his translations of bardic triads to 'some of the capital Booksellers, for their opinion and the opinion of their

[9] For details of Blake's relationship with Johnson, see Bentley, *The Stranger from Paradise*, pp. 108–17.
[10] Bodleian Library, Oxford, Abinger MSS, dep. e. 196–211, Godwin's Diary. Quoted by kind permission of the Bodleian Library, Oxford.
[11] NLW 21286E, Letter no. 1017, Iolo Morganwg to Joseph Johnson, 9 January 1795.
[12] Williams: *PLP*, I, p. xiii.

learned customers'. He went on: 'I was yesterd[ay] at Mr Johnson St Paul's Church yard and he told [me] that Dr Geddes, Dr Aikin, and others of the first literary abilities spoke well of it and expressed a wish that I shou[ld] soon publish it.'[13] The preface to the published *Poems* confirms that the triads were included 'at the desire of some friends, substituted in the room of the poems that were originally intended'.[14] Given that publishers regularly puffed their own products in reviews they owned, it may be significant that it is the Welsh bardic rather than English pastoral aspect of the collection that was emphasized in the *Analytical Review*. Known for mixing business acumen with generosity, Johnson obviously thought bardism would sell. It is no surprise then to find Johnson's name at the top of the list of those collecting subscriptions for the projected *History of the Ancient British Bards and Druids* advertised at the end of *Poems, Lyric and Pastoral*. During October 1793, the same month that Iolo was showing his triads to Johnson, Blake issued a prospectus announcing the advent of his illuminated books.[15] Presumably if this sheet was available anywhere, it was to be found in Johnson's shop: at exactly the time we know that Iolo was showing his triads there. Given that Blake's illuminated books were available to be seen there by September 1794, it seems unlikely that Iolo did not at least see them at some stage in the 1793–4 period. Likewise, it is hard to believe that Blake was not exposed to the Welsh antiquities Iolo was showing Johnson and his literary friends. Over a decade later, Blake was to quote a Welsh triad in the description of his painting 'The Ancient Britons' given in *The Descriptive Catalogue* (1809). There he claimed that 'the British Antiquities are now in the Artist's hands'.[16] Critics have assumed that Blake's knowledge of 'the British Antiquities' was primarily limited to this later period, the most likely source being William Owen Pughe, a patron of Iolo, of course, but also the person who commissioned Blake's painting some time around 1806.[17] Arthur Johnston, for instance, pointed out that the triad quoted by Blake had not previously been published in English, but Iolo's letter (unknown it seems to Johnston) shows that manuscript translations of the triads were circulating around Johnson's circle in 1793. Johnston in fact suggested that Iolo had altered the triad in question by 1791, noting that he was the one Welshman

---

[13]   NLW 21285E, Letter no. 822, Iolo Morganwg to Margaret Williams, 30 October 1793.
[14]   Williams: *PLP*, I, p. xx.
[15]   Erdman (ed.), *Complete Poetry and Prose*, p. 692.
[16]   Ibid., p. 542.
[17]   See Johnston, 'Blake and "The Ancient Britons"', and Bentley, '"The Triumph of Owen"'. Bentley claims that, prior to 1800, Blake focused mainly on Christian and biblical history, but notes an interest in Gray's 'The Bard' from as early as 1780. Whether or not Iolo is the source, at the very least the representation of 'the Stone of Night' in Europe, for instance, was clearly derived from writings on Stonehenge and Druid ritual. On Blake and druidism more generally, see Jon Mee, *Dangerous Enthusiasm: William Blake and the Culture of Radicalism in the 1790s* (Oxford, 1992), pp. 89–100, 121–2.

who knew it intimately at this time.[18] Although not included among the triads published in the second volume of *Poems*, it seems perfectly possible, likely even, that Blake would have seen it in manuscript in 1793–4. Iolo had plenty of material of this sort which he did not include in the two published volumes of poetry. Circumstantial it may be, but the evidence suggests that Blake and Williams at the very least knew what each other was doing in the period 1793–5.

Both Iolo and Blake were presenting themselves as contemporary manifestations of ancient bardic genius. Blake also pointedly announced himself as 'printer' as well as 'author' on the title-page of *Songs*. Iolo identified his work as the 'unsophisticated productions of the *self-tutored Journeyman Mason*'.[19] Both men would have interested antiquarians such as Douce as manifestations of 'native genius', that is, bards who retained the authenticity associated with 'uneducated poets'. Iolo noted that it 'is a matter of no less *curiosity* than of *wonder* that it should not have been long ago noticed; but the *Ancient British Bardism* has for ages been in the hands of those who ranked not with the higher classes'.[20] Oral tradition had kept the bardic tradition alive in times of persecution. Over the previous decade, the radical antiquarian Joseph Ritson had been developing a theory that authentic British culture resided in the oral traditions of the people. Iolo knew Ritson. Blake, for his part, had engraved eight plates after Thomas Stothard for Ritson's *Select Collection of English Songs* (1783), another Johnson publication that Douce owned. Just like Iolo's Welsh bards, Ritson claimed his illiterate popular singers had been persecuted.[21] Unsurprisingly, coverage of Iolo in the *Analytical Review* also stressed this political aspect: 'These bards were sons of truth and liberty, and of course became offensive in ages of tyranny and superstition.' Iolo's claims to be a native genius in the line of popular tradition were confirmed:

> The author of these poems, though of humble birth, and by occupation a mason, ranks himself among the successors of the ancient British bards; and as far as a love of truth, natural sentiments, easy language, and harmonious versification can support the claim, his title is good. From the simple stock of his own observations, he writes pleasing pastorals, songs, and descriptions of nature; moralizes agreeably; and sometimes pours forth animated strains in the cause of freedom.[22]

---

[18] Johnston, 'Blake and "The Ancient Britons"', 309.
[19] Williams: *PLP*, I, p. xiii.
[20] Ibid., II, p. 161.
[21] See Joseph Ritson, *A Select Collection of English Songs* (3 vols., London, 1783), I, p. lii. For Ritson and Blake, see Mee, *Dangerous Enthusiasm*, pp. 112–16. There is a brief discussion of Iolo and Ritson on pp. 119–20, but at that stage I did not know that Iolo himself actually knew Ritson. I am grateful to Mary-Ann Constantine for this information.
[22] *Analytical Review*, XVIII (1794), 196–200.

In a sense Blake and Iolo were competing during this period for the same crowded space in London's expanding print culture. If Iolo posed as a Welsh character in the drawing rooms of the literary elite, Blake, too, seems to have adopted the English equivalent of this role in Harriet Mathew's salon in the early 1780s. The preface to *The Poetical Sketches* (1783), brought out at the expense of his patrons, describes him as 'untutored'.[23] In the *Gentleman's Magazine* letter, Iolo described himself as 'remarkably sober and temperate . . . cheerfully contented with his lot'.[24] Obviously he was alert to the fact that those who seemed to presume beyond their social station might be dismissed as 'impatient of honest industry', as Francis Jeffrey later dismissed Iolo's friend John Thelwall's poetic aspirations.[25] Anna Seward's response to Iolo's request for a subscription in July 1792, for instance, sounded precisely this note of warning in its 'concern that Nature made you the fatal present of a spirit, & an imagination so raised above the sphere in which you were destined to move'.[26] With Johnson there were presumably fewer pressures, but probably still an expectation of the appropriate 'bardic' performance. Yet, if both Iolo and Blake sometimes conformed to the cultural expectations of their social superiors, they were equally given to truculent declarations of independence. Neither man can have been easy to deal with on a personal level, given what we know of their temperaments, but the question of their self-fashioning in the context of an expanding print market will concern us later.

First, more needs to be said in detail by way of comparison of the creative engagement with the idea of the bard. Although bards are mentioned twice in Blake's early *Poetical Sketches* in a manner that suggests the influence of Gray, this aspect became much more prominent from *c*.1793 when Iolo was circulating his Welsh antiquities around Johnson's friends. In 1794 'The Voice of the Ancient Bard' of *Songs of Innocence* was supplemented by the 'Introduction' to 'Songs of Experience':

> Hear the voice of the Bard!
> Who Present, Past, & Future sees
> Whose ears have heard,
> The Holy Word,
> That walk'd among the ancient trees.
>
> Calling the lapsed Soul
> And weeping in the evening dew:

---

[23] See the discussion in Bentley, *The Stranger from Paradise*, pp. 73–5.

[24] *Gentleman's Magazine*, LIX, Part 2 (1789), 976–7.

[25] For Jeffrey's comment on Thelwall, see *Edinburgh Review*, II (1803), 200. On Iolo and Thelwall's friendship, see Damian Walford Davies, *Presences that Disturb: Models of Romantic Identity in the Literature and Culture of the 1790s* (Cardiff, 2002), pp. 136, 143, 164, 306–7.

[26] NLW 21282E, Letter no. 459, Anna Seward to Iolo Morganwg, 12 July 1792.

That might controll,
The Starry pole;
And fallen fallen light renew!

O Earth O Earth return!
Arise from out the dewy grass;
Night is worn,
And the morn
Rises from the slumberous mass.

Turn away no more:
Why wilt thou turn away
The starry floor
The watry shore
Is giv'n thee till the break of day.[27]

The plaintive call for a renewal of primal energy here has some close parallels with a stanza from Iolo's 'Escape from London':

Thus, tuning high prophetic strains,
Of *Heav'n* obey'd from pole to pole,
Whilst through my song the transport reigns,
Be this no dream to cheat my soul
Throng'd in my breast what wishes burn!
O! days of INNOCENCE! Return!
No more in vain let Nature call.[28]

The same note, but with a more pronounced political edge, is heard in Iolo's 'Ode on Converting a Sword into a Pruning Hook':

Aloud the trump of Reason calls;
The nations hear! The worlds attend!
Detesting now the craft of Kings,
Man from his hand the weapon flings;
. . .
Long has this *earth* a captive mourn'd,
But *days of old* are now return'd.[29]

Iolo's notes to these lines comment: 'the *Ancient of days* in the *Prophet Daniel* may, with some plausibility, be supposed to mean no more than the restoration of the primeval state of *Innocence*, *Peace*, and *Benevolence*'.[30] The design now called 'The Ancient of Days' is probably the best known of any image engraved

---

[27] Erdman (ed.), *Complete Poetry and Prose*, p. 18.
[28] Williams: *PLP*, II, pp. 44–5.
[29] Ibid., II, pp. 166–7.
[30] Ibid., II, p. 167.

by Blake. J. T. Smith claimed that Blake had a vision of the figure at the top of his staircase in Lambeth.[31] Presumably this was *c.*1793–4 because Blake first used it as the frontispiece to his prophecy *Europe* (1794). More explicitly political than the 'Introduction' to 'Experience', *Europe* offers a history of priestcraft which ends with a vision of its imminent destruction as the spirit of revolution spreads from 'the vineyards of red France'. Los, 'the immortal Bard' as he is called in *Jerusalem*, concludes the poem with what might be called a militant version of the call to renewal from the 'Introduction' to 'Songs of Experience':

> Then Los arose his head he reard in snaky thunders clad:
> And with a cry that shook all nature to the utmost pole,
> Call'd all his sons to the strife of blood.[32]

What really unites Iolo and Blake at this stage is this idea of the bardic spirit of liberty being available in the present: the urgent call to renewal that Blake's 'Introduction' and *Europe* share in their differing registers with Iolo's 'Escape from London' and the 'Ode'. Iolo uses the word 'renew' four times in his collection. It echoes through Blake's work of 1793–4, especially in *America* (1793), where Orc seeks to 'renew the fiery joy, and burst the stony roof'.[33] This does not mean that Blake borrowed from Iolo or vice versa. Rather, their poetry participated in a discourse of regeneration common to radical circles at the time, particularly those associated with Johnson's shop. Iolo insisted that 'the renovated state of religion, and of every thing else . . . is entirely subversive of all the present establishments in *Church and State*'.[34] These establishments were precisely the church's 'stony roof' that Orc sought to destroy in *America*. This idea of the bardic role being available as a political position in the present was the one that really distinguished them from many of the literary appropriations of northern antiquities at the time.

Poets such as Gray, whom Iolo detested for his conflation of what he regarded as the savagery of Scandinavian mythology with pure Welsh antiquities, treated the simple, sublime values and honest emotions they valued in northern antiquity as unavoidably locked in the past. Such qualities were a melancholy cost of progress. Despite the obvious attraction that Gray's primitivism held for Blake from very early on, he tended to go beyond its nostalgia for a lost past and look to the idea of a renewal in the present and future. The primitive style which Blake developed in the 1790s, moving away from the derivative forms of his *Poetical Sketches*, announced itself as a creative refoundation of the inspirational art of the past in his own time. 'Eternity' was a term

---

[31] Bentley, *The Stranger from Paradise*, p. 150.
[32] Erdman (ed.), *Complete Poetry and Prose*, p. 66.
[33] Ibid., p. 54.
[34] Williams: *PLP*, II, p. 162.

in Blake's lexicon that defied temporal limits: 'O Earth O Earth return!' Neither
described nor circumscribed; Eternity was fixed neither in the past nor in any
distant 'allegorical abode' (as he called it in *Europe*). The brief view we get of
Eternity at the beginning of *The Book of Urizen*, for instance, suggests a space
of infinitely active energies:

> Earth was not: nor globes of attraction
> The will of the Immortal expanded
> Or contracted his all flexible senses.
> Death was not, but eternal life sprung.[35]

These lines call to mind the account of the ultimate state of the bardic
metempsychosis in the *Heroic Elegies* which William Owen Pughe published
with Iolo's help: 'No finite beings can possibly bear the infinite tedium of
eternity. They will be relieved from it by continual renovations.'[36] Iolo later
wrote of God's ability 'to reform and renovate every thing without causing the
loss of it'.[37] So Los in Blake's poem *Milton* declares:

> I in Six Thousand Years walk up and down: for not one Moment
> Of Time is lost, nor one Event of Space unpermanent
> But all remain: every fabric of Six Thousand Years
> Remains permanent.[38]

Certainly both Iolo and Blake came to see the 'continual renovations' of the
bardic spirit as creating possibilities for utterance in the present. Blakean
'Eternity' could be characterized as a space in which the reader is invited to
join in the recreation of original vision. The content of Iolo's bardic vision
certainly bears striking similarities to the kinds of ideas circulating around
Johnson's shop at the time. Unitarianism frequently presented itself as
Christianity cleansed of the corruptions of priestcraft. Iolo presents the
'*Patriarchal Religion* of ANCIENT BRITAIN' in similar terms as a pure form
of belief 'no more inimical to CHRISTIANITY than the religion of NOAH,
JOB, or ABRAHAM'. Strange though it may sound, Iolo's 'divestigating, or
purifying, *Metempsychosis*' is compatible with David Hartley's *Observations of
Man*. Iolo states:

> The ultimate states of HAPPINESS are eternally undergoing the most delightful
> *renovations* in endless succession, without which no *Finite Being* could ever, consistent
> with happiness, endure the *taedium* of ETERNITY. These *renovations* will not, like
> the deaths of the lower states of existence, occasion a suspension of memory and
> consciousness of self-identity.[39]

---

[35] Erdman (ed.), *Complete Poetry and Prose*, p. 71.
[36] William Owen Pughe, *The Heroic Elegies and other Pieces of Llywarç Hen* (London, 1792), p. lix.
[37] Williams: *PLP*, II, p. 246.
[38] Erdman (ed.), *Complete Poetry and Prose*, p. 117.
[39] Williams: *PLP*, II, p. 194; I, p. xxi, and II, p. 197.

Ultimately for Hartley the doctrine of associations would draw all souls towards a union with God: 'all become . . . new sets of senses, and perceive powers, to each other, so as to increase each other's happiness without limits'.[40] Many of the principles set out in Blake's *The Marriage of Heaven and Hell* (1790–3) also seem congenial to this brand of religious thinking. 'The voice of the Devil' declares in Blake's book that 'Energy is Eternal Delight', just as the Printer's Devil intervenes to make subversive comments in several notes to Iolo's *Poems*. The Devil's perspective in *The Marriage* seems confirmed when Blake's Isaiah says:

> I saw no God. nor heard any, in a finite organical perception; but my senses discover'd the infinite in every thing, and as I was then perswaded. & remain confirm'd; that the voice of honest indignation is the voice of God, I cared not for consequences but wrote.[41]

In a similar way the essay that prefaced *Heroic Elegies* insisted on the synonymy of 'poetical genius', the 'Holy Spirit' and what the Welsh tradition called 'Awen' (Muse).[42] The thinking of neither poet can be neatly organized under any specific -ism, the eclecticism of their thought reflecting the instability of a period when all kinds of fundamental ideas seemed open for debate. One recalls the dinner mentioned in Godwin's diary in 1795 when Iolo and others associated with the Johnson circle gathered to 'to talk of God'.[43]

Quite apart from the content of their ideas, the urgency in Iolo and Blake's writing *c.*1793–5 could only have been intensified by the millenarian spirit abroad in London. The biblical aspect of both men's writing is important. For both of them, in this period and later, London often figures as a version of the Babylonian city of corruption overthrown to make way for the New Jerusalem in Revelation. Blake's 'London' in 'Songs of Experience', for instance, is an elliptical and nightmarish vision of a city where 'the hapless Soldiers sigh/ Runs in blood down Palace walls'.[44] Iolo's 'Escape from London' also imagines a scene 'drench'd in human gore'.[45] In 1799, writing to his friend George Cumberland as he was about to quit the city for the first and only time in his life, Blake used a very similar phrase to describe the city:

> Behind me at London resists every beam of light: hanging from heaven and Earth
> Dropping with human gore. Lo! I have left it! I have torn it from my limbs
> I shake my wings ready to take my flight! Pale, Ghastly pale: stands the City
>   in fear.[46]

---

[40] Quoted in Richard C. Allen, *David Hartley on Human Nature* (New York, 1999), p. 355. Allen draws numerous parallels with Blake's thinking in his impressive study.

[41] Erdman (ed.), *Complete Poetry and Prose*, pp. 34, 38.

[42] Pughe, *Heroic Elegies and other Pieces of Llywarç Hen*, p. lxiv.

[43] See note 10.

[44] Erdman (ed.), *Complete Poetry and Prose*, p. 27.

[45] Williams: *PLP*, II, p. 44.

[46] This letter has only recently been discovered. It was published for the first time in Robert N.

For both poets 'human gore' was strongly associated with the war policies of what Blake called 'State Religion'. Ironically, after 1800 this idea of perverted and deformed religious institutions became fixed in Blake's imagination with the idea of druidic sacrifice, but the more general idea of London as a place of enslavement and human sacrifice seems to have come to Blake's imagination between the publication of *Songs of Innocence* and 'Songs of Experience'. To a certain extent we can also see a darkening away from the pastoral in Iolo's *Poems, Lyric and Pastoral*, especially in his 'king-flogging notes'. The anti-monarchical flavour of these notes is shot through with the millenarian rhetoric ubiquitous in London between 1793 and 1795, especially in relation to the expectation of an apocalyptic destruction of the established church. Events in France were widely regarded as 'Signs of the Times' and even the rationally minded Unitarians associated with Joseph Johnson were alert to their millenarian significance. The most controversial figure at this period, however, was the so-called Paddington prophet Richard Brothers, who published a series of prophecies in 1794 warning the government against pursuing the war against France and prophesying the destruction of London through the wrath of God if it persisted in its policy. Iolo seems to have defended Brothers to Pitt. Joseph Johnson himself appears to have been interested in his fate. Although it was deeply sceptical as to self-proclaimed visionaries and prophets such as Brothers, usually regarding them as regrettable signs of unenlightened popular enthusiasm, the *Analytical Review* covered millenarian publications of all kinds closely in its reviews. For both popular and scholarly dissenting constituencies, two facts loomed large in the identification of London with Babylon: its involvement in the trafficking in slaves and its role in the military alliance of continental despots against France. The conjunction was a staple of the prophecies which made Brothers notorious in 1794–5. For both Iolo and Blake, too, the slave trade and 'the English Crusade against France' were deformations of the British spirit of liberty that provided contemporary equivalents of the children of Israel pursuing false gods and bloodthirsty idols.[47] Their role as self-proclaimed bard-prophets was to call their countrymen back to the true patriarchal religion untainted by the corruptions 'King & Priest'.[48] Iolo's interest in London's millenarian print culture continued even when he was trying to set up his own bookshop in Wales. In November 1795 he wrote to London to ask not only for the works of Tom Paine and a catalogue of Johnson's latest publications, but also one of the earlier classics of English millenarianism.[49] His request was for Garnet Terry's 1793 edition of Robert

---

Essick and Morton D. Paley, '"Dear Generous Cumberland": A Newly Discovered Letter and Poem by William Blake', *Blake Illustrated Quarterly*, XXXII (1998), 4–13.

[47] Erdman (ed.), *Complete Poetry and Prose*, p. 613.

[48] Ibid., p. 615.

[49] NLW 21414E, Letter no. 17a, Iolo Morganwg to (?) Joseph Johnson, 11 November 1795.

Fleming's *Apocalyptical key, an extraordinary discourse on the rise and fall of papacy.* Originally published in 1701 as an attack on Louis XIV, it was one of many seventeenth-century texts republished in various forms in the 1790s. Most of these were virulently anti-Catholic and represented the French monarchy as the epitome of Antichrist. The British war effort to restore the French monarchy was confirmation that Pitt's government was pushing the country towards Armageddon. Terry claimed that his edition had been published in response to popular demand 'on account of the Predictions it contains (tho' delivered near One Hundred Years since) respecting the Revolutions in France; the Fate of its Monarch; the Decline of the Papal Power: Together with the Fate of the surrounding Nations'.[50] Terry had been a failing engraver before becoming a bookseller-publisher and he drew and engraved the key that came with his copy of Fleming's predictions himself. Eventually Terry seems to have set up his own independent meeting house to expound his particular brand of Christianity. To an extent, like Blake and Iolo, he can be seen as a man of humble origins fired to think of himself as in a prophetic light. The broad sense of the career open to talents that inspired so many individuals of the lower ranks during the eighteenth century gained a particular, fierce impetus in the heady years of 1793–5. For men and women from humble social origins, such as Blake, Iolo and even Terry, the idea of a prophetic spirit that could manifest itself again in the present provided further encouragement for self-expression in an expanding print culture.

Publishing achieved a spectacular take-off in the early 1780s, precisely when both men seemed to have imagined careers as authors for themselves. Instead of a steady pattern of growth, there was a sudden explosion that sucked into London many of those who took literally the idea of the republic of letters. The bardism of Blake and Iolo perhaps represents a specific aspect of this literalism. What was, we might say, only a trope in Gray's poetry, incapable of becoming a practice in the present, becomes a form of energy that is capable of being exploited in self-fashioning by 'untutored' poets. As autodidacts, their authority as writers came from the continuing possibility of the bardic spirit being available to the 'natural genius'. Many seem to have believed with Edward Williams, when he sent his poems to magazines in the 1770s and 1780s, that there 'was nothing to stop anyone who can feel from springing into verse'.[51] Earlier in the same volume as Iolo's letter to the *Gentleman's Magazine*,

---

[50] Robert Fleming, *Apocalyptical Key: An Extraordinary Discourse on the Rise and Fall of Papacy; or the Pouring Out of the Vials, in the Revelation of St. John, Chap. XVI* (London, 1793). Terry makes his claim on the wrapper of the edition in the Bodleian Library at 101999.2.37 (20). This copy also includes the engraving of the 'Key'. For further information on Terry and his relations with Huntington, see Jon Mee, 'Is there an Antinomian in the House? William Blake and the After-Life of a Heresy' in Steve H. Clark and David Worrall (eds.), *Historicizing Blake* (Basingstoke, 1994), pp. 43–58.

[51] Judith Pascoe, *Romantic Theatricality: Gender, Poetry, and Spectatorship* (Ithaca, 1997), p. 79.

for instance, another contributor commented: 'A few years back a self-taught bard would have been looked upon by the publick almost as a prodigy, but of late they grow so fast upon us, that few think them worthy their regard.' Even so, the contributor decided 'notwithstanding which, I am now preparing to add one to the number, who, I am half persuaded, has equal claim to the patronage of a generous publick as a Burns or a Yearsley'.[52] Obviously Blake and Iolo also believed that there was still room for one more. Buoyed by this faith, Edward Williams was eventually able to transform himself into Iolo Morganwg. William Blake the engraver becomes a prophet able to recapture the spirit of patriarchal religion in his illuminated books. This point about self-fashioning is not primarily about literary creation in a narrow sense. Access to print culture in whatever form offered the prospect of real mobility. Iolo's re-creation of himself as a Welsh bard gave him access to the elite of the literary world and the prospect of making his fortune through subscription publishing. The writing of both men was frequently prickly with the sense of independence and ultimately social and artistic aspiration. Many of those drawn to London in the 1790s by their literary aspirations responded with predictable if changeable enthusiasm to a fast-developing political situation, but also – as again with Blake and Iolo – often read these events as a sign of a time of the imminent renovation of an ancient state of liberty.

'Energy' indeed was a keyword in the writing of this period. Blake's *The Marriage of Heaven and Hell* proclaimed it 'Eternal delight': 'Energy is the only life and is from the Body and Reason is The bound or outward circumference of Energy.'[53] The idea of metempsychosis at the heart of Iolo's bardic religion also suggested a universe of perpetually circulating energies, continually taking on embodied forms: 'the soul is an inconceivably minute particle of the most refined matter, is necessarily endued with life, and never dies'.[54] Again and again the idea of an open circulation was celebrated in the poetry and prose of radical opinion between 1789 and 1794. For Edmund Burke this writing celebrated a principle of energy for its own sake: opinion rather than knowledge, he feared, was becoming the lifeblood of the nation. Looking at the thematic ubiquity of 'energy' in the radical writing of the period, we can see the source of his fears. Robert Merry's anniversary ode at the meeting of the 'Friends of Liberty' at the Crown and Anchor in 1791, for instance, provides a case in point:

> Fill high the animating glass,
> And let the electric ruby pass
> From hand to hand, from soul to soul;

---

[52] *Gentleman's Magazine*, LXI, Part 2 (1789), 36–7.
[53] Erdman (ed.), *Complete Poetry and Prose*, p. 34.
[54] Williams: *PLP*, II, p. 201.

> Who shall the energy controul.
> Exalted, pure, refin'd,
> The Health of Humankind![55]

Universal benevolence was imagined by Merry as an 'energy' that could communicate itself beyond all barriers, that is, what Burke feared as a virus capable of making 'a kind of electrick communication everywhere'.[56] Horace Walpole traced Merry's ideas back to Joseph Johnson's best-known author Joseph Priestley at 'the new Birmingham warehouse of the original Maker'.[57] There may be little in Merry that would interest the serious Priestley scholar, but there is no doubt that the idea of an animated universe driven by electrical energies was what many writers from this period took from Hartley and Priestley (often extending to a literal interest in the animating power of electricity explored in Priestley's scientific writings). Iolo's version of metempsychosis in terms of Unitarian ideas of the progress of the individual towards God would seem to be another example of the same reflex derived ultimately from Hartley's theory of association: 'All animated beings originate in the *lowest point of existence* (ANNWN), whence, by a regular gradation, they rise higher in the scale of existence till they arrive at the highest state of *happiness* and *perfection* that is possible for finite beings.' '*Eternal Misery*', Iolo believed with Hartley, 'is a thing impossible.'[58] Samuel Taylor Coleridge, who at the time was a fervent disciple of Hartley's thinking, owned a copy of *Poems, Lyric and Pastoral*, which he annotated. His various negotiations with the Unitarian tradition in his poetry of the 1790s were also part of an attempt to think of a universe in motion towards God, though as the decade went on he was to become increasingly concerned that the valorization of energy in radical writing was in danger of collapsing the Creator into his creation. Another aspect of the same conservative reflex which developed in Coleridge was his anxiety at the proliferation of authors, upstart pretenders to what he deemed the authentic power of the Imagination. Even at his most sympathetic, Coleridge tended to refer to Iolo in a patronizing tone as 'poor Williams' or 'the poor Welch bard'.[59] Coleridge's later anxieties about the degeneration of literary culture were anticipated by Burke's reaction to the energies released by events in France. Burke's *Reflections* were a clarion call for a cultural retreat.

---

[55]   Robert Merry, *Ode for the Fourteenth of July, 1791* (London, 1791), pp. 6–7.
[56]   Edmund Burke, *The French Revolution 1790–1794*, ed. L. G. Mitchell (Oxford, 1989), pp. 97–8.
[57]   Lewis Bettany (ed.), *Edward Jerningham and his Friends: A Series of Eighteenth-century Letters* (London, 1919), p. 50.
[58]   Williams: *PLP*, II, pp. 195, 197.
[59]   For a full discussion of relations between Iolo and Coleridge, see Walford Davies, *Presences that Disturb*, pp. 167–76, though he sees Coleridge's response to Iolo more sympathetically than I do in terms of a 'poignant human focus of competing ethical and political ideologies', p. 174.

The prospects held out to men such as Iolo and Blake of a career open to talents were in part the casualties of this reaction.

Of course, the literary market place may have seemed to be an open public sphere that encouraged people of talent from whatever background, but it had always been strewn with invisible barriers of class, education and manner. These barriers were imposed with a new vigour reinforced by the coercive institutions of the state in the 1790s. From 1792 John Reeves and his Association against Republicans and Levellers, the target of Iolo's vituperation on more than one occasion, saw to that, but self-fashioning had never been simply a matter of free will. Even in more liberal circles, collectors such as Douce, whatever their politics, were prone to present such men as specimens, and in order to gain access to a polite subscribers one often had to conform to ideas of literary style and social deference, as Mary-Ann Constantine's chapter in this volume reveals. Both Iolo and Blake at different times in their lives complained of 'friends' and patrons who were really enemies to their creativity. Writing after the poems came out to John Walters on 21 January 1794, Iolo suggested that he had muzzled his opinions to gain the approbation of the great and the good (and the patronage of the Prince of Wales in particular). He spoke of a desire 'to abet the cause of truth, Justice, and humanity, a cause to which I long to be a martyr', but he seemed anxious about whether radical 'impudence' was more or less likely to gain him financial reward:

> Tom Paine ran in six months thro' more than twenty editions, but I am not Tom Paine yet, and for the sake of my little Children to whom a father will, for a little while, be better than money, I will not endeavour to be so till I am in America; and there I will publish my Kingcraft versus Christianity.[60]

Only four years after Iolo wrote this letter, Blake, siding with Tom Paine against Richard Watson, bishop of Llandaf, described Paine as 'a worker of miracles' for the success of defeating 'all the armies of Europe with a small pamphlet'. By 1798, however, Blake was convinced that the 'Beast & the Whore rule without controls'. Joseph Johnson was arrested in 1798 and imprisoned for publishing an anti-war tract written by Iolo's friend Gilbert Wakefield. No wonder that Blake believed that 'to defend the Bible in this year 1798 would cost a man his life'.[61] How different things had seemed when he announced the project of the illuminated books in 1793. Blake obviously proudly believed he had found of way of circumventing the middle man which did not involve the compromises of subscription publishing: 'No Subscriptions for the numerous great works now in hand are asked, for none

---

[60] NLW 21285E, Letter no. 826, Iolo Morganwg to John Walters, 21 January 1794.
[61] Erdman (ed.), *Complete Poetry and Prose*, pp. 617, 611.

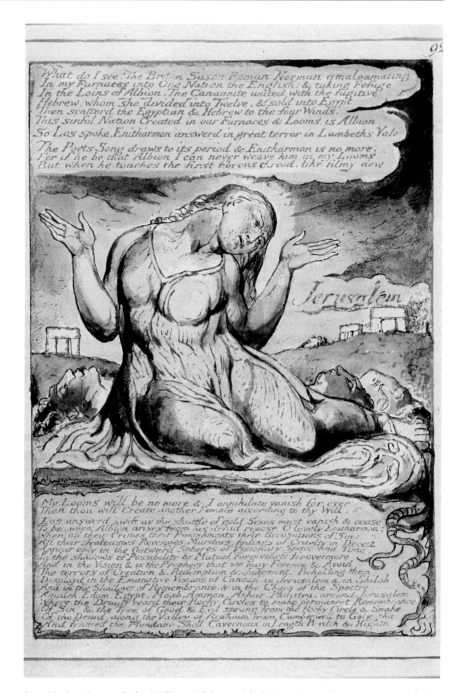

Fig. 10 A print made by William Blake, entitled 'Jerusalem: The Emanation of The Giant Albion'. A relief etching with black ink and grey wash, 1804.

are wanted; but the Author will produce his works, and offer them to sale at a fair price.'[62] The sense of infinite possibility captured in the confident rhetoric of the 1793 prospectus, however, was not to last out the decade. No less than Iolo, Blake was to come to feel that political circumstances in general and the publishing trade in particular were making London a dark dungeon. Even Joseph Johnson, Blake believed in 1799, was too inclined to encourage him to stick to what he knew – his trade as an engraver – rather than aspire to the status of bardic artist:

> As to Myself about whom you are so kindly Interested. I live by Miracle. I am Painting small Pictures from the Bible. For as to Engraving in which art I cannot reproach myself with any neglect yet I am laid by in a corner as if I did not Exist & Since my Youngs Night Thoughts have been publishd Even Johnson & Fuseli have discarded my Graver.[63]

In 1803 he was to complain to his patron Thomas Butts that Johnson had wanted to keep him to the 'mere drudgery of business', that is, to keep to his trade of engraving rather than aspiring to be a poet and painter.[64]

Yet, by taking the publishing process entirely into his own hands and printing the illuminated books for himself, Blake may have given himself more freedom to experiment than Iolo. Mary-Ann Constantine has remarked on the derivative nature of much of the poetry in *Poems, Lyric and Pastoral*. Iolo may have experienced London as a nightmare, but 'Stanzas written in London in 1773', for instance, do not have the same kind of apocalyptic ellipsis that makes Blake's 'London' such a powerful poetic statement. Perhaps it is unfair to compare a poem from 1773 with Blake's great poem of 1794, but Iolo probably revised his right up to the eve of publication. Certainly 'Stanzas' seems to express the despair Iolo often felt about London after 1792, but without communicating the stark sense of dread which pervades Blake's night-marish poem. Possibly, as Constantine suggests, Iolo was too aware of the taste of English literary figures such as Anna Seward and Hannah More in his subscription list to give himself the kind of freedom he seems to have taken for himself in his Welsh writing. For all we know, the Johnson circle, on the other hand, may have found Blake's poetry too innovative. Their house journal, the *Analytical Review*, could praise Iolo's 'simple stock of pleasing pastorals and songs' but, strangely, given that they were on display in Johnson's shop, the

---

[62] Ibid., p. 693.
[63] Ibid., p. 704.
[64] Ibid., p. 724. To be fair to Johnson, he remained solicitous of Blake's welfare. He wrote to William Hayley on 4 January 1802 to say that 'since I have had a connection with Mr Blake I have wished to serve him & on every occasion endeavoured to do so. I wish him to be paid for what he is doing now a fair & even a liberal price'. Quoted in Bentley, *The Stranger from Paradise*, p. 108.

Analytical Review never gives any of Blake's poetry any mention.[65] They may have been deemed too singular to live up to what was expected of the 'untutored' poet. Writing to a puzzled clergyman in August 1799, Blake told him that 'you ought to know that What is Grand is necessarily obscure to Weak men. That which can be made Explicit to the Idiot is not worth my care. The wisest of the Ancients considerd what is not too Explicit as the fittest for Instruction because it rouzes the faculties to act'.[66] By deliberately insulting a potential patron, Blake here showed little of the flickering spirit of compromise found in Iolo's letters to Hannah More.

Both poets represented themselves in their collections of 1794 as seeking a new enlightenment to dispel the clouds and darkness of the past. This familiar combination of metaphors recurs in both *Poems, Lyric and Pastoral* and *Songs of Innocence and of Experience*, but the clouds that obscure the truth are never 'clouds of reason' in Iolo's poetry as they are in Blake's 'Introduction'. For Blake, from early on in his writing, there is sense of the way that even the Enlightenment commitment to Reason and Truth could perpetuate what it was meant to be dispelling and become merely a new form of mystification. Blake's antagonism to system was founded on the perception that any truth could ossify into error where it was convinced of its own certainty. Both men strove in a sense to create their own systems in resistance to what they saw as the dungeon of state religion centred in the prison-house of London. Iolo went so far as to forge documents to support his version of Welsh antiquity. In the epic poem *Jerusalem*, Blake has Los declare:

> I must Create a System, or be enslav'd by another Mans
> I will not Reason & Compare: my business is to Create.[67]

Yet Los himself frequently becomes entangled in his own creations and continually has to renew the struggle against his own tendency towards self-righteousness. System for Blake was, therefore, both enabling and potentially enslaving. The incorporation of the 'British Antiquities' in his later work played off this idea in the tension between a druidic code of religion and the freedom of the bardic imagination. Although he could imagine Druids and bards as almost synonymous, the former were strongly associated with the priestly appropriation of the visionary imagination.[68] For Iolo, on the other hand, 'the *Patriarchal Religion* of ANCIENT BRITAIN' was venerated as a template for the 'renovated state of religion'. Iolo contrasted the '*rational, sublime,* and *congenial*' forms of druidism with 'the *superlatively barbarous* and *bloody Theology* of

---

[65] *Analytical Review*, XVIII (1794), 196.
[66] Erdman (ed.), *Complete Poetry and Prose*, p. 702.
[67] Ibid., p. 153.
[68] See the discussion of this point in Mee, *Dangerous Enthusiasm*, pp. 90–1.

the EDDA, which *some depraved imaginations* are so charmed with'.[69] Druidism kept alive a spirit of rational religion against 'the Church of Rome' and its persecuting spirit. So, for Iolo, it was opposed to priestcraft: it was simply the branch of bardism concerned with religion and ceremonies according to the *Heroic Elegies* volume.[70] The content of much of Iolo's thinking seems very close to that of Blake, but the latter seems to have remained much more fundamentally opposed to any religious institutions as such:

> The Bible or <Peculiar> Word of God, Exclusive of Conscience or the Word of God Universal, is that Abomination which like the Jewish ceremonies is for ever removed & henceforth every man may converse with God & be a King & Priest in his own house.[71]

From this perspective, Blake seems to have been much less obsessed with the founding authority of a particular tradition than Iolo:

> Read the Edda of Iceland the Songs of Fingal the accounts of North American Savages (as they are calld) Likewise Read Homers Iliad. he was certainly a Savage. in the Bishops sense. He knew nothing of God. in the Bishops sense of the word & yet he was no fool.[72]

'Druid Temples' become the holy places of an authoritarian code of war that demands human sacrifice in Blake's later prophecies, a code perpetuated in the judicial victims of the eighteenth century sacrificed to the state at 'Tyburn's Fatal Tree'. Although there is no explicit connection with the Druids in Blake's work *c.*1793–4, the account of the 'Stone of Night' in *Europe* has some parallels to the description in the *Heroic Elegies* of the druidic '*Stone of the Assembly*'.[73] In fact, the parallel between the human sacrifices carried out by the Druids and the eighteenth-century criminal code was also made by Iolo. The essay which William Owen Pughe wrote with Iolo's help pointed out that 'the human sacrifices were criminals, to appease divine justice. These victims are still devoted, perhaps in greater numbers, in *London*, and other great towns'.[74] Yet it is not obvious whether this comment was meant to be a defence of druidism or an indictment of eighteenth-century justice. The rest of the note implies the former: 'most authors have always unaccountably added the epithet *horrid* to these druidical sacrifices, whenever they have had occasion to mention them, seemingly without ever thinking of its propriety or otherwise'.

---

[69] Williams: *PLP*, II, pp. 194–5.
[70] Pughe, *Heroic Elegies and other Pieces of Llywarç Hen*, p. xxxviii.
[71] Erdman (ed.), *Complete Poetry and Prose*, p. 615.
[72] Ibid.
[73] Ibid., p. 64 and Pughe, *Heroic Elegies and other Pieces of Llywarç Hen*, pp. xlvi–xlviin.
[74] Pughe, *Heroic Elegies and other Pieces of Llywarç Hen*, p. xxxin.

There could be no propriety to judicial murder for Blake: 'Adam was a Druid, and Noah; also Abraham was called to succeed to the Druidical age, which began to turn allegoric and mental signification into corporeal command, whereby human sacrifice would have depopulated the earth.'[75] He seems to have agreed with Iolo that druidism was originally identical with the religion of the patriarchs, but that it fell into priestcraft and barbarity when it substituted 'forms of worship' for 'poetic tales'. Druidism for Blake was increasingly associated with an oppressive scriptural certainty rather than a more discursive and metaphorical ('allegoric and mental') approach to truth.

Iolo argued that:

> Truth was held so sacred by the ancient British Bards and Druids, that they would never admit into their poetical compositions any thing whatever of a fictitious nature; their fundamental maxim was to search for truth, and to adhere to it, with the most rigid severity.

He went on to declare that 'we meet not with a single poem founded on fiction; and, singular as it may appear, contrary to the practice of all other nations, the most authentic histories of the *Welsh* are in *verse*, and all their *fabulous* writings in *prose*'.[76] Iolo was obsessed with tradition to the extent that he was willing to invent it to give authority to his own powerful imagination. The literalism of Iolo's idea of truth would have been uncongenial to Blake, who wrote:

> I cannot concieve the Divinity of the <books in the>Bible to consist either in who they were written by or at what time or in the historical evidence which may be all false in the eyes of one man & true in the eyes of another but in the Sentiments & Examples which whether true or Parabolic are Equally useful as Examples given to us of the perverseness of some & its consequent evil & the honesty of others & its consequent good This sense of the Bible is equally true to all & equally plain to all. none can doubt the impression which he recieves from a book of Examples.[77]

Unlike Tom Paine, Blake believed that the Bible's status as a work of imagination did not undermine its truth. He used the 'British Antiquities . . . now in the Artist's hands' to create both the imaginative history of 'The Ancient Britons' and the mythic narrative of his epic *Jerusalem*. Neither pretended to give the literal truth of ancient Britain or of any other times. Blake's historical imagination was suspicious of any forgetting that 'All deities reside in the human breast'.[78] Iolo, in contrast, increasingly presented druidism as the only authentic version of patriarchal religion. Not only did he forge triads to prove

75 Erdman (ed.), *Complete Poetry and Prose*, pp. 542–3.
76 Williams: *PLP*, II, p. 2.
77 Erdman (ed.), *Complete Poetry and Prose*, p. 618.
78 Ibid., p. 38.

the historical veracity of his account of bardic mythology, he also instituted in the Gorsedd of the Bards a new church of rites and rituals which he claimed enshrined the true druidic religion. In *Jerusalem*, by way of stark contrast, the iconoclasm of Jesus destroys 'the whole Druid Law', a phrase that by this stage had become a synecdoche for the tyranny of 'state religion'. When comparing Blake with Iolo in this respect, one recalls the disillusionment with Swedenborg set out on Plate 21 of *The Marriage of Heaven and Hell*: 'Swedenborg boasts that what he writes is new; tho' it is only the Contents or Index of already publish'd books.' 'The Whole of the New Church', he wrote in some angry marginalia to Swedenborg's *Divine Love*, 'is in the Active Life & not in Ceremonies at all.' Swedenborg fulfilled the archetype of the reformer who became convinced of his own infallibility: 'It is so with Swedenborg; he shews the folly of churches & exposes hypocrites, till he imagines that all are religious. & himself the single One on earth that ever broke a net.'[79] Blake increasingly revisited this theme in terms of the bardic fall into druidic religion. Without suggesting that this development is in any way a commentary on Iolo himself, Blake was alert to the way that the inventions of the imagination, even in their declarations of a spirit of renewal, could harden into new forms of scriptural authority. If Blake was not without a tincture of monomania in his own writing, he was less inclined than Iolo to present his imaginative insights as literal 'images of truth new born'.

---

[79]   Ibid., pp. 223, 42, 605, 43.

III. Iolo's Preoccupations

9

*Iolo Morganwg: Stonecutter, Builder, and Antiquary**

RICHARD SUGGETT

'To Edward Williams, carver, at Mr Brooks, Iron Monger & Carpenter, near the Long Church, Wells, Somersetshire' (1785); 'To Mr Edward Williams, stone-cutter, statuary etc., Flimston' (1798); 'To Edward Williams, marble-mason at Flimston' (1803). It was only latterly that Iolo Morganwg's letters were addressed to Edward Williams, bard, at Bardic Lodge, Flimston. Posterity knows Edward Williams of Flemingston (or Flimston) as Iolo Morganwg, bard, radical and Romantic. A few scholars knew Iolo as Mr Williams the antiquary, but to most of his Glamorgan contemporaries he was simply Ned Williams the stone-cutter. Iolo was a mason and for much of his working life a tramping artisan. The best-known depiction of him shows a sturdy pedestrian clasping a tall walking-stick, with a large satchel for tools and papers draped over one shoulder. Ned the mason supported Iolo the writer until sensitivity to the stonecutter's fine dust forced him to lay aside the mason's mallet and chisel; in later life the asthmatic Iolo could find sleep only in a chair.[1] The late eighteenth century was a period of high craft skills and the discipline of Iolo's mason's work may be contrasted with the apparent chaos of his literary and antiquarian side. This was part of the tension between building castles in the air and erecting cottages on the rock, to which Prys Morgan has directed our attention.[2] Iolo constantly used building metaphors in his poems, and to describe his literary labour, most poignantly in his own mock epitaph: 'In memory of Edward Williams . . . mason, whose building lies here in ruins.'[3] To understand Iolo the poet, we also have to know Edward Williams the mason.

---

[*] The many facets of Iolo's character and the sheer quantity of his manuscripts can be overwhelming, but I have been fortunate to benefit from the research of the Iolo Morganwg Project team at the University of Wales Centre for Advanced Welsh and Celtic Studies. I am indebted to G. J. Williams's *Iolo Morganwg: Y Gyfrol Gyntaf* (1956), as well as to contributions to specialist themes by Howard Thomas and Prys Morgan. I am very conscious that part of this paper covers ground which Prys Morgan has discussed in an unpublished lecture entitled 'Cestyll yn yr Awyr: Castles in the Air', and I thank him for his interest in this chapter.

[1] *RAEW*, p. 23.

[2] Morgan: *IM*, chapters I, II.

[3] Cathryn Charnell-White, *Barbarism and Bardism: North Wales versus South Wales in the Bardic Vision of Iolo Morganwg* (Aberystwyth, 2004), pp. 23–4.

Iolo self-consciously described himself as Edward Williams, 'Journeyman Mason', in proposals for publishing his poems in English.[4] A journeyman was qualified to work for another for a daily wage; the journeyman had generally served an apprenticeship and, with luck and perseverance, he eventually became a master with a workshop. Within the masons' craft there were numerous trades: rough-masons (who erected walling), freestone masons, and the letter-cutters, marble-masons and statuaries who specialized in inscriptions, carved ornament and sculpture.[5] These were trades of increasing skill and remuneration. Iolo aspired to be a letter-cutter and carver, but did not serve a formal apprenticeship. He and his three younger brothers were brought up in the masons' trade by their father, Edward William(s) Senr., a farmer's son, who had completed his own apprenticeship in 1738.[6] In the building trades, craft skills were often family-based and might extend over several generations. Edward William's surviving accounts show that he ran a family firm, often working on local estates with his four sons, an apprentice or journeyman, and sometimes employing his brother Rowland ('Rowley') as a workman. They undertook all types of building work: new building, repairs, plastering, limewashing, as well as making and inscribing tombstones.[7]

Iolo had an aptitude for letter cutting and carving. By his own account, he learned the alphabet by seeing his father inscribe gravestones, and by the age of nine he began to work with him and to 'cut letters on stone, attempted carving etc'.[8] There seems no reason to doubt that the carved head still at Flemingston (reset on a nineteenth-century farm building) derived from Edward William's workshop and is probably Iolo's own work.[9] The carving is an unfinished version of a winged cherub, ubiquitous on eighteenth-century memorials, and among the first motifs that Iolo would have mastered, as indeed some early pencil drawings show.[10]

---

[4] NLW 21392F, p. 66; NLW 13106B, p. 141.

[5] The indispensable guide to the building crafts in the eighteenth century is James Ayres, *Building the Georgian City* (London, 1998).

[6] NLW 21410E, no. 2.

[7] Williams: *IM*, p. 108; see accounts in NLW 21412E, esp. nos. 2–7. When working at day-rates, Edward William's charges were 1s. 6d. for himself as master, 1s. 4d. for his sons and the workman, and 8d. for the apprentice.

[8] NLW 21387E, no. 2.

[9] As suggested by Aneirin Talfan Davies, *Crwydro Bro Morgannwg. Cyfrol I* (Abertawe, 1972), p. 64. The farm building was a granary belonging to Gregory Farm and was built on or near the site of Iolo's cottage. It has been converted to a house called 'Church Barn' and the head reset over the new front doorway.

[10] There are several early pencil drawings of memorials with winged cherubs in NLW 21417E, nos. 20–1, 23. A winged cherub in the same style as the Flemingston head, with some interesting vernacular decorative motifs, is carved on the Wathan family memorial on the south wall of Llantwit Major parish church, and was presumably carved in Edward William's workshop.

Fig. 11 A carved head re-set over the doorway of Church Barn, a former farmbuilding at Gregory Farm, Flemingston, built on the site of Iolo Morganwg's cottage. The head is not a self-portrait by Iolo, as is sometimes supposed, but a trial carving of the winged cherub motif often used on tombstones.

In 1770, when Iolo was twenty-three, his mother died and, three years later, he 'endeavoured to fly from sorrow by flying from home' to London, where he studied buildings and architecture, especially 'knowledge of sculpture which I had attempted in Wales'.[11] He began a period as a tramping artisan which was to last intermittently for some twenty years until he returned permanently to Glamorgan sometime after the publication of *Poems, Lyric and Pastoral* (1794). In the extraordinary preface to this anthology, Iolo the poet wrote: 'It is of no importance to any one to know how many stones I hewed, or on how many grave-stones I have inscribed vile doggrel.'[12] On the contrary, this period is fascinating to the architectural historian because there are so few biographical accounts of the itinerant mason, the backbone of the Georgian building trades. Georgian craftsmen are generally just names that appear and disappear in

---

[11] NLW 13106B, pp. 175–6; Williams: *PLP*, I, p. xvi; cf. Williams: *IM*, p. 166.
[12] Williams: *PLP*, I, p. xvii.

building accounts. Any connected account of a craftsman's working life is a rarity, and the biographical materials for Iolo the mason are exceptionally rich.

The compressed chronology in *Poems, Lyric and Pastoral* of Iolo's early adult working life can be refined and amplified from his letters. In 1773 Iolo and his brothers went to London to master their trades and to see something of the world. It was the beginning of much travelling that led to the brothers going their separate ways. Iolo 'rambled' (a favourite term) between Bristol, Bath, London, Kent, Dorset, Devon and Somerset, sometimes meeting up with his brothers and returning to Glamorgan. The Severn estuary offered easy communications between south Wales and the West Country quarries and workshops. Bath and Bristol, as well as London, were centres of fashionable and skilful statuary work, where experience with many different types of stone could be acquired. 'In my trade', Iolo remembered, 'I was always pushing forward. Having acquired what knowle[d]ge of one branch that I though[t] necessary, I would aspire to something higher. This passion kept me always poor.'[13]

It is not improbable that Iolo found work in one of the statuary workshops clustered at Hyde Park Corner. Stone carving was carried out in 'shops' (rather than on site), where numerous journeymen and apprentices worked under masters and their foremen. We should imagine Iolo in a 'shop' at his 'banker' (stone bench) with a mallet and chisel producing dressed-stone work at piece-work rates.[14] But he found himself 'continually among a vile debauched race of men' at odds with his 'love of sobriety and tranquillity'. His fellow-masons 'were continually committing depredations either on their masters, their fellow workmen or at the houses where they were sent to work'. Iolo refused to join in these thefts, and as a consequence some of his workmates 'seldom failed to bring on a misunderstanding, between me and my master'.[15] In 1773–4 he made his way to Kent, where he remained for three years, and found his passion for poetry revived with 'a return to rural objects'.[16] Iolo worked in Dover, but moved on to the workshop of Mr Davison, a stonecutter at Sandwich, where there were many hands at work. Iolo amused himself by satirizing the 'red-headed sons of Kent' in scatological *englynion*, but complained that he had little real leisure: 'At night I have so much writing work, and somtimes drawing, for my Master, that I have no time to do any thing for my self.'[17]

[13] NLW 21387E, no. 35.
[14] Plain work was paid for at 1s. per foot; mouldings at 3s. per foot. Cf. NLW 21417E, nos. 27, 33.
[15] NLW 21387E, no. 33.
[16] NLW 13106B, pp. 175–6; Williams: *IM*, p. 223.
[17] NLW 21285E, Letter no. 773, Iolo Morganwg to Edward William[s], 13 September 1774. NLW 13150A, pp. 3–4, has memoranda concerning Iolo's work in Kent (Lynsted, Sittingbourne, Queenborough) in May of an unspecified year.

We should not accept Iolo's account of his difficulties with other journeymen without also remembering that his song-writing talent would have made him a popular companion, even if he had reservations about the sociability of the tavern. There were accordingly 'many pressing invitations to join the pot-companionships of persons in his own humble sphere', though he claimed to have remained abstemious in the public tap-room.[18] His 'Stonecutter's Song', possibly written to entertain the Hyde Park Corner masons, begins in jolly fashion:

> A young stonecutter once did in Westminster dwell,
> Who for mirth and good humour did many excel,
> No lad more expert wielded chisel and mallet,
> He could sing a good song and eke make a new ballet.

The cheerful stonecutter is:

> Content in his station as great as a king
> And liberty always inspired him to sing.
> But the polish of bliss sad misfortune will fret
> Like Plaister of Paris exposed to the wet.

The stonecutter is smitten by 'a smart dory' called Celia: 'Her skin like Carara so white and so sleek/ The blush of the Jasper enamel'd her cheek'; her eyes were glossier than agate, 'more black than Vamure'. Tragedy ensues.[19] The sentimental depiction of the mason is maintained in Iolo's 'Cân y Maensaer, neu'r Maensaer mwyn' (The Stonemason's Song, or the gentle Stonemason), a song Iolo claimed as traditional.[20] However, Iolo's published 'Song . . . *for the Use of a little select* SOCIETY OF JOURNEY-MEN MASONS' has a radical edge. This 'rational' drinking song was apparently written in 1785 for journeymen masons who met weekly 'to spend a cheerful Hour at the moderate, and restricted, expence of fourpence'. The journeymen gathered in the tavern after work:

> The day was quite cold, and our toil very hard,
> But purse-cramming masters pay little regard,
> Yet night is our own, it gives freedom and rest,
> Come, ruby-fac'd landlord, a pot of your best.

The tone of the song becomes more radical: the masons sing 'Though poor in this world, we're of honest report;/ I wish it were thus with some *great ones* at

---

[18] Benjamin H. Malkin, *The Scenery, Antiquities, and Biography, of South Wales* (London, 1804), p. 128. Cf. also the song and rules for 'The Drive Away Care Club', Faversham, 1775: NLW 21421E, no. 13.

[19] NLW 21392F, no. 73. Unfortunately, many of the stanzas are rather faint.

[20] Printed in *CRhIM*, pp. 45–7.

Court.' The masons 'know nothing of Kings', but toast only those that have 'brighten'd the gloom of our lives'.[21]

Journeymen were expected to be able to read and write instructions, and to draw up accounts. Iolo was, of course, supremely literate, but the correspondence between the Williams brothers shows the practical importance of literacy to the travelling craftsman as a means of retaining links with home and gaining news of jobs. Sometimes the correspondents needed to be cautious. Thomas asked Iolo in 1785 to write all 'secrets' in Welsh since a letter describing a (business) disappointment at Devizes had been opened by one William Hegins (possibly a rival carver), who 'continually watched for letters'.[22] Thomas sent several letters from Moor Crichel, near Wimborne, Dorset, where he was working on the rebuilding of Crichel House for Humphrey Sturt between 1776 and 1780. At Crichel, as with other large country house projects, there would have been interaction between architect, contractor, and craftsmen. The building work at Crichel House was undertaken by the famous Bastards of Blandford, mason-builders, probably to the designs of James Wyatt, who was engaged to provide the decorative scheme. Craftsmen, presumably including Thomas Williams, were recruited in 1776 by advertisements placed in *The Salisbury Journal*.[23] Thomas's letters show that he expected to be involved with the geometrical stair and to fetch stone from Portland. He erected a chimney-piece in the bathing-house which gave Sturt and his family 'great satisfaction', and also laid a floor (for which he was apparently not paid). Iolo was familiar with the work at Crichel House and, certainly in 1780, he was measuring his brother's freestone work in Dorset.[24] A few years later Thomas had established a workshop at Wells, Somerset.

Most journeymen, we may suppose, were ambitious to become a master with a workshop, but the step could be precarious. Iolo hoped to set up as a marble-mason in south Wales, where there was little competition. He made several attempts, beginning at Flemingston in 1779, and then, having married, at St Mary Church and Cowbridge. In 1783 he leased a derelict site in Cardiff, intending to erect a workshop for his business as a marble- and freestone mason. The workshop was never built, however, and in 1785 Iolo took over his brother's business in Wells. He laid in a small stock of country marble for tombstones and advertised for business, using his brother's established name,

---

[21] Williams: *PLP*, II, pp. 80–4. The song was probably radicalized for publication.

[22] NLW 21285E, Letter no. 718, Thomas Williams to Iolo Morganwg, 14 October 1785. An undated letter from Thomas Williams says that Iolo could have work in the 'marble way' at Devizes for 15s. a week: NLW 13159A, pp. 131, 140.

[23] John Cornforth, 'The Building of Crichel' in *Design and Practice in British Architecture: Studies in Architectural History presented to Howard Colvin, Architectural History*, 27 (1984), 268–9; H. Avray Tipping, 'Crichel, Dorset: The Seat of Lord Allington', *Country Life*, LVII (1925), 766–74, 814–23, 874–81.

[24] Williams: *IM*, pp. 351–2; NLW 21284E, Letter nos. 710–16.

but the venture did not prosper. Soon Iolo was back in Glamorgan, leaving the rent unpaid and, in August 1786, he was arrested for debt and legal costs and confined to gaol for a year as an insolvent debtor.[25] An inventory of tools seized at Iolo's Cowbridge workshop is surprisingly modest: the grits, polishers, marble carving tools, freestone firmers, saws, compasses and rules, as well as the banker or workbench (7s. 6d.) and Darley's 'Book of Ornaments for Carvers' (3s. 6d.), amounted to just under £2.[26] Deprived of his tools, Iolo would have been reduced to the status of a day labourer. In this period he had boxes of tools and papers and small caches of materials, scattered between Kent, Somerset and Glamorgan. There were unpaid debts, of course, but Iolo was also owed money from jobs as a carver and stonecutter in Somerset (Shepton Mallet), Devon (Bideford), Dorset (Moor Crichel) and Glamorgan.[27]

The best way to appreciate the range of Iolo's mason's skills is to examine his advertisements. Once he had established a workshop, Iolo, like many other Georgian artisans and shopkeepers, produced small handbills (5in. x 6in.), a substitute for the engraved trade cards used by established tradesmen.[28] In his first handbill, dated 1779, Edward Williams Jr., advertised himself as a marble-mason specializing in 'all sorts of chimney-pieces, monuments, tombs, headstones' in marble and freestone. Iolo offered to clean and polish old marble tables and chimney-pieces at reasonable terms, and to cut inscriptions on old monuments or tombs. The new chimney-pieces and monuments were fashionable – 'in the newest and neatest manner'. Iolo emphasized that he had for many years 'regularly followed this Trade in London and other capital Towns under the best Masters'. Moreover, he could supply these articles on terms cheaper than those masons 'who profess the Trade without ever having followed it where any tolerable Knowledge of it could be acquired'.[29] Some years later, Iolo (one assumes) drafted a handbill for his brother Thomas which 'respectfully acquaints the inhabitants of Wells and its vicinity' of similar services, informing them that Thomas Williams had 'served many Years under the most eminent Masters in England, which has enabled him to excel most of his Profession'. In Wales, Iolo had announced that as 'various Sorts of good *Marble* [were] found in many Parts of Glamorgan', carved articles 'may be had very cheap'. Similarly, at Wells Iolo's brother announced that he had discovered in Somerset a variety of stone 'which takes a very beautiful *Polish*, and which he can render cheap'.[30]

[25] NLW 21389E, *passim*; the petition for discharge from gaol is in NLW Great Sessions P/2751 (August 1787); Williams: *IM*, pp. 348–9, 441–53.
[26] NLW 21389E, no. 45.
[27] NLW 21389E, nos. 8–9, 40.
[28] On trade cards, see Maurice Rickards, *The Encyclopedia of Ephemera* (London, 2000), pp. 334–6.
[29] NLW 21420E, no. 1.
[30] NLW 21420E, no. 4.

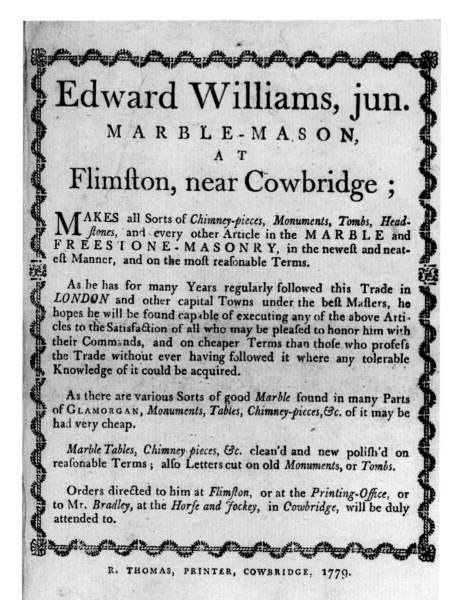

Fig. 12 A handbill, printed at Cowbridge in 1779, advertising the services of Edward Williams Jr. (Iolo Morganwg), marble-mason, at Flimston (Flemingston), near Cowbridge (NLW 21420E, no. 1).

Some of Iolo's tombstones and monuments are known to have survived, and other examples await identification. Draft inscriptions are found among his papers and include, affectingly, several alternative memorial inscriptions for his father, who died in April 1795.[31] Iolo critically assessed memorials in his locality, advising clients to commission headstones of a certain size: 'a Tomb less than the size I recommend would appear but a very trifling and pitiful object'. Words were cut and painted at 2d. per letter, edge mouldings cost 1s. per foot, and a few neat sculptured ornaments could be supplied for half a guinea. Iolo had strong views on what was appropriate: 'everything on a Tombstone or monument should, in my opinion, always have a very solemn and significant meaning and represent some lesson of piety or of Wisdom'.[32] Iolo's commissions included substantial ledger stones, sometimes (as at Cogan) set vertically as a wall monument and dignified with a dressed-stone pediment and moulded border.[33] Iolo's special skill as a marble-mason is still apparent from a few attributable wall-tablets, and the fortunate survival of several alternative designs for the Spencer monument at St Athan.[34] The undated, but signed, oval wall-tablet with draped urn commemorating Anthony Jones of Llantwit Major, erected about 1800, is (as Gunnis has pointed out) 'exactly like the contemporary work of T. King of Bath', who figured among the best provincial marble-masons.[35]

Iolo's claim to have served under some of the best masters was probably true. Subscribers to *Poems, Lyric and Pastoral* included several master statuaries (makers of chimney-pieces and sculptural monuments), who were among the best craftsmen of the period.[36] The most prominent was the largely self-taught London sculptor John Bacon RA (1740–99). West Country subscribers included Thomas King of Bath (d. 1804), 'the most prolific and popular of all the West Country statuaries', and John Ricketts of Bath (*fl.* 1787–96), a member of the Gloucestershire family firm (*fl.* 1729–95) of statuaries and masons. The Ricketts' monuments have quite carefully carved detail and are 'above the provincial level'. The firm had Glamorgan commissions for monuments (St Brides Major, 1756; Llantwit, 1767), and it is possible that the Williamses had dealings with them. Sometimes a direct connection can be

---

[31] NLW 21418E, no. 2.

[32] Williams: *IM*, pp. 346–8; Iolo's comments on the dimensions of local tombstones are in NLW 13136A, pp. 1–3. His transcripts of memorial inscriptions include a *memento mori* verse at St Mary Hill attributed to his grandfather ('Edwd. Mathews ai cant'): NLW 131504, p. 44.

[33] Details of the Cogan ledger tomb and monument are in NLW 21417E, no. 11.

[34] NLW 21417E, nos. 1–7.

[35] Rupert Gunnis, *Dictionary of British Sculptors, 1660–1851* (rev. edn., London, 19[64]), p. 432, s.n. 'Williams, Edward'.

[36] They are listed as Mr Bacon, statuary; Mr King, statuary, Bath; H. Marsh, statuary, Bristol; Mr Rickets, statuary, Bath, etc.; Mr John Rickets, statuary; Mr Thomas Rowland, statuary, Bristol; Mr Thomas Stackhouse, statuary. Identifications from Gunnis, *Dictionary of British Sculptors*.

Fig. 13a–b A wall-tablet in memory of Anthony Jones in the nave of St Illtud's Church, Llantwit Major, signed 'E. Williams, Cowbridge', probably *c.*1800.

demonstrated between Iolo and these master statuaries. Iolo was employed by Marsh of Bristol to erect the monument in Ross-on-Wye church to the memory of John Kyrle, the 'Man of Ross'. This monument, erected in 1776, is executed in coloured marbles with a medallion portrait, and (in Gunnis's judgement) is as good as London work.[37] Before Thomas Williams sailed for Jamaica he asked his brother Iolo to persuade Mr Marsh of Bristol to recommend him to John Bacon in London, who was preparing a monument to be shipped to Spanish Town.[38]

Iolo and his brothers were tramping artisans, moving from place to place and job to job, returning home only occasionally. The wear and tear of the mason's life and the weariness of living in lodgings are apparent in several wistful letters from Thomas. Those engaged in the building trades, even established masons, were often resident in a town for a short period only. Trade directories reveal that there was a greater turnover of masons than might be expected. Of twenty-five masons recorded in Bath in 1800, only twelve remained in 1805. In other words, even in centres of the building trade only half the resident masons were still resident after five years. Kenneth Hudson noted that if a mason's name disappeared he may have been dead, may no longer be a householder or retain a workshop, or may have moved to set up as a mason or builder elsewhere, with the reputation of having worked in Bath to help him; or he may have emigrated.[39] This mobility is detectable in the careers of the Williams brothers. They gained experience in some of the centres of the trade, and tried to establish themselves elsewhere. John and Miles emigrated to Jamaica in 1778, five years after leaving Glamorgan. Thomas persevered as a carver in England until 1785, sometimes sick at heart, before joining his brothers in Jamaica. Although often tempted to emigrate, Iolo was the only one of the four brothers to come home to practise his trade.

In 1795 Iolo returned permanently to Glamorgan. The author and antiquary Benjamin Heath Malkin, who travelled through south Wales in 1803, encountered Iolo 'buried' in Flemingston and fell under his spell:

> It is much to be lamented, that his talents, in the line of his profession, have been buried where they could not possibly emerge from their obscurity. Had they been noticed in early life, the public would probably have gained an eminent architect or sculptor.[40]

As it was, Iolo continued to work as a stonecutter and letterer after returning to Glamorgan, and the stonemason's craft was the bedrock of his working life. In due course, his son Taliesin began working with him, as he himself had

---

[37] *RAEW*, p. 107n.
[38] NLW 21284E, Letter no. 722, Thomas Williams to Iolo Morganwg, 10 November 1785.
[39] Kenneth Hudson, *The Fashionable Stone* (Bath, 1971), pp. 49–50.
[40] Malkin, *The Scenery, Antiquities, and Biography, of South Wales*, p. 129.

worked with his own father. A handbill drafted *c*.1805–10 advertises the services of Taliesin and Edward Williams, father and son, 'stone-cutters at Flimston and at their shop in Gileston', who 'make Monuments, Tombs and Head-stones in the best and newest Taste'. Letters are neatly cut on grave-stones, painted on 'Shop-boards, Coffin Breast plates, wagons and carts'.[41]

Working with stone absorbed Iolo intellectually as well as physically, and he became involved in every aspect of stoneworking, from quarrying to construction. He was fascinated by geology and his detailed knowledge of workable stone in Glamorgan was summarized in his 'General View of the Agriculture of Glamorgan' (1796).[42] The prospect of exploiting new sources of stone excited Iolo, though he complained that he had not received the slightest recompense from his discovery of valuable quarries on some local estates. This produced in him, as Malkin noted, 'an angry disposition to withhold the remainder of his knowledge on that subject'.[43] Iolo's resentment may have been fuelled by the failure of his own quarrying venture. In 1780 he had opened a quarry on the Margam estate at Pyle, hiring workmen to remove the overburden in order to reach the freestone, but the venture had collapsed owing to Iolo's frequent absences from Glamorgan.[44] Iolo also tried his hand at lime-burning, taking over a limekiln at Cardiff following the death of one Mr Roberts, a builder.[45] When imported marbles became virtually unobtainable during the Napoleonic Wars, Iolo considered exploiting the harder limestones as a substitute for the marbles used in statuary work. He had a collection of 'many beautiful specimens' of local 'marbles', which took a very high polish. Some Anglesey limestone were said to be whiter than Carrara marble and, in 1799, Iolo planned to investigate the quarries and if the stone was suitable for statuary he proposed bringing it to Swansea in copper-ore boats.[46]

Like his father, Edward William Senr., Iolo undertook much general work as a mason and builder.[47] His familiarity with the different branches of the building trade is apparent from his untitled essay on building.[48] It has sections

[41] NLW 21418E, no. 13ᵛ; Williams: *IM*, p. 358.

[42] NLW 13114B, pp. 54–7.

[43] Malkin, *The Scenery, Antiquities, and Biography, of South Wales*, pp. 129–30.

[44] NLW 21280E, Letter no. 791, Iolo Morganwg to unnamed recipient, 17 June 1782; Williams: *IM*, p. 369.

[45] NLW 21420E, no. 7, is a draft advertisement for the lime-burning business. There are accounts in NLW 21412E, *passim*.

[46] Williams: *IM*, p. 348.

[47] The earlier work, for which there are references, include repairs to the tower at Rumney parish church (NLW 21389E, no. 9); extensive repairs to St John's church, Cardiff, which seem to have included the replacement of one of the tower pinnacles (NLW 21416E, nos. 43–4); and the building of a barn at Roath (NLW 21416E, no. 37). Cf. Williams: *IM*, p. 351.

[48] NLW 13116B, pp. 346–59, probably written *c*.1785–7, according to Williams: *IM*, pp. 364–7, who printed the sections on 'ashlar fronts', 'stones' and 'mortar floors'. See also the undated

on cob walling, clay ashes and coal ashes (used in mortar), roughcast, rough-stone walling, ashlar fronts, the qualities of different stones, mortar, pointing, outside plastering and mortar floors. The essay is unfinished and there are references to missing sections on constructing ovens and furnaces, a branch of a mason's work in which Iolo seems to have had special expertise; it borrows its arrangement and themes from several well-known practical manuals on building. Like Neve's *Builder's Dictionary*, the text was partly a manual for workmen and partly 'fit for Gentlemen's use'.[49] Iolo delved fairly deeply into the mysteries of several crafts, but also directed some remarks at those who were commissioning buildings: 'Every gentlemen that intends building should give orders for keeping as much coal ashes as possible' for use in mortar; 'it is a common error in Glamorgan to make walls too thick, thereby putting gentlemen to an unnecessary expence of lime and stone'; and so on. There are comparisons with building practice in parts of England. The wet method of roughcasting in Devon was more durable, more beautiful and cheaper than the 'frippery dry' roughcast so common in Glamorgan; on the other hand, the price of rough-stone walling in Glamorgan was more reasonable than in most places; Glamorgan freestone was as cheap as Bath stone, but greatly superior to it in texture, colour and durability.

Iolo understood the different building trades and undertook work as a measurer and surveyor, pricing the work of masons, tilers and plasterers. This work could be undertaken only by those respected by other craftsmen, and its arcane complexities, full of customary variations and terminology, probably appealed to Iolo. London prices differed from provincial prices; different crafts estimated work in different ways; local 'customary' measures were used rather than standard imperial measures unless there was an agreement otherwise; some work was paid for at piece rates, or at day rates or by contract. Some of Iolo's notes on prices and measures have been preserved. Digging clay and stone, for example, was priced by the 'cranock'; a tiler and a thatcher's work was measured by 'the square'; rough-stone walling was measured by the customary perch of eighteen feet; Iolo sold lime by the 'pedoran' (quarter).[50] Memoranda record Iolo's conscientious measurements of a sea wall at Barry, building work at St Athan and work done at Newton Nottage parish church by William Williams, a tiler and plasterer. In 1806 Iolo helped estimate unfinished work at Cowbridge Bridewell, apparently an 'unpleasant business', and in

---

fragment 'Essay on Mortar, plaister, stucco &c also on Brick and artificial stone by Edward Williams': NLW 21417E, no. 36.

[49] Richard Neve, *The City and Country Purchaser, and Builder's Dictionary* (1726 edn.; Bath, 1969), 'Advertisement'.

[50] NLW 21416E, no. 26; NLW 13116B, p. 350. Cf. also NLW 21416E, no. 52, 'London prices of Journe[y]man's work'. Iolo owned a copy of William Salmon's *The London and Country Builder's Vade Mecum*, which gave price guides: NLW 13136A, p. 143.

1810 he made a reassuring survey of the arcade at Cowbridge church amid fears that it was collapsing.[51]

Drawing was an essential element of the work of the surveyor and mason-architect. Iolo had learned to draw as a marble-mason. The schedule of his effects at his bankruptcy – a bitterly humorous document – included one small portable desk which Iolo considered an instrument of his trade, 'being necessary for writing and for keeping drawings and other papers, and which in my trade cannot well be dispended with'.[52] Some of Iolo's surviving drawings shed light on his craft as a stonecutter, and include details of mouldings sketched during his days as a mason in London and Kent.[53] Like many antiquarians, Iolo favoured the Gothic style and claimed to have made a particular study of this 'noble species of architecture' during his 'rambles', maintaining that there were few who grasped its 'true principles'.[54] He considered that the classical orders were 'so many varieties of one order of architecture' and was scornful of those 'wise fellows' who argued that it was impossible to add a sixth order to the five of the classical world.[55] Iolo played with a new 'British Order' that would 'comprehend all the Beauty's of the others as well Gothic as Roman, Grecian, Chinese'.[56]

Many of Iolo's surviving plans relate to farmhouses and cottages. His 'General View of the Agriculture of Glamorgan' (1796) shows how thoroughly he understood the requirements of the farmer. In a chapter on buildings Iolo discussed in great detail the plan and construction of farmhouses, cottages, and farm buildings.[57] The farmhouses were often ancient structures, large and roomy, 'but not on plans of convenience such as recent times have conceived'. Cottages were similarly well built, comfortably commodious, but old-fashioned. Iolo described the plan: on the ground floor beyond the kitchen were generally two small rooms, one serving as a bedroom for the cottager and his wife, the other fitted up as a pantry. Stone steps at the side of the kitchen fireplace led to bedrooms for children in the upper storey. Most cottages were thatched, 'which is here done uncommonly well and neat'. A series of drawings

---

[51] NLW 13157A, pp. 198–9, 210–11; NLW 21415E, nos. 54–9; NLW 13089E, p. 181; Cowbridge Bridewell: NLW 13150A, pp. 216–17; NLW 21411E, nos. 34–40; Cowbridge Church: NLW 13094E, p. 181.

[52] NLW 21389E, no. 8. The inventory includes a mouse trap, a Toby jug – 'empty', three spoons – 'not silver', and 'one Munkin' – 'I know not what this is, but ask my wife.'

[53] Iolo sketched a 'Gothick Cornish in St Martins Lane' on a letter from his father dated 5 December 1773: NLW 13106B, p. 135; NLW 21417E, passim, esp. no. 17, for drawings of window tracery by 'Iorwerth Gwilym' and, on the dorse, 'Gothic sketches by Davison'.

[54] NLW 21387E, no. 10. Iolo praises as authorities ('more knowledge . . . than all besides I have met with') James Bentham's The History and Antiquities of the . . . Cathedral Church of Ely (Cambridge, 1771) and 'Mr King on Ancient Castles', probably a part work by Edward King collected as Monumenta Antiqua (c.1796).

[55] NLW 21387E, no. 10.

[56] NLW 21417E, nos. 15–16.

[57] NLW 13114B, pp. 54–80.

of 'snug cotts' illustrate the variations in plan; they include a plan and elevation of Iolo's own thatched cottage at Flemingston.[58] More generally he drew up a list of 'peculiarities of common Welsh houses in Glamorgan' which included details of the plan (ground-floor beds), decoration (frequent whitewashing outside and inside) and furnishings.[59] The architectural features of farmhouses and cottages in Glamorgan – waterproof walls, stone stairs, dressed-stone doorways, windows and fireplaces – were 'obvious copies' from castle architecture. Iolo viewed castles as embodiments of feudal tyranny, thanking God that they had become ruined, but conceded that with military architecture had come knowledge of the arch, mural stair, vaulted roof, chimney and stone bridge.[60]

Iolo believed that modern cottages, apart from their greater external symmetry, were generally much inferior to ancient houses. They were built on a more contracted scale, partly because of the increasing cost of timber, and were less comfortable and convenient than the ancient cottage. Iolo proposed building convenient modern houses two or three storeys high, using the ancient technique of stone vaulting. The vaulted roof would provide secure foundations for a pleasant roof garden, with pots, flower beds and tubs of flowering shrubs, green-painted seats and alcoves, and an area for drying clothes.[61] Unfortunately, these all-stone houses – a mason's delight – were never built. More conventionally, Iolo proposed building cottages of back-to-back type which saved timber as well as stone, redrawing designs for a pair of hipped cottages from Nathaniel Kent's *Hints to Gentlemen of Landed Property* (1775). Careful costings suggest that the cottages may have been commissioned, presumably by a local estate.[62] A particularly interesting plan shows Iolo's conception of a comfortable and convenient small farmhouse or large cottage. The house is of central-entry type with a heated parlour and kitchen at the front. A pantry and a cellar partly occupy the back, alongside externally entered recesses for garden tools and a pigsty. The garden and the pig were, of course, essential to the cottagers' economy. Iolo was particular about the appropriate disposition of furniture within a house. Integrated within the plan of the house were recesses for closets and furniture, including a dresser, table, buffets and a traditional ground-floor cupboard bed. Like many carvers of stone, Iolo may have been able to work in wood, and his interest in furniture is apparent in a few surviving designs.

[58] NLW 21416E, no. 14.
[59] NLW 21413E, no. 16. Furnishings include cupboard beds, a dresser and pewter, chimney corners and ledges ornamented with 'bright iron and brass ware', and Ewenny ware (including 'ffiolid ddolen', i.e. a lugged wassail bowl).
[60] NLW 13150A, pp. xi, xiv.
[61] NLW 13106B, p. 179. Iolo envisaged using artificial stone for the 'arches' (vaults) manufactured 'in Dr Higgins manner using dry coal ashes instead of bone ashes'.
[62] NLW 21416E, no. 2.

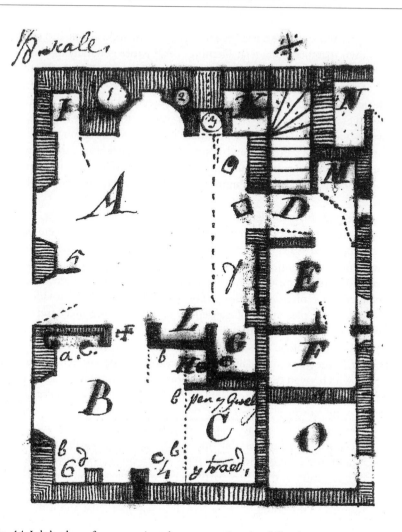

Fig. 14 Iolo's plan of a convenient house contains the following annotations: A–O: Rooms and Closets. 'A. Kitchen, B. Parlour, C. Bedcloset, D. stairs passage, E. Pantry, F. Cellar, G. Recess for Kitchen utensils H. Closet in the parlour for Book case cloaths press etc. I. Closet in the Kitchen J. landing [over] the copper place L. Closet in the Kitchen or place for shelves to serve for a dresser with a case of dresser drawers, or table below. M. Closet in the stairs passage to come out no farther than the facia of the second step or middle of the tread of ditto that more light may come to the stairs. N. Garden closet for Garden utensils. O. hogstye opening to a small back yard of the same length & breadth with the stye.' Nos. 1–6: fixtures and furniture. '1. larger oven. 2. small ditto. 3. Copper or furnace. 4. recess in the parlour for a small dressing table, with a small book case in the upper part. 5. board or wainscoat to keep of[f] the wind, and to make better room for a table or chair between it and the window. 6. Beaufet [buffet].' (NLW 21416E, no. 9).

Fig. 15 Iolo Morganwg's undated design for an ideal writing cabinet. He did not like unnecessary ornament. The cabinet is plain, apart from a shaped pediment rising from a dentillated cornice (NLW 21416E, no. 25).

Several designs suggest that Iolo may have nursed building schemes more ambitious than his plans for improved farmhouses and cottages. These were not entirely constructional daydreams. Improvements to public buildings provided considerable opportunities for mason-builders and architects during the second half of the eighteenth century. As early as 1782 Iolo prepared several alternative schemes for an extension to the town hall at Cowbridge that would accommodate new jury rooms and a prothonotary's office over the ground-floor market. His designs included carefully executed geometrical elevations, drawn in ink with grey washes in the conventional eighteenth-century style. As one would expect, the masonry detail was carefully considered: fine limestone or stone ashlar was proposed for the pillars and arches, freestone for the rustic quoins, window cases, and moulded cornice. A gothic fanlight provided the only flamboyant touch to a dignified stone building. Iolo's scheme was not approved, and he does not seem to have designed further buildings of this type; architects, rather than mason-builders, increasingly dominated the field of public buildings.[63]

[63] Ibid., nos. 31–5.

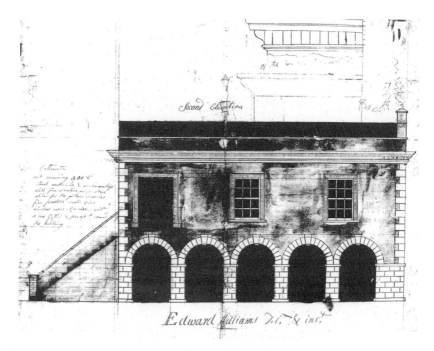

Fig. 16 'Plann and Elevation of a new additional building to the town hall in
Cowbridge', designed and drawn by Iolo Morganwg, 8 August 1782. Ink drawing with
grey washes (NLW 21416E, no. 31).

Like many of the period with an antiquarian cast of mind, Iolo was attracted
by the Gothic style and the idea of towers. An intriguing ink and wash drawing
of a finialed Gothic summer house notes that the work was to be prepared in
London under Iolo's supervision, and was intended for a gentleman in Canada
'40 miles higher up than Quebec'.[64] It is not clear whether this or any other
elaborate scheme was actually built, though Iolo bombarded potential patrons
with building proposals.[65] In 1810 Iolo congratulated Sir Watkin Lewes on
recovering an estate, and promptly offered his services as a superintendent of
buildings and repair.[66] He suggested quite detailed building schemes to the
owners of estates and country houses. Thomas Johnes tactfully declined Iolo's
proposal to embellish Hafod with a tower after a disastrous fire had destroyed
Nash's work, though he sought his advice about sources of marble.[67] The Hon.

---

[64] Ibid., no. 60.
[65] Other designs include a 'Summer house for Mrs Morgan', and a sketch of an octagonal
      meeting-house: NLW 13157A, pp. 118, 298.
[66] NLW 21285E, Letter no. 885, Iolo Morganwg to Sir Watkin Lewes, 27 July 1810.
[67] Letters printed in R. J. Moore-Colyer (ed.), *A Land of Pure Delight: Selections from the Letters
      of Thomas Johnes of Hafod, Cardiganshire (1748–1816)* (Llandysul, 1992), pp. 164–5, 180–1,
      227–8.

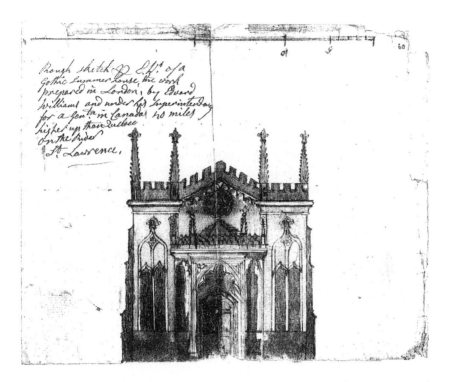

Fig. 17 An undated 'Rough sketch' of a Gothic summer house by Iolo Morganwg. Ink and grey wash (NLW 21416E, no. 60).

Thomas Mansel Talbot received an unsolicited letter from Iolo suggesting that a 'lofty tower' ('a much larger tower than that in Cotham Park' near Bristol) would have a noble effect at Margam Park. Iolo enticingly outlined a scheme that would make Margam Abbey and its environs a kind of 'earthly paradise'. Having heard that Talbot proposed improving the landscaping around Margam Abbey by removing Margam village, Iolo suggested rebuilding the estate buildings in a picturesque way: some in the antique Grecian taste, others in the Chinese or in a good Gothic taste, each having 'some elegant peculiarity in its structure'. No designs have survived, but we have Iolo's aesthetic judgement that there is nothing 'more essential to beauty than a Judicious and well managed variety'. Iolo, the mason, used his early pseudonym I[orwerth] G[wilym], fearing that he had 'presumed too far' to sign his real name.[68] Presumably he hoped that the scheme would be considered on its architectural merits, but there is no record of a reply from Talbot.

---

[68]   NLW 21285E, Letter no. 788, Iolo Morganwg to Thomas Mansel Talbot, 23 August 1780; Williams: *IM*, pp. 422–3.

Rather surprisingly, Iolo did not have much to say about contemporary architects. This is unexpected, given that Iolo witnessed the Georgian rebuilding of Bath, Bristol and London, and saw country-house rebuilding on a grand scale at Crichel House. In Glamorgan, according to Malkin, there were 'few better judges' than Iolo 'of design or execution in architecture'. Iolo briefly noted many of the new country houses and villas in Glamorgan, but did not name their architects, even when he was critical of the designs, as at Hensol Castle (rebuilt 'in a Heavy modern (of course misunderstood) Gothic stile'), or when he admired buildings like Adam's Wenvoe Castle ('recently built in the Castle stile') or Johnson's Penrice House ('an elegant freestone building').[69] Iolo ignored Nash, Jernegan and the other contemporary architects working in south Wales, apart from William Edwards, the celebrated bridge-builder, but he – like Iolo – was Glamorgan born and bred.[70]

Iolo may not have acknowledged the work of named contemporary architects, but he certainly showed an interest in past masters. In 1789 he compiled a list of seventeenth-century buildings in Glamorgan which might be attributed to the celebrated Inigo Jones, including 'the fine porch at Bewper'.[71] By 1797 Iolo attributed the porch to Richard Twrch, a name conjured out of his imagination, and communicated the 'tradition' to antiquaries. There were, of course, tangential glimpses of Iolo's own biography in the romantic story (discussed below) of the construction of the porch, which was essentially a celebration of native-born genius. Iolo sometimes described himself as 'self taught', and he compiled lists of self-taught persons in Glamorgan which included ingenious artisans whose practical inventiveness Iolo admired and sometimes tried to emulate.[72] The story of Beaupre porch was also perhaps a critical commentary on the growing celebrity of architects and the diminishing responsibilities and opportunities of the mason-builders; the unknown artisan is depicted as being at least as good as, if not better, than the celebrated court architect. Like other would-be provincial artisan-builders, Iolo was at a disadvantage in the increasingly professionalized world of late-Georgian architecture. However, as an antiquarian, he turned his apparent provincialism to

---

[69]   NLW 13114B, pp. 60–3; Williams: *PLP*, I, pp. 116–17.

[70]   Iolo must have known something of Nash through his connection with John Edwards of Rheola. Cf. Richard Suggett, *John Nash, Architect in Wales: John Nash, Pensaer yng Nghymru* (Aberystwyth, 1995), p. 100.

[71]   NLW 13115B, p. 285; Williams: *IM*, pp. 273, n. 33.

[72]   NLW 13157A, p. 158. They included the bridge-builder William Edwards, and the engineers Watkin George and William Aubrey. Elsewhere Iolo has biographical notes on 'Ingenious Jay' of Penmark, 'a man of almost miraculous ingenuity', and the Revd Edward Pritchard of Flemingston, a mathematician and, according to Iolo, a friend of Isaac Newton, whose cottage Iolo later occupied: NLW 13161A, p. 6; NLW 13152A, pp. 447–51. Iolo's papers include ingenious ideas with sketches for an improved wheelbarrow and a 'wheel-oared' boat: NLW 13093E, pp. 43–8; NLW 13114B, p. 233.

great advantage, claiming unique knowledge in certain esoteric matters and proclaiming the importance of oral tradition.

Iolo's 'Cursory remarks' on reading Camden's *Britannia* (Gibson's 1695 edition) parade his intimate knowledge of Glamorgan, much of it gained on the tramp as a working mason in his native county. There are notes on castles, churches, camps (generally considered Roman), Roman roads and archaeological discoveries. There are also anecdotes which may or may not be authentic traditions: Owain Glyndŵr is said to have taken refuge at Mynydd y Glew ('Hero's Down'), where he lived as an anchorite under the unlikely name of 'John Goodfellow' (Siôn Gwdfellow). The defacing of medieval churchyard crosses at Porthceri, and elsewhere in the Vale, was attributed by Iolo to another stonecutter, William Morrice, an Anabaptist who 'not many years ago', demonstrated his aversion to Popery 'by defacing this beautiful remain of Gothic sculpture'. In Iolo's topography of Glamorgan, anecdote and observation were often intertwined.[73]

Iolo's observations on antiquities were summarized in numerous lists of monuments of different types. There are lists of archaeological features: *cromlechau*, tumuli, stone circles, camps, 'druidical altars'. Architectural monuments include thirteen buildings attributed to Inigo Jones, 'church houses' and town halls (56), castles (82), ancient houses in the Gothic style (24) and ruined chapels (19).[74] Antiquarian and natural history miscellanea include named centenarians, the names of rivers, mountains and caves, rare plants, and an astonishing compilation of 147 varieties of apple found in Glamorgan and Gwent.[75] Historical esoterica informed by oral tradition include lists of autodidacts and 'freebooters' in Glamorgan, which preserve the arresting names of 'Captain Pudding' and 'Corri's Gang'.[76] The twenty remarkable self-educated persons in Glamorgan included William Thomas of Michaelston-super-Ely whose diary provides another, but very different, perception of the social life of Glamorgan in the second half of the eighteenth century.[77] Scattered throughout

---

[73] NLW 13089E, pp. 128–31; cf. also the list of 32 natural and historical curiosities, headed 'Glamorgan Topography' in NLW 13117E, pp. 43, 52.

[74] NLW 13129A, p. 528 (where Beaupre porch has been deleted from the edifices attributed to Inigo Jones); NLW 13153A, pp. 286–90 (tumuli, circles, *cromlechau*, ruined chapels); NLW 13130A, pp. 245–52.

[75] NLW 21413E, nos. 37–8 (apples), 42 (centenarians); NLW 13089E, pp. 64–9 (apples, pears, rivers, mountains).

[76] NLW 13114B, p. 191. Captain Pudding was 'a banditti supported by the Royalist party'. The existence of 'Corri's Gang' is confirmed by references to 'Corry men' in R. T. W. Denning (ed.), *The Diary of William Thomas of Michaelston-super-Ely, near St Fagans, Glamorgan: 1762–1795* (Cardiff, 1995), pp. 128, 170.

[77] NLW 13157A, p. 158. William Thomas of Roughbrook, Michaelston-super-Ely, is called 'Will Ysgolhaig Rhychbrwg'. William Thomas's diary does not mention Iolo Morganwg, but Iolo evidently knew of William Thomas. Perhaps Iolo made his ledger tomb, with its subtle memorial *englyn*, which still survives at Michaelston-super-Ely.

Iolo's manuscripts are the compressed topographical notes on which his lists were based, sometimes jotted on long strips of paper.[78] The accuracy of many of Iolo's topographical observations can still be demonstrated, and his record of vanished monuments is accordingly all the more valuable.[79]

Occasionally Iolo planned archaeological sites; it may have become a preoccupation in his later years. In 1814 (when he was 67) he proposed surveying Mynydd Baeden camp with a compass and tape-line.[80] The plan has not survived, but attention has been drawn to Iolo's plans of three earthworks at Llantwit Major (Llanilltud Fawr), intended for publication in the *Gentleman's Magazine*, as well as a stone circle at Mynydd Twmpathyddaear at Stormy Down.[81] In 1813 Iolo carried out a disciplined excavation (rather than treasure hunting or barrow cracking) at Dunraven camp to determine the structure of the defences. Iolo the mason admired the composition of the mortar used to cap the rampart – 'lias lime and sea sand used in very proper proportions' – which was still remarkably hard after two thousand years. Iolo sketched the stratigraphy for Taliesin; it is perhaps the earliest section of an archaeological site in Wales and an extension of Iolo's interest in geological strata.[82] Iolo could measure and draw, and it is a pity that he did not plan more archaeological sites. He did not, of course, have the leisure of the gentleman antiquary, and he was only able to record monuments between his literary labours and his work as a mason. A sketch-plan of a stone circle at Newton Down has the telling note that it was 'as correct as I was able to make in my late, of course, hurried hour'.[83] Iolo often recorded in haste, but he has been justly championed as a reliable pioneer field archaeologist.[84]

Iolo probably intended using some of this archaeological information in a projected 'complete and superb' history of Glamorgan in 1806.[85] His ill-tempered criticisms of the 'so nick-named' *History of the County of Brecknock* (1805–9) by Theophilus Jones reveal that his idea of a county history was much

---

[78]   For good examples, see NLW 21413E, no. 23 (notes on Barry, Cwmcidi, Sully (Sili), Lavernock (Larnog), Dinas Powys).

[79]   H. J. Thomas, 'Iolo Morganwg Vindicated: Glamorgan's First Field Archaeologist', *Glamorgan–Gwent Archaeological Trust Annual Report*, 1983–4 (Swansea, 1985), pp. 149–57. Iolo's observations on castles were incorporated in RCAHMW's Glamorgan Inventory volumes on *The Early Castles* (London, 1991) and *The Later Castles* (Aberystwyth, 2000), index, s.n. 'Iolo Morgan(n)wg'.

[80]   NLW 21285E, Letter no. 914, Iolo Morganwg to Taliesin Williams, 31 March 1814.

[81]   NLW 13114B, p. 173; NLW 21285E, Letter no. 899, Iolo Morganwg to Taliesin Williams, 6 November 1813, with extracts in *RAEW*, pp. 175–6; Thomas redrew several plans in 'Iolo Morganwg Vindicated', figs. 52–4, 57.

[82]   NLW 21285E, Letter nos. 648, 899, cited by Thomas, 'Iolo Morganwg Vindicated', p. 153, with a redrawn section, fig. 56; cf. RCAHMW, *An Inventory of the Ancient Monuments in Glamorgan, Vol. I, Part 2: The Iron Age and The Roman Occupation* (Cardiff, 1976), pp. 11, 14, 38b.

[83]   NLW 13089E, p. 173, cited by Thomas, 'Iolo Morganwg Vindicated', p. 151.

[84]   Thomas, 'Iolo Morganwg Vindicated'.

[85]   NLW 21413E, no. 21. Iolo hoped to write the county history, supported by an annual benefaction contributed by subscribers. Cf. also NLW 13114B, pp. 134–9.

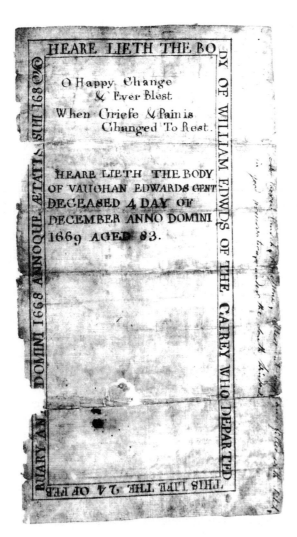

Fig. 18 The tombstone of William Edwards (aged 168!) and Vaughan Edwards, Caerau, Glamorgan. This is one of several fair drawings by Iolo of a memorial inscription. Iolo noted: 'At Caerey Church, limestone, letters cut deep and filled with pitch, in good preservation under the south window.' The tombstone has been destroyed (NLW 21418E, no. 5).

broader than the conventional parish-by-parish description of antiquities and landowners' mansions; his would also include language and literature, song and custom.[86] Another related historical project was a collection of monumental

---

[86] NLW 13136A, pp. 96–7.

inscriptions. In 1801 a correspondent optimistically asked him about the book he planned to publish on 'curious monumental inscriptions' in Glamorgan. Transcripts of inscriptions are scattered throughout Iolo's manuscripts, but an orderly collection of fair copies was brought together by Taliesin.[87] Perhaps the ideal literary vehicle for Iolo's magpie-like observations on antiquarian, agricultural, industrial, literary and social matters would have been a tour combining the accuracy and curiosity of Stukeley and Pennant with the radicalism and polemic of Cobbett's *Rural Rides*. Iolo had strong views on the superficiality of Welsh tours, and did indeed contemplate publishing a Tour of Glamorgan, listing some twenty-four significant and original topics to be discussed.[88] As it is, his manuscript journals of expeditions to different parts of Wales are brilliant compendia of observations and opinions.[89]

Iolo's records of antiquities are usually concise, but he also wrote a few sustained parochial accounts influenced by 'statistical accounts' of parishes published in the *Gentleman's Magazine* and elsewhere, which included information on antiquities, manufactures, agriculture and population. Iolo's 'Rough Sketch of a Topographical and Statistical Account' of Penmark parish may have been prompted by Nicholas Carlisle's questionnaire for information for his *Topographical Dictionary* (1811). The fair copy of Iolo's parochial history, apparently presented to Robert Jones of Fonmon, contains information on the parish church and its monuments ('one of them truly superb of the richest varieties of Italian marble'), the ruined chapels of ease, the stonework at Penmark Castle, the vaulting of the associated dovecote ('what masons call cave-work'), and much else besides. The parish name was explained by a tradition attributed to a Mr Jones of Broadclose, 'who would for many hours, and indeed for many days relate such tales'. The tone is measured, but Iolo allowed himself a gibe at the 'Methodistical nocturnal conventicle' attended by young people of both sexes 'for the purpose of nightly assignations', and discussed the merits of the parish revel or *gwylmabsant*.[90] Iolo kept other antiquarian papers 'always in sight', including 'Anecdotes of Llantwit Major', a 'Sketch of Dunraven' and 'Longevity in Glamorgan', which he hoped to publish.[91]

---

[87] A note on an inscription at Llanfechan ('No 22 in a series of inscriptions brought together by TW'), NLW 21284E, Letter no. 770, William Phillips to Iolo Morganwg, undated; NLW 21280E, Letter no. 32, Revd J. Bowen to Iolo Morganwg [1801].

[88] NLW 21413E, no. 14. The topics included proposals for a county infirmary and a fraternity to support shipwrecked sailors.

[89] Tecwyn Ellis, 'Ymweliadau Iolo Morganwg â Meirionnydd 1799 ac 1800', *JMHRS*, V, part 3 (1967), 239–50; Elizabeth Williams, 'Iolo Morganwg in Denbighshire: Extracts from his Itinerary in 1799', *TDHS*, 16 (1967), 82–99.

[90] There is a fair copy in GRO, D/D F, vol. 34. The 'Topographical Anecdotes' in NLW 13161A, pp. 1–16, are dated 1808 and include a copy of Nicholas Carlisle's questionnaire (addressed from the Society of Antiquaries), with queries for compiling descriptive and historic data relating to a parish.

[91] NLW 21413E, no. 43. The essay on longevity was partially published in the *Gentleman's*

In his 'General View of the Agriculture of Glamorgan' (1796) Iolo observed that farmers in the Vale generally lived in villages rather than in dispersed farmhouses. Village residence increased sociability and convenience, and Iolo identified 'lone cottages better suppressed' among several listed 'nuisances in Glamorgan'.[92] The distinctiveness of the Vale of Glamorgan, according to Iolo, partly lay in its numerous villages and hamlets, many with origins in the Anglo-Norman settlement of the Vale. 'Go which way you want', Iolo maintained, 'villages are everywhere found',[93] and he listed all the settlements in the Vale and Gower, counting seventy villages and forty parish churches within a seven-mile radius of Llantwit Major alone.[94] Iolo collected statistical information on the population of the villages around Flemingstone, listing over a hundred householders and finding that one in four households had 'infants under the age of 16'.[95] By listing ruined and uninhabited houses, he estimated that the population in the area had decreased by some 500 persons. Iolo attributed this depopulation to farm engrossment, which had reduced the population more effectively than the 'Robespierrean sword', leaving a trail of abandoned dwellings as if an invading army had passed through.[96]

Many Vale settlements had an air of departed glory, none more so than the 'tottering town' of Llantwit Major. In his 'Antiquities of Llantwit Major', Iolo explained that Llantwit – Llanilltud – owed its origin to a monastic settlement established by St Illtud, an early centre of learning. He collected information about the traditions and buildings of Llantwit, the natural features, the agriculture and the geology of the town and parish.[97] 'The many broad and direct roads leading towards Lantwit Major . . . like the Radii of a wheel . . . the extraordinary size of its church & the churchyard surrounding it, & the

---

Magazine in February 1794, but material on Llantwit Major may have been declined by the editor (cf. NLW 21413E, no. 2: draft of a letter to Mr Urban). Iolo's long-promised 'Collections for the History of Dunraven Castle' was presented to Mrs Wyndham in 1818: NLW Dunraven Documents 187B; NLW 13114B, pp. 165ff. Other parochial accounts were contemplated, but Iolo only got as far as writing skeletal outlines. That for Flemingston concludes with the heading (possibly added by Taliesin), 'Bedd Iolo Morganwg': NLW 13144A, p. 193.

92 NLW 21413E, no. 17. Other nuisances were bandy playing (a competitive form of hockey), 'low public houses' and houses that harboured vagrants.

93 NLW 13114B, pp. 78–9. There are further extracts in Williams: *IM*, pp. 25–6.

94 Williams: *IM*, p. 21. There are lists of villages in NLW 13116E, pp. 438–9.

95 NLW 13095B, pp. 87–92. The list for Flemingston (p. 89) duly includes 'Edward Williams no infants'.

96 NLW 13152A, pp. 233–8. In Flemingston Iolo noted that his own house was 'now vacant'. Cf. Thomas, 'Iolo Morganwg Vindicated', pp. 155–6.

97 NLW 13158A, pp. 147–60, 243–85; see also NLW 13153A, 13114B, 13116B, *passim*. Cf. also 'Antiquities of Llantwit Major and Boverton' collected from various authors and manuscripts by Henry Tucker, Llantwit, 1820, Royal Irish Academy 12.N.4, pp. 595–636 (I owe this reference to Dr Stephen Briggs). Tucker, a parish clerk, made a fair copy of Iolo's papers, including the spurious chronology of the abbots of Llantwit attributed to David Nicholls, 1719.

number of human skulls, which from time to time have been dug up in the gardens & in the fields' proved it to have been a place of much consequence. Iolo located the ruins of the monastery, the monastic gatehouse and the abbey barn, and depicted these and other antiquities in a rough but highly informative sketch-plan of Llantwit which exists in several states and may have been worked up into a finished drawing.[98]

Iolo devoted particular attention to inscribed monuments at Llantwit Major, adding to those described in Edward Lhuyd's additions to Camden's *Britannia* (1695), but apparently unaware that others had already been described in *Archaeologia*.[99] In 1797 he communicated a careful record of the inscriptions to Richard Colt Hoare in a letter bursting with learning.[100] Iolo claimed to have discovered – and what a discovery! – Abbot Samson's Pillar-cross, one of the most significant early Christian stones in Wales. The circumstances of the discovery were remarkable. Iolo had been told by one Richard Punter, 'a shoemaker of some literary and much traditionary knowledge', that, many years before, an ancient inscribed stone called the 'King's Stone' had toppled into the newly dug grave of an extraordinarily tall lad, called 'Will the Giant', and had remained there undisturbed. During harvest-time in 1789 curiosity got the better of Iolo while stonecutting in the churchyard; he dug deeply into Will the Giant's grave and uncovered the fallen stone. Returning harvesters helped him lift the stone, and the inscription commemorating Iuthahelo Rex was revealed on the 'King's Stone'.[101]

Iolo instanced this story as an illustration of the veracity and tenacity of local tradition. Still more remarkable was the story of the brothers Twrch, a tradition 'pretty common amongst the Glamorgan masons and stonecutters' ('of which last trade I am myself'). Iolo informed Colt Hoare that he had taken the most authentic tradition from Richard Roberts, whose family claimed descent from Richard Twrch and had worked the Bridgend freestone quarries in hereditary fashion until the family died out in 1780–6. The Twrch brothers jointly worked

---

[98] NLW 13089E, pp. 86–9; NLW 21413E, no. 2b.

[99] John Strange, 'Remarks on the Reverend Mr William Harris's Observations [etc.]', *Archaeologia*, VI (1783), 21–4.

[100] Cardiff 3.332, Letter from Iolo Morganwg to Sir Richard Colt Hoare, 18 August 1797, enclosing transcripts of the inscriptions at Llantwit Major. Extracts from a fair copy signed by Iolo and dated 1798, preserved in the Fonmon Library, were published by J. Romilly Allen, 'Iolo Morganwg's Readings of the Inscriptions on the Crosses at Llantwit Major', *AC*, 5th ser., X (1893), 326–31. Iolo hoped that another version in a letter sent to David Thomas of Bath, dated 20 October 1798, would be shown to Richard Warner, author of the well-known *A Walk through Wales . . . 1797* (Bath, 1798): NLW 13114B, p. 105.

[101] Did Iolo really discover the Abbot Samson's Pillar-cross? It certainly seems possible since there are no references to it before Iolo's letter to Colt Hoare. However, the story of Will the Giant's grave was one of Iolo's romances probably spun around his discovery in the parish register of the entry for the burial on 9 April 1724 of 'Wm. Williams called the Giant' (NLW 13153A, p. 229). Cunningly, Iolo refrained from citing the entry; no doubt it could be 'discovered' at a later date as a corroborative detail.

the famous Sutton ('Seaton') quarry, but quarrelled over a sweetheart. Richard Twrch then made his way to London and worked under an Italian master, accompanying him to Italy 'where he acquired an uncommon proficiency in the arts of masonry, sculpture, and architecture'. Twrch eventually returned to Glamorgan and to the freestone quarries (his brother having died some years previously) and 'executed his work in so masterly a fashion that he was much noticed' by the gentry. Sir Richard Bassett commissioned him to build the chapel and porch at Beaupre. Iolo went on to argue that when the date of the chapel entrance (1586) and the porch (1600) are considered, 'we must allow them to be amongst the very first samples of Greek architecture in this Kingdom, perhaps the very first by a native'. He pointed out that Inigo Jones was generally thought to have been the first to introduce Greek and Roman architecture into England, but he did nothing before 1620.[102]

What can one make of this romance communicated to Colt Hoare, which many after him swallowed hook, line and sinker.[103] Iolo was generally reliable in matters of antiquarian observation, but when he produced an 'authentic' tradition it could be pure invention. One is forced to admire the different levels that gave plausibility to the deceit: the disingenuous ('Of what Authenticity these Traditions are must be left to Judgments greatly superior to mine'), the artfully verifiable circumstantial detail, and the humour of the invented surname Twrch (hog). Iolo enjoyed posing as the self-educated letter-cutter who was simply a conduit for popular traditions whose significance those more sophisticated than he would be better able to judge. Just as Iolo's literary forgeries purported to be transcripts of lost manuscripts, so were his historical anecdotes attributed to named artisans who had passed away and could no longer be interrogated. Iolo believed in the importance of oral transmission, but felt constrained to produce remarkable instances of the veracity of tradition. His compilation of instances of longevity in Glamorgan was partly a paper parade of tradition-bearers, reaching back through hoary bards to the age of the saints. Iolo's research notes on his centenarian contemporaries, however, revealed the patchy actuality of oral tradition. While some, for example, remembered the battles and social dislocation of the civil wars, others teased Iolo or related traditions that did not actually interest him.[104]

---

[102] Cardiff 3.316, Letter from Iolo Morganwg to Sir Richard Colt Hoare, 17 August 1797. See Williams: *IM*, pp. 272–3, for further references.

[103] Cf. Malkin, *The Scenery, Antiquities, and Biography, of South Wales*, pp. 119–24.

[104] NLW 21413E, no. 42; NLW 13152A, pp. 407–71. John Harry, 'a lying old Devil', swore that he was 118 years old and remembered King David! Iolo ascertained his true age from the parish register (p. 436); Catherine Rees alias Jenkin, an 'illiterate rustic', could give no interesting account of anything that had happened in her days 'only that women . . . were in the general habit of smoking and of singing smutty songs when by themselves and remembered Morris dancers by women all in breeches contending with men' (p. 452). Extracts from Iolo's papers on longevity were used by Malkin, *The Scenery, Antiquities, and Biography, of South Wales*, pp. 624–33.

Iolo's emphasis on the importance of 'oral tradition' – he appears to have been one of the first to use the term – has a surprising apparent modernity, but it was closely related to his bardo-druidic vision and a growing antiquarian interest in popular customs that might preserve otherwise lost ancient modes of thought. Iolo believed that faithful oral transmission was closely related to song and poetry. A love of poetry and song was still to be found in Glamorgan, and elsewhere in Wales, and Iolo proposed including a collection of traditional songs in his 'History of Glamorgan'. He pointedly claimed that the Welsh, 'humble of station as they are, still endeavour in most parts of Wales to keep up in uninterrupted continuance their ancient customary meetings', which had a benign effect on the intellect.[105] He pointed out that 'before the use of letters was known, the best expedient for fixing and perpetuating oral tradition was song or verse'.[106] The Druids and bards had embodied their philosophy in a series of triads which had been transmitted orally until their late preservation in manuscript.

Oral triads breathed life into desiccated archaeological remains. Iolo's druidic archaeology was in the tradition of William Stukeley, the eighteenth-century antiquary who had accurately planned Stonehenge and Avebury. As a journeyman mason in the 1770s, Iolo had viewed Silbury Hill and Stonehenge, and other sites on Marlborough Downs, interpreting a concentration of sarsen blocks ('The Grey Withers') as a 'stupendous' *carnedd*, 'the grand seat of the Druids before the Roman invasion'.[107] Iolo's reaction to these monuments was primarily in terms of Stukeley's druidic theories. Stukeley (following Aubrey but contra Inigo Jones) had argued that Stonehenge and other stone circles were pre-Roman, and were indeed the temples of noble Druids who had led the resistance to Roman occupation.[108] Iolo's references to 'The *Patriarchal Religion* of ANCIENT BRITAIN, called Druidism' in *Poems, Lyric and Pastoral* (1794) show his indebtedness to Stukeley's view of druidism as a kind of proto-Christianity.[109] Iolo's innovation was to make the Welsh bards the inheritors of druidic wisdom, and to give primacy to the bards of Glamorgan as preservers of the tradition.[110] He himself inherited the mantle of a patriarch by claiming to be the last of 'the old regularly admitted bards', according to a custom evidently derived from the Druids.[111]

[105] NLW 13089E, p. 324.
[106] Ibid., p. 434.
[107] Jon Cannon and Mary-Ann Constantine, 'A Welsh Bard in Wiltshire: Iolo Morganwg, Silbury and the Sarsens', *Wiltshire Archaeological and Natural History Magazine*, 97 (2004), 78–88.
[108] Stuart Piggott, *William Stukeley: An Eighteenth-Century Antiquary* (rev. edn., London, 1985), chapter IV.
[109] Williams: *PLP*, II, p. 194.
[110] This theme will be discussed in Cathryn A. Charnell-White's forthcoming study of the bardo-druidic vision of Iolo Morganwg.
[111] NLW 21387E, no. 2.

Iolo's bardo-druidic vision strengthened his interest in the archaeological monuments associated with druidism. Henry Rowlands's *Mona Antiqua Restaurata* (1723), which had influenced Stukeley, claimed a druidic origin for chambered tombs – interpreted as druidic stone altars – and for standing stones – said to be 'unhewn idols'.[112] Iolo's Glamorgan – like Rowlands's Anglesey – had a landscape studded with druidic remains. Iolo listed fifty-nine 'druidic altars' in Glamorgan, as well as several rocking-stones and stone circles.[113] The two druidic altars (chambered tombs) near Dyffryn Golych – the Vale of Worship – were particularly impressive, with room enough for the stabling of five or six horses beneath the altar stone (capstone). Iolo was astounded by the huge erratics on Newton Down, which he believed had been brought together, like the sarsens on Marlborough Down ('we know not [by] what art'), to form rough circles. One stone alone, 'could we cut or break it', would produce as many stones 'as compass the whole of Stonehenge'. It was understandable that Iolo should link one of Glamorgan's massive druidic altars and Stonehenge as 'mighty achievements in the Isle of Britain' in one of his spurious ancient triads.[114] He disputed the primacy of the druidic landscape in Anglesey and rejected some of the 'groundless conjecture' of *Mona Antiqua Restaurata* in characteristically forthright terms. Druidic vestiges on Anglesey were considered 'paltry', and it was particularly disabling that the island lacked stone circles.[115] For Iolo, following Stukeley's interpretation of Stonehenge, the stone circle was a druidic temple, but – and this was Iolo's contribution – it was also a bardic circle. The stone circle became of central importance in Iolo's vision of bardo-druidism and his creation of the Gorsedd. As Iolo put it in *Poems, Lyric and Pastoral*:

> The *Welsh Bards* always meet in the open air whilst the Sun is above the horizon, where they form a circle of *stones*, according to this ancient custom . . . In these days, however, it is formed only of a few very small stones, or pebbles, such as may be carried to the spot in one man's pocket; but this would not have been deemed sufficient by those who formed the stupendous *Bardic Circle* of *Stone-Henge*.

In the middle of the bardic circle was the '*maen gorsedd* [presidial stone]; by all but the *Bards* called an *Altar*'.[116]

Although Iolo never published his history of the bards, his ideas circulated

---

[112] Charnell-White, *Barbarism and Bardism*, pp. 4–5.

[113] NLW 13159A, pp. 38–9 (druidic altars in Glamorgan); NLW 13153A, pp. 285–90 (incomplete lists of *cromlechau*, tumuli, stone circles, and ruined chapels).

[114] *MAW*, II, p. 70, triad 88. On Maen Cati, see Taliesin Williams and Thomas Price (eds.), *Iolo Manuscripts: A Selection of Ancient Manuscripts* (Llandovery, 1848), p. 473.

[115] NLW 13130A, p. 292; William Owen Pughe, *The Heroic Elegies and other Pieces of Llywarch Hen* (London, 1792), p. xlvi, n†.

[116] Williams: *PLP*, II, pp. 39n*, 215n*.

by correspondence and conversation. By 1806, when Colt Hoare had completed his annotations of Giraldus, Iolo's ideas had passed into the antiquarian
mainstream. Colt Hoare published notes on bardism communicated by
William Owen Pughe, which described in terms derived from Iolo the importance of the 'oral record' of the triads, the solemn meetings within stone circles,
and the three orders of bards, druids and ovates. It was important to bring to
the public's notice that the bardic system was 'still preserved as to the general
principles within a small district of Glamorganshire'. Without the oral record
preserved by the Chair of Glamorgan, 'we should have probably nothing left
of Bardism or Druidism except in scattered ruins, of which nothing satisfactory
could now be made out'.[117]

Archaeology linked history and literature in a meaningful way in Iolo's
bardic vision. It helped him to negotiate the problem of historicity and physically to ground his bardo-druidic mythology. We can take our leave of Iolo,
mason, poet and antiquary, with his 'Vision written in an ancient Bardic circle
on Morlais Hill near Merthyr Tidvil', confident that his historical mythology
approached the truth:[118]

> Frequenting still this hallow'd place
> In airy forms a gentle race
> Meek sons of truth, to Nature dear
> Britannia's ancient Bards appear.
>
> . . .
>
> They stand beside yon central stone,
> These first to Britains Isle were known
> Still offic'd, as of days of yore
> Conservators of bardic lore.
> To these of ancient right belong
> Truth's oral tale, the skill of song.

Within the circle is the self-educated bard (like Iolo himself), 'nobly favour'd
by the muse':

> Detesting error's haggard form
> He soar'd above her warring storm,
> Forsook the fervent joys of youth,
> To walk the toilsome roads of truth,
> Dangers that made all others quake,
> He nobly suffered for her sake.
> Self-taught he bridged th'imperil'd way
> That oe'r the bogs of error lay.

---

[117] Richard Colt Hoare, *The Itinerary of Archbishop Baldwin through Wales, A. D. MCLXXXVIII*
(2 vols., London, 1806), II, pp. 317–18.
[118] NLW 13094E, pp. 80–2; cf. also NLW 13117E, pp. 20–2.

10

Iolo Morganwg and the Welsh Rural Landscape

DAVID CERI JONES

Unlike many of the Enlightenment figures with whom Iolo Morganwg regularly rubbed shoulders, it is difficult to subject his writings to systematic examination. Like many autodidacts, his interests were wide ranging and his voluminous manuscripts are full of essays, tracts and notes on a remarkable array of subjects, only a fraction of which have seen the light of day. Like his near contemporary and fellow enlightened thinker, Robert Owen, Iolo's lack of formal intellectual training meant that he lacked many of the disciplines which would have enabled him to present a consistent argument.[1] To approach his writings in the expectation of finding a logical and internally consistent presentation of his thoughts on any given subject may therefore be unrealistic. While Elijah Waring may well have been overstating the case when he called him *'sui generis'*,[2] the sheer breadth of Iolo's interests and his undoubted idiosyncracies have made it difficult for historians and literary critics to unravel his reflections in a convincing manner.

Throughout his life Iolo maintained a remarkable interest in matters relating to mankind's relationship with the natural world. He read and wrote about subjects as diverse as geology, farming, gardening, rural life and customs, industry, urban development and architecture. His most distilled thoughts on many of these subjects are to be found in the material which he amassed on the counties of Glamorgan and Carmarthen during 1796 in the hope that he would be appointed a surveyor by the Board of Agriculture. Most of what Iolo penned was written with the specific remit of the Board in mind and it therefore focused narrowly on the agricultural improvements which had been carried out in south Wales. However, this material does not adequately reflect the breadth of Iolo's interests or the depth of his analysis of the socio-economic conditions in Wales during the era dominated by the Napoleonic

---

[1] For similarities in the thought-processes of both men, see Geoffrey Powell, '"They shall no longer see as through a glass darkly": Robert Owen and the Welsh Enlightenment', *MC*, 91 (2003), 53–4.

[2] *RAEW*, p. 34.

Wars. His manuscripts are full of notes on a diverse range of related subjects on this theme which enables us to trace some of the principal influences on his thought and to make some intriguing connections between him and some of the leading social and economic theorists of his day. While it would be too ambitious to claim that Iolo formulated a completely integrated vision of the rural landscape, it is possible to identify several themes and influences, albeit apparently contradictory, which run through his writings on subjects related to the rural economy and landscape. This chapter will examine Iolo's writing on rural affairs in a number of contexts. It will begin by looking at Iolo's considerable experience of rural life, before briefly looking at his espousal of a pastoral and picturesque view of nature, particularly during the period up to the publication of his *Poems, Lyric and Pastoral* in 1794. It will then analyse some of Iolo's comments on economics, which were informed by his reading of many of the leading theorists of the day during his four-year sojourn in London between 1791 and 1795. However, the bulk of the chapter will focus on the material which Iolo initially prepared for the Board of Agriculture in 1796, but which was later incorporated into Walter Davies's *General View of the Agriculture and Domestic Economy of South Wales* (1815). It was in this material that Iolo focused specifically on the introduction of agricultural improvements into Glamorgan and Carmarthenshire.

The Enlightenment revolutionized the way people related to the natural world by setting in motion a long process whereby influential thinkers redefined the place of mankind within the created order. The earth, it was suggested, was neither intrinsically evil nor divine, but a stable entity governed by the immutable laws of nature. It was therefore the responsibility of mankind to harness these laws and execute the biblical mandate to subdue and replenish the earth in a radically new way.[3] Among many other things, this opened the way for a new approach to agriculture which acknowledged that nature would pay handsome dividends if the principles of good husbandry were implemented in an environmentally sensitive manner. Improvement, by which was meant the management and cultivation of land to make it more profitable, became the watchword of those concerned with the appropriate utilization of the natural world, underlined as it was by the characteristic eighteenth-century ideology of progress.[4] Between roughly 1780 and the 1830s the rural territory of England and Wales underwent significant change as increasing amounts of land were brought under cultivation, and the use of efficient agricultural

---

[3]   For more on these developments, see R. W. Harris, *Reason and Nature in the Eighteenth Century* (London, 1968); Keith Thomas, *Man and the Natural World: Changing Attitudes in England, 1500–1800* (London, 1983); Roy Porter, *Enlightenment: Britain and the Creation of the Modern World* (London, 2000), pp. 295–319.

[4]   David Spadafora, *The Idea of Progress in Eighteenth-Century Britain* (New Haven, 1990), pp. 312–13, 328–9, 371–7.

Fig. 19 An oil painting, 1825–6, by Hugh Hughes of the antiquary and poet, Walter Davies (Gwallter Mechain), whom Iolo held in some esteem.

practices was championed on a much larger scale than ever before. These developments were given greater impetus after the outbreak of the Napoleonic Wars when a series of poor harvests, aggravated by the restrictions of the wars themselves, led to widespread grain shortages which were acutely felt by the rapidly growing population.[5]

These far-reaching economic changes were a daily reality to Iolo Morganwg. As a highly skilled stonemason, Iolo was deeply embedded in the commercial world of the Vale of Glamorgan, with its strong trade links with Bristol, Bath and other lucrative markets in south-west England.[6] During much of the 1770s, too, he travelled widely in England, finding work as a journeyman mason in Somerset, Devon, Dorset and Kent, as well as on the leading gentry estates in and around the Vale of Glamorgan. Having married in 1781, he began using his commercial contacts to become, as he styled himself, 'a piece of [a] marble and freestone mason . . . [a] piece of [a] builder and piece of a farmer, and a lime burner for the use of the public'.[7] Iolo, the budding entrepreneur, acquired a small sloop – grandly dubbed the *Lion* – which traded regularly between Aberthaw and Bristol. In the mid-1780s he attempted to extend his commercial interests by taking over his brother Thomas's workshop at Wells in Somerset.[8] Later, following his attempts to establish himself as a labouring-class poet in the cut-throat London literary scene, he sought to revive his commercial interests in 1795 by opening a bookshop and a general store in Cowbridge.[9] Even when this venture folded he continued to explore money-making opportunities; at one point he invited Owen Jones (Owain Myfyr) to help him set up a small business manufacturing pencils from lead he had extracted from a local quarry.[10]

Interspersed with these ventures were longer periods when Iolo attempted to farm the twenty acres which he had inherited from his father-in-law, Rees Roberts, at Rumney. His determination to make a success of the farm led him to rent additional land at Llandaf in 1783.[11] However, the financial burden of these additional commitments, together with debts he had inherited from his

[5]   The impact of the Napoleonic Wars on British agriculture is dealt with in considerable detail in Alan Armstrong, *Farmworkers in England and Wales: A Social and Economic History* (Ames, Iowa, 1988), pp. 44–60.
[6]   W. E. Minchinton, 'Bristol: Metropolis of the West in the Eighteenth Century' in Peter Clark (ed.), *The Early Modern Town: A Reader* (London, 1976), p. 297; Philip Jenkins, 'Wales' in Peter Clark (ed.), *The Cambridge Urban History of Britain, Volume II, 1540–1840* (Cambridge, 2000), p. 133.
[7]   BL Add. 15024, ff. 196–9, Iolo Morganwg to Owain Myfyr, 20 September 1783.
[8]   NLW 21289E, p. 8; Williams, *IM*, p. 349.
[9]   NLW 21282E, Letter no. 397, John Reed to Iolo Morganwg, 20 January 1796; Letter no. 401, Samuel Reed to Iolo Morganwg, 31 January 1796; Letter no. 402, Samuel Reed to Iolo Morganwg, 3 February 1796.
[10] BL Add. 15030, ff. 14ʳ–15ᵛ, Iolo Morganwg to Owain Myfyr, 9 July 1800.
[11] NLW 21389E, p. 8.

father-in-law, led to his incarceration for a year in Cardiff prison from August 1786.[12] Yet, there can be little doubt that Iolo was a moderately successful farmer. He did not lose his farms because of incompetence or misman-agement, but because he had taken on the onerous burden of his father-in-law's debts. We know from his manuscripts that Iolo was an avid reader of many of the leading improving agricultural writers of his day. He was familiar with the ideas of William Marshall and made copious notes on many of Arthur Young's writings, including *The Farmer's Kalendar* (1770) and the *Annals of Agriculture* (1784–1815). He steeped himself in many of the reports of the Board of Agriculture,[13] though his opinion of them was not high. He was scathing about John Fox's *General View of the Agriculture of Glamorgan*, published early in 1796. He believed it to be a 'glaring imposition on the public' and confessed to having been 'in some things led astray by it for some time as it suggested to me suppositions that I afterwards found to be very delusive'.[14]

Iolo was also determined to practise what he had read and to farm his land according to enlightened principles. In one of his letters to William Matthews, the secretary of the Royal Bath and West Agricultural Society, he informed him of the experiments he had carried out with two strains of Indian corn (maize) given him by Captain Murray, an otherwise anonymous loyalist soldier who had settled near Cowbridge following the outbreak of the American War of Independence. Iolo's account, interspersed with comments on several recently published works on the cultivation of Indian corn, included a detailed discussion of the consistency of the soils in which the two strains had been grown, the fertilizers used, and some of the variations in the microclimate at each site, before proceeding to make recommendations based on his empirical research. Contrasting his ideas with those carried out by two other local agricultural improvers, Robert Key, an agent at St Fagans, and John Bradley, the proprietor of the Angel Inn in Cardiff, Iolo reckoned that the abundant crops of Indian corn which they had been able to harvest, strongly suggested that it was an ideal fodder crop for cattle, sheep and horses.[15] Iolo was fully aware of advanced contemporary thinking on farming practices and was suffi-ciently in tune with the desire of the Board of Agriculture to encourage agricultural improvements to lead him to believe that it would be delighted to engage his services as a surveyor in south Wales.[16] Indeed, such was Iolo's opinion of his skills as an agriculturalist and a commentator on economic

[12] Ibid.; Williams: *IM*, pp. 442–50.
[13] For an indication of the range of books on agriculture and other aspects of the natural sciences which Iolo read, see NLW 13147A, pp. 293–412.
[14] NLW 21413E, no. 50.
[15] NLW 21285E, Letter no. 856, Iolo Morganwg to William Matthews, 18 July 1796.
[16] For a detailed consideration of Iolo's relationship with the Board of Agriculture, see David Ceri Jones, '"Mere Humbug": Iolo Morganwg and the Board of Agriculture', *THSC*, 10 (2004), 76–97.

affairs that he deigned to rebuke William Pitt on issues relating to taxation and offer his services as an adviser on Welsh affairs.[17]

Up until the mid-1790s much of Iolo's energy was devoted to securing the publication of the pastoral poems that he had been composing since the early 1770s, and the four tortuous years that he spent in London, between 1791 and 1795, trying to raise enough subscribers to enable him to realize this ambition exacted a heavy toll. The view of the countryside that emerges from *Poems, Lyric and Pastoral* is very different from that which Iolo was later to adopt in his work for the Board of Agriculture. Pastoral poetry had come back into vogue during the middle years of the eighteenth century.[18] Within the context of the growth of towns and cities and widespread industrialization, pastoral poetry became a form of escape literature in which poets extolled the virtues of the simple rural life. It reflected, in John Goodridge's words, the 'apparently universal, pre-conscious, human desire for an ideal and simple world',[19] and the trope of the Garden of Eden was often employed to reflect this longing for primitive simplicity. Yet there was not necessarily any contradiction between aggressive commercial farming and idyllic views of nature: to enlightened minds, enclosure and progressive agriculture were both appropriate forms of environmental superintendence. To Iolo, farming was one of the highest callings to which people could aspire: those engaged in tilling the land were at the forefront of efforts to 'restore . . . this world [to] the Eden it has been driven out of'.[20] In *Poems, Lyric and Pastoral* he eulogized ploughmen, shepherds and reapers,[21] and in a poem dedicated to the Glamorgan Agricultural Society he sharply contrasted the lives of those 'that abide in the filth of a town'[22] with the lot of the happy farmer:

> How happy the life of an innocent swain,
> That dwells with his hands and his flocks on the plain;
> Who labours abroad on his farm all the day,
> Now turning his fallows, now tedding his hay;
> Here cattle in fields of rich clover we view;
> Here lambkins in meads of a beautiful hue;
> And here the rich fruits of his labours we find,
> Where the wheat's golden curls gently wave in the wind.[23]

---

[17]   The National Archives, PRO 30/8/190/83LH, Iolo Morganwg to William Pitt, 16 December 1796.

[18]   For pastoral poetry, see Judith Haber, *Pastoral and the Poetics of Self-Contradiction: Theocritus to Marvell* (Cambridge, 1994); Terry Gifford, *Pastoral* (London, 1999).

[19]   John Goodridge, *Rural Life in Eighteenth-Century English Poetry* (Cambridge, 1995), p. 3.

[20]   NLW 21285E, Letter no. 857, Iolo Morganwg to William Matthews, 19 July 1796.

[21]   Williams: *PLP*, I, pp. 6–13.

[22]   Ibid., p. 59.

[23]   Ibid., p. 60.

Despite being well received, poetry of this type was becoming unfashionable by the end of the eighteenth century and was effectively abandoned by the Romantics. Wordsworth's pastoral poems probably mark the culmination of the genre, but even he preferred a view of nature charged with visionary power rather than the submissive, idyllic and inoffensive countryside which Iolo chose to eulogize in his volumes of poetry.[24]

Pastoral views of the countryside were supplemented by Iolo's interest in the picturesque. As a result of the neo-classical revival which occurred in art and literature towards the end of the eighteenth century, and which was popularized by Edmund Burke and William Gilpin, lovers of the picturesque often reacted against the formality introduced into the rural landscape by the proponents of commercial farming.[25] Although there is no evidence that Iolo had read the works of Uvedale Price, there seem to be clear parallels between the advice which he offered to landlords in south Wales who sought his counsel on refashioning their estates and the models which Price outlined in his highly influential *Essay on the Picturesque* (1794). Objecting to the uniformity which professional landscape gardeners like Capability Brown had introduced, Price celebrated the intricacy and variety of the British countryside and championed the contribution of the amateur gardener by harking back to individuals like William Shenstone and Charles Hamilton, who had created gardens in keeping with local conditions. He recommended that gardeners study the paintings of Claude, Poussin and Salvator Rosa, who had popularized the practice of setting their paintings within classical landscapes, in order to recreate similar vistas on their own estates.[26]

In 1780 Iolo ventured to advise Thomas Mansel Talbot on the refurbishment of his estate at Margam. Having recently completed the ambitious building of an impressive Georgian villa on his estate at Penrice, Gower, Mansel Talbot had begun drawing up similar plans for Margam. Iolo made several recommendations in a long and detailed letter, the most ambitious and fanciful of which, based on a similar edifice he had seen at Cotham Park near Bristol, was a plan to build a four- or five- hundred foot ornamented tower on the summit of one of the hills on the estate, which would 'be by far the highest in Britain or perhaps in the world and would have an appearance uncommonly novel, beautiful and originally grand and majestic'.[27] Less ambitious, but still

[24] Wordsworth's view of nature is discussed in Alan Bewell, *Wordsworth and the Enlightenment: Nature, Man, and Society in the Experimental Poetry* (New Haven, 1989).

[25] Thomas, *Man and the Natural World*, pp. 261–2.

[26] For more on Price's ideas, see Malcolm Andrews, *The Search for the Picturesque: Landscape, Aesthetic and Tourism in Britain, 1760–1800* (Aldershot, 1989), pp. 56–66; Stephen Daniels and Charles Watkins, 'Picturesque Landscaping and Estate Management: Uvedale Price at Foxley, 1770–1829', *Rural History*, II (1991), 141–69.

[27] NLW 21285E, Letter no. 788, Iolo Morganwg to Thomas Mansel Talbot, 23 August 1780.

aesthetically sensitive, were Iolo's plans for the rebuilding of Margam village along picturesque lines:

> Suppose a number of elegant farm houses and cottages were to [be] erected at a convenient distance, but within view, to the northwes[t] and north east of Margam Abbey, or any where else where it might be necessary to hide a disagreeable object in or enliven a dead part of the landscape, and that they be built a little detached from each other which would give them a more picturesque appearance than if built in continued rows, especially if they were interspersed with orchards, gardens, and plantations of fir, pine, larch, cedar, abele, lime, elm &c &c and the houses to be yearly white washed, according to the neat custom which prevails in and is almost peculiar to Glamorgan. Barns, stables, cowhouses and such buildings may be so order'd as to be cover'd from view by being placed behind the dwelling houses that too great regularity (which always has an air of stiffness) be avoided in the structure of these houses, nothing being more essential to beauty than a judicious and well managed variety. Accordingly, I would propose that some of these houses be built in the most modern taste, i.e. the antique Grecian taste, others in Chiness and other in a good Gothic taste and each of these houses to have some elegant peculiarity in its structure, especially those that are in the strongest view from the abbey. By this means, Sir, you could make Margam Abbey and its environs a kind of earthly paradise and induce many genteel families to settle in the neighbourhood which would be the means of greatly improving your estate.[28]

Iolo's interest in the picturesque did not fade as he became increasingly involved in collecting information for the Board of Agriculture. Indeed, as late as 1807 he discussed with Thomas Johnes plans for the rebuilding of the Hafod mansion following the devastating fire of March that year.[29] He advised Johnes regarding appropriate marble for the building of classical Italianate columns and returned once more to the idea of erecting a tall tower at an appropriate location on the estate.[30]

Iolo's plans reflected the revived interest in wild and picturesque Wales. These were the years when travellers and tourists visited Wales in unprecedented numbers, though the Wales they wished to see was increasingly becoming vulnerable to the onward march of industrialization and urban growth.[31] On the surface, Iolo's espousal of pastoral and picturesque views of the rural landscape stands in sharp contrast to his later commitment to agricultural improvement and the enclosure of common land. When viewed in

---

[28] Ibid.

[29] R. J. Moore-Colyer (ed.), *A Land of Pure Delight: Selections from the Letters of Thomas Johnes of Hafod, Cardiganshire (1748–1816)* (Llandysul, 1992), pp. 19–25.

[30] NLW 21281E, Letter no. 218, Thomas Johnes to Iolo Morganwg, 18 January 1808.

[31] Prys Morgan, 'Wild Wales: Civilizing the Welsh from the Sixteenth to the Nineteenth Centuries' in Peter Burke, Brian Harrison and Paul Slack (eds.), *Civil Histories: Essays presented to Sir Keith Thomas* (Oxford, 2000), pp. 276–7.

isolation, his ideas in each of these domains seem reasonable and consistent, but it is almost impossible to bring these disparate elements together into a coherent whole. Iolo seems to have been able to compartmentalize his thought with apparent ease, juxtaposing what appear to be contradictory opinions, without ever feeling the need to reconcile them or temper his language.

This lack of consistency may also be seen in some of Iolo's comments on economic matters. As he immersed himself in London's exciting and dangerous 'radical underworld' in the early 1790s,[32] Iolo came into contact with a bewildering array of individuals and ideas. He seems to have borrowed physiocratic notions about the value of agriculture and natural resources and combined them with more traditionalist mercantilist ideas, especially regarding the regulation of trade. Mercantilists, particularly those who followed the doctrines of Thomas Mun, believed that a positive trade balance could only be achieved by closely supervising foreign trade. By the seventeenth century this was interpreted in protectionist terms as mercantilists called on governments to support national manufactures.[33] Referring to the agricultural community, Iolo argued in favour of supporting and protecting indigenous farmers and manufacturers rather than depending on the uncertain profits of foreign trade. He wrote:

When Spain becomes as wise as ourselves and manufactures her own superior wool, when every other country in Europe does the same, when the East Indies and other countries will become determined not to export an ounce of cotton, silk &c unmanufactured, when iron, steel &c can no longer be obtained from Sweden, Russia, America &c b[eing] manufactured into the curious articles that now employ the ten of thousands at Birmingham, Sheffield, &c then we mu[st] bid adieu to our national wealth if it consists in nothing permanent. When nations and communities that have been [hither]to in a state of infancy attain to that of manhood, to which n[one] of them now approach very fast, when all Europe, Asia, Africa and America attain to this age of maturity we may still manufacture for home consumption but not for many countries besides. When the greatest part of the world becomes as skilful as ourselves, when most countries become our rivals, we shall not have many places whereunto we may send our laden ships, we must send hard cash for most of the articles that we want from abroad, wherever we may find those that will still buy our woollen, hard, and pottery wares &c that will be many other nations equally wise and skilful as ourselves endeavouring to undersell us and such a time must come infallibly sooner or later. But the agriculturalist is the eternal friend of the community. If he introduces an animal, a fruit, a grain, a root, a dye, a timber, a fibrous plant . . . that will bear our climate it is ours forever. It will in its culture and

[32] See Jon Mee, *Dangerous Enthusiasm: William Blake and the Culture of Radicalism in the 1790s* (Oxford, 1992); Iain McCalman, *Radical Underworld: Prophets, Revolutionaries and Pornographers in London, 1795–1840* (Oxford, 1993).

[33] For introductions to mercantilist economics, see Lars Magnusson, *Mercantilism: The Shaping of an Economic Language* (London, 1994); Gianni Vaggi and Peter D. Groenwegen, *A Concise History of Economic Thought: From Mercantilism to Monetarism* (Basingstoke, 2003), pp. 15–22.

preparation employ numbers of our fellow inhabitants as long as our wants call out.[34]

But it is in his commitment to the fundamental importance of agriculture within a modern and prosperous economy that the strongest overtones of physiocratic economics appear in Iolo's writings. The physiocratic school originated in France and was most closely associated with the thought of François Quesnay and the Marquis de Mirabeau who argued that, since all true wealth derived ultimately from the land, only agriculture could provide a real return on investment and that, if allowed to circulate freely, wealth derived from agriculture would sustain the economic life of society.[35] Investment in agriculture and the stimulation of demand for agricultural produce should therefore be the bedrock of government policy.[36] The extent to which physiocratic ideas had taken root in Britain by the end of the eighteenth century is difficult to ascertain. Some of Mirabeau's works had been translated into English and his son had translated Richard Price's *Observations on the Importance of the American Revolution* (1784) into French. Extracts from physiocratic writers had also appeared in the *Monthly Review* from time to time and we know that Iolo read the journal on a regular basis.[37] It is tempting to cite Richard Price as one of the sources from which Iolo might have assimilated physiocratic ideas. A severe critic of urban life, Price believed that agriculture should be enthusiastically promoted and that some inhabitants of towns and cities should be forced to return to the countryside.[38] Iolo entered this radical Dissenting culture, which focused around Joseph Johnson's printing house and various Dissenting academies,[39] when he arrived in London in 1791, and from then onwards the likes of John Aikin and George Dyer remained his most reliable contacts with radical Dissenting circles, particularly after he returned to Wales.[40] It is not difficult to find echoes of physocratic opinions in Iolo's writings. Since 'nature seems to have pointed out agriculture as the only source of wealth in Britain',[41] he wrote in one of his long political essays, the experimental farmer was the foundation of the success of the economy and the

[34] NLW 21285E, Letter no. 857, Iolo Morganwg to William Matthews, 19 July 1796.

[35] Peter France (ed.), *The New Oxford Companion to Literature in French* (Oxford, 1995), p. 622.

[36] Ronald L. Meek, *The Economics of Physiocracy: Essays and Translations* (London, 1962), pp. 22–7.

[37] NLW 13120B, pp. 132, 134; NLW 13129A, pp. 393–415, 441–56; NLW 13131A, pp. 159–60; NLW 13138A, pp. 247–53; NLW 13145A, pp. 350–6; NLW 13147A, pp. 225–45.

[38] George Claeys, 'Virtuous Commerce and Free Theology: Political Economy and the Dissenting Academies, 1750–1800', *History of Political Thought*, XX, no. I (1999), 164.

[39] For Johnson's circle, see Helen Braithwaite, *Romanticism, Publishing, and Dissent: Joseph Johnson and the Cause of Liberty* (Basingstoke, 2003).

[40] NLW 21280E, Letter no. 1, John Aikin to Iolo Morganwg, undated; Letter 132, George Dyer to Iolo Morganwg, 1794; Letter no. 136, George Dyer to Iolo Morganwg, 16 April 1801; Letter no. 141, George Dyer to Iolo Morganwg, 19 April 1798.

[41] NLW 21323B, p. 52.

prosperity of the country. Nevertheless, Iolo was not necessarily a critic of the urban and industrial development of south Wales. His career straddled the period when Wales made the transition from being a largely rural economy, reliant on agriculture, to one with a very sizeable proportion of people living in urban areas and employed in the rapidly growing copper, iron and coal industries. While Wales did not have any cities in this period, it could boast a large number of small but lively towns which performed similar functions to those of much larger towns in England.[42] Iolo had a foot in both rural and urban worlds. The Vale of Glamorgan was on the periphery of the rapidly growing industrial heartlands of south Wales and his trade as a mason regularly took him to some of these areas, as well as to larger commercial centres like Bristol and London. Later, his Unitarian contacts with places like Neath and Bridgend and his frequent visits to his son, Taliesin, who became a school-master in Merthyr Tydfil, meant that he acquired first-hand knowledge of the nature and problems of urban life.

Physiocrats despised what they referred to as the 'city spirit' which destroyed society from within, ruining the economy, corrupting morals and spreading idleness.[43] Iolo, too, could be scathing in his condemnation of towns and all that was associated with them. 'Great cities', he once wrote, 'are destructive of population, life, health [and] morals.'[44] He believed that London was 'totally unfriendly to the human constitution' and was so 'destructive of life and health'[45] that it 'ruins everyone'.[46] Economically, cities like London had exercised an adverse effect on the rest of the country 'by drawing as by magnetism, all trade and science into one spot, [leaving] remote and interior parts in a state of barbarity, ignorance, want of employment, and destitution'.[47] He was deeply critical of the culture of politeness and the preoccupation with luxury which characterized many English towns and cities. Echoing elements of Joseph Priestley's critique of luxury, he deplored the 'two great objects pursued in great cities ... pleasure and interest'.[48] Some of Iolo's most outspoken remarks about London can be attributed to the damaging effects of the four years he spent in the capital from February 1791 until June 1795, a period scarred by the death of his daughter, deep depressions and even thoughts of suicide as he worked tirelessly to secure the publication of *Poems,*

[42] For a discussion of the importance of functional, rather than strictly numerical, definitions of urban areas, see Peter Borsay, *The English Urban Renaissance: Culture and Society in the Provincial Town, 1660–1770* (Oxford, 1989), pp. 4–11.

[43] Pierre Rosanvallon, 'Physiocrats' in François Furet and Mona Ozouf (eds.), *A Critical Dictionary of the French Revolution* (Cambridge, MA, 1989), p. 765.

[44] NLW 21323B, p. 57.

[45] Ibid., p. 56.

[46] NLW 21285E, Letter no. 812, Iolo Morganwg to Margaret Williams, 27 October 1792.

[47] NLW 21323B, p. 57.

[48] Ibid., p. 51.

Lyric and Pastoral. But his views also offer an insight into the way in which many enlightened thinkers found it difficult to reconcile their idealized concepts of true virtue with the equally important pursuit of wealth and the encouragement of commerce.[49] His comments were held in tension with other more positive remarks in the material which he later collected for the Board of Agriculture. In a Welsh context Iolo was considerably more discerning in his observations on some of the major towns of Glamorgan and Carmarthenshire, particularly those associated with the growth of industry. Visiting Swansea in 1796, he observed that the town had 'improved amazingly'[50] over the course of the previous quarter of a century and that it now enjoyed 'a very great coal-trade, large copper works, [and] a pottery equal, as some say to Mr Wedgewood's'.[51] Three miles further inland he visited Sir John Morris's new settlement at Morriston and reckoned that his plan of laying out the town, consisting of 'houses stand[ing] detached from, but near to, each other, with good gardens, [and] the streets wide',[52] was the best he had witnessed in any part of Wales or further afield. Further west, Carmarthen also earned his praise for its trading links with London and Bristol, the good quality of its houses and its thriving markets.[53]

Accounting for the apparent contradictions in Iolo's views about urban life is difficult. Among the most bitter critics of urbanization and industrialization there existed a tacit acceptance of the reality of the commercial world. Richard Price, for example, could recommend repatriating urban dwellers to the country-side as well as recognize the economic advantages of towns of a moderate size.[54] Such towns usually fulfilled a vital function even within a predominantly rural landscape, whether as natural markets for agricultural produce or as centres of sociability.[55] The problem of interpreting Iolo's comments may also lie in the mind of the historian used to working within the context of a strict demarcation between urban and rural worlds. It may well be that this conflict was not as keenly felt in the eighteenth century, and that pre-industrial depictions of rural and urban life often did not accentuate the differences.[56] Iolo's views seem to reflect one of the most readily observable

---

[49] This tension is explored in more detail in relation to Joseph Priestley by Vilem Mudroch, 'Joseph Priestley in Morals and Economics: Reconciling the Quest for Virtue with the Pursuit of Wealth', *Enlightenment and Dissent*, XX (2001), 45–87.

[50] NLW 13115E, p. 37.

[51] Ibid.

[52] Ibid., p. 100.

[53] Ibid., p. 56.

[54] Claeys, 'Virtuous Commerce and Free Theology', 163.

[55] Paul Glennie and Ian Whyte, 'Towns in an Agrarian Economy, 1540–1700' in Clark (ed.), *The Cambridge Urban History of Britain*, II, pp. 173–80.

[56] Saree Makdisi, *Romantic Imperialism: Universal Empire and the Culture of Modernity* (Cambridge, 1998), pp. 71–6.

fault-lines in his character. While he often portrayed himself as a 'plain Welsh rustic',[57] a rural figure on the margins of national life, he also jealously craved the acceptance of urban elites and rather enjoyed the cut and thrust of urban life, whether it was in a small, but vibrant, market town like Cowbridge or a metropolis like London or Bristol.

Iolo's return from London in early 1795 marked a turning-point in his life and brought about a readjustment in his priorities. He did not envisage another protracted period away from home and therefore returned to his mason's trade to provide his family with a more secure and stable income. It was at a time when these changed priorities were uppermost in his mind that he came across an advertisement from the Royal Bath and West Agricultural Society who had been instructed by the Board of Agriculture to secure the services of an appropriate individual to undertake a survey of the agriculture and domestic economy of south Wales.[58] The Board of Agriculture was the institutional expression of the drive for agricultural improvement during the years dominated by the Napoleonic Wars.[59] The idea of a board of agriculture had first been suggested by William Marshall in *The Rural Economy of the Midland Counties* (1790),[60] but it was Sir John Sinclair, who had already invested considerable time and money in his ambitious *Statistical Account of Scotland* (1791–9), who eventually made the Board a reality in 1793. The Board of Agriculture drew heavily on the progressive agrarian ideas of Sinclair, Arthur Young and William Marshall, though the latter refused to cooperate with it once Young had been appointed the Board's first permanent secretary.[61] The Board of Agriculture differed from the improvers of the past[62] by calling for a more thorough reorganization of the mechanisms of production along lines which reflected its three watchwords: profit, innovation and productivity. Much of its attention was therefore directed towards the activities of a relatively small but progressive and highly motivated agrarian elite which would become the catalysts for more far-reaching change. But rather than sponsor experiments and fund improvements directly, Sinclair's Board commissioned separate surveys on each of the counties of England and Wales. First conducted in 1793 on a county-by-county basis, these surveys were so poorly conducted that Sinclair was

57 NLW 21285E, Letter no. 858, Iolo Morganwg to the Board of Agriculture, 28 July 1796.
58 NLW 21413E, no. 65.
59 Maureen McNeil, *Under the Banner of Science: Erasmus Darwin and his Age* (Manchester, 1987), p. 178.
60 William Marshall, *The Rural Economy of the Midland Counties* (London, 1790), pp. 88–9.
61 G. E. Mingay, 'William Marshall', *ODNB*; G. E. Fussell, 'William Marshall, Self-appointed National Farm Surveyor', *Journal of the Land Agent's Society*, 52 (1953), 485–90.
62 For their activities, see Pamela Horn, *William Marshall (1745–1815) and the Georgian Countryside* (Abingdon, 1983); Joan Thirsk, 'Plough and Pen: Agricultural Writers in the Seventeenth Century' in T. H. Aston, P. R. Cross, Christopher Dyer and Joan Thirsk (eds.), *Social Relations and Ideas: Essays in Honour of R. H. Hilton* (Cambridge, 1983), pp. 206–13.

forced to recommission them in 1796, at which stage financial considerations prompted him to abandon the notion of producing individual county reports for Wales, and to replace them with just two reports, one for the north and the other for the south.[63]

Sir John Sinclair believed that it was essential that individuals appointed to compile these surveys were entirely in sympathy with the Board's aims and ethos. Following the Baconian insistence that theory and practice should go hand in hand, surveyors were selected because of their practical experience of 'practical husbandry',[64] along with their willingness to record the activities of improving farmers and to demonstrate how backward farming practices could be effectively rooted out. There is no evidence to suggest that Iolo had any difficulty with the Board's remit or agenda in 1796. Initially he held the Board in 'high respect' and believed that it was a 'highly beneficial national insti-tution'.[65] Moreover, by 1796 he had travelled widely in Wales in search of liter-ary manuscripts and, more significantly, as he informed William Matthews, he had 'long been in the habit of making observations on whatever exites my attention in the frequent journeys that the nature of my situation in life occasions into the various parts of the kingdom'.[66] Coupled with his extensive experience of commercial life in south Wales and his efforts to become an improving farmer himself, Iolo, at least on the surface, seemed to be an ideal candidate for the Board.

Agrarian historians have traditionally taken a pessimistic view of the state of farming in Wales at the end of the eighteenth century. Compared with progressive parts of the south of England and East Anglia, farming in Wales was poverty stricken. Modern systems of crop rotation were almost unheard of, farms were often uneconomically small, too much land remained unenclosed, and the implements in regular use had remained unchanged for centuries.[67] This pitiful state of affairs persisted until the eve of the Napoleonic Wars, and certainly nothing approaching an agricultural revolution occurred in the Welsh countryside during the last third of the eighteenth century.[68] Yet there were glimmers of hope and indications that in some areas there were a few

[63] Rosalind Mitchison, 'The Old Board of Agriculture (1793–1822)', *EHR*, LXXIV (1959), 48–51.

[64] NLW 1808Ei, Letter no. 1326a, Sir John Sinclair to Walter Davies, 9 May 1797.

[65] NLW 21285E, Letter no. 858, Iolo Morganwg to William Matthews, 28 July 1796.

[66] Ibid.

[67] David W. Howell, *The Rural Poor in Eighteenth-Century Wales* (Cardiff, 2000), pp. 5–6.

[68] Historians of agriculture in eighteenth-century Britain have debated the existence of an agricultural revolution for many years. Wales has tended to be subsumed within these larger narratives. For introductions to the debate, see G. E. Mingay, *The Agricultural Revolution: Changes in Agriculture, 1650–1850* (London, 1977); Mark Overton, *Agricultural Revolution in England: The Transformation of the Agrarian Economy, 1500–1800* (Cambridge, 1996); Tom Williamson, *The Transformation of Rural England: Farming and the Landscape, 1700–1870* (Exeter, 2002).

resourceful and ambitious farmers who were prepared to implement the latest agricultural knowledge. Iolo became an assiduous recorder of their activities and his notebooks reveal that there was cause for some optimism in certain parts of Wales, especially those which could boast the most fertile agricultural land. However, not all farmers were eager to speak to Iolo. Whether his eccentric ways or his reputation for outspokenness deterred them is impossible to tell, but at Llan-non, Carmarthenshire, for instance, Iolo found that farmers were so truculent that he 'got but little information, only in general terms that wheat would not succeed in their part of the country'.[69]

Naturally, in both Glamorgan and Carmarthenshire there were plenty of primitive agricultural practices which Iolo took great relish in recording, though it must be noted that his criticism of farmers in Glamorgan was considerably more muted than that meted out to their Carmarthenshire counterparts. Despite being slow to adopt many of the progressive agricultural techniques of the day, he believed that Glamorgan had 'certainly made greater advances than any county in Wales'.[70] However, the problems which he highlighted were similar for both counties: the ignorance of the agricultural community, the lack of ambition and a deeply rooted reluctance to experiment with scientific farming practices. Even though he had still to be officially engaged by the Board of Agriculture, Iolo embarked in June 1796 on a tour of the two counties. He began with a detailed description of the state of farming in his parish of Flemingston. He chose not to focus on improvements, preferring instead to criticize local farmers for their excessive use of lime.[71] Liming had become a popular practice in the Vale of Glamorgan by this time. For instance, John Perkins, a gentleman farmer and a neighbour of Iolo at nearby Llantrithyd, had invested heavily in the production of lime by building a kiln and employing a small team of lime-burners to operate it.[72] It is possible that some of Iolo's more critical comments were aimed at Perkins, for we know that he later composed a bitingly satirical song in which he questioned Perkins's abilities as a farmer:

> Bestir them my muse, and I prithie be brief,
> There's Perkins of each awkward farmer the chief
> Some say he'll pass muster, I know not in what
> It is not in farming, full well I know that.[73]

---

[69]   NLW 13115B, p. 46.
[70]   NLW 13147A, p. 157.
[71]   NLW 13115B, pp. 8–11.
[72]   William Linnard, 'John Perkins of Llantrithyd: The Diary of a Gentleman Farmer in the Vale of Glamorgan, 1788–1801', *Morgannwg*, XXXI (1987), 31–2.
[73]   Cardiff 4.304, pp. 112–16.

Iolo blamed the farmers of the Vale for their reluctance to accept that the quality of their pastures was often the direct result of over-dependence on lime rather than, as many of them assumed, their dogged determination to persist with outmoded rotations.[74] According to R. J. Moore-Colyer, the use of lime was one of the more important indicators of agricultural progress in the eighteenth and nineteenth centuries,[75] and Iolo's concentration on its uses in Glamorgan, despite his criticisms, is evidence in itself that there had been at least some improvement in the practice of farming in the county.

In his reflections, Iolo's agricultural concerns overlapped with his interest in mineralogy. The founding of the Board of Agriculture coincided with the birth of the science of geology, which was institutionalized by the founding of the Geological Society in 1807.[76] Iolo drew a direct connection between his trade as a mason and his ability to comment on geological matters,[77] but he also kept abreast of the work of some of the leading geologists of his day and felt sufficiently well-qualified to offer lessons on the subject at his son's school in Merthyr Tydfil in 1816.[78] In 1802 he recommended that the Glamorgan Agricultural Society institute a scheme for a miners' borer which farmers could share among themselves and use to drill their land while searching for 'minerals of fossil manures'.[79] Later he discussed with Walter Davies the possibility of including a detailed geological map in Davies's survey of south Wales.[80] The material which Iolo collected for this purpose did not find its way into Davies's survey, but it was almost certainly utilized later by Conybeare and Phillips in their *Outline of the Geology of England and Wales* (1822).[81] Yet it would be a mistake to believe that none of Iolo's geological knowledge found a place in Davies's survey. Although he was also a keen mineralogist, Davies was able to draw on Iolo's unrivalled knowledge of the geology of Glamorgan when he began to frame the section of his report which dealt with this aspect of the county's natural history.[82] For Iolo, mineralogy was an intensely practical subject which was relevant to farmers everywhere. After visiting the Coed Gwili slate quarries near Brechfa, for example, he wrote: 'I am fully convinced

---

[74] NLW 13115B, pp. 9–10.

[75] R. J. Moore-Colyer, 'Of Lime and Men: Aspects of the Coastal Trade in Lime in South-West Wales in the Eighteenth and Nineteenth Centuries', *WHR*, 14, no. 1 (1988), 69.

[76] For the growing popularity of geological study in the eighteenth century, see Roy Porter, *The Making of Geology: Earth Science in Britain, 1600–1815* (Cambridge, 1997); David Oldroyd, *Thinking about the Earth: A History of Ideas in Geology* (London, 1998).

[77] NLW 13115B, p. 214.

[78] *Cambrian*, 20 January 1816.

[79] NLW 21285E, Letter no. 868, Iolo Morganwg to the Revd Mr [?], 1 September 1802.

[80] NLW 1808Eii, Letter no. 1526, Iolo Morganwg to Walter Davies, 12 August 1806; NLW 13221E, pp. 143–6.

[81] Mary-Ann Constantine, *Combustible Matter: Iolo Morganwg and the Bristol Volcano* (Aberystwyth, 2003), p. 6.

[82] Davies, *A General View of the Agriculture and Domestic Economy of South Wales*, I, pp. 27–94.

that a knowledge of the substrata, and of their properties is very necessary . . . Thus should we collect data whereas to ground subsequent agricultural studies.'[83] Wherever he went Iolo recommended that farmers study the substructure of their soils closely in order to ensure that the farming methods they adopted were in tune with the latest knowledge about the interrelationship between agriculture and geology.[84] There are striking parallels in his writings with those of James Hutton. Although Hutton had considerably wider interests than Iolo, taking in chemistry, botany, meteorology and geology, his studies were motivated by his desire to serve the purpose of the ordinary farmer who was, after all, the key figure in the rural economy.[85]

In Iolo's view the greatest engines of agricultural change were the agricultural societies and the ability of gentleman farmers like John Perkins to invest in new varieties of seeds, improved strains of livestock and the latest agricultural implements. William Williams, Llanishen, and the Revd William Willis, rector of Gileston, were complimented for their experiments with the latest crop rotations,[86] while an anonymous Gower farmer was praised for his wise use of lime.[87] Much of the activity of these farmers was either initiated or supported by the Glamorgan Agricultural Society, which had been founded at a meeting at the Bear Inn, Cowbridge, in October 1772.[88] Although Malkin believed that the Society was unreceptive to new ideas and was too busy constructing complex agricultural systems of no practical relevance,[89] Iolo reckoned it had 'done much good'.[90] By the time of the Napoleonic Wars the activities of local agricultural societies had been revitalized. A booming agricultural sector meant that many gentleman farmers had greater disposable income which could be used to promote some of the improving schemes which had failed through lack of capital in previous years. Iolo could consequently draw attention to the work of the Society in encouraging the growth of turnips, clover and sainfoin, and to its successful sponsorship of the cultivation of wheat in some of the more inhospitable upland parts of the county.

However, this did not blind him to some of the deficiencies of the Society and he was not slow to recommend that it should encourage the more widespread cultivation of burnet and parsley alongside clover, as, for example,

---

[83] NLW 13115B, pp. 60–1.
[84] See, for example, ibid., p. 14.
[85] Jean Jones, 'James Hutton's Agricultural Research and his Life as a Farmer', *Annals of Science*, 42, no. 6 (1985), 573–601.
[86] NLW 13115B, pp. 260–1, 264–5.
[87] Ibid., p. 284.
[88] T. J. Hopkins, 'Two Hundred Years of Agriculture in Glamorgan' in Stewart Williams (ed.), *Glamorgan Historian*, VIII (Barry, 1982), 70–2; Richard Colyer, 'Early Agricultural Societies in South Wales', *WHR*, 12, no. 4 (1985), 568, 570.
[89] Benjamin H. Malkin, *The Scenery, Antiquities, and Biography, of South Wales* (London, 1804), pp. 59–61.
[90] NLW 13115B, p. 42.

Thomas Edwards, Llandaf, had done with some success.[91] To some extent, his criticisms of the conservatism of the Glamorgan Agricultural Society reflected many of the general problems which hampered the development of Welsh farming. Several of their chief supporters were farmers who had already attempted to put progressive ideas into practice but whose efforts had often fallen on deaf ears among a tenantry whose lack of capital left them 'shrouded in a miasma of inertia'.[92] The kind of improvements being implemented on the home farms of many landlords seemed largely irrelevant to those tenants whose profit margins were wafer-thin and who failed to grasp the local relevance of innovatory practices. The activities of many landlords therefore appeared paternalistic and little more than 'a palliative to compensate the smaller tenant and labouring man for being on the lower rungs of the economic ladder'.[93]

When he crossed the border into Carmarthenshire, Iolo predictably found much more to criticize.[94] He decided on a route that took him directly from Llangyfelach, north of Swansea, to Carmarthen. He organized his comments on a parochial basis and went into considerable detail in the case of the parishes of Llan-non and Llanddarog. He spent a week with his close friend Thomas Evans (Tomos Glyn Cothi) at Brechfa, where he collected detailed notes about the agricultural practices he witnessed in that parish. For the most part, he found Carmarthenshire people 'very intelligent in everything but agriculture',[95] a defect he attributed to lack of improvements and the apathy of the peasantry. In the parish of Llanddarog, for example, he asked a group of farmers why they did not grow wheat. In reply they informed him that it had been tried, but that it had suffered from a 'blast that is locally peculiar to these parts'. When he came to record the details of this conversation in his notebook, he was suitably scathing:

> I can hardly believe this as I can see no reason for it. The country, in the disposition of its surface, gentle risings and fallings, is in that respect the most favourable to agriculture; the soil is a strongish and fertile loam on limestone, there are no stagnating waters, at least of any consequence, no large woods or deep dales that generate crude and cold airs &c whence then, and what, may be the cause of such a blast, does not yet occur to me.[96]

---

91 Ibid., pp. 43–4.
92 Moore-Colyer (ed.), *A Land of Pure Delight*, p. 26.
93 Colyer, 'Early Agricultural Societies in South Wales', 571.
94 Some of Iolo's comments on Carmarthenshire have been transcribed by Muriel Bowen Evans, '"Sir Gaeriaid": Some Comments on Carmarthenshire and its People by Iolo Morganwg', *CA*, XXIV (1988), 33–55. However, many of Iolo's more detailed comments on farming practices in the county have been heavily truncated and in some places omitted altogether.
95 NLW 13115B, p. 53.
96 Ibid.

Such lack of enterprise was even more prevalent in the northern parts of Carmarthenshire: 'No wheat, no orchards, no hop ground, nothing of improvement. I am angry! What a stupid country! – to look at Carmarthenshire, upon the whole it seems equal in fertility to any county in the kingdom.'[97]

However, his strictures were clearly exaggerated. We know that improvements had occurred in parts of north Carmarthenshire and that several well-to-do farmers had begun to experiment with the new farming. While criticizing farmers in the parish of Llanddarog, Iolo failed to pay tribute to the activities of William Davies, Glynogwyr, who had been using lime and farmyard manure as fertilizers and had even introduced potatoes as a break crop between successive crops of wheat and as a winter fodder.[98] Similarly, he made no mention of the work of Carmarthenshire's most famous progressive farmer, George Rice of Newton, near Llandeilo, who had been praised by Arthur Young in the *Annals of Agriculture* for bringing in a Berkshire man to act as his farm-bailiff in order to instruct his tenants in both turnip and cabbage cultivation.[99] Perhaps still more surprisingly, Iolo made no mention of the efforts of the Carmarthenshire Agricultural Society, which had been founded at the instigation of Watkin Lewis, Abernant-bychan, in 1772, the same year as its much better-known counterpart in Glamorgan. Between 1787 and 1790 the premiums claimed had increased from £51. 3s. to £308. 5s., which indicates that the Society had been actively involved in sponsoring modern farming techniques, however piecemeal those efforts might have been.[100]

The reasons for the lack of rigour in some of Iolo's comments on north Carmarthenshire undoubtedly stemmed from his unfamiliarity with the area. Ironically, he was later to claim that only those who resided in a particular county were adequately qualified to compile an agricultural survey of the county in question.[101] His comments on north Carmarthenshire, therefore, stand in sharp contrast to those on Glamorgan, which were illustrated throughout with reference to examples of improving farmers. Yet, the general tenor of Iolo's comments on Carmarthenshire were not wholly inaccurate. Thirty years later, Kennedy and Grainger, in the *Present State of the Tenancy of Land in Great Britain* (1828), also found that the farmers of north Carmarthenshire were 'not aware of the march of improvement in other quarters, whilst they are jealous of the interference of others with their long cherished

---

[97] Ibid., p. 54.
[98] Ibid., p. 276. See also R. N. Salamon, *The History and Social Influence of the Potato* (Cambridge, 1949); Overton, *Agricultural Revolution in England*, pp. 102–3.
[99] Arthur Young, *Annals of Agriculture and Other Useful Arts*, VIII (1793), p. 42.
[100] E. Wyn Jones, 'The First Carmarthenshire Agricultural Society', *CA*, III, no. 1 (1959), 155.
[101] NLW 13221E, Letter no. 19, pp. 95–8, Iolo Morganwg to William Owen Pughe, 19 March 1803.

prejudices, being fully persuaded that their own system is in every respect the best'.[102]

During his stay with his fellow Unitarian Thomas Evans (Tomos Glyn Cothi) at Brechfa, Iolo took the opportunity to reflect on the practice of agriculture in that locality in more detail than he had done in many other parts of the county. He returned to one of his favourite subjects, the growth of wheat, and found that farmers in the area were far too reluctant to grow it because they believed that the soil was too poor and the climate too cold to sustain it.[103] Following several excursions with Tomos Glyn Cothi, he concluded that the soil in the parish was in fact 'light and healthy',[104] bearing a remarkable resemblance to the soil found in some of the hillier parts of Glamorgan, where, just outside Merthyr Tydfil, he had witnessed the successful cultivation of red lammas wheat in September 1793.[105] The reluctance to experiment was further exemplified by the dogged determination of farmers to persist with their own strains of barley, which they were convinced made better malt and commanded higher prices than was the case in other counties, a notion which Iolo was swift to dismiss.[106]

Yet his observations were not entirely negative. At a house near the village of Brechfa he commended some flourishing apple trees, which he believed could supplement the income of the farmers and provide them with an invaluable additional source of food.[107] He also praised the quality of the livestock around Brechfa. While the sheep were ripe for improvement, the cattle were ideally suited to the terrain and soil type, and the 'hardy, sure-footed, tho' not large breed of horses answer their purposes well enough'.[108] But it was not until Iolo left Brechfa and turned towards Glamorgan once more, taking a route through the southern parts of Carmarthenshire, that he presented a more positive picture of farming in the county.

Immediately south of Carmarthen Iolo encountered evidence of the recent enclosure of wasteland. This was one of the few occasions on which he mentioned enclosure, even though the Board of Agriculture was determined to secure a General Enclosure Act.[109] Parliamentary enclosure in Wales was a slow process which reached its peak c.1810.[110] Despite his much-vaunted radical

---

[102] L. Kennedy and T. B. Grainger, *The Present State of the Tenancy of Land in Great Britain* (London, 1828), p. 170. Quoted in David W. Howell, 'Rural Society in Nineteenth Century Carmarthenshire', *CA*, XIII, no. 18 (1977), 74.

[103] NLW 13115B, p. 67.

[104] Ibid.

[105] Ibid., p. 68.

[106] Ibid., p. 75.

[107] Ibid., p. 76.

[108] Ibid.

[109] Rosalind Mitchison, *Agricultural Sir John: The Life of Sir John Sinclair of Ulbster, 1754–1835* (London, 1962), p. 181.

[110] John Chapman, 'Parliamentary Enclosure in Wales: Comparisons and Contrasts', *WHR*, 21, no. 4 (2001), 762.

credentials, Iolo remained a persuasive advocate of enclosure.[111] The language of common rights was largely absent from his discussion of the subject and he does not seem to have been aware of the arguments of those who opposed enclosure on the grounds of its adverse impact on small tenant farmers who often relied on access to common lands in order to keep cows and obtain fuel. The loss of these rights invariably led to extreme hardship and became one of the main contributory factors which forced farmers to quit their lands and move to the new industrial communities.[112] Iolo preferred to comment on the impetus that enclosure had given to the improvement of farming practices in the area immediately south of Carmarthen. The farmland was 'fine and very fertile', lime was readily available, new farmhouses had been built, old ones had been left to decay and the roads were wider and better maintained than those of Glamorgan.[113] Further east in the parish of Llangyndeyrn, despite seeing very little evidence of modern husbandry, he was heartened to discover a large field of thriving white lammas wheat[114] and, in the adjoining parish of Llandyfaelog, evidence of the use of clover.[115]

By the mid-1790s, however, the general backwardness of farming was exacting a heavy toll on the county. Many tenant farmers, unable to make a success of agriculture, were already beginning to move to the burgeoning industrial communities in the eastern part of the county and especially in Glamorgan. Even at this early date Iolo observed that 'half the hands employed in collieries, copper works, and iron works . . . are from Carmarthenshire'.[116] It should come as no surprise therefore that some of his most interesting comments on the parishes of south Carmarthenshire were reserved for the activities of a Dublin-born stonemason who, taking advantage of the excellent quality black marble that was available locally, had established a small manufactory in which he cut marble and exported it as far afield as Bristol and London.[117] Iolo took great pleasure in singling out the activities of such individuals since they were exemplars of his vision of a self-sustaining rural economy.

With characteristic shrewdness, Iolo also addressed one further critical problem. The Board of Agriculture had recognized that one of the most formidable obstacles in its path was getting its material into the hands of

---

[111] See his extended comments quoted in NLW 1806E, Letter no. 706, Owain Myfyr to Walter Davies, 7 February 1804.

[112] For the social and economic impact of enclosure, see David J.V. Jones, *Before Rebecca: Popular Protests in Wales, 1793–1835* (London, 1973), pp. 40–50; J. M. Neeson, *Commoners: Common Right, Enclosure and Social Change, 1700–1820* (Cambridge, 1993).

[113] NLW 13115B, pp. 89–90.

[114] Ibid., p. 92.

[115] Ibid., p. 93.

[116] Ibid., p. 62.

[117] Ibid., pp. 90–1.

hard-pressed tenant farmers.[118] Conscious that most of them were unable to read English or had neither the time or perhaps the inclination to read the Board's lengthy reports, Iolo recommended that an inexpensive treatise 'on those parts of natural philosophy that are useful for [the farmer] to know',[119] entitled 'Agricultural Philosophy', 'The Philosophy of Agriculture' or 'The Farmer's Useful Companion', should be produced and disseminated. At this stage he gave no indication that it would best be produced in Welsh, though he had earlier recommended to the Board that:

> The Welsh greatly want a few cheap tracts on husbandry in their language; hitherto they have had nothing of the kind worth mentioning, and the Welsh peasantry are more generally able to read their own language than the same class in England. The Board of Agriculture (if consistent with their institution and design) would do well in furnishing the Welsh with a treatise on agriculture.[120]

Nor did he give any indication that he was prepared to write such a volume, though it is highly likely that he would have seized the opportunity.

The manuscript account of this tour concludes with an intriguing account of a conversation Iolo had with a drover returning from a fair at Newcastle Emlyn. The encounter has the air of a light-hearted debate in which the two men seek to outwit each other as they make the case for the superiority of their respective counties. The drover was confident that the barley grown in Carmarthenshire was the best in Wales, but Iolo preferred Glamorgan barley. Iolo also thought that Carmarthenshire farmers should use more lime, like their Glamorgan counterparts, and should grow wheat.[121] On the morality of the inhabitants of the two counties, Iolo rounded on the young women of Carmarthenshire because of the county's reputedly high rates of illegitimate births.[122] Insisting that his comments were totally unbiased, Iolo proudly proclaimed to the drover that although much work was still required, Glamorgan, unlike Carmarthenshire, had 'made considerable progress in modern improvements, and at the same time retains in tolerable purity the ancient Welsh manners and simplicity'.[123] The history and antiquity of Glamorgan played a central role in Iolo's imagination and it could be argued that his overwhelming desire to demonstrate the superiority of the county was the one common theme which permeated the whole of his work.[124] Iolo's readiness to welcome

---

[118] Nicholas Goddard, 'Agricultural Literature and Societies' in G. E. Mingay (ed.), *The Agrarian History of England and Wales, Volume VI, 1750–1850* (Cambridge, 1989), pp. 361–70.

[119] NLW 13115B, p. 118.

[120] Ibid., p. 78.

[121] Ibid., pp. 109–12.

[122] Ibid., p. 113.

[123] Ibid., p. 116.

[124] This is developed further in Cathryn Charnell-White, *Barbarism and Bardism: North Wales versus South Wales in the Bardic Vision of Iolo Morganwg* (Aberystwyth, 2004).

the improvement, urbanization and industrialization of Glamorgan conveniently corresponded with his wish to enhance the reputation of the county as the most dynamic instigator of modern economic practices.

By the end of the summer of 1796 Iolo had invested a considerable amount of time in collecting material for his intended survey of south Wales and there was little in the manuscript that he sent to William Matthews which could be construed as controversial or which contradicted the avowed aims of the Board. Indeed, Iolo's account was remarkably conservative and was strongly supportive of the capitalistic system of agricultural production favoured by the leading figures of the Board of Agriculture. There was no sustained engagement, for instance, with some of the radical agrarian ideas of Thomas Spence, who advocated distributing within communities the bulk of wealth derived from agriculture,[125] or of the ameliorative version of improvement favoured by Wordsworth,[126] or, slightly later, of William Cobbett's desire to make the agricultural worker a self-sufficient producer.[127] Iolo did not venture to criticize enclosure or speak up for the common rights of the peasantry, even though Wales was no stranger to agrarian unrest in these years.[128] For those who know of Iolo as the radical Unitarian,[129] the detachment of his comments and his self-discipline in resisting every temptation to rail against 'tyrants and priests'[130] was remarkable. Sir John Sinclair's refusal to employ him is therefore all the more extraordinary and must surely have been attributable to the radical reputation that Iolo had acquired during his time in London.[131]

Like so much of his writings, Iolo's reflections on the rural landscape are an admixture of apparently contradictory elements. Despite his reputation as a forger and fantasist, Iolo proved himself a highly professional, hard-headed, indeed scientific agricultural observer and, while some of his comments lacked intellectual sophistication, on the whole his depiction of rural life in south Wales at the close of the eighteenth century was extremely balanced and well informed. The fastidious Walter Davies had no difficulty in accepting the veracity of his judgements, and much of what was included on Glamorgan in

---

[125] For Spence's ideas, see Malcolm Chase, *The People's Farm: English Radical Agrarianism, 1775–1840* (Oxford, 1988).

[126] Anne Janowitz, 'Land' in Iain McCalman (ed.), *The Oxford Companion to the Romantic Age: British Culture, 1776–1832* (Oxford, 1999), p. 159.

[127] Cobbett's views on the agricultural labourer are discussed in Ian Dyck, *William Cobbett and the Rural Popular Culture* (Cambridge, 1992), pp. 102–6.

[128] Jones, *Before Rebecca*, pp. 13–34.

[129] For Iolo's radicalism, see Damian Walford Davies, *Presences that Disturb: Models of Romantic Identity in the Literature and Culture of the 1790s* (Cardiff, 2002), pp. 136–52; Geraint H. Jenkins, 'The Bard of Liberty during William Pitt's Reign of Terror' in Joseph F. Nagy and Leslie E. Jones (eds.), *Heroic Poets and Poetic Heroes in Celtic Tradition: A Festschrift for Patrick K. Ford. CSANA Yearbook 3–4* (Dublin, 2005), pp. 183–206.

[130] NLW 21281E, Letter no. 276, William Matthews to Iolo Morganwg, 6 October 1796.

[131] This is discussed further in Jones, '"Mere Humbug"', 88–90.

his published two-volume survey of south Wales bears the unmistakable stamp of Iolo's researches.[132] Iolo's analysis of the rural landscape reveals that he was a serious student of enlightened attitudes to the natural world and that he interacted with a diverse, and often mutually exclusive, range of ideas without ever seeking to reconcile some of the more obvious inconsistencies. Since the audience for whom Iolo was writing was usually crucial in determining the opinions which he adopted, viewing Iolo's writings through post-industrial eyes can be misleading. In seeking to encourage improvement in farming and to maximize the use of industrial resources, he was voicing an ambitious desire to civilize the landscape and to demonstrate, above all, that his beloved Glamorgan was at the forefront of modern developments in both town and country.

---

[132] For further discussion of Davies's debt to Iolo's writings and notebooks, see David Ceri Jones, 'The Rural Society and Economy of Wales between 1790 and 1815 with Special Reference to the Manuscripts of Walter Davies (Gwallter Mechain)' (University of Wales Board of Celtic Studies Research Project Report, 2000–1), pp. 104–8; idem, 'The Board of Agriculture, Walter Davies (Gwallter Mechain) and Cardiganshire, c.1794–1815', *Ceredigion*, XIV, no. 1 (2001), 79–100.

11

Iolo Morganwg and Welsh Historical Traditions

PRYS MORGAN

It is striking that Iolo Morganwg should have been the subject of not one, but two, biographies in the mid-nineteenth century, one in English by Elijah Waring and the other in Welsh by T. D. Thomas. The former was published in 1850, the latter in 1857, at around the time the Welsh, challenged by the Blue Books on Welsh Education (1847), were facing the prospect of having to shunt the Welsh language and their history into the sidings of national life. In these works Iolo appears as a bard, a Dissenter, a radical and, above all, as an eccentric, a 'character'. He is not, of course, portrayed as a historian, though Waring included Iolo's grandiose plan for his history of Wales in an appendix, with a good deal more of Iolo's historical material. His druidic vision of the ancient British past was seen as a background to his bardistry, while his unfulfilled plan to find the descendants of Madoc's followers in the American mid-West was viewed as a zany, perhaps naive, example of Iolo's eccentricity.[1]

Yet, as far back as April 1781, John Walters, the son of Iolo's mentor, John Walters of Llandough, had written to him as follows: 'Cultivate your poetical talents, and forget not the history of Glamorgan, – Sculptor, linguist, poet, antiquarian – which is your favourite title?'[2] At least one side of his polygonal genius was at that time discerned as historical. Iolo's modern biographer, Griffith John Williams, included many references to the way history was a passion which drove him relentlessly. Iolo's reading as a young man was often about history; he borrowed books on English history and world history, and all his life he amassed historical notes and manuscripts on Glamorgan and on Welsh history. He told Owen Jones (Owain Myfyr) that one of the main aims of circles of Welsh scholars should be 'to bring our national history out of obscurity' – an echo of the aims of Lewis Morris, the leading figure of the previous generation of Welsh scholars.[3] The posthumously published collection

---

[1] *RAEW*, pp. 181–5 for his proposed History of Wales, and pp. 210–11 for his 'philosophy of history'; T. D. Thomas, *Bywgraffiad Iolo Morganwg B.B.D., sef Edward Williams, Diweddar Fardd a Hynafiaethydd o Forganwg* (Caerfyrddin, 1857).

[2] NLW 21283E, Letter no. 523, John Walters Jr. to Iolo Morganwg, 13 April 1781.

[3] G. J. Williams, 'Hanes Cyhoeddi'r "Myvyrian Archaiology"', *JWBS*, X, no. 1 (1966), 2–12.

of his notes, *Iolo Manuscripts*, were claimed to be materials for a 'new history of Wales'. In 1800 Iolo presented the Gwyneddigion Society with a plan for collecting historical lore and materials from all parts of Wales, and himself offered to take care of garnering data in Glamorgan.[4] Some of Iolo's enemies saw him as mounting an attack on accepted Welsh history: in 1806 William Williams (Gwilym Peris) informed David Thomas (Dafydd Ddu Eryri) – who formed a kind of 'northern alliance' against Iolo – that there seemed to be no one brave enough to confound the theories concocted by William Owen Pughe and Iolo, who had bewitched the minds of ordinary people and cast down 'all accepted history' ('bob hanes derbyniol') to such a degree that it might be as well to burn all history books. The nonsense, he continued, of the London Welsh would have to be stopped before it ruined the native language and 'destroyed our accepted histories' ('i ddiddymu ein derbyniol hanesion').[5]

G. J. Williams, however, said of Iolo: 'There are many people who have talked about the history of Glamorgan, but he is the only one who could hear the voice of the past' ('Y mae llawer o bobl wedi bod yn traethu ar hanes Morgannwg, ond ef yw'r unig un a allai glywed llais y gorffennol').[6] He believed that Iolo was the chief authority in his day, even on broader Welsh history and, while discussing Iolo's grandiose scheme of publishing a six-volume history of Wales, he argued that Iolo 'doubtless saw himself as a historian' ('diau fel hanesydd y syniai amdano ei hun').[7]

The aim of this chapter is threefold: to ascertain the Welsh historical traditions; how Iolo Morganwg acquired these traditions; and how he deployed them. The oldest and deepest historical tradition was that represented by the Triads of the Isle of Britain, a large corpus of historical lore, the core of which dealt with the Welsh as the primary people of these islands, their arrival here and their naming of all the parts, followed by the ruin and destruction wrought by various waves of invaders, and the exploits of a succession of heroes who fought against the conquests. The great mass of facts was to be memorized by learned bards and sages, and put into conveniently mnemonic form comprising three linked sentences, the form determined by the fact that they were for centuries transmitted orally from generation to generation, and committed to manuscript in the later medieval period.[8]

A second layer of the tradition was 'The Matter of Britain', again a tradition

---

[4]   W. D. Leathart, *The Origins and Progress of the Gwyneddigion Society of London* (London, 1831), pp. 32–3.

[5]   John Jones (Myrddin Fardd) (ed.), *Adgof uwch Anghof: Llythyrau Lluaws o Brif Enwogion Cymru, Hen a Diweddar* (Caernarfon, 1883), pp. 92–5.

[6]   Williams: *IM*, p. 158.

[7]   Ibid., p. 307.

[8]   Rachel Bromwich, *Trioedd Ynys Prydein: The Welsh Triads* (Cardiff, 1961); eadem, '*Trioedd Ynys Prydain*' in *Welsh Literature and Scholarship* (Cardiff, 1969).

of the early history of the Welsh as masters of the island, and how their hold upon it was lost. Part of this tradition came from Gildas, who believed that the sins of the Welsh had brought this loss upon themselves, part came from the work of authors lumped together in the name of someone called 'Nennius', who viewed the loss as caused by stupidity and internecine strife among the Welsh, and much of it came from the celebrated twelfth-century chronicle of Geoffrey of Monmouth, *Historia Regum Britanniae*, with its tales of King Arthur and his knights, and the theme of the messianic return of a Welsh king to restore the Welsh to their ancient place as rulers of Britain. The 'Galfridian' tradition was attacked as a baseless myth by Polydore Vergil and others in the sixteenth century, but despite much English scorn and mockery – perhaps because of it – Welsh scholars stoutly defended it even in the eighteenth century.

A third layer of the tradition was that which might be called 'The Protestant myth' of Welsh history. Welsh historians of the early modern period argued that since Henry Tudor, enthroned in 1485, was a Welshman who claimed to be descended from the last Welsh ruler of Britain, Cadwaladr the Blessed, the messianic prophecy of 'The Matter of Britain' had been fulfilled. But simultaneously, other Welsh historians argued that, although the Welsh had lost their mastery of the Isle of Britain, the son of Henry VII had given the Welsh something far more valuable, namely the Protestant Reformation, and a release of each Welshman from the bondage to Catholic Rome, and Henry's daughter, Elizabeth, had in turn, given the Welsh the Bible in their own language. They emphasized that the Protestant Church should regard the Welsh as its most important communicants, since they alone represented continuity with the ancient British Church, founded soon after the crucifixion when Joseph of Arimathea sailed to Britain, effectively founding a church which antedated the papacy, the liberties of which were later suppressed by the Norman conquest. This was a kind of 'Norman Yoke'.[9] Dafydd Glyn Jones has recently drawn attention to the great power of the Galfridian myth and its later Protestant version over the Welsh mind, even as late as the early nineteenth century, in many works, including *Prydnawngwaith y Cymry* (1822), a history of the Later Middle Ages by William Williams of Llandygái, a contemporary of Iolo Morganwg.[10]

The fourth layer of Welsh historical tradition was rather different: this was the antiquarian history which, as far as Iolo's Glamorgan was concerned, was begun by sixteenth-century historians such as Rees Merrick (Rhys Meurig) of

[9] Glanmor Williams, *Religion, Language and Nationality in Wales* (Cardiff, 1979), pp. 1–33, 71–86, 119, 134.

[10] Dafydd Glyn Jones, *Agoriad yr Oes: Erthyglau ar Lên, Hanes, a Gwleidyddiaeth Cymru* (Talybont, 2001), *passim*; idem, *Un o Wŷr y Medra: Bywyd a Gwaith William Williams, Llandygái (1738–1817)* (Dinbych, 1999), esp. pp. 294–309.

Cotrel, near Bonvilston, Glamorgan. Elizabethan and early Stuart antiquaries were concerned with recording and preserving as much as possible of the ancient things of each locality: local lore, customs, words, traditions, remains of barrows, monuments, forts, Roman remains, milestones, early Christian crosses, early graves and so on. The connecting link between English antiquaries and the Welsh was Edward Lhuyd at the end of the seventeenth century.[11] His most active patrons were Glamorgan gentry, who greatly encouraged him to publish *Archaeologia Britannica* in 1707. Philip Jenkins has shown that Glamorgan had several lively circles of local antiquarians, often in the service of old families of native gentry, up to the mid-eighteenth century. Such families died out or were replaced by English incomers during the course of the century, and their kind of antiquarianism was replaced by that of more middle-class families and, by the later eighteenth century, by lower class craftsmen, who were often Dissenting radicals. Approaching the antiquarian tradition from a different standpoint in his *Traddodiad Llenyddol Morgannwg*, G. J. Williams traced the continuity between Welsh bardic scholar-antiquaries of the early eighteenth century and Dissenting radicals of craftsman stock in the latter half of the century.[12] By this period Welsh antiquarianism to some extent partook of the spirit of English popular antiquarianism: it disliked metropolitan standards and the accepted canon of royal, aristocratic and establishment state history, its central institutions, its standardized language (to be found in Samuel Johnson's dictionary), and it delighted, by contrast, in the popular, the demotic, the subversive, the riotous, the ribald – an antiquarian tradition very different from that espoused by the older Glamorgan gentry and their friends. The older antiquaries had often been medievalists, studying the ruins of castles and abbeys, protecting and transcribing medieval charters, or piecing together monuments destroyed and muniments dispersed during the civil wars. The later popular antiquarians were also interested in the rediscovery of the life of the people – their games, feasts, fairs, jokes, japes, music – a pulsating popular culture which often shocked the stiff periwigs of the eighteenth-century establishment.[13]

It was not merely antiquarianism and its popular extension which changed Welsh historiography in the eighteenth century, but also other elements such as Celticism and druidism. As soon as Latin texts such as Caesar's 'Gallic War' became known to readers in the sixteenth century, the ancient Druids began

[11] Philip Jenkins, 'From Edward Lhuyd to Iolo Morganwg: The Death and Rebirth of Glamorgan antiquarianism in the eighteenth century', *Morgannwg*, XXIII (1979), 29–47; idem, *The Making of a Ruling Class: The Glamorgan Gentry c.1640–1790* (Cambridge, 1983), pp. 234–9.

[12] *TLlM*, pp. 228–318.

[13] Marilyn Butler, 'Antiquarianism (Popular)' in Iain McCalman (ed.), *An Oxford Companion to The Romantic Age: British Culture, 1776–1832* (Oxford, 1999), pp. 328–37.

to bewitch the imagination. English antiquaries like Leland and Bale identified a vague resemblance between the priestly class of the Druids (which had, of course, been killed off by the Romans and by the coming of Christianity) and the medieval Welsh order of bards (which still existed in the Tudor period), both of which provided examples of an influential native learned elite. By the early eighteenth century, interest in 'Ancient Britain' had grown considerably. John Aubrey, for example, claimed that Stonehenge and other megalithic remains were the temples of the ancient Druids, while Henry Rowlands of Llanidan developed the genuine tradition that Anglesey had been the headquarters of druidism in Britain and Gaul by discovering evidence of the presence of Druids in Welsh place-names and in the ancient megaliths of Anglesey.[14] When the London Welsh founded their own antiquarian society in 1751 – the Cymmrodorion Society (the word referred to the Welsh as the 'earliest natives' or the 'aborigines' of Britain) – they chose a Druid and St David as the two supporters of their arms on their ceremonial banner.[15] Writers like Linda Colley have reminded us that English patriotism in the eighteenth century had a strongly 'Ancient British' dimension: the English themselves sought an antiquity that lay beyond the Anglo-Saxon invasions, and found in 'Ancient Britain' and the Druids a basis for drawing together each of the four peoples of the British Isles into a common history, and thus, perhaps, a common struggle against France and Spain.[16] Welsh historians certainly took advantage of this new-found Britishness in order to raise the profile of Welsh history. In any case, writers and intellectuals, both English and Welsh, were attracted to the Druids as a learned class which had long ago commanded immense respect, and which, though they had never borne arms, had led resistance in Gaul and Britain against the might of Rome.[17]

At the end of the seventeenth century Edward Lhuyd had tried to create a local network of antiquarians throughout Wales to collect lore of all kinds. His major published work *Archaeologia Britannica* (1707), far from being antiquarian, was a deeply and, at the time bafflingly, learned description of the ancient languages of Britain – Irish, Gaelic, Manx, Cornish, Welsh, together with Breton – and the philological links between them. A year earlier, an English translation from French had appeared of the work of Paul-Yves Pezron, a Breton antiquary, entitled *The Antiquity of the Nation of the Celts*. In a highly enthusiastic but unscholarly way, Pezron had identified the Welsh and the Bretons with their remote ancestors in antiquity, the Celts, who had,

[14]   Henry Rowlands, *Mona Antiqua Restaurata* (Dublin, 1723).
[15]   R. T. Jenkins and Helen Ramage, *A History of the Honourable Society of Cymmrodorion, and of the Gwyneddigion and Cymreigyddion Societies, 1751–1951* (London, 1951).
[16]   Linda Colley, *Britons: Forging the Nation, 1707–1837* (London, 1992).
[17]   Sam Smiles, *The Image of Antiquity: Ancient Britain and the Romantic Imagination* (London, 1994), pp. 75–112.

centuries before Christ, roamed Europe and Asia Minor, threatening Greece and Rome. Lhuyd had read the French original in 1703 and had hoped that an English translation would fire the imagination of the Welsh gentry and spur them to develop Welsh studies. For their part, the monoglot literate Welsh could read about this thrilling story in Theophilus Evans's popular history book *Drych y Prif Oesoedd* (1716). Lhuyd never used the word 'Celtic', but it gradually took hold as a useful adjective to describe everything that was 'of Ancient Britain'. It also added a new dimension to Welsh history, linking the Welsh to the other peoples of Britain (and Brittany) and also to antiquity right across Europe as far as Galatia in Asia Minor.[18]

Another consequence of this new-found Celticism was the enhanced prestige of the Welsh language, whose predecessor, Ancient British, was not only a language of antiquity, just like Hebrew or Greek, but, according to some eighteenth-century propagandists, probably the language of the ancient patriarchs. Some even went so far as to claim that if Welsh words were dissected neatly into particles and compared to bits and pieces of other more modern languages such as English, Welsh might be found to lie at the root of all languages. Moonshine it may have been, but it greatly boosted the Welsh language and its study; in particular, it spurred many to compose dictionaries of the language, among them Iolo's early mentors, Thomas Richards of Coychurch and John Walters of Llandough near Cowbridge, and his London-based colleague, William Owen Pughe. One of the youthful Iolo's pathways into history was probably the study of ancient wordlists and the invention of new words for John Walters's dictionary.[19]

All in all, then, by the end of the eighteenth century the Welsh had discovered a long and complex historical tradition which played a central part in the cultural revival of the times. Recent surveys of Welsh historiography in that period by Dafydd Glyn Jones and Geraint H. Jenkins have revealed a considerable variety of works in English and Welsh: Wotton's edition of the Laws of Hywel Dda, local histories such as those by Edmund Jones 'The Old Prophet', historical topography by Thomas Pennant and others, histories of Wales and of the world in Welsh, denominational histories such as that by Joshua Thomas on the Baptists, county histories like those of Richard Fenton and David Williams, editions of family histories such as that by Sir John Wynn of Gwydir, translations of the texts of Giraldus Cambrensis, reprints of older Welsh history books by David Powel and William Wynne, all of which point to a burgeoning enthusiasm for Welsh history among the upper, middling and lower classes in both the English and Welsh languages. Iolo Morganwg was

---

[18] G. J. Williams, *Edward Lhuyd ac Iolo Morganwg* (Caerdydd, 1964).

[19] Caryl Davies, *Adfeilion Babel: Agweddau ar Syniadaeth Ieithyddol y Ddeunawfed Ganrif* (Caerdydd, 2000), esp. pp. 267–92.

thus the heir rather than the creator of the Welsh historical revival of the eighteenth century.[20]

Iolo was deeply aware of all these aspects of the Welsh historical tradition: he had read a wide range of history books as a young man, books (including Lhuyd's *Archaeologia Britannica*) which he had borrowed from the library at Cowbridge. He knew through clerical friends and mentors such as Thomas Richards and John Walters of the detailed empirical work of Glamorgan antiquaries in preserving local lore and manuscripts. As a young adult he was taught bardistry by the craftsmen-bards of the hill country, such as Lewis Hopkin, and he became familiar with all the old, sometimes medieval, manuscript collections of the county. From these local antiquarians he learned to record his discoveries as he travelled to his daily work. He asked all and sundry for information about the ancient houses, castles and churches, any strange ancient monuments, dialect words and verses, local fairs, games and pastimes, thus becoming a local antiquary at the same time as he became a Welsh poet and a budding lexicographer. Later, when he worked in England, he made similar notes, and when he was paid to discover and transcribe Welsh manuscript collections in different parts of Wales he gradually amassed a vast collection of notes of an antiquarian nature. Like the popular antiquarians in England, Iolo as a young man was deeply interested in medieval life and culture and copied everything he could of the work of the Welsh medieval poets. For several years he collected material for the Board of Agriculture and this gave him a further reason for embarking on long journeys to all parts of Wales. Naturally, he seized the opportunity to assemble all kinds of antiquarian lore and information, and to add them to the notes on geology, farming and the economy, which he was paid to collect. He retained the habit of note-taking throughout his long life, and since he seldom rode a horse or rode in a carriage, he had an intimate knowledge of the country.

Because of his reading, Iolo was always aware of the broader picture of the development of the Welsh historical tradition. As he collected manuscripts and made copies of others, he became aware of the great antiquity of the triads of the Isle of Britain, the medieval chronicles and other works which formed the basis for the ancient triadic history of Wales and Britain, the Galfridian history and the Protestant myth of the early modern historians.[21] As the eighteenth century advanced, and as he became increasingly acquainted with London Welsh poets and antiquarians, the followers of the Morris circle, and then

---

[20] Dafydd Glyn Jones, *Agoriad yr Oes, passim*; Geraint H. Jenkins, 'Historical Writing in the Eighteenth Century' in Branwen Jarvis (ed.), *A Guide to Welsh Literature, c.1700–1800* (Cardiff, 2000), pp. 23–44. See also Geraint H. Jenkins, *Facts, Fantasy and Fiction: The Historical Vision of Iolo Morganwg* (Aberystwyth, 1997), *passim*.

[21] Rachel Bromwich, 'Trioedd Ynys Prydain: The *Myvyrian* Third Series', *THSC*, Part 2 (1968), 299–338; Part 1 (1969), 127–56.

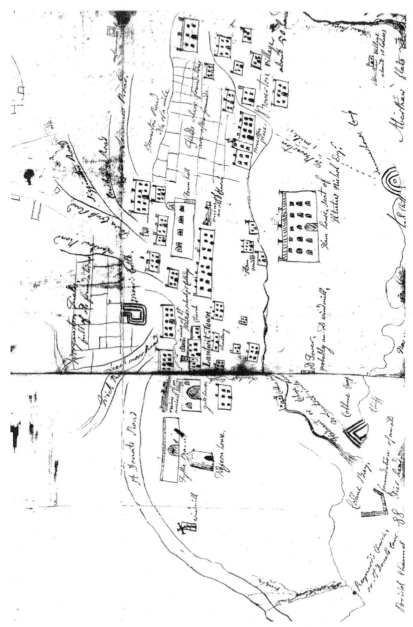

Fig. 20 A sketch map drawn by Iolo to illustrate his account of antiquities in Llantwit Major, Glamorgan, c.1800.

Owen Jones (Owain Myfyr) and William Owen Pughe, he became more aware of the newer aspects of Welsh history, the fashionable concern for Celticism and druidism, the Romantic concern for primitivism, the sense of unbroken continuity from his own day to that of the ancient Britons and the possibility of rediscovering the pure undefiled language of ancient times. It was also perhaps a Romantic passion which drove Iolo and his colleagues to search for the descendants of Madoc in the American mid-West in order to discover a pure and ancient Welsh society far from modern European corruptions and entanglements. When he was in London in the early 1790s he became involved in the 'Madoc fever' of the day. He forged documents about the legend and even announced his intention of emigrating to America to search for the Madogwys, the descendants of Madoc.[22] During the same period he discovered radical politics, which led him, for various reasons, to disapprove of the Galfridian tradition, with all its kings and knights, and its eventual link with the rise to power of the Tudors. He also disliked the 'Brutus myth' of the so-called Trojan origins of the Britons. Although he had been brought up in the Anglican faith, Iolo was strongly influenced by his teachers, the bards of the uplands of Glamorgan, who were usually strong Dissenters and, since one of his historical hobby-horses was the persecution of early Dissenters in the hills of Glamorgan, he could only accept parts of the Protestant myth of Welsh history. He was delighted by the idea of the early British Church, and cherished his collection of the lives of the early saints and especially their genealogies.

The Romantic Celticism of his contemporaries was expressed by Iolo mainly in his delight in the origins of languages, a preoccupation which created in him the notion of the central importance of a culture and of a language within that culture. Romantic druidism was an even more profound influence on him: it probably dated from a youthful reading of the work of Henry Rowlands in English and Theophilus Evans in Welsh, the works of John Aubrey and William Stukeley on English megalithic remains, and his own visits to Avebury and Stonehenge: indeed, he was familiar from childhood with megaliths in the Vale of Glamorgan, such as the Tinkinswood burial chamber near St Nicholas. But once he had discovered the current fashion for 'Ancient Britain' and ancient heroes such as the Druids he became obsessed with the subject and remained so for the rest of his life.[23]

Iolo, it is argued in this chapter, was a historian who worked on two different levels, especially in the latter half of his life. On one hand he was an antiquarian, and on the other a historical visionary. Antiquarianism occupied

---

[22] Gwyn A. Williams, 'John Evans's Mission to the Madogwys, 1792–1799', *BBCS*, XXVII, Part 4 (1978), 569–601; idem, *Madoc: The Making of a Myth* (London, 1979).

[23] Stuart Piggott, *The Druids* (Harmondsworth, 1974), pp. 243–50, and *passim*; Smiles, *The Image of Antiquity*, pp. 75–112.

much of his time all his life, but most of his work remained in manuscript, except when he supplied materials to other historians such as David Williams and Benjamin Heath Malkin.[24] Mythical and visionary history made him famous, though even here his material was often edited and published by others, notably his son, Taliesin ab Iolo, and John Williams (Ab Ithel). Since the antiquarian activity began much earlier in his life, it should be described first.

In several places in his biography G. J. Williams referred to Iolo's lifelong ambition of publishing a history of Glamorgan; he had clearly collected materials for what would have been a detailed cultural and social history.[25] Lewis Morris had attempted something similar for the Creuddyn area of Cardiganshire, Edmund Jones had written a history of Aberystruth and Thomas Pennant had done the same for Whitford and Holywell. But Iolo's materials were far more extensive: he collected all kinds of lore about long-lived inhabitants, dialects, songs and sayings of the common people, games and pastimes, the foods and dishes associated with the old rural calendar, trees and plants, including a long list of varieties of Glamorgan apples, with their Welsh names. He described tools and implements, farming customs, the furnishings and designs of farms, old manor houses, ruined chapels, hamlets, coasts and harbours, and all kinds of topographical details.[26] He also collected information about old hundreds and lordships, the descent of manors, the genealogies of old families – this seems to have been a topic of conversation between Iolo and his mother when he was young. Naturally some of the notes arose from his own trade as a stonemason, but it would be also true to say that his craft gave him an added skill to that of the antiquary, namely a sharp eye for any building or the remains of a building half hidden in fields. Unlike the gentleman antiquaries of his day, he was perfectly prepared to get his boots and hands dirty by involving himself in archaeological fieldwork. His accurate measurements have been confirmed by modern archaeologists in Glamorgan, as well as his conclusions, and, in the case of monuments which have been eroded or have partially disappeared, his evidence is particularly valuable.[27] Other Welsh scholars were influenced by Romantic antiquarians, notably Edward Jones, 'Bardd y Brenin', but Iolo's interests were far wider than mere harp music and verses for the harp. It is not surprising, therefore, that he should have expressed his hope that a corresponding academy might one day be established to enable antiquaries like himself to report their findings and seek comparative material from others. G. J. Williams also emphasized that Iolo

---

[24] David Williams, *History of Monmouthshire* (London, 1796); Benjamin H. Malkin, *The Scenery, Antiquities, and Biography, of South Wales* (London, 1804).

[25] Williams: *IM*, pp. 38–40.

[26] Ibid., pp. 334–8 for the names of fruit trees.

[27] H. J. Thomas, 'Iolo Morganwg Vindicated: Glamorgan's First Field Archaeologist', *Glamorgan–Gwent Archaeological Trust Annual Report*, 1983–4 (1985), pp. 149–57.

foresaw the urgent need of what would today be called a 'folk museum' to preserve the artefacts and records of a way of life which was disappearing in the face of industrialization.[28]

Another aspect of eighteenth-century antiquarianism was the urge to publish ancient materials, fables, proverbs, local dialects and sayings, songs and stories. Throughout the British Isles, several collections of ancient songs and stories were published towards the end of the eighteenth century. Part of Iolo's mission in helping to edit *The Myvyrian Archaiology of Wales* – the very name *Archaiology*, meaning a work of history, is surely significant here – was to provide the public with a corpus of ancient Welsh poetry and prose, and, as he put it, 'to reanimate the genius of our country', and to show the public 'the very beautiful ethics of our remote ancestors'.[29] This also seems to have been the aim of the editors of a posthumous selection of his papers, the *Iolo Manuscripts*, which contained a huge mass of tales and sayings which resembled the folkloric material collected by antiquaries.[30] Iolo never got beyond the stage of planning his ambitious history of Glamorgan, but he did offer material to other historians, and his son Taliesin supplied music and verses for the pioneering Glamorgan and Gwent song-book of Maria Jane Williams in 1844.[31] Notes which appeared to be of literary interest were bound together in Iolo's collection of manuscripts and these found their way to the Llanover collection, but the vast mass of non-literary antiquarian materials remained in private hands until the mid-twentieth century, so that the variety and breadth of Iolo's interests as an antiquarian have only become known fairly recently.

While it is true that Iolo remained until fairly late in life an antiquarian and an archaeologist, it is clear that from the 1780s onwards he was increasingly obsessed by a quite different sort of history: a visionary, mythological, Romantic history, based almost entirely on historical material which he himself forged. Druidism had already become a fad and a hobby for intellectuals throughout Britain and, in the form of 'Celtomania', it was *à la mode* in France as well. The Celtic scholar and Deist, John Toland, an Irishman resident in England, had warned in the early eighteenth century that no continuity existed between ancient Druids and medieval bards, but nevertheless went on to establish a club or a society in 1717 entitled the Druid Universal Bond. Better known was the friendly society set up in London in 1781, the Ancient Order of Druids, with which William Blake was long associated. Despite Toland, in his celebrated published tours in Wales, Thomas Pennant wrote

[28] Williams, *Edward Lhuyd ac Iolo Morganwg*, pp. 17, 26–7; Ceri Lewis, 'Iolo Morganwg' in Jarvis (ed.), *A Guide to Welsh Literature, c. 1700–1800*, pp. 126–67.

[29] *MAW*, I, pp. xv, xix.

[30] Taliesin Williams (ed.), *Iolo Manuscripts* (Llandovery, 1848).

[31] Daniel Huws, Introduction to the facsimile edition of Maria Jane Williams, *Ancient National Airs of Gwent and Morganwg* (Cymdeithas Alawon Gwerin Cymru, 1988); idem, *Caneuon Llafar Gwlad ac Iolo a'i Fath* (Cymdeithas Alawon Gwerin Cymru, 1993).

about the Caerwys eisteddfodau in the sixteenth century, hinting vaguely at
the association between Druids, bards and the eisteddfod. There was also a good
deal of speculative writing in the mid-eighteenth century about primitive,
patriarchal and druidic religion. All these matters were in the air which Iolo
and his contemporaries breathed.

Iolo became deeply interested in the whole question in the late 1780s and
the early 1790s. During the period in London when he saw his poems through
the press, he also worked in the British Museum on his projected 'History of
the Bards'. It is important to add at this point that Iolo had become addicted
to laudanum, and it is generally agreed that his fantastical view of Welsh history
in this period must surely have been connected to his addiction.[32] He knew of
the current interest in Druids in England and also of the tradition, stretching
back to the sixteenth century, of seeing a resemblance between the Ancient
Druids and the medieval Welsh order of bards. Between about 1788 and 1792
he evolved a new Welsh historical philosophy, based on the principle that true
history was that of a culture, not that of state institutions. He claimed that the
Welsh were the true heirs of the Ancient Britons, that their language gave
direct access to the language of the primitive times, that the Druids had not
been entirely extirpated, but had survived, as a Christianized order, and had
taken the form of bards during the Middle Ages, the examinations to the order
being held at eisteddfodau. Despite recurrent waves of persecution, druido-
bardism survived, ultimately only in the mountain fastnesses of Glamorgan,
where the ancient lore and learning of the Druids were preserved in the form
of collections of triads which had been passed on from bard to bard in
apostolic succession until only two genuine Druids were left, Edward Evan of
Aberdare and, of course, Iolo Morganwg himself. He now believed that the
time had come to reveal the arcane secrets of the ancient Druids to the whole
world.[33] For Iolo, history was archaism, but it was also continuity. The idea or
the ideal of preserving the past was transferred into his new visionary history
from his older antiquarianism.

It appears that Iolo first publicized the secrets of bardism in an article
published in the *Gentleman's Magazine* in 1789.[34] The vehicle for this new
historical fantasy was the Gwyneddigion Society, and in 1792 Iolo and his
friends organized a druidic moot in London, for which Iolo had devised the
name Gorsedd (throne, or summit). At the summer solstice he held a Gorsedd
on Primrose Hill, London – the only full description we have is of the second

[32]   Geraint H. Jenkins, 'Cyffesion Bwytawr Opiwm: Iolo Morganwg a Gorsedd Beirdd Ynys
       Prydain', *Taliesin*, 81 (1993), 45–57; Geraint Phillips, 'Math o Wallgofrwydd: Iolo Morganwg,
       Opiwm a Thomas Chatterton', *NLWJ*, XXIX , no. 4 (1996), 391–410.
[33]   Williams: *IM*, pp. 182–5, 231, 321, 340, 462–3; Lewis, 'Iolo Morganwg' in Jarvis (ed.), *A Guide
       to Welsh Literature, c. 1700–1800*, pp. 156–62.
[34]   Williams: *IM*, pp. 464–5 for the full text of the article.

Gorsedd, held at the autumnal equinox of the same year. Iolo took advantage of William Owen Pughe's edition of the poems of Llywarch Hen[35] by adding a long section to the introduction which gave his version of the Gorsedd of the Bards of the Isle of Britain. The second volume of Iolo's English verse, published in 1794, also contained several bardo-druidic poems, with extensive pseudo-historical footnotes. He returned to Wales to hold Gorseddau in various parts from 1795 onwards, in which he claimed that the religion of the Druids had always been a form of pacifism, and even to some extent resembled Unitarianism. His aim in setting up such an institution – the first national institution in modern Wales – was to teach people their history through poems and songs, in other words to gain publicity for Welsh history; but he also clearly hoped that it would become a champion of the language, culture and history of Wales, and that from it would stem a national museum, a library, a folk museum and so on. He succeeded in associating the Gorsedd with the revived institution of the eisteddfod at Carmarthen in 1819, and during the last decades of his life he spent much of his time composing a vast mass of documents about druidic bards, explaining their ceremonial, liturgy, politics, morals, philosophy and theology.

Iolo died in 1826, leaving his son Taliesin to carry on his work as the leading Welsh Druid. Taliesin was a totally faithful disciple: spurning all the criticism of his father's system, he maintained that had his father been a dishonest forger he would have been exposed by his former friend William Owen Pughe, who had become estranged from Iolo following a bitter quarrel.[36] In 1829 Taliesin published his father's *Cyfrinach Beirdd Ynys Prydain*. The title, 'Mystery of the Bards', which conveyed the essence of an exclusively protected skill, purported to be a sixteenth-century Glamorgan manuscript describing how Glamorgan bards had disputed the classical Welsh prosody agreed upon at the Carmarthen eisteddfod in the mid-fifteenth century, and showing how a different set of rules had always been maintained by them. This was a fabrication by Iolo, based to some extent on the genuine fact of the greater popularity of non-*cynghanedd* verse in south Wales. It formed part of the bogus evidence invented by Iolo to prove to the Welsh public that Glamorgan possessed the richest and liveliest tradition of bardistry, a claim which made his pose as the last of the ancient Druids all the more plausible.[37]

In 1840 Taliesin ventured to publish, again from his father's papers, *Coelbren y Beirdd*, meaning in this instance the 'Alphabet of the bards'.[38] This was a kind

---

[35] William Owen Pughe (ed.), *The Heroic Elegies and other Pieces of Llywarç Hen* (London, 1792), pp. xxi–lxxx.

[36] Thomas, *Bywgraffiad Iolo Morganwg*, p. 101; Glenda Carr, *William Owen Pughe* (Caerdydd, 1983), pp. 9, 113–14, 164, 135–9, 235, for Iolo's attacks on William Owen Pughe.

[37] Taliesin Williams (ed.), *Cyfrinach Beirdd Ynys Prydain* (Abertawy, 1829).

[38] Taliesin Williams, *Traethawd ar Hynafiaeth ac Awdurdodaeth Coelbren y Beirdd* (Llanymddyfri, 1840).

of runic alphabet which Iolo fathered on the Druids. One of its most striking uses was to enable the druidic bards of Wales to communicate with one another by carving runes on the slats of an elaborate abacus-like writing frame, which could be manipulated in order to convey the bardic secrets at times when the Welsh were forbidden to use pen and parchment by their English conquerors. Iolo had frequently referred to these things during his lifetime, and such a frame appeared as part of the archdruid's paraphernalia in the *Costume of the Original Inhabitants of the British Islands* (1815).[39] Iolo's runic alphabet was used on monuments and on the gravestones of bards, on the prizes (the chairs and crowns, for example) and the scrolls of the National Eisteddfod well into the twentieth century. All this balderdash fitted neatly into Iolo's version of Welsh history since it purported to show that the bards were still using an alphabet inherited from the ancient Druids. This served to emphasize immemorial continuity and to remind his countrymen of the survival of bardism in the teeth of persecution. This was a theme of powerful conquerors and resourceful resisters which Iolo had long admired in the early triads of the Isle of Britain and which he believed to be central to the whole course of Welsh history.

Taliesin ab Iolo died in 1847 and the task of completing the translation and publication of the entertaining and influential volume *Iolo Manuscripts* was left to other editors. This material represents Iolo's own extensions or variations upon the different periods of Welsh history, including stories about heroes such as Arthur or Owain Glyndŵr, but most of them contain some slight twist which attached all the great heroes and events of Welsh history directly or indirectly to Glamorgan. The fabrications were highly readable – many were in the form of folk-tales or fairy stories – and since mid-nineteenth century Glamorgan was becoming such a populous and important county the people of south Wales swallowed the forgeries with pride and pleasure.

Those manuscripts considered to be of literary interest and importance were purchased by Benjamin and Augusta Hall, and scholars were encouraged to study them at their home at Llanover Court, Monmouthshire. One who seized the opportunity was John Williams (Ab Ithel), a Flintshire cleric who published several volumes of Iolo's materials, two of which are of importance in this context: *Barddas* (1862; 1874).[40] His preface stoutly defended Iolo against accusations of forgery, and the first volume purported to be a translation from Iolo's manuscripts of the symbols, theology and wisdom of the Druids, while the second volume dealt with the privileges and usages of the Gorsedd of the

---

[39] Piggott, *The Druids*, cover illustration; Smiles, *The Image of Antiquity*, p. 132, plate 10.

[40] John Williams (Ab Ithel), *Barddas: or a Collection of Original Documents, Illustrative of the Theology, Wisdom and Usages of the Bardo-Druidic System of the Isle of Britain* (2 vols., Llandovery, 1862; London, 1874); idem, *Druidism* (Tenby, 1871). For Ab Ithel, see G. J. Williams, 'Ab Ithel' in Aneirin Lewis (ed.), *Agweddau ar Hanes Dysg Gymraeg* (Caerdydd, 1969), pp. 253–77.

Bards. These were claimed by Iolo to have been derived from the sixteenth-century manuscript of a perfectly genuine copyist, Llywelyn Siôn of Llangewydd, Glamorgan. The strange texts, many of them in the form of triads, supposedly memorized by initiates to the order of Druids from antiquity onwards, adumbrate a kind of rational society in which the Druids were almost 'philosopher kings', a theme which caught the imagination of many of the Welsh in the nineteenth century.

Despite the criticisms of poets from north Wales from *c.*1800 onwards, Iolo succeeded in grafting his Gorsedd of the Bards on to the institution of the eisteddfod from 1819 onwards. Indeed, provincial and local Gorseddau co-existed throughout Wales, and members eagerly read the revelations of the oracle from Flemingston. It is in a way curious that Iolo should have been concerned with druidic ceremonial because he appears to have sympathized with the Quakers before becoming a Unitarian from the 1790s onwards. One of his biographers notes that he was always fond of returning to church services, and it may be that he simply enjoyed the ceremonies.[41] It was Iolo, after all, who forced the eisteddfod to become a permanent and popular feature of Welsh culture. The Gorsedd of the Bards, of course, remained a separate organization, but it greatly enhanced the eisteddfod and, while the eisteddfod tended in the later nineteenth century to compromise with the forces of modernization and Anglicization, the Gorsedd of the Bards remained strictly faithful to Iolo's vision of the absolute, overriding importance of the Welsh language. It remained throughout this period the only Welsh national institution, and its liturgy, invented by Iolo, ensured that the Welsh nation met in public in Welsh.

It is notable that both Taliesin ab Iolo and John Williams (Ab Ithel) were troubled by the accusations of forgery against Iolo. As we have seen, Dafydd Ddu Eryri and other poets from north Wales, who had initially welcomed Iolo's Gorsedd in the mid-1790s, had their doubts about its authenticity by 1800. This was partly because the doctrines of Iolo's druidism resembled some of the more 'disagreeable' aspects of the French Revolution, and were therefore reckoned to be dangerous and to be avoided, but partly also because they were seen by many as an affront to the traditional history of Wales. Edward Jones, 'Bardd y Brenin', disliked Iolo's politics, and although he printed some of Iolo's verses in *The Bardic Museum* in 1802, he always clung to the conventional version of Welsh history.[42] Edward Davies, rector of Bishopston, who wrote on druidism in 1809, attacked Iolo's notions without ever being able enough to disprove his theories. This remained a fundamental difficulty until the gradual growth by the mid-nineteenth century of more scientific notions, higher scholarly standards in the fields of philology, history and archaeology, and a

---

[41] Thomas, *Bywgraffiad Iolo Morganwg*, p. 118.
[42] Tecwyn Ellis, 'Bardd y Brenin, Iolo Morganwg a Derwyddiaeth', *NLWJ*, XIII (1963–4), 147–56, 224–34, 356–62; XIV (1965–6), 183–93, 221–9, 424–36; XV (1967), 177–96.

more rigorous use of authentic documents.[43] One of Iolo's fellow-Unitarians, Thomas Stephens, a chemist from Merthyr Tydfil, gradually came to suspect that much of Iolo's history was bogus, and his debunking of the Madoc forgeries by Iolo and others caused an uproar at the eisteddfod of Llangollen organized in 1858 by John Williams (Ab Ithel). Stephens's attack on *Coelbren y Beirdd* followed in 1872,[44] and thereafter attacks upon the whole structure of Iolo's history grew apace, even though the *Iolo Manuscripts* were reissued in Liverpool in 1888. By this stage, the nature of Welsh culture and its attitude to Welsh language and literature had changed following the controversy provoked by 'The Treachery of the Blue Books' in 1847.[45] The three commissioners – had Iolo been alive, he would perhaps have called them 'a triad of commissioners' – who arrived in Wales to assess the state of education had been horrified to discover that the Welsh were ignorant of English history, which in itself is not surprising in the light of the popularity of all kinds of books about Welsh history published over the previous fifty years. For instance, when it became fashionable to set up workmen's friendly societies in the early nineteenth century, the Order of True Ivorites (Urdd y Gwir Iforiaid) took their name from Ifor Hael, who was one of Iolo's heroes, since he was reputed to be Dafydd ap Gwilym's greatest patron. When the three English commissioners published their animadversions on Welsh education in 1847, their report was satirized as 'The Treachery of the Blue Books' (Brad y Llyfrau Gleision) on the model of 'The Treachery of the Long Knives' (Brad y Cyllyll Hirion), in the knowledge that the public would immediately understand the reference to the fifth-century plot against the Welsh by Hengist and Horsa. Despite the satire, the Blue Books were a withering blast which led to a decline in the prestige of the Welsh language and Welsh history which Iolo had done so much to bathe in a radiance of brilliant publicity in order to give them class and distinction. It was fortunate from the Welsh point of view that the eisteddfod still survived through this period, and that the Gorsedd of the Bards clung resolutely to Iolo's vision of the importance of history and the Welsh language.

What, then, may be said in conclusion about Iolo the historian? The first and rather obvious feature is that all his work was vitiated by the great mass of forged documents he produced. His work cannot therefore be relied upon as

---

[43] Edward Davies, *Celtic Researches on the Origin, Traditions and Language of the Ancient Britons* (London, 1804); idem, *The Mythology and Rites of the British Druids* (London, 1809).

[44] Thomas Stephens, *The Literature of the Kymry* (2nd edn., London, 1876), esp. the life of the author by B. T. Williams, and pp. xxxvii–xl for the uproar at Llangollen in 1858 regarding the impact of Stephens's critique of Madoc. Stephens's attack on *Coelbren y Beirdd* is in *AC*, IV, Part 3 (1872), 181–209.

[45] Prys Morgan, 'From Long Knives to Blue Books' in R. R. Davies, Ralph A. Griffiths, Ieuan Gwynedd Jones and Kenneth O. Morgan (eds.), *Welsh Society and Nationhood: Historical Essays presented to Glanmor Williams* (Cardiff, 1984), pp. 199–215.

a source for ancient or medieval history. This aspect of his work should not trouble historians in our days, however, since his forgeries were detected around eighty years ago. It is thus possible for us today to stand back and see Iolo and his work as a part of Welsh history, as illustrations of the Welsh mind in the late eighteenth century.[46] He worked both as an antiquarian and as a visionary historian. Whenever he collected material of a detailed, empirical and antiquarian nature, its accuracy can often be corroborated from other sources, and all the indications are that he was extremely reliable. Whenever he wore the mantle of the visionary historian, he took materials from the past and offered his own variations (and improvements) on the theme. As Rachel Bromwich has commented in relation to his invention of additional sets of bardic triads, since he knew that the medieval bards had adapted oral tradition as they came to write down the ancient triads, he felt entitled to do likewise in adapting them to the concerns of his own age.[47] Iolo's druidic visions were probably prompted by the fantastic dreams induced by his drug addiction in the 1790s. He subsequently felt the need to support his visions and make them more real by embellishing or inventing new texts. He could see that the Welsh enjoyed and appreciated these extraordinary fantasies, and his Gorsedd of the Bards became a genuinely Welsh national institution which, in turn, gave vigour, life and continuity to the eisteddfod; indeed, it made it the central cultural institution of the Welsh for many decades.

His two kinds of history illustrate other aspects of the eighteenth-century mind. At least part of his antiquarian studies was devoted to preserving the colourful life of the peasantry, as a reaction against metropolitan and official standards and incipient industrialization. Iolo's mythical history, with its long pageant of heroes countering waves of invaders, and subsequently its heroic lines of bards defending an ancient culture and language, was truly Romantic in the sense that it was a reaction against the official British history – state and institutional history, kings, governments, foreign policy and all those elements which remained dominant in 'English History' up to the mid-twentieth century.[48] More precisely, the druidic vision, as developed by Iolo, illustrated an ideal society ruled by poet legislators, who had opinions not dissimilar to the Unitarian radicalism espoused by Iolo himself. But even if one sets that particular radical message aside, Iolo's history was in itself a kind of political statement, affirming the importance of the remote periphery against the

---

[46] Geraint H. Jenkins, 'The Cultural Uses of the Welsh Language, 1660–1800' in idem (ed.), *The Welsh Language before the Industrial Revolution* (Cardiff, 1997), pp. 399–402; idem, *Facts, Fantasy and Fiction*, p. 1.

[47] Bromwich, '*Trioedd Ynys Prydain*' in *Welsh Literature and Scholarship*, p. 46.

[48] Gwyn A. Williams, 'Romanticism in Wales' in Roy Porter and Mikuláš Teich (eds.), *Romanticism in National Context* (Cambridge, 1988), pp. 9–36, where Iolo is described as the 'arch-demon' and the 'demiurge' of Welsh Romanticism.

metropolis, and the role of the people and their culture, as against that of governments. It is not argued here that he created a historical revival in Wales, for he was clearly only one of an army of scholars and writers who published in Welsh and English during his lifetime. But, whereas most of them tended to write monographs about single aspects of Welsh history, Iolo perceived all the aspects as part of a whole, a colourful popular pageant stretching back to Celtic 'Ancient Britain' which, at that time, was the ultimate limit of knowable history. He also believed that it was still a living tradition: when he visited the 'sacred ground' of Gwernyclepa, near Newport, he saw Ifor Hael's hall lying in ruins all about him, yet he felt the Welsh muse was still pulsating vigorously.[49] He succeeded in conveying, by fair means and foul, this sense of the vitality and viability of the Welsh language and its history to the Welsh people. Thus, despite all the forgeries and inventions, he was himself a remarkable historical phenomenon.

---

[49]   Williams: *IM*, p. 432.

12

The Unitarian Firebrand, the Cambrian Society and the Eisteddfod

GERAINT H. JENKINS

Sometime during the third week of October 1818, at the invitation of Thomas Burgess, bishop of St David's, Iolo Morganwg set off on foot from his daughters' home at Cefncribwr in Glamorgan for the bishop's palace at Abergwili in Carmarthenshire. The frail septuagenarian deposited his indispensable travelling companions – pens, notepads, drafts of manuscripts, a spare shirt, a mallet and a chisel (in case his skills as a mason were called upon en route) – in his satchel before heading west. He had mixed feelings about visiting a county whose inhabitants were past masters at 'low Cunning and Knavish arts'[1] and he was particularly apprehensive about spending a night at an episcopal residence which he had once disparaged as 'this grovelingly great place'.[2] But his enthusiasm for Welsh literature and his natural curiosity had got the better of him, and the prospect of playing a decisive role in the formation of the proposed Cambrian Society was an irresistible incentive. Over the years the great survivor had been forced to compromise many times when the occasion demanded, and in his reply to Burgess he had expressed his satisfaction at being summoned to be 'a Witness to and partaker of your Lordships noble exertions in favour of Welsh Literature'.[3] To fit the occasion, Iolo – normally the most unkempt of travellers – had bought a bright new coat with gilt buttons, and a buff-coloured waistcoat. So resplendent was he that when he passed through Neath his friend Elijah Waring teased him over his uncharacteristic sartorial elegance.[4] Given Iolo's reputation as a Unitarian and an *enfant terrible*, it is surprising that Burgess was eager to involve him in initiatives by his clergy to rejuvenate Welsh letters and especially the eisteddfod, and it is highly likely that

---

[1] NLW 13156A, p. 84. It should be pointed out that Iolo's views of different counties and their inhabitants varied wildly according to his mood at any particular time.

[2] NLW 13115B, p. 58. This comment was made as he passed Abergwili in June 1796.

[3] NLW 1895Ei, no. 80. The invitation from Burgess is in NLW 21280E, Letter no. 43, Thomas Burgess to Iolo Morganwg, 27 August 1818.

[4] *RAEW*, p. 124. Iolo, who seldom liked being teased, replied that 'as he was going to visit at a palace he was minded to keep up appearances accordingly'.

Fig. 21 Thomas Burgess, bishop of St David's 1803–25. A stipple engraving by Thomson, 1825.

representatives of the 'old literary parsons' ('yr hen bersoniaid llengar'), notably Thomas Beynon, archdeacon of Cardigan, had persuaded the bishop that Iolo's knowledge of Welsh antiquities was unsurpassed and that his advice was indispensable.[5] It is remarkable how many distinguished people over the years had genuflected before the venerable Welsh bard, and when he arrived at Abergwili, chest wheezing and joints creaking, Iolo was cordially greeted by the bishop with a smile memorably likened by Burgess's biographer to 'a ray of sunshine, lighting up the serene beauty of an autumnal landscape'.[6] Perhaps unwisely, Burgess offered his guest unrestricted access to his library. During the small hours, the bishop's servants, terrified by the sound of heavy footsteps, tumbled out of their beds and peeped over the staircase to find that the culprit was the Glamorgan bard, who was 'pacing to and fro in the Hall, with a night-cap on

[5]   NLW 21280E, Letter no. 21, Thomas Beynon to Iolo Morganwg, 19 October 1818; Mari Ellis, 'Thomas Beynon, Archddiacon Ceredigion 1745–1833', *Ceredigion*, XIII, no. 1 (1997), 54–5.
[6]   John S. Harford, *The Life of Thomas Burgess, DD* (London, 1840), p. 303.

his head, a book in one hand, and a candle in the other'.[7] As Burgess would soon discover to his dismay, Iolo was still capable of behaving unpredictably and revelling in the spotlight.

Traditional accounts of the foundation of the Cambrian Society and the celebrated Carmarthen eisteddfod of July 1819 have highlighted the special role played by Thomas Burgess and a coterie of enthusiastic Welsh clerics and have viewed the whole initiative in a cultural context.[8] This chapter calls this conventional wisdom into question by arguing that the prelude to, as well as the events of, the Carmarthen eisteddfod were much more complex than has previously been allowed and can only be properly understood within the context of Rational Dissent. In spite of his public persona in his twilight years as an artless Welsh bard, Iolo was no more favourably disposed towards leaders of the established church than was the sweet-smiling Burgess towards champions of heterodoxy. Only three months before his visit to Abergwili, Iolo had informed the Unitarian, Lant Carpenter of Bristol, that 'those Titles which are solely or exclusively bestowed on Religion, or rather on the Ministers of Religion, as Revd Lord Bishop, right revd most revd His Holiness his Grace, etc etc are names of Blasphemy, and utterly inconsistent with the magnificent simplicity of the transcendently sublime and beautiful Christian Religion'.[9] Equally, fears of revolution and the alarming growth of Dissent within his see preyed so heavily on Burgess's mind that he had a reputation for hounding Rational Dissenters. Cultural, religious and political tensions simmered below the surface, and this theme warrants further consideration.

Iolo Morganwg was born and bred in the bosom of what was fondly known in the eighteenth century as the 'mother' church. He was baptized at Llancarfan Church on 13 March 1747, he married his wife Margaret (or Peggy) at St Mary Church on 18 July 1781, and each of his four children (one of whom, Elizabeth (Lilla), died in infancy) was baptized by local clergymen.[10] He acquired his expertise in Welsh lexicography and grammar from gifted local clergymen, especially Thomas Richards of Coychurch and John Walters of Llandough, and his craft as a stonemason meant that he spent long hours chiselling in cold and draughty churchyards in Glamorgan. His friend Evan Evans (Ieuan Fardd), the coiner of the term 'Esgyb Eingl' (Anglo Bishops), coloured his view of the Church by fulminating against prelates who openly

[7] *RAEW*, p. 124.
[8] Bedwyr Lewis Jones, *Yr Hen Bersoniaid Llengar* (Gwasg yr Eglwys yng Nghymru, [1963]); Mari Ellis, 'Cyfeillion Awenyddgar', *Y Casglwr*, 59 (1997), 11, 13; Hywel Teifi Edwards, *The Eisteddfod* (Cardiff, 1990), pp. 16–17; idem, 'The Eisteddfod Poet: An Embattled Figure' in idem (ed.), *A Guide to Welsh Literature c. 1800–1900. Volume V* (Cardiff, 2000), pp. 30–1.
[9] NLW 21286E, Letter no. 964, Iolo Morganwg to Lant Carpenter, 6 July 1818.
[10] GRO, P/36/CW/1, Llancarfan PR 1747; NLW 13141A, p. 111; GRO, P/23/CW/2, St Mary Church PR 1782; P/10/CW/1, Flemingston PR 1786, 1787, 1790.

despised the native tongue and promoted English-speaking sycophants and place-hunters at the expense of deserving Welsh-speaking clergymen.[11] Some of the poems which Iolo composed and sang in masonic circles in Cowbridge reveal that, certainly by the late 1780s, he believed that the established church had decayed into a moribund institution, staffed by idle absentee bishops, greedy sinecurists and sottish priests. Among them are the sharply satirical 'The Marshfield Shepherd, or Parson of Parsons', sung to the tune 'The Devil and Bishop of Canterbury', and 'Something to stare at', a thwacking indictment of the unreformed Church:

> The Priestcraft religion of Parsons and kings
> Unsanction'd by Liberty's law.
> To many a proud knave a fat Benefice brings
> Or keeps the dull vulgar in awe.[12]

Even before his conversion to Paineite radicalism after 1791, Iolo was expressing grave doubts about how established religions sustained the hypocritical lifestyles of clergymen and their tyrannical superiors.[13] Another powerful influence on his anti-clericalism was the weaver and dyer John Bradford of Betws Tir Iarll, whose reputation as a 'great Disbuter and a Nominated Deist, or a free thinker'[14] fostered the growth of anti-trinitarian views among those well-read farmers, artisans and craftsmen in upland Glamorgan whom Iolo liked to call 'Gwŷr Cwm y Felin' (Men of Cwm y Felin). These figured among the main agents through whom heterodox ideas, as well as druidic mythology, were circulated in south Wales among those, like Iolo, who had been denied formal schooling and the opportunity to attend Dissenting academies in which free enquiry was encouraged.[15] Like many autodidacts of craftsman stock, he read avidly and came to believe that knowledge was power and that careers should be open to all talents.

In the year of the outbreak of the French Revolution Iolo began to assimilate an even wider range of progressive ideas and to project himself as a writer. Poems which he sometimes wrote under the pseudonym 'Christopher Crabstick' underpinned the programme advanced by Glamorgan freeholders in the county election of 1789.[16] He began to read the philosophers of the Enlightenment, especially Voltaire, to adopt an anti-Calvinist liberal stance, to flirt with Quakerism and to seek out places where he could be the centre of attention and

---

[11] Geraint H. Jenkins, 'Yr Eglwys "Wiwlwys Olau" a'i Beirniaid', *Ceredigion*, X, no. 2 (1985), 139–44; idem, *The Foundations of Modern Wales: Wales 1642–1780* (Oxford, 1987), pp. 342–7.

[12] NLW 21328A, pp. 198–200, 222–32; NLW 21335B, pp. 6–9.

[13] NLW 21414E, no. 9. See also NLW 13089E, p. 382.

[14] R. T. W. Denning (ed.), *The Diary of William Thomas of Michaelston-super-Ely, near St Fagans Glamorgan 1762–1795* (Cardiff, 1995), p. 339.

[15] NLW 13121B, pp. 335–8; NLW 13138A, pp. 104–8. See also Williams: *IM*, p. 73.

[16] NLW 21402F, nos. 1, 2, 3, 5, 6.

where he could indulge his gift for conversation and interrogation. He believed that the French Revolution held out the promise of a new golden age, of a reformed and enlightened society in which the Paineite view of the world – that God had created people free and equal – would prevail.[17] During these years Iolo kept a close eye on the efforts of the Gwyneddigion Society to revive the largely dormant eisteddfodau, held mostly in the market towns of north Wales, in which substantial prizes were awarded for poetry, prose and music.[18] The progressive elements within London-Welsh circles firmly aligned themselves with the new enthusiasm for political change. 'Liberty' ('Rhyddid') and 'Truth' ('Gwirionedd') were the subjects of the *awdl* (ode) competitions in 1790–1, and the impressive medals were designed by Augustin Dupré, the celebrated goldsmith, medallist and engraver-general of coins of the First French Republic. The likes of Iolo and William Jones, the 'Welsh Voltaire' from Llangadfan, enter- tained fond hopes that inviting 'old brothers' from south Wales would not only invigorate the proceedings but also turn the eisteddfod into a truly national institution.[19] It soon became clear to Iolo, however, that the loyalist compos- itions of David Thomas (Dafydd Ddu Eryri) and Walter Davies (Gwallter Mechain) were voicing Burkean rhetoric rather than the natural rights and liberty of the people. Irked and disillusioned by the political stance of conser- vatively minded Gwyneddigion, Iolo turned elsewhere.

Increasingly, therefore, during his fraught four-year sojourn in London from 1791 – a time in which he was haunted by social, religious and political anxieties – Iolo threw in his lot with Rational Dissent and especially with Unitarianism, which was its most distinctive outcome. Although Unitarian worship remained illegal until the Trinity Act of 1813, by the early 1790s Unitarians in the metropolis and elsewhere were increasingly prepared to declare themselves and to lobby for change. Grayson M. Ditchfield has shown how the Unitarian Petition of 1792 (which was rejected by the House of Commons in May) offered an opportunity for Unitarianism to define itself, raise its public profile and play its part in the rapid expansion in print culture.[20] Later in life Iolo claimed to have attended Theophilus Lindsey's celebrated Unitarian chapel at Essex Street from its inception in 1774,[21] but his involvement with the liberal Dissenting community in London probably

---

[17]   See Geraint H. Jenkins, 'The Bard of Liberty during William Pitt's Reign of Terror' in Joseph F. Nagy and Leslie E. Jones (eds.), *Heroic Poets and Poetic Heroes in Celtic Tradition: A Festschrift for Patrick K. Ford. CSANA Yearbook 3–4* (Dublin, 2004), pp. 183–206.

[18]   G. J. Williams, 'Eisteddfodau'r Gwyneddigion', *Y Llenor*, XIV–XV (1935–6), 11–22, 88–96; Prys Morgan, *The Eighteenth Century Renaissance* (Llandybïe, 1981), pp. 63–6.

[19]   NLW 1806E, p. 777, William Jones to Walter Davies, 28 June 1789.

[20]   G. M. Ditchfield, 'Anti-trinitarianism and Toleration in Late Eighteenth-century British Politics: The Unitarian Petition of 1792', *Journal of Ecclesiastical History*, XLII, no. 1 (1991), 39–67.

[21]   NLW 21286E, Letter no. 988, Iolo Morganwg to Mr Christe, 29 April 1822; G. M. Ditchfield, *Theophilus Lindsey: From Anglican to Unitarian* (London, 1998).

dates from after the Birmingham riots in July 1791 when one of his principal heroes, Joseph Priestley, was forced to seek refuge in the capital. He rubbed shoulders with Priestley, David Williams, the nephews of Richard Price (George Cadogan Morgan and William Morgan) and others who promoted popular reform societies and celebrated the ideals of the French Revolution at the Crown and Anchor tavern.[22] While seeking subscriptions for his *Poems, Lyric and Pastoral* (1794) he found himself on the fringes of the literary and political Unitarian circle which developed at 72 St Paul's Churchyard around the radical publisher and bookseller Joseph Johnson and which included the physician and writer John Aikin, his sister Anna Laetitia Barbauld, William Godwin and Mary Wollstonecraft.[23] Cambridge-trained Unitarians like George Dyer and Gilbert Wakefield, whom Iolo entertained in the company of William Owen Pughe, were passionately committed to the cause of individual liberty, peace, anti-slavery and justice.[24] He campaigned for constitutional reform, thrived on theological debate, and wrote scores of unpublished essays and poems, some of which were tinged with apocalyptic expectations, designed to show that established religions served the interests of 'Tyrants priests hypocrites knaves & fools'.[25]

Celebrating his supposed Cromwellian roots and his growing reputation as the 'Bard of Liberty', Iolo had little interest in 'that rascally thing called Prudence'.[26] Having escaped from the stifling discipline of trinitarianism and subscribed to the Enlightenment aspiration of self-improvement as well as the post-1789 flowering of human rights, he revelled in the opportunity to take part in the struggle against the 'tyranny' of state religion, to encourage scepticism and to promote material which was both disruptive and subversive.[27] It was not unexpected at this time that a Welsh journeyman-mason with a sceptical cast of mind and social and literary ambitions of his

[22] H. McLachlan, *Letters of Theophilus Lindsey* (Manchester, 1920), p. 16; Damian Walford Davies, *Presences that Disturb: Models of Romantic Identity in the Literature and Culture of the 1790s* (Cardiff, 2002), chapter 4.

[23] J. E. Cookson, *The Friends of Peace: Anti-War Liberalism in England 1793–1815* (Cambridge, 1982), p. 89; R. K. Webb, 'The Unitarian Background' in Barbara Smith (ed.), *Truth, Liberty, Religion: Essays Celebrating Two Hundred Years of Manchester College* (Oxford, 1986), pp. 3–30; Ruth Watts, *Gender, Power and the Unitarians in England 1760–1860* (London, 1998), pp. 68, 92–3. For Johnson, see Gerald P. Tyson, *Joseph Johnson: A Liberal Publisher* (Iowa City, 1979) and Helen Braithwaite, *Romanticism, Publishing and Dissent: Joseph Johnson and the Cause of Liberty* (Basingstoke, 2003).

[24] NLW 13221E, p. 49, Iolo Morganwg to William Owen Pughe, 20 May 1795; George Thompson, *Slavery and Famine, Punishments for Sedition . . . with preliminary remarks by George Dyer* (London, 1794), pp. v–vi; *Monthly Repository*, new ser., I (1827), 582.

[25] NLW 21414E, no. 9. For a millennial gloss, see NLW 13136A, pp. 165–83.

[26] NLW 21344A, marginal note inside the cover.

[27] For the background, see Knud Haakonssen (ed.), *Enlightenment and Religion: Rational Dissent in Eighteenth-Century Britain* (Cambridge, 1996) and Martin Fitzpatrick, 'Enlightenment' in Iain McCalman (ed.), *An Oxford Companion to the Romantic Age: British Culture 1776–1832* (Oxford, 1999), pp. 299–311.

own should have become one of the most forthright critics of one of the handmaidens of the state, the universities. To Iolo, Oxford was a 'filthy den of iniquity', a moribund, corrupt institution where students spent more time drinking and whoring than sharpening their minds. It spewed out clerical graduates whose 'superlative vices' poisoned the minds and morals of the people they were meant to serve.[28] Deaf to the cry of freedom of expression and to the spirit of Nature, Reason and plain common sense, academics manufactured 'a locust swarm of Ignorant Pedants that only jabber like parrots what they remember'.[29]

The bitingly sceptical language Iolo employed in his writings, much of it couched in the spirit of Voltaire rather than the more guarded sentiments of the Friends of Peace, reveals that he had become convinced that all established religions were inimical to the principles of truth, justice and morality. That which he liked to call 'the sublimely beautiful column of Christianity'[30] had been undermined by kingcraft and priestcraft. Principles of 'genuine Christianity' were outlawed by self-seeking bishops and clerics who pandered to the 'great ones of the Earth' at the expense of meek, humble commoners.[31] In a flurry of unpublished drafts written for the benefit of the 'swinish multitude', he did not spare those who displayed 'the insolence of modern Parsoncraft':

> From Tyranies frown, stifling Freedom's debate,
> From brazen-faced Parsoncraft's infidel prate,
> And from making the Church a vile Engine of state,
>   Good Lord deliver us.[32]

In skittish vein, he threatened to publish a work advocating the abolition of Christianity on the grounds that it was inconsistent with the principles of kings, archbishops, bishops, priests and Belzeebub himself,[33] while his 'Push at the Pillars of Priestcraft' was signed by 'Citizen Sans-culotte' and bore the address 'Sign of the kings head, Guillotine Court'.[34]

Nothing infuriated Iolo more than discovering trophies of war in cathedrals and churches.[35] To him, the notion of a Christian warrior was an oxymoron and, by identifying themselves with what he called the 'blood trade', churchmen were feeding on human blood.[36] During vigorous debates held

[28] NLW 13174A, pp. 2ᵛ, 3ᵛ, 4ʳ⁻ᵛ; NLW 13115B, p. 346.
[29] NLW 13117E, p. 164.
[30] NLW 21396E, no. 33.
[31] NLW 13089E, p. 382.
[32] NLW 21401E, nos. 1–3; NLW 13089E, p. 451.
[33] NLW 13162A, p. 319.
[34] NLW 21400C, nos. 28, 28 a–b.
[35] NLW 13120B, pp. 360–3.
[36] NLW 21401E, nos. 18, 19, 22, 24, 25.

under the auspices of the Caradogion (Caractacan) Society in London his stance was unambiguous: 'No priest, no parson: truth, peace and liberty', and he was not averse to coupling appellations like 'His Most Sacred Majesty' and 'His Grace of Canterbury' with blasphemous terms like 'The Great Whore'.[37] In an extraordinary unpublished address to George III, in which he furiously decried his warmongering, he distanced himself entirely from all forms of established religions. Here we see Iolo at his most irascible, seeking new forms of expression as he sought to reshape the whole basis of ecclesiastical society:

> Do you think Sir that I am or ever will be of this Religion? No Sir. I will remain a convert to the religion of that place, tho it be hell it self, where there are no Babylonian kings, no antichrist priests no Graces of Canterby (holinesses of Rome may be admitted for without holiness no one shall see the Lord) no right rev.d father in God of human manufacture, no Grace bestowed, given, or confessed by a blasphemous earthly worm of a monarch, not even by Emperor of America, – but surely the place where these are not to be found can never be hell. It is that place where S.t John tells us all are kings and priests – i.e. all are equal in the divine love and estimation. Of course this place may be with strictest propriety be called the Land of Levelling – and as thus described by an inspired writer, it must be a heaven indeed. What a heaven where I shall no longer be trodden by Kings Priests etc.[38]

It has been argued that Iolo always couched his political views in universalist terms, without ever adapting them to specific Welsh concerns.[39] No such charge could be levelled against him regarding his assessment of the performance of the established church in Wales. Indeed, he was only too willing to reveal how ill-equipped it was to serve the spiritual needs of the Welsh people. Dogged by its outdated parochial structure, the absenteeism of its bishops and the poverty of its clergy, as well as by the divisive effects of language, the established church was in crisis.[40] For around a century and a half after 1727, no native Welsh speaker held a bishopric in Wales, and those with un-Welsh names like Claggett, Lowth, Smallwell, Sydall and Yorke who took up appointments in Wales were for the most part remote, distant figures, out of sympathy with their Welsh-speaking flocks and prone, as one world-weary cleric put it, to fly off at the earliest opportunity to a warmer and more lucrative nest.[41] They had few compunctions about rewarding their friends and ensuring that English bounty-hunters were able to leapfrog over more deserving Welsh-speaking candidates who silently seethed with resentment. Never one

---

[37] NLW 21433E, nos. 1, 3.
[38] NLW 21396E, no. 11.
[39] D. O. Thomas, *Ymateb i Chwyldro / Response to Revolution* (Cardiff, 1989), pp. 81–2; Lewis: *IM*, pp. 139–40.
[40] Walter T. Morgan, 'The Diocese of St David's in the Ninteenth Century: The Unreformed Church (III)', *JHSCW*, no. 28 (1973), 18–55.
[41] NLW 22131C, p. 55, Lewis Evans to John Evans, 27 January 1801.

to bite his tongue, Iolo fulminated against an institution which had become not only 'a forcer of conscience, a filcher of property [and] a system of Pride and Tyranny',[42] but also an alien imposition upon Welsh speakers. 'The Bishops of Wales', he thundered, 'are not Welsh Bishops . . . they know nothing of the Language of the Welsh Bible.'[43] Such men, in his eyes, were a disgrace to the memory of those Elizabethan prelates who had been at pains to ensure that Welsh became the language of Protestantism in Wales. Although he diligently sought subscriptions from several Welsh bishops for his *Poems, Lyric and Pastoral*, he excoriated them in private. Dotted throughout his papers are pungent references – in the form of proverbs, triads and verses – deriding bishops and clerics as proud, greedy, vain and mendacious: 'Saer Celwydd, a Bishop, a Parson' (A Barefaced Liar, a Bishop, a Parson) and 'Myned fel offeiriad tua'r nef. Gerfydd ei dîn' (Like a parson going to heaven. Arse foremost).[44] Among the hundreds of triads which he composed, a particular favourite – often recited in Gorsedd circles – was 'Parsonism, Kingism, and Devilism, the three grand curses of the world'.[45] On one occasion, while referring to the covering of a coffin on a bier, he was reminded of 'that other kind of dead body called an archbishop'.[46] By the end of the eighteenth century there is abundant evidence of popular hostility towards bishops and clergy, but no Welsh writer in this period linked as effectively as Iolo a range of objections to the authority of priests. While plodding past the palace of the bishop of St David's at Abergwili in June 1796, he exploded with rage as he pondered the benefits which would accrue if only the consciences of the godly could be liberated from the tyranny of their ecclesiastical superiors:

> God made man in his own image, we are told; but why were we not cautioned by the same writer that the Devil made also at Abergwily a brute animal resembling man in his own image; the Bishop of St Davids lives at Abergwily. I feel indignant!!! . . . o! that I could consign this Parish, Bishops and all, for a while, to the slave traders! I had almost said, to the D—l.[47]

Nor was Iolo loath to vent his disapproval of individual prelates. For instance, it seemed to him that Samuel Horsley, bishop of St David's (1788–93), deserved nothing but scorn. During the early 1790s, at a time when small groups of Welsh Arians and Unitarians were launching vociferous attacks on orthodox religion, a furious pamphlet war broke out between Horsley and

---

[42] NLW 13136A, p. 182. See also NLW 21400C, no. 276 and NLW 21401E, p. 5.

[43] NLW 13160A, p. 365.

[44] NLW 13146A, p. 432; NLW 13221E, Letter no. 12, pp. 67–70, Iolo Morganwg to William Owen Pughe, 8 June 1800.

[45] NLW 13174A, p. 21.

[46] NLW 13142A, p. 399. On another occasion, he disparaged every cleric who aspired to a bishopric, for which 'he may be enormously paid for doing of nothing'. NLW 21401E, p. 5.

[47] NLW 13115B, pp. 57–8, 362–3.

those whom he dubbed 'the Vulcano men'.[48] David Jones of Llandovery, an exceptionally able writer who assumed the pen name 'The Welsh Freeholder', published a flurry of polemics portraying Horsley as an inveterate enemy of human rights and as the epitome of blind anger and persecution. Pulling no punches, he voiced the readiness of anti-trinitarians to raise 'our little banners in opposition to your Lordship's towering standard',[49] and, as a reminder to the bishop that he had a special obligation to serve Welsh-speaking people, he pointedly included a Welsh epigram on the title-page of each rejoinder to Horsley.[50] It would not have escaped Horsley's attention that a Brechfa weaver – Thomas Evans (Tomos Glyn Cothi) – had become the first Unitarian minister in Wales and had deigned, in printed sermons published as early as 1792–3, to use the dreaded Welsh words 'Undodiaid' (Unitarians) and 'Undodiaeth' (Unitarianism).[51] Evans took no delight in the malice of Horsleyites and, following his lead, Iolo deplored the 'boisterous Horsleyan Taliho' which he believed was deliberately designed to deny individuals the freedom to work out their own salvation.[52]

By championing in outspoken language the cause of a small, despised group who were associated in the public mind with subversion, Iolo clearly risked the hazards of persecution. 'Church and King' loyalist associations were strong and William Pitt was determined to curb radical enthusiasm.[53] Iolo was interrogated by the Privy Council on more than one occasion and had he not played the role of the guileless Welsh bard and taken the precaution of removing his seditious writings to a safe place he might well have been locked away for a considerable time. Other Unitarians were not so fortunate. In 1793, in a travesty of justice, the Scottish Unitarian ministers, Thomas Muir and Thomas Fyshe Palmer, were sentenced to transportation to Botany Bay for fourteen and seven years respectively. To his credit, Iolo corresponded with Palmer and sent him a copy of his published poems, a gesture which the Scotsman acknowledged in a poignant letter.[54] Undeterred by such setbacks, on his

---

[48]   Anon., *Answer to a Letter from a Welsh Freeholder . . . By a Clergyman of the Diocese of St David's* (London, 1790), p. 15.

[49]   David Jones, *A Letter to the Right Reverend Samuel, Lord Bishop of St David's, on the Charge he Lately Delivered to the Clergy of his Diocese* (London and Carmarthen, 1790), p. 18.

[50]   See David Jones, *The Welsh Freeholder's Farewell Epistles to the Right Rev. Samuel Lord Bishop (lately, of St David's)* (London, 1794). See also the advertisement publicizing, in Welsh and English, the appearance of *Reasons for Unitarianism*, in the *Bath Chronicle*, 22 March 1792. For Horsley's arguments, see F. C. Mather, *High Church Prophet: Bishop Samuel Horsley (1733–1806) and the Caroline Tradition in the Later Georgian Church* (Oxford, 1992), chapter 9.

[51]   *GPC*, s.v. Undodiaid, Undodiaeth.

[52]   NLW 13145A, pp. 343–4.

[53]   E. C. Black, *The Association: British Extraparliamentary Political Organization, 1769–1793* (Cambridge, MA, 1963); Hywel M. Davies, 'Loyalism in Wales, 1792–1793', *WHR*, 20, no. 4 (2001), 687–716.

[54]   NLW 21282E, Letter no. 376, Thomas Fyshe Palmer to Iolo Morganwg, 12 September 1795.

return to Wales in 1795 Iolo continued to smite bishops, clergymen and every other enemy of religious freedom and toleration. Ever the showman, he advertised at his bookshop in Cowbridge 'Church-and-king sweets for the lovers of blood', 'Cowper's king-flogging Talk' for spies and informers and Paine's *Rights of Man* for 'lovers of Truth', and held a regular round of politically motivated Gorseddau on local hilltops and even in the fastnesses of north Carmarthenshire where Tomos Glyn Cothi was an enthusiastic ally.[55] He was genuinely concerned about the lot of the poor and, like his friend George Dyer, he protested even to the prime minister about soaring levels of taxation, the profligacy of government and the excesses of the rich.[56] But from 1797 onwards, following the mutinies at the Nore and Spithead, the French invasion at Fishguard and the rebellion of the United Irishmen, the Gwyneddigion eisteddfodau succumbed to popular patriotism, and Rational Dissenters like Iolo became marked men. Local magistrates and the Cowbridge Volunteers kept Gorseddau under such close and intrusive surveillance that Iolo was forced to postpone them indefinitely.[57] Gilbert Wakefield, a fiery Unitarian whom Iolo greatly revered, was incarcerated for two years for seditious libel in 1799, while in the same year Benjamin Flower, the outspoken editor of the *Cambridge Intelligencer* (which Iolo and Tomos Glyn Cothi regularly and avidly thumbed), found himself behind bars for calling the bishop of Llandaf 'a time-server and apostate'.[58] A thrill of horror spread through the whole Dissenting fraternity in south Wales when, in August 1801, the Unitarian minister Tomos Glyn Cothi was arraigned for singing seditious songs, a trumped-up charge which condemned him to be pilloried and imprisoned for two years,[59] a sentence which George Murray, bishop of St David's, reckoned was far too lenient for someone dedicated to the uprooting of prelacy.[60]

Small wonder that Iolo, alarmed by 'the fury of the Great Dragon',[61] set himself the task of protecting the interests of the small and beleaguered groups of Unitarians in south Wales. Once Tomos Glyn Cothi had been frogmarched to Carmarthen prison, he immediately assembled leading Unitarians who had

---

[55]   NLW 21410E, no. 299.

[56]   The National Archives, PRO 30/8/190/83LH, Iolo Morganwg to William Pitt, 16 December 1796; G. M. Ditchfield, 'English Rational Dissent and Philanthropy, c.1760–c.1810' in Hugh Cunningham and Joanna Innes (eds.), *Charity, Philanthropy and Reform from the 1690s to 1850* (Basingstoke, 1998), p. 196.

[57]   Geraint Bowen, *Golwg ar Orsedd y Beirdd* (Caerdydd, 1992), p. 6.

[58]   Michael R. Watts, *The Dissenters. Volume II: The Expansion of Evangelical Nonconformity* (Oxford, 1995), pp. 354–5.

[59]   Geraint H. Jenkins, '"A Very Horrid Affair": Sedition and Unitarianism in the Age of Revolutions' in R. R. Davies and Geraint H. Jenkins (eds.), *From Medieval to Modern Wales: Historical Essays in Honour of Kenneth O. Morgan and Ralph A. Griffiths* (Cardiff, 2004), pp. 175–96.

[60]   The National Archives, PRO HO 42/66, pp. 74–5.

[61]   NLW 21285E, Letter no. 861, Iolo Morganwg to Theophilus Lindsey, 10 February 1797.

come to Carmarthen to support their controversial minister and persuaded them that the only way in which they could protect themselves against the law, disseminate their doctrines effectively, and recover a sense of dignity and self-confidence was by establishing a regional society in the name of Unitarianism. Fifteen interested parties vowed to support this venture and, following this statement of intent, the South Wales Unitarian Society was formally established at Gellionnen on 8 October 1802.[62] To suppose that the Flemingston piper called the tune in determining the nature of this Society would be to oversimplify the situation. His self-conceit meant that he probably exaggerated his own role in his unpublished papers, but it is also true that he had few serious rivals. Josiah Rees, an able and well-respected Unitarian minister and journal editor, was more disposed to compromise than Iolo and certainly would not have picked a quarrel with him. Tomos Glyn Cothi was languishing in prison and Charles Lloyd, a learned but tempestuous figure, returned to England shortly after establishing in 1802 two Unitarian causes at Capel-y-groes and Pantydefaid in south Cardiganshire.[63] There was no one else with the necessary personal or political capacity to stand in Iolo's way, and the rules and regulations of the newly formed Society, which Iolo translated into Welsh, bore his stamp.[64] He styled himself 'Bard to the Theo-unitarian Society of south-Wales', persuaded William Owen Pughe to include his Welsh translation of the word Theo-Unitarians – 'Dwyfundodiaid' – in his celebrated dictionary, and defied trinitarians to do their worst:

> There are but one, and one is three,
> And those who think not so with me
> Are damned to all eternity.[65]

David Davis, son of Dafydd Dafis, the legendary Arian minister and academy tutor at Castellhywel, became secretary of the Society. He worshipped Iolo, often greeting him as 'our Father', and urged him never to abandon his radical and democratic programme: 'Perish K—gs and Emp———s; but let the Bard of Liberty live.'[66] Partly because of the sheer force of his personality and partly *faute de mieux*, Iolo became the mouthpiece of the new movement.

During the early decades of the nineteenth century, therefore, this tiny minority of worshippers appeared, at least to their opponents, to be more

[62]   NLW 13152A, p. 350; NLW 13221E, pp. 87–8, Iolo Morganwg to William Owen Pughe, 25 October 1802.

[63]   D. Elwyn Davies, '*They Thought for Themselves*' (Llandysul, 1982), pp. 43–4, 56–7.

[64]   *Rheolau a Threfniadau Cymdeithas Dwyfundodiaid yn Neheubarth Cymru* (Llundain, 1803).

[65]   NLW 13145A, p. 450; *Monthly Repository*, II (1807), 444; NLW 21327A, p. [62].

[66]   NLW 21280E, Letter nos. 100, 104, David Davis to Iolo Morganwg, 12 February 1803, 26 October 1805. For Davis, see T. G. Davies, *Neath's Wicked World and Other Essays on the History of Neath and District* (West Glamorgan Archive Service, 2000), pp. 109–24.

numerous and threatening than they actually were. Unlike Methodists, they did not seek to make windows into men's souls or move people in large numbers. Yet, as John Seed has emphasized, Unitarianism should be viewed 'neither as a disease nor an imposter',[67] but rather as a denomination which grew organically among groups who welcomed its liberal gospel and political stance. Unitarianism appealed to people who enjoyed reading, who could cope with demanding and unorthodox religious concepts, who had enquiring minds and who believed that the inherent right of revolution lay with the people. From the anti-trinitarian fiefdom in south Cardiganshire, stigmatized as 'The Black Spot' (Y Smotyn Du), to the 'labyrinth of flames' which circled the swiftly industrializing town of Merthyr Tydfil in Glamorgan,[68] there emerged small groups of farmers, craftsmen, artisans, shopkeepers and ministers of religion who had a modest stake in property and who aspired to playing an active role in public and spiritual life. In spite of the relative smallness of their congregations, the very presence of Unitarians, and the determination of their ministers, unsettled orthodox Christians. Guided, egged on and often intimidated by Iolo, members busied themselves in distributing books, organizing lecture tours, petitioning Parliament and debating different theological standpoints. Iolo had the ear of leading Unitarians in Bristol and London, and his friendship with the likes of Theophilus Lindsey, Thomas Belsham, John Prior Estlin and Lant Carpenter stood the Society in good stead. As a hymnologist Iolo proved to be even more productive than William Williams Pantycelyn, and he travelled far and wide in order to set up, advise and maintain Unitarian causes.[69] He was particularly effective in identifying dormant or feeble causes and using peripatetic Unitarian missionaries to revive them. When Richard Wright, a labourer's son and a former General Baptist minister at Wisbech, travelled to south Wales in the summer of 1816 to embark on an 800-mile preaching campaign, Iolo walked twenty miles to meet him at Neath and spent a week in his company. Wright was enchanted by him: 'He had no small degree of eccentricity; his feelings were remarkably independent; and he was enthusiastically fond of liberty.'[70]

[67] John Seed, 'Theologies of Power: Unitarianism and the Social Relations of Religious Discourse, 1800–50' in R. J. Morris (ed.), *Class, Power and Social Structure in British Nineteenth-century Towns* (Leicester, 1986), p. 114.

[68] D. Elwyn Davies, *Y Smotiau Duon* (Llandysul, 1981); idem, *Cewri'r Ffydd: Bywgraffiadur y Mudiad Undodaidd yng Nghymru* ([Aberdâr], 1999); Gwyn A. Williams, 'The Making of Radical Merthyr, 1800–1836', *WHR*, I, no. 1 (1961), 161–92; idem, 'The Merthyr Election of 1835', ibid., 10, no. 3 (1981), 359–97; Chris Evans, *'The Labyrinth of Flames': Work and Social Conflict in Early Industrial Merthyr Tydfil* (Cardiff, 1993), chapter IX.

[69] For an introduction to these themes, see D. Elwyn J. Davies, 'Astudiaeth o Feddwl a Chyfraniad Iolo Morganwg fel Rhesymolwr ac Undodwr' (unpubl. University of Wales Ph.D. thesis, 1975) and Geraint H. Jenkins, '"Dyro Dduw dy Nawdd": Iolo Morganwg a'r Mudiad Undodaidd' in idem (ed.), *Cof Cenedl XX: Ysgrifau ar Hanes Cymru* (Llandysul, 2005), pp. 65–100.

[70] Richard Wright, *A Review of the Missionary Life and Labors* (London, 1824), pp. 372–3.

In a fulsome paean dressed up as a biography, John S. Harford referred to the tenure of his chosen subject, Thomas Burgess, bishop of St David's 1803–25, as a period through which the good bishop 'glided on in a peaceful flow of serene happiness'.[71] Mercifully, such weasel words were written long after the death of Iolo Morganwg who, as one might expect, lost few opportunities to remind Burgess that those who had unshackled themselves from the chains of priestcraft would continue to assert rights of conscience and make his life as difficult as possible. In several respects Thomas Burgess was not much different from the long succession of 'Anglo-Bishops' who had reluctantly taken up Welsh sees. Hampshire-born, he spoke no Welsh and had no illusions about finding himself in what he rightly, but still uncharitably, called 'this very dilapidated part of the Church of England'.[72] Yet, unlike most of his predecessors, he did not prove to be a bird of passage. He served the diocese for twenty-two years, long enough for Dissenters to recognize him immediately, even though exchanging pleasantries in Welsh defeated him. Without a grasp of Welsh he was singularly ill-equipped to carry out essential duties and when, on one occasion, he confirmed groups of monoglot Welsh-speaking children at Aberystwyth, the bemused confirmands went away convinced that the reiteration of the phrase 'more and more' was somehow a reference to the sea (Welsh: *môr*).[73] The linguistic issue was simply one symptom of the extent to which the established church was rapidly losing its appeal. Both Methodist societies and Dissenting congregations were offering a more welcoming and reassuring alternative in terms of worship and pastoral care. Among these dissidents were increasingly bold and aggressive groups of Unitarians whom Iolo was determined to protect. He left Burgess in no doubt that, in spite of antagonisms and repression, these churches were here to stay:

> I had a humble and very Subordinate hand in the building of these Churches. I look at them with complacency, with a high degree of satisfaction and pleasure, and clearly see that the Gates of Hell, even should your Lord Bishopship sit as Supreme Judge in those Gates, will never prevail agst. Them.[74]

Burgess, however, was a tougher nut than Iolo had imagined. He was only too ready to do battle with Dissenting assertiveness and, like Iolo, he enjoyed drawing up plans. Determined to promote Christian knowledge, unity and fellowship within the diocese of St David's, on his arrival in 1803 he immediately established a Society for Promoting Christian Knowledge and Church

---

[71]   Harford, *Life of Thomas Burgess*, p. 292.
[72]   Thomas Burgess, *Peculiar Privileges of the Christian Ministry Considered in a Charge Delivered to the Clergy of the Diocese of St David's* (Durham, 1805), p. 36.
[73]   Morgan, 'The Diocese of St David's', 20; D. T. W. Price, *Yr Esgob Burgess a Choleg Llanbedr/ Bishop Burgess and Lampeter College* (Cardiff, 1987), pp. 35–7.
[74]   NLW 13145A, pp. 344–5.

Union which was made responsible for distributing saving literature among the poor, promoting Sunday schools and establishing libraries for the clergy. Probably mindful of what the likes of Iolo were writing, he warned the clergy against those who endeavoured to 'degrade religion by calling it priestcraft, and superstition; or a state-engine to keep the world in awe'.[75] With the benefit of hindsight, we can see that the greatest numerical threat to the established church was the prodigious rate at which orthodox Dissent was growing, notably in the period following the secession of Calvinistic Methodism from the 'mother' church in 1811. But Burgess was obsessed by the fear that his diocese was about to be engulfed by a rising tide of Arianism, Unitarianism and unbelief. As a result, whereas Iolo Morganwg agitated for the removal of religious disabilities, Burgess actively discouraged such initatives. Matters came to a head when the Trinity Act of 1813 removed penalties against anti-trinitarians. Passed, with delicious irony, on the anniversary of the Birmingham riots on 14 July, it put a spring into Iolo's step and he marked the occasion by noting on the inside cover of one of his manuscripts the day on which Unitarians 'became Freemen in their Native Land: on which day Men of Sincerity and of tender consciences were admitted as honest men to the Rights and Privileges of loyal subjects'.[76] Fifteen years would pass before the Test and Corporation Acts were repealed, but for the moment Iolo and his jubilant colleagues had every reason to rejoice. By contrast, Burgess was incandescent with rage when he learned that the Act had been passed without debate or opposition. By mounting a concerted campaign to annul the repeal of the Blasphemy Act, he declared war on the anti-trinitarians – 'apostates' and 'blasphemers', as he called them (according to 'A Lay Seceder') – of south Wales.[77]

Judging by the flurry of pamphlets which followed, grave issues were clearly believed to be at stake. In pulpit and press, Burgess went on the offensive in a desperate bid to counteract the propagators of 'infidelity'. In sermons preached before nervous clergymen in the archdeaconries of Cardigan and Carmarthen, he urged them to re-establish regular catechizing and set up parochial schools to instruct poor people in the principles of the established church.[78] Doubtless most members of the audience would have agreed that no Christian country should grant Unitarianism legislative sanction, but they would also have known in their hearts that Wales had already become a pluralist society and that the principal threat to Anglicanism was the serious haemorrhage of

[75] Burgess, *Peculiar Privileges of the Christian Ministry*, p. 2.
[76] NLW 21344A, marginal note inside the cover.
[77] 'A Lay Seceder', *A Letter to the Bishop of St David's, on some extraordinary passages, in a Charge delivered to the clergy of his diocese, in September, 1813* (London, 1814), pp. 5–6.
[78] Thomas Burgess, *The Truth to which Christ came into the world to bear witness* (Carmarthen, 1815), *passim*.

worshippers to Calvinistic Methodist, Independent and Baptist causes rather than to numerically small groups of Unitarians.

Not everyone felt as threatened by the growth of Rational Dissent as Burgess did, but, as a bishop, he had every right to consider the matter in deadly seriousness since it affected the immortal souls of his people. In his eyes, the two religions – Anglicanism and Unitarianism – were '*littora littoribus contraria* . . . as different as light from darkness, as God from Belial; and, consequently, to believe one, must be to deny the truth of the other'.[79] In a series of pamphlets he insisted that the religion of the established church was firmly rooted in the Scriptures, the doctrines of the primitive Church and the Protestant Reformation. By contrast, Unitarianism was not a Christian faith. Simply by denying the trinity, Unitarians were wilful heretics and blasphemers who mutilated and corrupted biblical teachings and disseminated 'audacious falsehoods' which were likely to encourage the growth of impiety and undermine received wisdom regarding authority and obedience.[80] He vowed to do all within his power to curtail their activities and to campaign strongly against the repeal of the old law. Welsh Unitarians were not surprised to find Burgess mounting a vigorous defence of episcopalianism, but they were clearly taken aback by the asperity of his language. It is almost certain that Iolo Morganwg was enlisted to orchestrate formal rebuttals. Thomas Belsham, Lindsey's successor at Essex Street, London, was persuaded to respond to 'those extraordinary effusions which have of late issued so copiously from the Dark Gate of Carmarthen',[81] and although his reply lacked the depth of learning which characterized Burgess's argument he was perfectly happy to trade insults. Iolo's friend, John Prior Estlin, also joined the fray, expressing surprise that a dignified servant of God 'should discover so much want of candour and of Christian liberality'.[82] Another anonymous commentator (possibly Iolo himself) sourly observed that a more fitting seat for Burgess would be on 'the episcopal bench of Spain, under the patronage of the beloved Ferdinand, and in the neighbourhood of the Inquisition'.[83] As usual, Iolo relished the opportunity to provoke the enemies of Christian and civil liberty. In August 1814 he presided over a Gorsedd ritual on the Rocking-stone (*Y Maen Chwŷf*) at Pontypridd and began to consider the possibility of incorporating druidic ceremonies within a newly revived eisteddfod. In May 1817 he registered his

---

[79] Thomas Burgess, *A Brief Memorial on the Repeal of so much of the Statue 9. and 10. William III as relates to persons denying the doctrine of the Holy Trinity* (London, 1814), p. v.

[80] Thomas Burgess, *An Address to Persons Calling themselves Unitarians* (2nd edn., Carmarthen, 1815); idem, *A Second Address to Persons Calling themselves Unitarians* (Carmarthen, 1815); idem, *A Third Address to Persons Calling themselves Unitarians* (Carmarthen, 1815).

[81] Thomas Belsham, *A Letter to the Unitarian Christians in South Wales* (London, 1816), p. 81.

[82] *Monthly Repository*, X (1815), 446–7.

[83] Ibid., X (1815), 508–9.

daughters' house at Cefncribwr as a place of Unitarian worship, used the offices of the magazine *Seren Gomer* at Swansea to print and distribute radical literature, including *Vox Populi Vox Dei!* (1818), and duly informed Burgess that the episcopal polity which he represented was 'a system of Idiotism, of madness or of villainy'.[84] Still hostile to dogmatism, privilege and priestly control, the Unitarian bard had no intention of drawing in his horns.

In the light of the running battle recounted above, it is impossible to believe the recent assertion that Iolo and Burgess had become close friends.[85] It could scarcely have been expected that Iolo would have forgiven the bishop for his truculent outbursts, and Burgess, for his part, was too shrewd to believe that the 'Bard of Liberty', whose teachings he loathed with every fibre of his being, had mellowed into a harmless icon. It was surely an extremely wary – and weary – Unitarian who arrived at the bishop's palace at Abergwili in October 1818 to be greeted by his equally distrustful adversary. Nevertheless, both men contrived to appear civil and cooperative, and fixed their attention on matters relating to the cultivation of Welsh literature.

There is little doubt that Burgess's 'conversion' to the cause of Welsh letters and the eisteddfod movement had been relatively recent. On his arrival in 1803 he had been opposed to setting up Welsh-language schools for the poor, and over the years he had made a pretty poor fist of learning Welsh. Although Walter Davies consoled himself by believing that Burgess was 'purely Welsh in heart, though English in tongue',[86] several of his fellow 'literary parsons' feared that he had done little either to rid the established church of its unflattering image as an agent of Anglicization or to arrest the growth of Dissent. Among these clerical luminaries were John Jenkins (Ifor Ceri), vicar of Kerry in Montgomeryshire, W. J. Rees, vicar of Casgob and Heyope in Radnorshire, David Rowland (Dewi Brefi), curate of St Peter's, Carmarthen, and Walter Davies (Gwallter Mechain), vicar of Manafon in Montgomeryshire, all of whom were well-read, lively and convivial champions of Welsh-language culture. Indeed, the patronage which John Jenkins offered to poets, minstrels and harpists at Kerry was so lavish that he was likened to Ifor Hael, the supposed medieval patron of the peerless Dafydd ap Gwilym. Sometime in January 1818 David Rowland mooted the idea of establishing a cultural society which, by promoting bardism and the eisteddfod, would render the established church more attractive to the Welsh. Burgess was much taken by the idea and, over time, he came to believe that he was the chief instigator of what became known as the Cambrian Society, a fiction which the Anglican literati assiduously cultivated by pandering to his vanity. 'When you speak of

---

[84] NLW 21406E, nos. 1 a–c, 38; NLW 21404F, nos. 38–41.
[85] Morgan: *IM*, pp. 19–20.
[86] NLW 1914C, p. 17.

the origin of the Cambrian Society', wrote Jenkins to Rees in April 1820, 'you ought carefully to avoid the taking of the credit of it from the Bishop. The subject must be handled with great delicacy indeed.'[87]

Nevertheless, it was Burgess, working through his intermediary Thomas Beynon, archdeacon of Cardigan, who summoned interested parties, including Iolo Morganwg, to a public meeting to be held at the White Lion, Carmarthen, on 28 October 1818.[88] Of the twenty-one who attended, Iolo was the only Dissenter, and he soon began to weave his own peculiar brand of magic. Having hoodwinked the literati of the Gwyneddigion Society with his superbly fabricated versions of the *cywyddau* of Dafydd ap Gwilym, a wordsmith like Iolo had no difficulty in gaining a sympathetic response for his ambitious prospectus from Anglican squires and clergymen who were in awe of the legendary Welsh bard. The blueprint agreed upon at this round-table conference bore the unmistakable imprint of Iolo's long-held dreams. The new Society, which Burgess was determined to call the Cambrian Society (though the Welsh press stubbornly referred to it as 'Y Gymdeithas Gymröaidd'), was not only designed to revive and promote the Welsh eisteddfod on a provincial basis but also to raise funds to ensure the completion of a complete catalogue of all Welsh manuscripts in Wales and England and on the Continent. A competent scholar was to be charged with the task of visiting libraries, transcribing the material and placing the transcripts in the British Museum. A copy of all Welsh printed books was to be deposited in the Welsh School at Gray's Inn Lane, London, and Iolo himself would receive grants to enable him to reside in Carmarthen for part of the year to supervise the printing of the Society's publications and to instruct young students in Welsh poetry and prose (and, covertly no doubt, Unitarian principles). It was also resolved that the Society would publish a prospectus of Iolo's grandiose six-volume 'New History of Wales'.[89] The whole proceedings, conducted without acrimony or dissent, strikingly illustrate the way in which Iolo was able to cast a spell over people who did not share his religious and political principles. Disarmed and enthused by his literary mission, as well as by the prodigious and unrewarded efforts he had hitherto made, the assembled churchmen gave him a hearty vote of confidence.

As the foremost living authority on Welsh poetry, Iolo was appointed one of the adjudicators for the Carmarthen eisteddfod scheduled for July 1819. Characteristically, he made bold attempts to force the pace by urging Dissenters to compete and by airing trenchant views on fellow-adjudicators

---

[87]   Jones, *Yr Hen Bersoniaid Llengar*, p. 18.

[88]   NLW 1898D, Letter no. 27, John Jenkins to David Rowland, 2 September 1818; NLW 21280E, Letter no. 21, Thomas Beynon to Iolo Morganwg, 19 October 1818.

[89]   For full details, see the minutes of the meeting and a printed prospectus of the Cambrian Society in NLW 1949E.

and competitors who had had the misfortune to be born in north Wales. A month before the eisteddfod he informed the secretary, David Rowland, that he had read the poetic entries carefully ('if calling them poetry be not blasphemy'), that Robert Davies, Nantglyn, was not competent to be a fellow-adjudicator, and that he had not met any scholar in north Wales 'who has a competent skill either in the rules of versification and in poetry, or in the language itself of which they boast so much'.[90] Only after conferring with his fellow 'umpires', as John Jenkins sportively called them,[91] did he relent, and when the first of the 'Cambrian Olympiads' was held on 8–10 July 1819 Iolo dragged his gout-ridden body to Carmarthen.

To Iolo at least, it was entirely appropriate that Carmarthen should have been the venue for one of his finest hours. In several ways Carmarthen was the fountain-head of radical Dissent in Wales and there were also significant cultural resonances associated with the town which would not have been lost upon Iolo. For instance, he was deeply unhappy about the metrical system established by Dafydd ab Edmwnd at the Carmarthen eisteddfod of c.1453, an initiative which prompted him to describe the event as 'that mountain which brought forth a mouse'.[92] Since then, and especially from Tudor times, Carmarthen had developed into the unofficial capital of south-west Wales: it was an administrative focus, a municipal borough and a major commercial and shipbuilding centre. It was very much on the tourist route, and visitors often referred to it as a 'polite' town, by which they meant that its grammar school, academy, assembly rooms, theatres, bookshops, libraries and inns were both bilingual and congenial. Iolo Morganwg himself believed that, at Carmarthen, 'English is more purely spoken than in most Towns in England'.[93] In short, Carmarthen, with a population of 7,275 in 1811 (not far short of that of Swansea), was a thriving intellectual centre. Its Dissenting academy, established in 1704, was the oldest institution of higher education in Wales and it had gained a reputation for lively heterodox ideas and as a breeding-ground for Rational Dissent.[94] By 1820 it had 2,500 books in its library, probably the largest collection of printed volumes to be found anywhere in Wales.[95] There

---

[90] NLW 1895Ei, Letter no. 81, Iolo Morganwg to David Rowland, 14 June 1819.

[91] NLW 1898D, Letter no. 34, John Jenkins to David Rowland, 4 June 1819.

[92] D. J. Bowen, 'Dafydd ab Edmwnt ac Eisteddfod Caerfyrddin', *Barn*, 142 (1974), 441–8; BL Add. 15030, Letter no. 2, ff. 3–4, Iolo Morganwg to William Owen Pughe, 13 August 1799.

[93] NLW 13115B, p. 363. For an overview of Welsh towns, see Philip Jenkins, 'Wales' in Peter Clark (ed.), *The Cambridge Urban History of Britain. Volume II. 1540–1840* (Cambridge, 2000), pp. 133–49.

[94] R. T. Jenkins, 'Nonconformity after 1715: Methodism' in J. E. Lloyd (ed.), *A History of Carmarthenshire* (Cardiff, 1939), pp. 185–263; David Wykes, 'The Dissenting Academy and Rational Dissent' in Haakonssen (ed.), *Enlightenment and Religion*, pp. 99–139.

[95] Brian Ll. James, 'Academic Libraries in Wales to 1914' in Philip Henry Jones and Eiluned Rees (eds.), *A Nation and its Books: A History of the Book in Wales* (Aberystwyth, 1998), p. 308.

had been a printing press in the town since 1721, but not until the arrival of John Ross, an enterprising Scot, in the 1760s was it acknowledged that printing presses therein needed to modernize and expand. Together with rival firms run by John Evans and John Daniel in the middle of the town, Ross turned Carmarthen into the printing capital of Wales. Not surprisingly, too, it had a reputation for political turbulence and thuggish behaviour. The first masonic lodge in Wales had been established in Carmarthen in 1726[96] and, even as wistful champions of the Stuart cause recognized that theirs was a lost cause, Toryism-cum-Jacobitism metamorphosed into Wilkite radicalism, a cause which was zealously defended by agitators like Sir Watkin Lewes (lord mayor of London in 1780) and Robert Morris of Clasemont, both of whom Iolo knew.[97] In the year of the French Revolution the ruling oligarchy in the town became the butt of scorn: burgesses were depicted as blackguards, knaves and fools, and, as the economy took a turn for the worse in the mid-1790s, small farmers took the standard Winchester corn-measure from the market place to the Dark Gate and tore it to pieces.[98] Although it was often drowned by loyalist chants, the language of atheism, sedition and sans-culottism was to be heard in the town's sixty taverns and inns, and the militia were kept on constant alert.[99] Memories of the harsh treatment suffered by Tomos Glyn Cothi did not fade, and dissidents in Carmarthen, as we have seen, continued to participate in heated religious controversies and, whenever the opportunity arose, to engage in rough-and-tumble politics during election years. Meanwhile, Iolo Morganwg, still heavily involved in cultural initiatives and political Dissent, was poised to work his magic once more. Indeed, what follows leaves us in no doubt that the radical Unitarian bard had by no means shot his bolt.

To the sound of trumpets, the newly instituted Cambrian Society, which hosted the Carmarthen eisteddfod at the Ivy Bush Inn, began its proceedings on Thursday morning, 8 July 1819.[100] In the unavoidable absence of the president, Lord Dynevor, Bishop Thomas Burgess took the chair, and the assembled throng of up to 300 well-to-do guests watched intently as Iolo

---

[96] J. P. Jenkins, 'Jacobites and Freemasons in Eighteenth-Century Wales', *WHR*, 9, no. 4 (1979), 396. Cf. Peter Clark, *Sociability and Urbanity: Clubs and Societies in the Eighteenth Century City* (Leicester, 1986).

[97] J. E. Ross, *Radical Adventurer* (Swansea, 1971); *DWB*, s.v. Lewes, Sir Watkin; David W. Howell, *Patriarchs and Parasites: The Gentry of South-West Wales in the Eighteenth Century* (Cardiff, 1986), p. 120.

[98] David J.V. Jones, *Before Rebecca: Popular Protests in Wales 1793–1835* (London, 1973), pp. 20–1, 25–6; Leslie Baker-Jones, 'Princelings, Privilege and Power . . .': The Tivyside Gentry in their Community (Llandysul, 1999), p. 272.

[99] Geraint Dyfnallt Owen, *Thomas Evans (Tomos Glyn Cothi)* (n. pl., 1963), pp. 23–32.

[100] NLW 1860B; *Carmarthen Journal*, 9 July 1819; *Cambrian*, 17 July 1819; *Seren Gomer*, 28 July 1819, 229–35; D. L., *Awen Dyfed* (Caerfyrddin, 1822), pp. 97–106.

Morganwg hobbled into the room, leaning on the shoulder of the young Cardiganshire poet Daniel Evans (Daniel ab Ieuan Ddu). Following a brief and unexceptional address by Burgess, Iolo slowly rose to his feet to deliver a peroration deftly calculated to appeal to the public-spirited gathering. By focusing on the distinctive literary identity of the Welsh people and the privileged position of Carmarthen as host to the celebrated eisteddfod held under the auspices of Dafydd ab Edmwnd c.1453, as well as hinting at some of the dividends provided by the resplendent druidic tradition, Iolo confirmed his reputation as one of the most captivating orators of his age. A précis of this extraordinary presentation survives in Iolo's papers and deserves to be cited in full:

> Poetry has been the original vehicle of knowledge amongst all nations. It has been the incipiency of Literature. At an early period of the World the Cymmry (Kimmeri) became civilized by the moral, sentimental, and instructive songs of their Bards, and 'in the light of the song' became united in a social and civilized compact. The remains of their ancient and druidical learning are to this very day amongst us, and exhibit such high attainment of genuine wisdom as cannot be generally found amongst the Nations of this World. Poetry has preserved to us our original language to this day, and in all its pristine purity. At a period when a dark cloud had involved us in a winter night of ignorance Caermarthen had the highly merited honour of being as it were a morning star preceding the dawn of a glorious Morning that soon afterwards appeared. Some clouds have since appeared, but again at Caermarthen the sky clears up. We see the clouds beginning to disperse, and we hope that a glorious Summers day of Bardic and of every other description of Literature morality virtue and Religion will ensue.[101]

Thunderous, prolonged applause followed and, although Burgess and others might have wondered whether the cryptic reference in the final sentence to 'morality virtue and Religion' was a portent of things to come, Iolo had clearly won the confidence of the affluent, conservatively minded guests.

Iolo and his fellow-adjudicators then recited a series of Welsh *englynion* and, in order to stiffen the attention span of non-Welsh-speakers, four harpists were set to work to entertain them. That inveterate competitor, Walter Davies, walked off with three of the five major literary prizes and, since he was one of the few people who never fell out with Iolo, there are good grounds for believing that the latter knew the identity of the winning poet long before it was publicly revealed. To loud acclaim Davies recited his winning *englyn* on the subject the 'Harp New Strung' and was duly seated in a handsome oak chair as the Poet Laureate of the eisteddfod. At this point Iolo wilfully stole the scene. Having pinned a blue ribbon to Davies's right arm, he approached the

---

[101] NLW 21430E, no. 15.

unsuspecting Bishop Burgess, informed him that he was empowered to admit him to the druidic order and then audaciously affixed a white ribbon to his right arm. Although clearly alarmed, Burgess did not respond, but he must have regretted giving a champion of rational religion and civil liberty the opportunity to bring him into the druidic fold.[102] Even by Iolo's standards, this was a major coup: a leading Welsh prelate had been admitted to an institution dedicated (at least in the eyes of its founder) to achieving universal freedom.

Iolo had one more rabbit to pull out of his capacious hat. Bishop Burgess had been determined to present to the public an image of the eisteddfod as 'a priestly foundation',[103] but Iolo was equally bent on ensuring that his beloved druidic moot should become an integral part of the proceedings. In a scroll which he himself had written and declaimed, an open invitation had been issued to bards of all religious persuasions.[104] Wrong-footed once more, Burgess was forced to witness (with palpable disdain) a formal ceremony of the Gorsedd of the Bards in the garden of the Ivy Bush Inn on Saturday, 10 July. As the officiating bard, Iolo marked out a circle with pebbles. Revelling in the occasion, he instituted several new bards, each of whom, from within the circle, unsheathed a sword held by the sword-bearer Thomas Williams (Gwilym Morganwg), a poet steeped in the arcana of druidism. Iolo then held the point of the scabbard as he enjoined the new recruits to observe druidic traditions. In particular he reminded them that accredited Welsh bards were ministers of truth and heralds of peace: 'Bardism . . . breathes an invincible Spirit of Liberty . . . it has ever been the warm advocate of Rationality and Liberty.'[105] Appalled by the unfolding scene, Burgess tried to intervene, urging Iolo to dispense with the initiatory rituals. He flatly refused and only then did it finally dawn on the bishop that he had been completely hoodwinked by this Unitarian druid and firebrand. The round of applause reserved for Burgess at the end of this colourful, but subversive, pageant somehow carried a hollow ring.

Having undermined the politico-religious principles on which the Cambrian Society was based, Iolo had every cause to be deeply satisfied as he tramped homewards. Burgess was furious, and in a letter to Edward 'Celtic' Davies, rector of Bishopston and one of Iolo's many *bêtes noires*, he fumed: 'If you had been there, we should, probably, have escaped the nonsense of the Bardic degrees on Saturday . . . which had some considerable improprieties in it (to say the least of it).'[106] Pouring oil on troubled waters, Davies assured

---

[102] *Seren Gomer*, 28 July 1819, 230.

[103] *Seren Gomer*, VI, no. 88 (1823), 43–4; Bowen, *Golwg ar Orsedd y Beirdd*, p. 14.

[104] NLW 854D, pp. 5, 8–9; Dillwyn Miles, *The Royal National Eisteddfod of Wales* (Swansea, 1978), *passim*.

[105] NLW 13097B, pp. 287–8.

[106] Cardiff 3.82, Thomas Burgess to Edward Davies, 25 August 1819.

Burgess that the Glamorgan bard was a complete stranger to plain unvarnished truth and that he was determined to use Gorsedd ceremonies as a means of rooting up 'every sound principle of Politics & Religion'. He feared that Iolo's malign influence over the proceedings of the Cambrian Society had made a 'very unfavourable impression upon the minds of very respectable individuals' and urged the bishop to counteract the effects by publishing a firmly worded printed rebuttal.[107] Although he did not act on this advice, Burgess used his good offices to prohibit the holding of Gorsedd ceremonies at the Wrexham eisteddfod of 1820. As Taliesin ab Iolo warned his father: 'He is more your enemy than friend.'[108]

To sum up. The Carmarthen eisteddfod of 1819 has rightly been depicted as a seminal event in the annals of the eisteddfod movement. In the cultural sphere, Iolo Morganwg scored a great success not only with his memorable peroration but also by replacing the constricting twenty-four metres as codified by Dafydd ab Edmwnd in the Carmarthen eisteddfod of *c.*1453 with the more 'democratic' and allegedly 'superior' Glamorgan metres which he had devised in order to enhance the cultural reputation of his native country.[109] But in order to appreciate the full significance of the politico–religious successes which Iolo achieved we must view this eisteddfod within the context of the long and fierce rivalry which existed between the established church and Rational Dissent and, in particular, between Bishop Thomas Burgess and Iolo himself. Having invited a venerable figure who claimed to be the heir of a long and honourable bardic tradition in the hope that, on this special occasion, he would jettison his traditional hostility towards tyrants and prelates, the bishop of St David's and Welsh literary parsons found themselves hoist with their own petard. At every turn, the irascible Unitarian was able to outmanoeuvre them. Even in his dotage the Bard of Liberty was prepared to fight for truth, liberty and justice, and to harness the original, and potentially subversive, ideals of his beloved Gorsedd of the Bards to the cultural programme of the provincial eisteddfodau. The ceremonies which Iolo had inaugurated on Primrose Hill, London, in 1792 had never been a frivolous undertaking designed to bewitch a romantic and credulous public. They were meant to

---

[107] Cardiff 3.86, Edward Davies to Thomas Burgess, undated.

[108] NLW 21284E, Letter no. 684, Taliesin Williams to Iolo Morganwg, 26 January 1821. Burgess's fears were encapsulated in a minute recorded by the Cambrian Society: 'At this season of peril, when the signal of revolution is sounded over the land, and sedition and infidelity, treason and atheism stalk around us in all their naked deformity . . . it can not but be consolatory to contemplate those enlightened associations, which have, for their peaceful aim, the promotion of literature and of science.' *Cambro-Briton*, I (1819), 71–2. For the subsequent role of the provincial eisteddfodau, see Hywel Teifi Edwards, 'The Welsh Language in the Eisteddfod' in Geraint H. Jenkins (ed.), *The Welsh Language and its Social Domains 1801–1911* (Cardiff, 2000), chapter 10.

[109] NLW 13141A, pp. 127–33.

persuade his countrymen to sweep aside Old Corruption and promote civil and religious liberty. Iolo's breathtaking coup in the summer of 1819, carried out a matter of days before the anniversary of the fall of the Bastille, was thus a symbolic attempt to keep the old druidic-Jacobin tradition alive.

13

'Uncontaminated with Human Gore'? Iolo Morganwg, Slavery and the Jamaican Inheritance

ANDREW DAVIES

Iolo Morganwg's biographer Elijah Waring once famously claimed that Iolo had advertised the sugar which he sold at his Cowbridge shop from the mid-1790s as '*East India Sweets, uncontaminated with human gore*'.[1] By virtue of plausibility, as well as its frequent quotation, this catchy phrase has passed into the already voluminous body of Iolo Morganwg folklore: anecdotes, for which there is little hard evidence, but which appear at least possible on the basis of what we know with certainty about Iolo. A somewhat credulous and uncritical biographer, Waring took his cue from his subject in producing what has become a familiar and enduring portrayal of Iolo and his views on the question of slavery. He depicted the Glamorgan bard as an unremitting idealist and an unbending abolitionist who '[o]n the question of slavery . . . would admit no compromise, – no arguments of expedience, of an evil necessity, or temporary policy'.[2] This is an image that would appear to befit the self-styled Bard of Liberty, the irreverent social critic and the author of anti-slavery verse who proudly and ostentatiously listed 'Humanity's Wilberforce' among the subscribers to his *Poems, Lyric and Pastoral*.[3]

Nevertheless, in spite of Iolo's avowed and undoubtedly heartfelt opposition to what he called the 'most horrid traffick in human blood',[4] the thorny issue of slavery would make frequent and unwelcome intrusions into his life. From the late 1770s until the end of the 1810s the subject posed a severe moral challenge. It is well known that his three younger brothers, John, Miles and Thomas, accumulated considerable wealth in Jamaica through the use of slave labour. They also, so Iolo claimed, made several offers of financial assistance to their frequently penniless brother, all of which, Iolo also claimed, were flatly refused. Several critics, among them Iolo's twentieth-century biographer

---

[1] *RAEW*, p. 108.

[2] Ibid., p. 60.

[3] Williams: *PLP*, I, p. xxxviii. The words 'Humanity's Wilberforce' appear at the head of the page in large capitalized type.

[4] NLW 21387E, no. 8.

G. J. Williams, have since examined the relationship between Iolo and his brothers during their time in Jamaica in the 1780s and 1790s. Refusing to accept uncritically either Iolo or Waring's version of events around this time, he cast doubt on the veracity of certain claims made by both of them and boldly declared that he would present proof in the second volume of his biography which, sadly, was never published.[5] Williams's conclusions on the subject were subsequently furiously attacked by Brinley Richards[6] and more soberly explored by Clare Taylor.[7]

The first part of this chapter will re-evaluate ground already covered by these critics in the light of a close reading of the Iolo Morganwg correspondence, and shed new light on the nature of the relationship between Iolo and his brothers and the veracity of his claims about them. Since little attention has been paid to the period after the death of each of Iolo's brothers and the subsequent fate of their estates, the second part will therefore consider the implications of several revealing letters dating from the 1810s, especially those concerning the estate of John Williams, which have not yet played a part in this debate. This correspondence renders wholly unsustainable the simplistic account of the views and deeds generated by Iolo himself and later amplified by Waring. The evidence which arises from Iolo's later letters in fact reveals that his actions were at times considerably more ambiguous and disconcerting than either he or his nineteenth-century biographer would allow.

Iolo's views on the subject of slavery are first discernible in the early 1790s around the time of his first engagement with abolitionists such as Hannah More[8] in Bristol, as well as with radical circles in London.[9] By this point the abolitionist movement had been hugely successful in mobilizing support and influencing public opinion throughout Britain.[10] Following the establishment of the Society for the Abolition of the Slave Trade in 1787, the petition movement, which began in 1788, gathered significant momentum and, by the last decade of the century, it had become a popular cause among the British middle classes. As J. R. Oldfield has pointed out, this opposition was both a metropolitan and a provincial phenomenon: agents and area committees all

---

[5] Williams: *IM*, pp. xxxi–xxxii, 231–6.

[6] Brinley Richards, 'Iolo Morganwg', *Y Faner*, 20 January 1978, 8–11, and idem, *Golwg Newydd ar Iolo Morganwg* (Abertawe, 1979), pp. 86–7.

[7] Clare Taylor, 'Edward Williams ('Iolo Morganwg') and his Brothers: A Jamaican Inheritance', *THSC* (1980), 35–43.

[8] NLW 21285E, Letter no. 797, Iolo Morganwg to Margaret Williams, 19 February 1791.

[9] For Iolo's contacts with radical circles in London, see Damian Walford Davies, *Presences that Disturb: Models of Romantic Identity in the Literature and Culture of the 1790s* (Cardiff, 2002), pp. 139–59.

[10] For a summary of the links between the anti-slavery movement and political radicalism in the late 1780s and early 1790s, see J. R. Oldfield, *Popular Politics and British Anti-Slavery: The Mobilisation of Public Opinion against the Slave Trade, 1787–1807* (2nd edn., London, 1998), pp. 42–3.

over the country had sprung up and begun to organize protests at local level. During the petitioning campaign of 1792 it has been estimated that some 400,000 people put their names to petitions, a figure which represented around 13 per cent of the adult male population of England, Scotland and Wales.[11]

Iolo's first expressions of opposition to slavery also occurred at a point when peoples perceived as being displaced, 'uncivilized' or colonized were likely to have been foremost in his mind. He was so heavily involved in the first wave of the mania surrounding the 'Madoc affair'[12] that he collected evidence to support the legend surrounding the alleged existence of a settlement of Welsh-speaking 'Indians' in the American mid-West.[13] Caroline Franklin has noted that the credibility enjoyed by the Madoc legend allowed 'the marginalised Welsh to romanticise themselves as a lost tribe',[14] while Prys Morgan has pointed out that Iolo, around this time, was cultivating his own exotic ethnic and cultural persona in polite society: 'In English drawing rooms Iolo posed as a Celtic Noble Savage.'[15] In the early 1790s Iolo had also taken a keen interest in the tales of his friend David Samwell (Dafydd Ddu Feddyg) of the native peoples of Tahiti, as well as in the explorations of Captain James Cook, to whom Samwell was surgeon.[16] It is unsurprising, therefore, that, in this context of sympathetic interest in and advocacy for various cultural and ethnic groups, Iolo entered the anti-slavery debate by deploying his talent for fierce invective.

Characteristically, given his newly forged contacts with abolitionist circles in Bristol, Iolo's first remarks on the subject were bound up with attempts to establish himself as a poet in the English language and to garner financial support in south-west England. In 1791, a year in which Iolo divided his time between London, Bath and his home at Flemingston gathering subscriptions for *Poems, Lyric and Pastoral* (1794), anti-slavery sentiments first appeared in his correspondence. At some point before August that year, he wrote to several Bristol printers and booksellers, among them William Bulgin, who had been collecting the names of Bristolean subscribers to *Poems, Lyric and Pastoral*. Iolo complained that the city's close connection with the slave trade would make it impossible for him to accept subscriptions from some of the city's well-heeled citizens:

[11] Ibid., pp. 7–8, 47, 113–14.
[12] Gwyn A. Williams, *Madoc: The Making of a Myth* (London, 1979) and Caroline Franklin, 'The Welsh American Dream: Iolo Morganwg, Robert Southey and the Madoc Legend' in Gerard Carruthers and Alan Rawes (eds.), *English Romanticism and the Celtic World* (Cambridge, 2003), pp. 69–84.
[13] Morgan: *IM*, p. 14; Franklin, 'The Welsh American Dream', pp. 75–6. Iolo's 'evidence' was published in a series of letters in the *Gentleman's Magazine*, LXI, no. 1 (1791), 612–14; no. 3 (1791), 796–7; no. 5 (1791), 1000.
[14] Franklin, 'The Welsh American Dream', p. 79.
[15] Morgan: *IM*, p. 14.
[16] Ibid.; *Gentleman's Magazine*, LXI, no. 1 (1791), 612–14.

I shall not be able to accept of many, if any, of them [the subscriptions], for it is my fixed resolution not to disgrace my list with the names of any who villainously abet the slave trade, and who so exultingly rejoiced lately in your City on the failure of the humane Mr Wilberforce's Bill for the abolition of this inhuman traffic, for which Bristol is, and always has been so remarkably infamous.[17]

Indeed, it is not difficult to detect faint traces of Iolo's growing preoccupation with slavery in his *Poems*,[18] and it is clear from his manuscripts that he had been reading tracts on the slave trade at some point prior to 1794.[19] Later that year he proposed, probably to the publisher Joseph Johnson, writing a treatise on the abolition of the slave trade entitled 'A New and Equitable Plan for the Abolition of Slavery. Addressed to Parliament of Great Britain'.[20] Although the publication never appeared, Iolo jotted down several of his recommendations in the margins of a draft of a letter, written in the early 1790s, to the 'Bristol milkwoman', Ann Yearsley, poet and protegée of Hannah More:

No Planter to buy a slave for more than 7 years.
Every liberated Slave to marry, according to Law.
Laws properly constrictive to enforce good order; industry and conjugal fidelity.
Establishments with plantations on the coast of Guinea, to regulate the trade and support missions.[21]

Outside the intoxicating world of literary society, Iolo also appears to have worn the badge of abolitionism in his daily life as a Cowbridge shopkeeper

[17]   NLW 21400C, Letter no. 24, Iolo Morganwg to William Bulgin, undated [prior to 20 August 1791]. A scathing reply, probably written by Bulgin under the pseudonym 'Jacobus Placo', was sent to Iolo in August 1791. See NLW 21282E, Letter no. 382, 'Jacobus Placo' [William Bulgin] to Iolo Morganwg, 20 August 1791. This incident also echoes another unverifiable anecdote recounted by Elijah Waring regarding Iolo's first visit to Bristol to look into his Caribbean affairs. After hearing the peal of the city's bells, Iolo learned that the celebration was occasioned by the defeat of one of Wilberforce's anti-slavery bills. Waring relates how Iolo, 'smitten with horror and disgust', turned on his heel and 'shook off the unhallowed dust of the city from his feet'. *RAEW*, p. 61. Waring does not specify which bill he was referring to, but given that Iolo recounted the anecdote in the letter to Bulgin quoted above and that this letter itself elicited a reply on 20 August 1791, it was probably the bill presented to Parliament by Wilberforce which was defeated on 18 April 1791. See R. G. Thorne, *The House of Commons 1790–1820* (5 vols., London, 1986), V, p. 558.
[18]   The word 'slave' is used liberally throughout the work, normally to delineate the submission of will and reason to other forces such as love ('Advice to Whining Lover' and 'Love Triumphant', 'Liberty'), flattery ('Inscription in a Grotto, To the Memory of the Late Earl of Chatham') and religious oppression ('On Religion'). Williams: *PLP*, I, pp. 54–7, 64–6, 103, 104–8, 132–4. His most overt reference to slavery in *Poems* occurs in his 'Address to the Inhabitants of Wales, Exhorting them to emigrate, with William Penn, To Pennsylvania', in which he referred to the Britain of the pilgrims and, by unwritten implication, contemporary Britain as '*Slavery's* realm'. Ibid., II, p. 59.
[19]   See Iolo's 'Catalogue of Books at London', a list of the books he owned in May 1794: NLW 13136A, no. 145.
[20]   NLW 21400C, no. 8.
[21]   NLW 21286E, Letter no. 1045, 'Tom 'O Bedlam' (Iolo Morganwg) to Ann Yearsley, undated.

from the mid-1790s. In September 1795 he was granted a licence to sell tea, coffee and chocolate from a shop in the centre of this lively and prosperous market town,[22] and it was around this time he was deemed to have advertised the sugar he sold as 'uncontaminated with human gore'. He also made similar claims in an entertaining piece of verse advertising his exotic merchandise:

> There are currants and raisins, delicious French plums,
> The Christian free sugar from East India comes,
> And brought from where Truth is not yet in the bud,
> Rank Church-and-king sweets for the lovers of blood.[23]

The increasing dependency of British society on imported sugar produced by slaves in the Caribbean in order to make tea, as well as other foodstuffs, palatable has been well-documented and renders its position as an area of abolitionist protest unsurprising.[24] Carole Shammas[25] has shown how the eighteenth century witnessed a fourfold increase in the consumption of sugar, fuelled by the emergence of tea-drinking as a truly popular national pastime and one which transcended social boundaries.[26] Iolo's gesture can be read, on the one hand, as a piece of canny niche-marketing calculated to appeal to the conscientious middle-class consumer,[27] but it also clearly demonstrated a moral commitment to the cause of abolitionism and his persistent eagerness to politicize his livelihood, be that in the subscription list of his *Poems* or in the more unlikely context of Cowbridge High Street.

Nevertheless, these public declarations of opposition to slavery tell only half the story. By the time that Iolo was making his living selling radical poetry and 'Christian free sugar', his three brothers had all emigrated to Jamaica and were in the process of making their own fortunes on the basis of slave labour. All were younger than him and none shared his passion for literature, antiquarianism and radical politics, though the youngest of them, Thomas, is said to have been similar to Iolo in temperament.[28] Miles and John, both of whom Iolo misleadingly described as bricklayers, moved to Jamaica in 1778 and Thomas, who, like Iolo, was a stonemason, joined them in 1785.[29] None of them found their early years in Jamaica easy: although John and Miles were able to free

---

22 For details, see NLW 21410E, no. 28. The licence was granted for one year and seems not to have been renewed. Iolo had also been granted a similar licence in 1785 when he appears to have traded from his cottage in Flemingston. See NLW 21410E, no. 20.

23 NLW 21410E, no. 29 (a).

24 James Walvin, 'Slavery' in Iain McCalman (ed.), *An Oxford Companion to the Romantic Age: British Culture 1776–1832* (Oxford, 1999), pp. 58–60.

25 Carole Shammas, *The Pre-Industrial Consumer in England and America* (Oxford, 1990), pp. 82–6.

26 James Walvin, *Fruits of Empire: Exotic Produce and British Taste, 1660–1800* (Basingstoke , 1997), pp. 16–31.

27 Oldfield, *Popular Politics and British Anti-Slavery*, pp. 7–20.

28 Williams: *IM*, p. 103.

29 NLW 21387E, no. 8; Taylor, 'Edward Williams ('Iolo Morganwg') and his Brothers', 36.

themselves from their indentures early on,[30] there is evidence in the early letters to Iolo of illness, shortage of money and provisions, and substantial losses of property caused by a hurricane.[31] In 1786, a year after his arrival on the island, Thomas wrote to Iolo complaining of the enormous difficulties he faced in grinding out a living there: 'belive Me Brother Jamaica is like all other placies pav.d with Gold till known, then found to be poor nurishment for the Body . . . I wish I never had Sean the Place'.[32]

Yet, in spite of these initial difficulties, the brothers seem to have slowly succeeded in establishing themselves as masons and afterwards as coffee growers. In the late 1790s they worked on a prestigious civic commission, helping to construct the setting for a monument by John Bacon to Admiral Rodney which commemorated the defeat of the French at the battle of Saints in 1782.[33] By the end of their lives they had each amassed considerable wealth, mostly in property and slaves. According to one conservative estimate, between them John and Miles, the two elder brothers, 'could muster' around £15,000 to £20,000 in 1803,[34] and a copy of John Williams's will, made in 1811, includes a crude breakdown of his property, which amounted to £7,676.[35] Thomas, too, died with some money to his name which appears to have passed to Miles.[36]

Their use of slaves, however, clearly troubled Iolo. In an undated autobiographical fragment, the brotherly admiration he expressed for their obvious hard work and eventual success yields to a tone of resigned disappointment and shame:

> My Brothers Miles & John are Bricklayer[s] they went over to Jamaica in 1777, where they soon by exertions of industry got into a good line of business. My Brother Thomas, a Stone Mason, went also to Jamaica in 1785. He has also been successful. I believe at least hope that they still retain their habits of sobriety which has done so much for them. I am however sorry to hear that they are slave-holders

[30] NLW 21283E, Letter no. 617, Miles and John Williams to Edward Williams, Thomas Williams and Iolo Morganwg, 15 February 1779.
[31] NLW 21283E, Letter nos. 619, 623, John Williams to Iolo Morganwg, 24 September 1785, 24 November 1785; NLW 21284E, Letter no. 724, Thomas Williams to Iolo Morganwg, 14 July 1786.
[32] NLW 21284E, Letter no. 724, Thomas Williams to Iolo Morganwg, 14 July 1786.
[33] NLW 21283E, Letter no. 631, Miles Williams to Iolo Morganwg, 11 November 1798; NLW 21283E, Letter no. 632, John Williams to Iolo Morganwg, 22 November 1798; Taylor, 'Edward Williams ('Iolo Morganwg') and his Brothers', 39–40.
[34] NLW 21283E, Letter no. 487, William Thomas to Iolo Morganwg, 7 October 1803.
[35] NLW 21285E, Letter no. 887, Iolo Morganwg to David Davis, 31 January 1811. Iolo also noted in this letter that John appeared to have owned property not accounted for in this copy of his will.
[36] There seems to have been a pact between the three brothers in Jamaica that he who survived longest would inherit the property of the others, a gentleman's agreement which was undermined by the will of John Williams. See NLW 21283E, Letter no. 488, William Thomas to Iolo Morganwg, 6 February 1808 and NLW 13221E, Letter no. 25, pp. 123–6, Iolo Morganwg to William Owen Pughe, 14 February 1805.

... they will greatly dishonour the memory of a mother whose maxims of virtue and humanity once strongly impressed on their minds, qualified them for that advancement from a very humble to (as far as wealth can effect it) very respectable situation in life which they have experienced.[37]

The exact nature of Iolo's relationship with his brothers during their years in Jamaica is, however, extremely difficult to determine. Iolo (and Waring after him) made three significant claims about the brothers and their time in Jamaica: the first was that Iolo had remonstrated with them regarding their use of slaves; secondly, that they had severed contact with him because of his anti-slavery views and protestations; and thirdly, that he had, probably at some point during the 1790s, shunned their offer of an equal portion of their profits and later of an annual benefaction of £50 or £60. The first dated appearance of these claims[38] occurs in a frequently quoted letter to an unidentified Miss Barker in March 1798, in which Iolo includes a long, but suspiciously simple, account of his relationship with his brothers:

I abominate the slave trade. This gives great offence. I believe that there are but few, that on this subject can give proofs of their disinterestedness equal to mine. I have nothing to live upon but the produce of manual labour . . . yet I have three very rich Brothers in Jamaica supposed to be worth Sixty thousand pounds. Mr Bryan Edwards knows them well, and you madam probably know him or some that know him. I understand that my Brothers [w]ho carry on business in Partnership have upwards of two hundred and [f]orty slaves! They have no children none but my children to inherit their [w]ealth. They have many times urged me to come over to Jamaica, offering [m]e gratis an equal portion with themselves of the business and property . . . I have not been able to accept of this. Instead of doing so, I have warmly [re]monstrated with them against the diabolical traffic, have sent them the most [stro]ngly argumentative publications that have appeared against it, have urged [them] to give liberty to the poor wretches and with a sufficiency for their lives [?———]ould remain retire from their infernal business: they have at last [taken] offence, have declined writing to me for some years.[39]

Much of the information about his brothers in this letter is as accurate as Iolo could have been at that particular time, given that contact with his brothers during the 1790s had, for whatever reason, been very sparse: the sporadic bursts of letters were largely occasioned by major family events such as the death of Iolo's father in 1795 and the death of John Williams in 1803. There were also varied accounts of how wealthy the brothers actually were.[40] But what are we

---

[37] NLW 21387E, no. 8. See also Williams: *IM*, pp. 231–2.

[38] Iolo also claimed in the undated autobiographical fragment quoted above (NLW 21387E, no. 8) that he had expressed his disapproval of his brothers' use of slaves and that they had severed contact with him as a result.

[39] NLW 21285E, Letter no. 862, Iolo Morganwg to Miss Barker, 26 March 1798.

[40] See NLW 21283E, Letter no. 487, William Thomas to Iolo Morganwg, 7 October 1803.

to make of the three claims made here by Iolo? It is fair to say that there is no firm evidence that the first two claims made by Iolo provide a wholly truthful account of his actions or those his brothers: namely that he had protested to them on the issue of slavery and that they had severed contact with him as a result. While it is difficult to imagine him exercising the kind of stoic restraint which would have prompted him to maintain a discreet silence regarding their use of slaves, none of the surviving letters demonstrates that Iolo had voiced his misgivings with them over this issue, or that they had severed contact with him on account of such criticism. Indeed, the picture that emerges from the surviving correspondence suggests a very different pattern of events.

The first discernible reference to the brothers' involvement in slavery occurs in a letter sent by John to Iolo in September 1785 in which he, rather mundanely and unselfconsciously, stated that 'all Our Negroes perfectly Recover'd from the small pox'.[41] Significantly, there was subsequently very little correspondence between the brothers from around this point until the mid-1790s. G. J. Williams also questioned Iolo's claim, made in his letter of 1798 to Miss Barker, that his brothers had refused to write to him for several years on account of his alleged condemnation of their use of slaves.[42] We know that John and Miles had in fact written to Iolo on three occasions in 1795,[43] each time complaining about the lack of contact by him. John claimed that he had written to Iolo eight times over the previous five years,[44] but had been denied 'the Pleasure of Receiving a Scrape of a Pen in Answer'.[45] In another letter sent in the same year he could find no reason for Iolo's silence: 'It is a long time since I have the pleasure of receiving A letter from you I have wrote you frequently but have reced no answer, for what reason I Know not.'[46] It seems likely, given the pattern and content of the correspondence from 1785 to 1795, that Iolo was responsible for the lack of contact which prevailed for most of this period and that his brothers were unaware that the issue of slavery was the likely cause of his silence.

There were also, however, more visible tensions between the brothers. Following the publication of *Poems, Lyric and Pastoral* in 1794, Thomas had written to Iolo furiously criticizing him for listing John and Miles's occupations as bricklayers in his subscription list:[47]

---

[41] NLW 21283E, Letter no. 619, John Williams to Iolo Morganwg, 24 September 1785.
[42] Williams: *IM*, p. 233.
[43] NLW 21283E, Letter no. 626, Miles Williams to Iolo Morganwg, 8 March 1795; NLW 21283E, Letter nos. 627, 630, John Williams to Iolo Morganwg, 5 July 1795, 27 September 1795.
[44] In fairness to Iolo, however, it is worth pointing out that the eight letters sent by John have not come to light.
[45] NLW 21283E, Letter no. 630, John Williams to Iolo Morganwg, 27 September 1795.
[46] NLW 21283E, Letter no. 627, John Williams to Iolo Morganwg, 5 July 1795.
[47] See Williams: *PLP*, I, p. xxxviii.

I am sorry you wrote My Brothers names as they are as the have no More Bricklayers then any other part of the Building Branch. What they have aquiard they have a Juster Claime to then he who is Born to a title or Estate and Should think you aught to be the last Man that wished to degrade then ... belive I differ from you in point of insulting with out Caus for it as far as posible a man Can — Sooner then in Sult a man as you do them — I would Murder a Man that insulted Me.[48]

In 1804 William Thomas, a friend of the family who had himself been in Jamaica, wrote to Iolo following John Williams's death hinting that Iolo had made unflattering remarks about John's second wife Ann Williams (who later remarried and became Ann Duncan) who would play a prominent role in subsequent events.[49]

Regarding the third claim referred to above, namely that Iolo was offered a share of his brothers' businesses and an annual benefaction, some evidence offers the tantalizing possibility that Iolo was indeed offered a portion of his brothers' trade and an annuity on two separate occasions. In a letter of June 1783 John hinted to his eldest brother that an offer of financial benefaction had been made to Iolo by John and Miles, but that he had not responded:

Since our ariveal in Jamicia one [letter] in purticuler by Mr Sanders the aturny at Law upon who [word] [I] dependend to deliver it into you own hands and flatterd my Self with being Shuer of a answer from so favorable an opertunity. But receving we Conjectord that you were not in the Cuntry other times we thought that we hade so much ofended you by our abrqubt departor that you were determind not to write at all.[50]

Moreover, in 1800 Iolo wrote to the lexicographer William Owen Pughe, with whom he was at that time engaged in editing the *The Myvyrian Archaiology of Wales*, on the same subject, claiming that his brothers had, on several occasions in their correspondence, offered him an annual benefaction of £50 or £60 per annum:

My Brothers in Jamaica have several times offered to settle fifty pounds a year upon me for life I have never noticed this to them in my letters, so that I wonder they have not taken offence. Last year whilst I was in Anglesea a Mr Harriot, a Gentleman from Jamaica, came over to England. He came to Cowbridge, enquired for me, and told my wife that he had been by my brothers legally authorized to execute a deed which would settle 50, or 60, £ a year on me for life, and he wrote to me at Anglesea the same thing. The answer that I gave him was that if my Brothers would first liberate their Slaves and settle on each of them 50£. P ann for life I could then accept of their offer, and not till then.[51]

[48] NLW 21284E, Letter no. 736, Thomas Williams to Iolo Morganwg, 10 February 1794.
[49] NLW 21283E, Letter no. 487, William Thomas to Iolo Morganwg, 7 October 1803; NLW 21283E, Letter no. 629, Miles Williams to Iolo Morganwg, 27 September 1795; NLW 21283E, Letter no. 630, John Williams to Iolo Morganwg, 27 September 1795.
[50] NLW 21283E, Letter no. 618, Miles and John Williams to Iolo Morganwg, 17 June 1783.
[51] NLW 13221E, Letter no. 13, pp. 71–4, Iolo Morganwg to William Owen Pughe, 8 September 1800.

In February 1799 Thomas had indeed written to Iolo asking that an acquaintance of his with a similar name be accommodated by Iolo, and urging him to
seek £40 or £50 from Thomas if he needed money:

> The gentleman that Bring⁵ you this is is a perticuler acquaintance of mine Since my
> First arival in this Country. I shall be perticuler thankfull to Show him that attention
> it may be in your power, as he may posibly wish to remain in the naiborwood should
> this take place. I have promised Mʳ Harriet to request you to let him have the House
> at Gilestone till I come home, which God willing I hope to Come next yeare for
> Good . . . If you should be in Surcomstance that forty or fifty pounds Starling would
> be of Great Servis Draw on me to that amount at thirty days.[52]

The issue resurfaced in September 1803 in a letter from James Robins, a
friend of the brothers in Jamaica and a fellow native of Glamorgan who had
returned that year to Wales. Robins hinted that the issue of providing Iolo with
an annual benefaction had occurred to the youngest brother Thomas, who, by
this stage, was prospering on the island. Robins maintained that Thomas 'can
afford to give you 20 or 30 pounds, and that anually if he chose to do it'.[53] It
is a matter of judgement whether we accept Iolo's claims or entertain the
possibility that they were made, or perhaps exaggerated, in order to enhance
his reputation as a conscientious abolitionist. It is perhaps significant that a
critic as thorough and judicious as G. J. Williams, in both *Iolo Morganwg a
Chywyddau'r Ychwanegiad* (1926) and in the first volume of his biography of
Iolo in 1956, believed that Iolo's version was 'wholly misleading' and that he
would refute it in the proposed second volume of his biography.[54]

As far as the correspondence of Miles, John and Thomas is concerned, it is
difficult to gauge whether there is any substance in Iolo's claims. There is also
little evidence about how they viewed their eldest brother's political stance, if
they were aware of it at all. For their part, the brothers' views on questions of
race, such as they were, appear to have been more sophisticated than one might
immediately assume. Miles and Thomas are known to have lived with so-called
'free women of colour' and to have fathered children with their respective
partners.[55] Iolo also pointed out, in the letter quoted above to Miss Barker, that
his brothers were known to the merchant Bryan Edwards, historian of Jamaica
and a supporter of amelioration.[56] Edwards was also a subscriber to *Poems, Lyric*

---

[52] NLW 21284E, Letter no. 738, Thomas Williams to Iolo Morganwg, 10 February 1799.
[53] NLW 21282E, Letter no. 441, James Robins to Iolo Morganwg, 4 September 1803.
[54] *IMChY*, p. 204 and Williams: *IM*, pp. xxxi–xxxii. In an article, published in *Y Faner* in 1978,
      Brinley Richards questioned G. J. Williams's assertion that Iolo's letter to Miss Barker was
      misleading, and in the process mounted an impassioned defence of Iolo's reputation. Richards
      warned, with some justification, that speculating about what Iolo may or may not have
      written to his brothers regarding their use of slavery was a dangerous exercise, especially since
      his letters to his brothers had not been found. Richards, 'Iolo Morganwg', 8–11.
[55] Taylor, 'Edward Williams ('Iolo Morganwg') and his Brothers', 38–9.
[56] NLW 21284E, Letter nos. 726, 727, 730, 735, Thomas Williams to Iolo Morganwg, 27
      September 1793, 6 October 1793, 8 November 1793, 31 January 1794.

and Pastoral.[57] Indeed, in 1783 John was living on an estate called Nonsuch in St Mary which came to be owned by Edwards,[58] and several letters from Thomas to Iolo in 1793–4 suggest that Thomas had undertaken some work for Edwards.[59] It is less clear, however, whether any of the brothers shared his pragmatic and (by the standards of the time) progressive views on slavery. Further reference to Edwards was made by Iolo in a letter to Thomas in October 1793 in which he stated that he had read Edwards's *History of Jamaica* and, on account of Edwards's defence of the Creation, he believed its author to be 'a believer in the doctrines of Christianity'. However tempting it may be to read this remark as an endorsement of Edwards's views on slavery, especially given the tendency of Iolo and the abolitionist movement in general to portray slavery as the antithesis of Christianity, it is extremely unlikely that this was the case.[60]

Certainly Thomas, the youngest brother and a morose and wayward character who was frequently compared to Iolo, indicated that he initially regarded the use of slaves as an act of oppression. In the letter of 1786 quoted above, in which he complained of his early difficulties on the island, he wrote:

> My Brothers are Both at work hear as hard as at Home only this I deall advantage of being plaugᵈ with ignorant Blockeds that they Call theyer Slaves. But in My opinion they are in a great Measher Slaves to them. You Can have no Ideas of the perfect ignorance of New Negros. They are of greater Servis to planters then trades Men as it requiers less Merit opretion is hear the Ruling Pation the the laws are hear as at home in fact the Godess Justis never yet visited this Isle. Power and opretion only are Rulers hear.[61]

Nevertheless, by 1803 it is clear from the aforementioned letter from James Robins to Iolo that Thomas, having overcome his misgivings, was renting a coffee plantation, and possessed around '20 Negroes of his own'.[62]

No such scruples, however, are apparent in the communication from the two middle brothers, John and Miles: their letters to Iolo are mostly notable

---

[57] Williams: *PLP*, I, p. xxviii. Although Edwards subscribed to six sets, according to Miles, they never reached Jamaica. NLW 21283E, Letter nos. 631, 633, Miles Williams to Iolo Morganwg, 11 November 1798, 28 June 1799.

[58] NLW 21283E, Letter no. 618, Miles and John Williams to Iolo Morganwg, 17 June 1783; Taylor, 'Edward Williams ('Iolo Morganwg') and his Brothers', 37.

[59] NLW 21284E, Letter nos. 726, 730, 735, Thomas Williams to Iolo Morganwg, 27 September 1793, 8 November 1793, 31 January 1794.

[60] NLW 21285E, Letter no. 821, Iolo Morganwg to Thomas Williams, 26 October 1793. Iolo wrote of Edwards: 'I have seen Bryan Edwards History of the West Indies, it is an extremely well-written work. And what pleases me most of all, he is a believer in the doctrines of Christianity, and in his observations on the Theory of the Earth he, in a very masterly manner, attacks and refutes, Busson and other infidel writers who have endeavoured to invalidate the scriptural account of the Creation.'

[61] NLW 21284E, Letter no. 724, Thomas Williams to Iolo Morganwg, 14 July 1786.

[62] NLW 21282E, Letter no. 441, James Robins to Iolo Morganwg, 4 September 1803.

Fig. 22 'A slave hung from a gallows': an illustration by William Blake, published by Joseph Johnston in 1796.

only for their conspicuous lack of reference to the politics of abolitionism so passionately upheld by their eldest brother. The only discernible political comment was made by John in a letter to Iolo in 1795 in which he gave an account of the Maroon insurrection in Trelawney that year. John recounted the uprising of around 300 free-born Maroons in the town and how they had been influenced by what he called the 'Diabolical and Informose politicks of the French revolution'.[63] Miles also recounted in the same year that he had undertaken militia duty following the Trelawney uprising,[64] an event recorded by Bryan Edwards. It is, in fact, highly probable that Miles was one of the eighty militia men mentioned in Edwards's account who were dispatched on 19 July 1795 to defend the town against the Maroons.[65] Yet, at no point did John or Miles appear to have been aware that their Jacobin brother would, even by 1795, have taken a markedly different view on both the freedom of the Maroons and the politics of the French Revolution.

These unresolved, and potentially unresolvable, issues have dominated accounts of Iolo Morganwg's attitude towards slavery and the issue of his brothers' actions in Jamaica. Yet, as noted above, very little critical attention has been focused on the fate of the estates of his brothers. Even though he was the eldest of the brothers, Iolo survived them all and lived until 1826. As a result, he became, late in life, the likely inheritor of some of the wealth amassed by his Jamaican-based brothers.

Having briefly examined the financial legacy left by Iolo's brothers, Clare Taylor concluded that Iolo and Taliesin were unlikely to have received a penny.[66] Certainly Iolo had become increasingly adamant in his refusal to consider accepting his brothers' money, be it as a proportion of profits, annuity or legacy, in his frequent letters to William Owen Pughe between 1799 and 1808. Although their friendship would later cool following a dispute between Iolo and his patron Owen Jones (Owain Myfyr), at this stage their correspondence was honest, good-natured and respectful. But whenever the subject of his brothers and their wealth arose, Iolo was prone to embark on intemperate rants and to use unconvincing hyperbole. He may well have been playing to the gallery, feeding Pughe with an exaggerated picture which would in turn have been relayed to his associates in London, thereby further enhancing his reputation as a committed abolitionist. On one occasion he declared that he would rather benefit from the proceeds of highway robbery than partake of a portion of his brothers' wealth,[67] and in 1803 he wrote to Pughe, in typically overstated fashion, on the subject of his children being the legitimate heirs to his brothers' fortunes:

> I consider it as a most dreadful misfortune that my Children are their only heirs at Law, estates got by the infernal traffic in human blood, by slave-holding; God deliver

[63] NLW 21283E, Letter no. 630, John Williams to Iolo Morganwg, 27 September 1795.
[64] NLW 21283E, Letter no. 629, Miles Williams to Iolo Morganwg, 27 September 1795.
[65] Bryan Edwards, 'Account of the Maroon Uprisings in Trelawney-Town in July 1795', *The Proceedings of the Governor and Assembly of Jamaica, in regard to the Maroon Negroes* (London, 1796), p. xli.
[66] Taylor, 'Edward Williams ('Iolo Morganwg') and his Brothers', 43.
[67] NLW 13221E, Letter no. 13, pp. 71–4, Iolo Morganwg to William Owen Pughe, 8 September 1800.

my very poor children from ever having a single farthing from such estates. May the vast Atlantic ocean swallow up Jamaica, and all other slave-trading and slave-holding Countries, before a boy or a girl of mine eats that single morsel that would prevent him or her from perishing of hunger, if it is the produce of slavery.[68]

In these letters Iolo certainly lived up to the image portrayed in Waring's account, admitting no arguments of expedience, of evil necessity, or temporary policy.

For all this bluster, however, it is also fair to say that Iolo was able to justify his views with a philosophical conviction which makes it difficult to believe that his position was simply abolitionist bravado. In 1800 Pughe argued, quite persuasively and perhaps mischievously, that in refusing to accept money from his brothers Iolo was only objecting to one 'particular sort of bondage':

> the bulk of the [peasants] of Clas Meidyn are virtually as great slaves, an[d] essentially in worse condition than the negroes in the West Indies. The peasantry are tied to the land in Russia and so they are effectually to the plwyv in Clas Meidyn, and where is the real difference, that you should expose one, more than the other.[69]

Iolo responded with a pithy rejoinder which cut through Pughe's seductive argument. While acknowledging the difficult conditions faced by much of the underclass in Britain, he maintained that their suffering 'does not entail eternal slavery on their posterities'.[70] In spite of his somewhat exaggerated posturing, the issue appears to have been more than a social question: it was one of basic humanity and Christianity. Similarly, Waring recounted a plausible exchange on the subject between Iolo and the Boverton schoolmaster, Thomas Redwood.[71] The exchange opened with Iolo responding to a remark made by Redwood on the subject of his brothers' wealth:

> 'Sir! *The Almighty Himself* could not make me take that money.' Mr Redwood, in his own calm impressive manner, protested against so extravagant an assertion, asking him what he could possibly mean by calling in question the Divine Omnipotence. 'I meant what I said,' was the prompt reply. 'The Almighty can do nothing contrary to his attributes; Justice and Mercy are his great attributes, and both are violated by slavery; but both are upheld by my objections. Therefore, sir, I assert, The Almighty could not make me take that money, because it would be contrary to his attributes

---

[68] NLW 13222C, Letter no. 12, pp. 173–6, Iolo Morganwg to William Owen Pughe, 25 August 1803.

[69] NLW 21282E, Letter no. 343, William Owen Pughe to Iolo Morganwg, 21 November 1800.

[70] NLW 13221E, Letter no. 14, pp. 75–8, Iolo Morganwg to William Owen Pughe, 19 December 1800.

[71] Notwithstanding the unreliability of his work, the tone and content of the exchange reported by Waring sound reasonably plausible, given the similar way in which Iolo wrote to Redwood in 1817 in order to explore some of his theological ideas. See NLW 21286E, Letter no. 960, Iolo Morganwg to Thomas Redwood, 18 December 1817.

to do so.' The theorem was admitted, and the subject dropped in favour of something less argumentative.[72]

Nonetheless, Iolo's public declarations, however heartfelt, inflated or philosphically convincing, again do not tell the full story. Clare Taylor rightly pointed out that, on a few occasions during the 1790s and 1800s, Iolo received small amounts of money from his brothers.[73] For instance, in 1803 he was sent £20 by Thomas via James Robins.[74] As usual, Iolo did not acknowledge the gift – he seldom did when sent money – but the letters which accompanied the two banknotes, one of which was a Bristol bank bill for £10, survive and would therefore appear to confirm that he had received the bills.[75] One cannot help but wonder how he could reconcile receiving money acquired through slavery which had been channelled through a bank in the city of Bristol which he had earlier decried for its links with this 'inhuman traffic'.[76]

The following year the saga took a decisive turn when Iolo learned, through another letter from Robins, of the death of his brother John in December 1803.[77] A flurry of letters followed, several of which noted that John had left Iolo and his three children, Taliesin, Ann (Nancy) and Margaret (Peggy), individual legacies of £100 each.[78] John left the remainder of his estate to his second wife Ann Williams (later Ann Duncan) for the duration of her life or until such time as she chose to sell the property. Following either outcome, the estate or the proceeds from its sale were to go to Iolo's children. A copy of John Williams's will, made in 1811, demonstrates his wishes and the extent of his estate:

I John Williams of the Parish of St Catherine in the County of Middlesex in the Island of Jamaica Mason, being of sound &c . . .

give unto my elder brother Edwd Williams of the Parish of Flemingston in the County of Glamorgan in South Wales the sum of one hundred pounds sterling

---

72 *RAEW*, p. 63.
73 NLW 21284E, Letter nos. 727, 730, 731, Thomas Williams to Iolo Morganwg, 6 October 1793, 8 November 1793, 11 November 1793; Taylor, 'Edward Williams ('Iolo Morganwg') and his Brothers', 41.
74 NLW 21282E, Letter nos. 441–6, James Robins to Iolo Morganwg, 4 September 1803, 12 December 1803, 13 January 1804, 8 February 1804, 1 May 1804, 4 September 1804; NLW 21284E, Letter no. 639, Taliesin Williams to Iolo Morganwg, 27 March 1804; NLW 21284E, Letter no. 739, Thomas Williams to Iolo Morganwg, 17 May 1803.
75 NLW 21282E, Letter nos. 443–4, James Robins to Iolo Morganwg, 13 January 1804, 8 February 1804.
76 NLW 21400C, Letter no. 24, Iolo Morganwg to William Bulgin, undated [prior to 20 August 1791].
77 NLW 21282E, Letter no. 445, James Robins to Iolo Morganwg, 1 May 1804.
78 Ibid.; NLW 21283E, Letter no. 634, Miles Williams to Iolo Morganwg, 4 May 1804; NLW 21284E, Letter no. 640, Taliesin Williams to Iolo Morganwg, 8 May 1804.

money of Great Britain &. If the said Edwd Williams should die before me, it is my will that the said sum of money be paid to his widow . . .

I give and bequeath the said sum of one hundred pounds sterling unto and among all and every the lawfully begotten children of my said brother Edward who may be living at the time of my decease, in equal proportions . . .

I give devise and bequeath all the rest residue and remainder of my Estate, real and personal unto my dearly beloved wife Ann Williams to hold the same unto my said Wife and her assigns during the term of her natural Life . . . and after the decease of my said Wife I give devise and bequeath my said residuary Estate unto the lawfully begotten Children of my said Brother Edward their heirs and assigns for ever as Tenants in Common and not as Joint Tenants if more than one but in case there shall be no Children or Child of my said Brother Edward living at the death of my said Wife then and in that Case I give devise and bequeath my said residuary Estate unto the right Heirs of my said Wife absolutely for ever . . .

Docket of the Inventory of John Williams deceased returned into office 19th July 1804, Lib. 102, folio 19.

Amount of houshold furniture horses &c	£754. 12. 5
D.º of Negroes	3880. 0. 0
11 Negroes run away and detained by Miles Williams} not valued}	3041. 18. 7½
Book Debts	£7676. 11. 0½[79]

During the years before the death of John Williams relations seem to have soured between the three brothers in Jamaica. According to a later account by Walter Pollock, an attorney in Jamaica, 'the three brothers lived in a state of law warfare',[80] while another independent observer noted that John lived under the 'petticoat government' of his wife Ann Williams.[81] When John left Miles and Thomas legacies of just £10 apiece from the proceeds of his large estate,[82] Miles wilfully took possession of a dozen of his deceased brother's plantation slaves.[83]

Around this point, shortly after the death of John Williams, a marked change occurred in Iolo's actions and in his attitude towards his brother's property, a change which has hitherto been overlooked. In 1804 he consulted Theophilus Jones, the Breconshire historian who practised law, about the possibility of

[79] NLW 21285E, Letter no. 887, Iolo Morganwg to David Davis, 31 January 1811.

[80] NLW 21282E, Letter no. 383, William Basset Popkin to Iolo Morganwg, 30 July 1812. See also NLW 21284E, Letter no. 738, Thomas Williams to Iolo Morganwg, 10 February 1799.

[81] NLW 21283E, Letter no. 488, William Thomas to Iolo Morganwg, 6 February 1808.

[82] A codicil to his will, however, notes that Miles Williams was to receive the deeds to an unspecified mountain. See NLW 21285E, Letter no. 887, Iolo Morganwg to David Davis, 31 January 1811.

[83] NLW 13221E, Letter no. 25, pp. 123–6, Iolo Morganwg to William Owen Pughe, 14 February 1805. The evidence in the copy of John's will appears to confirm that Miles had seized some of his dead brother's property. See NLW 21285E, Letter no. 887, Iolo Morganwg to David Davis, 31 January 1811.

emigrating to Jamaica to take control of his brother John's estate.[84] In 1805 he sent a power of attorney to Jamaica in the hope of settling outstanding legal impediments to taking possession.[85] His motives were twofold: the first was that his immediate family had put pressure on him to secure the legacy, if not for his own benefit, then for the sake of his children. In 1804 Taliesin had written to his father, strongly urging him to contact his brother Thomas to determine whether John had bequeathed anything to Iolo and his family, and adding that he suspected Miles and Thomas of concealing the truth.[86] Indeed, in marked contrast to his earlier declarations that he would prefer his children to starve than inherit his brothers' wealth, Iolo wrote to William Owen Pughe in 1808 deploying significantly less hyperbole than on previous occasions and revealing a softer position on the matter: 'I cannot answer for my Children, notwithstanding that they appear to be well fix'd in the Principles which I have endeavored to inculcate and impress upon their minds.'[87] Taliesin was close to his twenty-first birthday and would therefore soon be eligible to collect his legacy. Secondly, Iolo, and later Taliesin,[88] may well have harboured genuine hopes of freeing the brother's slaves, selling off the remaining assets, and emigrating to America.[89] In 1804 Iolo had written to William Owen Pughe:

> I wish I could get into possession of some of [my] late Brother's Negroes, that I might exhibit an example of such [?] conduct as should be intended by me to shame those who have it in their power to lead the way in liberating from their long miseries and captivity the large portion of human beings that groan under the [?] of oppression.[90]

Sometime before April 1805, Iolo had also written to the Bristol Quaker and agriculturalist William Matthews, proposing the establishment of a Society for General Liberation and expressing his concern about the fate of his brother's

---

[84] See NLW 21281E, Letter nos. 261–2, Theophilus Jones to Iolo Morganwg, 17 October 1804, 16 November 1804.

[85] NLW 13222C, Letter no. 17, pp. 195–8, Iolo Morganwg to William Owen Pughe, 20 February 1805.

[86] NLW 21284E, Letter no. 639, Taliesin Williams to Iolo Morganwg, 27 March 1804; NLW 21284E, Letter no. 742, Thomas Williams to Iolo Morganwg, 10 November 1804. In 1810 Ann (Nancy) also urged Iolo to write to Jamaica in order to ascertain whether or not Miles was still alive. She also relayed William Thomas's view that it would be of great advantage for Iolo to re-establish contact with Miles. NLW 21283E, Letter no. 536, Ann Williams to Iolo Morganwg, 13 May 1810.

[87] NLW 21285E, Letter no. 881, Iolo Morganwg to William Owen Pughe, 27 April 1808.

[88] NLW 21284E, Letter no. 666, Taliesin Williams to Iolo Morganwg, 21 April 1815.

[89] NLW 21282E, Letter no. 375, William Owen Pughe to Iolo Morganwg, 18 May 1808.

[90] NLW 13221E, Letter no. 26, pp. 127–30. Iolo Morganwg to William Owen Pughe, 28 April 1805. In 1815 Taliesin seriously considered going to Jamaica to wind up the estates because he was 'fully convinced that the only good in our power is to diminish the means of oppression in the hands of others'. NLW 21284E, Letter no. 666, Taliesin Williams to Iolo Morganwg, 21 April 1815.

slaves.[91] Nevertheless, his plan to emigrate was shelved when legal advice received from Theophilus Jones suggested that Iolo might have more than a little difficulty shaking off his still numerous creditors.[92]

Several years went by during which nothing of any substance appeared in the correspondence about the Jamaican affair. Meanwhile Miles and Thomas died, the former having endured poor health for a number of years and the latter 'giving himself up to the bottle', according to a much-quoted account.[93] A letter from William Basset Popkin[94] in 1812, however, resurrected the issue. Through the aforementioned lawyer Walter Pollock, Popkin informed Iolo that he would receive nothing from either estate since their value had been consumed by other legacies and unpaid debts. Taliesin, however, had inherited what Pollock called a 'worthless' house, some coffee pasture and so-called 'negroes grounds'.[95] Around this time, the ever-resourceful Iolo made enquiries in Bristol in order to discover whether there was a market for a 'great quantity of coffee'.[96] Pollock recommended that Iolo's family should seek to come to terms with the widow, Ann Williams, who was by now known as Ann Duncan, in order to recover their legacies and the lands or proceeds from it. He also warned that 'the Lady has more Law in her head than even Blackstone[97] or all the Judges in Jamaica'.[98]

In 1814 Ann and her husband John Duncan returned from Jamaica to live in Bath. Soon afterwards John Duncan wrote to Iolo stating that he was keen to arrange the settlement of the legacies,[99] and in September Iolo went to Bath to meet him. He was not as warmly received as he would have hoped. He was kept waiting for several days: Ann Duncan claimed her husband was in London, but Iolo was convinced he was hiding indoors.[100] He finally lost patience and returned to Cowbridge, stopping off en route at the 'unhallowed' city of Bristol, where he sought the counsel of another lawyer. Iolo's representative at this

---

[91] NLW 21281E, Letter no. 278, William Matthews to Iolo Morganwg, 11 April 1805.

[92] NLW 21281E, Letter no. 261, Theophilus Jones to Iolo Morganwg, 17 October 1804.

[93] NLW 21283E, Letter no. 488, William Thomas to Iolo Morganwg, 6 February 1808.

[94] William Basset Popkin was the grandson of John Popkin (*fl.* 1759–1824), a Methodist and Sandemanian exhorter. D. Emrys Williams, 'The Popkin Family', *CA*, VII (1971), 129.

[95] Sometime around 1819 Taliesin appears to have inherited £500, the proceeds from the sale of a house in Kingston owned by his uncle, Miles Williams. NLW 21282E, Letter no. 383, William Basset Popkin to Iolo Morganwg, 30 July 1812; NLW 21286E, Letter no. 962, Iolo Morganwg to Taliesin Williams, undated.

[96] NLW 21283E, Letter nos. 534–5, Rickett Willett to Iolo Morganwg, 26 April 1812, 17 August 1812.

[97] This refers to the barrister Sir William Blackstone (1723–80), who became the first Vinerian professor of common law at Oxford and was best known for his hugely influential *Commentaries on the Laws of England* (4 vols., Oxford, 1765–9), which, for many years, was regarded the standard textbook for students of English law. *ODNB*.

[98] NLW 21282E, Letter no. 383, William Basset Popkin to Iolo Morganwg, 30 July 1812.

[99] NLW 21280E, Letter no. 127, John Duncan to Iolo Morganwg, 16 August 1814.

[100] NLW 21285E, Letter no. 921, Iolo Morganwg to Taliesin Williams, 31 March 1814.

stage of the protracted case was Alfred Estlin, the second son of his old friend and Unitarian minister, John Prior Estlin.

It is worth pausing for a moment to reflect further on Iolo's attitude towards his brothers' money at this stage in his life. The impassioned and high-minded tirades against the 'diabolical traffic'[101] which had appeared in his earlier letters had now given way to sober pragmatism. Whenever the subject of his brothers' money was raised, the vocabulary of morality disappeared entirely from his letters and was replaced by legal jargon. For example, in February 1815 he wrote to Taliesin regarding the imminent settlement of the legacies. The following extract is worth quoting in its entirety more for its revealing vocabulary and tone than for its its legal content, which was only incidental to the process under way at that time:

> My plea for setting the Will aside is founded on a very different point from what you conceive it to be. It is on that point in Law expressed thus in Latin *Voluit et contradixit*, or *voluit sed contradixit*, by willing a thing to be done in a stated manner and immediately contradicting it. This is a proof in Law that the Testator was *non compos mentis*. And Duncan has been frightened by this into compliance with my requisition to pay the Legacies, without any reference to the reversionary claims – My Brother John says that it is his will that his widow should have the use for life only of the Chattle property, and immediately afterwards says that it is to be at her own free and entire disposal. This is to Will that it shall be so and that it shall not be so in the same case and at the same time – *Voluit et contradixit*. Duncan will, with all his affected Stubborness yield to almost any thing if by so doing he may be able to obviate those things with which I have threatened him. I wrote to him the day after you left us, and in consequence thereof he is now proposing to pay the legacies and no longer proposes that we should convey and release unto him the reversionary claims. If the will should be proved at Drs Commons he now understands that we shall be able to arrest him for the Legacies. And if we set the Will aside he will have only the Widowhood claims of his wife, which having no child by My Bro^r John, will be only half the annual profits and for her life only, and then the whole to us.[102]

After some inevitable complications, Alfred Estlin, who worked assiduously on the case, finally succeeded in securing from the Duncans 5 per cent interest per annum on each legacy for every year since John's death in 1803. In his next letter, on 21 February 1815, Estlin wrote to Iolo enclosing the amount which was legally due to him from the estate of his brother John:

> I have the sincere pleasure of inclosing you a Bankers' Draft for £146. 10., being the amount of your Legacy and Interest . . .
> I have sent Mr Taliesin Williams, his Legacy, and the same post also brings your Daughters theirs . . .

---

[101] NLW 21285E, Letter no. 862, Iolo Morganwg to Miss Barker, 26 March 1798.
[102] NLW 21286E, Letter no. 928, Iolo Morganwg to Taliesin Williams, 1 February 1815.

> Allow me to offer You my sincere Congratulations on the receipt of this Legacy
> . . .[103]

There is little to add to the convoluted chain of events which culminated in the receipt of the above sum from his brother's estate. Yet, it is unclear what happened to the money after it was drawn. Iolo had claimed in July 1814 that he was as deeply in debt as he had ever been, quoting figures of between £60 and £80.[104] He also wrote to Taliesin, shortly after the bankers' drafts had been sent to him, to inform him that he was contacting London to ensure that that 'every thing may be ready by the time the money becomes payable', adding that 'our Creditors are very clamorous as the affair has taken wind'.[105] Some days later Iolo received a cheque for just £11 from Taliesin, who had drawn the legacies at Neath. This curious turn of events raises several possibilities. It may have been the case that Iolo had paid off his creditors and that the £11 received from Taliesin represented the remainder of his legacy. It is also possible that Iolo's share of John's estate went directly to his children, whose own legacies appear to have been invested in securing a livelihood for each of them. Taliesin's legacy from the estate of John Williams almost certainly funded the establishment, in February 1816, of his 'Commercial School' at Merthyr Tydfil.[106] It is also probable that Peggy and Nancy's milliner's shop and general store at Cefncribwr, which opened in the same year, was funded by their uncle's legacy.[107]

Whatever the fate of Iolo's own legacy, it is abundantly clear that, by the mid-1810s, he was determined to acquire the money owed to him and his children. Why did his attitude change? Why was he apparently prepared to accept money that, a decade earlier, he considered to have been the fruits of 'the infernal traffic in human blood'.[108] We must search for answers in the context in which this apparent change of heart occurred, both on a personal and political level. During the years leading up to his acceptance of the bequest Iolo was, as ever, in a financially precarious situation. From 1810 onwards there

---

[103] NLW 21281E, Letter no. 151, Alfred Estlin to Iolo Morganwg, 21 February 1815.

[104] NLW 21285E, Letter no. 917, Iolo Morganwg to John Herbert Lloyd, 1 July 1814.

[105] NLW 21286E, Letter no. 930, Iolo Morganwg to Taliesin Williams, 2 March 1815.

[106] NLW 21286E, Letter no. 934, Iolo Morganwg to Taliesin Williams, 27 April 1815. This letter from Iolo to Taliesin reveals that the money eventually used to establish Taliesin's school was at this point invested in government funds. Several documents pertaining to the estate of John Williams demonstrate that the Williams family's legacies were also invested in such funds. NLW 21282E, Letter no. 383, William Basset Popkin to Iolo Morganwg, 30 July 1812; NLW 21285E, Letter no. 887, Iolo Morganwg to David Davis, 31 January 1811; NLW 21285E, Letter no. 921, Iolo Morganwg to Taliesin Williams, 16 September 1814. For Taliesin's school at Merthyr, see Brynley F. Roberts, 'Mab ei Dad: Taliesin ab Iolo Morganwg' in Hywel Teifi Edwards (ed.), *Merthyr a Thaf* (Llandysul, 2001), pp. 61–4.

[107] Neville Granville, *Cefn Cribwr: Chronicle of a Village* (Barry, 1980), pp. 75–7.

[108] NLW 13222C, Letter no. 12, pp. 173–6, Iolo Morganwg to William Owen Pughe, 25 August 1803.

are frequent references to poverty and debt in numerous letters to would-be benefactors.[109] His London-based acquaintances, including Evan Williams, the well-known bookseller in the Strand, and Richard Fenton had made represen- tations to the Literary Fund on his behalf,[110] and late in 1814 Elijah Waring, aware of Iolo's penury, secured £15 for him from the Gurneys, a prosperous Quaker family from Norfolk.[111] For much of 1814 Taliesin had been a tutor in Neath at the school of the Unitarian minister David Davis (the son of Dafydd Dafis, Castellhywel). By October, however, his health had begun to deteriorate and disagreements arose between him and Davis. In his frequent letters to his father in 1814–15 he became increasingly desperate about his failing health and his desire to leave the school: in March 1815 he grimly noted that 'Neath has shortened my days'.[112] It was against this backdrop that the final stages of the legal wranglings between Iolo and the Duncans were played out. It is highly likely that Iolo was under pressure from his family to accept money he was entitled to. Although it was only a small proportion of John's estate, £140 was a considerable sum and would have gone some way to relieving Iolo's debts and providing him with a more comfortable retirement.

In the political context, of course, the slave trade had been abolished as a result of the efforts of Wilberforce in 1806–7. We also know from other letters that Iolo's brother's lands were free of slaves by 1815, though exactly what happened to the land is unclear. David Davis had written to Iolo in 1807 to celebrate the abolition of the slave trade with the words: 'Allow me to congrat- ulate you most heartily on the abolition of the nefarious traffic in human flesh, which has, for ages, been the great national sin of Britain – you are, I hope, by this time pretty well cured of the heart-ache.'[113] Who knows what private anguish Iolo, the fervent abolitionist, had endured by this point and what was to follow if indeed he later accepted 'the contaminated gains of that *detested slave-trade*'.[114]

---

[109] NLW 21285E, Letter no. 917, Iolo Morganwg to John Herbert Lloyd, 1 July 1814; NLW 21286E, Letter no. 927, Iolo Morganwg to an unknown recipient, undated [November 1814].

[110] NLW 21283E, Letter no. 580, Evan Williams to Iolo Morganwg, 11 February 1812.

[111] NLW 21284E, Letter no. 661, Taliesin Williams to Iolo Morganwg, 7 November 1814.

[112] NLW 21284E, Letter nos. 660–2, 665, Taliesin Williams to Iolo Morganwg, 15 October 1814, 7 November 1814, 10 November 1814, 24 March 1815; NLW 21286E, Letter no. 926, Iolo Morganwg to Taliesin Williams, undated.

[113] NLW 21280E, Letter no. 105, David Davis to Iolo Morganwg, 3 April 1807.

[114] *RAEW*, p. 59.

14

Iolo Morganwg and the Dialects of Welsh

RICHARD CROWE

In the latter part of the eighteenth century the expression of political radicalism in the linguistic field was characterized by a far greater respect for the spoken language. The lexicographer Noah Webster argued in *Dissertations on the English Language* (1789) that spoken English should be the model of grammar.[1] Most grammars of European languages had formerly sought to contort vernacular tongues into Latin and Greek grammatical systems. Gradually, however, grammarians began to realize that it was not possible to describe the vernacular, or even to prescribe correct grammatical forms, on the basis of a foreign language. Some authors suggested that the usage of 'refined' and educated speakers should become the model for grammar, and in this belief lay the germ of the doctrine of usage. Radical thinkers in England and America feared that traditional grammars were socially divisive because the accepted grammatical norm of the language was so far removed from daily usage. Joseph Priestley, with whose work Iolo Morganwg was familiar, advocated a kind of linguistic democracy whereby the speakers of a particular language would standardize and freeze their language by selecting from it all the possibilities and by practising the most popular.[2] Correctness was no longer believed to be the sole monopoly of the educated classes, but the true nature of the language as it was spoken would become the standard if radicals had their way. Burgeoning interest in geographical and sociological varieties was reflected in the appreciable number of popular works on dialects and slang published in the latter half of the eighteenth century. These often took the form of dialogues, and dictionaries of urban slang were also compiled.

In many fields of knowledge during the latter years of the eighteenth century and the beginning of the nineteenth century, collecting became something of a mania. Collections of all sorts were amassed, sometimes in order to prove a point, but mainly because words and languages lent themselves to being collected. Languages which had previously been considered worthless,

---

[1] Olivia Smith, *The Politics of Language 1791–1819* (Oxford, 1984), p. 40.
[2] Joseph Priestley, *The Rudiments of English Grammar* (3rd edn., London, 1772), p. xvii.

uncouth or barbaric suddenly became worth collecting and recording. Iolo Morganwg was fascinated by words and he collected them wherever he went. He could not go for a stroll without jotting down unfamiliar words and phrases, and nothing interested him more than peculiarities, oddities, 'barbarisms', antiquated forms and the like.

Iolo's interest in the spoken language and in the nature of linguistic studies in the eighteenth century meant that he devoted considerable attention to vernacular words and phrases. As early as 1776 he claimed that he had in his possession a collection of eight to nine thousand Welsh words which he had compiled from the works of the ancient bards, as well as around a thousand dialectal forms. With great pride, he informed Owen Jones (Owain Myfyr): 'I think I may safely say that I have the greatest collection of Welsh words of any man living.'[3] In 1806 he declared that his collection had swollen to some 25,000 words, over 5,000 of which were from the Gwentian (the dialect of south-east Wales) or from other Welsh dialects.[4]

Early Welsh lexicographers and grammarians had noted dialectal variations in printed dictionaries and grammars without attempting to describe the dialects in any systematic way. In the late Stuart period the Celtic scholar Edward Lhuyd went a step further by including a question on local words and expressions in a questionnaire which he sent to every parish in Wales. Although Iolo made observations on aspects of the dialects which we would now consider under the headings of phonology, syntax and morphology, often taking a comparative approach by contrasting features in two different dialects (usually the Venedotian (the Welsh of north Wales) and the Gwentian) in tabular form, these did not form a cohesive whole. They merely constituted some striking features which had caught his attention. He may have collected this material simply because he had developed the collecting mania and found his discoveries utterly fascinating, though he did note some specific reasons why he believed that words and phrases were worth collecting. One of them was his awareness that vernacular words sometimes dropped out of use. As the number of printed books in Welsh increased, for instance, Iolo believed that 'the Welsh language becomes daily more uniform. in every part of Wales the language of writers drives out of use many local words and dialectical expressions'.[5] However, it seems that this was not a purely conservational motive. Iolo

---

[3]   BL Add. 15024, ff.183ʳ–4ʳ, Iolo Morganwg to Owain Myfyr, 25 January 1776.
[4]   NLW 13221E, p. 145, Iolo Morganwg to William Owen Pughe, 12 January 1806. See also Richard M. Crowe, 'Diddordebau Ieithyddol Iolo Morganwg' (unpublished University of Wales Ph.D. thesis, 1988); idem, 'Iolo Morganwg: An Eighteenth-century Welsh Linguist' in Cyril J. Byrne, Margaret Harry and Pádraig Ó Siadhail (eds.), *Celtic Languages and Celtic Peoples* (Halifax, NS, 1992), pp. 305–14; Caryl Davies, *Adfeilion Babel: Agweddau ar Syniadaeth Ieithyddol y Ddeunawfed Ganrif* (Caerdydd, 2000), chapter 11.
[5]   NLW 13155A, p. 8.

noted in several places that he was anxious to improve the modern standard literary language by collecting dialectal variations, rejecting what he considered to be corruptions and 'barbarisms', while preserving the pure and beautiful aspects and combining them in order to enrich the standard language. Everything suggests that the radical Iolo was determined to bring the standard written language closer to spoken varieties and to achieve this in a democratic spirit by drawing on the resources of all dialects. Even so, Iolo's notes on Welsh dialects concentrated mainly on his own dialect, the Gwentian (or Silurian dialect). Whenever he mentioned other dialects, he often did so in order to contrast them with the Gwentian dialect. As well as collecting words and phrases, he noted aspects of phonology, morphology and syntax.

One of the most salient aspects of the phonology of the dialects of Glamorgan is provection. Iolo observed this, and in his papers he offered examples of its occurrence without attempting to explain the phenomenon. For example, he noted that: 'the Silurian dialect is apt to have C, P & T for G, B & D, thus macu for magu, Epol for Ebol, petar for pedair'.[6] Iolo did not approve of this feature, however, and noted that Dissenters in Glamorgan, i.e. educated speakers, had an 'improved pronunciation'. He probably objected to provection because the pronunciation masked the true etymology of the word, and since Dissenters were more likely to be literate in Welsh they would have received greater exposure to standard written Welsh. Iolo was aware that differences in pronunciation could be attributed to different groups in society and set himself the task, among many others, of making a comparative study between the Welsh used by Dissenters in Glamorgan and that used by the common people at fairs and markets.[7]

The modern dialects of east Glamorgan, in common with the Welsh of north-west Wales, realize the final unaccented -e as -a, for example, llyfra (books) where other dialects have llyfre and the standard written form is llyfrau. Once again, Iolo condemned this feature, this time by means of a letter attributed by him to Edward Gamage, vicar of St Athan at the beginning of the eighteenth century, in which he maintained that it was true that e was sounded as a in Glamorgan in words such as llawan, bachgan, bachgenas, cyfeillas (for llawen, bachgen, bachgenes, cyfeilles), but that this was a 'great fault' and as great a 'corruption' as the pronunciation of -aidd as -edd in north Wales.[8]

Another feature of the Gwentian dialect of which Iolo disapproved was the tendency to palatalize /d/ into /dʒ/ when preceding semi-consonantal /i/.

---

[6] NLW 13091E, p. 148.

[7] For lists of popular proverbial and figurative expressions or phrases in Welsh, see ibid., pp. 93–148.

[8] Ibid., p. 284. The pronunciation of -aidd as -edd in the modern dialects of north Wales occurs in the north-east, whereas -add occurs in the north-west.

He noted the following examples as 'corruptions of pronunciation in the Silurian Dialect' (representing /dʒ/ with /dz/):

> Ymprydzio – for ymprydio
> Ysgrydzio – ysgrydio
> Rhodzio – rhodio
> Cydzio – cydio
> Bydzio – bydio
> Trambydzio – Trambydio.[9]

He added *dziawl* (for standard *diawl*) and *dziangyd* (*diengyd*) to show that this feature could occur in an initial position.

In the tables which he devised to reveal the value of the letters of his bardic alphabet, *Coelbren y Beirdd*, Iolo noted that the letter corresponding to *chw* in standard written Welsh was pronounced /xw/ in the Welsh of north Wales, but /hw/ in the Welsh of south Wales.[10] He did not regard the latter pronunciation as faulty on this occasion, but rather as the logical pronunciation because, so he argued, no word should begin with a guttural sound.[11] Since the modern dialects of Glamorgan typically realize *chw* as /w/, if Iolo's evidence is to be believed the Welsh of Glamorgan in his day shared the pronunciation /hw/ with south-west Wales, and only weakened to /w/ in later times.

It is well known that the classic distribution of rounded /ɪ/ in north Wales and corresponding /ɪ/ in south Wales, represented orthographically as *u* and *y*, is too simplistic in the light of the evidence of the dialects of Glamorgan. There is evidence that some twentieth-century speakers of Glamorgan Welsh would use a rounded /ɪ/ in the same situations as a native of north Wales would. Iolo recorded that the letters *u* and *y* were pronounced as *i* in many parts of Wales, including the counties of Brecon, Merioneth, Montgomery and Carmarthen, and he noted the examples 'Din, Diw, biwch, hinn, iw and hidd' for 'Dyn, Duw, buwch, hynn, yw, hydd'.[12] He did not include Glamorgan and Monmouthshire as a non-rounded area, but neither did he include Pembrokeshire, Cardiganshire or Radnorshire in his description. In another set of notes on the same subject, however, a list entitled 'Peculiarities of the Dimetian Dialect', he specified the southern parts of Merioneth, Montgomeryshire, Radnorshire and Breconshire as regions in which *u* and *y* were pronounced as *i*.[13] Iolo's observations suggest that non-rounded /ɪ/ was a feature of mid-Wales, especially

---

[9] NLW 13095B, p. 200.
[10] NLW 13087E, p. 15; see also NLW 13087E, p. 21; NLW 13093E, p. 163; NLW 13093E, p. 155.
[11] NLW 13087E, p. 21.
[12] NLW 13098B, p. 181.
[13] NLW 13162A, pp. 301–3.

those counties on the border with England, while the north and the south retained the rounded form.

One of the most characteristic morphological features of the dialects of Glamorgan is the third person singular preterite verbal suffix -*ws*. Surprisingly, however, Iolo had little to say about it. In a note comparing the Gwentian 'Pwy welwys hynny' with the Venedotian 'Pwy a welodd hynny' (Who saw that?) the point of the comparison, as is made clear in other examples in the list, was the lack of the relative particle *a* in the Gwentian example, rather than the differing verbal suffixes.[14] The presence of this verbal suffix in medieval Welsh manuscripts drawn from all parts of Wales led Iolo to believe that the Gwentian dialect was Wales's first standard literary dialect of Welsh. He claimed that he had not discovered any example of the verbal suffix -*odd* in the works of the poets of north Wales in the period between Meilyr Brydydd Mawr (*fl.* 1100–37) and the death of Llywelyn ap Gruffudd in 1282, while the suffixes -*ws*, -*wys*, -*es*, -*is*, -*as* were abundant.[15] He overstated the case, however, for the suffix -*odd* is to be found in the works of the *Gogynfeirdd* (though he may not have seen the whole corpus), but the sigmatic suffixes are indeed the predominant third person singular preterite markers.

Iolo recorded examples of the first person preterite of the verbs *mynd* (go), *dod* (come), and *gwneud* (do) in their typical Gwentian forms, that is 'euthof – or eutho, Deuthof – deutho, Gwneuthof – gwneutho' rather than the standard forms of 'aethum, Daethum, Gwnaethum'. However, he added that the more standard forms were used just as commonly in Glamorgan,[16] predominantly, one suspects, among educated speakers.

Another way in which Iolo believed that the Gwentian dialect differed from the Venedotian was in the latter's usage of what he considered to be unnecessary suffixes. This was to be seen in the formation of the imperative. He claimed that in the Venedotian dialect the second person singular imperative was formed by adding the suffix -*a* to the verbal root, whereas the Gwentian used the verbal root alone. He compared, for example, the Venedotian *cladda* (bury), *lladda* (kill) and *darllena* (read) with the Gwentian *cladd*, *lladd* and *darllen*.[17] Imperative forms in modern dialects seem to be more of a mixed pattern than Iolo's description. Forms with and without the imperative suffix -*a* are to be found in descriptions of the Welsh of north-west Wales and Glamorgan.[18] However, there is a general tendency for the conservative

---

[14] NLW 13142A, p. 225.

[15] NLW 13129A, pp. 493–4.

[16] NLW 13142A, p. 62.

[17] NLW 13128A, p. 212.

[18] The imperative second person forms *lladd* and *darllan* (but not *cladd*) were recorded by O. H. Fynes-Clinton in *The Welsh Vocabulary of the Bangor District* (Oxford, 1913), pp. 74, 339. Ceinwen Thomas discussed the imperative forms in her study of the Welsh of Nantgarw (*Tafodiaith Nantgarw: Astudiaeth o Gymraeg Llafar Nantgarw yng Nghwm Taf, Morgannwg*

dialects of south Wales to favour forms without the suffix -*a*, whereas the northern dialects use it.[19]

Iolo noted that the Venedotian dialect had a predilection for adding verb-noun suffixes, whereas the Gwentian dialect contented itself with the verbal stem. For example, speakers of Gwentian used *agor* (open), *cwrdd* (meet) and *adfer* (revive), while the Venedotian used *agoryd*, *cwrddyd*, and *adferyd* or *adferu*. The evidence of modern dialects suggests that Iolo may have observed a general tendency correctly: for example, *agoryd* and *agor* are attested in the Welsh of the Bangor district, while only *acor* is attested in Nantgarw.[20]

Iolo believed that the adjectival suffix -*us* was more common in the Gwentian dialect than in the Venedotian. Gwentian adjectives such as *tesus*, *rhywus* and *naturus* corresponded to the Venedotian *tesog* (warm), *rhywiog* (kindly) and *naturiol* (natural), but he added that the Venedotian forms were also to be found in Glamorgan.[21] There seems to be little evidence to support these claims.

Time after time Iolo claimed that Gwentian forms were unique to the territory of the dialect, but that Venedotian forms, presumably as a result of the dissemination of books, were also known in the territory. He explained the presence of the diminutive suffix -*os* in the Gwentian dialect, for example *perthïos* (hedges), *plantos* (children) and *gwrageddos* (wives) as basically Venedotian forms that had become familiar in south Wales through the literary language. He contended that -*ach* was the corresponding suffix in the Gwentian. In the modern literary language –*ach* has a derogatory meaning, while -*os* is used to convey endearment.

Iolo had little to say on syntax, which is hardly surprising since linguistic studies in the eighteenth century centred on individual words rather than words in relationship to one another. Interestingly, he did not comment on one of the most obvious syntactical features of the modern dialects of east Glamorgan, that is the verbal construction in which the pronoun precedes the verb and agrees with it, for example 'fi welas y gath' (I saw the cat), where standard Welsh would have 'gwelais i'r gath'. However, he did claim that the Gwentian dialect did not require concord between a plural noun and its adjective, for example *merched bach* (little girls), *brethynnau cul* (narrow cloths), *pethau mawr* (big things), *dynion drwg* (bad men), *dynion da* (good men).[22] He

(Caerdydd, 1993)), and showed that both forms consisting of the verbal stem alone and the verbal stem with the suffix –*a* exist in the dialect and are formed according to type, though speakers sometimes use both forms.

[19]   Peter Wynn Thomas, *Gramadeg y Gymraeg* (Caerdydd, 1996), p. 67.

[20]   See Fynes-Clinton, *The Welsh Vocabulary of the Bangor District*; Thomas, *Geirfa Tafodiaith Nantgarw*.

[21]   NLW 13089E, p. 344.

[22]   NLW 13098B, pp. 177–89, 'Miscellaneous collections for the Analytical Dissertation on the Welsh Language'.

did not compare this feature with any other dialect. In any case, *bach*, *drwg* and *da* do not have plural forms and so only *brethynnau culion* and *pethau mawrion* were possibilities. It is difficult to understand why he made this claim since he himself used the plural forms of adjectives in his writing, and various plural forms have been attested in the modern dialects of east Glamorgan.

Iolo made many more observations on features of the dialects of his day, including several on the Venedotian and Dimetian (south-west Wales) not mentioned here. Even when all these notes are considered together, however, they do not present a detailed and comprehensive account of the dialects since they focus mainly on aspects of the Gwentian dialect, which differed from other dialects. Compared with the collections of dialectal words and phrases, these observations on phonological, morphological and syntactical features form only a small part of his work on Welsh dialects.

G. J. Williams believed that Iolo Morganwg's lists of vocabulary contain important material for lexicographers and students of the history of the dialect of Glamorgan.[23] He also reckoned that these lists contained many more words which Iolo had heard on his travels in Glamorgan than he had believed genuine when he first examined them while preparing *Iolo Morganwg a Chywyddau'r Ychwanegiad* (1926). Having published the volume, he showed some of the word-lists to Dr Ceinwen Thomas, a native of Nantgarw in east Glamorgan, who informed him that many of the words contained in them were familiar to her mother and others from Nantgarw.[24] In an introduction to a list of words from Nantgarw, Dr Thomas explained that G. J. Williams had invited her to examine a list of words which he had compiled from Iolo Morganwg's word-lists in order to see how many of them formed part of the present-day dialect of Nantgarw. She enlisted the support of her mother and Mr Bromley Edmunds, who was described as a 'literate old man' in her later study of the dialect. The list which she published constitutes words used by Iolo which were familiar to Dr Thomas's mother and to Mr Edmunds, together with words used in Nantgarw which differed from those in Iolo's word-list but which had retained the same meaning. Dr Thomas's list reveals that at least some of the words which Iolo claimed were a part of the vocabulary of the Welsh of Glamorgan were still part of the vocabulary of Nantgarw. Some of the words Iolo claimed to be part of the Gwentian dialect may have no modern attestations, but that does not necessarily mean that his claims were false. When one bears in mind the enormous linguistic changes brought about in Glamorgan by the industrial revolution and the migration of Welsh speakers from other parts of Wales, as well as the Anglicization caused by the in-migration of monoglot English speakers, many words had clearly disappeared

---

[23] Williams: *IM*, p. 149.
[24] Ceinwen H. Thomas, 'Tafodiaith Nantgarw', *BBCS*, XVI, part 1 (1954), 95–102.

as a result of lexical erosion. Other words not attested by studies of the dialect could have been literary words given the status of vernacular words by Iolo, or indeed words which he himself had created.

Iolo Morganwg is well-known as the forger of many of the poems which appeared in the appendix of the edition of the poetry of Dafydd ap Gwilym published in 1789. Not until G. J. Williams published an article in *Y Beirniad* in 1919 and a much fuller discussion in *Iolo Morganwg a Chywyddau'r Ychwanegiad* in 1926 was it revealed that Iolo had forged numbers 70 and 80 of the poems in the main body of the work and the majority of the poems in the appendix. One of the methods used by G. J. Williams in detecting these forgeries was linguistic analysis. He discovered that the forgeries not only contained many words not previously attested in the Welsh language but that these apparently newly coined words also seemed to share common features and patterns. For example, Iolo appeared to have a predilection for certain prefixes, such as *gos-* (for example *gosgel, gosgan, gosgwydd*), suffixes, such as *-ineb* (for example *mosineb, gloesineb, brwsineb*) and other elements, such as *-tardd* and *-pwyll*, from which he formed untranslatable words such as *ffrwythlondardd* and *cyweirbwyll*. However, not all the words Iolo coined found their way into his forgeries. He sometimes coined terms openly in order to allow science, history, philosophy and other branches of learning to be treated in Welsh. Some of them, such as *amlen* (envelope), *blaenor* (elder) and *canolog* (central) have become an integral part of the modern Welsh language.

In his discussion of Iolo's word-lists, G. J. Williams reproduced one list in full. Entitled 'Words collected in Blaenau Morganwg, Anno 1770', it is of particular interest since Blaenau Morgannwg (Uplands of Glamorgan), and the year 1770 are mentioned.[25] Some 30 per cent of the words in this list are attested in the modern dialects of Glamorgan, 37 per cent have literary attestations predating 1770 (and thus could be examples of words used both in the spoken and written language, or literary words to which Iolo gave dialectal status), while the remaining 33 per cent are not attested in modern dialects and do not predate 1770. These may have been created by Iolo, but they may also be genuine dialectal words which perished before being recorded by another person.

An analysis of another word-list, 'Welsh Agricultural Terms, in Glamorgan' yields slightly different results.[26] Of these words 41 per cent were attested in modern-day Glamorgan dialects, 17 per cent had literary attestations predating Iolo's period, but no modern colloquial usage in Glamorgan, while 42 per cent had no literary attestations predating Iolo's period and no modern colloquial usage. Two of the words undocumented in modern colloquial Glamorgan

[25]   Williams: *IM*, pp. 147–8.
[26]   NLW 13098B, p. 247.

Welsh appear to be loan-words from English. The verb *bago*, which Iolo described as being a process connected to peas and beans, was almost certainly a borrowing from a dialectal English verb 'to bag', meaning 'to cut corn, peas, beans, etc close to the ground with a bagging hook'. The word was used in English counties bordering Wales and is also recorded in the English of Radnorshire. Another word, *bwtt*, is listed among different sorts of vehicles and is most likely to be a borrowing from the English 'butt', 'a type of cart'. The word was used in Somerset and Devon and we know that there was considerable migration of people between Glamorgan and these two English counties. Iolo himself was a familiar figure in the West Country.

Many of the words in this list which have no other evidence apart from that of Iolo are variations on an authentic original. For example, the verb *aru*, 'to plough, till land, cultivate' is first attested in a poem by Tudur Aled (*c.*1465–*c.*1525), but the derivative forms, *blaenaru*, *eilaru* and *croesaru*, have no such pedigree. The same pattern can be seen with *âr*, 'ploughed land, tilth', which dates back to the thirteenth century, but the derivatives *blaenar*, *eilar*, *croesar* and *attar* have no such history. The elements *blaen* (fore), *eil* (second, re-) and *croes* (cross) appear to have been added in order to create new compounds from *aru* and *âr*. This embellishment of authentic material, of filling in the gaps and providing more of the same, was Iolo's classic method of forging, and these derivative forms might well be the fruit of his imagination. However, the situation may be more complicated. The list contains a long section of words describing different kinds of land, all of which are compounds of the word *tir* (land). Of twenty-four, twelve predate Iolo and are to be found in the works of the *Cywyddwyr*. Eleven have no previous evidence for their existence, but three of them, *cleidir*, *tondir* and *mawndir*, are documented in studies of contemporary Welsh in Glamorgan, and one of those predating Iolo, *tywottir*, is also recorded as a vernacular word in Caernarfonshire. It cannot be claimed that Iolo had seen thirteen of these words, such as *marldir*, *gweirdir* and *meilliondir* in old manuscripts, attributed them to the Gwentian dialect and coined new ones following the same pattern, because similar forms have been recorded as part of the speech of Glamorgan in the twentieth century.

On the basis of his own observations on Welsh dialects, and the information he gleaned from Welsh dictionaries and grammars, Iolo was able to calculate how many dialects existed and where they were spoken. He was not the first to pay attention to dialectal variations in Welsh. The major divide was reckoned to be the difference between the Welsh of south Wales and that of north Wales. This, for example, was the basic division used by Edward Lhuyd in his *Archaeologia Britannica* (1707). Words marked as S[outh] W[ales] accounted for nearly half the dialectal words included, while N[orth] W[ales] was used for around a quarter of the words, and other descriptions were used for the remainder. Traditionally, the geographical distribution of dialectal words beyond

Fig. 23 A cartographic representation, based on Iolo Morganwg's writings, of the dialects of the Welsh language.

the basic north/south classification was described by using the names of counties and old administrative units either singly or in combination, for example 'Caernarvonshire and Meirionnydd', 'Glam. & Brec.', 'Monmouthshire and Herefordshire', and even 'the Counties of Monmouth, Hereford, Brecknock, and Glamorg'. Iolo clearly followed in this tradition in thinking about the relationship of dialects with one another and in denoting their geographical distribution. The dual division between the Welsh of north Wales and that of south Wales is evident in his writings, but he went further in differentiating between the Welsh of south-east Wales (the Gwentian or Silurian dialect) and that of the south-west (the Dimetian dialect). Iolo recalled the names of the ancient tribes and territories of the Silures and the Demetae in his nomenclature. It appears that he conceived of a triple division of the dialects – the Gwentian, the Dimetian and the Venedotian – from an early period. Whenever he discussed the history of the dialects and their relationship with the standard literary language, this triple division was central to his thinking. As we have seen, Iolo believed that the Gwentian dialect had served as Wales's first standard literary language and that it was used throughout Wales until the beginning of the fourteenth century. Thereafter, and until Iolo's own period, the Dimetian, or rather the Dimetian mixed with the Gwentian, formed the basis of the standard. Although William Morgan, the translator of the Bible into Welsh, was a native of north Wales, he had used the standard admixture of Dimetian and Gwentian, though he had allowed a few 'Northwalian Barbarisms' to slip through.[27]

Iolo described the geographical extent of the dialects by using county boundaries.[28] Gwentian was spoken in Glamorgan, Monmouthshire, the Welsh part of Herefordshire, and the southern part of Breconshire. Dimetian was spoken in Carmarthenshire, Cardiganshire, Pembrokeshire, parts of Breconshire, and Gower (in Glamorgan). Venedotian was spoken in north Wales. This triple division constituted a significant development in the history of dialect studies in Wales. It is true that Giraldus Cambrensis had considered the language of Cardiganshire a little different from that of north and south Wales, a sentiment repeated by Humphrey Llwyd in his *Breuiary of Britayne* (1573).[29] As we have seen, however, Edward Lhuyd went into some detail in noting the geographical extent of the Gwentian dialect, and his description, so similar to that by Iolo quoted above, must surely have played an important part in awakening Iolo's interest in the field of dialect studies.[30] Yet, as far as is known, Iolo Morganwg was the first to form a tripartite division of Welsh dialects. In this classification, the north remains as one unit, but the south is divided between the Gwentian dialect in the south-east and the Dimetian dialect in the south-west.

The description of the geographical extent of the Gwentian dialect appears to be the most complete. The greatest difficulty arises in seeking to draw the northern boundary of the area, since we cannot know with any certainty what Iolo meant by southern and eastern Breconshire. In another set of notes

[27] NLW 21419E, nos. 3, 19.
[28] Ibid., no. 19.
[29] Gerald of Wales, *The Description of Wales* (Harmondsworth, 1978), trans. Lewis Thorpe, p. 231; Humphrey Llwyd, *The Breuiary of Britayne* ([London], 1573), trans. Thomas Twyne, f. 75ᵛ.
[30] Edward Lhuyd, *Archaeologia Britannica* (Oxford, 1707), p. 227.

describing the most congenial places in which to collect information about different dialects, Iolo included Defynnog within the territory of the Gwentian dialect.[31]

In his description of the Dimetian dialect Iolo included Gower, though this may have been a reference to the cantref of Gower rather than the peninsula alone. Breconshire is problematic since it is impossible to ascertain which part of the county he planned to include within the territory of the Dimetian dialect. Glyn E. Jones's recent study of the spoken Welsh of Breconshire suggests that two main dialectal divides run through the county, one between the Defynnog area and Epynt, and the other between Epynt and the Llanwrtyd area.[32] These areas correspond closely to the old cantrefi of Cantref Mawr (the Defynnog area), Epynt in the Comos commote in Cantref Selyf, and Llanwrtyd in Cantref Buallt. Elements of the Welsh of Glamorgan continue into Breconshire, especially in the Defynnog area, and those elements common to the Welsh of mid- and north Wales begin in Breconshire, typically in the Llanwrtyd area, with the Epynt area acting as a link zone between the two.

Iolo located the Venedotian dialect in north Wales, but we do not know how he defined the north. It certainly contained the counties of Anglesey, Caernarfon, Denbigh and Flint, and a large part of Merioneth and Montgomery (presumably the northern parts). We know from the other set of notes previously mentioned that Machynlleth and Llanidloes were located in territory which we may refer to as a sub-dialect of the Venedotian dialect, namely the Powysian dialect. Thus, the southern boundary of the Venedotian dialect area can be drawn somewhere to the north of those towns. Corwen in Merioneth was noted as a collecting point for the Venedotian dialect.

The Powysian sub-dialect is interesting since it shows how three dialects became four. Although it is mentioned above as being in some sense part of the Venedotian dialect, in the draft of a linguistic questionnaire drawn up by Iolo he included a question seeking information on the different dialects of Welsh such as the Gwentian, Dimetian, Venedotian and Powysian dialects.[33] Here, the Powysian dialect did not appear as sub-dialect but rather as a dialect on equal footing with the other three. In a letter to William Owen Pughe, sent in 1805, Iolo expressed his desire to see collections of Welsh proverbs made in Cardiganshire (for the Dimetian dialect), Anglesey or Caernarfonshire, or

---

[31] NLW 13162A, p. 227. For the Venedotian dialect, he recommended Beddgelert, Corwen, Llannerchymedd or Aberffraw; for Powys: Llanidloes and Machynlleth; for the Dimetian dialect: Llanbadarn Fawr, Castellnewydd Emlyn, Whitland and Llandeilo; for the Silurian: Aberdâr, Defynnog, Gelli-gaer, Blaenau Gwent, Basaleg, Llancarfan and Ewyas (in Herefordshire).

[32] Glyn E. Jones, *Iaith Lafar Brycheiniog: Astudiaeth o'i Ffonoleg a'i Morffoleg* (Caerdydd, 2000), pp. [140], 147.

[33] NLW 13162A, p. 175.

within the confines of Arfon and Merioneth, or in the Iâl area for the Venedotian dialect.[34] He marked out the *cantrefi* of Arwystli and Maelienydd (roughly Montgomeryshire and north Radnorshire) as an area worthy of attention since the Silurian, Venedotian and Dimetian dialects met here in the Powysian dialect. This, he maintained, rendered the Powysian dialect particularly rich and 'peculiarly useful towards embellishing our literary dialect'.[35] This comment on the Powysian dialect as a meeting point for the other three main dialects corresponds in substance to Glyn E. Jones's depiction of Breconshire as a transitional zone.

In his proposed plans for the systematic collection of dialect material, discussed in greater detail below, Iolo revealed his eagerness to concentrate on areas where dialects were in their purest state. Dialectology has historically taken this stance, focusing on the language of elderly speakers in rural areas rather than on young urban speakers.

In a letter sent to William Owen Pughe in January 1806, Iolo mentioned dialectal variations in Welsh.[36] For south Wales he singled out as worthy of attention the Gwentian dialect, the dialect of the *cantrefi* of Emlyn, Cemais and Pebidiog (north Pembrokeshire) and that of Cardiganshire. The Welsh of Carmarthenshire, he complained, 'is so impure as to be of no use at all'.[37] He made similar remarks in another set of notes, praising the 'country Welsh' of Cilgerran, Cemais and Pebidiog for being 'equal in purity to that of any other part of Wales', and Cardiganshire Welsh for being 'not inferior to it'.[38] These are the dialects which, in his view, came closest to the modern literary dialect. The Welsh of Carmarthenshire, however, was condemned as being 'the most corrupt of any excepting that of the Northwalian borderers on Cheshire, Shropshire, &c.'.[39] The comparison with the Welsh spoken by people living on the northern borders with England suggests that the corruption he referred to was the influence of English upon Welsh. It is difficult, therefore, to understand why he should have had such a low opinion of Carmarthenshire Welsh. In yet another set of notes, he claimed that the Dimetian dialect of Cardiganshire and the Welsh hundreds of Pembrokeshire was 'justly considered as the Standard of the modern Literary dialect'.[40] Yet, in an earlier letter to William Owen Pughe, written in 1800, Iolo argued that the Welsh of Cardiganshire was not purely Dimetian and that it contained many features of the Venedotian dialect.[41]

---

[34] NLW 13224B, p. 37, Iolo Morganwg to William Owen Pughe, 23 September 1805.
[35] Ibid.
[36] NLW 13221E, pp. 151–4, Iolo Morganwg to William Owen Pughe, 9 January 1806.
[37] Ibid., p. 153.
[38] NLW 13121B, p. 477.
[39] Ibid.
[40] Ibid., p. 478.
[41] NLW 13222C, p. 143.

In his use of the names of the old *cantrefi* to specify an area smaller than a whole county, as with Emlyn, Cemais and Pebidiog above, Iolo followed in the footsteps of Edward Lhuyd and other lexicographers. However, he made relatively little use of these descriptors. For example, he used the descriptor 'Glam[organshire]' over a thousand times in his collections, the combined descriptor 'Monmouthshire and Glamorganshire' sixteen times, and the second most widely used combined descriptor, 'Gwent and Glamorganshire', six times. Despite the relatively low occurrence of these descriptors, it is evident that Iolo understood that the boundaries of dialect areas do not always follow county boundaries neatly and that variations can occur within and across boundaries.

In the case of the Gwentian dialect Iolo sometimes linked Monmouthshire (or more particularly the western part of it) with Glamorgan, particularly its eastern parts. While the Dimetian (with the exception of Carmarthenshire Welsh) came closest to the modern literary dialect, Iolo claimed that 'the Dialect of Monmouthshire and East Glamorgan come[s] the nearest of any of the present vernacular Dialects to the Ancient literary dialect'.[42] In the same manuscript, he wrote more specifically of 'monmouthshire and the North eastern parts of Glamorgan'. Particularly interesting are the examples of words which Iolo claimed were in use in east Glamorgan and Monmouthshire and whose meanings, or synonyms, he compared with other parts of the Gwentian region. For example, he claimed that 'coethi' was used in the Vale of Glamorgan in the sense of fluency of speech, but that the word meant 'to evaporate' in Monmouthshire.[43] As well as the contrast between east and west Glamorgan, Iolo also offered evidence of differences in pronunciation between the north and the south of the county; for example, the word 'creulosg' (unattested anywhere else, but said to mean 'charcoal') was pronounced as 'croelosg' in the Vale of Glamorgan and as 'creulosg' in the rest of the county.[44] The emerging pattern was that a contrast existed between (a) an area which included east (or north-east Glamorgan) and the Welsh-speaking eastern parts of Monmouthshire (that is Gwynllwg and Gwent Uwch Coed) and the rest of Glamorgan; (b) between the Blaenau, or the Uplands (the north) and the Vale (the south); (c) between the west and the Vale. Recent work on the dialects of Glamorgan appear to support these three basic divisions.[45] Glamorgan can be

---

[42] NLW 13121B, p. 477.

[43] NLW 13103B, p. 158. According to *GPC*, 'coethi' (evaporate) dates from the sixteenth century, but it is not recorded by anyone other than Iolo as being a Monmouthshire word. Thomas Richards noted in 1753 that 'coethi' meant 'to prate, to be pert and talkative, in Glamorg'. Thomas Richards, *Antiquae Linguae Britannicae Thesaurus* (Bristol, 1753), sig. MI[r-v].

[44] NLW 13098B, p. 266.

[45] Peter Wynn Thomas, 'Glamorgan Revisited: Progress Report and Some Emerging Distribution Patterns', *Cardiff Working Papers in Welsh Linguistics*, 3 (1984), 119.

split into two major regions: east and west. Within the east, the region can be split into north-east, south and the Nedd area. The west can also be divided into three: Dulais, Tawe–Llwchwr Isaf, and the west.

If we were to take all of Iolo's observations into account, a map of the dialects of Welsh would reveal four main dialect areas: Gwentian in the south-east; Dimetian in the south-west; Powysian in mid-Wales; and Venedotian in the north. The Gwentian dialect area can be divided into three: east Glamorgan and Monmouthshire, south Glamorgan and west Glamorgan. The Dimetian can also be divided into three: Cardiganshire, north Pembrokeshire and Carmarthenshire. There is less evidence that Iolo perceived any significant differences within the Venedotian region, but it was divided into three for the purposes of collecting material: Anglesey and Caernarfonshire, Denbighshire and Flintshire, and (northern) Montgomeryshire and Merioneth. The Powysian dialect was located in south Merioneth, Montgomeryshire and north Radnorshire.

On the basis of his reading and observations, Iolo Morganwg succeeded in formulating a surprisingly complex view of the geographical distribution of the Welsh dialects. Like Iolo Morganwg, John Rhŷs (1840–1915) divided Welsh dialects into the same basic four and illustrated this on a map.[46] It is true that Rhŷs delineated the areas more precisely than Iolo and that his conclusions were based on more objective evidence than that of Iolo, but it is also fair to say that Iolo had reached the same basic conclusions nearly a century before Rhŷs undertook his work. In his *Linguistic Geography of Wales* (1973) Alan R. Thomas refined the classification further, indicating that six main areas could be distinguished: the north-west, the north-east, west Midlands, east Midlands, the south-west and the south-east.[47]

Iolo collected his dialect material on his own. He described his method to William Owen Pughe:

> I have rambled over all Wales with all my ears open to every local word, idiom, peculiarity of pronunciation, of construction and have attended more than perhaps ever any one did before to the language in every part of the Country.[48]

Although the fruit of his rambles suggest a haphazard approach, he had a plan in mind and his work in collecting data was conducted in a serious manner: 'I can, amongst other things, give the peculiarities of our several dialects better than most, for I have rambled deliberately over all Wales with all my ears open to every word and sound of the language.'[49] However, Iolo was also aware of

---

[46] NLW 2473C, p. 1.
[47] Alan R. Thomas, *The Linguistic Geography of Wales: A Contribution to Welsh Dialectology* (Cardiff, 1973).
[48] NLW 13222C, p. 162, Iolo Morganwg to William Owen Pughe, 15 February 1803.
[49] NLW 13224B, p. 32, Iolo Morganwg to William Owen Pughe, 15 August 1805.

his own limitations and saw the advantages of collecting material in a wider and more systematic way. He suggested several different plans which involved local teams working in collaboration. These plans had three elements in common: they made use of amateurs, involved cooperation, and required external sponsorship.

The first of these plans was mooted by Iolo Morganwg to Owen Jones (Owain Myfyr) in April 1800.[50] In effect, it was a plan to collect folklore of all kinds. Iolo's intention was to have one person, preferably a native, in each county and that these collectors would then use their personal networks to gather information. The work would be conducted under the auspices of the Gwyneddigion Society based in London, and a prize of five to ten guineas would be offered for the best collection in each county. He suggested beginning in the north, no doubt in order to win the support of the largely northern-based members of the Gwyneddigion, before moving southward. He named potential collectors, among them Walter Davies (Gwallter Mechain), Robert Davies (Bardd Nantglyn), Peter Bailey Williams and William Williams, Llandygái.

Iolo was so greatly excited by this idea that he wrote another letter on the subject five days later, this time to William Owen Pughe.[51] He hoped that Pughe would urge Owain Myfyr to put the scheme into practice, and in his letter he offered further detail regarding the organization of the collecting. He suggested dividing the north into three regions and allowing three years for the work to take place. A prize of £5 would be given to the best collection in each region, £3 to the runner-up and £2 to the third. By taking one region each year the whole of north Wales could be covered within three years, and the south could be divided in similar fashion and could either be covered after all the collecting in the north had been completed or a region in the north could be studied alternately with a region in the south. The total cost would be £60 over a period of six years (assuming that the south would be divided into three regions). Iolo generously and freely offered his own collections as a spur to others.

The Gwyneddigion Society apparently showed no interest in these schemes, and Iolo wrote five years later to William Owen Pughe outlining a similar kind of project. In this letter Iolo expressed his desire to see that collections of proverbs were made in various parts of Wales in order to provide excellent examples of dialects and enable 'any Common Welshman, that can read and write tolerably' to bring the plans to fruition.[52]

Perhaps the most interesting of Iolo's collecting schemes was outlined in a draft of a treatise on 'corruptions' in Welsh.[53] The collection plan was similar

[50]   BL Add. 15024, f. 310ʳ, Iolo Morganwg to Owain Myfyr, 10 April 1800.
[51]   NLW 13224B, p. 17, Iolo Morganwg to William Owen Pughe, 15 April 1800.
[52]   NLW 13221E, pp. 131–4, Iolo Morganwg to William Owen Pughe, 23 October 1805.
[53]   NLW 13129A, pp. 113–15.

to those mentioned above, but this time the Gwyneddigion Society was not involved. Instead, Iolo suggested that the collections or reports be presented to a committee, which would form the basis of a Welsh academy. Its full name would be 'The Welsh Corresponding Academy for the Restoring to its Pristine Purity the Ancient British or Welsh Language'. It would have a fixed number of elected members to represent the regions where different dialects were spoken. On the basis of the research, the academy would decide which dialectal words or features would be admitted into the standard literary language and ensure that the prejudices of individuals in favour of or against different dialects would not hold sway. This was possibly the first ever blueprint for collective corpus planning on behalf of the Welsh language. Not least among the many faces of Iolo Morganwg, therefore, was his acute sensitivity to the resources of expression of vernacular languages and, in particular, his attempt to standardize the Welsh literary language on the basis of spoken dialects.

15

Iolo Morganwg and Traditional Music

DANIEL HUWS

Traditional music was never more than a marginal interest for Iolo Morganwg, and writing it down appears to have been his habit for little more than a decade, *c.*1795–1806. Yet the fruit of this interest during these few years, even though it amounted to a mere sixty tunes or so, is sufficient to earn Iolo credit as the first collector of Welsh folk-songs. This assertion must be qualified by the observation that the words of what are clearly Welsh 'folk-songs', and *penillion*, are commonly found in manuscripts from the mid-sixteenth century onwards, but without music, while a few isolated cases of words with their music occur before 1800.[1] Iolo's surviving notations, moreover, have the virtue of being, so far as one can be sure in these matters, faithful ones, given the limits of his skill as a notator. With one or two possible exceptions, they are free of the suspicion which taints many of the literary texts that came from his hand. The tunes reflect what we might call Iolo's Aristotelian mode – that which gave scope to his acute powers of observation – as opposed to his Platonic mode – that of a codifier of a constitution for his bardic republic. We arrive at the curious fact that, whereas publications of Welsh music before and during Iolo's day come in heavy druidical garb (as, after his time, did Breton ballads, in La Villemarqué's *Barzaz-Breiz*), his own contribution – not that it was ever published – steps out in rustic innocence.

There are collections of music made to go out into the world simply for the benefit of performing musicians; there are others which carry with them a satchel of tracts. In Wales the Robert ap Huw manuscript, written in 1613, and which contains a repertoire of late-medieval harp music, stands, in relation to later collections, beyond an unbridgeable chasm.[2] Apart from a few Welsh airs

---

[1] *Penillion* (stanzas) or, usually, in modern Welsh, *hen benillion* (old stanzas), generally free-standing, often epigrammatic, 'floaters', are an integral part of the folk-song tradition. Many folk-songs incorporate *penillion*, while some consist of little more than a *mélange* of *penillion*. It is because of their association with 'canu gyda'r tannau' or 'canu penillion', the old Welsh custom of singing extempore stanzas to the harp, that *penillion* tend to be treated apart. This custom, as will appear below, is what gave *penillion* special status in the eyes of antiquaries.

[2] The best survey of traditional Welsh music is W. S. Gwynn Williams, *Welsh National Music and*

printed in *Aria di Camera* (*c*.1727), from the eighteenth century we have two precious Welsh manuscript collections of fiddle music, that of John Thomas, *c*.1752, and of Maurice Edwards, 1778, and three mid-eighteenth-century collections made by harpers.[3] All these are collections made for personal use or perhaps for other musicians. The well-known published collections, however – those of John Parry (the earliest in 1742) and Edward Jones – came with doctrinal baggage. The genesis of the doctrine seems to lie in Edward Lhuyd's *Archaeologia Britannica* (1707), in which he published three of the 'Juvencus' *englynion* from the earliest surviving manuscript to contain Welsh poetry.[4] His view was that the form of these *englynion*, the *englyn milwr*, was the earliest verse-form in the Brittonic languages, and that ''twas in this sort of meeter the Druids taught their disciples'.[5]

Lewis Morris's sharp eye saw the implications of Lhuyd's discovery. In 1738, as a New Year gift for his patron, Owen Meyrick of Bodorgan, he wrote his essay 'On the Cambro British Musick', which he described as 'a small tract on our British custom of singing with the harp'. He elaborated on the metres of the *penillion*, including the *englyn milwr*, and maintained:

> Those that were time-proof were transmitted to us by oral Tradition being sung to the harp from age to age and seldom if ever committed to writing. This is one of y[e] plainest marks I can see of y[e] remains of druidical Learning left among us perhaps not to be met with in any other nation. This observation opens a new and pleasant scene of things unheard of in our age, which like a distant Landskip appears pretty enough to persons concerned.[6]

A few years later, in 1742, the first published collection of Welsh music appeared: John Parry and Evan Williams's *Antient British Music*. Its full title was: *Antient British Music or, a Collection of Tunes, never before published, which are retained by the Cambro-Britons, (more particularly in North-Wales) and supposed, by the learned, to be the Remains of the Music of the Antient Druids, so famed in Roman History*. In 1741 Evan Williams had asked Lewis Morris for help in connection with this publication.[7] We can, on the good authority of Richard Morris in his

---

Dance (London, 1932), supplemented by the article 'Wales: Traditional Music' in Stanley Sadie (ed.), *The New Grove Dictionary of Music and Musicians* (29 vols., 2nd edn., London, 2001). On the Robert ap Huw Manuscript, see the special issue of *WMH* 3 (1999).

[3] John Thomas's manuscript has been admirably edited by Cass Meurig, *Alawon John Thomas: A Fiddler's Tune-book from Eighteenth-century Wales* (Aberystwyth, 2004); Maurice Edwards's collection is UWB, Bangor 2294; on the harpers' manuscripts, see Daniel Huws, 'Tair o Lawysgrifau Telynorion', *Welsh Music / Cerddoriaeth Cymru*, 4, no. 9 (1975), 24–32.

[4] Edward Lhuyd, *Archaeologia Britannica* (Oxford, 1707), p. 221.

[5] Ibid., p. 250.

[6] Hugh Owen (ed.), *Additional Letters of the Morrises of Anglesey (1735–1786)* (2 vols., London, 1947–9), I, p. 74.

[7] J. H. Davies (ed.), *The Letters of Lewis, Richard, William and John Morris of Anglesey, (Morrisiaid Môn) 1728–1765* (2 vols., Aberystwyth, 1907–9), I , p. 60.

copy of *Antient British Music*, attribute to his brother, Lewis, the 'Historical Account' prefixed to the collection.[8] This, 'An Historical Account of the Rise and Progress of Music among the Antient Britons; wherin the Errors of Dr Powel, and his Editor Mr Wynne, on that subject, in their History of Wales, are pointed out and confuted; and the whole set in its own true and proper Light', provided justification for the title. The 'error' to be confuted was the assertion that Welsh music, for the most part, 'either came over from Ireland, with the said Prince [Gruffudd ap Cynan] and his Irish musicians, or was composed by them afterwards'. Lewis Morris thought the British music 'to be entirely our own, and a Remains of Druidism'. The key to his thinking is revealed in these words: 'The peculiar Air of their Music, and Method of Singing, plainly shews it, even at this distance of Time.'[9] If the *englyn milwr* and *triban* were survivors, he reasoned, so, too, was the transmission of learning and wisdom in such verse-forms, and so, too, the accompanying harp music. *Penillion*-singing, so vigorous a tradition in Anglesey at that time, so beloved by Lewis Morris and his family, was thus a legacy of the Druids (we can hear Iolo's snort!). In later years, Lewis Morris would have expressed himself more guardedly.

John Parry's second volume devoted to Welsh music, *British Harmony* (1781), eschewed the druidic claim by describing itself on the title-page simply as 'a Collection of Antient Welsh Airs the traditional Remains of those originally sung by the Bards of Wales'. But three years later the most influential work of Welsh music before Victorian times, *Musical and Poetical Relicks of the Welsh Bards* (1784), was published by Edward Jones. This was a large collection of Welsh harp music, introduced by a 29-page 'historical account of the Welsh bards and their music and poetry', and containing a further section on 'Welsh pennillion'. A revised and much expanded edition appeared in 1794 and another in 1808. The iconic frontispiece, found in all editions, is an engraving of a painting by Philippe de Loutherbourg of a harper, with a triple harp, on a crag above a river, accompanied by the quotation which inspired the painting, from Thomas Gray's poem *The Bard*: 'On a rock whose haughty brow/ Frowns o'er old Conway's foaming flood . . . loose his beard, and hoary hair.'[10] Gray's poem had, in turn, been inspired by his hearing the playing of John Parry.[11]

Edward Jones, 'Bardd y Brenin', harper to the Prince of Wales, was a touchy, sensitive and reclusive bachelor.[12] His reading was wide, his research painstaking;

8   BL Add. 14939. Added in Richard Morris's hand at the beginning of the printed text of *Antient British Music* (1742) is 'By Lewis Morris Esq.' (p. 1) and at the end 'L. Morris' (p. 6).
9   John Parry and Evan Williams, *Antient British Music* (London, 1742), p. 3.
10   Roger Lonsdale (ed.), *The Poems of Thomas Gray, William Collins, Oliver Goldsmith* (London, 1969), pp. 177–200.
11   Ibid., p. 179.
12   On Edward Jones, see Tecwyn Ellis, *Edward Jones Bardd y Brenin, 1752–1824* (Caerdydd, 1957); on his use, and rejection, of Iolo's ideas, see idem, 'Bardd y Brenin, Iolo Morganwg a

in discussing the Druids and *penillion*, he assembled in his long introduction the received antiquarian thinking of the time. He was scrupulous to the point of pedantry, and ponderous in style. The few examples in the *Relicks* of Welsh words accompanying the music are single stanzas, mostly *penillion*.[13] Nothing suggests that Edward Jones regarded other forms of folk-song, whether lyric folk-songs, *carolau* (carols) in the Huw Morys tradition (still then immensely popular in north Wales) or ballads, as venerable enough to be considered 'relicks'. He was again following received opinion. But with regard to the music, as distinct from the words, he had no received opinion to guide him. The *Relicks*, therefore, is a good representation of the repertoire of north Wales harpers of the generation or two preceding Edward Jones, and of a few singers.[14] As is now well recognized, many of the tunes are no older than the eighteenth century; some are of English or Continental origin; the manner is more Welsh than the roots.[15] Although Edward Jones was musically educated and a gifted performer, his uncritical cast of mind extended to music. The musically uneducated Iolo, as we shall see, because of his understanding of Welsh prosody had a surer feeling for what was primitive. The later editions of the *Relicks*, and Edward Jones's other collections of Welsh music, *The Bardic Museum* (1802) and *Hen Ganiadau Cymru* (1820 and 1825), reveal the cumulative influence of Iolo's druidic ideas, which had reached him through the credulous mediation of William Owen Pughe.

Iolo had been known in Welsh circles in London since 1773 (Edward Jones arrived in 1774–5). Like other London Welshmen of literary bent, he became familiar with Richard Morris's collection of manuscripts, which included a large part of his brother Lewis's collection. He was probably aware of the attribution to Lewis Morris of the 'Historical Account' prefixed to *Antient British Music*. Iolo's relationship to Lewis Morris could, if one chose, be viewed in terms of 'anxiety of influence'. Like Iolo, Morris was an extraordinarily gifted man; like Iolo, he was torn between literary and scholarly ambition; and, like Iolo, he died with his great dreamed-of *opus* far from complete. Iolo's reaction to Lewis Morris became extreme: no good could be said of him. This reaction

---

Derwyddiaeth', *NLWJ*, XIII (1963–4), 147–56, 224–34, 356–62; XIV (1965–6), 183–93, 321–9, 424–36; XV (1967), 177–96.

[13]   In the 1794 edition we find, besides six *penillion*, three other short stanzas: the first verse of a ballad, 'Cerdd yr hen wr o'r coed' ('The song of the old man of the wood'), of 'Dadl dau' ('Flaunting two'), and 'Suo-gân' ('The lullaby song').

[14]   Among his few named sources are the harper Evan Tynwern, Edward Jones of Mold and Richard Owen of Trawsfynydd, 'who was a very old man and is since dead. From his playing I wrote down several of the best Welsh tunes, and from several of the old singers in different parts of Wales'. See Ellis, *Edward Jones*, p. 86 and idem, 'Bardd y Brenin', *NLWJ*, XIII, 234, n. 40.

[15]   Ellis, *Edward Jones*, pp. 88–90; Joan Rimmer, 'Edward Jones's Musical and Poetical Relicks of the Welsh Bards: A Re-assessment', *The Galpin Society Journal*, 39 (1986), 77–96, reprinted in *CG*, 10 (1987), 26–42.

might alone have been sufficient to immunize Iolo against associating Welsh music with the Druids, even if this association, in connection with *penillion* (of which Iolo was a connoisseur) had not been taken up by Edward Jones in the introduction of the *Relicks*. Iolo was among those who had provided Edward Jones with information for this introduction. While he showed little interest in the musical contents, the introduction dealt with matters after Iolo's own heart. Probably already in 1784, and certainly by 1794, Iolo had a more profound and subtle knowledge of the Welsh bardic tradition than any of his contemporaries. His own ideas were well formed. Edward Jones, in his introduction to the *Relicks*, had occupied ground which Iolo regarded as his own and had thereby queered his pitch. Seizing on the excuse that Jones had failed to acknowledge his help (given at the request of John Walters) and that he had not been sent his promised copy of the 1784 edition, Iolo turned his venom on the harper.[16] Edward Jones became 'Humstrum Jones', an object of unfailing mockery and scorn;[17] he joined, as Edward Davies would later, the long-dead Lewis Morris, Henry Rowlands and Moses Williams in Iolo's gallery of rogues, trespassers on his domain.

In 1791 Iolo went up to London. His main aim was to collect subscriptions for his proposed volume of English poems and to arrange for their publication. After the productive years of 1777–81, during which he had written much of his best Welsh poetry, Iolo had married and entered a period of hardship. The seeker of fame who went up to London in 1791 was not young, and once there, things moved slowly. He remained in London, with short breaks, until 1795. These were years of the propagation of many of his cultural ideas among the London Welsh, of political radicalism, years in which the bardic ceremonies were held on Primrose Hill and years also of depressions and perhaps of over-indulgence in laudanum. *Poems, Lyric and Pastoral* was eventually published in two volumes in 1794. The work in which so much hope had been invested brought recognition, if not fame, but not what Iolo needed most: money.[18] He returned to Glamorgan in 1795 a disappointed man. At this point in his life, turning his back on the capital and its false allure and returning to his first trade, like Robert Burns before him, and John Clare after him, he decided to collect folk-songs.

---

[16]   There is evidence that his copy was in fact sent: see Ellis, *Edward Jones*, p. 23.

[17]   Iolo had no doubt taken his cue from Edward Jones's solemn words in his section on the musical instruments of the Welsh: 'I am sorry I can give no certain account of those two incomparable instruments, the Salt-Box and the Hum-Strum, or Hurdy-Gourdy; but it is reasonable to conclude, that the first was usually performed on at festivals, and the other at funerals, and on serious occasions.' Edward Jones, *Musical and Poetical Relicks of the Welsh Bards* (London, 1794), p. 107.

[18]   For a full account of these years in London and the publication of *Poems, Lyric and Pastoral*, see chapter 6 above.

Robert Burns's good fortune was to be born in Scotland. Eighteenth-century Scotland enjoyed a peculiar literary gusto and had become accustomed, even before the dawn of Romanticism, to seeing traditional songs, and their tunes, in print. Burns would have come to know the collections of Allan Ramsay's songs, the tunes in *Orpheus Caledoneus* (1725), David Herd's large collection of traditional song (without music), *Ancient and Modern Scottish Songs* (1776), and Patrick Macdonald's *A Collection of Highland Vocal Airs* (1784); he later plundered the last two for his own ends.[19] Inspired by Herder, Germany saw collections of folk-song in print before 1800. In England and France, on the other hand, however great the impact of Romantic literature, however diligent the searches of antiquaries for ancient national epic and narrative song, and however ready the literary public was to enthuse over ancient song from the fringes of civilization, such as the Celtic west, indigenous folk-song remained more or less invisible for another half century. It took the disturbed genius of two poets, John Clare (1793–1864) in England and Gérard Nerval (1808–55) in France, to uncover its richness. An influential article by Nerval in 1842 with a plea that France begin to emulate other countries and collect its folk-songs was answered in 1852 when, in best French fashion, a committee was set up, by imperial decree, to collect the nation's folk-songs.[20] John Clare's discovery, in contrast, remained secret, and his collection of words and of music, like that of Iolo, languished in manuscript until the twentieth century.[21] Meanwhile, folk-song collecting in England made its belated and hesitant start.

While Burns, as will be seen, played a direct role in Iolo Morganwg's story, the other poets, younger men, did not. But before we leave them it may be illuminating to dwell on some similarities. Just as Burns could be called the first collector of Scottish song and Iolo of Welsh song, so could Clare be called the first collector of English folk-song.[22] These three run counter to the common-place that the typical collector of the music of a country (or of dance or oral literature or folklore) is an outsider, of different nationality or class. The three poets – each the child of poor parents, each brought up to follow his father's calling, each turning to poetry while young and showing a marked gift for both satire and pastiche, and, for a while, enjoying recognition in his capital city as a peasant poet, each with a radical streak – all came from within the traditions

---

[19] See Francis Collinson, *The Traditional and National Music of Scotland* (London, 1966), chapter IV; James Kinsley, 'The Music of the Heart' in D. A. Low (ed.), *Critical Essays on Robert Burns* (London, 1985), pp. 124–36.

[20] On Nerval and folk-song, see Paul Bénichou, *Nerval et la chanson folklorique* (Paris, 1970).

[21] On Clare in this context, see George Deacon, *John Clare and the Folk Tradition* (London, 1983) and Jonathan Bate, *John Clare: A Biography* (London, 2003), chapter 5.

[22] On the grounds that literary circles in Newcastle were closer in spirit to those of Edinburgh than London, this ignores the rightful claim of John Bell (1783–1864), whose collection, *Rhymes of Northern Bards*, was published in Newcastle in 1812. Bell also collected tunes, which survived in manuscript.

whose songs they collected. They were, indeed, so much part of their own traditions that the boundaries between their roles as collector, editor and poet often
dissolved. There was one great difference between them: Burns, because of the
encouragement he received from Edinburgh publishers, saw into print most of
the songs he collected, as he did his own poetry. The songs collected by Iolo and
John Clare, like most of their own poetry, remained unpublished.[23]

Nerval, well-born, highly educated, moving among the intelligentsia of
Paris, proclaiming the poetry in folk-song but collecting only the words, is a
different case. Yet he, too, may help us understand something of Iolo's complex
mind. Nerval, like Clare, began in later life to suffer periods of madness and
became obsessed with memories of childhood love. He went wandering in the
Valois of his youth, recording his experiences, describing the lost world
conjured up by the old songs. Iolo, like Burns, preserved his sanity. But to what
degree was his poetic inspiration rooted, like that of Clare and Nerval, in
memories of a vanished Eden? Besides songs and customs, both Iolo and Clare
delighted in recording the games of childhood.[24]

The first collection of the poems of Robert Burns, published in Kilmarnock
in 1786, was a sensation. One frequently reprinted review, which the ever-alert
Iolo must have read, spoke of the 'heavenly-taught ploughman' and invoked
the name of Shakespeare.[25] Editions were published the following year in
Edinburgh and London. Burns was famous and his fame never lapsed. But he
soon grew disillusioned with Edinburgh society and returned to the country.
He had begun to collect traditional songs as early as 1785, but it was after his
return from Edinburgh that he threw himself into collecting: 'I have been
absolutely crazed about it, collecting old stanzas, and every information
remaining, respecting their origin, authors, etc.'[26] In Edinburgh he had met
James Johnson, a music publisher, who was on the point of bringing out the
first volume of his *The Scots Musical Museum* (1787–1803), an ambitious
collection of songs and music. Johnson roused Burns's enthusiasm for his publication. From 1787 until his death in 1796 Burns collected, composed and, to
a large degree, acted as editor of the songs in the later volumes of *The Scots
Musical Museum*. Providing material for Johnson's collection became the main
focus of his creative life. In the process he increasingly turned to the songs and
the language of his upbringing. 'These English verses gravel me to death', he

---

[23] Much of Iolo's poetry first saw print in Tegwyn Jones (ed.), *Y Gwir Degwch: Detholiad o
Gywyddau Serch Iolo Morganwg* (Bow Street, 1980), a collection of Iolo's poetry in strict metre,
and in *CRhIM*. The comprehensive five-volume edition of the poetry of John Clare under
the general editorship of Eric Robinson has recently been completed (Oxford, 1984–2003).
The common ground shared by Burns, Iolo and Clare is surveyed in more detail in Daniel
Huws, *Caneuon Llafar Gwlad ac Iolo a'i Fath* (Cymdeithas Alawon Gwerin Cymru, 1993).

[24] Deacon, *John Clare and the Folk Tradition*, pp. 283–96; Williams: *IM*, pp. 35–72.

[25] D. A. Low (ed.), *Robert Burns: The Critical Heritage* (London, 1974), pp. 67–71.

[26] J. De Lancey Ferguson and G. Ross Roy (eds.), *The Letters of Robert Burns* (2nd edn., 2 vols.,
Oxford, 1985), I, p. 168.

commented when asked by Thomson, another music publisher for whom he provided words, for songs in English rather than Scots.[27] The six volumes of *The Scots Musical Museum*, completed in 1803, contained over 600 songs. Burns had been responsible for more than a third of them, as collector, author or polisher.[28] He also provided over a hundred songs for the five volumes of Thomson's *A Select Collection of Original Scottish Airs for the Voice* (1793–1818). By his contributions to these two collections Burns had, within some ten years, changed the face of the folk-song tradition in Scotland.

The observant Iolo could not have failed to notice the sudden fame of the ploughman poet and the way in which Burns had drawn on his native tradition of song. Among books which Iolo had possessed in London in 1794 were a volume of Burns's poems and two, if not three, volumes of Scottish songs.[29] In a list of 'Subjects for New Songs, Odes &c by E W', dated 1791, Iolo noted a song in the metre of 'Auld Lang Syne', which had appeared in the first volume of the *Musical Museum*.[30] For his own *Poems, Lyric and Pastoral*, Iolo took Burns's collection as a model.[31] When Iolo read the biography of Burns by James Currie, published in 1800, he copied from it into a notebook several quotations, among them 'Burns usually composed while walking in the open air' (clear self-identification) and 'There is no species of Poetry . . . so much calculated to influence the morals as well as the happiness of a people, as those popular verses which are associated with national airs.'[32]

A recurrent theme in Iolo's writing about Welsh literature was the difference between the traditions of north and south Wales.[33] In asserting the superiority of the southern tradition he constantly emphasized the flourishing there of *canu teuluaidd* (domestic song) – more civilized, one might almost say more romantic – beginning in the twelfth century with Rhys Goch ap Rhicert (one of Iolo's most inspired literary fictions), and coming down to Wil Hopcyn and Dafydd Nicolas in the eighteenth century, poets whose songs were in oral circulation in Iolo's own day and which were preserved in his manuscripts. Iolo more than once compared this tradition of *canu teuluaidd* with Scottish song: for instance, 'Some of the South Walian popular songs have all the beautiful simplicity of the Scottish popular poetry.'[34] As so often, he had hit upon a truth

---

[27] Ibid., II, p. 318.

[28] Introduction to Donald Low (ed.), reprint of *The Scots Musical Museum* (Aldershot, 1991); C. T. Davie, 'Robert Burns, Writer of Songs' in Low (ed.), *Critical Essays on Robert Burns*, pp. 157–85.

[29] NLW 13136A, pp. 137–57. The volumes were: 'Burn's Poems' and 'Scots Songs and Ballads', both 8vo, and 'Musical Miscellany, Scots, etc.' and 'Select Poems (Glasgow)', both 12mo.

[30] NLW 13136A, pp. 87–94.

[31] See chapter 6 above.

[32] NLW 13146A, p. 4.

[33] This is explored in Cathryn Charnell-White, *Barbarism and Bardism: North Wales versus South Wales in the Bardic Vision of Iolo Morganwg* (Aberystwyth, 2004).

[34] NLW 13138A, p. 71. See also the comment quoted in Williams: *IM*, p. 61, n. 49.

and, as usual, had clothed it with his own preconceptions and theories. Scottish songs, with their directness and freshness, could favourably be compared to most contemporary English poetry, and so, in much the same way, could popular south Wales songs familiar to Iolo, such as 'Bugeila'r Gwenith Gwyn' (Watching the White Wheat) or 'Y Ferch o'r Sger' (The Maid of Sker), be compared to the laboured *awdlau* (odes) and *cywyddau* and the long, intricate *carolau* still favoured by most north Wales poets. Iolo's perception was acute, but his argument was skewed. What to us is interesting about its poetry and music is that south Wales had remained more or less immune to developments in the north; it was conservative. Ancient but uncanonical metres, and associated tunes, were still current; the tradition of *carolau* (the tradition popularized by Huw Morys) with its host of appropriated English tunes, had scarcely taken hold; nor had the triple harp, which had been prevalent in north Wales since the early eighteenth century.[35] The triple harp got Iolo into particular difficulty: it was already so firmly the national instrument that he could hardly vaunt the much older one, the single harp, still played in Glamorgan. The tradition that the triple harp had been introduced into Wales by Elis Siôn Siamas of Llanfachreth in the reign of Queen Anne was recorded from a north Wales harper by Iolo himself: to this he felt bound to add that his own mother had told him that when she was young a harper of that name had played the triple harp in the houses of the Glamorgan gentry.[36]

A correspondent who shared Iolo's interest in tunes and *penillion* was William Owen Pughe,[37] the son of an able *penillion*-singer from Merioneth, a county regarded even in the eighteenth century as the chief home of that art. Pughe's son, Aneurin, the later editor of Welsh law texts, was also a collector of Welsh music. In 1802, at the height of his period of interest in music, Iolo sent Pughe some *penillion* with their tunes.[38] In response, he suggested that Iolo prepare 'a little publication consisting of some of our old singular Tunes', to which Iolo replied that he had not the time.[39] In 1803 Iolo sent his friend a copy of the words of 'our favorite (at least in Glamorgan) Welsh song of Ffanni Blodau'r Ffair', adding that he had promised to help with

> a little volume of South-Walian Songs to be published at Merthyr Tudfyl. Ffanni Blodau'r Ffair will be one. I shall be able to furnish about 30 or 40 very decent songs from the time of Henry the 7th (and three or four perhaps that are older) down to

---

[35] On the absence of the triple harp and survival of the single harp, see John Thomas (Ieuan Ddu), 'The Harps and Harpers of Gwent and Morganwg', *Cambrian Journal*, II (1855), 191–202.

[36] NLW 13144A, p. 277; NLW 13146A, pp. 417–18.

[37] We are fortunate to have an excellent biography by Glenda Carr, *William Owen Pughe* (Caerdydd, 1983).

[38] NLW 13221E, pp. 91–4, Iolo Morganwg to William Owen Pughe, 19 December 1802, quoted in Williams: *IM*, pp. 61–2.

[39] Ibid., p. 100, Iolo Morganwg to William Owen Pughe, 7 June 1803.

the present time . . . I will also prepare a little collection of Pennillion, which will give a pleasing variety to such a work . . . We are three or four engaged in it.[40]

This collection (for which we have no other evidence) was probably not planned as one to include music. That same year, Pughe was informed about another of Iolo's plans: 'I have attempted 5 or 6 little English songs adapted to some ancient South Walian tunes for the purpose of introducing the music with them in the second edition of my Poems.'[41] The year 1806 brought the last reference to songs in the correspondence. 'What think you', Iolo wrote to Pughe with regard to possible contributions to *Y Greal*, a journal of which the latter was editor,

> also of collecting old Welsh Tunes &c? What of collecting *Pennillion* as you *Deudneudwyr* call them, but which we the *hwyntwyr* term caniadau bychain, and in Glam *canuau'r Cathreiwr, canuau Buarth*, because usually sung to the chants of the Ploughboy and Milkmaid. I have however none myself to give you, for though I have collected all that I could in this part of Wales, or all that I thought worth preserving, yet I have used them as a supplement to my collection of popular proverbs which I have greatly improved since I brought it with me from London.[42]

Five lists of tunes made by Iolo survive.[43] All can probably be dated to the period 1795–1805.[44] The longest of them, containing forty-three titles, is endorsed by him: 'Ancient popular melodies collected in South Wales by E. Williams B.B.D.'. The force of Iolo's 'collected' should probably be taken as meaning 'might be brought together'. A second list contains 21 titles, a third lacks its beginning and contains titles numbered 12–25, while a fourth contains 20 and a fifth 29. There are no corresponding collections of tunes in Iolo's hand, nor indeed any hint that a collection of any kind ever existed, unless the unidentified manuscript 'Peroriaeth Morganwg', listed by Iolo among his books in London in 1794, contained music.[45] Iolo's collection of tunes was, to use his own expression, one of his 'castles in the air'. There is a degree of

---

[40]   Ibid., p. 105.
[41]   Ibid., p. 108, Iolo Morganwg to William Owen Pughe, 11 October 1803. One which he may have had in mind was his English song to the tune 'Mi yw'r bachgen ifangc ffol' (I am the foolish youth): NLW 21392F, p. 46.
[42]   NLW 13221E, pp. 152–3, Iolo Morganwg to William Owen Pughe, 9 January 1806. See Williams: *IM*, pp. 60–1.
[43]   The lists are in NLW 21426E, nos. 17, 18; NLW 13099B, p. 227; NLW 21410E, p. 49ᵛ, and printed in L. J. Hopkin-James and T. C. Evans (eds.), *Hen Gwndidau, Carolau, a Chywyddau* (Bangor, 1910), pp. lviii–lx. This last is said to come from 'Llanover, Book No. 35', i.e. Llanover C35, now NLW 13122B. This list is no longer in situ.
[44]   The fixed dates in Iolo's active period of collecting are: *c*.1795–1800 (dated watermarks in NLW 13146A); 1796 (NLW, IAW 145, f. 10); 1802 (NLW 13174A); *c*.1802 (NLW 13127A, p. 530); 1802–6 (references in his correspondence with William Owen Pughe); 1805 (date on the cover of NLW 21375A).
[45]   NLW 13136A, p. 157.

overlap in all the lists; they give the impression of having been written on the spur of the moment. The tunes that survive in Iolo's hand, some sixty in all, are scattered throughout his notebooks or found in loose papers or papers that were originally loose; but of this sixty or so, only nine occur in his lists of tunes (some, it must be said, are without titles). Under half the tunes are accompanied by words. The five lists of tunes are consolidated in the Appendix to this chapter.

Iolo had learnt when young to play the flute (Burns and Clare played the fiddle) and later he studied music.[46] Burns and Clare, to judge by their notation, were both abler musicians than Iolo. Even so, Burns observed: 'I am not scholar enough to prick down my tune properly',[47] while Clare, who notated a large number of dance-tunes (mostly printed by Deacon), referring to song-tunes, confessed: 'I wish I had skill enough in music to prick them down.'[48] The problems which gave rise to these remarks by Burns and Clare doubtless lay in the difficulties sometimes encountered when trying to notate from singers rather than instrumentalists, of registering the tonality and rhythm of traditional songs, difficulties which could still arise today. What was true of Burns and Clare would be even more so of Iolo (the last person to admit to any weakness). Iolo's notation is limited: he rarely gave time signatures; the barring, if present at all, followed the rhythmic units of the words rather than the musical ones; he seldom gave a key signature (if he did, one can guess that he was copying from a printed or written source), but indicated the g-clef by a *g* on the line, evidently taking *c* or *g* as the tonic. One possible symptom of Iolo's relative inability to notate is that most of the tunes which he recorded were short. A generation later, both Maria Jane Williams and John Thomas (Ieuan Ddu), in collections made in the 1830s, included many long and complicated Glamorgan tunes. For only two songs by Wil Hopcyn and Dafydd Nicolas did Iolo record a tune: 'Pebyll Penon' (Penonned tents), to the words 'Bugeila'r Gwenith Gwyn' (a song by Dafydd Nicolas, not Wil Hopcyn, according to Maria Jane Williams's informant) and Wil Hopcyn's *tribannau* to Llanbedr-ar-fynydd.[49]

We must also look on the positive side. Thanks to Iolo's custom of fixing the tonic, combined perhaps with his lack of thorough musical training, he inadvertently preserved several modal melodies, dorian (ray mode) or aeolian (lah mode).[50] These are melodies that later musically trained collectors would

---

[46] Williams: *IM*, pp. 215–16.

[47] Quoted by C. T. Davie, 'Robert Burns, Writer of Songs', p. 165.

[48] Deacon, *John Clare and the Folk Tradition*, p. 17.

[49] NLW, IAW 145, f. 7, and NLW 13146A, p. 173.

[50] 'Down by a meadow', 'Nutbrown maid', one 'Rhupynt Hir' and two 'Cywydd deuair fyrion' tunes, 'Tri Thrawiad' ('Hen garol Nadolig'), 'Y fuwch wynebwen lwyd' (The grey white-faced cow), 'Dawns triban deublig' (the double triban dance), and 'a glywais mewn eglwys ym Mrycheiniog' ('which I heard in a Breconshire church') (NLW, IAW 145, f. 14). See below.

probably have 'corrected': John Jenkins (Ifor Ceri), the compiler of the most orderly early collection of Welsh song-tunes, would have done so unfailingly, and Maria Jane Williams and John Thomas, both of whom struggled with modal tunes, quite probably.[51] Among these modal tunes are some which figure among Iolo's most valuable finds.

There are very few recorded songs in the Welsh tradition whose origin can confidently be placed earlier than 1700. The great bulk of recorded Welsh folk-song dates from the eighteenth and nineteenth centuries. While Iolo's musical knowledge was that of an amateur, his knowledge of Welsh bardic metres was profound. Almost alone in his day, he realized that Dafydd ab Edmwnd, in his codification of the 24 metres of Welsh prosody, had excluded simpler early metres, some of them still current in south Wales. No one could have been more aware of the significance of the several versions he recorded of tunes which he labelled 'Cywydd deuair fyrion' or 'Hen gywydd deuair' or 'Tôn deuair'. The medieval metre *cywydd deuair fyrion o'r hen ganiad* (rhyming couplet of four- or five-syllable lines), spurned by the professional bards, was widely used for the *cwndidau* popular in Glamorgan and Gwent in the sixteenth and early seventeenth centuries. Meredydd Evans has published these tunes and made a revealing analysis of their primitive musical structure.[52] He shows that the only survival of *deuair fyrion* tunes in later tradition was in ritual seasonal songs associated with hunting the wren and with *Dydd Calan* (New Year). Such songs are often the last refuges of ancient tunes. The medieval *cyhydedd hir* (a couplet of nineteen syllables containing eight beats) survives in a song associated with the ritual of the *Mari Lwyd* (Blessed Mary, a Christmas season ritual associated with the skull of a horse), for which Iolo collected two versions.[53] Two other seasonal songs in early metre are 'Mesur Carol Haf' (invariably associated with May Day carols) and 'hen garol Nadolig Morganwg' (old Glamorgan Christmas carol) in the metre of *tri thrawiad* (three beats).[54] An added interest of the *deuair fyrion* tunes is that some of them preserve what to the ear sound like what was once the accompanying instrumental symphony: see, for example, the final strains in Fig. 24a–b.[55] These may provide further evidence of how instrumental symphonies transmuted into repeated lines or half-lines of verse, as they did in the case of the *triban* (triplet), where they

---

[51]   On John Jenkins's editing, see Daniel Huws, 'Melus-Seiniau Cymru', *CG*, 8 (1985), 32–50; 9 (1986), 47–57; on that of Maria Jane Williams and John Thomas, see Maria Jane Williams, *Ancient National Airs of Gwent and Morganwg* (Llandovery, 1844), ed. Daniel Huws (facsimile edn., Cymdeithas Alawon Gwerin Cymru / Welsh Folk Song Society, 1988), p. [xxxv].

[52]   Meredydd Evans, 'Deuair Fyrion ac Alawon', *CG*, 8 (1985), 16–31, reprinted in Ann Ffrancon and Geraint H. Jenkins (eds.), *Merêd: Detholiad o Ysgrifau* (Llandysul, 1994), pp. 271–87.

[53]   NLW, IAW 145, f. 10, and one uncatalogued.

[54]   NLW, IAW 145, f. 15ᵛ ('Carol haf'), f. 10 ('Tri thrawiad').

[55]   Evans, 'Deuair Fyrion ac Alawon', nos. 4 and 1. My suggestion is that in the latter the final repeated words have replaced the symphony.

Fig. 24a 'Cywydd deuair fyrion' (NLW 13089E, p. 253). Reproduced, by kind permission of Dr Meredydd Evans, from 'Deuair Fyrion ac Alawon'.

Fig. 24b 'Cywydd deuair: Morganwg', Iolo's notation (NLW, Iolo Aneurin Williams MSS, uncatalogued).

further transmuted into nonsense syllables.[56] We are perhaps as close as we ever may be to one style of Welsh sixteenth-century performance.

The *deuair fyrion* is the metre of over half the known *halsingod*, religious songs widely sung in the Teifi valley and the surrounding area in the seventeenth and eighteenth centuries; these were late survivals of the tradition of the Glamorgan *cwndidau*.[57] In one of his many valuable observations on Welsh music, Iolo made the following teasing comment (*alsain* is his form of *halsing*): had something developed analogous to the singing of Gaelic metrical psalms (here with instruments)?

the Alsain is . . . a loose recitative kind of verse sung with a Cathedral-like Chant, the instrument playing some solemn piece of devotional music, with which the

---

[56] See Phyllis Kinney, 'Vocal and Instrumental Interaction in Earlier "Canu penillion"', *CG*, 7 (1984), 28–38. Iolo also preserved an instrumental symphony (which he termed *goslef*) for 'Y ferch o'r Sger', NLW, IAW 145, f. 9.

[57] On *halsingod*, see Geraint Bowen, 'Yr Halsingod', *THSC* (1945), 83–108; see also Meredydd Evans, 'Cainc ar gyfer Halsingod: Nodyn', *CG*, 18 (1995), 45–7.

singers keep their Chant as much as possible in concord, attempting at the same time as much melody as possible. The Alsain versification is the most simple, rude, and, for these reasons, doubtless the most ancient kind of Welsh Verse. It is still used very much in Caermarthen and Cardiganshire, and was not long since very common in Glamorgan.[58]

Among those which succeeded the vanishing medieval metres was one that became known as 'Y Dôn Fechan' (The Small Tune). Like the *triban* it had a long life and varied use. It was the metre of much of the poetry of Rees Prichard, of scores of ballads, particularly mournful ones, and of hundreds of *penillion*. Versions of 'Y Dôn Fechan' are myriad. Among versions collected by Iolo is one which he called 'hen erddigan Morganwg . . . gynt yn arferedig ym Morganwg, yn yr Eglwysydd . . . [i] ganu amryw o ganiadau'r Hen Ficar' ('formerly used in Glamorgan in the churches to sing various songs of the Old Vicar [Rees Prichard]').[59] Another, which he called 'Cainc y Cathreiwr' (the Song of the Ploughman), an ox-driving song, was sent to William Owen Pughe in 1802.[60] Iolo's disapproving comment (who else made this observation so early?) on what is nowadays one of the surviving traits of Welsh folk tradition, 'the practice of singing religious songs in public houses and companies of topers', referred perhaps to hymns sung to more recent folk melodies such as found favour with the early Methodists.[61]

Iolo did not admire the manner in which *penillion* were sung in north Wales:

> a kind of chaunt which is to this day retained, and it is adapted to every kind of verse and Stanza . . . nothing better than a tollerable drone to the harp. The South Walian Music has much of the Scotish manner, and is more lively than the No Wal.[n] which has in it something grand. In South Wales the manner of Singing is for the instrument to play the song's appropriate tune which, and not a chaunt, the singer also uses.[62]

He nevertheless acknowledged its antiquity, noting that Welsh poetry 'down to the 14th or 15th centurie can never be adapted to any kind of tune but those chaunts'. Referring to *penillion*-singing in north Wales, he further remarked: 'this N. W. chant has intruded its cadences into all the tunes of that country':[63] an exaggeration, but a truth that can be demonstrated in scores of north Wales

---

[58] NLW 13118B, p. 134.
[59] NLW 21421E, no. 4.
[60] John Jenkins (Ifor Ceri) acquired a copy from William Owen Pughe and included it in his collection, *Melus-seiniau Cymru*, from which the tune was printed in the second volume of John Parry's *The Welsh Harper* (2 vols., London, 1848), under the title 'Cainc yr Aradwr'. On *Melus-seiniau Cymru* and the relationship of these collections, see Huws, 'Melus-Seiniau Cymru'.
[61] NLW 13138A, p. 63.
[62] NLW 13118B, p. 136. For a fuller extract, see Williams: *IM*, pp. 60–1, n. 49.
[63] Williams: *IM*, p. 136.

tunes collected subsequently. Iolo was the first to make clear the distinction in *penillion*-singing between north and south which, to later generations, was recognized in the terms 'Dull y Gogledd' (Northern Style) and 'Dull y De' (Southern Style). How much further back the distinction went is a moot point. But Iolo again provides precious evidence in his recording of tunes sung to another metre of medieval origin, one which is still very much alive today, *triban Morgannwg* (Glamorgan triplet). *Penillion* in this metre were popular throughout Wales, but particularly so in Glamorgan. Hundreds of examples were recorded in the nineteenth and twentieth centuries, several of them as ox-driving songs.[64] Iolo recorded a dozen *triban* tunes. One of them shows the interplay of voice and instrument which is also found in examples recorded by William Jones of Llangadfan, *c*.1790, and John Jenkins (Ifor Ceri), *c*.1820.[65] These provide invaluable evidence of south Wales *penillion*-singing to the harp in a manner not recorded by later collectors.

An early commentator on Burns's songs was the English scholar Joseph Ritson, an acquaintance of Iolo. He wrote in 1794:

> Mr Burns, as good a poet as Ramsay, is it must be regretted an equally licentious unfaithful publisher of the performances of others. Many of the original, old, ancient genuine songs inserted in Johnson's *Scots Musical Museum* derive not a little of their merit from passing through the hands of this very ingenious critic.[66]

The same could have been written of traditional songs in the manuscript collections of Iolo Morganwg and John Clare, as indeed it could of many famous national songs, of epics even, throughout the world. Of all three poets it could be said that there are songs about which it is hard to say whether the words are wholly traditional, partly traditional and partly by the poet, or wholly by the poet.[67] All three in their youth were already composing songs in traditional idiom before they had become fully aware of metropolitan standards. Ritson's purist strictures were understandable, but inapposite. Iolo's role has been hotly disputed in the case of Wil Hopcyn, who was elevated by Iolo into a major lyric poet, but who is now a shadowy figure.[68] To what extent were Wil's songs composed by Iolo? The truth lies beyond us: almost all surviving poems attributed to him are in Iolo's own manuscripts. The same would be true also of Dafydd Nicolas were it not for Maria Jane Williams's

---

[64] Tegwyn Jones, *Tribannau Morgannwg* (Llandysul, 1976), includes a large selection and a comprehensive introduction.

[65] Ibid., pp. 211–12; Huws, *Caneuon Llafar Gwlad*, p. 17. For a discussion, see Kinney, 'Vocal and Instrumental Interaction', 31–2.

[66] Quoted in Low (ed.), *Robert Burns: The Critical Heritage*, p. 98.

[67] The notes of James Kinsley in his edition, *The Poems and Songs of Robert Burns* (3 vols., Oxford, 1968), record his frequent doubts in this respect. Deacon, *John Clare and the Folk Tradition*, p. 77, outlines the difficulties he faced in the case of Clare.

[68] The case is clearly set out in *TLIM*, pp. 251–9.

Ancient National Airs of Gwent and Morganwg (1844). This volume, the first published collection of Welsh folk-songs, contains five songs attributed to Dafydd Nicolas, including 'Callyn Serchus' (Lovely Kate), 'Ffanni Blodau'r Ffair' (Fanny Blooming Fair) and 'Bugeila'r Gwenith Gwyn', besides 'Y Deryn Pur' (The Gentle Dove), also credited to him by tradition.[69] The same volume contains two songs by Edward Evan, the last, according to Iolo (apart from Iolo himself) of the ancient bardic order of Glamorgan, one attributed to Wil Hopcyn, and two which Jane Williams heard sung by Iolo himself, 'Ffoles Llantrisant' (The Merry Girl of Llantrisant) and 'Cerais Ferch' (I loved a Maiden).[70] In editing her volume, Jane Williams enlisted the help of Taliesin ab Iolo, who supplied versions of the words of many songs from his father's manuscripts. In this way the touch of Iolo's improving hand came to lie on a number of songs derived from *Ancient National Airs* which soon became Welsh 'national airs', as did that of Burns on hundreds of Scottish airs. The commonly published words of 'Ffanni Blodau'r Ffair', 'Bugeila'r Gwenith Gwyn' and 'Y Ferch o'r Sger' all bear the stamp of Iolo's 'improvements'.[71]

The question of Wil Hopcyn is no more than a symbol of a larger one. Iolo's manuscripts contain scores of other songs that could be placed in the tradition of *canu teuluaidd*, some no doubt traditional, at least in part, others Iolo's own work.[72] Most of this poetry has been edited by P. J. Donovan,[73] whose texts and variant readings show how time and again Iolo adapted traditional words or incorporated them in new songs, after the manner of Burns. The effect can be of over-polishing: the slight awkwardness, part of the charm of most oral texts, is absent. Several songs in Donovan's edition, however, have their counterparts in recovered oral tradition.[74] Two stanzas from one example must suffice: a four-stanza song attributed by Iolo to Thomas Llywelyn but which, Donovan argued, was in fact his own. The model was clearly a version of the popular *penillion*, 'Diofal yw'r aderyn' (Carefree is the bird).

> Gwyn fyd y bêr fwyalchen
> Sy'n ddigrif ar y gangen
> Heb awr ofalus yno bydd
> Drwy gorff y dydd yn llawen.

---

[69] See the notes on these songs in Williams, *Ancient National Airs* (facsimile edn., 1988).

[70] By Edward Evan, 'Y ferch fedydd' (The god-daughter) and 'Mab addfwyn' (The gentle swain); by Wil Hopcyn, 'Pryd o'wn ar ddiwarnod' (When on a day returning).

[71] See Williams, *Ancient National Airs* (facsimile edn., 1988), notes to these songs.

[72] Williams: *IM*, pp. 297–304.

[73] *CRhIM*.

[74] Ibid., no. 3, see 'Pan o'wn yn rhodio mynwent eglwys' (When I was strolling in the church graveyard), e.g. *JWFSS*, I, 71 and II, 275; no. 24, see 'Ow! Mab wyf fi' (Oh! I'm a young man), *JWFSS*, IV, 34; no. 86 (two stanzas printed below), see *JWFSS*, III, 208, and for the words, e.g. T. H. Parry-Williams, *Hen Benillion* (Aberystwyth, 1940), nos. 273–5; no. 88, see 'Y deryn du sy'n rhodio'r gwledydd' (The blackbird which travels the lands), e.g. *JWFSS*, I, 123–5, 194.

Ni chais na hau na garddu
Na meddwl am yfory,
Ond myned fyth wrth iâs ei ben
O bren i bren dan ganu.[75]

(Blessed is the sweet-sounding blackbird/ Which is delightful on the branch,/ With no anxious time, that's where he'll be,/ Happy all day long.

He does not attempt to sow nor cultivate a garden,/ Nor think about tomorrow,/ But always follows his whim/ From tree to tree, singing.)

Tunes know no frontiers. Although in Iolo's day the Welsh language in Glamorgan was at a high tide, having re-established itself in areas from which it had once retreated, English was widespread. Iolo's tune lists included English titles. Some were associated with Welsh words. Of *The Nutbrown Maid*, he noted: 'In Welsh it is called Y Fynachlog (The Abbey) and was formerly much used as a psalm-tune but is now oftener applied to elegaic songs.'[76] Probably copying from Edward Jones's *Bardic Museum* (1802), he recorded 'Cornish May Song', an early version of the Helston Furry Dance, with its opening words from a Robin Hood ballad.[77] Unfortunately, he did not write down the music of the English song 'Away from my window', described as an 'old song commonly sung in Glam'.[78] This was a version of a song which can be traced back to the sixteenth century and was recorded from oral tradition in the West Country at the end of the nineteenth century.[79] Iolo's six-verse version preserved the fullest set of words to have been recorded. 'Away from my window' is given particular Welsh interest by its relationship to the Welsh song 'Rhybydd i'r carwr' (The lover's warning), recorded in Ceredigion, and the lullaby, 'Si hei lwli 'mabi' (Hush, my baby).[80] Evidence of the early arrival in Wales of the English song is provided by the fragment added in the early seventeenth century to the margin of a manuscript of Welsh poetry from the Cydweli area.[81] Other English songs are scattered in Iolo's manuscripts.

---

[75] *CRhIM*, no. 86, pp. 134, 163.
[76] NLW, IAW 145, f. 17.
[77] NLW, IAW 145, f. 16. Another version, with the title 'Morris dance tune', is in NLW 13089E, p. 419.
[78] NLW 13129A, p. 65.
[79] For versions from English oral tradition under the title of 'Go from my window', see S. Baring-Gould et al., *Songs of the West: Folk Songs of Devon and Cornwall* (3rd edn., London, 1905); W. A. Barrett, *English Folk-Songs* (London, 1891); James Reeves, *The Everlasting Circle* (London, 1960), p. 122. For early versions, see Claude M. Simpson, *The British Broadside Ballad and its Music* (New Brunswick, NJ, 1966), pp. 257–9.
[80] For 'Rhybydd y Carwr', see David de Lloyd (ed.), *Forty Welsh Traditional Tunes* (London, 1929), no. 29, and Phyllis Kinney and Meredydd Evans (eds.), *Canu'r Cymry II* (Cymdeithas Alawon Gwerin Cymru / Welsh Folk Song Society, 1987), no. 25; for 'Si hei lwli 'mabi', *JWFSS*, III (1930), 29. See also Mary-Ann Constantine and Gerald Porter, *Fragments and Meaning in Traditional Song: From the Blues to the Baltic* (Oxford, 2003), pp. 6–7, 164–6.
[81] BL, Stowe 959, f. 17ᵛ: 'Go from my window goe/ go from my window my deere/ the wind

A favourite hobby-horse of the London Welsh in the 1790s was the alleged existence of the Welsh American Indians, the Madogwys. Iolo was a fervent advocate. At this time he wrote down an unremarkable tune which must come under suspicion: 'Symlen ben bys, as in Glamorgan, an old Welsh tune', below which he added another tune 'said to be a North American Indian tune, is remarkably like the above old Welsh tune'.[82] We are alerted by his further note: 'The Welsh tune is from a MS prior to the discovery of America by Columbus.' Iolo would have been aware that Edward Jones had included in the *Relicks* a tune called 'Symlen ben bys' (The simple fingertip tune) and that Rhys Jones, in *Gorchestion Beirdd Cymru* (1773), had identified Dafydd ap Gwilym's *cywydd* 'Y gainc' (the tune) as 'Cywydd i'r gaingc a elwir Symlen Penbys'.[83]

The example of 'Symlen ben bys' raises questions about other tunes recorded by Iolo: can we accept them at face value? Iolo's ability as a musician may have been limited, but he died the composer of hundreds of tunes, tunes which survive among his papers.[84] These, dating from *c*.1810, are hymn-tunes composed for the use of Unitarian congregations in south Wales. None, it must be added, took hold. Could Iolo also have been the composer of some of the folk-tunes he recorded? This seems unlikely. With tunes, as opposed to literary texts, there was not the same incentive to deceive. There was no audience. As far as we know, Iolo shared his interest in tunes with no one else except, briefly, William Owen Pughe. Yet, positive evidence of the authenticity of his tunes is provided by the occurrence among them of versions of otherwise well-known tunes: 'Y Ferch o'r Sger', 'Morgan Jones o'r Dolau Gwyrddion' (Morgan Jones from Dolau Gwyrddion), 'Hob y deri dando' and several *triban* tunes. We should not ignore the apparent warranty of notes such as 'gynt yn arferedig ym Morganwg yn yr eglwysydd' ('formerly used in Glamorgan in the churches') and 'a glywais mewn eglwys ym Mrycheiniog' ('which I heard in a Breconshire church').[85] Iolo habitually signed his hymn-tunes and also, occasionally, secular tunes 'I. M.': it thus appears that he distinguished his own compositions.[86] But perhaps we should remain wary, and never altogether discount his playfulness.

The impression left on reading letters written by Iolo in later life is of overriding selfishness, obsessiveness, only the rarest hint of warmth, and

---

and the raine hath turnd him back againe/ thow canst not be lodged heere.' These words were to be sung to 'the tune of Irish Shaen o Neal'.

[82]   NLW, IAW 145, f. 17A.

[83]   Rhys Jones, *Gorchestion Beirdd Cymru* (Amwythig, 1773), p. 18.

[84]   Among the uncatalogued papers.

[85]   NLW, IAW 145, f. 14.

[86]   For example, in NLW, IAW 145, f. 8, is the tune 'Hengoed', followed by another 'yr un mesur I M' ('the same metre IM'), and on f. 22, 'Triban. Pont y Ty Pridd', followed by 'Triban. I. M.'. NLW 13145A, p. 433, contains 'Cân yr angylion' (The angels' song), a Christmas carol, with a tune, signed 'I. M. cân a chainc ai cant' ('I.M. composed song and tune').

vindictive envy. The poet in him had been stifled by the supervention of other ambitions, by his heavy use of laudanum or by innate traits in his personality – we are free to speculate. Burns had died young before any such fate could befall him; the muse of Clare and Nerval had remained true to them, at the terrible price of madness. In Iolo's case, while his desire to collect folk-songs may have been inspired by the example of Burns, and while his pursuit of it may for a time have been linked to literary ambition, there was a deeper impulse, akin to that which had moved Clare and Nerval. Returning from England in 1802, Iolo reached Caerffili and wrote in pencil in a small pocket diary:[87]

> Vale of Glamorgan opens to view. One of its songs and tunes occurs. There is something strange in the powerful effect of these provincial, or local, things. The Swiss have their mal de pays. So have the Glamorganians. I mentally sung the following old popular Stanza to the ancient tune in two parts of Triban Morganwg and felt my eyes Streaming with tears.

> Mi wela'r mor yn amlwg
> Mi wela Fro Morganwg
> Pan fwyf yn hon am bwthyn bach
> Mi fydda'n iach fy ngolwg.

(I see the sea clearly,/ I see the Vale of Glamorgan,/ When I am there and in my cottage/ I'll be healthy in appearance.)

He went on:

> There is no panegyric intended here. Nothing more than to observe the powerful effects of ideas that strongly associate with those of early youth . . . I have attempted a second Stanza thus

> Caf gwrdd am hen gyfeillion
> Caf rodio'r twynydd tirion
> Lle bu'm yn chware'n lencyn bach
> Caf fod yn iach fy nghalon.

(I shall meet my old friends,/ I shall roam the gentle hills/ Where I played as a small boy,/ I shall be healthy of heart.)

> But who can equal the old one? What would I not give to know the name and æra of its author? Any addition to this beautiful little thing can never have a good effect, will never establish it self. But if more singing is required this old stanza will bear a thousand repetitions at one sitting.

---

[87] NLW 13174A, pp. 90ᵛ–2ʳ. The words and tune are printed in Huws, *Caneuon Llafar Gwlad ac Iolo a'i Fath*, p. 17. On the words, cf. *CRhIM*, no. 11.

Can it be that even here, in the privacy of a scribbled pencil note in his pocket diary, Iolo was posing? It would be gratifying to believe that in writing down these words and their tune, as lovely as anything he ever recorded, he was for once being honest with himself and that the tears were genuine. But we cannot be sure. He may have been posing; even the first *triban* might be his own work (that *bwthyn bach* bears his stamp), but the tune was most certainly not.

APPENDIX

This appendix lists in alphabetical order, by name or opening words of songs, tunes that were notated by Iolo (asterisks signify notation), together with those listed by him in five tune-lists, designated A–E (A. and B., in NLW MS 21426E; C., in NLW 13099B; D., in NLW 21410E; and E., from L. J. Hopkin-James and T. C. Evans (eds.), *Hen Gwndidau, Carolau a Chywyddau* (Bangor, 1910), pp. lvii–lx. It does not include other tunes whose names occur *passim* in his manuscripts. Manuscript sources are given, as are, following a bold **P**, references to tunes in print. The list is expanded from that printed as an appendix to *Caneuon Llafar Gwlad ac Iolo a'i Fath* (Cymdeithas Alawon Gwerin Cymru, 1993). Iolo's orthography has been followed. Tunes noted by him simply under the names of Welsh bardic metres (e.g. 'Cywydd deuair byrion', 'Rhupynt', 'Triban') have been brought together under 'Mesurau'. Two untitled tunes are added at the end.

This appendix contains several references to 'IAW 145': this is a manuscript in the Iolo Aneurin Williams archive which has yet to receive its NLW number. There are also a few references to 'IAW uncat.': these are papers in the uncatalogued residue of the archive. The abbreviation *ANA* refers to Maria Jane Williams, *Ancient National Airs of Gwent and Morganwg*.

Away from my window B. (Words: NLW 13129A, p. 271).
Bailiff's daughter of Islington B.
Bedwen Cefn Panwr, *see* Cefn Pennar
Bendith Dduw'n dy ddau lygadyn A.
Betawn i'n [fachgen ieuanc llawen 'I.M.']★ A. NLW, IAW uncat.
Blin yw caru [pennill 8.8.8.8]★ NLW 21423E, no. 14 (×2).
Blodau coed afalau A.
Bore dydd Llun A.
Braw nhin y pannwr C., *see* Y pannwr
Breuddwyd Wil Hopkin B.
Breuddwyd y Frenhines D.
Brigant, *see* Frincum francum

Brithi i'r buarth★ (Cainc yr odryddes) NLW 13146A, p. 435; NLW 13221E, p. 93.

Bryniau'r Werddon D.

Bwbach darllain ('8 a 7 deublyg')★ NLW 13146A, p. 204; NLW 21419E, p. 56.

Cainc y Cathreiwr★ NLW 13146A, p. 436; NLW 13221E, p. 92. **P:** *Welsh Harper*, II, 18.

Cainc y Clych★ NLW 13146A, p. 413. **P:** *JWFSS*, V, 181.

Cainc yr odryddes, *see* Brithi i'r buarth

Calon drom D.

Cân bachgen y felin★ NLW 13146A, pp. 422–3. **P:** *JWFSS*, V, 182.

Cân crottyn y gwartheg, *see* Y fuwch wynebwen lwyd

Cân y cunnogyn (Triban Morgannwg) A., E.

Cân y maensaer★ NLW 13146A, pp. 424–5 (Words: *CRhIM*, no. 32).

Cân yr eos, *see* Eglwysnewydd

Canu 'ddwyf a bod yn llawen★ NLW, IAW 145, f. 10ᵛ. **P:** *ANA*, p. [25].

Canu gwasaela Morganwg, *see* Gwashaela

Canu'r crymman A., E. (Words: *CRhIM*, no. 90).

Canu'r ebol (Canu'r ebol gwinau) A.

Canu'r lleuod [unclear] A.

Canu Wil Tabor, *see* Twm taro tant

Carchar caeth yw Ciwpyd A., B.

Cario cŵd★ B. NLW 13146A, p. 386. **P:** *JWFSS*, IV, 19.

Cefn Pennar★ (Bedwen Cefn Pennar, Cefn Panwr, Toriad y dydd) A., D., E. NLW 21392F, f. 51ᵛ (Words: *CRhIM*, no. 19).

Cerais ferch, *see* Canu 'ddwyf

Cobler Coch o'r Hengoed★ NLW, IAW 145, f. 8 (×2).

Coed y glyn★ NLW, IAW 145, f. 11.

Cof Gwenllian★ NLW, IAW 145, f. 19.

Cofia di'n wastad C.

Colinetta A.

Cornish May Song★ NLW, IAW 145, f. 16; NLW 13089E, p. 419 ('Morris dance tune').

Crimson Velvet B., D.

Cywydd deuair hirion, *see under* Mesurau

Dawns triban deublyg★ NLW, IAW 145, f. 10 *see* Triban

Delw Llandaf E.

Dili dwd, *see* Cario cŵd

Dolau Gleision★ (Morgan Jones) NLW, IAW uncat. (Words: NLW 13030A, p. 209).

Down by a meadow there runs a stream★ NLW, IAW uncat.

Dydd da i chwi Gwen lliw'r lili A.

Dyfod diwarnod ar daith A. (Words: *CRhIM*, no. 91).

Dyri hir C.

Eglwysnewydd A., C., D., E. (Words: *ANA*, pp. [29–31])

Ei di'r deryn penfelyn C.

Etifeddes y Coety, *see* Nutbrown maid

Ffoles Llantrisant★ **P:** *ANA*, pp. 24, [12]

Frincum francum (Brigant)★ B. NLW 13146A, p. 451. **P:** *JWFSS*,V, 183.

Fy nhad★ NLW 13146A, p. 229. **P:** *JWFSS*,V, 181.

Glan y môr A., D.

Glyn Heligon A.

Gwashaela★ A. NLW, IAW 145, f.10; NLW, IAW uncat.

Gweddus yw'r gwedd-dod A., E.

Gwegil y fwyall A., E.

Gwel yr adeilad A.

Gwen lliw'r lili E.

Gweno fach dos yn iach C.

Gwrandewch bawb C.

Hai diofal calon fach B.

Helicon (Helygen) D.

Hen erddigan Morganwg★ NLW 21421E, no. 4.

Hen ficar A.

Hen gainc gwasaela Morganwg, *see* Gwashaela

Hen garol Nadolig (Tri thrawiad)★ NLW, IAW 145, f. 10.

Hen grofan A.

Hen ŵr dall a'r angau A., B.

Hen ŵr o'r coed A. NLW, IAW 145, p.12^v (×2).

Holl feibion da dewrion E.

Holl ientyd glân clywch gân ar goedd C.

Holl ientyd glân o blwyf Ll[   ] C.

Hun Gwenllian★ NLW, IAW 145, f. 1.

Hwp y deri dando★ NLW, IAW 145, ff. 6, 12, 21 (Words: NLW 13099B, pp. 199–200).

Leave Land D.

Llanbedr ar fynydd★ (Triban) B. NLW 13146A, p. 173. **P:** *JWFSS*,V, 180.

Lliw rhosyn yr haf C., E.

Llwyn ynn D.

Llywydd y lleuad A., E.

Mae gennyf fi gettyn★ NLW, IAW uncat.

Mae hyn o achos Gwen A.

Melwefus D.

Mentra Gwen A.

Merch brenin Ffrainc D.

Merch brenin Twrci A.

Mesurau

    Mesur byr★ NLW 21421E, no. 4.

Tri thrawiad, *see under* Mesurau

Triban Morganwg, *see under* Mesurau

Twm taro tant★ (Twm o'r Coety, Canu Wil Tabor) NLW 21319A, pp. 260–1.

Y cadno coch, *see* Y daear fochyn

Y cardotyn, *see* Cario cŵd

Y cler mae rhai'n eu galw A.

Y cobler coch, *see* Cobler Coch o'r Hengoed

Y daear fochyn★ (Cadno coch) E. NLW, IAW 145, f.15ᵛ.

Y deryn du ar dro C.

Y fedel (fedle) fawr D., E.

Y fedwen★ NLW, IAW 145, f. 13.

Y feindwf fun★ NLW 21423E, no. 13 (Words: *CRhIM*, no. 24).

Y ferch benfelen A., C., D.

Y ferch o'r Scer★ NLW, IAW 145, f. 9.

Y forheulan D.

Y fun euraidd fwyn C.

Y fuwch benfelen E.

Y fuwch wynebwen lwyd★ NLW 13146A, p. 421. **P:** *JWFSS*, III, 78.

Y fynachlog, *see* Nutbrown maid

Y mwya' gar fy nghalon★ NLW, IAW 145, p. 11; NLW 21423E, no. 14.

Y pannwr★ NLW, IAW 145, f. 18 (cf. NLW 13146A, p. 426).

Ymhennydd ci a llygoden B.

Yr ebol coch mawr C., D. cf. Canu'r ebol.

Yr het helyg★ NLW, IAW 145, f. 25.

Untitled

    'a glywais mewn eglwys ym Mrycheiniog'★ NLW, IAW 145, f. 14.

    'hen gaingc ym Morganwg' NLW, IAW uncat.

IV. Iolo's Friends and Enemies

16

Women and Gender in the Private and Social Relationships of Iolo Morganwg

CATHRYN A. CHARNELL-WHITE

Although women figured prominently in Iolo Morganwg's extraordinary life and writings, little scholarly work has been done on this theme. Just as Iolo's relationship with a wide circle of male acquaintances was fraught, ambiguous and contradictory, so too was it in the case of women. Iolo's views of and attitude towards women, at least on the surface, were riddled with ambiguity. He dismissed women as 'silly things' intent on 'deep ensnaring acts' and obsessed with fashion,[1] but he also commended them for being 'in general more temperate than [men], more moderate, in every thing more virtuous'.[2] Profound compassion compelled him to petition on behalf of poor and destitute women in Glamorgan but, at the other extreme, he wrote much overtly anti-feminist ephemera replete with sniggering clichés about old maids, scolding wives, gossips and women of dubious virtue. This chapter focuses on five particular aspects: his views on the political rights of women; his domestic role as a son, husband and father; his paternalistic support for female paupers; his dealings with female correspondents, patrons and subscribers; and the misogynist sentiments about women which he aired in male circles.

First of all, we must ask: was the self-styled Bard of Liberty a champion of the political rights of women? The period which he spent from 1791 to 1795 in post-revolutionary London was undoubtedly one of the most stimulating in his life. Encountering the ferment of republican, radical and anti-slavery ideas, via the London-Welsh and Joseph Johnson's circle, broadened his horizons and encouraged him to look beyond the publication of his poems, *Poems, Lyric and Pastoral* (1794), to a much broader literary and political career. He planned to publish several polemical tracts, but none of them was devoted to feminist

---

[1]   NLW 21328A, no. 18, 'Song of Liberty'. These comments were omitted from *Poems, Lyric and Pastoral*. See Williams: *PLP*, I, pp. 132–6; NLW 21323B, pp. 41–7. See also his derogatory comments about fashionable Carmarthenshire women: NLW 13115B, pp. 53–4.
[2]   NLW 21285E, Letter no. 862, Iolo Morganwg to Miss Barker, 26 March 1798.

issues.[3] To that extent Iolo was entirely in tune with the climate in which he wrote. The French 'Declaration of the Rights of Man and the Citizen' of 1789 had been primarily concerned with the universal rights of men, irrespective of their social standing or privilege. In the enthusiastic levelling of hierarchy and social injustice, women and their rights had initially been overlooked until Olympe de Gouges, Théroigne de Mericourt, Condorcet and Mary Wollstonecraft argued that women, too, merited full citizenship: equal education, equal civic status and equal legal and political rights. Even Wollstonecraft, an icon of radical feminism, penned *A Vindication of the Rights of Men* (1790) before turning her attention to women in *A Vindication of the Rights of Woman* (1792). Despite their industry, radical feminists failed to inaugurate a feminist revolution: in France, the plight of women in the post-revolutionary age was worse than that under the *ancien régime*,[4] and feminism in Britain was prematurely stunted by the reaction to events in France and posthumous revelations of Wollstonecraft's unconventional private life. So, when Iolo, in an untitled and unfinished treatise on the ideal form of government (which echoed the function of the Gorsedd of the Bards), outlined a model within which the 'rights and duties of man' would be enshrined and 'the personal suffrage of every [male] individual' ensured, his marginalization of women was wholly consonant with the Enlightenment *Zeitgeist*.[5]

Feminism and radicalism were most notably intertwined in the 'revolutionary' feminism of Mary Wollstonecraft and Catharine Macaulay.[6] Wollstonecraft was in France and Scandinavia during most of Iolo's sojourn in London in the early 1790s, but he could not have avoided her virtual presence.[7] Her active participation in the pamphlet war, and in the 'revolution debate' directed against Edmund Burke, positioned her alongside Richard Price, Tom Paine and William Godwin as an instrumental force in the shaping of the Jacobin ideology of the day. Iolo was in London in the year *A Vindication of the Rights of Woman* (1792) was published and Wollstonecraft's books and ideas were no doubt hotly debated in the circles in which he moved, particularly that of Joseph Johnson, her publisher and mentor, who also features in Iolo's story as an important conduit for literary and radical ideas. We know that Iolo dined

---

3   These are listed in NLW 21400C, no. 9.

4   Joan B. Landes, *Women and the Public Sphere in the Age of the French Revolution* (London, 1988), *passim*.

5   NLW 21396E, no. 8.

6   Gary Kelly, *Revolutionary Feminism: The Mind and Career of Mary Wollstonecraft* (London, 1992), *passim*; Jennifer Loach, *Mary Wollstonecraft: The Making of a Radical Feminist* (Oxford, 1990), pp. 75–89. For Macaulay, see Bridget Hill, *The Republican Virago: The Life and Times of Catharine Macaulay, Historian* (Oxford, 1992).

7   For Wollstonecraft, see Janet Todd, *Mary Wollstonecraft: A Revolutionary Life* (London, 2000); Barbara Taylor, *Mary Wollstonecraft and the Feminist Imagination* (Cambridge, 2003); Caroline Franklin, *Mary Wollstonecraft: A Literary Life* (London, 2004), pp. 85–111.

with Godwin, Wollstonecraft's future husband, and shared other contacts in common with her, among them Richard Price, Tom Paine, George Dyer, Joseph Priestley and Anna Barbauld (née Aikin). But although Iolo maintained that both Wollstonecraft and Macaulay 'would have figured to greater Advantage in the House of Lords than half the wooden headed peers in the kingdom',[8] he never, at least in the writings which survive, engaged with their ideas. In the light of these connections, the paucity of writings of a political nature is disappointing. One might have expected Iolo to demonstrate more overtly feminist sympathies, like his friend, the Unitarian George Dyer, with whom he dined and corresponded sporadically between 1794 and 1811, and who sympathized with the well-established feminist topos that deficient education and social customs were 'degrading to the female character'.[9]

Although women and their rights are largely incidental in Iolo's unpublished papers, it is still possible to form a composite portrait of his attitudes towards them in relation to marriage, celibacy and citizenship. For instance, in his correspondence with Miss Mary Barker in 1798, Iolo voiced 'strong objections to universal suffrage' which he considered too 'dangerously unwieldy, fatiguingly cumbersome' in a large state.[10] Carefully negotiating the subject, while rejecting the 'entire exclusion' of women 'from any part or voice in the Legislature', he espoused a system of elective suffrage which would be 'very [no]vel' and 'considerably assertive of the RIGHTS of LADIES'. Mindful of Barker's own sensibilities, he avoided echoing *A Vindication of the Rights of Woman*: '[Let] this madam put you in good humour. My ideas go not the length of [Mary] Wollstonecraft's but implicated if not active rights your sex madam have [in m]y opinion a just claim to.'[11] Tradition or 'ancient prejudice' prevented him from admitting women into the legislative body though, in order to maintain a semblance of inclusivity, he contrived the notion of 'joint suffrage', whereby only married men were considered part of the legislature:

> Yet I will not so far wound ancient prejudice (who is a very obstinate fellow,) as to propose admission of Women into the Legislature, but let every voice in elections and all other legislative proceedings be always considered as the joint suffrage of a man and woman legally connected in Matrimony. By this means the woman's voice is implied. She becomes virtually represented in that without her the man has no voice.[12]

---

[8] NLW 21396E, no. 8.

[9] George Dyer, *Poems, by G. Dyer* (London, 1792), quoted in Claire Tomalin, *The Life and Death of Mary Wollstonecraft* (rev. edn., London, 1992), p. 143.

[10] NLW 21285E, Letter no. 862, Iolo Morganwg to Miss Barker, 26 March 1798. This may have been the novelist, Mary Barker, author of *A Welsh Story* (1798).

[11] NLW 21396E, no. 8; NLW 21285E, Letter no. 862, Iolo Morganwg to Miss Barker, 26 March 1798.

[12] NLW 21396E, no. 8. See also ibid., no. 10.

In a few exceptional circumstances – sickness or unavoidable absence from home – a wife could be allowed to vote on her husband's behalf, but the language of 'joint suffrage' only serves to reinforce the marginalization and passivity of women in the public sphere. Iolo's scheme for 'the personal suffrage of every individual' was nothing more than a rhetorical sleight of hand in which women became 'virtually', but not 'actually', represented.[13]

The arguments which Iolo presented in favour of 'joint suffrage' offer insights into his views on the role of marriage within society. He believed that marriage equipped a man to contribute to the running of a state since, as husband and father, he had, through his descendants, invested in society and secured its continuance: 'A man by matrimony becomes a link in the political chain of perpetuity by contributing to the main strength which is population of the State. He, being a Parent has a warm interest in the Welfare of posterity.'[14] His stake in society as a parent would guide his actions in matters of legislation and election 'for the good of posterity'.[15] Unlike the selfishly driven celibate, Iolo argued that the married man possessed feelings which equipped him to empathize with women and thus care for them:

> The married man knows experientally all the feelings of the Lover, the Husband, the father of daughters, the other sex are dear to him he feels [w]armly for them, he will take their causes, their wrongs, their weaknesses, [?] to glowing consideration, he will be their advocate, redresser, and affectionate helper. The Celibate has no feeling, no sentiment, but such as are vile and ungenerous towards the other sex.[16]

In a passage bearing a Coleridgean emphasis,[17] Iolo's politics converged with the culture of sensibility for, in arguing that legislators and electors alike should be married men, he seemed to equate a heightened capacity for feelings with heightened moral character.[18] Indeed, he required all titled men, judges, justices of the peace, clergymen and moral teachers to be married men.[19] The celibate were deemed incapable of altruism, were emotionally defective and were more inclined to be disrespectful and hateful to women.

---

[13] NLW 21285E, Letter no. 862, Iolo Morganwg to Miss Barker, 26 March 1798.
[14] NLW 21396E, no. 8. In a religious context, he reiterated these ideas, stating that conjugal and paternal feelings better equip a man to grasp the 'idea of the divine attribute'. NLW 13112B, p. 275.
[15] NLW 21396E, no. 8. This view was given a different, more inclusive, meaning when addressed to a woman, Miss Barker: 'The married Couple constitute a link in a nation or Community's [ch]ain of perpetuity, and contribute to give it eternity of duration. The Celibate breaks this chain, interrupts the line of population, and all acting as he acts, would [in] a short time annihilate a Community.' NLW 21285E, Letter no. 862, Iolo Morganwg to Miss Barker, 26 March 1798.
[16] NLW 21285E, Letter no. 862, Iolo Morganwg to Miss Barker, 26 March 1798.
[17] Damian Walford Davies, *Presences that Disturb: Models of Romantic Identity in the Literature and Culture of the 1790s* (Cardiff, 2002), p. 172.
[18] NLW 21285E, Letter no. 862, Iolo Morganwg to Miss Barker, 26 March 1798.
[19] They are required to be 'matured into a perfect man [?] becoming susceptible of all our sensibilities'. Ibid. See also NLW 13159A, pp. 400–9; NLW 13088B, p. 74.

Iolo reiterated these conclusions in an unfinished treatise entitled 'Welsh Ideas of Celibacy',[20] a pseudo-historical and pseudo-intellectual treatise in the same mould as William Hayley's three-volume study of old maids, *A Philosophical, Historical, and Moral Essay on Old Maids* (1786), a work which possibly influenced him.[21] Like Hayley's work, which was facetiously dedicated to the eminent bluestocking, Elizabeth Carter, Iolo's stereotypical condemnations of old maids and bachelors were supported by popular rhymes and proverbs. Echoes of Hayley's language are audible as Iolo mocks the 'sisterhood' of old maids: prudish and coquettish, they are veritable man-haters and, likewise, bachelors are misers or debauchees and confirmed woman-haters, a point he expanded upon in a veiled allusion to homosexuality, a practice which he believed confirmed the 'defects in their affections'.[22]

In his polemical writings which touched on issues of gender Iolo was therefore by no means a progressive voice. However, radical feminism was not the only feminism with which Iolo would have been familiar in the latter decades of the eighteenth century. The prevalence of sensibility in Iolo's writings on gender points to a familiarity with feminism within the culture of sensibility, especially bluestocking sensibility. The cult of sensibility found expression in his private and public relationships with women and sheds considerable light on his domestic travails. We turn next, therefore, to his relationship with his mother, his wife and his children.

Ann Matthew, Iolo's mother, had married the stonemason Edward William at St Athan church on 8 November 1744.[23] Following the death of their first-born, a daughter named Ann,[24] their son Edward (Iolo Morganwg) was very much an *enfant gâté* and he remained his mother's favourite despite the arrival of three further siblings: John, Miles and Thomas: 'I was . . . her favourite and am happy in the thoughts of having never, for any considerable time, left her.'[25] The daughter of Edward Matthew of Ty'n caeau, Coychurch, Iolo's mother was a member of the relatively new gentry, the Matthews families of Llandaf and Radyr.[26] When she was nine, her mother died and her father sold his

---

[20] NLW 13118B, pp. 100–4.

[21] William Hayley, *A Philosophical, Historical, and Moral Essay on Old Maids. By a Friend to the Sisterhood* (London, 1786).

[22] 'And let it be remembered that it is Batchelors in ninety nine out of every hundred instances, that are notoriously addicted to the most shocking filthy and unnatural of all the evil propensities incident to human nature.' NLW 13118B, p. 101. This is a rare example of a passionate outburst by Iolo on sexual morality in a period which held ambivalent attitudes towards homosexuality. See Barry Reay, *Popular Cultures in England 1550–1750* (London, 1998), pp. 26–9. For Iolo, sexuality was only acceptable within the safe confines of marriage.

[23] Williams: *IM*, pp. 81, 94.

[24] NLW 21319A, pp. 11–13.

[25] NLW 21387E, no. 10.

[26] Williams: *IM*, p. 86; Philip Jenkins, *The Making of a Ruling Class: The Glamorgan Gentry 1640–1790* (Cambridge, 1983), p. 64.

inheritance, leaving her to be raised in a sizeable mansion at nearby Boverton by her dead mother's sister, who had married into the Seys family, an old Glamorgan dynasty.[27]

This semi-privileged upbringing and his mother's very genuine aristocratic roots deeply scored the literary persona which Iolo presented to the literary world, even though his slightly affected mother was absent from the first posthumous biographical account of Iolo by Elijah Waring.[28] All subsequent biographers and critics, however, have pointed to this formative relationship as the key to Iolo's quixotic psyche.[29] His irrepressible egotism as an adult, his class-inflected inferiority complex and his creative nostalgia for the past have all been attributed to his strong identification with his mother. In the light of her importance, Ann's absence from Waring's volume is surprising, especially since the biography bears all the hallmarks of an authorized version. Elsewhere, notably in the introduction to *Poems, Lyric and Pastoral* (1794) and in other stray manuscript pieces, Iolo tellingly focused on the influence of his mother who, because of her own innate sensibility, was the only person able to relate to the budding Romantic poet. Iolo portrayed her death when he was twenty-three as a defining moment in his life and expressed his ensuing vulnerability in Freudian terms: 'I was when she died as ignorant of the world as almost a new born child.'[30] Always conscious of his audience and their expectations, it is clear that Iolo's various accounts of the mother-son relationship is highly fictionalized. He represented his mother as a stoic, physically fragile Gothic heroine who had been 'ever since I can remember asthmatic & consumptive with very weak nerves'.[31] Her centrality is again underlined by his account of his extreme reaction to her death:

> In August 1770, my Mother died, and how irreparable was the loss of her to me! I had for seven weeks sat up with her with[out] ever taking a moments rest in bed. She would not suffer me to quit the room. Her disorder was a consumption. I had anticipated the fatal moment long before it arrived. My grief was extreme, but its effects were singular I believe. A deep melancholy would for awhile seize me than [*sic*] followed often an odd kind of extravagant laugh which some deemed mirth, and blamed me for, but little did they know of the matter.[32]

Elsewhere, he claimed that, inconsolable with grief, he left Glamorgan for Bristol, Bath and London and became interested only in architecture, 'especially Gothic',[33] thereby echoing the subtle Gothic touches in the

27 Williams: *IM*, p. 91; Jenkins, *The Making of a Ruling Class*, p. 29.
28 *RAEW*.
29 Williams: *IM*, pp. 109, 166; Lewis: *IM*, pp. 20–2; Morgan: *IM*, pp. 1–2; Walford Davies, *Presences that Disturb*, pp. 170–3.
30 NLW 21387E, no. 9.
31 NLW 21387E, no. 2.
32 NLW 21387E, no. 10.
33 NLW 21387E, no. 9.

narrative of his mother's protracted death and his devoted attendance upon her. Not only do these details serve to highlight Iolo's own heightened emotional and moral faculties, but their pathos is designed to engage the senti-mental impulse of the reader.

These statements were, of course, intended for the public arena and were designed to maximize the emotional and moral sympathy his youthful loss might evoke among the adherents of sensibility. In contrast, his private expres-sions of grief were less contrived. 'On My Birth day', written *c.*1780, hinges on the notion that marking the day of his birth recapitulates his grief for the woman who gave birth to him:[34]

> Why? was I doom'd to taste this cup of woe
> This tide of grief that must incessant flow,
> Why part I not from that Dear Mother's womb
> To, where she's now at rest, the peaceful tomb.
> Ten years are past, since she, from pinching grief,
> Fled to that place where anguish finds relief.
> Yet still for her the spring of sorrow flows
> And memory awakens all my woes.

A decade later, in 1790, his grief found expression in a sonnet to her memory.[35] But Ann Matthew's psychological inheritance to her son also involved a class dynamic which brings into focus the complex and sometimes bewildering interplay between class and gender in the eighteenth century, an interplay which also found expression in the concept of sensibility.[36] The fictionalized account of his mother's death not only vouched for Iolo's own commitment to the concept but also suggests that it was an inherited trait.[37] Iolo depicted his mother as an exponent of sensibility, and also claimed that she was responsible for nurturing this faculty in her son:

> Safe in thy care I pass'd through feeble youth;
> Unschool'd beside, I, tutor'd at thy knee,
> Caught from thy lips the sacred lore of truth.[38]

His impressionable mind had been stimulated by books from her library, which included copies of the *Spectator* and the *Tatler*, the foremost purveyors

---

[34] NLW 21422E, no. 2.

[35] 'Sonnet, written in 1790, *To the Memory of my Mother, who died Aug. 20, 1770*', Williams: *PLP*, II, p. 97.

[36] Leonore Davidoff and Catherine Hall (eds.), *Family Fortunes: Men and Women of the English Middle Class 1780–1850* (rev. edn., London, 2002), p. 73; Landes, *Women and the Public Sphere in the Age of the French Revolution*, p. 13.

[37] In writings of a political nature he boasted of his descent from Welsh princes and identified in particular with Rhita Gawr, a suitable role model, since having 'dethroned so many Despots that he made a long trailing Robe of their Beards', Rhita strengthened rather than undermined Iolo's radical sympathies, NLW 21323B, p. 41.

[38] Williams: *PLP*, II, p. 97.

of sensibility in the early eighteenth century.[39] Adherence to sensibility was therefore represented as a feature of her gentility which, in her lifetime, had set her apart from her boorish neighbours:

> Let the Reader pardon my filial partiality, and allow me to say that she was a woman of uncommon mental abilities. Her taste in polite literature was uncommonly, but unperceived by those amongst whom it was her destiny to pass thro' life. She had a dignity of mind which kept aloof from many.[40]

His mother, and his fictionalized relationship with her, was thus a useful tool with which Iolo shaped his public persona. Not only did he interpret the notion of sensibility as an equalizing social force, 'a meritocracy of feeling not necessarily coinciding with the hierarchy of birth',[41] but he also strengthened his sentimental credentials with references to his mother's gentility. But for his maternal grandfather's profligacy, Iolo would have been the social equal of those to whom he was required to defer in order to gain their financial assistance. By identifying with his 'aristocratic' and emotionally susceptible parent, was he seeking to reclaim that heritage, perhaps under the illusion that by doing so he would be better positioned to negotiate the class-ridden networks of patronage and salon life? This, allied with his curious status as last of the genuine 'British bards', provided valuable leverage against the rigid class divides of high culture which he so despised. In addition, perhaps, the tantalizing proximity of this lost superiority, of which Boverton House was a physical reminder, may have been a motivating factor in Iolo's lifelong quest to recapture the lost literary and druidic glory of Glamorgan?

As well as fictionalizing his relationship with his mother, Iolo also fictionalized his parents' relationship by framing it in terms of a literary motif: that of the high-born woman and the low-born man. This was the theme of one of his most famous poetic reworkings, 'Bugeila'r Gwenith Gwyn' (Watching the White Wheat), and in his own courtship with women, notably his infatuation with Kitty Deere, the daughter of a high sheriff.[42] She features only once in his correspondence, in a postscript to John Walters which contains a joyous series of *englynion* in which Kitty features as 'Haul Awen a Seren Serch' (The Sun of Inspiration and Love's Star), while in a *cywydd* he cites her as his poetic muse.[43] Some of Kitty Deere's poetry is copied in Iolo's manuscripts, but no

---

[39] Janet Todd, *Sensibility: An Introduction* (London, 1986), p. 19; G. Barker-Benfield, *The Culture of Sensibility: Sex and Society in Eighteenth-Century Britain* (London, 1992).

[40] NLW 21387E, no. 10.

[41] Todd, *Sensibility: An Introduction*, p. 13.

[42] Morgan: *IM*, p. 8; The Deere family was a newly elevated gentry family in the eighteenth century. Jenkins, *The Making of a Ruling Class*, pp. 37, 93, 184.

[43] NLW 21285E, Letter no. 771, Iolo Morganwg to John Walters, 1 November 1772; NLW 13087E, pp. 335–6. The expressions of love are purely conventional, relying on conventions of courtly love such as sickening with unrequited love, a notion much favoured by his idol, Dafydd ap Gwilym.

correspondence survives from her to Iolo. Based on the extant written material, it is fair to assume that their relationship was less a romantic fact than a romantic fiction and that Iolo's amorous expressions were no more than poetic conceits.

According to his effusive love-poetry, his one true love was Margaret (Peggy) Roberts, or 'Euron' (Golden One) as he called her. Margaret and Iolo were married by the Revd John Walters at St Mary Church on 18 July 1781, and their union produced four children: Margaret (Peggy), Taliesin (Tally), Ann (Nancy) and Elizabeth (Lilla). Unlike Iolo's mother, who is known to us through his own fictionalized and highly partisan account, his wife's voice is entirely her own and survives unedited in nine letters in her hand. Margaret's voice is authentic, not least because her phonetic orthography conveys the cadences of her Welsh-inflected English dialect. The only fictional aspect, perhaps, was Iolo's insistence that he had been attracted to her natural sensibility:

> your sensibility, innocent simplicity, delicate modesty, and unaffected sweetness of temper, are the very beauties which my soul can taste, even the few weaknesses of human nature that I find in you contribute as much as your virtues to render you amiable in my eyes.[44]

The correspondence between Margaret and Iolo belongs to the period from February 1791 to June 1795 when Iolo lived mostly in London and Margaret remained in Flemingston, raising four small children and nursing her elderly father-in-law.

Margaret's poignant letters to Iolo provide testimony to the strength of her resolve as well as her love for him. G. J. Williams acknowledged that Margaret was a remarkable woman, and it is clear from her correspondence that she knew how to handle her volatile husband. Notwithstanding the uniqueness of her personal circumstances, her letters provide an insight into female vulnerability: her fears and frustrations are those of a wife and mother left to provide for her family with minimal economic and emotional support from her 'imperious husband'.[45] Every letter speaks of hardship and poverty, though Margaret's tone ranges from a feisty attempt to disarm her husband with humour and verse to pitiful cries for help and brutal denunciations of his behaviour. Towards the end of 1791, desperately in need of money, she complained that her family had consumed its last piece of bread:

> My life has bin one continuall and very painful strugule for the last nine Months such expressions fills me wi[t]h terror after your late behaviour in leveing us upwards

---

[44] NLW 21285E, Letter no. 789, Iolo Morganwg to Margaret Williams, undated.
[45] NLW 21285E, Letter no. 817, Iolo Morganwg to Margaret Williams, 6 April 1793. Iolo chided Margaret on this description.

of three-weeks by half a guinea . . . how you Could enjoy rest is w[h]at I cannot gess.[46]

Uncertainty made their hardship all the more unbearable: infrequent correspondence and scant information about his progress meant that she could not keep track of her errant husband: 'onley let me know my fate', she pleaded, 'unsertinty for the nexte maks me miserable'.[47] Lonely, isolated and forced to second-guess Iolo at every step, she sought to save face by hiding her distress from neighbours.[48] Iolo exacerbated Margaret's sense of isolation by excluding her from his parallel life in London. He could be horribly callous at times, belittling her intelligence as a diversionary tactic.[49] This undercurrent took on insidious gendered and social dimensions in one instance when, clearly responding to one of Margaret's vitriolic letters, he portrayed her as the stereotypical irrational female:

> great harshness of temper, and violent and inconsiderate rage that you often put yourself into before you know whether you have a good reason – if you will not do this, you will be the ruin of your self, of me, and all others dependant on us. – for if you come to London which, by what I have now in view, must be the case – your uncivilized temper will be detested by all, except the inhabitants of Billingsgate, Broad St. Giles, and some other curious places inhabited by those of your cast.[50]

The implication was clear: Margaret's persona was inimical to that which prevailed in the literary salons of London. No matter how convincingly he cultivated his image, the poverty and unrefinement which his wife represented was a painful check on reality for him: she compounded his own keen sense of exclusion and relative insignificance in London's fickle, market-driven world of publishing:

> the prevailing customs of London are such that a man must know much of them to know how they affect a person in my situation, and of my proffessed pursuits. Amongst other inconvencies the great and rich so deeply intrench themselves here that [?] it is hardly possible to get access to them, I have written twenty letters of recommendation, which I have long ago been determined not to deliver, I will subject myself no more to their superciliousness.[51]

Rather than accept responsibility for their fragile situation, his response was one of transferral, as is made clear in a letter to his twelve-year-old daughter, Margaret (Peggy):

[46]   NLW 21283E, Letter no. 603, Margaret Williams to Iolo Morganwg, 22 September 1791.
[47]   Ibid.
[48]   NLW 21283E, Letter no. 604, Margaret Williams to Iolo Morganwg, 1 January 1793: 'and none put your self knows of our distres which is more then I can manidg believe the truth I know not how to find bread for your children a nother week'.
[49]   NLW 21285E, Letter no. 835, Iolo Morganwg to Margaret Williams, ? February 1794.
[50]   NLW 21285E, Letter no. 800, Iolo Morganwg to Margaret Williams, undated.
[51]   NLW 21285E, Letter no. 811, Iolo Morganwg to Margaret Williams, 9 August 1792. See also Letter nos. 808–9, Iolo Morganwg to Margaret Williams, 5 May, 20 June 1792.

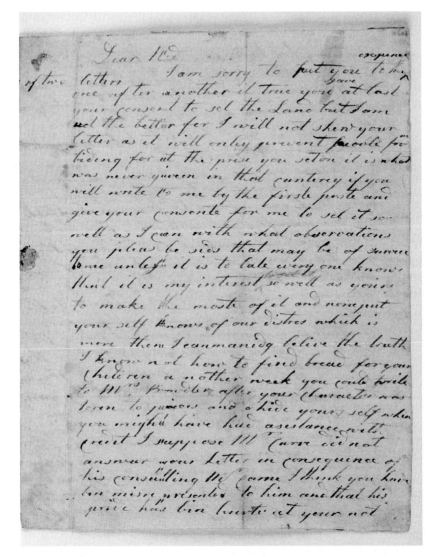

Fig. 25 A letter, dated 1 January 1793, from Margaret (Peggy) Williams to her husband, Iolo Morganwg (NLW 21283E, Letter no. 604).

I hope that you and your sister Nancy and Tally your Brother is well. and that your Mother is well also. Tell her that she has done me a very material injury by writing her last letters she has always been my ruin by her want of a proper knowledge of human nature. letters of this kind throw mystery and Suspicion on a person's character, I have no doubt but that she will at last completely ruin me.[52]

[52] NLW 21285E, Letter no. 844, Iolo Morganwg to Margaret Williams Jr., 29/30 October 1794.

As 1794 drew to a close, Margaret appealed to Iolo's paternal instinct in the hope that his profound grief for their daughter Elizabeth, who had died in April 1793, would prompt him to return to his family. In syntax which cracks under the strain, she concluded that Iolo should give up his futile quest for fame and fortune:

> returne to reason and your fameley who will gladly receive you with all your errors Dear Ned do not Suffer your aspireing Spirit and violent pationess to ruing you and yours . . . it is better late than ever for God's sake return to your Chil[n], by deceiving me you onley deacive your self whe youre efford will do more towards retrieving our affairs then reserve disast[er] and violent opposition will do for you or your children.[53]

Having appealed to Iolo's paternal instincts, Margaret also questioned the sanctity with which Iolo regarded their marriage, a Christian sacrament:

> I have suffered my self to be to long tantalised by you for my childrens good for it has deprived them of all put the name of a Mother[.] tell me sincearly do you look upon the Engagement we have ententered into sacred enough to entille me to the priveleg of being with you where and as you are . . . don insult my misery with false pretences that will not bare excommunication for the anxiety of my mind such as will eyther through me into som disorder that will put a period to my wretched existence or end in a fixt malencoly if it has not don so already I now flater my self that I would recover could I put see you perhaps I may faile and should it be so you will find yourself ansarable for my life to God and my Children . . . If the want of an inclination to be with us is the cause of your apsence be candid and let me know it and I will never trouble you againe . . . I [?know] not what to think nor to say[.] all that I [?wish] for is to be with you aney where and all that I feare is to be longer apsent from you . . . all my complaints has not made the last impression as yet on your minde . . . and consequently I must strougle for my self eyther with or without your assistance.[54]

But while Margaret's letters are testimony to her precarious position, they also reveal a hard-nosed pragmatism. Falling on his mercy, which she stingingly described as having 'fallen very short of my expectations',[55] she begged him to allow her to sell some land and, by February 1795, she brought Iolo down to earth by demanding power of attorney.[56] As well as revealing Margaret's wretchedness, resilience and pragmatism, however, her letters also attest to her abiding love for her deeply flawed husband. He eventually returned home in June 1795, racked with guilt, especially in the wake of the death of his

---

53 NLW 21283E, Letter no. 608, Margaret Williams to Iolo Morganwg, 10 December 1794.
54 NLW 21283E, Letter no. 607, Margaret Williams to Iolo Morganwg, 11 October 1794.
55 Ibid.
56 Iolo answered that he was unable to grant her a letter of attorney since he could not afford the price of a stamp. NLW 21285E, Letter no. 814, Iolo Morganwg to Margaret Williams, 21 December 1792. In Letter no. 815, Iolo Morganwg to Margaret Williams, 29 December 1792, he permitted her to bargain for the sale of the land, but for no less than £700.

daughter Elizabeth, following which he had been 'utterly unable to do or think of any thing, for 8 or 9 months after'.[57] Deeply troubled at the time by feelings of inadequacy as a father and husband as well as a writer, he had contemplated suicide and his rambling meditations on the subject project a grim view of paternity and the joys of fatherhood:

> The principles that operate in forbiddance of suicide are, the injuries that another would suffer thereby. For instance having given existence to other beings without their own consent, and having the power or the least prospect of become able, to guard them from the evils which they are, without their own consent in consequence of my selfish enjoyment that gave them existence, unavoidably subjected to.[58]

Iolo's judgement here was certainly clouded by depression and laudanum because his tone belies the evident delight he took in his children and, later, in his grandchildren, to whom he was known as 'Daitta'.[59]

Iolo related well to his children, and commanded particular filial respect and love from his eldest daughter, Peggy, who ignored all his flaws in a mawkish elegy:

> He was a man with every virtue blest
> No vicious wish he harbour'd in his breast
> Blest with a heart benevolent and kind
> A heart from every earthly dross refin'd
>
> . . .
>
> How often with delight his voice I heard
> Whilst he was with me I no evil fear'd.[60]

Named after her mother, Peggy was a sickly child, blighted with congenital ailments: asthma, stomach complaints and terrible flatulence.[61] According to Elijah Waring, she was 'a very simple rustic Welshwoman, and not at all charming', but she was nonetheless an affectionate and loyal daughter.[62] She also inherited her father's fondness for poetry: twenty-seven sentimental poems survive in her own hand.[63] Both sisters ventured into the political arena,

---

[57] NLW 21387E, no. 21. See 'Bedd-bennill Lila fach' (Little Lilla's funerary-verse) and its conventional Christian consolation: she died before her soul could be corrupted and it was better that she reside with her heavenly Father than with her grief-stricken earthly father. NLW 13141A, p. 113.

[58] NLW 21433E, p. 5a. See also Geraint Phillips, 'Math o Wallgofrwydd: Iolo Morganwg, Opium a Thomas Chatterton', *NLWJ*, XXIX, no. 4 (1996), 391–410.

[59] NLW 21286E, Letter no. 998, Iolo Morganwg to Taliesin Williams, 30 May 1825. See also an endearing letter to the first of Taliesin's sons to be named Edward after their grandfather, 'Iolo Bach', Letter no. 993, Iolo Morganwg to Edward Williams Jr., 17 April 1823.

[60] NLW 21377B, pp. 4b–6b: 'on the [death of] my Father who died Dec 17th 1826'.

[61] NLW 21410E, p. 38a, outlines Peggy's medical history. Waring refers to her as an 'invalid daughter', *RAEW*, p. 115.

[62] *RAEW*, pp. 113–14. She was invited to accompany her father to the eisteddfod at Brecon. NLW 21282E, Letter no. 420, W. J. Rees to Iolo Morganwg, 28 January 1822.

[63] NLW 21377B.

composing poetry during the Glamorgan election in 1818.[64] Nancy, named Ann Matthews Williams after her paternal grandmother, went into service in 1810 and from 1816 onwards kept a milliner's shop with her sister Peggy at Cefncribwr.[65] Apart from the election poem, Nancy showed no leanings towards poetry, but some letters survive in her hand, about half a dozen of which are addressed to her father.[66] Lacking the intellectual fibre and curiosity of her brother Taliesin's correspondence with their father, Nancy's colloquial letters concentrate on matters of health and gossip, referring only in passing to Taliesin's poetry and pressing issues such as the Jamaican legacy.

As far as his children were concerned, the London period was a blot on an otherwise unblemished record, for Iolo otherwise seems to have undertaken his paternal duties seriously, educating his children and endeavouring to provide for them to the best of his ability. They received a basic education which consisted of reading (Welsh and English), writing and arithmetic. Ensuring his daughters' education was a relatively progressive step on his part and may indicate his adherence to the principles of Reason and Nature, and a respect for education as an essential tool towards the improvement of the individual and of society. It is more likely, however, that his aim was not to improve their minds or to free them from their prescribed female role, but rather to equip them properly for their domestic responsibilities.[67] In this sense, Iolo's attitudes towards the education of his daughters were closer to those of Hannah More, a great detractor of Wollstonecraft, than to Wollstonecraft herself.[68] In 1802 Iolo visited Birmingham to research the possibility of opening a stationery shop and a circulating library for his eldest daughter at Bridgend, Neath or Swansea. While at Bromwich and Westbury, the sight of 'a very pretty young woman working at the anvil very handily' sent him on a sentimental flight of fancy. It is worth quoting this section at length since this effectively private record reveals that sensibility for Iolo was more than a useful framework to be utilized in a public, printed arena:

> I felt hurt at the sight for a moment, but recollected that my feelings would have been more sorely wounded, if instead of having been brought in this line of

[64] *Vox Populi Vox Dei! or, Edwards for Ever!* (Swansea, 1818); NLW 6275E, pp. 7–8.

[65] Neville Granville, *Cefn Cribwr: Chronicle of a Village* (Barry, 1980), pp. 75–7. NLW 21286E, Letter no. 953, Iolo Morganwg to Taliesin Williams, 17 October 1816, suggests that their shop was a general store since the daughters were also licensed to sell tea and tobacco. By 1818 they were experiencing financial troubles: NLW 21284E, Letter no. 679, Taliesin Williams to Iolo Morganwg, 16 June 1818.

[66] NLW 21283E, Letter nos. 536, 538–9, Ann Matthews Williams to Iolo Morganwg, 13 May 1810, 28 July 1822, 4 April 1824. NLW 21284E, Letter no. 680, Taliesin Williams to Iolo Morganwg, 10 June 1819, includes a brief note to Ann as an addendum. Three further letters survive from Ann to her sister Margaret which allude to their millinery business: NLW 21283E, Letter nos. 537, 540–1, Ann Matthews Williams to Margaret Williams Jr., 21 February 1821, 13 July 1824, undated.

[67] Taylor, *Mary Wollstonecraft and the Feminist Imagination*, p. 47.

[68] Anne Stott, *Hannah More: The First Victorian* (Oxford, 2003), p. 221.

Industry, I should have seen her on the Town in London having been there a very useful and faithful servant but suddenly dismissed from her place by a capricious impudent purseproud or fashion-proud mistress of the Cockney mushroom dungsprung gentry, without a character, well deserving of a very good one, but denied it because she had committed a very trifling error. Or what to such trash would-be gentry, had dared to assert the dignity of her nature her innocence of a fault with which she had been unjustly charged . . . What can a young woman do in London without a character. What becomes of her when turned unjustly adrift in such a manner by such infamous wretches she asserts a truth boldly. What contradict me Betty? You saucy baggage will you contradict your Master? – Damn such stuff, and let my words be recorded in heaven Damn them, damn them . . . I feel warm, very warm, but it is a warmth from Heaven.[69]

Returning from this novelistic aside to the plight of his own daughters, Iolo regretted having cosseted them at home. For this reason, he feared that 'they are incapable of shifting for themselves', and that their accomplishments amounted to very little: 'A little at their needle my poor girls can do. Nothing else beyond the cookery and the general economy of a Welsh cottage.'[70] Despite their co-educational childhood, the girls did not attain the same intellectual level as their brother who, having worked in David Davis's academy in 1813–15, established his own Commercial School at Merthyr Tydfil in February 1816.[71]

Differences of gender come to the fore in the advice which Iolo imparted to his children regarding their employment, including Rousseauesque echoes in the only surviving letter written to his daughter Nancy in 1810. As she prepared to join the Llewelin household at Bridgend, Iolo exhorted her to abide by Nature. Because of the nature of her work, this letter has an interesting class, as well as gender, inflection: he urged her to fulfil her work 'diligently, faithfully and as well as you possibly can . . . one thing I will request . . . what I have always told you, adhere to truth on all occasions'.[72] This is a striking echo of the advice given to Émile by Rousseau,[73] and suggests that he may have read or heard such ideas reiterated in the work of Priestley,

[69] NLW 13174A, pp. 23–5.
[70] Quoted in D. Elwyn J. Davies, 'Astudiaeth o Feddwl a Chyfraniad Iolo Morganwg fel Rhesymolwr ac Undodwr' (unpublished University of Wales Ph.D. thesis, 1975), p. 192.
[71] See chapter 21 below.
[72] NLW 21285E, Letter no. 884, Iolo Morganwg to Ann Matthews Williams, 5 May 1810.
[73] 'Truth, they say, can never do a man harm. I think so too. My good youth, be honest and humble . . . keep steadfastly to the path of truth or what seems to you truth, in simplicity of heart, and never let yourself be turned aside by pride or weakness . . . It may be you will stand alone, but you will bear within you a witness which will make the witness of men of no account with you . . . Speak the truth and do the right.' Quoted in Davies, 'Astudiaeth o Feddwl a Chyfraniad Iolo Morganwg fel Rhesymolwr ac Undodwr', p. 438. This echo of Rousseau is discussed by Davies in the context of the free enquiry tradition which lay at the heart of the non-denominational religious societies that Iolo wished to establish and which would be dedicated to tolerance and the search for truth.

Wollstonecraft or Godwin. However, in her reply Nancy did not engage at all with her father's philosophical musings, and showed concern only for the fine view from her window.[74] It appears, however, that the notion of the child of nature fitted his daughter better than his son who had been groomed for a future in a respectable profession, for Iolo did not adhere as strictly to this model in the context of Taliesin's professional dispute with his employer, David Davis. While he urged Nancy to contradict her superiors 'in polite terms without flinching, whatever the consequences' if wrongly accused of anything,[75] his tone in the letter to Taliesin was conciliatory, urging him to compromise, not from obedience to hierarchy, but for the sake of friendship.[76]

Thirdly, we must consider Iolo's attitude towards the injustices and cruelty inflicted upon women by parochial administrators of poor relief. Pauperism had been increasing in Wales since the 1770s and was exacerbated by the food crises of the 1790s. This steady growth in demand for relief was met with hostility from parish vestries throughout Wales, many of which adopted under-hand ploys in order to avoid the financial burden of increasing pauperism.[77] One case which Iolo espoused is especially intriguing since its social and moral dimensions are overlaid with issues of gender and sexuality.[78] Following the death of her parents, Catherine Thomas, known locally as Cati Caerffili, was placed in the care of inattentive relatives at Caerffili, where she was sent to work in a woollen factory, only to be dismissed for stealing wool. Forced by poverty and destitution to wander between Caerffili and Flemingston, she was twice ill-used by Flemingston parish vestry. Rather than providing her with an appropriate education or apprenticeship, she had been employed in conditions and company thoroughly inappropriate for a girl on the verge of womanhood: collecting sticks, shovelling manure and collecting stones in the company of vulgar men. For Iolo, this impropriety was confirmed by the fact that she later turned to prostitution. Iolo believed that local magistrates had sought to rid the parish of its financial obligation to Catherine by withholding relief from her in order to force her into criminal acts for which she could legitimately be imprisoned or transported. And just as her own parish had failed in its moral and Christian duty of care towards her, so too had the ills of contemporary industrial society played a part in her downfall. Forced by her uncle to work in the woollen factories at Caerffili at a tender age, she inevitably succumbed to its morally corruptive influence:

[74] NLW 21285E, Letter no. 536, Ann Matthews Williams to Iolo Morganwg, 13 May 1814.
[75] NLW 21285E, Letter no. 884, Iolo Morganwg to Ann Matthews Williams, 5 May 1810.
[76] NLW 21286E, Letter no. 926, Iolo Morganwg to Taliesin Williams, 8 November 1814.
[77] David W. Howell, *The Rural Poor in Eighteenth-Century Wales* (Cardiff, 2000), pp. 81, 95, 97–9, 241.
[78] Cardiff 2.279, Iolo Morganwg to magistrates at Cowbridge, 13 March 1818.

This poor girl is only one of the very numerous instances that I have know[n], of poor families having been ruined for life by having been employed in these nurseries of lewd and idle females, the woollen, cotton, and other manufactories.[79]

Prison, too, was also depicted as a force for evil:

Alas! The ice had been broken in her first delinquencies of stealing wool; she sank deeper into depravity by having been urged to steal by the parish officers and vestries; and her confinement in Jail amongst very wicked characters of her own sex like a millstone about her neck sank her, I am afraid, into depths of depravity out of which nothing I fear but a miraculous interposition of Divine Providence can recover her.[80]

Iolo's sense of despair was made all the more acute because he himself had personally intervened. Impressed by the extraordinary fact that Catherine had taught herself to read both Welsh and English, he sought her recovery through formal education: 'she possesses Talents that, improved by education would have rendered her a female of very superior character'.[81] He believed that the parish vestry should have trained her 'to those employments that are proper to qualify young women for becoming good servants'.[82] Even though Catherine was sentenced to a month's imprisonment, Iolo continued to seek her moral redemption through education and was instrumental in securing a place for her in a benevolent institution in London, where young charges were educated and prepared for a trade. Alas, Catherine absconded before completing her training.

In an ironic twist, which highlights the interplay of gender and social bias, Iolo left the following instructions on an undated scrap of paper, presumably for the attention of his wife and daughters: 'Take care of Katty Caerfilly, and do not suffer her to sit in the house, do as much good as you can for her, but do not admit her into your company.'[83] Despite Iolo's compassion for her plight, ultimately Cati Caerffili was a threatening, albeit pitiful, spectre, tainted by sexual transgression and criminal deeds. The case of Catherine Thomas therefore highlights the tension between Iolo's philanthropy and his paternal concerns: as a destitute thief and prostitute, she was a potentially damaging

[79] NLW 21286E, Letter no. 968, Taliesin Williams to Iolo Morganwg, 12 August 1815.
[80] NLW 1895Ei, Letter no. 81, Iolo Morganwg to David Rowlands, 14 June 1819. In a memorandum regarding this case, Iolo argued that Cati Caerffili would have been better served had she been placed in solitary confinement where she could have considered her actions and repented; 'but to be amongst a rabble of wicked characters for nearly 6 months, has opened the way for seven devilst to enter where only one was before. The house of correction is thus become a house of corruption'. NLW 21286E, Letter no. 970, undated memorandum.
[81] Ibid.
[82] NLW 21286E, Letter no. 968, Iolo Morganwg to Judge Wingfield, 8 April 1819.
[83] NLW 21286E, Letter no. 970A, undated scrap in Iolo Morganwg's hand.

model for his own daughters, whom he had raised to be moral and virtuous.[84] It also highlights how unwise it was for him to be too closely associated with Catherine, since both men and women were vulnerable to sexual defamation.[85] As a coda to this cautionary tale, in 1824, in a hastily penned note to her sister Peggy, Nancy sent her regards to 'father mother you and Catherine Thomas and family'.[86] Was this the same Catherine Thomas or Cati Caerffili, redeemed after all and now possessed of a family of her own? If so, this was one project which Iolo completed satisfactorily.

Fourthly, we turn to the public sphere of Iolo's social relationships. The women with whom he associated were either patrons or subscribers, and were, to all appearances, drawn from a narrower social milieu than his male acquaintances and correspondents. Women who subscribed to his poems and who featured in his correspondence were predominantly bluestockings or Rational Dissenters: they included Elizabeth Montagu, 'Queen of the Blues' and her sister Sarah Scott, Hannah More and her protégée Ann Yearsley, Anna Seward, Mary Barker, Hester Thrale Piozzi,[87] Anna Laetitia Barbauld, Henrietta M. Bowdler[88] and Lady Elizabeth Brown Greenly.[89] Although many other women appear in the subscription list of *Poems, Lyric and Pastoral* (1794), Iolo actually corresponded with very few women. Elizabeth Montagu, for example, featured in Iolo's correspondence with Margaret his wife in the context of her loyal support in difficult circumstances, but no letters survive to attest to an active correspondence between them.[90] The female correspondence is generally fleeting as each woman either received or wrote, on average, only one letter. In the absence of a sustained exchange of letters with any one female correspondent, it is difficult to generalize about the nature of Iolo's relationship with individuals.

Within Iolo's correspondence, gender operated within the prescribed and safe confines of sensibility and the accepted norms of letter-writing. Stylistically, his obsequious deferring was a feature of his missives both to male and

84 NLW 13174A, p. 26ʳ.
85 Bernard Capp, *When Gossips Meet: Women, Family, and Neighbourhood in Early Modern England* (Oxford, 2003), pp. 252–6.
86 NLW 21283E, Letter no. 540, Ann Matthews Williams to Margaret Williams Jr., 13 July 1824.
87 Iolo described Hester Piozzi as 'a Welsh woman and speaks Welsh', NLW 21285E, Letter no. 814, Iolo Morganwg to Margaret Williams, 21 December 1792.
88 Miss Bowdler boasted of her Welsh connections to Iolo: NLW 21280E, Letter no. 28, Henrietta M. Bowdler to Iolo Morganwg, 17 August 1791.
89 Lady Greenly, a patron and composer, was associated with Brecon and the border county of Monmouthshire. She became one of the first members of Cymreigyddion y Fenni (Abergavenny Cymreigyddion Society) and the Welsh Manuscript Society which played a significant role in the transmission and reception of Iolo's work. Sian Rhiannon Williams, 'Llwydlas, Gwenynen Gwent a Dadeni Diwylliannol y Bedwaredd Ganrif ar Bymtheg' in Geraint H. Jenkins (ed.), *Cof Cenedl XV: Ysgrifau ar Hanes Cymru* (Llandysul, 2000), pp. 97–128.
90 NLW 21285E, Letter no. 814, Iolo Morganwg to Margaret Williams, 21 December 1792.

female correspondents and, in terms of content, Iolo's chameleon-like ability meant that his letters constitute a literary performance in which he wrote to order, tailoring his letters, views and tone for each implied reader. This is most clearly seen in his lengthy letter to Miss Mary Barker in 1798. Seeking her patronage as a result of flattering comments she had made about his poems, he responded with inordinate energy to her remark that a friend had warned her that he was a 'terrible Jacobin'. In an extended, but polite, defence of his 'misrepresented' political sentiments, Iolo outlined his views on democracy, church, suffrage, women, religion and slavery in order to prove that he was a 'reformist, but not what may be term[ed a] Jacobin'.[91] This was hardly necessary, since the mildly flirtatious tenor of Barker's letter suggests that she was excited by the frisson of danger and would not have written directly to such a 'terrible' reformer. But Iolo was not always so deferential, and similar accusations from Mrs Nicholl, who retracted her support of Iolo because of his alleged Jacobinism, elicited a very different response:[92] this time he offered an impassioned self-justification and mocked her by the sarcastic use of deferential titles, 'goody nichols', 'dame Nichols' and 'madam'.[93] Having vented his spleen in this, as well as in another unfinished diatribe against her, Iolo felt no compunction either about completing or sending them. The second draft was more venomous and had recourse to sexual defamation:

> It is this unbelief of the Christian religion that constitutes . . . a Jacobin so give me leave madam to call you a Jacobin, I will, if it will soothe your pride a little, call you a Lady-Jacobin. This will not be the greatest prostitution known of the once honourable term Lady now the designation of every common strumpet.[94]

Both women voiced accusations of Jacobinism, but class and politics rather than gender was the imperative behind Iolo's different responses. Clearly a woman of feeling, and perhaps of bluestocking pedigree, Barker was judged to be less deserving of castigation than a vicar's wife who, as Iolo's tirade reveals, was considered to represent the 'Church and Kingism' he so heartily despised.

Iolo's attack on Mrs Nicholl is quite exceptional because, as a rule, he responded graciously to criticism from women. For example, because their social standing and wealth raised them above the male stonemason poet, members of the Bowdler group who, from 1791 to 1794, provided much additional financial support towards the publication of Iolo's poems, felt able to advise him to abandon his plans in London and return to Wales.[95] Anna Seward provides another example of how harsh home truths may have been

[91] NLW 21285E, Letter no. 862, Iolo Morganwg to Miss Barker, 26 March 1798.
[92] NLW 21281E, Letter no. 297, Mrs Nicholl to Iolo Morganwg, 1 May 1794.
[93] NLW 21281E, Letter no. 224b, Iolo Morganwg to an Aristocratic Woman [Mrs Nicholl?], 1 January 1792.
[94] NLW 21326E, p. 50.
[95] NLW 21280E, Letter no. 31, Henrietta M. Bowdler to Iolo Morganwg, 13 December 1792.

considered more palatable from a female pen. Perhaps familiar with Ann Yearsley's problems with Hannah More,[96] Seward patronizingly warned Iolo that his opportunities of literary success were likely to be inhibited by his class as well as his acute sensibility:

> but permit me to express my concern that Nature made you the fatal present of a spirit, & an imagination so raised above the sphere in which you were destined to move; since in every Age they have much oftener proved great misfortunes than blessings to their Possessor.[97]

No reply survives to indicate Iolo's response, but since Seward subscribed to his poems he may have been satisfied with that single, yet significant, gesture of approval.

A further interesting feature of Iolo's letters to women is the way in which he constructed his persona. In his previously quoted letter to Miss Barker he carefully attributed his 'passion' and 'wild warmth' to his Welshness rather than to the politics he espoused. He also compounded this softer image of himself by claiming to be a Quaker, although several pages later, perhaps inadvertently, he acknowledged his Unitarian faith. Generally speaking, however, he softened his radicalism because the majority of the women with whom he corresponded were bluestockings. Unsurprisingly, his bardo-druidic persona was rarely disclosed in his letters to such women despite its prominence in the letter he penned to the *Gentleman's Magazine* in 1789, in the preface to *Poems, Lyric and Pastoral* (1794) and in his correspondence with others of a bardic or antiquarian persuasion. The persona presented in the letters to women was more rustic than bardic, except for a letter to an unknown female recipient (probably Hannah More) in which he stated boldly: 'I am a Druid in many of my principles.'[98] In letters to an unknown female correspondent and also to Barker,[99] Iolo aligned himself with the labouring-class poets Ann Yearsley and Robert Burns, a model which would have been familiar to bluestockings and, perhaps, more acceptable to them than the radical bardic persona. Thus Iolo may have considered this model, the genius of nature, a more profitable one in terms of procuring patronage from affluent, conservative females. He certainly made a play of his lack of sophistication. Yearsley and Burns, he pointed out, had never had occasion to disappoint anyone with their unrefined manners because they had the advantage of people to mediate with gentlefolk on their behalf:

---

[96] Stott, *Hannah More: The First Victorian*, pp. 70–8.

[97] NLW 21282E, Letter no. 459, Anna Seward to Iolo Morganwg, 12 July 1792.

[98] NLW 21286E, Letter no. 1025, Iolo Morganwg to an unknown recipient, undated. Anna Seward was initiated into the Gorsedd of the Bards as an Ovate, but the Gorsedd and the bardo-druidic vision are not mentioned in her letter to Iolo: NLW 21282E, Letter no. 459, Anna Seward to Iolo Morganwg, 12 July 1792.

[99] NLW 21285E, Letter no. 862, Iolo Morganwg to Miss Barker, 26 March 1798.

I never had the good fortune of Mrs Yearsley whose business of procuring subscribers and collecting the money was done all by other, and by those whose influence precluded disappointments, Creech the Bookseller of Edinburgh and others in Scotland did the same for Burns, I observe that those of the higher classes grant much to the requests of each other, more I firmly believe, from that modification of Pride and false (I had almost said diabolical) virtue called honour.[100]

He reinforced his labouring-class persona by emphasizing the unfair treatment he had received at the hands of less gracious people than his correspondents:

> To their inferiors (as we must be called) the Gentry &c (as they call themselves) behave with the most unfeeling cruelty (I was going to use the word indifference but it was too mild) how many hours have I shivered at the doors of great and opulent names waiting for the paltry sum of four shilling.[101]

The inherent class antagonism involved possibly accounts for the overall prominence of his bardic persona over that of labouring-class poet. The bardic persona was more liberating and, indeed, more viable in the male antiquarian and radical circles in which Iolo turned rather than in the class-bound structures of the bluestockings and their literary coteries.

This brings us finally to the male circles which Iolo frequented, notably the taverns of Cowbridge and the beery gatherings of the London-Welsh circle, which represented a culture diametrically opposed to that of the bluestockings and the polite-society culture of other correspondents. In these circles Iolo was better known by a series of bardic names which roughly corresponded with periods in his poetic and bardic development. Among the poets of his native Glamorgan from the late 1760s onwards he was known as 'Iorwerth Gwilym (or Gwilim)' while, under the influence of the London-Welsh in the early 1770s, he became known as 'Iorwerth Morganwg'. He espoused the more mature bardic pseudonym, 'Iolo Morganwg', *c.*1790, shortly before his second sojourn in London. These bardic names also correspond with two bardic personae, though the distinction is not a strict one. While the bardic name 'Iolo Morganwg' was identified primarily with the post-revolutionary 'Bard of Liberty' and the purveyor of bardism, the activity of 'Iorwerth Gwilym' and 'Iorwerth Morganwg' represented Iolo's early involvement with the Gwyneddigion Society and much, though not all, of his earthy material belongs to this period. Iolo became intoxicated by the Gwyneddigion while he was in London, and he sought to maintain the sense of camaraderie in his correspondence with several like-minded members upon his return to Glamorgan, among them Siôn Ceiriog (John Edwards), Robin Ddu (Robert Hughes), Owain Myfyr (Owen Jones) and Dafydd Ddu Feddyg (David Samwell), with whom he exchanged bawdy, scabrous material. Following the

---

[100] NLW 21286E, Letter no. 1025, Iolo Morganwg to an unknown recipient, undated.
[101] Ibid.

example of Lewis Morris, whose letters and manuscripts Iolo had perused at the Welsh School in London, the poems and squibs composed by the Gwynedd-igion were intended for mutual diversion and entertainment. Young bucks bandied around stock anti-feminist themes of the prevailing male sub-culture, including crude condemnations of old women, old maids and scolding wives.[102] In Iolo's hands, even the triad form, revered for its encapsulation of druidic learning, became a suitable conduit for misogynist humour: 'Tripeth sy'n gofyn eu porthi yn aml; Cywion mân, Plant bychain, a Chont Gwraig ifanc' (Three things that require frequent feeding; tiny chicks, small children, and a young wife's cunt),[103] and 'Tri pheth ni fyddys gwell o geisio eu gwneu-thur: piso'n erbyn y gwynt, dal llucheden, ag attal tafod gwraig' (Three things that one would not be the better for trying to achieve: pissing against the wind, catching lightning, and holding a woman's tongue).[104] That Iolo delighted in entertaining his friends is evident in the comments which accompanied his responses to the boasts made by Siôn Ceiriog and Robin Ddu of their sexual prowess. Most of this smuttiness focused on Morfudd, Dafydd ap Gwilym's most treasured lover, in 'Cân Morfydd i'r Gyllell Gig' (Morfydd's Song to the Meat Knife):[105] 'Ni sefais nemawr am iaith na reol yn un o'r ddwy gân yma, fy unig ofal oedd eu cael yn ddiymofal, i beri chwerthin canys dywedir ei fod yn ddigon gwir' (I did not bother much about language and rule in both of these songs, my only concern was to make them amusing, to cause laughter because it is said to be quite true.)[106] 'Nani Gamp aflan o Forfa Gwaunllwg' (Nani foul feat of Wentloog Marsh) and other earthy poems were couched in similar vein, and local gossips like Bessi Fingam were reviled by him as 'wry mouthed or peevish' women.[107]

It is fitting that this chapter should close with Iolo's links with the Gwyneddigion Society since this particular relationship casts light on the overall masculine nature of Iolo's *oeuvre*, and his most influential literary and cultural legacy, bardism. Constructed largely as a result of Iolo's involvement with the interest of the Gwyneddigion in Welsh poetry and antiquities, bardism owed its internal dynamic, which exalted south Wales above north Wales, to the dissolution of Iolo's friendship with Owain Myfyr and William Owen Pughe, two of the foremost members of the society. Iolo Morganwg's vision of Wales's bardo-druidic past was a thoroughly masculine construct: Iolo himself was its hub and the historical and mythological characters whom he enlisted to provide Wales and especially the county of Glamorgan with a

---

[102] NLW 13170B, p. 260; NLW 21331B, pp. 91–4; NLW 21413E, p. 42; NLW 13148A, p. 263; NLW 21424E, p. 63; NLW 21328A, p. 46.

[103] NLW 13133A, p. 69.

[104] NLW 21319A, p. 170. See also the bawdy triads in NLW 13087E, pp. 164, 249, 270.

[105] NLW 21390E, p. 22.

[106] NLW 21390E, p. 31.

[107] NLW 21391E, p. 6; NLW 13091E, p. 95.

venerable cultural pantheon were, without exception, male. Women were reckoned to be absent from bardism's past, though they were involved in its present and would also play an instrumental role in its future. In a postscript to a draft of 'A Short Account of the Ancient British Bards' Iolo noted that 'Women as well as men, may be admitted of all orders',[108] and both Sarah Elizabeth Owen (William Owen Pughe's wife) and Anna Seward, 'the Swan of Lichfield', were initiated into the Gorsedd of the Bards as Ovates during Iolo's lifetime.[109] After his death the formidable Augusta Waddington Hall (Lady Llanover or 'Gwenynen Gwent'), who had initially heard of Iolo through Lady Greenly, promoted the cause of the Gorsedd of the Bards and bardism through her association with Taliesin ab Iolo and her involvement with the Abergavenny Cymreigyddion Society and the Welsh Manuscript Society. It was also in her library at Llanover that the bulk of Iolo's voluminous manuscript collection was housed prior to being deposited in the National Library of Wales in the early twentieth century. Admitting women into the bardic orders was a new departure for Welsh poetry since the genuine professional poetic guild in Wales had always been closed to women, whose only access to strict-metre poetry had occurred through informal, and necessarily amateur, training. Iolo's innovation may have had more to do with seeking female patronage than asserting female equality, but it nonetheless ensured that his undisputedly masculine legacy also captured the female imagination and encouraged their active participation.

---

[108] NLW 13089E, p. 458.

[109] Sarah Elizabeth Owen was made an Ovate at Primrose Hill in 1792, though she may have received her honour *in absentia*: NLW 8540C; Geraint and Zonia Bowen, *Hanes Gorsedd y Beirdd* (Dinbych, 1991), p. 25.

17

The 'Cultivated Understanding' and Chaotic Genius of David Samwell*

MARTIN FITZPATRICK

In December 1798 an obituary for David Samwell appeared in the *Gentleman's Magazine* which concluded: 'He was a man of cultivated understanding and friendly disposition. In his profession he was justly esteemed skilful; and he is much lamented.'[1] On the other hand, Owen Jones (Owain Myfyr) probably summed up the feelings of his Welsh contemporaries when he remarked, 'where there's genius, there'll be chaos' ('os bydd Camp e fydd ystremp').[2] What are we to make of this? Does it represent the dual personality of the man and the different circles in which he moved? On the one hand, in polite English society he was remembered as a surgeon who, as the obituary noted,

> accompanied Capt. Cook in his last voyage to the South Seas; and, a few years ago, published an account of the circumstances attending the death of that celebrated navigator. He was likewise author of many short detached pieces of poetry, as well in his native Welsh as in the English language; several of which have appeared in our miscellany, and possess considerable merit. His little poem of 'The Negro boy' was favourably received by the publick.[3]

In this view, he was a man of modest but solid achievements. On the other hand, there was the David Samwell his Welsh friends knew: Black David the Doctor (Dafydd Ddu Feddyg), brilliant and wonderfully entertaining company, but with a volcanic temperament. Close friends and drinking

---

* I am grateful to Dr Grayson M. Ditchfield for his advice during the preparation of this chapter. I should also like to thank the editor of this volume and the research fellows working under his direction at the University of Wales Centre for Advanced Welsh and Celtic Studies – Dr Mary-Ann Constantine, Dr Andrew Davies, Dr David Ceri Jones, Dr Ffion Mair Jones and Dr Cathryn A. Charnell-White – for their expert advice and assistance.

[1] *Gentleman's Magazine*, LXVIII, Part 2 (1798), 1085.

[2] This translation, kindly provided by Daniel Huws, aims to capture the essence of the words of Owen Jones. William Ll. Davies, 'David Samwell (1751–1798): Surgeon of the "Discovery", London-Welshman and Poet', *THSC* (1926–7), 122. This article is the main source for Samwell's life. See also *ODNB* and Martin Fitzpatrick, Nicholas Thomas and Jenny Newell (eds.), *The Death of Captain Cook and other Writings by David Samwell* (Cardiff, forthcoming, 2006), chapter 1.

[3] Quoted in Davies, 'David Samwell', 71.

companions experienced his dazzling intelligence and his waywardness, and
not surprisingly some, like Owen Jones, believed that his death was a result of
excess – of drink and drugs. This was the man who, on occasion, supplied Iolo
with laudanum,[4] and who, like Iolo, moved in radical patriotic circles. He was
one-time vice-president of the Gwyneddigion Society and a member of the
Caradogion Society.

Seeing David Samwell as a man of dual personality, or indeed of several
identities, does not resolve the difficulties in understanding his character, for,
despite his many contradictions, his personality traits and abilities manifested
themselves in the various worlds he inhabited. It is hardly surprising that his
fierce temper and impetuosity were not confined to his Welsh relationships.
John Crosier, to whom he was apprenticed as a surgeon, thought that he would
go far, provided he kept his temperament in check. Samwell was aware of his
judgement.[5] Moreover, it was not only his Welsh friends who thought of him
as someone with special abilities. 'Rays of genius play over the paper', wrote
Anna Seward of one of Samwell's letters. She told him that critics reckoned
him worthy of the poet laureateship.[6]

When his friend John Edwards (Siôn Ceiriog) died in 1792, Samwell wrote:
'He was witty, satirical & humourous, a sensible well informed man but rather
too violent in his argument. He was fluent in his speech and very fond of
speaking.'[7] He could have been writing about himself. With friends like John
Edwards and Iolo Morganwg, Samwell seems less distinctive perhaps and the
essence of Samwell was his Welshness. He certainly participated in their enthusiasms not only for reviving ancient bardic traditions but also in the Madoc
fever of the 1790s. Indeed, almost all characterizations of Samwell emphasize
his Welshness; for example, J. C. Beaglehole described him as 'highly Welsh',
O. H. K. Spate as the 'rollicking Welsh surgeon' and, most recently, Nicholas
Thomas as a 'poet, antiquarian, and romantic Welsh nationalist'.[8]

There are, however, dangers in thinking that one can reconcile the difficulties in understanding him by portraying him as essentially Welsh. It does not
really provide a solution to understanding his many sides, and it can lead to a

---

[4] NLW 21282E, Letter nos. 458, 458a (lines sent by Samwell to Iolo Morganwg).
[5] LRO 920, Samwell Correspondence, Gregson Papers, GRE 2/17, Letter no. 13, 16 May
1776; Letter no. 17, 2 February 1780. Unless otherwise stated, all the letters in this correspondence are from David Samwell to Matthew Gregson.
[6] Archibald Constable (ed.), *Letters of Anna Seward written between the Years 1784 and 1807*
(6 vols., Edinburgh, 1811), III, pp. 139–40, Letter no. XXVII, Anna Seward to David Samwell,
12 December 1795. Seward was interested in the Welsh cultural revival. Samwell may have
been responsible for her investiture as an ovate of the Order of Welsh Bards in the autumn
of 1793. Davies, 'David Samwell', 119, n. 1.
[7] NLW 4582C, p. 5.
[8] J. C. Beaglehole (ed.), *The Journals of Captain Cook on his Voyages of Discovery* (4 vols. and a
portfolio, Cambridge, 1955–74), IV, p. 500; O. H. K. Spate, *The Pacific since Magellan, Volume
III: Paradise Found and Lost* (London, 1988), p. 238; Nicholas Thomas, *Discoveries: The Voyages
of Captain Cook* (London, 2003), p. 269.

Fig. 26 The naval surgeon and poet, David Samwell (1751–98): Dafydd Ddu Feddyg (Black David the Doctor). An engraving by Chretien after Jouquet, 1790.

lazy characterization whenever he appears on the wider stage. He is Samwell, the sexy and eccentric Welshman, the implication being that he is so because he is Welsh. And, of course, 'Welsh' is not seen in any sense as problematic, itself requiring interpretation. There are, moreover, alternative candidates for the 'essence' of Samwell.

For most of his adult life Samwell was at sea. From the time he was apprenticed as a naval surgeon to John Crosier in 1768, the longest period he was on land was four years, from November 1786 to October 1790.[9] We might therefore say that the clue to Samwell was that he was a sailor. Like many

---

[9] Davies, 'David Samwell', 90, gives the dates of his service as a surgeon at sea. Also, from the information he gives (p. 128) and Samwell's correspondence with Matthew Gregson, we know that in 1771–2 he was serving off Greenland.

sailors, he was disciplined aboard ship, and undisciplined and disorientated on land.[10] But that tends to reintroduce the notion of Samwell as a split person-ality. Moreover, it ignores the fact that he was no ordinary sailor, for his most important experience at sea was on Cook's third voyage, far different from the humdrum life of a sailor on patrol in the Western approaches or the North Sea.

Another way to view Samwell would be to see him as a marginal man, a natural inhabitant of the radical underworld which Iain McCalman has charted. He has shown how respectable Rational Dissent, which rested on deep philosophical and theological principles, shaded into a much less respectable world, where intellectual depth was replaced by daring bricolages of ideas, where millennial, utopian, and libertarian ideas swirled around in a melting pot heated by revolutionary sympathies.[11] But Samwell does not slot neatly into this pigeon-hole. He could indeed be swayed by his enthusiasms, but he was well educated and was no autodidact, dogmatist or mere intellectual adventurer. Among his friends were those who were anxious to promote a culture of sensibility. In the early 1770s he was a participant in such develop-ments in Liverpool. For such a thoroughly masculine type, it comes as something of a surprise to see him even remotely involved in a trend which is regarded as feminizing the world of manners and taste.[12]

It is clear that there is no simple key to understanding Samwell. In some cases, he changed his views as a result of experience, but in other respects we can detect what appear to be permanently contradictory elements in his make-up. In attempting to understand Samwell it might be worth spelling out in more detail some of the contradictions and paradoxes in his ideas and make-up before trying to put the parts back together again.

Samwell moved in radical circles. He shared radical aspirations. He was for the rights of ancient Britons, was against slavery and was anti-clerical. Like Richard Price, he welcomed the French Revolution and published an ode in 1790 in which he portrayed the revolution as the 'opening dawn of perfect liberty'.[13] He revered Tom Paine and kept the *Rights of Man* on board ship with him. He recorded in one of his letters how he refused to doff his hat to George III when passing him in Hyde Park.[14] Among the radicals, he supported John

---

[10] N. A. M. Rodger, *The Wooden World: An Anatomy of the Georgian Navy* (paperback edn., London, 1988), pp. 205–11.

[11] Iain McCalman, *Radical Underworld: Prophets, Revolutionaries and Pornographers in London, 1795–1840* (Cambridge, 1988).

[12] See G. J. Barker Benfield, *The Culture of Sensibility: Sex and Society in Eighteenth-Century Britain* (London, 1992), and Harriet Guest, *Small Change: Women, Learning, Patriotism, 1750–1810* (Chicago and London, 2000), esp. pp. 252–67; more specifically, H. A. Taylor, 'Matthew Gregson and the Pursuit of Taste', *Transactions of the Historic Society of Lancashire and Cheshire*, 110 (1958), 160.

[13] BL Add. 1495, f. 117.

[14] LRO 920 GRE 2/17, Letter no. 5, 25 June 1774. Samwell noted that 'His Majesty always looks as surly as a Bull at his subjects'.

Wilkes and, like Wilkes, his libertarianism had a sexual dimension. Samwell loved the nymphs. He pursued them relentlessly at every port of call and paid for their favours. For the most part, he did not seem to worry overmuch about the consequences of his liaisons. In 1788, he signed off a letter to Matthew Gregson with the casual remark that all his 'Bearns' were at 'Otahiete', noting slightly regretfully that they were being brought up 'little better than Heathens'.[15]

Despite his misogynist streak, Samwell was an admirer of women poets – he read the poems of, and possibly knew, Anna Laetitia Aikin (soon to become Mrs Barbauld) and corresponded with Anna Seward.[16] He knew Helen Maria Williams and stayed with her on arriving in Paris in 1798.[17] He also associated with Rational Dissenters, whose radicalism was more straightlaced than that of Wilkes. They refused to distinguish between public and private morality. Indeed, the morally wayward leader of the Whigs, Charles James Fox, came in for criticism from the Revd Richard Price in his *Discourse on the Love of our Country* (1789), though the criticism was omitted from the published version.[18]

Samwell's radicalism had an important Welsh dimension. He participated in the eighteenth-century Welsh renaissance. He was a companion of Iolo Morganwg and associated ancient British virtue with the bardic and druidic tradition, and particularly its pacific dimension.[19] Like Iolo, he might be described as a bardic Jacobin, to use Damian Walford Davies's classification.[20]

Samwell shared many of the assumptions of the improving sensibility of the

---

[15] Ibid., Letter no. 42, 15 October 1788. Samwell may have formed some closer relationships. When he left with Cook, he also left a woman with child. When he returned, he discovered that she had died in childbirth, as had the child. This caused him considerable grief. Much later there is a reference to a 'Mrs Meddyg Du' in a letter from Iolo Morganwg to William Owen (NLW 13224B, Letter no. 1, 23 December 1791). There is no other evidence that Samwell was married. Iolo's reference may have been jocular, and perhaps at the time Samwell did have a close female companion.

[16] LRO 920 GRE 2/17, Letter no. 5, 25 June 1774. Dr John Aikin, the father of Anna Laetitia (1743–1825), was a tutor at the Dissenting academy at Warrington. In 1774 Anna married Rochemont Barbauld, a graduate of the academy. In 1773 she had published her first volume of poetry, and Samwell was probably referring to this collection when he referred to her poetry as 'excellent indeed'.

[17] Ibid., Letter no. 54, 31 May 1798.

[18] North Riding Record Office, Wyvill Papers, 2FW 7/2/159/6, John Disney to Christopher Wyvill, 9 July 1803. *Discourse on the Love of our Country* (1789), in D. O. Thomas (ed.), *Richard Price: Political Writings* (Cambridge, 1991), p. 182: 'We must discourage vice in all its forms, and our endeavours to enlighten must have ultimately in view a reformation of manners and virtuous practice.'

[19] Davies, 'David Samwell', 98–102. Samwell was responsible for the account of the meeting of the Gorsedd of the Bards on Primrose Hill on 22 September 1792 in *Woodfall's Diary* and he may also have written the more substantial account in the *Morning Chronicle* in which it was stated that the bards 'were the heralds and ministers of peace'.

[20] Damian Walford Davies, *Presences that Disturb: Models of Romantic Identity in the Literature and Culture of the 1790s* (Cardiff, 2002), pp. 135–92.

late eighteenth century, but there remained a scatological and erotic aspect of his thought and writings which were far from polite. To an extent he kept this to himself and his close companions, but they were present in his poem, the 'Padouca Hunt', in which referred to his Tahitian adventures in the verse: 'Where, led by love's enchanting smile/ Among the tawney maids,/ We peopled more than half the Isle,/ With Welsh and Saxon blades.'[21]

Samwell was a man of the Enlightenment, a reader of Voltaire.[22] He was fascinated by things antiquarian, and believed that there were reasonable grounds for giving credence to the Madoc story; yet he was also gullible – he too easily identified the Shakespearean forgeries of William Henry Ireland as authentic – and he was also given to flights of imagination.[23]

Samwell's sympathies were not entirely radical. He admitted that there was a side to him which favoured absolute monarchy. He sympathized with the fate of Charles I.[24] He did not inveigh against Hanoverian oppression when visiting the site of Culloden.[25] He abandoned Wilkite patriotism and supported Lord North's conduct of the dispute with the American colonies.[26] Although he revered Paine, he did not want to see his ideas implemented.[27] He was a patriotic Briton, who loved nothing better than a fight with the French. This Welshman was a proud Jack Tar who could write: 'I glory in a Man of War not only as being the pride of every Englishman, I have always seen the sailors well treated on board, well fed & well clothed.'[28]

[21] William Ll. Davies, 'David Samwell's Poem – "The Padouca Hunt"', *NLWJ*, II, nos. 3–4 (1942), 150. The poem was published in 1799, shortly after Samwell's death, but he had already prepared it for publication with an elaborate series of notes. See also pp. 399–400.

[22] LRO 920 GRE 2/17, Letter no. 5, 25 June 1774. Samwell had been reading Voltaire's *Philosophical Dictionary*, but had found nothing exceptional in it even though it had been burnt in France, where it became one of the illegal bestsellers. Robert Darnton, *The Forbidden Best-sellers of Pre-Revolutionary France* (London, 1996), esp. pp. 60–74.

[23] See Fitzpatrick, Thomas, Newell (eds.), *David Samwell*, chapter 2.

[24] LRO 920 GRE 2/17, Letter no. 29, 31 December 1781, 'I cannot but lament the fate of the unhappy monarch.'

[25] Ibid., Letter no. 37, 16 September 1784.

[26] Ibid., Letter no. 10, 9 December 1775: 'As you know I was a flaming Patriot a while ago perhaps you may think that a place or pension has work'd my conversion, but may I accept of a place or pension in the higher regions from a Methodist parson if I have palmed a single Tester – or if aught hath worked my reformation, but a persuasion, (not indeed from positive Knowledge) that the present Administration mean well to this Country in particular & to the legal Liberty of its several Dependencies.' See also Letter no. 30, 16 May 1782, which reveals that he was a supporter of Lord North, that he disliked parties, and that he had 'sometimes been led to agree in favour of Absolute Government'.

[27] Ibid., Letter no. 44, 2 July 1792; Letter no. 49, 9 August 1795, Samwell described Paine as 'our Shakespear [*sic*] in Politics'.

[28] Ibid., Letter no. 42, 15 October 1788. There is nothing in Samwell's letters to Gregson to indicate the growing dissatisfaction in the navy with rates of pay, though he was always keen on gaining prize money.

Although he loved conflict, he accepted that war was wrong. Unlike many of his contemporaries, he did not see in victory a sign that providence favoured one's cause. It made no sense to Samwell that providence looked on the 'extirpation of the human race' with approval. The only battle which might be 'pleasing to his all seeing eye' was between lovers and their mistresses.[29] That was certainly the sort of conflict Samwell understood. With his fiery temperament he liked nothing better than contentious debate, and sometimes he came close to blows over bardic contests.[30] Yet, for all his disputatiousness, he was not a very public man. In writing to Matthew Gregson of debating societies, notably the Robin Hood Society, he admired the oratorical skill of his friend George Gregory, but self-revealingly wrote, 'for my part, was I ever so well qualified, I cou'd as soon fly as speak in those Societies'.[31]

Samwell was in some ways a typical example of the wayward son of a clergyman. He often treated religion with considerable levity. He was anti-clerical and anti-Catholic, and had no time for priestcraft, superstition and idolatry.[32] Yet he was not anti-religious. On at least one occasion he attended Theophilus Lindsey's new Unitarian chapel in Essex Street and approved of his revisions of the Book of Common Prayer.[33] In the South Seas he made careful notes of native religious practices, and was sympathetic to the priests in Hawaii.[34] Finally, we may infer that he admired religious faith and the strength derived from it. In his copy of the beautiful 1770 edition of the Welsh Book of Common Prayer he noted the last words of Louis XVI, in which he testified to the sustenance which his faith had given him and, more significantly, the comment of the enlightened statesman, Malesherbes, who would follow Louis to the guillotine: 'It is then true, that Religion alone can give sufficient force

---

[29] Ibid., Letter no. 31, 1 May 1782.

[30] Samwell quarrelled over the result of a bardic contest at Corwen in 1789, even to the point of 'demanding satisfaction'. When tempers cooled, he presented his preferred bard, Thomas Edwards (Twm o'r Nant), with a pen with the punning inscription, 'Gift from Dav. Samwel to Thomas Edwards (Nant) head Welsh Bard' (Rhodd Dav. Samwel i Thomas Edward (Nant) pen bardd Cymmru), *pen* meaning 'head' in Welsh. Although on this and at least one other occasion he championed his friend Twm o'r Nant over Walter Davies (Gwallter Mechain), he became firm friends with the latter. It is probable that the contentiousness of such occasions as well as the quality of the verse was affected by heavy drinking. The contest at Corwen, however, was decided by the Gwyneddigion Society in London, on which occasion Samwell lost his temper. Davies, 'David Samwell', 102–3; Geraint H. Jenkins, '"A Rank Republican [and] a Leveller": William Jones, Llangadfan', *WHR*, 17, no. 3 (1995), 378–9.

[31] LRO 920 GRE 2/17, Letter no. 11, 23 February 1776.

[32] Samwell described Popery as 'damnable'. See LRO 920 GRE 2/17, Letter no. 5, 25 June 1774; Letter no. 16, 22 October 1776.

[33] LRO 920 GRE 2/17, Letter no. 6, 14 September 1774. It may have been a coincidence that Samwell visited Lindsey's chapel soon after it was opened (17 April 1774) or it may be an indication of a real interest in liberal religion.

[34] See Marshall Sahlins, *How 'Natives' Think: About Captain Cook for example* (London, 1995), pp. 80, 200.

to enable the Mind of Man to support the most dreadful Trials with so much Dignity.'[35]

Even if the various aspects of Samwell cannot be reconciled, they can, to a degree, be understood, especially by focusing on the most important experience of Samwell's life, namely, serving on Captain Cook's third expedition. It took over three years of his life, introduced him to sailors of distinction and spirited him to exotic places. He kept a journal of his experiences, which is his most extensive writing, being over 140,000 words. The Liverpool bookseller, John Christie, had suggested he kept a journal and he subsequently regretted that he did not take his advice and keep it from the very beginning of the voyage.[36] The fact that it was a bookseller who made the suggestion might lead one to believe that the intention was that it would be published on his return. Yet there is no sign that Samwell wanted to publish it in his lifetime. It was not drawn on by Canon John Douglas in his official account, *Voyage to the Pacific Ocean* (1784), though, like all the other journals of the voyage, it had to be handed over to the Admiralty on the completion of the voyage. All these journals were available to Douglas for his official account. Indeed, Samwell's journal was much franker than would have been acceptable to a wider public. He would have been aware of the scandal caused by Hawkesworth's account of Cook's first voyage, which he read as soon as it was published,[37] and he may well have known that Cook himself had asked Douglas to omit the potentially scandalous parts of his journal of his second voyage which dealt with sexual commerce.[38] Samwell explained to Matthew Gregson that not only would publication affect his career in the navy but that it would dishonour the memory of his great hero, Cook.[39] His journal, therefore, is best viewed as one he kept for himself and his friends. It is this journal, supplemented mainly by his letters to his lifelong friend from Liverpool, Matthew Gregson, which is used here to try to understand the man.

Samwell joined Cook's expedition with no high-minded intent. He went with an eye to the main chance. There was a considerable element of sexual opportunism here. He was a philanderer who knew all about the sexual

[35] *Hyfforddiadau i Ymddygiad Defosiynol a Gweddus yng nghyhoedd wasanaeth Duw* (Caergrawnt, 1770), notes on the opening unnumbered page. The book is inscribed on the second inside page, 'Dafydd Samwell, 1797', but further on, 'Dafydd Samwell, Versailles, yn Ffrainc, Dydd Sul y Pasg, Ebrill 8, 1798' (in France, Easter Sunday, 8 April, 1798).

[36] LRO 920 GRE 2/17, Letter no. 23, David Samwell to John Christie, 17 December 1780.

[37] John Hawkesworth, *An Account of the Voyages . . . by Commodore Byron, Captain Wallis, Captain Carteret, and Captain Cook, in the Dolphin, Swallow and Endeavour* (3 vols., London, 1773); LRO 920 GRE 2/17, Letter no. 3, 24 June 1773; W. H. Pearson, 'Hawkesworth's Voyages' in R. F. Brissenden (ed.), *Studies in the Eighteenth Century* (Canberra, 1973), pp. 239–57; Thomas, *Discoveries*, pp. xxvi–xxvii.

[38] Thomas, *Discoveries*, p. 291.

[39] LRO 920 GRE 2/17, Letter no. 25, 26 February 1781.

accessibility of native women – he went well-stocked with nails – and had high expectations of their beauty. These were fulfilled and, like his fellow shipmates, he cleaned himself out. Writing in his journal of the Indian women of Nootka Sound, which the expedition visited in April 1778, he explained that many on the expedition had already exchanged all their available hatchets and nails for 'the beautiful nymphs' in the South Seas and so were driven to exchange their 'kitchen furniture' for the 'fair Americans'. He confessed: '*we enjoyed the present Day & left the Morrow to provide for itself* – & to provide us Tables & Chests to eat our Salt Beef & pork from instead of Plates' [my italics].[40]

Did this clergyman's son have any regrets for his behaviour? There is very little sign of that. The only evidence of regret he showed for his sexual activities in his letters to Matthew Gregson was not over his exploits in the South Seas but rather over a woman he had left pregnant in England before he left with Cook. In a letter to Matthew Gregson following the return, he wrote:

> Till you put me in mind of it, I had forgot yt I had mentioned a young cub to you – it is not living – and what has affected me exceedingly is that ye poor mother died along with it – my friends in whose care I left her shew'd her every degree of attention yt. I could wish, which is some satisfactn. to me – but still yt ye poor girl shd. be so unfortunate as loose her life continues to give me much uneasiness –[41]

As to the Pacific maidens, there is something refreshing about his candour in describing sexual commerce. Others in writing about it were more circumspect, but they indulged all the same. Probably only Captain Cook remained chaste. He only allowed sexual commerce because he could not prevent it, though he did his best to police it.[42]

The South Sea islanders paid a high price for the trade in sex through the spread of venereal disease. In his pamphlet on the introduction of venereal disease into the Sandwich Islands (the Hawaiian Islands), Samwell wrote that, if they had been responsible for introducing the disease into the Islands, then one would wish that the voyage had never been undertaken. That meant that he was going to produce one answer: they were not responsible.

Cook did his best to ensure that no infected member of the crew should go ashore and no women should come on board. Samwell claimed that none of those who had gone ashore subsequently showed symptoms of the disease. He went on to argue that there was insufficient proof to decide how the disease had reached the islands or whether it was indigenous. We know it was not indigenous and that Samwell's assumption that it could not have spread from

---

[40] Beaglehole (ed.), *The Journals of Captain Cook: III, The Voyage of the 'Resolution' and 'Discovery' 1776–1780*, Part Two (1967), Appendix II, 'Samwell's Journal', pp. 1094–6.
[41] LRO 920 GRE 2/17, Letter no. 25, 26 February 1781.
[42] Thomas, *Discoveries*, p. 237; Beaglehole (ed.), *The Journals of Captain Cook: III, The Voyage of the 'Resolution' and 'Discovery' 1776–1780*, Part One (1967), 'Journal of Captain Cook: The Third Voyage', pp. 61–2.

one island (Kauai) to another (Molokai) within the ten months between their visits was also false.[43] Perhaps his lack of candour on this issue owed something to an uneasy conscience, though there is nothing in the letters or the journal to suggest this. His tendentious discussion of the question appeared in a pamphlet which functioned as a postscript to his account of the death of Cook, and may be seen as an attempt to ensure that the memory of Cook was not sullied on this count. The best one can say is that he deceived himself and the public in order to preserve Cook's reputation. Nicholas Thomas's verdict is: 'Samwell was for the most part an honest, perceptive, and acute observer, but on this occasion these traits deserted him.'[44]

Samwell's sexual frankness should not divert attention from the considerable value of his journal. He was not entirely unprepared for voyaging. As noted already, he had read about Cook's first expedition in Hawkesworth's account. He had discussed the South Seas with his friends and took with him, among several other books, one of Lawrence Echard's geographical works.[45] Although he went with nails at the ready, not all his trade was for sexual favours. He brought back a sufficient number of artefacts to hold an auction of them in 1781.[46] His journal is of a zestful man, full of curiosity about the societies he encountered. Although educated, he did not travel encumbered by theory. Generally he did not rank the cultures he observed (though he did rank feminine beauty). If that led to some contradictory elements in his observations, it also indicates that he took native peoples as he found them. He did not try to fit them into a current theory about the stadial development of mankind, as the Forsters did in their accounts of the second voyage. His own superior in the *Discovery*, the surgeon William Andersen (who died in August 1778), having learnt from the Forsters on the second voyage, was a fine natural historian. Samwell's strengths were rather different. His narrative, as Nicholas Thomas has remarked, is notable for its attention to human interaction. He was

---

43   Samwell recorded in his journal that, on reaching the island of Kauai (21 January 1778), Cook insisted that there should be no sexual contact with native women and, in particular, that those sailors with symptoms of venereal disease should not be allowed ashore or women allowed on board. He also noted that this policy failed – some who went ashore had sexual relations with native women and some native women managed to board the *Discovery*, though not Cook's ship, the *Resolution*. Samwell's Journal, pp. 1083–4. Thomas notes that Samwell seemed to gain a vicarious pleasure from writing of the licentiousness of the native women. *Discoveries*, p. 358.

44   Fitzpatrick, Thomas, Newell (eds.), *David Samwell*, chapter 3.

45   LRO 920 GRE 2/17, Letter nos. 11 and 12, 23 February 1776, 25 March 1776.

46   Adrienne L. Kaeppler, 'Tracing the History of Hawaiian Cook Voyage Artefacts in the Museum of Mankind' in T. C. Mitchell (ed.), *Captain Cook and the South Pacific* (Canberra, 1979), pp. 173, 175, 188 pl. 96, 189, pl. 97. W. D. Leathart, in *The Origin and Progress of the Gwyneddigion Society of London* (London, 1831) p. 31n. maintained that part of Samwell's collection was eventually deposited in the library of Trinity College, Cambridge. However, Trinity College archivist, Jonathan Smith, has kindly informed me that no Samwell materials were deposited in the library.

an empirical traveller, who wanted to know all the facets of the life of native peoples: their appearance, and customs, disposition, social and political structures. Like Andersen, he was interested in language and also in music: he made the first serious transcription of Maori songs. His journal is of first-rate importance for anthropologists and ethnographers. It provides crucial evidence in the controversy over the native status of Cook and the significance of his death.[47] His account of the death of Cook, which would eventually be published separately and incorporated into Andrew Kippis's biography of Cook, was derived from the journal. Whatever its limitations, it is a detailed account of what had occurred and Samwell did his best to collect all the available evidence. After the voyage, Samwell visited Cook's birthplace to gather information for his portrait of Cook which formed part of his pamphlet (he was generally accurate, though he got Cook's date of birth wrong). Samwell's curiosity and interaction with native peoples were transmitted in his letters to Gregson. Here is just a sample:

> You must know Matt that the inhabts. of Sandwich Islands are of ye same sort of People as ye Othaiteans, the language is exactly the same, so is their manner of preparing their cloth, but you will perceive that their mode of staining is quite difft. – You ask whether they painted them so before they were visited by Europeans – we were the first Europeans who visited Sandwich Islands and I can assure you yt we employed our time to much better purpose than teaching them to paint cloth – we were quite amazed to see such an infinite variety of beautiful patterns among them & many of them so like our cottons – the colr is a vegtble dye which they lay on with a sort of brush made from ye stem of a plant it is all done by the women – I have more than once been called a painter of cloth among them when they have seen me writing & ye girls have very innocently taken ye pen out of my hand & shewn me that they were better skilled in ye art than I was for they thought but meanly of the confused irregular lines I made – & they said I had no notion of any thing yt was beautiful for I never employed any other colr. than black – they really believed that our writing was the same as their marking of cloth – I never remember to have seen them express greater pleasure & surprise than some of them did at my taking out a piece of this painted cloth of ours & repeating from it one of their own songs – they did not know what the Devil to make of it[48] & I am sure Matt it would have done thy heart good to have been in the Hutt along with me at the time – a kinder a more affectionate people than the natives of Sandwich Islands the Sun never shone upon – nor I dont suppose ever will.[49]

[47] The two main protagonists in the controversy, Marshal Sahlins and Ganeth Obeyesekere, make extensive use of Samwell's account. See Sahlins, *How 'Natives' Think* and Ganath Obeyesekere, *The Apotheosis of Captain Cook: European Mythmaking in the Pacific* (Princeton, NJ, 1992).

[48] See Samwell's Journal, p. 1187; Samwell noted that the girls came to realize that there was a purpose to his curious orthography.

[49] LRO 920 GRE 2/17, Letter no. 26, 7 April 1781. Samwell's letters to Matthew Gregson regarding the South Seas will be published in full in Fitzpatrick, Thomas, Newell (eds.), *David Samwell*.

Of course, it was impossible for Samwell to view the South Sea societies with a mind free of assumptions. He was not alone in this. Nicholas Thomas has observed in relation to the desire of Banks and Cook to assist native societies to develop their agriculture that this reflected nostalgia for an idealized past and current worries about the corrupting effects of luxury within a commercial society.[50] Like many of his contemporaries, there were primitivist dimensions to Samwell's thought which acknowledged that a simpler and more natural life was to be admired. Frank Holden recorded how, in many of his meetings with Samwell in the early 1780s, they discussed 'the comparative happiness of a savage and civilized [state] and we both seem to be of our friend Rousseau's sentiment'.[51] But Samwell was not a consistent Rousseauist. In February 1777 Cook's voyagers revisited the site at Grass Cove in Queen Charlotte Sound, where some of the crew members of Captain Furneaux's *Adventure* on the second expedition had been murdered by natives and subsequently eaten by them. He described the group of natives who were found consuming the sailors they had killed the previous day as 'infernal savages'.[52]

This is not the exception which proves the rule of native benevolence, even though Samwell leant in that direction. Samwell responded to what he found and did not seek a consistent view. Indeed he sought to discover as much as possible of what had happened in Grass Cove and provided alternative explanations for the tragedy (one that it was deliberate on the part of the natives, the other that it was accidental). He was in many ways a man of sympathy in the broad sense of the term defined by Adam Smith as 'our fellow-feeling with any passion whatever'.[53] His own contacts with natives were almost invariably favourable. He did not change his views despite the killing of Cook and the brutal treatment of his body. On his return he wrote to John Christie:

> The friendly intercourse that I have had with the Inhabitants of the South Sea Islands have interested me very much in their favour – they are a very happy innocent people and their behaviour towards us has been such as must ever inspire the warmest affection for them in every grateful and feeling mind.[54]

---

50   Thomas, *Discoveries*, pp. xxii–xxiii.
51   LRO, Roscoe Papers, 920 ROS 2065, Frank Holden to William Roscoe, 1 May 1781.
52   Samwell's Journal, pp. 998–9; for a discussion of the episode, see Thomas, *Discoveries*, pp. 302–6. Samwell does not mention the fact that Cook allowed Kahura, the chief culprit, aboard. See 'Journal of Captain Cook: The Third Voyage', p. 62, 13 February 1777.
53   Adam Smith, *The Theory of Moral Sentiments* (1759), ed. D. D. Raphael and A. L. Macfie (Oxford, 1976), I. i. I. 3.
54   LRO 920 GRE 2/17, Letter no. 23, 17 December 1780. In this same letter Samwell was anxious to assure Christie that, although the New Zealanders were cannibals, the two boys taken on board there as companions for Omai were 'wel disposed, truly good natured, & shew'd a warmth of affection towards us that made us all much regret their being left behind' (at Huahine).

Samwell accepted that there were many things they did not understand about native societies, mainly because of the problems of communication. Yet, he did not refrain from criticizing native practices, their religious idolatry and superstitions, and especially political and social structures which appeared repressive. In his assessment of the Tongans he condemned the 'exorbitant Power of the chiefs' and believed that the ordinary natives were completely in thrall to them.[55] In this he was broadly correct. His judgement differed from that of Cook, who admired the dignified manners and religiosity of the Tongans and the hierarchical and deferential social structure.[56] Later in his journal Samwell combined detailed descriptions of the religion of the Hawaiians with condemnation, notably of their 'many ludicrous obscene idols'. He also observed, without offering an explanation, that the very idols they regarded as gods were treated with little reverence.[57]

If there is a consistent ideal emerging from Samwell's journal, it comes not from his judgement of native societies, but from the figure of Cook. For he combined humanity, benevolence, order and liberality, knowledge and virtue:

> Nature had endowed him with a mind vigorous and comprehensive, which in his riper years he had cultivated with care and industry. His general knowledge was extensive and various: in that of his own profession he was unequalled. With a clear judgment, strong masculine sense, and the most determined resolution; with a genius peculiarly turned for enterprize, he pursued his object with unshaken perseverance: – vigilant and active in an eminent degree: – cool and intrepid among dangers; patient and firm under difficulties and distress; fertile in expedients; great and original in all his designs; active and resolved in carrying them into execution. These qualities rendered him the animating spirit of the expedition: in every situation, he stood unrivalled and alone; on him all eyes were turned; *he was our leading-star, which at its setting, left us involved in darkness and despair* [my italics].[58]

Cook ran his ship like a well-ordered and well-policed kingdom. He was regarded by Samwell as the perfect father figure, a man who most notably protected his crew from scurvy by ceaseless vigilance and enforcing dietary

---

[55] Samwell's Journal, pp. 1022–3, 1048. At the same time, Samwell noted that, 'From our scanty knowledge of their Language & short stay among them it is impossible that we should know anything circumstantial of their Government and policy.'

[56] Thomas, *Discoveries*, pp. 320–1.

[57] Samwell's Journal, p. 1185. Samwell accepted that he was ignorant of the content of the religion of the Hawaiians. He was unaware that the Hawaiians might ridicule their own idols during the Mahakiki season when ordinary rites were 'in abeyance'. Sahlins, *How 'Natives' Think*, p. 271.

[58] Andrew Kippis, *A Narrative of the Voyages round the World performed by Captain James Cook. With an Account of his Life, during the Previous and Intervening Periods* (1788, new edn., London, 1893), pp. 353–4. Samwell had written an account of Cook for Kippis, who encouraged him to publish it. The pamphlet was entitled *A Narrative of the Death of Captain James Cook. To which are added some particulars, concerning his Life and Character* (London, 1786). Kippis quoted from this verbatim, with acknowledgement, in his own *A Narrative*, published in 1788.

norms which were often not to the taste of the crew. Moreover, he was to be admired because he had become in effect a philosopher king and the benefactor of mankind through his own single-minded pursuit of knowledge and virtue. His character of Cook concluded with this glowing tribute:

> England has been unanimous in her tribute of applause to his virtues, and all Europe has borne testimony to his merit. There is hardly a corner of the earth, however remote and savage, that will not long remember his benevolence and humanity. The grateful Indian, in time to come, pointing to the herds grazing his fertile plains, will relate to his children how the first stock of them was introduced into the country; and the name of Cook will be remembered among those benign spirits, whom they worship as the source of every good, and the fountain of every blessing.[59]

The view that the voyages of discovery inaugurated a new age, which contrasted dramatically with earlier imperial ages (notably of the great Continental Catholic powers – Spain and Portugal) when conquerors terrorized and exploited native peoples, was common both to British and French thinkers. It was stated by Hawkesworth in the preface to his account of the first voyage. By the time of his death, Cook's achievements were such that he came to epitomize that belief. Samwell played an important role in this process. He venerated Cook and fervently believed in the benign consequences of discovery. His views were persuasive and were elaborated by Andrew Kippis in 1788 in his biography (the first) of Captain James Cook. It was dedicated in fulsome terms to George III:

> Without your Majesty's munificence and encouragement the world would have remained destitute of that immense light which has been thrown on geography, navigation, and the most important sciences. To your Majesty, therefore, a work like the present is with particular propriety addressed.[60]

Samwell, who had been quoted *in extenso* by Kippis, was aware that his feelings towards Cook might cloud his judgement:

> I hope . . . that even the great Veneration in which I hold the abilities and virtues of Captn Cook has not cast a mist before my eyes but that I have been able to see & honest enough to follow the Path that is enlightened by the Rays of Truth.[61]

Such enlightened pieties cannot hide the fact that Samwell always placed the most favourable construction on Cook's behaviour and rationalized his conduct even when it was at its most puzzling and deplorable. Nicholas Thomas notes that admirers of Cook among the crew were shocked by the cruelty of his punishment of Tongans for theft, including cutting crosses in a

[59] Kippis, *A Narrative of the Voyages*, pp. 354–5.
[60] Ibid., p. v.
[61] Samwell's Journal, p. 1201.

man's arm which penetrated to the bone.[62] Samwell, however, justified this 'Appearance of Cruelty' with the argument that if thefts were left unpunished they would eventually have to punish them with the penalty of death.[63] While it is undeniable that there is much in Cook's character and behaviour to admire, Samwell's veneration owed much to his setting up his captain as a paradigm for values which he, Samwell, already cherished, especially those associated with enlightened leadership.

On 4 June 1774 Samwell witnessed the firework celebrations of the king's birthday; this gave rise to the following generous reflections, which he recaptured in a letter to Matthew Gregson over a fortnight later:

> Being seated upon the Top of a House to view the Fireworks on the King's Birthday, I had a fine view of the prodigous concourse of the People beneath on Tower Hill, & as my carcase was elevated above the Croud so were the Ideas of my Soul, & looking around upon the myriad faces that presented themselves, I said to myself, happy Beings, was some Tyrant placed where I am, he never cou'd find in his heart to do you an Injury, at the sight of so many of his Fellow Creatures, the Patriot Passion wou'd expand his soul & tender Feeling of Humanity play around the heart, the poor (?) selfish considerations of the Pride or Interest of me, wou'd give way to the ardent wish for the happiness of the whole human Race, & his mind wou'd embrace you with that brotherly love which is an emanation of the Divinity.[64]

This is not untypical of the optimism of the day: that enlightenment was capable of converting tyranny into benevolent despotism. Such optimism represented an updating of the stoic notion of spreading circles of affection – embodied in the conclusion of Pope's 'Essay on Man' (1733–4), which Samwell would have known:

> Self-love but serves the virtuous mind to wake,
> As the small pebble stirs the peaceful lake,
> The centre moved, a circle straight succeeds,
> Another still, and still another spreads,
> Friend, parent, neighbour, first it will embrace,
> His country next, and next all human race;
> Wide and more wide, the o'erflowings of the mind
> Take every creature in, of every kind;[65]

---

[62] Thomas, *Discoveries*, p. 322. Like Samwell, Thomas suggests that Cook believed that the severity of punishment was to ensure that he did not have to punish theft, which was endemic, with the death penalty, but, unlike Samwell, he believes that Cook knew that his actions were dreadfully cruel. If Cook's action was deliberate and not the result of loss of temper, his dilemma reflected that of the domestic penal system where there was little intermediate punishment between whipping and branding for the first offence and the ultimate sanction of the death penalty. Cook pushed mutilation to its limits to avoid the latter. See Paul Langford, *A Polite and Commercial People: England 1727–1783* (Oxford, 1992), p. 158.

[63] Samwell's Journal, p. 1029.

[64] LRO 920 GRE 2/17, Letter no. 5, 25 June 1774.

[65] 'Essay on Man', Epistle IV, 360–70, in Bonamy Dobrée (ed.), *Alexander Pope's Collected Poems* (London, rev. edn. 1956, repr. 1961), pp. 214–15.

There is no doubt that Samwell saw himself as 'a Humanity man', a term he used in relation to his opposition to the slave trade.[66] Interestingly, the campaign for the abolition of the trade was one which gained support across the spectrum of political and religious sensibilities. Is this then the resolution (in so far as it is possible) of Samwell's contradictions? Humanitarianism, in theory and practice, drew on affections from the closest to the widest, from the local community, through the nation and nations, to the universal brotherhood of mankind; it drew on enlightened reason and sentimental sensibilities, and embodied elements of radical and conservative views. It assumed that all mankind were essentially the same, that differences of culture could be understood, and that tensions between nations could be resolved through greater knowledge of one another.

Undoubtedly it is in part. It accords with one aspect of Samwell's self-perception, and explains many of his ideas and actions, but not all. Like the spreading circles of affections, it is rather too neat. It does not explain the wilder imaginative side of Samwell, though it is not unconnected with it, for it has a powerful utopian dimension. For Samwell, being a humanity man required the employment of sympathy, a willingness to suspend ideological principles and making 'allowances for the failings of Humanity'.[67]

Voyagers journeyed with 'imaginations . . . heated up', as Samwell said of expectations of Tahiti, which he described as a new Cythera – as had Bougainville before him.[68] They envisaged a world of unsurpassable beauty, bountiful nature and pre-lapsarian virtue; a world free of guilt, where all the problems and dilemmas associated with Enlightenment beliefs in happiness as the end of existence would be resolved. As Samwell wrote of the Tongan island of Nomuka:

> Such enchanting prospects does this little Isle afford that it may be said to realize the poetical descriptions of Elysian Field in ancient writers, it is certainly as beautiful a Spot as Imagination can paint. It abounds with bread fruit trees, Cocoa nuts, yams, Plantains & tarroo root & is well stocked with Hogs and fowls.

And to cap it all, 'we found no difficulty in getting the Girls on board'.[69] Samwell wrote something similar about Tongapatu, portraying an idyllic pastoral scene. At the end of a very full description of Tongan dancing he noted that: 'As they withdrew each Nymph took the Chaplet of Flowers off her head & bestowed it upon her favourite Swain.'[70]

---

[66] LRO 920 GRE 2/17, Letter no. 41, 11 October 1788.
[67] LRO 920 GRE 2/17, Letter no. 29, 31 December 1781.
[68] Samwell's Journal, p. 1055. Jonathan Lamb, 'Fantasies of Paradise' in Martin Fitzpatrick, Peter Jones, Christa Knellwolf, Iain McCalman (eds.), *The Enlightenment World* (London, 2004), p. 522.
[69] Samwell's Journal, pp. 1014–15.
[70] Ibid., p. 1020.

This was an enchanted world which few could really believe unless they had experienced it. Later, when Samwell was locked in dispute over the belief that Madoc was the first to discover America, he reminded his fellow Welshmen that since the Pacific fantasy was fact, so might the legend of Madoc also be true. Parts of the relevant verses to the Padouca Hunt in which Samwell argued the case for Madoc have already been quoted, but are now provided in full:

And as to Môn's[71] profound reply,
'Gainst Madog's host so mighty,
He may with equal law deny
My trip to Otaheite.[72]

Where, led by love's enchanting smile
Among the tawney maids,
We peopled more than half the Isle,
With Welsh and Saxon blades.

But as that fact is clear enough,
Wherefore my friends should we
Seek for a stronger, plainer proof
That Madog went to sea?

And in America's wild plains
Rais'd up a mighty nation.
Which in *Padouca* still remains,
Of Cambrian generation.

If I, from Nantglyn, not long since[73]
Could reach Kamtshatka's shore,
Why might not Madog, glorious Prince,
America explore?

I deem the oath of honest men
Of sacred truth the organ,
And neither slight the historian's pen,
Nor doubt the faith of Morgan.[74]

Williams[75] and Owen,[76] to their praise,
From facts have us advis'd,
Traditions of the older days
Are not to be despis'd.

71 Ned Môn, i.e. Edward Jones. The notes, with this exception, are by Samwell.
72 In 1777.
73 In 1779.
74 The Revd Mr Morgan gave early intelligence of the Welsh Indians.
75 The Revd Dr Williams.
76 Mr William Owen Pughe.

And that prince Madog and his train
Th' advent'rous sail unfurl'd,
And, having cross'd the Atlantic main,
First found the western world.

Where following Nature's simple plan,
In climes where Nature smiles,
They quickly multiplied the man,
Like us among the isles.[77]

Yet, all was not sweetness and light in these faraway worlds. There was a dark side to the Pacific paradise which was not easy to explain. Samwell used the analogy of waking up from a dream world, quoting the lines, 'From Fancy's Visionary Realms he flies/ and Wakes to meet life's dull realities.'[78]

In the real world, even in the lovely unspoiled isles visited by Cook, human nature appeared depraved. It was all very confusing. Samwell wrote that the Tongan islanders themselves were not 'cruel, fierce and savage'. The reason for the barbarous treatment of the 'common People' lay in the exorbitant power of the chiefs which included that of life and death. Yet, power had not corrupted the humanity of all the chiefs. Of Powlohow he remarked that 'such is the humanity of his Disposition that he has never yet taken away the Life of any of his Subjects'.[79] One might therefore ask, if power had not corrupted him, why had it corrupted the others?

No doubt Enlightenment views on nature, human nature, superstition and arbitrary power helped Samwell to make sense of his experiences, and for the rest he could blame lack of understanding on the fleeting nature of contacts and the difficulty of communications. And he never gave up recording all the details of the encounters. His curiosity sustained him where his understanding was most stretched.

He was not alone in struggling to keep his sense of paradise intact. As Jonathan Lamb has noted in relation both to fictional and South Sea paradises: 'there is always something to spoil the completeness of the picture'.[80] For all Samwell's clinging on to notions of the beneficence of nature and the goodness of human nature, he knew this paradisial world was flawed, and not only by native customs and institutions. Whether or not he believed his own argument about the introduction of venereal disease into the Sandwich Islands, he knew full well that voyagers had brought it to the South Seas and of Cook's worries about the role of voyagers in spreading it. It was as if, as Jonathan Lamb

---

[77] South Sea Islands.
[78] Samwell's Journal, p. 1022. Beaglehole was unable to identify the source of the quotation. I have fared no better.
[79] Ibid.
[80] Lamb, 'Fantasies of Paradise', p. 523.

notes, they had acted out a satanic role in entering and ruining an Edenic world.[81]

Ultimately the sense one could make of voyaging could only be fleeting and uncertain. Nonetheless, Samwell had the time of his life. Voyaging, as Greg Denning has noted, was an end in itself. Herein lay the excitement, the adrenalin rush. The voyager probed 'eclectically into anything new'.[82] Indeed, no single theory could meld into a coherent view all the diverse experiences of voyaging, and no single personality could emerge from the experience entirely free of guilt. Jonathan Lamb has suggested that one way of organizing the ambivalences experienced in the South Seas was to formalize the qualities and experiences of Edenic paradise into a Utopia – 'a highly organized society operating in a contrived landscape and a definite architectural space'.[83] Such a Utopia may be fictional or aspirational: Tahiti and Mauritius were candidates for its location in the South Seas. One could add to this the notion of an ideal Pantisocratic community on the banks of Susquehanna which appealed to radicals and romantics in the 1790s. But this was an organized settler solution. It was the way of cultivated understanding, a way of resolving the ambivalences of paradise by taking out the worst – the disease, the savagery – and cultivating the best – nature's abundance and human benevolence. The flawed old world would be left behind in the creation of a perfect new one.

Another response, if not a solution, was a sceptical one. Life must be accepted as it is; it is too complex to make overall sense, too unpredictable to be organized into a system, and too enjoyable to be turned into a common-wealth of virtue. It was a journey with twists and turns. One could never know what lay around the corner, but one should travel enthusiastically, for there were always surprises in store. This was an appealing response to our 'chaotic genius'. He embodied many of the characteristics of an eighteenth-century traveller, real and fictional: wit, eroticism, sentimentalism. His exuberance, manifested in his letters to Matthew Gregson, resembles that of Lawrence Sterne:

> If you will look cunning into the last Sentimental Magazine you may perceive a most admirable Essay of mine signed Postqueer – If you do not say it is a damn'd clever thing I will say you are a damn'd Rascal who envy my superior, shining, towering, abilities.[84]

---

[81] Ibid.

[82] Greg Denning, 'The Theatricality of Observing and being Observed: Eighteenth-century Europe "Discovers" the ? Century "Pacific"' in Stuart B. Schwartz (ed.), *Implicit Understandings: Observing, Reporting, and Reflecting on the Encounters between Europeans and Other Peoples in the Early Modern Era* (Cambridge, 1994), p. 453.

[83] Lamb, 'Fantasies of Paradise', p. 529.

[84] LRO 920 GRE 2/17, Letter no. 4, 25 March 1774.

It is hardly surprising that Sterne was one of his heroes. In 1791 he even went on a pilgrimage with Iolo Morganwg to Sterne's grave, which proved to be the occasion for a sentimental poem, which Samwell published in the *Gentleman's Magazine*.[85] Like Sterne's Yorick, as a traveller, Samwell's aim was to experience everything and, like Tristram Shandy, he loved to ride his 'Hobby Horse'.[86] That is why he took the opportunity to journey with Cook. Yet, whatever he knew about Pacific voyaging beforehand, he could not really anticipate the impact it would have upon him. While in many ways it fortified his faith in human nature, and presented in Cook a model for mankind, it was not a model he could follow consistently. Life for him, like the voyage itself, was a fascinating but untidy experience. Ultimately, sympathy triumphed over reason, imagination over empirical observation, serious debate gave way to wit, sober reflection to *joie de vivre*. Life was to be lived in the moment; one should take opportunities as they arise, pursue one's passions and interests as one can and accept that the boundary between fact and fantasy was extremely slim. Samwell's life after he returned from the Pacific was unstructured. He was broadly content with what he had, loving the company of like-minded friends, occasionally regretting his lack of ambition, gaining at last a good job on land with an application which was offhand and perfunctory, and dying soon after he had been appointed. He would have appreciated the irony. Certainly he would have had no regrets. As he had written to Matthew Gregson in 1774: '– ah! my friend, life is a jest, and a short one, so let us act the jest as merry as we can –.'[87]

[85] Davies, 'David Samwell', 115.
[86] I have explored this theme in Fitzpatrick, Thomas, Newell (eds.), *David Samwell*, chapter 2.
[87] LRO 920 GRE, Letter no. 5, 25 June 1774.

18

Forgery and Patronage: Iolo Morganwg and Owain Myfyr

GERAINT PHILLIPS

> There mark what Ills the Scholar's Life assail,
> Toil, Envy, Want, the Patron and the Jail.
> Samuel Johnson[1]

By the spring of 1805 Iolo Morganwg may well have felt that he had experienced all the tribulations which, according to Samuel Johnson, afflict the aspiring scholar. A self-styled victim of 'the mean machinations of Envy',[2] he had already endured both penury and imprisonment. Now, as he approached his sixtieth year, relations with his patron, Owen Jones (Owain Myfyr), the prosperous London furrier and the unwitting publisher of his forgeries, were grinding inexorably towards a crisis. Writing to his friend and fellow-antiquary William Owen Pughe, in April 1805, Iolo inveighed against the traditional concept of literary patronage:

> Litterary encouragements are only seductions, litterary Patronage only a mere hum. I will no longer confide in any such things. Dr Johnson was perfectly right when he said that the only Patrons of Literature in this Country are the Booksellers who will certainly pay so much per sheet for whatever may be thought worth printing. Of all other kinds of literary Patronage his Lives of the English Poets prove what they are, and always have been in a very Melancholy manner.[3]

Iolo was bitter because Owain Myfyr had reneged on a promise to pay him a pension of £50 a year for life. Their friendship of over thirty years eventually came to an end in March the following year amid a storm of mutual recrimination. This chapter charts the vicissitudes of that friendship from its inception in 1773, when Owain Myfyr had neither wealth nor consequence. It also seeks

---

[1] 'The Vanity of Human Wishes', J. D. Fleeman (ed.) *Samuel Johnson: The Complete English Poems* (London, 1971), pp. 83–92.

[2] Williams: *PLP*, I, p. xi.

[3] NLW 13221E, p. 127, Iolo Morganwg to William Owen Pughe, 28 April 1805.

to cast some light on Iolo's complex attitude towards patronage and on the means by which he succeeded in publishing his forgeries.

By the second half of the eighteenth century there was a perception among many authors that the age of aristocratic patronage was in decline. Johnson's celebrated letter of 1755, rebuking his patron, Lord Chesterfield, for having failed to take an interest in the progress of his *Dictionary*, was seen as ushering in a new age of authorial independence. But, while the boom in print culture and the new market for books among the emerging middle class offered exciting possibilities, most authors still eked out a precarious existence and sought aristocratic patronage wherever they could find it. Even Johnson had to make do with commissions and beggarly piece-rates for booksellers until, at the age of fifty-two, he was rescued by a state pension of £300.[4]

In Wales the demise of patronage was compounded by the Anglicization of the gentry and their indifference towards the native literature. Yet, by raising subscriptions amongst the middling sorts – mainly craftsmen and humble farmers – enterprising publishers found that there were modest profits to be made from the sale of poetry. During the early 1770s, in a bid to emulate the success of two north Wales anthologies – Dafydd Jones's *Blodeu-gerdd Cymry* (1759) and Huw Jones's *Diddanwch Teuluaidd* (1763) – Iolo Morganwg conceived a plan of publishing a collection of Glamorgan poetry called 'Diddanwch y Cymry' (Entertainment for the Welsh). In 1773, following a successful subscription-raising tour of north Wales, he set off for London in search of work and further subscribers among members of the Cymmrodorion Society. His mentor, the Glamorgan lexicographer John Walters, who was engaged in a slow and painful struggle to publish an English–Welsh dictionary by subscription, warned him not to expect too much.[5] Soon after his arrival, however, Iolo informed Walters that a 'Mr Jones of Cannon-street' had volunteered to distribute the various numbers of the dictionary in London 'out of pure humanity and an affection for the work'.[6] This was Owen Jones, who took the name 'Owain Myfyr' from his native Llanfihangel Glyn Myfyr in Denbighshire. Born in 1741, the son of a yeoman, he had been sent to London early in life to work for a firm of skinners called Kidney and Nutt, of Cannon Street and Ducksfoot Lane. Thereafter, his visits to Wales were infrequent. Under the influence of the kindly Richard Morris – the last of the multi-faceted Morris brothers of Anglesey, and co-founder, along with his brother Lewis, of the Cymmrodorion Society – Owain Myfyr had developed a passion for Welsh antiquity and a zealous desire to see the earliest literature brought to light. 'To print all the scarce and valuable antient British Manuscripts, with

---

[4]   John Wain, *Samuel Johnson* (London, 1974), p. 179.
[5]   NLW 21283E, Letter no. 517, John Walters to Iolo Morganwg, 27 April 1771.
[6]   BL Add. 15030, f. 184, John Walters to Owain Myfyr, 8 March 1774.

OWAIN JONES, MYFYR.

Fig. 27 The affluent London-Welsh furrier and literary patron, Owen Jones (Owain Myfyr) 1741–1814. A lithograph, published by the Gwyneddigion Society in 1828, after a lost portrait by John Vaughan.

Notes Critical and Explanatory' was, nominally at least, one of the aims of the Cymmrodorion,[7] but its members had proved less than willing to bear the considerable financial burden of such an endeavour.

In 1770 Owain Myfyr and his friend, the poet Robert Hughes (Robin Ddu), had set up the more convivial (and at first exclusive to north Wales) Gwyneddigion Society. Yet they remained members of the Cymmrodorion and continued to look upon the older society as a kind of national academy, albeit a rather lethargic one. As assistant secretary of the Cymmrodorion during the mid-1770s, Owain Myfyr succeeded in introducing an annual levy of 10s. 6d. per head to pay for the printing of Welsh texts. He also corresponded with gifted scholars such as Evan Evans (Ieuan Fardd) and Richard Thomas, urging them to submit their work for publication. Evans promised to edit the Welsh proverbs and triads, while Thomas began work on the poetry attributed to Llywarch Hen.

Described in later life as a 'red hot Welshman',[8] Owain Myfyr was a genial, self-deprecating man. Exile had given him a simple vision of Wales and a romantic attachment to the Welsh past, while London had endowed him with energy, optimism and determination. Iolo was enormously impressed by his common sense and his practical patriotism. Straining for effect in his early correspondence with him, he declared himself willing to do more for Owain Myfyr 'than the mind of man can encompass' ('nag a ddichon meddwl dyn ei amgyffred').[9] Owain Myfyr's patriotism transcended the traditional rivalry between north and south Wales, and this made him especially receptive to Iolo's spellbinding descriptions of Glamorgan and its history. Writing to John Walters, he declared Iolo to be supreme in his knowledge of the Welsh language and its literature, but lamented the fact that he had no wealthy patron to encourage and direct his efforts: 'but what's the use, such things are contrary to the spirit of the age' ('eithr ni thal son, nid yw hynny yn gyttunol a xyneddfau'r oes').[10]

Iolo's knowledge of literature was deepened considerably during his stay in London by the opportunity to read the manuscript collections of the Morris brothers. Following the death of William and Lewis Morris, Richard had transferred their papers to the Tower of London, where he lived and worked as a clerk at the Navy Office. At a time when the finest Welsh libraries – notably those at Hengwrt, Wynnstay and Gloddaith – were largely inaccessible, the Morris collection was fast becoming a Mecca for scholars. Owain Myfyr also spent his leisure hours among these manuscripts. In 1768 he had transcribed Lewis and William Morris's extensive collections of the poems of Dafydd ap

---

[7]   *Gosodedigaethau Anrhydeddus Gymdeithas y Cymmrodorion* (Llundain, 1755), p. 29.
[8]   NLW 21280E, Letter no. 83, Walter Davies to Iolo Morganwg, 28 July 1806.
[9]   BL Add. 15031, f. 33, Iolo Morganwg to Owain Myfyr, 6 March 1779.
[10] NLW 15415E, p. 10, Owain Myfyr to John Walters, 9 January 1777.

Gwilym into a large, thick volume.[11] Incessantly thumbed by members of the Gwyneddigion, the volume had swiftly made Dafydd a cult figure within the society. Of the many manuscripts encountered by Iolo in London, this would prove to be the most influential. Its contents took a decisive hold over his imagination.

Iolo Morganwg was less than impressed, however, by the veneration accorded to that other icon of the Cymmrodorion and Gwyneddigion: Lewis Morris. At a Cymmrodorion meeting he found himself at odds with Richard Morris, having ventured to offer opinions which differed from those expressed in Lewis's 'Celtic Remains': 'he . . . disaproved of them without giving any other reason than that his Brother thought otherwise. And many times I have discovered the most malignant envy in his countenance'.[12] The northern hegemony in the Welsh republic of letters clearly rankled, and this marked the beginning of a lifelong hatred of Lewis Morris; he became, for Iolo, a symbol of north Wales hubris.[13] During his stay in London, however, Iolo's resentment and paranoia appear to have found expression only in his letters to John Walters.

Iolo's mercurial temperament and brilliant conversation made him a welcome guest among members of the Gwyneddigion Society. His earliest imitations of Dafydd ap Gwilym (works which he acknowledged as his own) were given a rapturous reception by Owain Myfyr, Robert Hughes and other members such as David Samwell and John Edwards (Siôn Ceiriog). They also delighted in his squibs and bawdy songs. Under the sway of such infectious high spirits, Iolo was capable, at least temporarily, of abandoning his prejudice against those from north Wales. The gatherings of the Gwyneddigion, amid the smell of beer, tobacco and toasted cheese, became a kind of refuge for him from the harsher, more alienating realities of London life. The city's populace – 'a vile debauched race of men'[14] – grated on his refined sensibility, and its fogs and smogs exacerbated his asthma, forcing him, in 1773, to resort for the first time to regular doses of laudanum.[15]

In the summer of 1774 Iolo left London for Kent and, with the onset of winter, he sank into a depression. There is, in fact, compelling evidence that he had suffered since adolescence from a form of manic-depressive illness. He would later describe himself as having been a 'pensive, melancholy' child, who was prone to be overtaken by cheerful fits of 'wild extravagance'.[16] His old teacher, John Walters, was familiar with his mood swings. Writing to Walters

---

[11]   UWB, Bangor 6.
[12]   NLW 21285E, Letter no. 779, Iolo Morganwg to John Walters, draft, c.1774.
[13]   Williams: *IM*, pp. 210–11.
[14]   Ibid., p. 220.
[15]   NLW 21387E, no. 10.
[16]   Williams: *PLP*, I, p. xvi.

from Sandwich in February 1775, Iolo confessed to having lapsed into his 'former habits of mind': 'indulging melancholy Ideas which you know are constitutional to me'. As a result, he feared that 'the Inclination I had once for poetry antiquities and the Welsh Language is almost worn out'.[17]

Iolo's long exile in Kent offered an opportunity to brood over his experiences in London. In January 1776 – when the south of England lay paralysed by snow – he penned his first letter to Owain Myfyr. Still smarting over Richard Morris's remarks, his letter was a rather petulant response to criticism. It certainly gives a strong indication of the direction in which Iolo's mind was moving, even though it was a curious mixture of egotism and uncertainty. One passage in particular was a forewarning of things to come:

> had I the abilities of an able writer I should have no other motive for writing Welsh than merely my own private amusement, with that of a few particular friends. But nothing could ever induce me to publish my works: perhaps I might deposit them in some public Library . . . Perhaps a more grateful posterity would call them from obscurity and oblivion: but whoever can well endure disencouragement and ill-natured reflections on his intentions and abilities, let him in this age be a Welsh author.[18]

Would forgery perhaps become for Iolo a way of eschewing criticism, while at the same time affording him some private amusement?

With the letter, he enclosed a copy of his Dafydd ap Gwilym-inspired 'Cywydd y Daran'. Although he urged Owain Myfyr and the Gwyneddigion to point out its 'imperfections' – its 'errors of Language and versification' – he felt it necessary to defend his use in the poem of Glamorgan dialect since 'the North Wales Poets [have] always taken a liberty, bordering on unwarrantable licentiousness, of us[ing] their local words and phrases, in their works, certainly a Silurian write[r] must be allowed the same priviledge'.[19]

Passing off his *cywyddau* as authentic works by Dafydd ap Gwilym would, of course, obviate the need for such justifications. Iolo ended his letter with a remarkable exhortation: 'P.S. do not show my letter to your acquaintance, for I thought it too long to write over a second time, and my first rough copy is always very incorrect.'[20] This was palpably untrue: an earlier draft of the letter has survived among Iolo's papers.[21] His anxiety possibly stemmed from an awareness of the canonical status conferred by the Gwyneddigion on the letters of the Morris circle. An unusually self-conscious writer, Iolo always found it extremely difficult, when writing under his own name, to give his productions a final form. Forgery, on the other hand, always came more easily.

---

[17] NLW 21285E, Letter no. 779, Iolo Morganwg to John Walters, draft, *c.*1774.
[18] BL Add. 15024, f. 183ʳ, Iolo Morganwg to Owain Myfyr, 25 January 1776.
[19] Ibid.
[20] Ibid.
[21] NLW 21285E, Letter no. 785, Iolo Morganwg to Owain Myfyr, undated draft.

It was as if attributing his compositions to others enabled him to shrug off the responsibility for any perceived weaknesses.

In the winter of 1776 Iolo began a circuitous journey home to Glamorgan. He called at Avebury and sent Owain Myfyr an impassioned description of the monuments he had seen, speculating wildly on their druidic connections.[22] Landscapes and places with specific historical associations would often evoke deep resonances within Iolo's psyche. He also stopped at Bristol and, with the authenticity of the 'Rowley poems' a hot topic of debate, he might well have visited the birthplace of the literary forger Thomas Chatterton. By the summer of 1777 he had returned to Flemingston. Contrary to expectation, Owain Myfyr received no word from him. John Walters confessed to being 'amazed at his not writing to you, and the more so, as he always professes the highest esteem and affection for you'.[23] Iolo eventually broke his silence in March 1779, claiming that since his return he had drafted several letters to him, but that none of them had been fit to send. A 'failure of nerve' ('gwanhyder') had prevented him from forwarding them.[24] With this particular letter, he enclosed:

[p]edwar Cywydd o waith Dafydd ab Gwilym (medd llyfr Sion Bradford) y rhai nid ynt yn eich llyfr chwi. Mae gennyf mwy etto a chwi a'u cewch o bryd i bryd.

(four *cywyddau* by Dafydd ap Gwilym (according to Sion Bradford's book) which are not in your book. I have others and you shall receive them from time to time.)[25]

Unfortunately, the four *cywyddau* have not been identified, but it seems likely that they marked the beginning of Iolo's public career as a forger.

Since early youth Iolo had been in the habit of embellishing existing poems with bogus couplets, but he had now progressed to forging entire poems. He also experimented with other genres besides *cywyddau*. One of his favourite pursuits was fashioning literary letters, in the manner of the Morris circle, and attributing them to recently deceased poets of the Glamorgan bardic revival, such as Rhys Morgan and Lewis Hopkin.[26] Iolo's main preoccupation, however, continued to be the work of Dafydd ap Gwilym, and over the next few years Owain Myfyr would receive many more *cywyddau*. Seeing no reason to doubt Iolo's character, he was delighted.

These were bleak years for Welsh scholarship. By 1780 Owain Myfyr's efforts to secure the publication of the earliest texts had come to naught. The brilliant, but erratic, Evan Evans had tumbled into a life of embittered destitution following a quarrel with his patron Sir Watkin Williams Wynn. And

[22] NLW 1808E, Letter no. 1519, Iolo Morganwg to Owain Myfyr, 12 January 1777.
[23] BL Add. 15024, f. 185, John Walters to Owain Myfyr, 29 January 1779.
[24] BL Add. 15031, f. 33, Iolo Morganwg to Owain Myfyr, 6 March 1779.
[25] Ibid. See *IMChY*, p. 4.
[26] Williams: *IM*, pp. 274–5.

tragically, Richard Thomas, the most promising scholar of his generation, had died, aged twenty-seven, in 1780. Moreover, with the death in 1779 of the charismatic Richard Morris, the Cymmrodorion Society had entered a period of terminal decline, losing most of the gentry support which Morris had worked hard to cultivate. Nevertheless, amid the gloom, Iolo offered fresh hope to Owain Myfyr. With 'Diddanwch y Cymry' long consigned to oblivion, he announced his plan for 'Dywenydd Morganwg' (The Happiness of Glamorgan), a quarterly magazine to be published by subscription: 'particularly intended to preserve as many as can be got of our ancient pieces.'[27] Owain Myfyr warmly welcomed the idea and, with an offer of a bed, a fire and a candle, he sought to entice Iolo back to London to pursue his studies.[28] But the circumstances of both men were about to change profoundly.

Through loyalty and hard work, Owain Myfyr had earned the trust of his employers, Benjamin Kidney and William Nutt. Such was their regard for him that, on quitting the trade, they decided to assign their business to his management. Thus, during the summer of 1780 – as London recovered from the turmoil of the Gordon Riots[29] – he took up residence in a large house above his shop at 148 Upper Thames Street. Over the next two years his letters to Iolo contained dark hints of an arduous struggle to become established in the world of commerce. He made a success of it and by 1782 he was trading under his own name.[30] In 1781, replying to Owain Myfyr's offers of assistance with 'Dywenydd Morganwg', Iolo confessed that there was little prospect of his coming to London. 'I have tied myself firmly to a post in Glamorgan', he said; 'in short, I have married a wife' ('yr wyf . . . wedi clymu fy hun yn ddiogel wrth Bost ym Morganwg, yn fyr yr wyf wedi priodi gwraig'). He had also acquired 'a patrimony of thirty acres' ('deg erw ar hugain o dir Treftadawl') at Wentloog, near Rumney. He then went on to give an idyllic account of married bliss in the Vale of Glamorgan.[31] But 'Dywenydd Morganwg' never materialized. Nevertheless, buoyed by a sense of financial security – perhaps even inspired by Myfyr's example – Iolo, too, launched himself into business. He acquired a cart and horses, a lime kiln and a sloop for trading on the Severn estuary. But, lacking Myfyr's acumen, he soon found himself floundering in debt. Eventually, in 1784, having ignored several writs from the Court of Great Sessions, he abandoned his concern and fled, with his wife and child, to Wentloog, now intent on becoming a farmer.

The area around Wentloog – a quiet former marshland intersected with

---

27 BL Add. 15024, f. 189, Iolo Morganwg to Owain Myfyr, 10 July 1780.
28 NLW 21281E, Letter no. 229, Owain Myfyr to Iolo Morganwg, 'Pumed Sul o'r Grawys', 1781.
29 Ibid., Letter no. 227, Owain Myfyr to Iolo Morganwg, 22 August 1780.
30 Henry Kent, *Kent's Directory for the year 1782* (London, 1782).
31 BL Add. 15024, f. 192, Iolo Morganwg to Owain Myfyr, 16 November 1781.

dykes – had close associations with Dafydd ap Gwilym. Dafydd's patron, the nobleman Ifor Hael, had held court at nearby Basaleg. Iolo had visited the place in 1780 in the company of Evan Evans and even claimed that this was the occasion on which Evans had composed his famous *englynion* to the ruins of Ifor's court, elegizing the age of aristocratic patronage.[32] Now, in 1784, as the shadow of penury lowered, Iolo, too, sought comfort in an idealized past. His obsession with Dafydd ap Gwilym reached its highest pitch of intensity. From Basaleg, on 8 August, he wrote:

> Y Myfyr Caredig,
> Y wyf yn awr yn ysgrifennu attad o fann ag yr wyf yn ei ystyried yn fath o dir Cysegredig. Hwnn yw'r tir a droediwyd lawer arno gan Ddafydd ab Gwilym, Morfydd, Ifor Hael a Nest wiwgoeth wenddoeth wynddaint . . . yma y prydawdd y melus Eosfardd lawer iawn o'i Gywyddau pereiddfwyn.[33]

> (Kind Myfyr,
> I now write to you from a place I consider a kind of Sacred land. This is the earth which was trodden upon a great deal by Dafydd ap Gwilym, Morfydd, Ifor Hael and the pure, wise and fair Nest of the sparkling teeth . . . here the sweet Nightingale-poet sang very many of his pleasant, melodious Cywyddau.)

It was here, too, that Iolo produced his most accomplished forgeries: mellow, sonorous *cywyddau* which celebrated the friendship of Dafydd and Ifor, poet and patron.[34] One might speculate that the process of forgery involved Iolo in a kind of identification with the medieval bard. He may even have sought in this identification a way of dealing with his personal crisis. His preoccupation at Wentloog with the figure of Ifor Hael certainly provides a fascinating backdrop to his own friendship with Owain Myfyr. By giving encouragement and offering practical assistance to Iolo, Owain Myfyr had already fulfilled many of the duties of a traditional patron. Iolo's earliest Dafydd ap Gwilym forgeries had been written specifically for Myfyr's perusal, just as Dafydd had composed *cywyddau* for Ifor's amusement. As Iolo's fortunes plummeted, those of Owain Myfyr continued to rise and, by 1784, the Londoner was in a position to offer his beleaguered friend a measure of financial assistance. For his part, Iolo began to look upon Owain Myfyr as a potential saviour.

But Iolo was too proud to make an explicit request for money. Rather, he chose to emphasize his depressed state of mind, hoping that Owain Myfyr would take the hint. On 13 September 1784 he wrote a pathetic, sombre letter to Siôn Ceiriog (at 148 Upper Thames Street), begging him to persuade Owain

---

[32] NLW 21390E, no. 24.

[33] BL Add. 15024, f. 199, Iolo Morganwg to Owain Myfyr, 8 August 1784.

[34] See Gwyneth Lewis, 'Eighteenth-century Literary Forgeries with special reference to the work of Iolo Morganwg' (unpublished University of Oxford D. Phil. thesis, 1991), pp. 147, 156.

Myfyr to send some words of comfort.[35] At this stage, the furrier was deeply entangled in legal wrangling over the ownership of his Dafydd ap Gwilym manuscript – the volume having been appropriated by the Dolgellau surgeon, Griffith Roberts.[36] He was also possibly inured by now to Iolo's bouts of melodramatic self-indulgence. Whatever the reason, he failed to respond. By 1785 it was too late. With the bailiffs closing in, Iolo and his family were forced to flee by night to the city of Wells, leaving no forwarding address.[37] In the summer of 1785 he spent a fortnight in London. But he stayed well clear of Owain Myfyr and the Gwyneddigion, having convinced himself that insolvency had made him a pariah in their eyes. When, in August 1786, Iolo became a prisoner for debt in Cardiff gaol, Owain Myfyr apparently knew nothing of his circumstances. Released in August the following year under the Act for the Relief of Insolvent Debtors, Iolo retreated to Flemingston to lick his wounds.

In the mean time Owain Myfyr had continued to prosper. By 1787 he was in a position to fulfil a long cherished ideal: the publication of the works of Dafydd ap Gwilym. Following the demise of the first Cymmrodorion Society in 1787, the Gwyneddigion looked upon themselves as the guardians of Welsh scholarship. Owain Myfyr was therefore eager to publish *Barddoniaeth Dafydd ab Gwilym* under the auspices of the Gwyneddigion, even though he himself would finance the entire enterprise, with little prospect of remuneration. By now he had engaged a willing assistant editor. In 1782 William Owen (later William Owen Pughe), a mild-mannered clerk, had emerged from six years of lonely obscurity in another part of London to demonstrate a rare enthusiasm for Welsh literature as well as a staggering capacity for hard work.[38] He became Owain Myfyr's confidant and his most trusted adviser on literary matters. Iolo would see in William Owen Pughe's naivety and untempered Romanticism a convenient means for propagating his deceptions.

In March 1788, William Owen Pughe began corresponding with Iolo in the hope of gaining his assistance with *Barddoniaeth Dafydd ab Gwilym*. Iolo was only too willing to oblige. He immediately forwarded a dozen forged *cywyddau*,[39] and seized the opportunity to air his grievances against Owain Myfyr, the fruit of much brooding between prison walls. Pughe found himself playing the part of conciliator, a role with which he was to become familiar over the years. Writing to Iolo on 28 March, he claimed that Myfyr had only been informed the previous week of Iolo's period in gaol, and that, on hearing the news, he

---

[35]   NLW 13087E, pp. 343–6, Iolo Morganwg to John Edwards, 13 September 1784.

[36]   Roberts had decided to keep the manuscript in lieu of some volumes of his own which Owain Myfyr had lost. The manuscript was eventually returned to Owain Myfyr in 1785. See G. T. Roberts, 'Robin Ddu yr Ail o Fôn', *BBCS*, VI, part 3 (1932), 240–3.

[37]   Morgan: *IM*, p. 9.

[38]   See Glenda Carr, *William Owen Pughe* (Caerdydd, 1983).

[39]   NLW 13221E, p. 11, Iolo Morganwg to William Owen Pughe, 12 March 1788.

had become visibly distressed, exclaiming: 'Had I known it was thus for Iorwerth I would have made him free' ('Be buaswn yn gwybod ei fod felly ar Iorwerth mi fuaswn i yn ei wneud yn rhydd').[40]

On 9 April, Owain Myfyr urged Iolo to drown his enmity in a quart of beer. Dafydd ap Gwilym, he said, was eagerly awaiting his attention.[41] In the event, Iolo's forgeries had to be incorporated into an appendix, where, on the book's appearance in 1789, their peculiarities of style attracted the attention of at least one shrewd critic, David Thomas (Dafydd Ddu Eryri). In later years, Owain Myfyr, too, claimed to have suspected their authenticity, declaring to Iolo that he had yielded to the 'obstinnacy of Wm Owen' in allowing them to be published.[42] For the time being, however, good relations between Iolo and Owain Myfyr had been restored, and in 1790 the latter sent Iolo the respectable sum of £10 in payment for his contribution to *Barddoniaeth Dafydd ab Gwilym*. Iolo was effusive in his thanks, but behind the bonhomie there would always lurk an ambivalence towards Owain Myfyr's money.

Seeing his forgeries in print gave Iolo proof of his own genius, and perhaps even a sense of having triumphed over Owain Myfyr and the Gwyneddigion. He resolved to return to London to publish a collection of English verse, *Poems, Lyric and Pastoral*, and earn a living as an author. This time he would be well armed against the condescension of Londoners from north Wales. Posing as an authentic Druid, the heir to arcane wisdom, he carried in his satchel a manuscript entitled 'Cyfrinach Beirdd Ynys Prydain' ('The Secret of the Bards of the Isle of Britain'), an ingenious forgery which purported to show that Glamorgan had a superior system of bardic learning to that developed in north Wales. He arrived in London in 1791, riding high on a wave of euphoria. An extended visit to the drawing rooms of Bath had brought him a dazzling list of subscribers and an initiation into 'many Mysteries of Authorship' in the company of fashionable poets such as Christopher Anstey.[43] He also gained permission to dedicate his poems to the Prince of Wales. In a letter to the Bath bookseller, William Meyler, Iolo now confessed to being ashamed of his connection with the 'barbarous Gwyneddigion', whom he dismissed as a collection of unlettered tradesmen. Even Owain Myfyr, despite his 'good sense', was 'no schollar, no judge of Poetry'.[44]

Iolo's Gorsedd ceremonies on Primrose Hill attracted a good deal of curiosity within both Welsh and English circles, but by the summer of 1792 his dream of becoming a London author was turning sour. The euphoria had evaporated and he was overcome by exhaustion and depression. The old uncertainty about

[40] NLW 21282E, Letter no. 307, William Owen Pughe to Iolo Morganwg, 28 March 1788.
[41] NLW 21281E, Letter no. 232, Owain Myfyr to Iolo Morganwg, 9 April 1788.
[42] NLW 21281E, Letter no. 260, Owain Myfyr to Iolo Morganwg, 11 March 1806.
[43] NLW 21285E, Letter no. 798, Iolo Morganwg to John Walters, 24 February 1791.
[44] Cardiff 3.104, vol. 6, no. 39, Iolo Morganwg to William Meyler, ? January 1792.

the quality of his writings also reared its head. When *Poems, Lyric and Pastoral* failed to appear by the appointed time he felt obliged to offer his subscribers an explanation:

> I was . . . conscious of the numerous defects and crudities of my pieces, which made me frequently linger over them before I would put them to the press, whilst a dejection thus occasioned disqualified me for making some amendments that I saw so very requisite.[45]

His asthma deteriorated in the smoky air and he took stupefying doses of laudanum. Gnawed by guilt over his failure to provide for his family, he penned a series of hysterical letters to his wife Margaret (Peggy), complaining, among other things, of the 'superciliousness' of London's 'great and rich', whose patronage he had failed to obtain.[46] He no longer found comfort in the persona of Dafydd ap Gwilym, as he had done at Wentloog eight years earlier. In London he sought out a more troubling alter-ego in a more harrowing landscape. Roaming the filthy side-alleys of Holborn, he found lodgings 'within a door or two' of where Thomas Chatterton, the archetypal victim of London's patronage system, had been 'obliged to force his way out of this good-for-nothing world'. Now Iolo, too, contemplated suicide. Only thoughts of his children saved him.[47]

As his family faced starvation, his wife Margaret successfully begged his permission to sell the farm at Wentloog.[48] She obtained £590 for it,[49] and a temporary solution to their difficulties. Despite his proximity to Iolo, Owain Myfyr had been – for the second time – unaware of the crisis. Pride, and perhaps even a lingering fear of rejection, had prevented Iolo from approaching him. Iolo came to regret his decision, confessing in 1793 in a draft of the preface to *Poems, Lyric and Pastoral* that had he mentioned his troubles to Myfyr 'my poems would have been long ago published'.[50] The poems eventually appeared in 1794 to fairly widespread acclaim, and Iolo immediately began collecting subscriptions for his *magnum opus*, 'The History of the Bards'. By now, however, he had become tired of London, and in 1795, despite Myfyr's offers of assistance with his new book, he walked home to Flemingston.

Owain Myfyr's business continued to flourish during the 1790s and, true to his early ideals, he had become an extraordinary benefactor to Welsh schol-arship. Without his drive and munificence, the London-based antiquarian

---

[45]   Williams: *PLP*, I, p. xii.
[46]   NLW 21285E, Letter no. 811, Edward Williams to Margaret Williams, 9 August 1792. See also Geraint Phillips, 'Math o Wallgofrwydd: Iolo Morganwg, Opiwm a Thomas Chatterton', *NLWJ*, XXIX, no. 4 (1996), 391–410.
[47]   NLW 21285E, Letter no. 811, Iolo Morganwg to Margaret Williams, 9 August 1792.
[48]   NLW 21283E, Letter no. 604, Margaret Williams to Iolo Morganwg, 1 January 1793.
[49]   Williams: *IM*, p. 452.
[50]   NLW 21387E, no. 9.

movement of the late eighteenth century could not have been sustained. Among many other things, he had paid for the printing of the final numbers of John Walters's *English–Welsh Dictionary*, and had financed the education at Oxford of Walter Davies (Gwallter Mechain), a talented young cooper from Llanfechain in Montgomeryshire. By 1797 Owain Myfyr had amassed sufficient wealth to embark upon his most ambitious project: the publication of the entire corpus of early Welsh literature from the Dark Ages to the end of the Elizabethan age. He was prevailed upon to call his venture *The Myvyrian Archaiology of Wales.*

Iolo gave the plan an ecstatic welcome, describing Owain Myfyr as 'the only real patriot that Wales has known since the days of Ifor Hael'.[51] He even allotted him a place in his bardic vision as the inaugurator of a new golden age of patronage:

> The name of Owen Myfyr must descend to future ages with transcendent fame. What our ancient Bards relate of Tydain Tad Awen as the restorer of the almost lost Barddoniaeth & Barddas of the ancient Gwyddoniaid & on whose principles our Trichyntefigion Beirdd Ynys Prydain formed our splendidly beautiful Bardic & Druidic System will be again verified in Owain Myfyr, from him a new aera will commence.[52]

But Owain Myfyr had little time for such encomia. For him, the *Archaiology* was primarily a rescue mission, an attempt to save the contents of the most important Welsh manuscripts for posterity. The news from Wales had been alarming, with reports that the Hengwrt collection was rapidly succumbing to thieves, rats and rainwater. The creation of an authoritative printed record of each of the early texts had thus become a matter of the utmost urgency. Commentaries and translations into English could follow at a later stage.

Owain Myfyr's plan was twofold. First, and somewhat naively, he expected to employ Iolo in London to assist William Owen Pughe with the task of editing the work. Myfyr himself – by now 'over head and ears in business'[53] – had little time to spare. Secondly, he expected to be able to persuade the owners of Welsh manuscripts to send items to London to be copied for the press. He had no difficulty in securing the cooperation of the most enlightened members of the Welsh gentry: Paul Panton of Plas Gwyn in Anglesey, whose father had purchased the transcripts made by the now deceased Evan Evans, immediately sent a wagonload of volumes to London,[54] while Thomas Johnes of Hafod in Cardiganshire, who had acquired the manuscripts of Edward Lhuyd, also showed a lively interest in the project. Petitions to Hengwrt, Wynnstay and Gloddaith, however, were rebuffed.

[51] BL Add. 15024, f. 274, Iolo Morganwg to William Owen Pughe, 29 September 1798.
[52] BL Add. 15030, f. 9, Iolo Morganwg to Owain Myfyr, 7 August 1798.
[53] NLW 1807iiE, Letter no. 1201, William Owen Pughe to Walter Davies, 15 February 1796.
[54] BL Add. 15030, f. 117ᵛ, Paul Panton to Owain Myfyr, 11 November 1798.

For his part, Iolo was profuse in his offers to procure Glamorgan manuscripts and to visit some of the Welsh libraries, but he remained vague on the subject of returning to London. In the summer of 1798 William Owen Pughe, already burdened with several other projects, began working alone on the *Archaiology*. Owain Myfyr felt increasingly uneasy – and perhaps even guilty about his own inability to help. Writing to Walter Davies, he confessed that 'Will is so much engaged with the School, Diction^y Cambrian Register &c that I am affraid that his health poor Fellow will be impaired ac nid oes yma un dyn a rydd law wrth yr Aradr [and there is no one here to lend a hand at the plough].'[55] By the winter of 1798 Owain Myfyr had tired of Iolo's prevarication, and had decided on a different strategy. Taking up Iolo's original offer, he invited him to embark on a brief fact-finding mission, first to Hafod, and then to Wynnstay, where Walter Davies (by now a curate at Meifod) was expected to assist him in gaining admission to the library. Owain Myfyr hoped that, having gathered his material, Iolo would feel obliged to come to London to report on his findings. He sent him £20 to cover his travel expenses and urged him to buy any manuscripts which he thought worth acquiring.

After further procrastination, Iolo arrived at Hafod in May 1799. 'Here at Havod', he informed Myfyr, 'I find invaluable Treasures.'[56] Thomas Johnes proved to be an amiable host, and even appeared willing to send his manuscripts to London. As the days passed, however, Iolo sensed a change of heart in the squire and a certain coolness towards him. When Johnes, in a letter sent to London, indicated a preference for having his manuscripts copied on the estate by William Owen Pughe,[57] both Myfyr and Pughe concluded that someone must have informed Johnes of Iolo's 'kingophobia'.[58] From Hafod, Iolo went on to Llanrwst, 'very much indisposed and quite in a fever'.[59] By now he was beyond the reach of Owain Myfyr's commands and the open road beckoned. Instead of going to London via Wynnstay, he spent the next five months wandering around north Wales and parts of England, walking up to forty miles a day in search of manuscripts and following his whims. Iolo's long absence from his family began to weigh heavily on Owain Myfyr's conscience and, as the weeks wore on, he became increasingly concerned for his welfare. He feared that Iolo might be short of money, but had no inkling where to send his payments. On 13 August 1799 Iolo wrote to Owain Myfyr from Beaumaris:

> I have for the last month nearly, at Bangor, Plas Gwyn and here been every day & almost every night, Sundays not excepted, writing continually, from four o'clock in

---

[55] NLW 1806E, Letter no. 694, Owain Myfyr to Walter Davies, 11 December 1798.
[56] BL Add. 15030, f. 7, Iolo Morganwg to Owain Myfyr, 28 May 1799.
[57] NLW 13222C, p. 613, Thomas Johnes to William Owen Pughe, 10 June 1799.
[58] NLW 21282E, Letter no. 335, William Owen Pughe to Iolo Morganwg, 14 June 1799.
[59] BL Add. 15024, f. 282, Iolo Morganwg to Owain Myfyr, 9 June 1799.

the morning till twelve at night & often later. I have exercised myself so little otherwise & have been so little in the open air that I feel the bad effects of it especially in the swelling of my ancles & legs like those of a man in the dropsy, but my journey home will remove this complaint.[60]

Fearing that Iolo was on the edge of nervous collapse, Owain Myfyr immediately sent him £2, informing him that a further £10 awaited him at Llanrwst:

I beg of you to take care of your Health I am much affraid that you are to[o] anxtious & exert Your Self too much . . . relax we have now a very good collection if we live next year we may visit those Treasures not yet explored they will do us an apendix to the Whole the object is preservation it will not be great consequence in what part of our depot.[61]

But instead of returning home, Iolo collected his £10 from Llanrwst and headed back to Anglesey. In October he held a Gorsedd at Dinorwig for the bards of Gwynedd.

Owain Myfyr was understandably incensed. The first two volumes of the *Archaiology* were due to be published in January but, without having seen the materials gathered by Iolo, William Owen Pughe was unable to continue with the editing. On 8 October Owain Myfyr sent Iolo a furious letter, rebuking him for neglecting his family and urging him to send his transcripts to London by coach as soon as possible.[62] Finally, as winter closed in, Iolo began his journey home, passing through Hafod on 14 November, 'after a most vexatious journey thro' bad weather, along roads dreadfully dirty . . . and with a very heavy luggage of 60lb weight at least'.[63] Stopping at Aberystwyth, he posted a large box of transcripts to Cowbridge and, towards the end of November, he staggered back to Flemingston, exhausted and depressed; his many months of frenetic activity were now taking their toll. Owain Myfyr sent him another £20, but no transcripts arrived in London, and *The Myvyrian Archaiology of Wales* failed to appear at the appointed time.

On 12 March 1800 Iolo informed Owain Myfyr that the transcripts posted in November at Aberystwyth had been stolen by an employee of the coach office at Carmarthen. Forced to retrieve his parcel, Iolo had carried it away on his back, 'not caring to leave it any longer amongst the Thieves of Caerm[n]'.[64] He had then placed his transcripts in a box, intending to send them to London via the Aberthaw boat to Bristol. But further complications had ensued, including a subpoena to be a witness at the Court of Great Sessions. The

60 BL Add. 15030, f. 5, Iolo Morganwg to Owain Myfyr, 13 August 1799.
61 NLW 21281E, Letter no. 242, Owain Myfyr to Iolo Morganwg, 22 August 1799.
62 NLW 21281E, Letter no. 243, Owain Myfyr to Iolo Morganwg, 8 October 1799.
63 NLW 13221E, p. 59, Iolo Morganwg to William Owen Pughe, 14 November 1799.
64 BL Add. 15024, f. 308, Iolo Morganwg to Owain Myfyr, 12 March 1800.

outcome of this improbable sequence of events was that the box was now stranded in Bristol: 'it lies now in the warehouse belonging to the Aberthaw boat, and before I can send to the Captain he will have left Bristol, and there is no forwarding direction on it . . . My management of this matter has been something unfortunate as things have turned out', Iolo confessed,[65] but Owain Myfyr, seething with anger, did not even trouble to respond.

It became clear over the following six months that Iolo had little inclination to rescue the box. His transcripts consisted mainly of medieval chronicles and works by the poets of the Welsh princes, literature which glorified war and bloodshed. Such things were out of keeping with Iolo's anti-war stance, and with the particular image of early Welsh society that he had wished to convey in *The Myvyrian Archaiology of Wales*. Much later, in 1805, he informed William Owen Pughe that he had

> always considered the bardic morality as the glory of our ancient Literature, a single sentence of which is worth a thousand volumes of such History as that of the infernally bloodthirsty princes of Wales . . . the Arts of Peace and civilization were cultivated in a very considerable degree [by] our wise ancestors, but how little of this is [g]enerally known?[66]

With his north Wales transcripts safely banished to Bristol, Iolo was now able to focus his attention on what he really wished to see published in *The Myvyrian Archaiology of Wales*: his own forgeries. Over the years he had created an enormous collection of proverbs and triads: 'the noble ruins of what was once very great and splendid in our language and Ethics'.[67] Throughout the spring and summer of 1800, without making any reference to the box at Bristol, Iolo sought to persuade Myfyr to devote a volume of *The Myvyrian Archaiology of Wales* to 'The Wisdom of the Welsh' ('Doethineb y Cymry'). As Myfyr's silence became increasingly ominous, Iolo begged him for an answer: 'such a letter will be a relief to my very much exhausted spirits'.[68]

On 8 May, William Owen Pughe sent Iolo a frantic letter claiming that Owain Myfyr was threatening to abort the entire venture: 'For goodness sake, do not be the means of his becoming tired of the path (to glory) wherein he now treads, for Welsh literature will not find another such a supporter.'[69] But Iolo simply withdrew further into the world of his forgeries. On 17 June, in a letter which offers a glimpse of the startling complexity of his mind, he even began to deal critically with his own fabrications. Fearing perhaps that the

---

[65] Ibid.
[66] NLW 13221E, p. 123, Iolo Morganwg to William Owen Pughe, 14 February 1805.
[67] BL Add. 15031, f. 31, Iolo Morganwg to Owain Myfyr, 15 April 1800.
[68] BL Add. 15024, f. 310, Iolo Morganwg to Owain Myfyr, 10 April 1800.
[69] NLW 21282E, Letter no. 339, William Owen Pughe to Iolo Morganwg, 8 May 1800.

anachronisms in his work were likely to arouse suspicion, he resorted to a strategy of double bluff:

> In my collection of the Proverbs of common use in Glamorgan . . . a great many of
> them are ancient. A great number also are obviously modern . . . ancient modes of
> speech will not, were we to attempt it, designate new modes of thought, whence the
> difficulty, I will say, impossibility, of imitating the ancients in language and stile
> beyond the power of detection, could we think precisely as the ancients did, we
> might perhaps hope to succeed in our attempts to write as they did. but this we
> never can possibly do.[70]

And then, as if daring Owain Myfyr to accuse him of having forged the work of Dafydd ap Gwilym, Iolo added: 'Dafydd ap Gwilym is comparatively a modern, but who can copy after him? not a man living.'[71]

At the end of June, thanks to William Owen Pughe's gifts of diplomacy, Owain Myfyr capitulated and agreed to include Iolo's bardic morality in the third volume of *The Myvyrian Archaiology of Wales*. Iolo immediately set off for Bristol to rescue his box and forward it to London. On seeing the first examples of Iolo's triads and proverbs, Owain Myfyr exclaimed to Pughe: 'These things are worth all that you have printed.'[72] He was hugely impressed by their homespun philosophy – much of which Iolo had derived from Benjamin Franklin's popular *Poor Richard's Almanac*. For him, they offered proof 'that our Ancestors were posessed of more extentive & corect Knowlege of things than modern times have allowed them'.[73] Iolo also succeeded in getting two forged chronicles – 'Brut Aberpergwm' and 'Brut Ieuan Brechfa' – as well as a series of triads, published in the second volume of *The Myvyrian Archaiology of Wales*, which eventually appeared, along with the first volume, in June 1801.

His faith in Iolo Morganwg now restored, Owain Myfyr began to hint at the possibility of paying him a pension of £50 a year in order to enable him to complete 'The History of the Bards'. Iolo, who was once more in financial difficulties, set off for London, arriving in March 1802. Finding themselves alone in the dining room at William Owen Pughe's house, Owain Myfyr informed Iolo: 'You shall never fag any more at your Trade, and be sure you do not let your family want.'[74] It was the high-water mark of their friendship, and Iolo indulged fantasies about opening small businesses in Glamorgan for his son and eldest daughter. But the cordiality proved to be short lived. Instead of assisting William Owen Pughe with *The Myvyrian Archaiology of Wales*, Iolo spent the remainder of his time in London advancing the Unitarian cause. Nonplussed, Myfyr began to regret making his promise.

---

[70] BL Add. 15030, f. 12, Iolo Morganwg to Owain Myfyr, 17 June 1800.

[71] Ibid.

[72] NLW 21282E, Letter no. 342, William Owen Pughe to Iolo Morganwg, 28 August 1800.

[73] NLW 9074E, Owain Myfyr to Paul Panton, 18 July 1807.

[74] NLW 21285E, Letter no. 880, Iolo Morganwg to Owain Myfyr, draft, 5 April 1806.

Further storm clouds gathered in July 1802 when Owain Myfyr informed Iolo that he had suffered grave financial losses and had been forced to suspend publication of *The Myvyrian Archaiology of Wales*.[75] His confidence was badly shaken by these losses and they wrought a curious change in his attitude towards Iolo. No longer willing to indulge his foibles, he began to suspect Iolo of taking advantage of his generosity. The situation deteriorated further when Iolo failed to honour a commitment to assist Walter Davies with the writing of a report on the agriculture of south Wales. Owain Myfyr had persuaded Davies to employ Iolo for the sum of £40 in the belief that he was likely to benefit from Iolo's visionary grasp of agricultural matters. Owain Myfyr himself had stumped up the £40, expecting to be repaid by Davies when the report was completed. But over the years he received a series of carping letters from Davies, complaining of Iolo's failure to cooperate. By March 1804, when Iolo returned to London, he had decided to withdraw his offer of a pension.

In letters to William Owen Pughe, Iolo made no attempt to disguise his utter loathing for Owain Myfyr. He claimed that his erstwhile benefactor had encouraged him to set aside his trade in Glamorgan, had lured him to London to publish 'The History of the Bards', had sent him on a 'foolish and useless Agricultural scamper' with Walter Davies and, then, having reduced him to penury, had forsaken him.[76]

In 1805 Owain Myfyr decided to resurrect *The Myvyrian Archaiology of Wales*. Writing much later to William Owen Pughe, Iolo announced that, in spite of Owain Myfyr's treatment of him: 'I do not intend to relax in any thing that I can do for the Archaiology it is for Wales, for the Welsh Nation, for the Welsh language and literature to . . . which I have sacrificed all the comforts of life.'[77] In August 1805 Walter Davies travelled to Flemingston to confront Iolo with the unfinished report. They reached a compromise and, on his return, Davies gave Owain Myfyr a tear-jerking account of Iolo's circumstances. 'Upon the representation you gave me of his distress', wrote Owain Myfyr to Davies, 'I remitted him Ten pds with a promise of further Assistance after I recvd the Forty pds from you.'[78] Sensing a glimmer of hope of reconciliation, William Owen Pughe urged Iolo to compromise with Owain Myfyr: 'as he is throwing all the past into oblivion, you also should come halfway'.[79] Owain Myfyr sent Iolo another two guineas on 30 October, with the warning: 'I have some Cas wîr [home truths] but shall wait another opportunity to thro back the stones you frequently pick up.'[80] In November, Pughe persuaded his friend,

---

[75] NLW 21281E, Letter no. 255, Owain Myfyr to Iolo Morganwg, 15 July 1802.
[76] NLW 13222E, p. 195, Iolo Morganwg to William Owen Pughe, 20 February 1805.
[77] NLW 13221E, p. 147, Iolo Morganwg to William Owen Pughe, 1 March 1806.
[78] NLW 1806E, Letter no. 709, Owain Myfyr to Walter Davies, 31 October 1805.
[79] NLW 21282E, Letter no. 366, William Owen Pughe to Edward Williams, 18 September 1805.
[80] NLW 21281E, Letter no. 257, Owain Myfyr to Iolo Morganwg, 30 October 1805.

the historian Sharon Turner, to donate £5 to Iolo to enable him to continue with 'The History of the Bards'. But Iolo's failure to acknowledge Turner's generosity prompted the following expostulation from Myfyr in a letter to Walter Davies: 'the man I mean Iolo as he conceitedly calls himself hath Talents and very valuable ones & is possessed of many articles of great worth to Welsh Literature but shocking that he is not possessed of few grains of integrity & gratetude'.[81] In a letter to Owain Myfyr in February 1806 Iolo delivered a withering attack on the 'barbarous ... becockney'd idiom' of the Gwyneddigion's new periodical Y Greal.[82] The attack was calculated to wound Myfyr where he was most vulnerable. His pig-headed decision to adopt William Owen Pughe's bizarre new orthography in Y Greal had already alienated most of its readers and had led to an acrimonious dispute between Owain Myfyr and his old friend, David Thomas. By anathematizing Y Greal, Iolo had gone too far. The storm was finally breaking.

On 11 March, Owain Myfyr sat down to write his last letter to Iolo: 'if this abuse will any longer be continued I must decline any or the least conection w.th Iolo Morganwg'.[83] There followed an unpunctuated catalogue of griev-ances relating mainly to Iolo's conduct with regard to The Myvyrian Archaiology of Wales. Owain Myfyr had never been an articulate man, and his grammar and syntax now buckled under the burden of his rage. Significantly, he accused the Glamorgan bard of having forged the poems published in the appendix to Barddoniaeth Dafydd ab Gwilym:

> Dd ddu Eryri with great Penetration remarked that the addition were more correct in cynghanedd &c but not with sufficient Taste to distinguished between the Poetry of D. G & Iolo Morganwg it was to the obstinnacy of W.m Owen that this impotition was Suff.d to Pass & tho perhaps there are not many that can detect the fraud.[84]

This, like other charges in the letter, was the product of long and bitter rumination. As far back as 1789, in his preface to Barddoniaeth Dafydd ab Gwilym, Owain Myfyr had demonstrated a special preoccupation with the use made by Dafydd of cynghanedd. He may well, at that time, have expressed reser-vations to William Owen Pughe about the cywyddau received from Iolo and suspected that a more rigorous use of cynghanedd marked them out as belonging to a later age. Following publication David Thomas had voiced similar concerns, but neither he nor Owain Myfyr had irrefutable grounds for doubting Iolo's integrity. By 1806, however, Owain Myfyr had been granted a piercing insight into Iolo's capacity for dishonest and unscrupulous behaviour. He now felt sufficiently confident to make this accusation. More than one of

[81] NLW 1806E, Letter no. 710, Owain Myfyr to Walter Davies, 18 December 1805.
[82] BL Add. 15029, f. 143, Iolo Morganwg to Owain Myfyr, 7 February 1806.
[83] NLW 21281E, Letter no. 260, Owain Myfyr to Iolo Morganwg, 11 March 1806.
[84] Ibid.

Iolo's contemporaries poured cold water on his druidic fantasies, but only Owain Myfyr accused him directly of committing literary forgery.

Ironically, at the time of the accusation, Owain Myfyr was engaged in publishing a significantly larger corpus of Iolo Morganwg's forgeries, but he was in no position to expose these forgeries because his own scholarship lacked the necessary depth and breadth. Dafydd ap Gwilym, on the other hand, was a special case: Owain Myfyr had immersed himself in his poetry since his early youth. Furthermore, perhaps he had allowed himself to be duped by Iolo's bardic-wisdom literature because, like many others, he wanted to believe that the ancient Welsh had anticipated the eighteenth-century Enlightenment.

Having read Owain Myfyr's accusations with mounting rage, Iolo seized his pen and endorsed the letter as follows: 'Rhyfedd! Rhyfedd! Rhyfedd! Rhyfedd! [Strange!]'. And then, like a man possessed, he set about preparing his reply – a febrile mixture of half-truths and selective quotations from Owain Myfyr's letters: 'I thank God that I carefully kept them to appear as evidences against you before the public.'[85] Iolo now believed that his benefactor's promise to pay him an annuity of £50 had been 'nothing but a coolly premeditated plan of delusion carried on for almost three years'.[86] As for the charge of having forged the work of Dafydd ap Gwilym, he could cite the manuscripts from which he had copied the poems: 'I thank God for it, for any one that may wish to examine them.'[87] In fact, he named only the source of the four authentic poems in the appendix. 'With you sir who have uttered such horrible untruths', he added, 'I cannot possibly hold any further correspondence . . . for what a number of years have I thought you of all the men in the world the least capable of such a conduct. Nid rhyfedd dim i ddyn trugainoed [nothing is strange to a man of sixty].'[88] The efforts of William Owen Pughe and Walter Davies to bring about a reconciliation proved fruitless.

The rift with Owain Myfyr effectively ended Iolo's long and formative association with the London Welsh. Yet – true to Dr Johnson's pronouncement – he was careful to maintain a connection with the London bookseller, Evan Williams of the Strand. They discussed various projects, including 'The History of the Bards', but, predictably, the book was never completed. Evan Williams also supplied Iolo with the occasional morsel of malicious gossip, declaring in 1813 that:

> Your once old friend Owen Jones is become one of the greatest misers in London – he Rolls himself up in fur & curses all Welsh Literature – & is turned pagan, he

---

85 NLW 21285E, Letter no. 880, Iolo Morganwg to Owain Myfyr, draft, 5 April 1806.
86 Ibid.
87 Ibid., Letter no. 879, Iolo Morganwg to Owain Myfyr, draft, 2 April 1806.
88 Ibid.

has married his maid servant – & no Venus, and she has brought him several young Bratts! & he is grown poor, pure & virtuous![89]

Owain Myfyr had, in fact, abandoned the cause of Welsh scholarship soon after his quarrel with Iolo. In 1807, with the appearance of the egregious third volume, *The Myvyrian Archaiology of Wales* came to a final halt.

The centre of gravity now shifted from London to Wales, and within a few years the work of publishing Welsh manuscripts had been taken up by a new movement: 'yr hen bersoniaid llengar' (the old literary parsons). Iolo found himself lionized at their provincial eisteddfodau and he also remained on good terms with Walter Davies, a leading light within the new movement. During the winter of 1814 Evan Williams informed Iolo that Owain Myfyr had died: 'we must now forget and forgive all his errors'.[90] But Iolo remained unforgiving and, even in advanced old age, the name of Owain Myfyr would occasion diatribes of extraordinary virulence from him.

---

[89] NLW 21283E, Letter no. 586, Evan Williams to Iolo Morganwg, 18 October 1813.
[90] NLW 21283E, Letter no. 587, Evan Williams to Iolo Morganwg, 15 November 1814.

19

'Mad Ned' and the 'Smatter-Dasher': Iolo Morganwg and Edward 'Celtic' Davies

MOIRA DEARNLEY

The fraught relationship between the schoolmaster cleric Edward Davies and the stonemason bard Edward Williams, otherwise known as Iolo Morganwg, provides a dramatic enactment, if not a *reductio ad absurdum*, of a key issue which lay at the heart of that frenetic late eighteenth-century activity devoted to ensuring the survival of the ancient language and literature of Wales – namely, the authenticity of its manuscript sources and the integrity of its scholarship. It is no accident that their acquaintance began soon after John Pinkerton made his notorious attack in 1788 on those who 'rather chuse to sicken the publick with their dreams concerning the Welch language and antiquities, than to acquire great fame by publishing the original authors'.[1] Both Davies and Iolo were ostensibly devoted to the notion of 'publishing the original authors'. Texts – whether 'copies on vellum', transcripts, translations or 'versions' – loom large in the story of their relationship. Yet, just as Sharon Turner's *Vindication of the Genuineness of the Ancient British Poems* (1803) was flawed as a result of his reliance on information derived from Iolo and William Owen Pughe, so was Davies's scholarship compromised by what his old school-friend Theophilus Jones referred to as 'the frauds and the tricks of Ned Williams'.[2] Although Davies was almost certainly hoodwinked in ways he never even suspected, he was by no means entirely innocent in the business: his delight in Iolo's version of the past occasionally overcame his scholarly instincts. Even so, he was clearly questioning Iolo's veracity, as well as Pughe's, when he suspected 'marks of gross misrepresentation, if not of absolute forgery',[3] and in so doing he began the arduous process, still incomplete, of ascertaining how far the creative imagination of Iolo Morganwg polluted the ancient sources of a nation's history and culture.

---

[1] Philistor [John Pinkerton], 'Letters to the People of Great Britain, on the Cultivation of their National History', *Gentleman's Magazine*, LVIII, part 1 (1788), 500.
[2] Cardiff 3.104, Letter no. 117, Theophilus Jones to Edward Davies, June 1807.
[3] Edward Davies, *The Mythology and Rites of the British Druids* (London, 1809), p. 33.

A native of Llanfaredd, Radnorshire, the Revd Edward Davies (1756–1831) began his 'darling study' of Welsh literature while he was living in exile in Sodbury, Gloucestershire, where he was master of the grammar school and curate of the neighbouring parish of Berkeley.[4] It was William Owen Pughe's 'elegant edition' of Dafydd ap Gwilym,[5] and his specimens of ancient poetry published in the *Gentleman's Magazine* in 1788–90 in response to Pinkerton's attack,[6] that quickened the desire which Davies had long cherished 'for the elucidation of our venerable bards'.[7] Inspired by Pughe's work, Davies produced his own 'Specimens of an English Metrical Translation of the Poems of the more ancient Welsh Bards, and of Dafydd ab Gwilym With an Introduction to Welsh Literature', which he sent to the Gwyneddigion Society in 1791.[8] He included translations of nine poems from *Barddoniaeth Dafydd ab Gwilym*, pointing out that these were quite new to English readers and that he had by no means exhausted his treasure:

> He has only announced his countryman, M[r] Dafydd ab Gwilym: if the public think proper, to cultivate an intimacy with him, he will answer them with a hundred and fifty elegant trifles, of equal merit with any in the following collection. I call them trifles, for we must not dignify this bard's lucubrations, with a title of importance; but the world cannot always be intent upon serious affairs; and Dafydd knows, when he thinks proper, how to trifle with a grace.[9]

Unfortunately, Davies was unaware that Iolo also knew how to trifle with a grace. Five of the nine poems translated by Davies from *Barddoniaeth Dafydd ab Gwilym* were in fact taken from the appendix to that work[10] – poems which are now recognized as forgeries, composed by Iolo himself.[11] Davies seems never to have questioned their authenticity and eventually his translations found their way into print. One version appeared in his novel, *Elisa Powell*

---

[4]   For biographical information about Edward Davies, see [W. J. Rees], 'Memoir of the Rev. Edward Davies', *Cambrian Quarterly Magazine*, III (1831), 408–36; Frank R. Lewis, 'Edward Davies, 1756–1831', *TRS*, XXXIX (1969), 8–23; Geoffrey R. Orrin, 'Edward "Celtic" Davies, Rector of Bishopston 1805–1831', *Gower*, XXXI (1980), 65–71.

[5]   Owen Jones and William Owen Pughe (eds.), *Barddoniaeth Dafydd ab Gwilym* (Llundain, 1789).

[6]   William Owen Pughe's contributions, over the signature Owain o Feirion, appeared in the *Gentleman's Magazine*, LVIII, part 2 (1788), 606–8, 821, 865–7; LIX, part 1 (1789), 30–2, 335–6; LIX, part 2 (1789), 603–5, 1077–8; LX, part 1 (1790), 214; LX, part 2 (1790), 989–90.

[7]   NLW 13222C, p. 281, Edward Davies to William Owen Pughe, 26 March 1792.

[8]   Cardiff 3.99. Another version, NLW 4360B, is entitled 'A Letter addressed to the members of the Gwyneddigion society'.

[9]   Cardiff 3.99, pp. 148–9.

[10] Davies translated LXX, CXLIX, CCVII and CCXXII from the main text of *Barddoniaeth Dafydd ab Gwilym*, and III, IX, XII, XIV and XVI from 'Y Chwanegiad' (The Appendix).

[11] See *IMChY*.

(1795),[12] and all five were printed anonymously in the *Cambrian Register* in 1818.[13]

As chance would have it, while Davies's 'Specimens' was in transit between Sodbury and London, William Meyler, a Bath bookseller, lent the manuscript to Iolo, who happened to be in Bath at the time. After reading it, Iolo wrote Meyler a letter in which he suggested rather ominously that he could provide Davies 'with a better copy of the British Triades than he seems to have' and had the effrontery to praise his translations of Dafydd ap Gwilym: 'true to, without being the slaves of, the originals. this is just what they ought to be, in my opinion, they are by far the best attempts that have yet appeared to put our old licencious Bards into an English dress'. Modestly, he did not refer to the modern bard that Davies had inadvertently put into English dress. He then turned to 'severe criticism': 'What in the name of Old Nick, for it cannot be in that of any other being, induced Mr Davies to address his book to the Gwyneddigion?'; and so began a famous diatribe against members of the society for their lowly origins, trades and aspirations. Advising him to find a patron 'who would receive no less honour from, than he would confer on, this performance', he humbly asked Davies's pardon if anything he had said could be constructed as being offensive, before signing off, 'With all possible respect, Your, and Mr Davies' most humble servant.'[14] Meyler dutifully passed on the letter to Davies.

Davies was eager to meet Iolo. Perhaps he had seen his pen-portrait in the *Gentleman's Magazine*, with an ode imitated from *Y Gododdin*.[15] On receiving the letter from Meyler, he rode to Bath, but was disappointed to find that Iolo had already left for London. On 19 January 1792 Davies wrote to Iolo, humbly apologizing for his 'intolerable blunder' in sending the 'Specimens' to the Gwyneddigion. He had withdrawn his manuscript and was already planning a more ambitious work. He begged Iolo to help him locate some essential texts

> which I know not where to find, unless they are in the possession of Mr William Owen. Do you think he will communicate? If you should speak to him, on the subject; present my compliments to him, and assure him of my warmest wishes for his success in his patriotic labours – I am quite impatient for the appearance of his dictionary.

He ended by asking whether Iolo had any copies of his forthcoming collection of poems still to be disposed of.[16] Davies was duly listed as a subscriber to

---

[12] Edward Davies, *Elisa Powell, or, Trials of Sensibility* (2 vols., London, 1795), I, pp. 161–4. See Moira Dearnley, *Distant Fields: Eighteenth-Century Fictions of Wales* (Cardiff, 2001), chapter 12.
[13] *Cambrian Register*, III (1818), 440–3, 455–68.
[14] Cardiff 3.104, vol. 6, Letter no. 39, Iolo Morganwg to William Meyler, undated.
[15] *Gentleman's Magazine*, LIX, part 2 (1789), 976–7, 1035–6.
[16] NLW 21280E, Letter no. 66, Edward Davies to Iolo Morganwg, 19 January 1792.

Poems, Lyric and Pastoral (1794), though his request for help with texts seems to have gone unanswered.

Davies began his correspondence with William Owen Pughe in March 1792 'without previous acquaintance or formal introduction',[17] and was soon entrusted with his collection of 'valuable and elegant manuscripts'.[18] Davies's transcripts[19] later proved useful for compiling *The Myvyrian Archaiology of Wales*.[20] In his letters to Davies, Pughe occasionally referred to Iolo's visits to London and discussed ideas that had originated (though this was generally unacknowledged) in his friend's fertile imagination. He sent Davies an account of the gradations and dress of the bards a few weeks after the Primrose Hill Gorsedd of June 1792,[21] and in December 1792 he posted off six copies of his edition of Llywarch Hen,[22] which included a seminal essay on bardism, with acknowledgements to Iolo for his 'communications and assistance'.[23] It is clear from a letter sent by the Revd John Walters to Davies on 10 May 1793 that at this early stage both men were already highly sceptical about Pughe's version of bardic history:

> I perfectly agree with You in your Sentiments of M[r] Owen's Bardism. It is a made Dish, cooked up from obscure scraps of the ancient Bards, and the Cabala (the pretended arcana) of the modern ones; a superficial acquaintance with the Metempsychosis; and these ingredients spiced with an immoderate quantity of wild Invention. It is a species of Free Masonry. It puts me much in mind of Dryden's description of Fame – Things done relates, not done she feigns, and mingles truth with lies. All that I shall further say on the Subject is – that Mr Owen and his Cöadjutor [Iolo] have not clubb'd their wits for nothing.[24]

Davies soon had access to Iolo's own notes on Bardism in *Poems, Lyric and Pastoral* (1794),[25] as well as his 'Account of, and Extracts from, The Welsh-Bardic Triades'.[26] On 19 November 1798 Pughe promised to send Davies a

17   NLW 13222C, p. 281, Edward Davies to William Owen Pughe, 26 March 1792.
18   NLW 13222C, p. 299, Edward Davies to William Owen Pughe, 31 August 1792.
19   Cardiff 4.140.
20   In his letter of 23 August 1798 Edward Davies offered to lend William Owen Pughe his 'collection of the old bards', specifying that this was based entirely on manuscripts borrowed from Pughe himself and the Revd John Walters. The volume was sent on 10 September 1798. NLW 13222C, pp. 511, 551.
21   Cardiff 3.104, vol. 6, Letter no. 12, William Owen Pughe to Edward Davies, 13 August 1792.
22   Cardiff 3.104, vol. 6, Letter no. 14, William Owen Pughe to Edward Davies, 8 April 1793.
23   William Owen Pughe (ed.), *The Heroic Elegies and other Pieces of Llywarç Hen* (London, 1792), pp. xxi–lxxx.
24   Cardiff 3.104, vol. 6, Letter no. 3, John Walters to Edward Davies, 10 May 1793.
25   Williams: *PLP*. See especially 'Ode to the British Muse', 'Ode on Converting a Sword into a Pruning Hook' and 'Ode on the Mythology of the Ancient British Bards', II, pp. 1–10, 160–8, 193–216.
26   Ibid., I, pp. 175–6; II, pp. 36n, 181, 217–56.

copy of the bardic alphabet,[27] now known to be another of Iolo's inventions.[28] In his reply of 26 November Davies's excitement was palpable:

> I anticipate a most delicious treat in the copy of the Real Ancient British Alphabet which you are so good as to promise me . . . from its general complection I am induced to believe that the ancient British alphabet, far from overturning my system will greatly assist me in the regulation of it.

Nevertheless, he did ask some sensible questions. Were there any ancient British manuscripts or inscriptions written in the alphabet and, if not, 'of what age is the author who has preserved the alphabet – What authorities does he quote, and what are his pretensions to credibility?'[29] But the spirit of scholarly enquiry began to evaporate when Pughe sent him the alphabet[30] and Davies found to his delight that it lent 'powerful support' to a theory of his own, though he was still anxiously waiting for any external testimony Pughe could adduce in its favour.[31] On 4 November 1799 he was cautiously enthusiastic about Pughe's plans to publish the bardic alphabet 'which appears from internal evidence to have been the original alphabet of Europe and I doubt not but you will be able to bring together such a mass of collateral evidence as will enable it to support its cause before the bar of sceptical criticism'.[32] That same year Edmund Fry included illustrations of the bardic alphabet in his *Pantographia*, with acknowledgements to Pughe,[33] and in 1803 Pughe included an illustration of 'Coelbren y Beirz' in *A Grammar of the Welsh Language*.[34] Abandoning 'sceptical criticism', Davies cited both Fry and Pughe in *Celtic Researches*, without reference to the 'mass of collateral evidence' he had initially looked for. In the mean time the publication in 1801 of two volumes of *The Myvyrian Archaiology of Wales*, with acknowledgements to both Edward Williams and Edward Davies, provided the latter with another haul of problematic triads for use in his first major work of scholarship.

Even before the publication of *Celtic Researches*, Davies was recognized as a poor curate whose scholarship marked him out as a worthy case for patronage. On 27 April 1799, during a period when Davies's health was affected by

---

[27] Cardiff 3.104, vol. 6, Letter no. 20, William Owen Pughe to Edward Davies, 19 November 1798.

[28] Glenda Carr, *William Owen Pughe* (Caerdydd, 1983), pp. 89–91.

[29] NLW 13222C, unnumbered loose page, Edward Davies to William Owen Pughe, 26 November 1798.

[30] Cardiff 3.104, vol. 6, Letter nos. 21, 23, William Owen Pughe to Edward Davies, 5 January, 18 July 1799. Letter no. 21 went astray.

[31] NLW 13222C, p. 581, Edward Davies to William Owen Pughe, 25 July 1799.

[32] NLW 13222C, pp. 623–4, Edward Davies to William Owen Pughe, 4 November 1799.

[33] Edmund Fry, *Pantographia; containing accurate copies of all the known Alphabets in the World* (London, 1799), pp. 305–7.

[34] William Owen Pughe, *A Grammar of the Welsh Language* (London, 1803), p. 5.

Theophilus Jones, author of the History of Brecknockshire
Obit Jan.y 15 . 1812 aged 54.

A very good likeness, taken a short time before his death, by me T. Price –

Fig. 28 Theophilus Jones (1759–1812), the lawyer who referred to Iolo Morganwg as 'Mad Ned'. A watercolour portrait by Thomas Price (Carnhuanawc), *c.* 1811.

'nervous disorders',[35] the Brecon lawyer Theophilus Jones informed his friend that he had written to Judge George Hardinge ('as inconsistent & eccentric as he is benevolent') on his behalf.[36] Part of the correspondence that ensued was later published as *Davies' Letters* (1802),[37] a work vigorously promoted by

---

[35]   [W. J. Rees], 'Memoir of the Rev. Edward Davies', 418–19.

[36]   Cardiff 3.104, vol. 6, Letter no. 72, Theophilus Jones to Edward Davies, 27 April 1799. Jones's letters to Davies are printed in Edwin Davies (ed.), *Theophilus Jones, F.S.A., Historian: His Life, Letters & Literary Remains* (Brecon, 1905).

[37]   *Davies' Letters: Fifteen Letters, in explanation of the Essay on the Art of Writing and the Nature and*

George Hardinge as an aperitif for the forthcoming *Celtic Researches*.[38] Even as the letters were being edited for publication, Hardinge was already trying to obtain a church living for Davies, though, as he informed William Pughe, 'he is too great a genius to act like other men . . . He is too Celtic for this world – but he is a noble creature & I admire him extremely as I ever shall'.[39]

It was in relation to *Davies' Letters* that Iolo twice suffered humiliations which continued to rankle for some time after the event, and any initial enthusiasm he may have felt for Davies's work waned rapidly. One might have expected Iolo to feel hostile to Hardinge after the proceedings at the Guildhall, Carmarthen, on 17 August 1801, when the judge had sentenced his friend Thomas Evans (Tomos Glyn Cothi) to two years' imprisonment for sedition. Iolo had certainly described the trial as 'a most lamentable occasion . . . a very horrid affair'.[40] Yet there can be little doubt that he found Hardinge's friendship for Davies extremely galling, perhaps feeling that he had prior claims on the patronage of a judge to whom he had once addressed a petition while incarcerated for debt in Cardiff gaol.[41] He remembered how Hardinge had once praised his conduct from the bench, and that he had been a liberal subscriber to *Poems, Lyric and Pastoral*.[42] Even more to the point, he, too, had once corresponded with Hardinge on scholarly matters.[43] As he later explained to Hardinge himself, it was during a visit to London[44] that he happened to see two or three of Davies's letters 'at the House of a friend' and found there 'some things that not a little surprized me, I could not well conceive what Mr Davies would be at'. On three occasions he tried to borrow the rest of the letters from Hardinge himself, but was eventually sent roughly on his way by one of the servants:

> I saw some glaring mistakes and instances of the profoundest ignorance in Mr Davies, even where he affected to appear uncommonly knowing and even learned.

Origin of Celtic Dialects (London, 1802). See Cardiff 3.79, 3.81, 3.91 for Davies's correspondence with Hardinge.

[38] Philo-Celticus [Hardinge] inserted a puff for *Davies' Letters* in the *Gentleman's Magazine*, LXXII, part 2 (1802), 990–1.

[39] NLW 13223C, pp. 505–6, George Hardinge to William Owen Pughe, undated.

[40] Geraint H. Jenkins, '"A Very Horrid Affair": Sedition and Unitarianism in the Age of Revolutions' in R. R. Davies and Geraint H. Jenkins (eds.), *From Medieval to Modern Wales: Historical Essays in Honour of Kenneth O. Morgan and Ralph A. Griffiths* (Cardiff, 2004), p. 190.

[41] NLW 21389E, no. 10.

[42] NLW 21286E, Letter no. 1038, Iolo Morganwg to George Hardinge. Internal evidence suggests that this letter, apparently intended for publication, was written to Hardinge (unnamed) *c*.1803. See also Williams: *IM*, pp. 452–3n, quoting a letter in which Iolo recalls that the judge spoke well of him when he appeared in court at Cowbridge:' "you sir highly approved of my conduct, and was pleased to declare your good opinion of my morals and principles in a very public man[n]er"'.

[43] Williams: *IM*, p. 453n.

[44] Pughe referred to Iolo's forthcoming visit in his letter to Davies. Cardiff 3.104, vol. 6, Letter no. 27, William Owen Pughe to Edward Davies, 15 February 1802.

I wished to set him right, conscious that I was able to do so, but could not do this well till I had seen more of his letters, he is a gentleman that I respect, he possesses genius and other abilities. I had then a little time on my hands, and should have transmited thro' your hand, to him, some corrections of his errors, in the most friendly manner that I possible could, the power of doing so, you Sir withheld from me.[45]

The following year brought further humiliation. By his own account, Iolo was in Cardiff, 'subpœna'd to attend the Great Sessions', when he was presented with a copy of *Davies' Letters* by Theophilus Jones. He immediately wrote to Hardinge, pointing out some of Davies's errors and offering to lend the clergyman all two hundred volumes of his Welsh manuscripts. He also left a specimen of the bardic alphabet at the judge's chambers. When Jones heard about this, he called on Iolo 'in a pett' to tell him that his intended civility was ill timed: Davies should not appear 'defective in knowledge' if he was to have any chance of gaining a living through Hardinge's interest (an idea calculated to fuel Iolo's resentment even further).[46]

Dedicated to George Hardinge, *Celtic Researches* appeared in 1804, with 'Jolo Morgwng' among the subscribers. It consisted of three substantial essays, the first tracing the separation of the Noachide after Nimrod's rebellion and the dispersal of his descendants to every region of the known world, taking with them the remains of what was once the one language of the whole earth. The second (in which Iolo's influence is pervasive) traced the descent of the Celtae from Japheth, Gomer and Ashkenaz, arguing that '*the fundamental principles of Druidism accompanied that nation, from its very source*',[47] and discussing their knowledge of letters. The third was a linguistic study of the Celtic language, exploring the relation between sounds and ideas and concluding that 'The *identity* of fundamental principles, which pervade the general mass of the old languages, *demonstrates*, that all of them sprung from one parent, – and that mankind are, what *Scripture* declares them to be – the children of one family.'[48]

Rachel Bromwich has demonstrated that, while the first two series of 'Trioedd Ynys Prydain' printed in *The Myvyrian Archaiology of Wales* in 1801 were derived from authentic manuscripts,[49] the third series of 126 triads was the work of Iolo Morganwg, 84 of which were elaborations of triads in the first series, the remainder his own fabrication.[50] Arguing in the second essay of

---

[45] NLW 21286E, Letter no. 1038, Iolo Morganwg to George Hardinge, undated.

[46] NLW 21286E, Letter no. 1039, Iolo Morganwg to Edward Davies. Internal evidence suggests that it was written *c*.1809.

[47] Edward Davies, *Celtic Researches, on the Origin, Traditions & Language, of the Ancient Britons; with some introductory sketches, on Primitive Society* (London, 1804), p. 122.

[48] Ibid., p. 547.

[49] Rachel Bromwich (ed.), *Trioedd Ynys Prydein / The Welsh Triads* (2nd edn., Cardiff, 1978).

[50] Rachel Bromwich, '*Trioedd Ynys Prydain*' in *Welsh Literature and Scholarship* (Cardiff, 1969), p. 18.

Celtic Researches that the Druids' method of instruction was by symbols and enigmas, and conjecturing that the triad was the general form of their moral and historical instructions,[51] Davies quoted extensively from the third series of 'Trioedd Ynys Prydain' and supplemented this material with items from other sources, including the 'Institutional Triads' which had appeared earlier in Iolo's *Poems, Lyric and Pastoral*.[52] In scholarly fashion Davies cited the manuscript authorities for his chosen triads,[53] blithely unaware of what Bromwich refers to as the 'elaborate verbal spider's web' woven by Iolo around his alleged sources.[54] He then used the triads as a basis for reconstructing druidic beliefs. No attempt can be made here to discuss Davies's intricate interpretations of what are essentially flawed texts, though it may be worth noting that, while his pacifist Druids would have been quite at home on Primrose Hill, the author himself predictably disapproved of their politics. In discussing the circumstances in which the sword might have been unsheathed, he admitted that 'In the hour of invasion, *Druids* could only withdraw from the field', making it clear that he disassociated himself from such unpatriotic behaviour: 'In favour of this institution, considered in a political view, little can be said. As our nature is constituted, it seems neither to have been calculated for the liberty of the individual, or the independence of the nation.'[55] His later attack on the radical politics inherent in Iolo's brand of bardism hardly comes as a surprise.

Davies's discussion of the bardic alphabet appears in Sections IV–IX of *Celtic Researches*, with an 'annexed plate' based on the copy sent to him by William Owen Pughe.[56] Davies postulated that the Druids used an arrangement of leaves and twigs as 'a *general system of tokens, or symbols*, which they not only used in their divinations, *by lot*, but applied, also, to the purpose of communicating ideas, and thoughts'.[57] He went on to argue that these hieroglyphic sprigs became the symbols of sounds as well as things:

> *our Druids possessed a kind of alphabet, which, according to their tradition, and their doctrine,*
> *was formed upon the system of their symbolical sprigs, or hieroglyphics, cut, or delineated, in*

[51] Davies, *Celtic Researches*, pp. 150–1.
[52] See especially the seventeen triads quoted in Davies, *Celtic Researches*, pp. 154–62.
[53] Davies claimed that the triads now referred to as the 'third series' were transcribed from a copy made in 1601 by Thomas Jones of Tregaron (ibid., p. 153). According to *MAW*, II, p. 57n, the transcription was made by Iolo from Thomas Richards's copy, lent to him by the Revd John Walters of Llandough. For the source of the institutional triads Davies cited Iolo's reference (Williams: *PLP*, II, p. 227) to a manuscript collection in the possession of Richard Bradford of Betws, near Bridgend, made by Llywelyn Siôn (Davies, *Celtic Researches*, p. 186n). For a corrective, see Ceri W. Lewis, 'The Literary History of Glamorgan from 1550 to 1770' in Glanmor Williams (ed.), *Glamorgan County History Volume IV: Early Modern Glamorgan* (Cardiff, 1974), pp. 582–4.
[54] Bromwich, *'Trioedd Ynys Prydain' in Welsh Literature and Scholarship*, p. 13.
[55] Davies, *Celtic Researches*, p. 172.
[56] Ibid., p. 272 and facing.
[57] Ibid., p. 246.

simple figures, and adapted, so as to represent the first principles, or the elementary sounds, of their language.[58]

He pointed out that he had inferred the existence of this alphabet before discovering that the actual characters still existed: 'My satisfaction was equal to my surprise, when *Mr Owen* presented me with a complete copy of it; and when I contemplated the magical sprigs of the *Druids*, which I had rather *wished*, than encouraged the *hope*, to discover.'[59] Citing William Owen Pughe, Fry and Iolo, Davies explained that, while the Druids guarded their secrets from the uninitiated, they 'left a regular chain of successors, in the *Welsh* mountains . . . [who] profess to have preserved the system of *Bardism,* or *Druidism*, entire, to this day'. Among other 'curious notices', these successors of the Druids had inherited a series of letters, which they distinguished by the name of '*Coelbren y Beirdd*, the *billet of signs, of the Bards*, or the *Bardic alphabet*'.[60] Despite the latent scepticism implicit in the word 'profess', Davies insisted that his opinion was not based on one preconceived hypothesis but was rather the result of enquiries, gradually formed and impressed by force of evidence: 'I cannot hesitate in concluding – *it is the evidence of truth*.'[61]

Not everyone agreed. On 11 March 1804 Theophilus Jones wrote to his old friend:

> I fear you have been imposed upon by Owen as to the Coelbren y Beirdd. I am very much mistaken if that Alphabet is not the manufacture of Ned Williams, & himself, and the Behav.[r] of Mad Ned at last Cardiff Assizes, when he heard that you had inserted those Letters in your Book, convinces me he fear'd detection . . . Owen is undoubtedly learned, & Williams has eccentric Talents, but both are System Mongers and I believe System Makers.[62]

'Mad Ned' fired off his own vigorous response to *Celtic Researches*. The letter he sent to George Hardinge from William Owen Pughe's London address on 29 May 1804 is densely written, continues around three sides of the 'Proposals' for a second edition of *Poems, Lyric and Pastoral*, and seems to have been accompanied by yet another specimen of the bardic alphabet. Iolo claimed that he regretted Davies's 'astonishing mistakes' in translating *Coelbren y Beirdd* as 'Bardic Lots, Magic Lots, Lots of Druidism &c' and reminded the judge that had he known Davies's address,

> I could have lent him Manuscripts that would have afforded him very interesting information. for of these my hundreds I venture to say it, are more numerous than

---

[58]   Ibid., pp. 266–7.
[59]   Ibid., p. 273.
[60]   Ibid., p. 270.
[61]   Ibid., p. 282.
[62]   Cardiff 3.104, vol. 6, Letter nos. 92–3, Theophilus Jones to Edward Davies, 11 March 1804.

his Units this I confidently affirm, not a man living has read the tenth part of the Welsh MSS. I have read except my friend Mr Wm Owen. Mr Davies exclusive of his unfortunate Mistakes, tells the world that what he calls Bardic Lots are known to the Welsh, but he does not inform us where he saw them, or on what manuscript Authority he gives them. I could have furnished him with all the information that has yet been obtained from our ancient MSS.[63]

He consoled himself that his own 'History of the British Bards and Druids' would not now appear to be plagiarized from Davies. He did not on any account undervalue Davies's book – indeed he would now be able to mention him as a very respectable authority – but he rejected Davies's 'fanciful system of trees, sprigs, reeds &c', preferring the mythological account given by the ancient bards whereby the three primary letters / | \ ,'whence all others spring', represent the ineffable name of the Deity, heard by Eniget the Great, who thence deduced the first alphabet. He reiterated his high opinion of Davies's learning, praised Hardinge's 'uncommonly liberal conduct in rescuing from distress a gentleman of his merit' and promised that if Davies's book came to a second edition, the manuscripts would still be at his service. He also promised that only his son would hear about this, with the strictest injunctions of silence, to caution him against what Iolo believed to be incorrect.[64] This effusion Hardinge coolly passed on to Davies. In a covering letter, which offered comfort to his 'dear & admired friend' following a lukewarm review in the *Gentleman's Magazine*,[65] Hardinge's contempt for Iolo was only too evident:

> The enclosed is a picture of all your enemies – you now can produce adversaries of more liberality than are possesst by this knave – I wish you could enable me to answer him well & without masking that you have seen his depraved & malevolent jealousy the sole motive to his work.[66]

Davies put Iolo's letter to good use in *The Mythology and Rites of the British Druids*.

More than a decade after Pinkerton's attack, the question of authenticity remained fundamental to the scholarly discussion of Welsh language and literature. Perhaps stung by the realization that in writing about the bardic alphabet in *Celtic Researches*, he had both been fooled and made a fool of himself (one reviewer commented that 'We have heard of trees suggesting the idea of Gothic arches; but here we first hear of *alphabetical* trees'),[67] Davies had begun to perceive, if only through a glass darkly, the threat posed by Williams and Pughe to scholarship that depended on '*the evidence of truth*'. Although he could

---

[63] Cardiff 3.104, vol. 6, Letter no. 41, Iolo Morganwg to George Hardinge, 29 May 1804.
[64] Ibid.
[65] *Gentleman's Magazine*, LXXIV, part 1 (1804), 434–6.
[66] Cardiff 3.104, vol. 6, Letter no. 40, George Hardinge to Edward Davies, undated.
[67] *Gentleman's Magazine*, LXXIV, part 1 (1804), 436.

have had no idea of the extent of the fraud he was dealing with, he suspected enough to launch a counter-attack. Theophilus Jones, who had befriended Iolo in the past, now encouraged hostilities. On 18 September 1806 a joking reference to 'Woods & woody writing' reminded him that 'that fellow Ned Williams is a strange fellow and all that can be said for him he is mad – he now finds fault with Owen'.[68] By sometime in June 1807 Jones was looking forward to Davies's new book with relish:

> I am very much pleased at your exposing and detecting the frauds and the tricks of Ned Williams adopted partly by choice and partly by combination by Owen but you have in one part of your book, accredited their mummeries by quoting Owen for the drawn sword placed at the Gorsedd – depend upon it all those monkey tricks exhibited at Primrose hill by Owen and others have no more foundation or pretence for antiquity than Williams's Chair of Glamorgan but however I shall explain myself further upon this and other parts of your book which must be published.[69]

On 28 July he assured his friend: 'I wish you much to correct the insolence of Ned Williams and I intreat that he may not be spared.'[70]

In *The Mythology and Rites of the British Druids* (1809), dedicated to Richard Watson, bishop of Llandaf, Davies set out to demonstrate that several early texts (principally the triads and poems of Taliesin, Aneirin and 'Merddin the Caledonian') provided new information about the ancient religion and customs of Britain. Although Davies had told the printer, John Booth, that he would 'combat some of the principles of Mess[rs] Williams and Owen, but not roughly',[71] Section I is devoted to a ferocious attack on Iolo, with sideswipes at Pughe. At pains to establish the authenticity of his sources, Davies pointed out that Sharon Turner had found the 'mystical' poems obscure only because he had been misled by Iolo and Pughe:

> That a critic, so candid, and so well informed, should have pronounced these poems, which peculiarly treat of Druidism, absolutely unintelligible; and especially, as he acknowledges the assistance of *Mr Owen* and *Mr Williams*, men who claim an exclusive acquaintance with the whole system of Bardic lore, may seem rather extraordinary: but the wonder will cease, when we shall have seen, that the information of these ingenious writers is drawn from another source; from a document which will appear to be, in many respects, irreconcilable with the works of the ancient Bards, or with the authority of the classical page.[72]

Here Davies was implicitly questioning the validity of the sources used by Pughe in his essay on bardism, with its account of the Chair of Glamorgan and

---

[68] Cardiff 3.104, vol. 6, Letter nos. 112–13, Theophilus Jones to Edward Davies, 18 September 1806.

[69] Cardiff 3.104, vol. 6, Letter no. 117, Theophilus Jones to Edward Davies, June 1807.

[70] Cardiff 3.104, vol. 6, Letter nos. 121–2, Theophilus Jones to Edward Davies, 28 July 1807.

[71] Cardiff 3.86, unnumbered draft, Edward Davies to John Booth, 21 June 1808.

[72] Davies, *The Mythology and Rites of the British Druids*, p. 5.

its list of presidents beginning with Trahaearn Brydydd Mawr and ending with Edward Williams. Davies went on to assert with brutal directness that 'a slight inquiry into the credentials of the society itself, will discover some marks of gross misrepresentation, if not of absolute forgery'.[73] In challenging the president to publish his manuscripts, Davies referred obliquely to Iolo's letter to Hardinge of 29 May 1804 (described as 'an unprovoked attack' on *Celtic Researches*):[74]

Mr Williams, whether he styles himself president, or sole surviving member, values himself highly upon his superior collection of Welsh manuscripts. Whatever he has, that can bear the light, I should be glad to see it produced to the Public; and I would cheerfully contribute my mite to facilitate its appearance. But he has no copy of a single British writer, more ancient, or better accredited, than those which I adduce in the course of my inquiry, and which the light, held forth from his chair, has certainly misrepresented.[75]

Davies preferred (misguidedly) to rely on the manuscript sources readily available in *The Myvyrian Archaiology of Wales*: 'I therefore appeal, from his whole library, to the authority of documents, which have been known for ages to exist; which are now accessible to every man who understands the language; and which, as I have already shewn, have been regarded as authentically derived from the Druidical school.'[76] Davies referred again to Iolo's letter in his discussion of druidical magic (an idea which 'it seems, has given umbrage to the present representative of Taliesin'),[77] exemplified in the story of Ceridwen's cauldron which he interpreted as a bardic account of the *awen* or inspiration. Iolo may have objected to the term 'magical lots' in connection with the bardic alphabet, but to Davies this appeared to be a genuine tradition of the Britons: 'and with them I connected the *letters*, which are called *Coelbreni, Omensticks, Lots*, or *Tallies*'.[78] He then announced, rather petulantly, that he would take no further notice of Iolo's letter:

My opinion, I thought, was innocent at least; but it produced from Mr Williams a severe philippic, together with an exposition of some curious mythology, upon the origin of letters and language, which is not to be found in any ancient British writer. This was put into the hands of my best friends: but I shall not take farther notice of *manuscript* or *oral* criticism. I only wish the author to publish it; when I see it in print, my answer shall be ready.[79]

[73]   Ibid., p. 33.
[74]   Ibid., p. 37.
[75]   Ibid., p. 36.
[76]   Ibid.
[77]   Ibid., p. 37.
[78]   Ibid., p. 43.
[79]   Ibid.

There were, however, other issues to deal with. Davies accused Iolo and Pughe of peddling a bardic philosophy which reflected their own radical convictions. Sharply reminding them that a society like the Chair of Glamorgan could not search the inextricable mazes of new philosophies, new politics and new religions in the 'pretended *search after truth*' while, at the same time, claiming to be the 'infallible repositories of *ancient tradition; ancient opinions,* and *ancient usages*',[80] he proceeded to druidical politics, referring with heavy-handed irony to their putative support for the radical cause in the English civil wars ('was not Druidism, *as far as this goes,* very popular amongst Britons and Saxons in the age of Cromwell?')[81] and the French Revolution:

> The principles here announced, seem to go rather beyond the levellers of the seventeenth century, and to savour strongly of a *Druidism* which originated in *Gaul,* and was from thence transplanted into some corners of Britain, not many ages before the year 1792, when the *memorial of Bardism* made its appearance. It were well, if the sages who prepared that memorial, would revise their extracts, and recal any *accidental inaccuracy,* that might otherwise mislead future antiquaries. They must know, as *well as I do, that this is not the Druidism of history, nor of the British Bards.*[82]

The reaction of 'the dictatorial Chair' to this onslaught can only be described as a howl of pain and anger. A drafted title-page among Iolo's manuscripts, 'Animadversions on a lately publish[ed] farago entitled The Mythology of the Druids. &c, In a series of Letters to its Author Edwd Davies, to which are added 3 Essays . . . By Edwd Williams',[83] suggests that he might even have intended to publish a reply. But in the undated fragments that appear to belong to the projected work, any attempt to defend bardism is subverted by personal invective, distress and indignation about the patronage Davies now enjoyed. In one fragment, headed 'Animadversions on Mr Davies',[84] he described Davies's book as 'More like the reveries of a Bedlamite than the lucubrations of a scholar', accused him of being

> clearly actuated by a rank malevolence that induced you in violation of Truths that were clearly before you, that stared you in the face. to strain all the nerves of premeditated wickedness to exert all that rancorous ebulition<s?> of a bad heart, in virulent endeavours to misrepresent my character and conduct . . .

and insulted him by addressing him without title: 'shame on such a character as you are Davies, you see that I am gradually dropping without respect to you the terms wherein gentlemen are commonly and properly addressed'. Another

---

[80] Ibid., pp. 35–6.
[81] Ibid., p. 56.
[82] Ibid., p. 57.
[83] NLW 21426E, no. 54.
[84] NLW 21425E, no. 11.

drafted letter, beginning peremptorily 'Edward Davies', refers to a 'Jumble of odd conceits, wild ideas, and presumptuous falshoods', with a note to explain that 'there may be some impropriety, and sometimes blasphemy' in adding epithets to proper names.[85] Elsewhere 'Edward (alias parson) Davies' appeared on a list of current *bêtes noires*, noticed 'by their proper names only', which included Owain Myfyr, William Owen Pughe and 'William (alias Hell-fire) Pitt'.[86]

Iolo fiercely objected to Davies's reference to his 'ingenious poems', revealing by his choice of metaphor how much the attack had wounded him:

> my ingenious poems you say. did you then feel conscious that you were doing me the greatest wrong, and that it would be prudent in you to apply something like a salve to the stabs that you were giving me? be that as it may. from a man of principle I should have been gratified by such a compliment. but from you sir on this occasion, I perceive nothing [but] hypocritical art.
> O! give me honest fame, or give me none.[87]

Similarly, in recalling his thwarted attempt in 1803 to lend Davies his manuscripts ('not one or a few of them, but all of them'), he revealed a painful sense of humiliation and rejection.[88] He had not forgiven Theophilus Jones for his intervention – so much is implicit in his tirade against Jones's *A History . . . of Brecknock* in which the author's 'selfconceit appears so great that nothing but that of his friend Edward Davies, and the infinite extensions of space can be greater'[89] – and he raged against 'the old netecclesiastic', deploring the patronage Davies had gained as a by-product of his scholarship.[90] He accused him of making 'enormous impositions' on 'numerous and illustrious Patrons', and was convinced that, for Davies:

> a Stall in Landaff Cathedral was a desireable object, and to attain to that another wild farago of wild invention of falshood, with an addition of the most unprincipled Calumnies must be dedicated to our venerable our Truth-loving, our greatly beloved, Watson of Landaff . . . O shame where is thy blush?[91]

There was, of course, more than a grain of truth in these accusations, for Hardinge was certainly complicit in Watson's offer of the living of Bishopston in 1805,[92] though it was scarcely a fat one, with a rectory so dilapidated that,

[85] NLW 21286E, Letter no. 1039, Iolo Morganwg to Edward Davies, undated.
[86] NLW 21419E, no. 54.
[87] NLW 21425E, no. 11.
[88] NLW 21286E, Letter no. 1039, Iolo Morganwg to Edward Davies, undated.
[89] NLW 21419E, no. 51.
[90] NLW 21286E, Letter no. 1039, Iolo Morganwg to Edward Davies, undated.
[91] NLW 21425E, nos. 11–12.
[92] See the letter from Bishop Richard Watson to Edward Davies, 27 April 1805, in *Anecdotes of the Life of Richard Watson, Bishop of Landaff* (2 vols., 2nd edn., London, 1818), II, p. 242; and the letter from Watson to Hardinge in Orrin, 'Edward "Celtic" Davies', 67.

after eventually moving to Gower, Davies was forced to live in Ilston for several years.[93] While there is no evidence that he ever obtained a stall in Llandaf, Davies certainly accepted the bishop of St David's offer of the prebend of Llangynllo following the publication of *A Series of Discourses on Church Union* (1811), and he later obtained the chancellorship of Christ College, Brecon, and the rectory of Llanfairorllwyn.[94] Iolo doubtless ground his teeth.

Iolo returned to the attack in a letter written to the editor of the *Cambrian Register* on 31 March 1811, ridiculing Davies as an ignorant outsider:

> The false ideas entertained of our ancient literature have never by native writers been corrected; – but they have long been heaping error upon error, blunder upon blunder, till an enormous pile has at length been raised. A very sensible old gentleman, with whom I was very intimately acquainted for the last forty years of his continuance in this world, called such self-conceited scribblers *Smatter-dashers*; who, with a very slight smattering of what they never could understand, dashed away through thick and thin at an uncommon rate; and *Smatter-dasher, Edward Davies* has recently performed wonders in this dashing line. His smattering knowledge of our language, our literary and Bardic antiquities, &c., has instigated him to publish what sooner or later will render him truly *ridiculous*.[95]

Seven years passed before the letter appeared in print, mischievously placed next to a letter from Davies himself, written over twenty years earlier when he had read the *Cambrian Register* with 'the eagerness of a British virtuoso'.[96] The same volume also included 'Observations on certain Discrepancies of Opinion among some of our modern Archaiologists, upon the Character of Druidism', which took the view that both parties had been 'hampered by strong and opposite prepossessions':

> One party [Iolo and Pughe] had seemingly a pretty strong predilection for druidism, and the other [Davies] an equally strong aversion to it. The former placed too much reliance on the institutes of the chair of Glamorgan, whose legitimacy is doubted, and the latter was, perhaps, equally influenced and misled by the Bryantian System of Mythology, which, like other systems, has evidently its weak parts, and may, in this investigation, have been often inapplicable. The former may also be said to have been carried too far by a strong attachment to liberty and the rights of man, and the latter by a dread of innovation, and a wish to perpetuate the present established order of things. Under such circumstances their accounts or disquisitions would necessarily prove defective, and like too many historical productions, afford the authors but a slender claim to the merit or praise of impartiality.[97]

---

[93] Orrin, 'Edward "Celtic" Davies', 67–8.
[94] Ibid., 68–9.
[95] *Cambrian Register*, III (1818), 382. See also NLW 13150A, p. 87, where Iolo objected to Davies's hasty publication: 'ac allan a hi yn fellt ynfyd heb gymmeryd amser' ('and out with it like mad lightning, without taking time').
[96] *Cambrian Register*, III (1818), 385.
[97] Ibid., 9.

Having listed inaccuracies on both sides, the anonymous writer grudgingly acknowledged their contribution to scholarship: 'After all, their labours, in general, are certainly very valuable, and have greatly contributed to increase the knowledge of British antiquities.'[98]

Doubts about the 'legitimacy' of the Chair of Glamorgan seem to have had little effect on the nascent Cambrian Society. In a series of notes appended to a letter to Thomas Burgess, bishop of St David's, drafted on 26 October 1818, Davies approved of the fact that the new society seemed to be avoiding the 'mummery' of modern bardism. He also agreed that the Chair of Glamorgan was a suitable topic for an essay competition, providing the bishop 'will insist upon evidence, and take nothing upon trust', reminding him that 'were it not for such communications as came either immediately from E.W. I never met with any thing in the course of my reading which would have given me the slightest notion of the Existence of any such Chair'. He admitted that there may be an obscure society, composed of infidels, freethinkers, fanatics, buffoons, republicans, anarchists and 'ev[er]y thing that a vain undisciplined imagination is calculated to produce', but this had no connection with 'the ancient and more respectable Bards, with whom alone we have any concern'. Hinting that unpublished documents in the Chair's library may 'have afforded E.W. an opportunity to root up ev[er]y sound principle of Politics & religion', Davies launched a devastating attack on Iolo's integrity:

> I should be sorry to detract one atom from the real merit of Iolo. He is certainly an excellent welsh scholar and it is not to be doubted that in his industry in collection he has amassed m[an]y scarce and valuable papers. His assistance would be of import-ance if he could be kept to the simple truth. But he certainly is not a man of literary integrity he presumes too much upon the ignorance of the public, and seldom scruples to sacrifice truth to his favourite system.[99]

Despite his misgivings, a letter from Davies was among those read out at the Bishop's Palace at Abergwili on 28 October 1818, 'containing the most cordial assurances of co-operation in forwarding the views of the Society'. His warnings seem to have gone unheard: the committee, which included Davies (presumably elected *in absentia*), was asked to consider inviting Iolo to instruct students in Welsh literature, to superintend the printing of the society's publi-cations, and to issue a prospectus for his History of Wales. Although these matters were not discussed at the committee meeting held on 25 November (Davies did not attend), a comparison between the bardic institutions of Carmarthen and Glamorgan was approved as an essay topic.[100] The following

---

[98] Ibid., 10.
[99] Cardiff 3.86, unnumbered draft, probably written in reply to Bishop Thomas Burgess's letter of 20 October [1818], Cardiff 3.82, unnumbered.
[100] NLW 21403E, no. 10.

year saw the Gorsedd linked for the first time to an eisteddfod, which was held in the garden of the Ivy Bush Inn in Carmarthen. In the mean time Davies dutifully paid a two-guinea subscription to the society.[101]

When Elijah Waring brought out his *Recollections and Anecdotes of Edward Williams* (eight years before Iolo's Gorsedd was officially integrated with the National Eisteddfod in 1858), he acknowledged that: 'It has been a fashion among Welsh antiquaries, who have adopted the Druidical theories of Edward Davies, and other writers of the same school, to tax the imaginative faculty of Edward Williams, with the authorship of assumed facts, in speaking or writing upon the arcana of Bardism.' However, he insisted that those who knew Iolo best would 'acquit him of any attempt at imposing forgeries of his own brain' on an oral tradition which he held in reverence: 'That his vivid fancy might give a colouring to some veracious records, which the stern hand of criticism would wipe off, may be admitted, without disparagement to his honesty of purpose.'[102] What Waring referred to as Iolo's 'vivid fancy', Davies preferred to call 'a vain undisciplined imagination', and there is perhaps a certain irony and even some poignancy in the fact that it was the fanciful stonemason, rather than the scholarly clergyman, who succeeded in making a permanent contribution to the cultural life of Wales. Yet, even as one recognizes the potency of the creative imagination which brought into being the ceremonial of the modern eisteddfod, it is perhaps only just to acknowledge Davies's flawed attempt to exercise the 'stern hand of criticism'. His own scholarship is now discredited ('his mistranslations are only a minor feature of so intricate an assembly of error and fallacy that its author's orchestration, as it were, is itself remarkable')[103] and he was cheated by Iolo in ways he almost certainly never even began to suspect. Even so, he undoubtedly deserves some recognition as a forerunner of the band of scholars who have since undertaken the 'search after truth' in respect of Iolo's writings.

---

[101] NLW 21403E, no. 11. See chapter 18 above.

[102] *RAEW*, pp. 147–8.

[103] Aidan L. Owen, *The Famous Druids: A Survey of Three Centuries of English Literature on the Druids* (Oxford, 1997), p. 216.

20

An Uneasy Partnership: Iolo Morganwg and William Owen Pughe

GLENDA CARR

In May 1776 a shy, quiet young man, not yet seventeen years old, arrived in London from his home in rural Merioneth. He was overwhelmed by what he saw: 'every thing seemed new, even the language'.[1] This was William Owen, later to become known by his adopted name, William Owen Pughe. He was a diligent youth and soon settled in his work as a solicitor's clerk. However, he admitted that he missed Wales and the Welsh language, and he turned to his books for comfort. His lonely existence continued for six years during which, inexplicably, he had no inkling that a flourishing Welsh community existed in London until, in 1782, he met another Welshman who was also a solicitor's clerk: Robert Hughes (Robin Ddu yr Ail o Fôn), who introduced him to the Gwyneddigion Society. There he found like-minded companions, an oppor-tunity to converse in Welsh and a collection of books and manuscripts. Through the society, too, he was to meet the men who were to play such an important part in his early work: Owen Jones (Owain Myfyr) and Iolo Morganwg.

Owain Myfyr was at this time a forty-one year old successful furrier and one of the founders of the Gwyneddigion Society. He had brought with him a rich cultural heritage from his native Hiraethog and followed his literary interests in what little spare time he had. The promising young William Owen Pughe soon caught his eye. In 1783 he wrote to Iolo Morganwg about 'the most skilful lad that I know' ('Llencyn cywreinia a'r adwaen i').[2] He praised Pughe's knowledge of the *Gododdin*, his grasp of Hebrew and his artistic talent. Myfyr had obviously found a new protégé and wanted to share his discovery with Iolo. It is difficult to pinpoint when exactly Iolo himself came to know Owain Myfyr. It is hard to believe Iolo's claim that he was in London as early as 1765,[3]

---

[1]   William Owen Pughe, *A Dictionary of the Welsh Language* (2 vols., London, 1803), Sig. B3ʳ. For a Welsh-language biography of Pughe, see Glenda Carr, *William Owen Pughe* (Caerdydd, 1983).

[2]   NLW 21281E, Letter no. 231, Owain Myfyr to Iolo Morganwg, 14 October 1783.

[3]   Williams: *IM*, p. 160.

but it is fairly certain that he was in the capital by the end of the summer of
1773. He had been travelling around north Wales, mainly pursuing his dialect-
ological interests, and had visited some of the private libraries in the area. He
had also heard from scholars such as Evan Evans (Ieuan Fardd) about the group
of Welshmen in London who shared his passion for collecting and copying
early Welsh poetry. Iolo certainly attended the meetings of the societies of the
Cymmrodorion and the Gwyneddigion in 1773–4 as the guest of one of the
members. He recalled these visits fondly in later years; writing to Owain Myfyr
in September 1783, he remarked on the 'mournful recollection of the great
happiness I once enjoy'd in their company and conversation'.[4]

Because of the itinerant nature of his occupation as a stonemason, Iolo's
visits to the Gwyneddigion were infrequent, whereas Pughe, now settled in
London, quickly became a prominent member: he was made a life member of
the council in 1783, secretary from 1784 to 1787, vice-president in 1788 and
again in 1803, and president in 1789 and again in 1820.[5] Iolo must have
known of Pughe's involvement with the society when he wrote a curious
letter to the bookseller William Meyler of Bath around the beginning of 1792.
Referring to the Gwyneddigion, he claimed:

> I was one of the very first members, in 1772; it was at first whimsical, became after-
> wards ridiculous, and is now detestable . . . M[r] William Owen has long ago left the
> Gwyneddigion, so has M[r] Samwell: What shall I say of the other members, about 40
> in number? Why, there are amongst them some very eminent Coal-heavers, Porters,
> Scavengers, Chimney-sweepers, &c. 'Knaves and Fools of ev'ry class'.[6]

This was Iolo at his most inexplicably devious. Not only was Pughe still
playing an active role in the society, but David Samwell was also as loyal a
member as his duties as a ship's surgeon allowed him to be; he was secretary in
1788 and vice-president in 1797. Even Iolo's claims about himself are untrue.
Since the society was founded in 1770, he could not have been 'one of the very
first members in 1772': his first official connection with the society occurred
when he was made a corresponding member in 1785.

The animosity towards the Gwyneddigion and the lies about Pughe are all
the more curious since they occurred at a time when Iolo seemed to be on
good terms with him. In August 1791, a few months before writing this letter,
Iolo was in London, where he met Sarah, Pughe's young wife. Pughe himself
was out of town, so Iolo, always in his element when describing symptoms of
illness and injury, sent him a progress report on the sore throat which had been
troubling Sarah, and noted the 'genuine appearances of conjugal affection' he

[4]   BL Add. 15024, ff. 196–7, Iolo Morganwg to Owain Myfyr, 20 September 1783.
[5]   W. D. Leathart, *The Origin and Progress of the Gwyneddigion Society of London* (London, 1831),
      pp. 101–4.
[6]   Cardiff 3.104, vol. 6, Letter no. 39, Iolo Morganwg to William Meyler, ? January 1792.

had observed in her when Pughe's name was mentioned.[7] Sarah's delicate constitution was to provide Iolo with an excuse for much advice and sententious comment over the years. In 1805 he wrote Pughe a letter full of such sentiments, ending on a note of rather heavy-handed banter:

> I am particularly glad to hear that M[rs] Owen has been benefited by Elixir of Vitriol. The most dangerous period of youth is from about 18 to 28 years of age, and of those that fall into and die of declines 99 out of every 100 go off before they are 28 years old. M[rs] Owen is now got over the age of danger, she is if I mistake not, about 34 or 35, of course we may hope that she will live in tolerably good health till turned of fifty, when a little care will carry her over a second dangerous period to 80 years of age, or more, at least I wish it to be so; but whether you wish it or not I cannot Swear, you may possibly have another lady in your eye, but all this is what I shall not concern myself with.[8]

What the uxorious and rather humourless William Owen Pughe made of this letter, we do not know. What we do know is that Sarah gained no lasting benefit from the elixir of vitriol: she died at the age of forty-four. Pughe survived her by nineteen years and never remarried. From all these letters, which are so full of intimate details, we see that Iolo was obviously on extremely friendly terms with the family, even staying with them during some of his visits to London.

During Iolo's visits to London in the early 1770s he had been much impressed by the collection of Dafydd ap Gwilym's work, which had been assembled by William Morris between 1740 and 1755,[9] as well as Lewis Morris's collection of Dafydd's poems.[10] These had come into Richard Morris's hands on the death of his brothers and so were later easily accessible to the London-Welsh societies. Owain Myfyr intended to publish the poems, using the Morris collections as the basis of the work, but he also hoped to incorporate the many lost poems he believed were lying unrecognized in libraries throughout Wales. In 1773 he appealed for help in tracking these down by advertising in local newspapers in Wales and the border counties. He also contacted Iolo Morganwg, who was becoming well known for his knowledge of Welsh manuscripts. In 1787 the Gwyneddigion announced their intention of publishing the work. By this stage Myfyr's main assistant in the task was William Owen Pughe. In March 1788 Iolo sent Pughe a bundle of poems, with a comment which, with hindsight, is extremely revealing: 'alas, had I but known earlier about your work in publishing D G, I could have sent you copies of many *cywyddau* (perhaps nearly a hundred), better ones than those in Myfyr's Book' ('och na buaswn yn gwybod yn gynt am eich gwaith yn argraffu

---

[7]   NLW 13221E, p. 33, Iolo Morganwg to William Owen Pughe, 1 August 1791.
[8]   BL Add. 15027, ff. 78–80, Iolo Morganwg to Owain Myfyr, 21 September 1805.
[9]   BL Add. 14932.
[10] BL Add. 14870.

D G, mi a allaswn ddanfon i chwi gopïau o lawer C^{dd} (f'allai'n agos i gant,) gwell na'r rhai yn Llyfr y Myfyr').[11] Iolo could hardly claim that he knew nothing of the projected work since Myfyr had already asked for his help. The poems sent by Iolo arrived too late to be included in the body of *Barddoniaeth Dafydd ab Gwilym*, which was published in 1789. Pughe wrote to Iolo to explain this, and apologised profusely for having to include them as an appendix at the end of the volume. Not until the early twentieth century were these proved to be skilful forgeries composed by Iolo himself. For whatever reason, he had already begun hoodwinking his compatriots, especially those from the despised north Wales.

William Owen Pughe was a gullible, and in many ways a rather innocent man. Utterly without guile or malice, he failed to suspect these failings in others. He was also ready to embrace new ideas and it was perhaps his misfortune to have lived in an age that bombarded him with such novelties. It was hardly surprising that he welcomed Iolo's bardic dreams with enthusiasm and he allowed Iolo to promote these at length in his essay on 'Bardism', which formed a preface to Pughe's own work *The Heroic Elegies and other Pieces of Llywarç Hen*, published in 1792. If *The Heroic Elegies* is read at all today, it is for Iolo's preface rather than for Pughe's clumsy and often incomprehensible translation of the Llywarch Hen text. In June 1792 Pughe had also attended a Gorsedd held by Iolo on Primrose Hill, where he was described as a *trwyddedog*, a mere novice, compared with Iolo's *bardd wrth fraint* (privileged bard). In September of the same year another Gorsedd was held with greater ceremony in which the superiority of Iolo's status was stressed even further:

> On this occasion the Bards appear'd in their insignia of their various orders. The presiding Bards were, David Samwell of the primitive and claimant of the Ovatian order. William Owen, of the ovatian and primitive Orders . . . Edward Williams of the Primitive and Druidic Orders.[12]

Iolo's preface to *The Heroic Elegies* not only promoted his bardic system but also introduced many of his radical ideas: the bards, he claimed, believed strongly in the equality of men and in 'everything supported by reason and proof'. In a later period Edward Davies, author of *Celtic Researches* (1804) and *The Mythology and Rites of the British Druids* (1809), remarked rather cynically: 'I do not recollect to have seen this doctrine, in its full extent, promulgated by any code before a certain period of the French Revolution.'[13]

Davies no doubt knew that the French Revolution had thrown the London

---

[11] NLW 13221E, pp. 11–12, Iolo Morganwg to William Owen Pughe, 12 March 1788.
[12] Thomas Shankland, 'Hanes Dechreuad "Gorsedd Beirdd Ynys Prydain"', *Y Llenor*, III (1924), 100. He quotes from a 'Memorandum, London 1792', a report by David Samwell found in Angharad Llwyd's papers.
[13] Edward Davies, *The Mythology and Rites of the British Druids* (London, 1809), p. 60.

Fig. 29 A watercolour drawing of William Owen Pughe (1759–1835) by Daniel Maclise.

Welsh into a frenzy of writing and debating: a new society, the Caradogion, was formed solely, according to Pughe, as 'a weekly spouting meeting'.[14] The Gwyneddigion set 'Liberty' as the subject of the chair and essay competitions in the eisteddfod which they sponsored at St Asaph in 1790, offering as a prize for the essay a silver medal designed by Dupré, who became famous as an engraver in the French Republic. Even the taciturn William Owen Pughe, known to the Gwyneddigion as 'Gwilym Dawel' (William the Silent), was excited by all these daring new ideas. When John Horne Tooke and other members of the London Corresponding Society were detained to await trial on charges of treason in 1794, Pughe, in a letter to Walter Davies (Gwallter Mechain), described them as 'a number of students of my way of thinking'.[15] When they were freed, enthusiastic celebrations were held at the Crown and Anchor tavern, with Iolo composing a special poem for the occasion.[16] Their radical sympathies brought Iolo and Pughe closer together.

Yet, those who spread radical propaganda were marked men. In 1793 William Winterbotham, a Dissenting minister from Plymouth, was given a two-year prison sentence and a fine of £200 for preaching sedition. Iolo Morganwg went to visit Winterbotham in Newgate gaol, giving his name as 'The Bard of Liberty' when accosted by the keeper. He returned a second time, accompanied by William Owen Pughe, only to be told that the only liberty allowed to him would be to walk out the way he came in.[17] By the time this episode was related to Iolo's biographer, Elijah Waring, it had been somewhat embellished. Iolo claimed to have told the keeper: 'O, very well, Mr Gaoler, by all means; and I wish no Bard of Liberty may ever meet with worse treatment, than being told to walk *out of* a prison.' Waring added: 'This smart and amusing colloquy is given verbatim from the Bard's lips.'[18] Pughe was obviously ready to be seen in the company of a well-known radical visiting another in prison. There was a great deal of boastful talk: Iolo wrote to Pughe on 20 May 1795, announcing his intention to visit him at his home 'to talk of Politics, republicanism, Jacobinisms, Carmagnolism, Sansculololisms, and a number of other wicked and trayterous isms against the peace of the Lords Kingism and Parsonism, their Crowns and dignities'.[19] However, for all their bravado in the early days of the French Revolution, Pughe and most of his friends were sobered and silenced by the atrocities of the Reign of Terror.

---

[14] Carr, *William Owen Pughe*, p. 14.

[15] G. J. Williams, 'Bywyd Cymreig Llundain yng nghyfnod Owain Myfyr', *Y Llenor*, XVIII (1939), 225. See also Emrys Jones (ed.), *The Welsh in London 1500–2000* (Cardiff, 2001), chapter 3.

[16] It was sold as a ballad on the streets of London; there is a printed copy in NLW 13221E, p. 1.

[17] Leathart, *The Origin and Progress of the Gwyneddigion*, p. 68.

[18] *RAEW*, pp. 47–8.

[19] NLW 13221E, p. 49, Iolo Morganwg to William Owen Pughe, 20 May 1795.

By around 1803–4 they had calmed down considerably. Napoleon had now become a very real threat, so much so that Pughe was inspired to join the Clerkenwell Loyal Volunteer Infantry when he feared that Britain might be invaded, and Iolo went as far as to write what has been misleadingly called 'a warlike song' for the Cowbridge Volunteers, thereby, according to Elijah Waring, whose political views were rather different from those of Iolo, 'showing how sincerely he repudiated those Gallican politics, whose glare he had formerly mistaken for glory'.[20]

Throughout the period when they were heavily preoccupied with radical politics, Iolo and his friends had another interest which also took up much of their time: the quest for the Padoucas or the Madogwys. These people were believed to be the descendants of Madoc ab Owain Gwynedd and his men who, according to legend, had sailed across the Atlantic and discovered America in 1170. Since the existence of Madoc himself is uncertain, his descendants, not surprisingly, were extremely elusive. But many believed that they were to be found conversing in remarkably unadulterated Welsh on the banks of the Mississippi and the Missouri. The Elizabethans had made good use of the Madoc story to strengthen British claims to territories in the New World and it flared up again in 1740 when Britain was involved in the War of Jenkins's Ear. The historian Theophilus Evans had joined the Madoc campaign by including some esoteric details about his voyage and the fate of the Madogwys in his second edition of *Drych y Prif Oesoedd*, which was published in 1740. By 1790 Britain and Spain were in dispute once more, this time over Nootka Sound. It was time to summon Madoc's aid again. A mysterious American calling himself 'General' William Bowles arrived in London, full of exciting tales about the Padoucas. Small wonder that Pughe, for whom etymology had never been a strong point, immediately decided that the name 'Padoucas' was derived from 'Madogwys'. Bowles claimed to be a chief of the Creek Indians but, in fact, he was an Irish American who had married a Creek woman and ingratiated himself with his in-laws. Pughe decided to investigate Bowles's claims and visited him in the company of that man of the world, David Samwell. They returned to the Gwyneddigion fully convinced of the existence of the Welsh Indians and managed to infuse their friends with fresh enthusiasm for the subject. Pughe shared this enthusiasm with the world in the columns of the *Gentleman's Magazine*, and the Caradogion Society decided to devote a whole meeting to the subject. This meeting was immortalized by David Samwell in his 'Padouca Hunt', a poem of ninety-six stanzas, in which he described the Caradogion as:

> Fully determined to decide
> This long disputed matter;

[20]   *RAEW*, p. 45.

> Did Madog cross th' Atlantic tide
> Or never take the water?[21]

It appears that the evening ended in drunken disarray, with no one much the wiser about the Madogwys.

Iolo, too, had a contribution to make to the quest for the Madogwys, and used the columns of the *Gentleman's Magazine* to gain support for an expedition to search for them. He claimed to have talked to a man called Binon, a native of Glamorgan naturally, who had met the Madogwys and had heard them speaking in Welsh 'with much greater purity than we speak it in Wales'.[22] Iolo was fascinated by the subject and gathered as much information as possible in south Wales, Bristol and Bath. He dreamed of going to America himself and prepared for this venture by camping out in the open air in all weathers and living off wild berries. He wrote to Pughe outlining his plans to explore the fur trade and to send furs over from America for Owain Myfyr's business: 'Castles in the air, you cry, – but the idea gives me pleasure.'[23] The Madogeion Society was set up to fund and support the quest in general. By this stage Iolo was expecting a travelling companion to accompany him, 'a young man from Caernarvonshire'.[24] This was John Evans of Waunfawr, who did indeed set off in 1792, without Iolo, and travelled further up the Missouri than any white man had done. He lived with the fair-skinned Mandan Indians for a while and it was they who no doubt gave rise to many of the so-called Madogwys sightings. Evans failed to discover the Madogwys, however, and died a disappointed and broken man in New Orleans in 1799. The Madogwys craze slowly fizzled out among the Gwyneddigion and other matters seized their attention. William Owen Pughe, who had also thought of venturing to America, wrote to Iolo after meeting William Bowles in 1791: 'If this had happened a year or two ago, this would have been a letter of adieu on my setting out, Iorwerth.'[25] Pughe, however, had married the frail young Sarah in 1790 and could no longer dream such dreams. Iolo was more reluctant to abandon his own ambition; as late as 1803 he confessed in a letter to Pughe: 'Old as I am growing, I have not yet given up the idea of going in quest of the *Madogwys*. You will say that I am romantic.'[26] And so he was, but he never ventured on that perilous journey.

[21] W. Ll. Davies, 'David Samwell's Poem – "The Padouca Hunt"', *NLWJ*, II, nos. 3–4 (1942), 144–52; idem, 'David Samwell (1751–1798), Surgeon of the "Discovery"', London-Welshman and Poet', *THSC* (1926–7), facsimile text between 112 and 113.

[22] *Gentleman's Magazine*, LXI, Part II (1791), 612–14. For the Madoc story, see Gwyn A. Williams, *Madoc: The Making of a Myth* (London, 1979) and idem, *The Search for Beulah Land* (London, 1980).

[23] NLW 13224B, p. 9, Iolo Morganwg to William Owen Pughe, 2 January 1792.

[24] NLW 9072E, p. 260, William Owen Pughe to Paul Panton, 10 May 1792.

[25] NLW 21282E, Letter no. 314, William Owen Pughe to Iolo Morganwg, 28 March 1791.

[26] NLW 13222C, p. 173, Iolo Morganwg to William Owen Pughe, 25 August 1803.

Their interest in politics and the Madogwys did not distract members of the Gwyneddigion Society from their literary pursuits. Like scholars in other Celtic countries, they had come to realize the value of their literary heritage and the importance of publishing the contents of their ancient manuscripts before it was too late. By the end of the seventeenth century, following the death of collectors and copyists such as Robert Vaughan of Hengwrt and William Maurice of Cefn-y-braich, much of the former interest in the manuscript collections had been lost, and they were in danger of being forgotten or destroyed from lack of care and conservation in the privately owned libraries. There was a surprising lack of knowledge about ancient texts. Humphrey Humphreys, bishop of Bangor and later of Hereford, a cultured and educated antiquary and genealogist, did not know what the *Mabinogi* were, and even the polymath Lewis Morris had little idea of the significance of the *Gododdin* until Evan Evans explained it to him. Both Lewis Morris and Evan Evans made an effort to improve the situation: Morris with the publication of *Tlysau yr Hen Oesoedd* in 1735 and Evans with *Some Specimens of the Poetry of the Antient Welsh Bards* in 1764. By the time that Iolo Morganwg, William Owen Pughe and Owain Myfyr – the trio who were responsible for *The Myvyrian Archaiology of Wales* – had embarked on the daunting task of collecting and publishing some of the contents of the early Welsh manuscripts, the way had been partly paved for them and the climate was favourable for such a venture. Each of them was well suited to the task.

Owain Myfyr was not the ignoramus who made his money talk for him, as he was often depicted. He had neither Iolo's genius nor Pughe's plodding scholarship, but he had already steeped himself in the poetry of Dafydd ap Gwilym whilst preparing the 1789 volume, copying out the whole collection in his distinctive florid hand.[27] He was genuinely interested in Welsh literature and had the money to finance the new venture but not the time to carry out the work. Instead, he bought the time of his two colleagues to carry out the editing and collecting. Pughe, who had endless patience and the interest if not the critical faculty of a scholar, was charged with the task of editing and organizing the material, while Iolo, who not only had a vast knowledge of the manuscript collections but also the stamina to trudge around the libraries of the great houses of Wales to seek them out, was invited to carry out the bulk of the collecting and copying. Iolo possessed sufficient stamina to enable him to spend hours copying manuscripts at the end of his many long journeys. He is said to have sat in a noisy inn in Beaumaris for fifteen hours a day copying Evan Evans's manuscripts. This activity was to damage his health: having sat for eight or nine hours a day in the British Museum and other libraries, he admitted in a letter to his wife that his sedentary lifestyle had caused him to be 'tormented and weakened' by a stone caused by 'retaining the Urine'.[28]

[27] UWB, Bangor 6.
[28] Williams: *IM*, p. 215.

Nothing could have been achieved, however, without the generous support of Owain Myfyr. He paid for the paper and printing 'without looking for a reimbursement from the sale of the books'.[29] He also supported his fellow-workers: we know that he made regular payments to Pughe and Iolo, and it was only reluctantly that he allowed his patronage to be acknowledged in the title of the work. While Iolo was travelling around Wales, it was Pughe who had the difficult task of keeping his nose to the grindstone, for Iolo would often disappear without trace for several weeks, pursuing his own literary researches as well as collecting material for *The Myvyrian Archaiology of Wales.* Iolo's wife was often as ignorant as Pughe about his movements. She wrote in desperation to him in June 1802 asking for news of Iolo, who had written to her from Oxford saying that he was 'very unwell'. She wanted him to know that their daughter's health had deteriorated since he was last at home.[30] She appealed to Pughe again in September 1802 for any news of his whereabouts. Iolo had a good excuse for his silence this time: he had been ill of a fever near Hafod Uchdryd in Cardiganshire on his way to the library there.[31] Iolo had been in Hafod Uchdryd, too, in 1799 when Pughe had written to him to complain about the slowness in printing *The Myvyrian Archaiology of Wales.* The material was obviously being fed in instalments to the printer. Iolo moved on to Llanrwst and Pughe wrote again, urging him to keep sending any contributions 'to keep Griffiths's Gwasg Malwen [Snail Press] a going, in order not to leave him any excuse for saying he stops on our account'.[32] The delays were not only impeding Pughe's work as editor, but he also feared that Iolo's 'dilatory spirit' would prompt Owain Myfyr to lose interest in the venture.[33]

By July 1799 Iolo was heading for Anglesey.[34] He stopped in Bangor on the way to see the Revd Richard Davies's collection and then stayed in Anglesey for a fortnight before making his way through Caernarfonshire and Merioneth again. Small wonder that he toyed with the idea of writing a book about his travels, 'a better Tour in Wales than has yet appeared'.[35] By the autumn he was back in Anglesey once more, this time at Tre-ffos. From there he went to Llanrug to see Peter Bailey Williams. By then, winter was upon him and he battled through heavy rains to Hengwrt and Hafod Uchdryd before returning home to Glamorgan. In an attempt to expedite the work and also, perhaps, to

---

[29] NLW 21282E, Letter no. 327, William Owen Pughe to Iolo Morganwg, 26 April 1798.
[30] NLW 13224B, p. 289, Margaret (Peggy) Williams to William Owen Pughe, 17 June 1802.
[31] Ibid., p. 207, Margaret (Peggy) Williams to William Owen Pughe, 1 September 1802.
[32] NLW 21282E, Letter no. 335, William Owen Pughe to Iolo Morganwg, 14 June 1799.
[33] NLW 21282E, Letter no. 339, William Owen Pughe to Iolo Morganwg, 8 May 1800.
[34] Tecwyn Ellis, 'Ymweliadau Iolo Morganwg â Meirionnydd 1799 ac 1800', *JMHRS*, V, no. 3 (1967), 239–50.
[35] BL Add. 15031, f. 22, Iolo Morganwg to Owain Myfyr, 12 June 1799.

satisfy his own curiosity about the manuscripts, William Owen Pughe also decided to visit the library at Hengwrt in July 1800.

Hengwrt library had suffered considerable neglect by the end of the eighteenth century, largely because the owners had been too tolerant of unscrupulous antiquaries and copyists. Countless volumes had been borrowed and never returned, while others had been lost or stolen. Having visited Hengwrt library in 1800, Walter Davies informed his friends in London: 'Hengwrt Library I am afraid has been too much pillaged to have anything curious in it.'[36] William Owen Pughe set off to see for himself and found the situation much changed. The owners had awoken to their losses and had clamped down on visitors to the library. Pughe was obliged to stay in Dolgellau, awaiting permission to visit Hengwrt. He decided to make good use of his time by enquiring what manuscripts were in private hands in the vicinity. He found a collection of 'annals and historical fragments' by John Jones, Gellilyfdy, genealogies collected by Robert Vaughan of Hengwrt and, unbelievably, 'the llyvyr du and llyvyr Taliesin [the black book and Taliesin's book], both of which are very curious and valuable'.[37] These treasures were too curious and valuable to be passing nonchalantly from hand to hand around Dolgellau. It is typical, too, of the attitude of Pughe and many other scholars of his day that he had decided not to bother copying much from the original text of the Black Book of Carmarthen since, so he claimed, a great deal of it had already been noted from other copies of the text. He lacked the critical faculty to realize that such copies were not always reliable. Iolo, to give him his due, had realized this, and had found fault with the transcriptions of Evan Evans: 'Evan Evans was not a fair copyist. I have detected him on several occasions copying according to his own ammendments.'[38] But there were other means of polluting the literary waters, as Iolo himself knew only too well. Having waited for some time for permission to use the Hengwrt library, and been fobbed off with excuses by the family, Pughe was smuggled in by the son of Dr Griffith Roberts of Dolgellau, a manuscript collector with whom he had dealt a great deal over the years. Once in the library, he realized that Walter Davies had not exaggerated its sorry state, but he could not loiter to do much copying because he was not supposed to be there. Moreover, another problem had arisen, as he explained in his letter to Owain Myfyr: 'After I had been in Dolgellau some days, Iorwerth also came there, which still heightened the disagreeableness of the business.'[39] To make matters worse, Hugh Maurice, Owain Myfyr's nephew, arrived in Dolgellau in the hope of visiting Hengwrt. Pughe swiftly realized that there was no hope that all three would gain access

[36] BL Add. 15030, f. 26, Walter Davies to William Owen Pughe, 1 June 1800.
[37] BL Add. 15030, f. 192, William Owen Pughe to Owain Myfyr, 31 July [1800].
[38] NLW 13221E, p. 76, Iolo Morganwg to William Owen Pughe, 19 December 1800.
[39] BL Add. 15030, f. 194, William Owen Pughe to Owain Myfyr, 11 August 1800.

to the library, and so they decided to call it a day and went off instead to climb Cadair Idris. Pughe gave Iolo a guinea to cover the expenses of his homeward journey, but the Glamorgan bard decided to press on and try his luck in the library at Gloddaith.

Such were the difficulties that Iolo, Pughe and other scholars faced in their pursuit of early Welsh manuscripts. However, they did manage to publish three volumes of *The Myvyrian Archaiology of Wales* between 1801 and 1807. This is not the place to record the great number of forgeries which Iolo managed to include in the *Archaiology*, but it is worth noting here that he also contributed a treatise, 'Review of the Present State of Welsh Manuscripts', which was published as a preface to the first volume, a work attributed by many to William Owen Pughe. As Iolo himself complained to Evan Williams, the bookseller and publisher: 'I have been by many, perhaps all, the subsequent Writer[s] who quote or refer to it, rob'd of the credit of being the Author of it; all ascribe it to Wm Owen.'[40] This misconception may have contributed to Iolo's burgeoning resentment towards Pughe, which, together with his grudge against Owain Myfyr, was soon to poison irreparably the relationship between the three men.

It was around this time that two momentous changes occurred in William Owen Pughe's life. In June 1803 he wrote excitedly to Iolo to inform him of the curious new influence which had recently entered his life. This is one of the earliest references to Pughe's involvement with Joanna Southcott, the celebrated Devon-born prophetess. In the letter he claimed that Joanna explained the scriptures 'more closely to the bardism of Wales than anyone else!' ('yn nes i varddas y Cymry no neb arall!').[41] This was probably a case of Pughe seeing what he wanted to see in Joanna's teachings. Nevertheless, he became part of her most intimate coterie, even acting as her amanuensis. Southcott saw in her own turbulent age a fulfilment of prophecies and portents mentioned in the Book of Daniel and the Book of Revelation, and she eventually became convinced that she was 'the woman clothed with the sun', described in the Book of Revelation as giving birth to a male child. This child is snatched away to heaven while the woman flees to the wilderness where a place had been prepared for her.[42]

Joanna Southcott has been much maligned by historians and often described as a fraud. However, from what we can gather from Pughe's writings and from the diary which he kept meticulously for the last twenty-four years of his life, she seems to have been a sincere, if deluded, woman who was a generous friend to him and his family. It is unclear how he came to know her, but it may have

---

[40]   NLW 21286E, Letter no. 971, Iolo Morganwg to Edward Williams, 17 April 1819.
[41]   NLW 21282E, Letter no. 357, William Owen Pughe to Iolo Morganwg, 30 June 1803.
[42]   Revelation 12.1, 2, 5.

been through his radical friends William Sharp, the engraver, and William Tooke Harwood, who were already followers of the prophetess. Southcott attracted many thousands of supporters in London, in her native Devon, and in the north of England. Although the vast majority of Southcottians were working-class people, Pughe would have found plenty of men who were his intellectual and social equals: among Southcott's followers were a member of parliament, a surgeon and several clergymen, for she remained loyal to the Church of England. Southcott had some notable successes in predicting various inconspicuous events, but she became increasingly obsessed with the woman clothed with the sun and, eventually, at the age of sixty-five and still a self-confessed virgin, she announced that she was with child, a 'Shiloh' who was to be some kind of leader or saviour. She was obviously suffering from pseudocyesis or a phantom pregnancy to such a degree that she deceived a great many leading physicians in London. Small wonder that poor, gullible William Owen Pughe was beguiled by Southcott and her prophecies. Her followers prepared frantically for Shiloh's birth: Pughe himself went to Charing Cross to buy a trumpet for the miraculous child. Southcott's 'pregnancy' proved to be a prolonged affair and eventually she sickened and grew weaker. The signs of pregnancy disappeared and she died on 27 December 1814. An autopsy was held, with Pughe being one of the privileged few allowed to wait in an ante-room to hear the verdict that there had been no child nor any other apparent cause of death. Pughe, too, was one of the handful who attended Southcott's clandestine funeral.

But all this lay in the future. In 1803 Joanna was still a novelty that Pughe was eager to share with his friends. Iolo, however, had a new religious interest of his own. In the autumn of 1802 he emerged as one of the founders of the South Wales Unitarian Society,[43] or, as he preferred to call it, 'Cymdeithas Dwyfundodiaid Deheubarth Cymru'. He explained the meaning of the Welsh appellation in a letter to Pughe in December 1802: 'You will perceive that the Appellation of our Society is a compound of Dwyf, the old Word for God (whence dwyfawl) and Undod, i.e. believers in, or holders of, the Divine Unity.'[44]

This was obviously not a propitious moment to awaken Iolo's interest in the teachings of an unknown prophetess, but Pughe persevered. Southcott used to give her loyal supporters a seal to indicate that they would figure among the elect when the judgements described in the Book of Revelation came to pass. Pughe appealed to Iolo's vanity not only by claiming that Southcott's teachings accorded with those of bardism, but also by assuring him that the Bards of the

---

[43] NLW 13145B, pp. 159–74, 296–8; NLW 21280E, Letter no. 99, David Davis to Iolo Morganwg, 17–18 January 1803.

[44] NLW 13222C, p. 157, Iolo Morganwg to William Owen Pughe, 23 December 1802.

Isle of Britain were definitely among the elect. It is obvious from a letter which Pughe wrote to his friend William Cunnington of Heytesbury in December 1804 that Iolo was singularly unimpressed:

> Perhaps you may not have heard anything about the divine Mission of Joanna Southcott the prophetess of Exeter; but it is a very remarkable circumstance that the great leading points of theology in her writings agree exactly, and often in the very expression, with our Druidical Triads of Divinity. Bard Williams was so struck with this similitude that he charged me, as a believer in her, with giving her the materials for those points.[45]

Iolo may have been right: it may be that hearing Pughe talking about the bards and their alleged beliefs had influenced Southcott. She was practically illiterate and depended heavily on Pughe to supply her with news of current affairs and the ways of the world in general. Once he realized that singing the praises of the prophetess had no effect on Iolo, Pughe turned to more desperate measures, even to menaces. He urged Iolo to make haste to join the sect since Southcott would shortly end her sealing of the elect; to refuse such an offer might lead to dire consequences:

> But I hope Iolo Morganwg, his wife and children will join the Prayer of Joanna . . . They must send their names so that I may receive them on the 11th instant. Three Clergymen, the most active opposers of the work going on have died suddenly in the same way within this fortnight here, according to signs given us to mark![46]

Iolo, who had embraced druidism and the Madogwys with such enthusiasm, was not to be persuaded by this fantasy. He found Pughe's infatuation irritating and, in a letter written in April 1805, he referred sneeringly to Southcott's prophecy of her impending death and that three years of judgements were about to begin:

> I do not hear that Joanna Southcott, as she once prophe[sied], died in last November. I do not understand that her predicted Judg[ements] have yet commenced tho' one of her three years is on the point of expiring, for whatever little calamities may be pointed out they are only such as have been common, and often in greater degree than any thing seen of late, to every year that this World has hitherto seen.[47]

Pughe was convinced that if Iolo could only hear Joanna for himself, all his doubts would vanish: 'Had you still remained in London, notwithstanding the violent tangents from this sphere of Joanna in which you so often flew, you

---

[45]   E. Vincent Evans, 'Letters to and from William Owen (Pughe), 1804–1806', *Y Cymmrodor*, XXXIX (1928), 202. For Southcott, see Frances Brown, *Joanna Southcott: The Woman Clothed with the Sun* (Cambridge, 2002).

[46]   NLW 21282E, Letter no. 361, William Owen Pughe to Iolo Morganwg, 6 January 1804.

[47]   NLW 13221E, p. 128, Iolo Morganwg to William Owen Pughe, 28 April 1805.

would ere now been a gently revolving satellite.'[48] He had now begun translating some of Southcott's bible commentaries into Welsh in an unsuccessful attempt to proselytize among his friends in Wales. The only one who seems to have shown any interest in Southcott and her mission was Robert Roberts, a Holyhead almanacker, who made some effort to win supporters in that town. Iolo, however, was Pughe's main target and he seems to have revelled in the challenge; he maintained that Southcott's teachings contained truths 'which will shake your Unitarian structure about your ears. What say you to that Iolo!!?'[49] Iolo had plenty to say, most of it scornful. He had obviously lost patience with Pughe by this stage and, in a letter to Walter Davies, he remarked that he was sure that Pughe would never awake out his 'wonderful Trance'.[50] Cracks were already appearing in the old partnership, but worse was to come.

The second important change in the life of William Owen Pughe occurred in 1806 following the death of a distant relation, the Revd Rice Pughe, rector of Nantglyn, in Denbighshire. It is difficult to establish the exact relationship between the two men: Pughe referred to the rector as 'my old and distant relation'. Since all of Rice Pughe's seven children had died before him, he had nominated William Owen, as he then was, as his heir. On his relation's death in October 1806, William Owen inherited a sizeable estate, mainly around Nantglyn, with some land in Merioneth, and even a farm in Essex. In gratitude to his benefactor, he added the surname Pughe to his own. The inheritance, though it was mainly tied up in land, certainly made a difference to his career. Hitherto, he had struggled to make a living from private tuition, teaching part-time in a girls' boarding school, and receiving payments from Owain Myfyr for work done on *The Myvyrian Archaiology of Wales*. His antiquarian friends rejoiced in his good fortune, hoping that he would now be able to devote more time to his literary pursuits. But Pughe had completed most of his important work before 1806 and the inheritance was often to cause him many financial and administrative worries. He managed the estate at a distance from his home in London, employing a bailiff to supervise the day-to-day organization in Nantglyn until his son Aneurin was old enough to assume such duties. It was not until 1825 that he eventually retired to Nantglyn. He seems to have adopted his new surname immediately and it was accepted at once by most of his friends and correspondents, with one notable exception: as late as 1819 Iolo claimed that he could never remember the name. In a letter to Evan Williams, he said: 'Can you favour me with Mr Owen's address . . . I said Mr Owen, a name familiar to me, but the Nick name of Pugh is seldom or never present to my memory.'[51] In another letter to Evan Williams a month later, Iolo's

[48]   NLW 21282E, Letter no. 362, William Owen Pughe to Iolo Morganwg, 23 January 1805.
[49]   NLW 21282E, Letter no. 375, William Owen Pughe to Iolo Morganwg, 18 May 1808.
[50]   NLW 1808Eii, Letter no. 1526, Iolo Morganwg to Walter Davies, 12 August 1806.
[51]   NLW 21286E, Letter no. 971, Iolo Morganwg to Evan Williams, 17 April 1819.

irritation was palpable: 'My wish to write to Mr O.P (let me not always omit the O.P.) was this.'[52] There was no doubt that the double-barrelled surname rankled, and Pughe's comfortable circumstances as a gentleman farmer were obviously a sore point.

Iolo grew increasingly resentful during the latter years of the work on *The Myvyrian Archaiology of Wales*. As early as 1801 Pughe had to remind him of his dependency on the patronage of Owain Myfyr. Iolo was told that both Pughe and Myfyr appreciated his literary talents so much that they were eager to foster them even after the work on the *Archaiology* project was finished. Owain Myfyr had admitted as much to Pughe who, unwisely, divulged this secret to Iolo:

> I consider that your life should be devoted to it – and that too is Myvyr's idea, and what he wants to effect by all means. Even if he dies he has made that certain; a confidential secret, which I am loath to make, and which you must bury in your own breast.[53]

Pughe's indiscretion was to have repercussions which lasted for the rest of Iolo's life. He was determined to hold Owain Myfyr to this promise, long after his patron was in no position to honour it, for he had suffered losses in his business, had married and begun to raise a family late in life. Iolo refused to acknowledge such difficulties and was still complaining about his alleged unfair treatment in a letter to Evan Williams in 1821, when he claimed that he had worked for Owain Myfyr for eight years: 'at the very inadequate annual sallery of £50 per ann, which O. Jones promised to settle on me for life, of which I received less that £80'.[54] He proceeded to attack Owain Myfyr vehemently, referring also to Pughe as Myfyr's 'cat's paw'. Admittedly this letter was written long after the events it described, when Iolo's resentment had been festering for several years, but his attacks on Owain Myfyr can also be seen in letters to his friends as early as 1806. There had been disagreements, too, about the contents and methodology of *The Myvyrian Archaiology of Wales* and all such distant grievances were mulled over and exaggerated in Iolo's mind over the years. Elijah Waring, too, heard these complaints, but found it hard to support Iolo entirely:

> It is difficult to conceive that two such old and formerly generous friends of the Bard, as Mr Owen Jones, and Dr Owen Pughe . . . should have concurred in deliberately wronging him in this matter. Some misapprehensions may have existed on both sides: but the painful impression was never removed from his mind.[55]

This was true: Iolo carried his grudges with him to the grave.

[52]   NLW 21286E, Letter no. 972, Iolo Morganwg to Evan Williams, 12 May 1819.
[53]   NLW 21282E, Letter no. 350, William Owen Pughe to Iolo Morganwg, 11 November 1801.
[54]   NLW 21286E, Letter no. 986, Iolo Morganwg to Evan Williams, 15 November 1821.
[55]   *RAEW*, p. 112.

The relationship between Iolo and Pughe had also cooled when work on the *Archaiology* ended, but at first there was no definite breach; it was a natural parting of their ways as Pughe became increasingly involved with Joanna Southcott and her activities. In 1819 Iolo received a letter from Evan Williams, upbraiding him for being so hostile to his old friend:

> You seem to be half angry with our old & mutual friend W. Owen Pughe. I see no reason why – as he Certainly was your friend and Benefactor formerly when you resided at his House, & forsooth he is still the same honest fellow as he was formerly, & a man of great worth & merit. But as for your old friend Owen Jones – he is under ground Long Since – & there let the fellow remain & rott in quiet – with all his Sins upon his head.[56]

Iolo was quick to defend himself: he claimed that Pughe had resolutely failed to answer his letters and that he could not really regard him as a benefactor because 'that most artful of all Scoundrels O. Jones, always told me that he defrayed Mr Owen for all expences incur'd on my account'.[57] He went on to claim that Pughe had been unaware of Myfyr's alleged duplicity and that he was probably embarrassed when he discovered it: 'hence his reserve towards me, unless my contemptuous opinion of Joanna Southcott occasioned it, but no matter what it was now'.[58]

Iolo was less than honest in this letter. There were other reasons for his being 'half angry' with William Owen Pughe, as he revealed later in the letter. Iolo, 'the Bard of Glamorgan', had been infuriated by the fact that Pughe was now publicly acclaimed as a poet. In 1819 he had published *Coll Gwynfa*, his virtually incomprehensible translation of Milton's *Paradise Lost*. For once, Iolo's angry attacks were justified:

> I had some time ago received a Ms specimen of his Paradise Lost (alas how truly lost) he has fallen away from Milton as much or more than Adam fell from God. – he knows not the principles of the Miltonic Blank verse or indeed of any kind of verse whatever.[59]

The fact that Pughe had ventured to trespass in the realm of poetry was enough to enrage Iolo, but the fact that he was praised and honoured for his feeble efforts was more than he could bear. Pughe, indeed, was honoured in the highest manner. In 1822, mainly through the influence of his friend John Jones (Tegid), who was chaplain of Christ Church College, Oxford, he was awarded the honorary degree of DCL by the University of Oxford.

---

[56] NLW 21283E, Letter no. 592, Evan Williams to Iolo Morganwg, 4 March 1819.
[57] NLW 21286E, Letter no. 972, Iolo Morganwg to Evan Williams, 12 May 1819.
[58] Ibid.
[59] Ibid.

It was this honorary doctorate which sparked the most virulent of Iolo's attacks on William Owen Pughe. Six months after the award Iolo wrote to Dafydd Dafis, Castellhywel, scornfully referring to Pughe's new title: 'that complete and utter fool the blessed Dr William Owen Pughe' ('[y] ffol Canmhlyg hwnnw y Doctor bendigaid *William Owain Pughe*'); 'the Doctoral Scoundrel W.O.P.' ('y Crasgoethyn Doctoraidd W.O.P.'); 'the uneducated Dr Southcott with his unbridled insolence' ('y Dr Southcott di ddysg ai Ryfyg yn anffrwynedig').[60] The letter was not only an attack on his poetic efforts but also his general publications on the Welsh language. Iolo also threatened to attack Pughe further in his forthcoming book *Cyfrinach Beirdd Ynys Prydain*, and when it eventually appeared he did indeed attack Idrison (Pughe's bardic name) by insisting that he knew no more about the rules of strict metres 'than a new-born pig knows of what materials a new moon is made when the old one has waned to nothing' ('nag a wyr mochyn newydd ei eni o ba ddefnydd-ion y gwneir lleuad newydd pan fo'r un hen wedi llwyr dreulio'n ddim').[61]

William Owen Pughe was now as much the object of Iolo's hatred as Owain Myfyr had been in the past. Soon, everyone knew that the old friendship was well and truly over. The versatile antiquary, J. W. Prichard of Plas-y-brain, Llanbedr-goch, remarked on the breach in a letter written in May 1822:

Yr wyf yn deall fod Iolo Morganwg a Gwilym Owain Pughe wedi syrthio allan a'u gilydd . . . Buasai yn dda i Mr G. O. Pughe pe na's gwelsai erioed wyneb Iolyn; dyn ar ddrygau bob amser, ac yn dyfeisio rhyw gelwyddau i geisio twyllo'r byd, ac wrth hynny, nid yn unig tynu dirmyg a gwaradwydd arno ei hun, ond fe barodd lawer o ddirmyg ac anfri ar enw Mr G. O. P. Och fi! Duw a'n gwaredo rhag syrthio i rwyd y cyfryw Anghenfil.

(I understand that Iolo Morganwg and William Owen Pughe have fallen out with each other . . . It would have been well for Mr W. O. Pughe had he never set eyes on Iolo, a man always up to mischief, and devising lies to try to deceive the world, and thereby not only bringing scorn and disgrace upon himself but also causing much scorn and disgrace to the name of Mr W. O. P. Woe is me! God protect us from falling into the clutches of such a Monster.)[62]

There was to be no reconciliation: the benign William Owen Pughe hardly mentioned Iolo thereafter. Iolo died in December 1826. On the last day of that year Pughe noted in his diary: 'a clywwn varw Iolo Morganwg y 17.ved' ('I heard that Iolo Morganwg died on the 17th').[63] That is all; a bleak comment to end what had once been a fruitful, if uneasy, partnership.

---

[60] NLW 21286E, Letter no. 992, Iolo Morganwg to David Davis, 3 January 1823.
[61] Edward Williams, *Cyfrinach Beirdd Ynys Prydain* (Caernarfon, n.d.), p. 126.
[62] 'Mr J. W. Prichard o Blasybrain', *Y Traethodydd*, XXXIX (1884), 29.
[63] NLW 13248Bii, p. 464.

21

'The Age of Restitution': Taliesin ab Iolo and the Reception of Iolo Morganwg

BRYNLEY F. ROBERTS

Given the renaissance of Welsh classical literature in the eighteenth century, it might be expected that the names of the *Cynfeirdd* should have achieved a degree of popularity in literary and scholarly circles in Wales and that Iolo Morganwg should have named his only son, and last-born child, Taliesin. For Iolo, however, naming his son Taliesin was far more than a gesture of regard for Welsh literary history, for it appears that this son, from the very beginning, was intended to play some part in Iolo's as yet unformulated plans.

Taliesin Williams was born on 9 July 1787, perhaps in Cardiff at a time when his father was in the debtors' prison.[1] Iolo was forty by then and experiencing one of his most unsettled periods. He had tried, with little success, to make a name for himself as a poet in London and he was gradually becoming addicted to laudanum, the drug which eased his physical discomfort but which also stimulated his imagination and mental energy, leaving him feeling even more unsettled. During Taliesin's boyhood years Iolo was away from home frequently, but on his visits to his wife and family in Flemingston he surely communicated to his son his vision of the true and radical literary history of Wales. These were the years when Iolo's fantasies were being brought into some sort of order and structure. The *Gentleman's Magazine* in November 1789 contained a letter from a certain 'J.D.' (probably Iolo himself) which asserted Edward Williams's claim to be 'one of only two persons who are the only legitimate descendants of the so-long celebrated Ancient British Bards' and that he had been admitted into a Congress of Bards 'after undergoing proper examination and being admitted also into their Mysteries, they are pleased to call them'.[2] 'A Sketch of British Bardism' appeared in the introduction to William Owen Pughe's *The Heroic Elegies and other Pieces of Llywarç Hen* (1792), while in the second volume of his own *Poems, Lyric and Pastoral* (1794) he gave an

---

[1]   According to the memorial tablet in Flemingston church, Taliesin Williams was born on 9 July 1787. The parish registers, however, note that he was baptized on 16 September 1787. GRO, P/10/CW1, Flemingston PR, p. 9; Williams: *IM*, pp. 450–1.

[2]   *Gentleman's Magazine*, LIX, Part 2 (1789), 976–7.

account of 'The Patriarchal Religion of Ancient Britain called Druidism but by the Welsh most commonly Barddas (Bardism), though they also term it Derwyddoniaeth (Druidism)' and included extracts from the 'Welsh-Bardic Triades'. The reinstitution of the 'ancient bardic order' was launched at the Gorsedd on Primrose Hill in London in June and again in September 1792; an ode recited there was annotated and published in the *Poems*. Taliesin was being brought up in this imaginative ferment of ideas and assertions.

The boy was further exposed to Iolo's religious and political radicalism when his father returned more or less permanently to Flemingston in 1795 to earn his living once more as a stonemason, a surveyor and a builder. Iolo ensured that Taliesin, like his sisters, received as good an education as possible at local schools. He seems to have been at Thomas Williams's school, somewhere in the vicinity of Gileston, from October 1796 until 1798 and then from November 1802 to October 1803, before becoming an assistant there from October 1804 to January 1805.[3] He may have left school then, as Iolo took him under his wing; together they set up a business as masons, stone-cutters and woodcutters, and surveyors.[4] The very nature of their trade must have obliged father and son to spend a great deal of time in each other's company as they worked side by side in churches, graveyards and farms as well as in the workshop, and there must have been many hours of conversation, expounding and listening as Iolo shared with this chosen vessel his views and ideas – the secrets of the bards of Britain, preserved by the last of them – and the genuine history of Wales. In the evenings Taliesin would have seen growing the mass of notebooks and folders, which his father was constantly writing, transcribing and annotating, and he may have heard some of the accompanying verbal commentary.

From his birth he was destined to be part of Iolo's ambition to present the authentic bardic history of Wales to the world: 'I hope my Taliesin will live to be the Editor and Translator of the works of his ancient name's sake.'[5] So spoke Iolo soon after his son's birth. A scholarly father's aspiration for his son, no doubt, but when one recalls that the 'ancient' Taliesin, in Iolo's version of bardic history, was the archetypal druidic bard, representing tradition retained in its purity in Glamorgan, the real significance of the boy's name becomes apparent. Iolo reiterated his son's role when, in 1788, he entered 'Taliesin ab Iorwerth' as a subscriber to William Owen Pughe's edition of the poetry of Dafydd ap Gwilym: 'Pwy a wyr na fydd fyw i fod mor enwog a Thaliesin Ben Beirdd? (Who knows but that he will live to be as famous as Taliesin Chief of Bards?).[6]

---

[3]   Iolo's accounts with Thomas Williams are in NLW 13112B, pp. 198, 203. I am grateful to Dr Cathryn A. Charnell-White for bringing this document to my attention.

[4]   NLW 13089E, p. 181.

[5]   NLW 13221E, p. 28. Iolo Morganwg to William Owen Pughe, 23 July 1788.

[6]   Ibid., p. 12. Iolo Morganwg to William Owen Pughe, 12 March 1788.

For his part, Taliesin seems (if his father is to be believed) to have responded to Iolo's teaching. On 23 April Iolo set out some of his plans in a letter to the publisher, Evan Williams, The Strand, London: 'My son is entering deeply into these studies and will, to my sorrow, become an author; will, most probably, like myself, "Fall on Evil Days and Evil Tongues."'[7]

In a later letter, dated 16 January 1810, he lavished praise on Taliesin's literary efforts:

> for he is fond of poetry, has written many pieces both in Welsh and English that have been well-spoken of by good judges, and, in each of these languages, he is, I really believe, the best poet in this county, at least; possibly the best in Wales. I have seldom met with thoughts more truly new and original than his very frequently are.[8]

Iolo was anxious to prevent his son from becoming 'infected with the *cacoethes scribendi*' and were he able to set him up in his trade as a stonemason, in which he had 'acquired a considerable proficiency . . . he would be, in a great measure, out of the way of literary poverty'.[9] Unfortunately, Taliesin's constitution was not strong enough to allow him to follow this path. Even during the years of their 'partnership' Iolo had sought a position for Taliesin as a writing master at David Davis's school in Neath; for a while, during 1811–12, he was at schools in Gileston and St Athan before he was appointed in 1813 an assistant at Davis's 'academy' in Neath, one of the best and most highly regarded schools in south Wales. David Davis was one of a notable family of Presbyterian teachers and ministers. His father, also David Davis (Dafydd Dafis), Castellhywel, kept an academy in Cardiganshire famed for its classical and liberal education. The elder son, David, was a minister and schoolmaster in Neath from 1800 to 1824 and Timothy, the second son, became an influential minister at Evesham. Iolo was a leading Unitarian in south Wales, a founder of the South Wales Unitarian Society in 1802 (Taliesin had been enrolled from the outset) and his collection of hymns, *Salmau yr Eglwys yn yr Anialwch*, was published in Merthyr Tydfil in 1812. Davis's academy could therefore be expected to be a congenial and appropriate environment for a young man brought up by an uncompromisingly radical father. In letters to his father and sister in July 1813 Taliesin revealed how happy he was in his new post. He praised Davis and his wife for their personal care and took full advantage of his widening educational horizons, enthusiastically reporting on the science lectures on 'light, vision and colours' and the 'optical museum' that a visiting lecturer had exhibited.[10] By October 1814, however, the pleasant atmosphere

---

[7]   *Cambrian Register*, III (1818), 373.
[8]   Ibid., 378.
[9]   Ibid. See also NLW 21285E, Letter no. 886, Iolo Morganwg to David Williams, 8 January 1811, for a version of the second letter.
[10] NLW 21284E, Letter no. 643, Taliesin Williams to Iolo Morganwg, 7 August 1813.

at the academy had changed as a result of a disagreement between Davis and Taliesin. Taliesin discounted the matter when he wrote to his father that month, simply informing him that the 'very bad state' of his health and 'some small disagreement' with Mr Davis had rendered his stay beyond Christmas highly improbable. The cause of the rift is not clear. It appears that Taliesin had been accused of some wrongdoing (in 1816 he referred to being cleared of the 'imputation' against him), but this may have been one of the first signs of the mental illness which was to afflict Davis and which led to his retirement in 1824 to a home in Evesham under the care of his brother Timothy. By November, Taliesin was urging Iolo to seek a new position for him and he felt obliged to resign in February/March 1815. He left Neath a bitter and despondent man. He was twenty-eight; not only had a promising career been shattered, but it must have seemed that the taste he had acquired for knowledge and literature beyond bardic history would remain cruelly unsat- isfied. He did not wish to be a burden on his parents and he was unable to undertake heavy work. There was nothing for him in Wales, so he claimed, but he was dissuaded from emigrating to his late uncle's sugar plantation in Jamaica ('madness', according to Iolo) and from seeking his living in London. Iolo remained supportive and sympathetic throughout this difficult period though, not surprisingly, his patience was sorely tried at times. His suggestions were not ones that greatly appealed to Taliesin – keeping school and a stationer's shop, or responding to the needs of a small congregation in Bridgend who were seeking a Unitarian, 'or at least a rational and liberal minister', and combining this with a school, as so many Unitarian ministers did. Taliesin had not freed himself from his experience at Neath, claiming to have 'an utter aversion to school-keeping',[11] but eventually, though he had claimed that Neath would be his last post of that nature, he was obliged to concede that there was no other avenue before him. Thus, in the *Cambrian* in January 1816, he advertised his new Commercial School in Merthyr:

> Wherein will be taught Reading, Writing, English Grammar & Composition; Arithmetic, Book-keeping, Geometry, Trigonometry, Mensuration, Geography, Navigation, Algebra &c. at One Guinea per Qtr . . . Sessions on the elements of Mineralogy will be given if required at such stated times as may appear expedient, by Edward Williams.[12]

The school duly opened in Bridge Street and migrated to various locations as Taliesin moved house. Taliesin was to spend the rest of his life in Merthyr and he died there on 16 February 1847.

[11]   NLW 21284E, Letter no. 666, Taliesin Williams to Iolo Morganwg, Letter nos. 660–8, dating from 15 October 1814 to 12 August 1815, regularly discussed Taliesin's predicament. Iolo's responses are in Letter nos. 926–38, to 14 September 1815.
[12]   *Cambrian*, 20 January 1816.

The fortunes of the school fluctuated according to the economic conditions of the town, especially in the early years, but it soon gained a reputation as the principal school in the district. Nevertheless, Taliesin's initial attitude towards his new venture was hardly encouraging and the 'aversion to teaching', to which he had confessed in 1815, may well have persisted. Certainly the cynicism which characterized comments to his father in May 1817 is not what one might have expected from a young man excited at the prospect of a new beginning: 'There is so much filth, ignorance and Blackguardism here that no person possessed of common sense would dream of sending a boy here from any distance.'[13] Circumstances improved over the years, however, and the school could reckon among its former pupils many who achieved distinction in their fields, including Rees Lewis, the printer and publisher, W. T. Lewis (Lord Merthyr), Charles Herbert James MP, his cousin Sir William James (Lord Justice James), Penry Williams, the artist, Joseph Edwards, the sculptor, and others who went on to English schools and universities. Taliesin Williams, 'the famous old school-master', as he later became known,[14] was held in high regard. Charles James wrote more than one account of his schooldays in Merthyr, from which we can gather that, in spite of his reputation as 'the pedagogue *par excellence* of his day in these parts',[15] Taliesin was a more conscientious than inspired teacher: 'a hard master but completely sound and skilled in what he taught' ('yn feistr caled ond yn hollol *sound* ac hyfforddus yn yr hyn a ddysgai');[16] 'Mr Williams had many good points about him, with many peculiarities.'[17] And although another writer praised his pupils' mastery of grammar, history and arithmetic, claiming that they were fond of talking about, and hearing others talk about 'their former fatherly Teacher' ('eu cyn Athraw tadol'),[18] Charles James's abiding memory was of the thrashings, sometimes rather absent-mindedly administered, 'till the blood came'.[19] Taliesin was praised for the effectiveness of his tuition, especially in literature and English, and there is no doubt that he laid stress on fluent reading and memorizing poetry:

> One of the institutions was a grand recitation every Christmas. For days beforehand all the schoolwork was suspended except learning the pieces for recitation, and

[13] NLW 21284E, Letter no. 675, Taliesin Williams to Iolo Morganwg, 20 January 1816.
[14] H. W. Southey, 'Reminiscences of Old Merthyr, 1919', *MH*, 14 (2002), 137.
[15] T. F. Holley, 'In Memoriam, Rees Lewis, Printer, 1886', ibid., 100.
[16] 'Charles Herbert James', *Yr Ymofynydd*, new series, no. 35 (1890), 253. Among other descrip-tions of Taliesin are: 'that universally-esteemed scholar and disciplinarian', 'A Biographical Account of Sir W. T. Lewis in the period 1837–1891', *MH*, 9 (1997), 43; 'not merely a skilled theoretical English and Welsh grammarian, but knew how to teach the science', ibid., 14 (2002), 90.
[17] Charles Herbert James, *What I Remember about Myself and Old Merthyr* (Merthyr Tydfil, 1892), p. 12.
[18] Anon., 'Mr Taliesin Williams (*Ab Iolo*)', *Y Wawr*, 1 (1850), 114–15.
[19] James, *What I Remember*, p. 15.

during a couple of days nothing was done but rehearsing for the great occasion. Great care was taken about our stops, our intonation, emphasis, &c., and the pieces were got up perfectly. I attribute much of the good reading of Tally's boys (and they did read better than average boys) to this thorough drilling which we got every Christmas.[20]

But this was in striking contrast to his method of teaching arithmetic: rather than correct errors, he merely pronounced them 'wrong', and sent unfortunate boys to try again and to discover the rule for themselves, however long that might take. Charles James's comment is a fair one: 'It worked a boy tremendously sharp . . . and possibly made them more sharp, but dull boys I am sure it disheartened to a most distressing degree.'[21] Notwithstanding the lighter moments, for 'Taliesin was a great stickler for old customs' and kept *nos galangaeaf* (Hallowe'en) with 'a good deal of jollity',[22] most accounts of his school-mastering are marked by a constant emphasis on his discipline: 'a severe master, but he had turned out good and capable men . . . Taliesin was so firm a believer in the efficacy of the birch that he would not have been able to sleep a night if he had not during the day given some one a good thrashing'.[23] Even in an age that believed in the cane as a necessary instrument of discipline, Taliesin's energetic enthusiasm evoked comment and this 'strongly-built, stern-faced man . . . [who] walked with a sedate, dignified gait, as became the man in whose mind was stored so much learning' may never have felt completely at ease in his profession.[24]

The close links between father and son, forged in these boyhood years, did not loosen over the passage of time and the changes of circumstances. They maintained a regular correspondence, each complaining so often when the other was tardy in responding that it is easy to believe that the contact and exchange of news and information were necessary props for both. Iolo, the inveterate walker, used to visit Taliesin both at Neath and then at Merthyr, or they would arrange to meet in one of the villages in the lowlands of Glamorgan. Iolo may have been enlisted to assist Taliesin at his school if he is the Edward Williams named in the original advertisement, though how capable he might have been must be doubted in the light of a description given by one of the pupils around 1817–18:

Iolo was at that time in advanced years, and although he was ensconced in an upper storey just above the students, it was very seldom that they could catch a glimpse of

[20] Ibid., p. 8.
[21] Ibid., p. 15.
[22] Ibid., p. 13.
[23] Holley, 'Rees Lewis, Merthyr Printer', 99. This is part of a description by Morgan Williams of Rees Lewis's schooldays; his remarks were greeted with loud laughter.
[24] Charles Wilkins, 'Mr Taliesin Williams (Ab Iolo Morganwg)', *Cymru Fu*, II, 18 January (1890), 115.

his venerable figure. Iolo pursued his researches with profound attention, and he rarely went out of doors. Paroxysms of coughing, too, and other painful symptoms of physical debility, perpetually harrassed him, and it was not without difficulty that he could at times get to the top of the stairs-landing to call out to his son with characteristic brusqueness, 'Tally, Tally'.[25]

A few years later Charles James recalled seeing on one occasion 'an old man and feeble' whom he assumed was Iolo.[26] But Iolo's compulsive desire to be Taliesin's tutor in literary matters was independent of any assistance he might be able to give at the school, and it never weakened. As early as 1809 he had hoped that the youth would arrange to print and publish his papers in order to safeguard the copyright, and even in 1817, when Taliesin was in the throes of establishing his new school in a town where there were already four such schools, Iolo sought to persuade him to undertake the printing of his papers.[27] However, he probably had good reason to believe that Taliesin was showing greater interest in his father's literary affairs during these years. While he was at Neath, around 1813, he had begun to compose *englynion* and turned to Iolo for assistance (as he would do again, more than once).[28] For his part, Iolo insisted on seeing Taliesin's translation of a *cywydd* claimed to be by Dafydd ap Gwilym in the Appendix to *Barddoniaeth Dafydd ab Gwilym* (1789), though this was not disinterest since he was, of course, the author of the poem. More significant is that Taliesin had become interested in the poets whom Iolo had claimed as the last witnesses for the bardic assemblies which had been safeguarded in Glamorgan – Lewis Hopkin, Edward Evan and the patriarchal William Moses, 'Gwilym Tew o Lan Taf', of Merthyr. Taliesin took the initiative from 1814 onwards by asking his father for information in his letters about Wales and her literature.[29] Iolo responded warmly and undertook to send a monthly letter, a correspondence course no less, on Welsh literature and antiquities, not so much in order to continue Tally's education but rather to equip him for his true mission:

> I have no doubt but that, if you properly qualify yourself in time for the under-taking, you may make a good deal of money of my papers and MSS. After I am gone out of your way, only I wish that your sisters may in some degree partake of the profits.[30]

25 Holley, 'Rees Lewis, Merthyr Printer', 90.
26 James, *What I Remember*, p. 6.
27 NLW 21286E, Letter no. 956, Iolo Morganwg to Taliesin Williams, 28 July 1817.
28 NLW 21284E, Letter no. 643, Taliesin Williams to Iolo Morganwg, 7 August 1813. For the *englynion*, see NLW 13134A, p. 197.
29 NLW 21284E, Letter no. 653, Taliesin Williams to Iolo Morganwg, 4 May 1814.
30 NLW 21284E, Letter no. 916, Iolo Morganwg to Taliesin Williams, 29 May 1814.

Like so many of Iolo's plans, nothing ever came of this particular scheme of instruction, but there is no doubt that the teaching continued – he was being urged in 1818 to study classical Welsh grammars by William Gambold and Siôn Dafydd Rhys – and that Taliesin would henceforth become ever more closely involved in his father's 'researches', not merely as the publisher of his papers, but as the recognized authority on their content, as is suggested by an unsent letter composed by Iolo in Taliesin's name in 1818, which indicates the role which he envisaged for his son: 'I am known by some friends to amuse myself with the perusal of my father's numerous Welsh MSS, and for that reason am supposed to be capable of giving some account of the origin of this silly custom [i.e. the Mari Lwyd].'[31] Taliesin as publisher and curator was intended to have a crucial place in Iolo's literary history. His name was full of signifi-cance in bardic history, but in Iolo's revisionist version of the fortunes of the Welsh language and its literature the messianic Taliesin was to herald a new age. Iolo set out the successive ages of Welsh in a planned 'Dissertation on the Welsh Language', c.1815:

1st Age – of Taliesin, Lib Land – Landaff Charter – Vocabulary.

2d In the Middle ages, Gogynfeirdd,

3d Age of D ab Gwilym.

4th Age of Henry 7th abounded more in subsequent times in English words, but still pure in Idiom.

5th Age of Elizabeth & James, very pedantic, Dr Tho. William's Preface, Henry & Wm. Salusbury, Henri Perry.

6. age of Charles 2d down to George 3rd (or age of Dr Davies, depurating age)

7. Age of Wm. Owen. or age of rebarbarization.

*8. Age of Taliesin yr Ail [the second], or age of Restitution.

all the above to include vocables, inflections, prepositives, Compounds, idioms, variations.[32]

Taliesin, the keeper of the archive and library, was charged with ensuring the acceptance of his father's vision; he was to be the medium of the restitution of the true history. His role was not to develop or even interpret his father's ideas, but rather to digest and present them.

This is not to say that Taliesin had no existence outside Iolo's own ambitions or that he was no more than his father's creature. His 'sedate, dignified gait' owed as much to his standing in public and cultural life in Merthyr Tydfil as to

---

[31] NLW 21414E, no. 26. The letter is dated 21 January 1818.

[32] NLW 13131A, p. 364. I am grateful to Dr Cathryn A. Charnell-White for drawing this document to my attention. Page 363 contains notes from a sermon by Joseph Turnbull, *Unbelief and Credulity: A Sermon Occasioned by the Death of Mrs Joanna Southcott* (Chard, 1815).

his learning. He came to Merthyr in 1815 at a time when the town and surrounding villages were embarking on that development which would create the largest urban settlement in Wales.[33] Over the years of Taliesin's residence the population increased from 7,705 inhabitants in 1801 to 22,083 in 1831 and thereafter by some ten thousand every decade until it reached 46,378 in 1851, a few years after his death. There is more here than the growth of industry and the subsequent rise in population, for these were the years when formal and informal structures of government and administration were created and circles of influence and power were established. Taliesin threw himself into the developing municipal life in which his colleagues were the burgeoning middle class – merchants, shopkeepers, businessmen (some of whom were also newspaper proprietors and editors involved in a swiftly growing local press), Dissenting ministers, lawyers, doctors, middle management – a sector with increasing influence in most aspects of Merthyr life and one into which Taliesin entered in 1821 when he married Mary Petherick, the daughter of the agent of Penydarren ironworks. Many of this middle class were Unitarians, heirs of an old intellectual radicalism which had strong roots in these Glamorgan uplands and which was nurtured in societies like the Cyfarthfa Philosophical Society of 1807. The tradition of free discussion and social ideals, now allied with the power to plan and act in a community which was searching for effective patterns of local government, was continued in the later societies described by Charles Wilkins, the historian of Merthyr, as associations where 'many liberal minds, comprising most of the respectable tradesmen of the place' came together to discuss 'the politics of the day, and advanced subjects of thought in the religious and scientific world'.[34] It was this middle-class grouping of radical Unitarians (and others) which set the tone of municipal life and society in Merthyr, a group within which Taliesin Williams was comfortable in his religious convictions and political sympathies, as well as in his social connections, not only by marriage and as the teacher of the children of many of his colleagues but also as a member of the structures of government (he was a member of the district committee of the local Board of Health).

Taliesin revealed something of his father's spirit soon after his arrival in Merthyr. In 1817, following the upheavals of the strike of the previous year, he stood with the reformers in rejecting proposed increased rates on workmen's cottages. Some years later, during the great debate on parliamentary reform in 1830–1, he was among local leaders who called public meetings and launched

---

[33] For the history of the town and the community, see Charles Wilkins, *The History of Merthyr Tydfil* (Merthyr Tydfil, 1908); Glanmor Williams (ed.), *Merthyr Politics: The Making of a Working-Class Tradition* (Cardiff, 1966); Joseph Gross, *A Brief History of Merthyr Tydfil* (Newport, 1980); Andy Croll, *Civilizing the Urban: Popular Culture and Public Space in Merthyr, c.1870–1914* (Cardiff, 2000).

[34] Wilkins, *History of Merthyr*, p. 385.

Fig. 30 A bust of Taliesin Williams (Taliesin ab Iolo) by Joseph Edwards, 1839.

a petition in support of the Reform Bill, meetings at which he spoke. Although
he was not part of the 1831 rising, his sympathies were made clear when he
joined others in preparing a petition to ameliorate the sentences passed on
Richard Lewis (Dic Penderyn) and Lewis Lewis (Lewsyn yr Heliwr).[35] A
footnote in the history, perhaps, but he is an exemplar, for Merthyr was his
home throughout the early years of the development of this industrial
community.

Most of the immigrants who swelled the population of the town during this
period were Welsh and they brought with them their Welsh-language culture.

---

[35]   *Cambrian*, 9 March 1831, 30 April 1831, 25 February, 12 March 1832; NLW 21271E, Letter
       nos. 392 and 392a–c, discuss the sentences and include a draft petition; Gwyn A. Williams, *The
       Merthyr Rising* (Cardiff, 1988), pp. 95–7, 182.

By the 1820s societies, bearing a variety of names but established to safeguard Welsh literary life, were common throughout Wales. They were intended as meetings where poets could regularly discuss their craft and develop their skills, examine one another's work and hold eisteddfodau. It is not surprising that societies of this kind should have been established so early in Merthyr Tydfil, for here most of all there was a venue for Iolo's Gorseddau and Unitarian radicalism. The minister of the Unitarian meeting-house at Aberdare until 1796 was Edward Evan, the sole survivor, besides Iolo himself, of the allegedly genuine ancient Welsh bards, and one of his successors from 1811 was the redoubtable Thomas Evans (Tomos Glyn Cothi). Taliesin had been instituted a Druid by his father at the Carmarthen eisteddfod in 1819 and was one of the prime movers in setting up in 1821 the literary Cymdeithas y Gwladgarwyr (Society of Patriots), which met in the Patriot tavern, the home of one of the old freethinkers' societies, and where the first eisteddfod at Merthyr is recorded on 19 April 1820. As in the case of the Carw Coch literary society in neighbouring Aberdare, a close correlation existed in these early years between the membership of radical and literary groups. Under Taliesin's guidance a Welsh literary society could not merely be a Cymdeithas Gymreigyddol but, more importantly for him, one of Iolo's reinstituted bardic assemblies: Cymdeithas Cadair Merthyr Tudfyl, ym mraint Cadair a Gorsedd Pendefigaeth Morganwg, a Gwent, ac Erging ac Euas, ac Ystrad Yw (The Society of the Chair of Merthyr Tydfil, in the privilege of the Chair and Gorsedd of the Nobility of Glamorgan and Gwent, and Ergyng and Ewias, and Ystrad Yw), which was formed in September 1821, 'as conformable as possible to genuine ancient usage', according to the advice Taliesin had sought from his father.[36] The Cymreigyddion was very much Taliesin's society: he served and guided it over the years as *prifardd* (chief poet), chairman, recorder, 'sergeant', adjudicator and correspondent. It was not only a means of propagating Iolo's ideas, for here were nurtured Taliesin's bardic and eisteddfodic ambitions which brought him into contact with other literary figures throughout south Wales. They also provided him with an entry-point into the group of Anglican and gentry supporters of Welsh literature who established the Abergavenny Cymreigyddion Society and its influential series of eisteddfodau, under the dominant patronage of Augusta Hall, Lady Llanover, with which Taliesin was associated from their inception in 1833. Small wonder, therefore, that he achieved status as a Welsh cultural authority as well as becoming an important figure in Merthyr's intellectual community, both Welsh- and English-language.

The 1820s and 1830s were crucial years in Taliesin's development as a

---

[36] For the Merthyr literary societies, see E. G. Millward, 'Merthyr Tudful: Tref y Brodyr Rhagorol' in Hywel Teifi Edwards (ed.), *Merthyr a Thaf* (Llandysul, 2001), pp. 9–56; Williams, *The Merthyr Rising*, pp. 85–7.

literary figure. His status as a poet was assured with his winning ode on the Druids at the Cardiff eisteddfod in 1834. He presided over the *Maen Chwŷf* (Rocking-stone) bardic assemblies in Pontypridd in the same year, and served as president (together with the likes of Sir John Guest, Sir Charles Morgan and Sir Benjamin Hall) and adjudicator at the Abergavenny eisteddfodau. He won prizes not only for his poems but also for essays on antiquarian themes at Abergavenny, Pontypridd and Merthyr. These were also the years when he appears actively to have begun to study his father's papers and adopt his ideas. One of his pupils (probably in the early 1830s) recalled how they would go to his house to copy 'some old manuscripts. I remember we were told to copy them exactly as they were. "Ye" stood for "the", "yt" for "that", and many other abbreviations that I have forgotten'.[37] For his part, Iolo appears to have been prepared to entrust editorial work to Taliesin, a significant gesture from one who normally brooked no interference in his compositions. Father and son cooperated in 1824 in preparing a second edition of Iolo's collection of hymns, *Salmau yr Eglwys yn yr Anialwch* (1812), which appeared in 1827 after Iolo's death, and a second collection by Taliesin in 1834. More crucial, both for Taliesin's acceptance into the wider, national literary community and for his growing familiarity with Iolo's papers, was his visit to Kerry in January 1821, in place of his father, to discuss the publication of *Cyfrinach Beirdd Ynys Prydain*, a visit which introduced him to an influential group of Montgomeryshire 'literary parsons', among them John Jenkins (Ifor Ceri), W. J. Rees of Casgob, John Jones (Tegid), Walter Davies (Gwallter Mechain), David and Thomas Richards, and others from different parts of Wales. Taliesin's circle of correspondents and associates expanded to include not only the local literary societies and their eisteddfodau and the wider world of the provincial eisteddfodau with their national ambience but also antiquaries and historians among the south Wales clergy and gentry – Thomas Price (Carnhuanawc), J. M. Traherne, J. B. Bruce, Austin Bruce Knight, Octavius Morgan, the Williams family of Aberpergwm and Lady Augusta Hall of Llanover and her husband among them – who were often supporters of eisteddfodau and who combined the enthusiasm and culture of local historians with their own more academically based studies. Increasingly, Taliesin was called upon to respond to queries from a wide range of correspondents in Wales and further afield on Welsh literature, history and antiquities, and to provide translations of Welsh texts for some of them. One indication of his standing was his role during 1838–43 in mediating the very different views and attitudes of Maria Jane Williams and Augusta Hall towards the words to appear in the former's collection, *Ancient National Airs of Gwent and Morganwg* (Llandovery, 1844), for which she had been awarded first prize at the Abergavenny eisteddfod in 1837. Both women tried to bring the

---

[37] James, *What I Remember*, p. 16.

weight of Taliesin's cultural influence to bear on the other and both sought his help, the one (Maria Jane Williams) to prepare 'corrected' and English versions of the words of some songs, the other to produce traditional and composed ('appropriate and authentic') Welsh words only. In the event, Taliesin contributed 'corrections', together with verses taken from Iolo's papers, and thus unwittingly gave circulation to some of his father's free-verse poetry as well as to some traditional verse.[38] In the public view Taliesin was 'esteemed as an eminent Welsh scholar, philologist and critic, as well as a bard'.[39] The coming together of the gentry and leaders of Welsh literary life which led to the establishing of the prestigious Abergavenny eisteddfodau from 1833 to 1853 also inspired the creation in 1837 of the Welsh Manuscript Society. Taliesin's status within the professional, urban middle class and his role as a cultural consultant and poet gave him a unique opportunity to bridge the worlds of the bardic literary societies and the gentry with their historical, antiquarian and folkloric interests. In all this, though his own commitment to contemporary literary activity in south Wales in both English and Welsh was real enough, there is no doubt that being 'ab Iolo' was important for his own standing and for the authoritative link which he provided with Iolo and his vision. Taliesin accepted his role as keeper, voice and, as the need arose, defender of Iolo's papers, claiming and being afforded 'ownership' of them not merely in the legal sense but as the most knowledgeable authority upon them, while his respected place in the complex interweave of business, education, municipal life, Welsh literary circles and English antiquarianism meant that Iolo was taken seriously by diverse groups.

By inclination and talent Taliesin was more a 'researcher' than a poet, and his own literary efforts owed much to his familiarity with Iolo's papers. This is especially true of his Walter Scott-type narrative poems, 'Cardiff Castle' (1827) and 'The Doom of Colyn Dolphin' (1837), his ode 'Y Derwyddon' (The Druids), and his eisteddfod essay on the history of the Vale of Neath (1839, but published in 1886). He claimed a historical basis for these, and his explanatory notes to his narrative poems, many of them taken from 'the Writings and Collections of my late Father', and Henry A. Bruce's annotated translation of the ode on the British Druids (1835), did as much as anything to give credence to Iolo's intricate forgeries outside the Welsh bardic community, even though Taliesin felt constrained to add defensively: 'With regard to the information derived from my Father's papers, I leave the credit due to it in the protection of the numerous tributes of respect paid to his genius and knowledge,

[38] For the disagreement, see Allan James, 'Maria Jane Williams' in Hywel Teifi Edwards (ed.), *Nedd a Dulais* (Llandysul, 1994), pp. 95–130; Daniel Huws, Introduction and Notes, *Ancient National Airs of Gwent and Morganwg* (facsimile edn., The Welsh Folk-Song Society, 1988), pp. xxx–xxxvi.

[39] Joseph Harris (Gomer) in the *Cambrian,* 19 November 1831.

by writers of the highest authority.'[40] At this time, too, he felt obliged to defend
Iolo's scholarly reputation by reprinting in 1836 'A Short Review of the
Present State of Welsh Manuscripts written by E. Williams', which had
appeared anonymously in the first volume of *The Myvyrian Archaiology of Wales*
(1801) and which was being ascribed, according to Taliesin, to William Owen
Pughe rather than to Iolo as the sole author.

   All this, however, is the acceptance of Iolo by implication. More directly
relevant are the three publications for which Taliesin was responsible: *Coelbren
y Beirdd* (1840), *Cyfrinach Beirdd Ynys Prydain* (1829) and *Iolo Manuscripts*
(1848). Iolo's accounts of *Barddas* and Welsh literary history were already in
circulation by word of mouth and through the medium of his extensive correspondence and his own writings. A new body of 'medieval' literature had been
presented in the appendix to *Barddoniaeth Dafydd ab Gwilym* in 1789 and in the
collection of triads and historical documents in the third volume of *The
Myvyrian Archaiology of Wales* (1807), many of which were being translated as
examples of 'bardic wisdom' in journals like *Cambrian Register* (1818) and
Cambro-Briton (1820–2). Not everyone was convinced by this 'new' literature.
Some, like Edward Davies in 1809 and Peter Bailey Williams in 1828, doubted
the historicity and context of the whole construct;[41] others took issue with
specific items, either in doubt or in sheer puzzlement at the inconsistencies
they discovered. Since its first appearance, the so-called bardic alphabet,
Coelbren y Beirdd, had been under suspicion – by Walter Davies, for instance, as
early as 1793[42] – and these doubts persisted. In 1829 Thomas Price,
'Carnhuanawc', urged Taliesin not to publish it until he could quote his
authorities for the text:

> you mention your authorities for Coelbren y Beirdd. I should certainly like to see
> them. I have no doubt of them being genuine to a certain degree, satisfactory that
> is by inference only, for as to your being able to produce proof I am still rather
> sceptical. And under this impression if I might take the liberty, I would recommend
> you to withold any publication respecting them until you have re-considered the
> subject.[43]

   Indeed, much of Carnhuanawc's correspondence with Taliesin is shot
through with scepticism. A few years later, the poet and scholar John Jones
(Tegid), was more pointed in his comments – 'But the public have not yet been

---

[40] 'Explanatory Remarks and Historical Notices', *Cardiff Castle: A Poem* (Merthyr Tydfil, 1827),
     p. 24. Cf. *The Doom of Colyn Dolphin: A Poem* (London, 1837), p. 81.
[41] Edward Davies, *The Mythology and Rites of the British Druids* (London, 1809), p. 60. See
     Damian Walford Davies, *Presences that Disturb: Models of Romantic Identity in the Literature and
     Culture of the 1790s* (Cardiff, 2002), p. 166.
[42] See Caryl Davies, *Adfeilion Babel: Agweddau ar Syniadaeth Ieithyddol y Ddeunawfed Ganrif*
     (Caerdydd, 2000), pp. 282–4.
[43] NLW 21274E, Letter no. 397, Aneurin Owen to Taliesin Williams, 16 November 1829.

informed from what source Mr Edward Williams received the bardic alphabet'
– though he was willing to refer to Iolo as 'the promulgator; not to say the
inventor' of this relic.[44] Taliesin attempted to defend the *coelbren* in his essay at
the Abergavenny eisteddfod of 1830, 'Hendra ac Awdurdodaeth Coelbren y
Beirdd' (The antiquity and authority of *Coelbren y Beirdd*), but the doubts of
the critics, who were now referring to the text as a forgery and who had
'chosen to accuse the old Bard of having himself invented much of what he
transmitted', were in no way assuaged. In 1840 Taliesin published *Traethawd ar
hynafiaeth ac awdurdodaeth Coelbren y Beirdd*, an essay designed to defend his
father's name with some ardour ('yn lled-danbaid'). The essay reveals both his
strengths and deficiencies as a scholar. He could present the arguments of his
critics and his own counter-arguments clearly and logically, even convincingly,
but since his knowledge of medieval Welsh literature was superficial, his
discussion was entirely based on essays, triads and poems found in Iolo's papers.
As a result, his arguments turn upon themselves, one set of forgeries becoming
the evidence to sustain another. Taliesin's essay was thoroughly rebutted by his
fellow Unitarian and neighbour, the pioneering scholar and critic, Thomas
Stephens,[45] but the damage had already been done and the use of the *coelbren*
became fashionable among poets of the second half of the nineteenth century,
especially following the publication of *Barddas*, a comprehensive collection of
bardic documents, in 1862.

In itself *Coelbren y Beirdd* was not particularly important; it could never be
more than symbol of, perhaps evidence for, arcane bardic practice. What gave
it appeal and status was its context of the poets' culture and learning as a whole,
and the circumstances of their preservation as these were explicated in what
would be the authoritative statement of Welsh bardic philosophy, usage and
history, *Cyfrinach Beirdd Ynys Prydain*. Two or three manuscript copies of this
crucial document – 'Athrawiaeth ar y farddoniaeth Gymraeg a'i pherthnasau
yn ôl trefn a dosparth y prif feirdd gynt ar y gelfyddyd wrth gerdd dafod' (The
Secret of the Bards of the Island of Britain – Teaching on Welsh poetry and its
appurtenances according to the order and system of the first poets of old on
the art of poetry) – were circulating (with Iolo's permission) and were being
studied by interested groups like the 'literary parsons' in Montgomeryshire. At
their eisteddfod in Kerry at Christmas 1820 they expressed their desire to see
the document printed and published 'immediately', and thus invited Iolo to
visit them to discuss the possibility. Winter weather prevented his making the
journey but, as we have seen, he was prepared to entrust this responsibility to

---

[44] John Jones (ed.), *Gwaith Lewis Glyn Cothi: The Poetical Works of Lewis Glyn Cothi* (Oxford, 1837), p. 260.

[45] Thomas Stephens, 'Stephens o Ferthyr ar y nod cyfrin a myvyryddiaeth', *Yr Ymofynydd*, VII, no. 77 (1854), 11–13; idem, 'An Essay on the Bardic Alphabet called "Coelbren y Beirdd"', *AC*, III (1872), 181–210.

Taliesin, who went to Kerry in January 1821. The encouragement which Iolo received led to the publication of proposals in 1821 which stated that the book was at the press and would be published shortly with all possible haste. It was advertised in the *Cambro-Briton* in January 1821 and during the following year Iolo sought subscribers for the work, 'extracted from a manuscript written in the time of Queen Elizabeth', a substantial part of which had been printed; only the introduction remained to be completed. Iolo died in 1826 and it was left to Taliesin to bring out the *Cyfrinach*, which was finally published in 1829. In spite of Iolo's protestations, Taliesin had clearly been unable to discover his father's introduction and had thus been obliged to write his own on the basis of Iolo's notes. He was right, therefore, to claim authorship, though he made his role as editor unambiguous. The book had been part of Taliesin's life for the best part of a decade; he had discussed it with his father since his visit to Kerry, listened to his characteristic complaints against Job Jones, his printer, and had conveyed, as best he could, excuses for the delay in the appearance of the work to an impatient group who had been collecting subscriptions for a book promised for 1822. His, too, was the task of seeing the book through the press of the new printer, John Williams, who set up the introduction and printed the whole at Swansea. Over these years Taliesin mastered Iolo's archive and became the recognized authority on the 'Iolo tradition'. For the literary community, and as far as his influence on the direction of Welsh poetics for the rest of the century is concerned, *Cyfrinach Beirdd Ynys Prydain*, which was reprinted in *Geiriadur y Bardd* (1874) by Robert Ellis (Cynddelw), was probably Iolo's most important document.

It was, however, an esoteric text since its relevance and appeal were to a specific section of the community in Wales. The volume which was to reveal the riches and diversity of Iolo Morganwg's invented cultural tradition was *Iolo Manuscripts*, published by the Welsh Manuscript Society, formed in 1837 with the intention of 'transcribing and printing the more important of the numerous unpublished Bardic and Historical Remains of Wales'.[46] The nature of Iolo's bardic philosophy and system was already familiar and his collection and transcripts of 'old' manuscripts were sufficiently well known to be held in high regard and judged suitable for inclusion in the society's plans. Taliesin was obviously the only editor who was capable of editing and translating a selection from the papers. He accepted a commission of £200 to undertake the task and began work on what had been Iolo's hope (and ambition for his son in 1810 and 1817) in January 1840. The society acted honourably, and

---

[46] The society published seven volumes between 1840 and 1862. See Brynley F. Roberts, 'Scholarly Publishing 1820–1922' in Philip Henry Jones and Eiluned Rees (eds.), *A Nation and its Books: A History of the Book in Wales* (Aberystwyth, 1998), pp. 221–36. The faith shown in Iolo's documents undermined the work of the society, which became a means for John Williams (Ab Ithel) to publish several of Iolo's compilations. See G. J. Williams, 'Ab Ithel', *Y Llenor*, XII, no. 4 (1933), 216–30.

faithfully paid its instalments of the commission, but Taliesin's health was deteriorating and he was unable to complete his task. It was an enormous undertaking and the labour which it entailed should not be underestimated – the selecting and copying of material, commenting on manuscript sources, translating and annotating. Nevertheless, he succeeded in preparing all the Welsh material he had selected – sections on Welsh history, bardic history, church history, folk-tales and anecdotes, together with a large number of poems – and in annotating and translating most of it. The society showed much patience and forbearance but, as time passed, Taliesin came under increasing pressure from the officers and members close to him, including Maria Jane Williams, Lady Augusta Hall and Carnhuanawc, and from the printer of the volume, D. R. Rees of Llandovery, who complained that the book was already too long and too costly and that the press was crying out for copy. In 1845 the society made it clear that it could brook no further delay. Taliesin resigned in August, having completed up to page 494 of the printed text, and arrange-ments were made to complete the work by others. The book, over 700 pages in length, appeared in 1848, a year after his death.

Taliesin's procrastination, however, was not the only reason for the unease among some members of the Welsh Manuscript Society. Carnhuanawc was particularly critical of the editor's annotations not simply because they added to the size of the book but because this was contrary to the policy of the society:

> I do not in the least blame you for maintaining your own opinions, but I do not think you are equally justified in persisting in making the work a vehicle for those opinions, in direct opposition to the wishes and entreaties of the Committee . . . The Society was formed for the publication of M.S.S. and not for the promulgation of opinions whether correct or erroneous.[47]

Running through his correspondence with Taliesin, however, is a deeper vein of criticism of the substance of the annotations, and the new editors distanced themselves from some of Taliesin's comments when the book was published. No doubts, however, were expressed about the genuineness of these documents. *Iolo Manuscripts* was greeted as a continuation of *The Myvyrian Archaiology of Wales*, the fulfilment of one of the plans of the Gwyneddigion Society and of the second Cymmrodorion Society in the 1820s, while the imprint of the Welsh Manuscript Society gave it authority as a collection of primary materials for the history of Wales, both at home and elsewhere.[48] Taliesin's unrivalled and detailed knowledge of the Iolo papers was manifest,

---

[47]   NLW 21275E, Letter no. 590, Thomas Price to Taliesin Williams, 30 July 1844.
[48]   G. J. Williams's comment that this book did more harm to nineteenth-century Welsh schol-arship than any other is testimony to Taliesin's faithful labours and to the status of *Iolo Manuscripts*. Williams, 'Ab Ithel', 219.

and his editing and annotations were scholarly in style. He noted mistakes and doubtful readings in the text, drew attention to inconsistencies within the collection and in other sources, and even raised questions about the genuineness or authority of some pieces. The notes display an orderly mind and logical argument, and it is very likely that such sober writing was an important element in the reception of the book and thus of Iolo's forgeries. The crucial fault in his editing was not so much his attitude to scholarship or his methods as his lack of critical judgement. For all his standing in literary circles, Taliesin was not really knowledgeable in medieval Welsh literature. He rarely ventured outside the bounds of Iolo's papers and he was unable to place the genuine pieces of medieval Welsh literature which Iolo had used so astutely in their true context.

Iolo Manuscripts gave the stamp of authenticity to Iolo Morganwg's creations and ensured that they were acceptable to different audiences. Political and church historians were given a body of new documents, the poets and bards of the literary societies and eisteddfodau could authenticate the claims and the regulations of their chairs and rites; the section 'Prydyddiaeth' continued and, indeed, enriched the collection of medieval poems in *The Myvyrian Archaiology of Wales*. The section which was probably of greatest interest to the ordinary reader and antiquarian alike was the entertaining collection of fables (*chwedlau*), 'traditions' and other folklore. This was to the taste of the new generation of folklorists, but required no particular expertise to be enjoyed generally. This material remains a major puzzle in the critical examination of Iolo's sources and methods, for it is not clear how much of it was created by Iolo, how much is his manipulation of tradition, and how much, especially the anecdotes of poetic tradition, represents his sources more or less faithfully.

Iolo Manuscripts, which was reprinted by Isaac Foulkes in 1888, contributed to the romantic portrayal of Wales and her exotic history and literature, in Wales and more generally. Taliesin showed their possibilities in his own English narrative poems. But more importantly, even critics unconvinced by the excesses of bardic philosophy represented by John Williams's (Ab Ithel's) edition of *Barddas* (1862, 1874), and able to recognize spurious elements in the documents, were sufficiently impressed by the whole to accept Iolo's good faith. Thomas Stephens, the shrewdest Welsh literary historian of the nineteenth century, made it clear that he did not accept all of Iolo's assertions or believe in the bardic philosophy, but although he was able to reveal that some texts could not be medieval (the forgeries were of the sixteenth century), he warmly acknowledged Iolo's major and unique contribution to Welsh literature and antiquities[49] and even used 'evidence' he had read in *Iolo Manuscripts*

---

[49]   Stephens wrote a 'biography' of Iolo in Welsh which portrayed him as a rather eccentric but knowledgeable scholar. See *Yr Ymofynydd* (1852–4). This view contrasted sharply with his low opinion of Taliesin, as recorded by Wilkins, 'Mr Taliesin Williams', 117.

in his highly regarded and internationally influential *The Literature of the Kymry*.[50] In his own literary works and by loyally publishing and defending of his father's papers and reputation, Taliesin was a key figure in the reception of Iolo Morganwg. When his father's papers had been safely housed in Llanover and made available to a new generation of devotees,[51] his own standing and publications, notably *Iolo Manuscripts*, taken in conjunction with the popular folklore figure that 'old Iolo' had become in Elijah Waring's biography and in the popular biographies of the latter half of the nineteenth century,[52] served to reinforce the attitudes of an audience already predisposed to accept Ioloism eagerly.

---

[50] Thomas Stephens, *The Literature of the Kymry* (Llandovery, 1849). A second edition was published in London in 1876. See also Albert Schulz, *Geschichte der Wälschen Literatur vom XII bis zum XIV Jahrhundert* (Halle, 1864).

[51] Williams: *IM*, pp. xiii–iv, for the history of the papers.

[52] For example, T. D. Thomas, *Bywgraffiad Iolo Morganwg, B.B.D., sef Edward Williams, Diweddar Fardd a Hynafiaethydd o Forganwg* (Caerfyrddin, 1857); *Iolo Morganwg: Y Bardd, yr Hynafiaethydd, a'r Anianydd Gymreig* (Caernarfon, n.d.); A. Emrys Jones, *The Life and Works of Edward Williams (Iolo Morganwg), The Bard of Glamorgan* (London, 1889).

22

Myfyr Morganwg and the Rocking-Stone Gorsedd

HUW WALTERS

The concluding verdict on Iolo Morganwg by John Morris-Jones, in his foreword to *Iolo Morganwg a Chywyddau'r Ychwanegiad* by G. J. Williams, is well known:

> Yr ydym yn araf ymysgwyd o'i faglau; ond wedi cael yn rhydd o un twyll, byddwn yn aml yn ein cael ein hunain yn rhwym mewn un arall. Ac y mae lle i ofni y bydd ein llên a'n hanes am oes neu ddwy eto cyn byddant lân o ôl ei ddwylo halog ef.[1]

> (We are slowly liberating ourselves from his snares; but having freed ourselves from one deception, we often find ourselves ensnared in another. And we have good reason to believe that another age or two will pass before our literature and history will be cleansed from the vestiges of his soiled hands.)

It is common knowledge that Iolo composed *cywyddau* which he appropriated to Dafydd ap Gwilym and others; he also fabricated pedigrees and manuscripts, and created illusory characters. Yet, his most bizarre creation was unquestionably the Gorsedd of the Bards of the Isle of Britain, the first assembly of which was held on Primrose Hill in London on 21 June 1792. Twenty-seven years later, in July 1819, the Gorsedd became associated with the Dyfed provincial eisteddfod held in Carmarthen and by the end of the nineteenth century it had become an integral part of the festival.

Druidism, bardism and the genesis of the Welsh language were integral parts of Iolo's world and of his posthumous influence. Among his most devout disciples in Glamorgan throughout the first quarter of the nineteenth century was Thomas Williams (Gwilym Morganwg). He was born in 1778, the son of a miller from Llanddeti, Breconshire, though his family had settled at Cefncoedycymer, near Merthyr Tydfil, by 1781.[2] At the age of seven he began work as a collier boy in a coal level owned by his father and he later worked at the Cyfarthfa ironworks. Following a brief period in London he returned

---

[1] John Morris-Jones, 'Rhagymadrodd', *IMChY*, p. xvi.

[2] O. V. Williams, 'Gwilym Morganwg', *Glamorgan Family History Society Journal*, 30 (1993), 8–11; 31 (1993), 6–7.

to Cefncoedycymer, where he served his apprenticeship as a stonemason with Rhys Hywel Rhys of Faenor. However, he had already settled at Pontypridd by 1807, where he remained landlord of the New Inn public house until his death in 1835.[3] For a short period he was associated with the printing business of John Jenkins, a Baptist minister at Hengoed, when they established *Argraffdy'r Beirdd* (Poets' Printing-house) at Merthyr Tydfil in 1819.[4] Gwilym Morganwg became one of the most prominent figures in the eisteddfod movement in south Wales during his lifetime. He competed unsuccessfully at the Llangefni eisteddfod of 1816 and the Carmarthen eisteddfod of 1819.[5] It is also known that he held eisteddfodau at the New Inn, where members of the Merthyr Tydfil Cymreigyddion Society and the folk-poets of the outlying districts frequently met to compete at bardic congresses. Unsurprisingly, when he died in 1835, Gwilym Morganwg was elegized by many of his fellow-poets in the columns of the Welsh-language periodical press.[6]

Like most of his contemporaries Gwilym Morganwg accepted Iolo Morganwg's theories regarding the Gorsedd without question, and the Rocking-stone or *Y Maen Chwŷf*, as it was called by Iolo, became a popular meeting-place for Gwilym Morganwg, Taliesin ab Iolo and other poets of Pontypridd and district who were heavily under Iolo's influence. The stone, which still exists, is of Pennant sandstone, measures a hundred square feet and weighs nine and a half tons. According to geological evidence, it was deposited on the hillside of Coed-pen-maen by glacial movements dating from the Ice Age. It is described in an article, probably written by Taliesin ab Iolo, in 1835:

> The stone, known in Welsh as Y Maen Chwyf (the Rocking Stone), is situated on the western brink of a hill called Coed-pen-maen, in the parish of Eglwysilan, Glamorganshire, above the turn-pike road from Merthyr to Cardiff, and nearly equidistant from both towns . . . The name of the hill, Coed-pen-maen (viz. the Wood of the Stone summit), is, doubtless, derived from this stone, which, in primitive ages, under the Druidic theology, was venerated as the sacred altar on which the Druids offered 'in the face of the sun and in the eye of the light', their orisons to the Great Creator. The ground immediately around the stone is at present a bare sheep-walk, but the higher ground to the east is still covered with wood. The superficial contents of this stone are about 100 square feet, its thickness varying from two to three feet; it contains about 250 cubic feet. It is a sort of rough agrillaceous

---

[3]   [Taliesin] ab Iolo, 'Gwilym Morganwg', *Merthyr Guardian*, 22 August 1835. Reprinted in Taliesin Williams (Taliesin ab Gwilym) (ed.), *Awen y Maen Chwŷf, yn cynnwys awdlau, cywyddau, caniadau ac englynion gan y diweddar Dderwyddfardd Thomas Williams B.B.D. (Gwilym Morganwg)* (Merthyr Tydfil, 1890), pp. v–viii.

[4]   J. Ifano Jones, *A History of Printing and Printers in Wales to 1910* (Cardiff, 1925), pp. 265–6.

[5]   Geraint and Zonia Bowen, *Hanes Gorsedd y Beirdd* (Abertawe, 1991), pp. 48, 65–6, 88.

[6]   See, for example, Iolo Mynwy, 'Marwnad Gwilym Morganwg', *Seren Gomer*, XIX, no. 248 (1836), 145; Gwilym Grawerth, 'Cân Goffadwriaeth Gwilym Morganwg', ibid., XIX, no. 246 (1836), 83.

sandstone, which generally accompanies the coal-measures of this part of the country. A moderate application of strength will give it considerable motion, which may be easily continued with one hand. The underside slopes around towards the centre or pivot, and it stands nearly in equilibrium on a rock beneath, the circumstance which imparts to it its facility of motion.[7]

Iolo Morganwg had held some kind of Gorsedd ritual on the Rocking-stone on 1 August 1814, during which Gwilym Morganwg and Taliesin ab Iolo were initiated in druidic practices by Iolo himself. 'The first Gorsedd that was held on the Rocking Stone, in my recollections was in the year of the general peace', wrote Gwilym Morganwg to Taliesin ab Iolo in November 1834. 'Iolo Morganwg presided at the time; and it was then and there I was invested with my Bardic Order.'[8] Iolo held a similar ceremony on the Rocking-stone on 21 December of the same year and another, three years later, in 1817, but it was at the Dyfed provincial eisteddfod of 1819 that the Gorsedd ritual became associated with the eisteddfod movement for the first time. It was at this eisteddfod that Gwilym Morganwg came to prominence as the Gorsedd 'swordbearer'. His influence and enthusiasm cannot be underestimated; indeed, he encouraged and nurtured the poets of Pontypridd and district, and was influential in establishing Cymdeithas Cymreigyddion y Maen Chwŷf (the Rocking-stone Cymreigyddion Society) in the early 1830s. The Society held its own eisteddfodau at which Aneurin Jones (Aneurin Fardd), Thomas Evans (Gwilym Llanwynno) and Evan Richards (Meudwy Glan Elái), among others, were regular competitors.[9]

Pontypridd became an important centre of druidism in Glamorgan, mainly as a result of the activities of Evan Davies (Ieuan Myfyr), who was born in Cornel Du farmhouse in the parish of Coychurch on 6 January 1801 (though he himself claimed that he was born on Christmas Day 1800). His father, Thomas, had died tragically in the presence of two of his sons when Myfyr was a child. According to Owen Morgan (Morien):

> They were engaged in Tregroes Park, by the permission of the Thomas family, in gathering cones from the trees, and the father had climbed up into one of the trees for the purpose of shaking the branches that the cones might fall for his sons to gather them, when he fell close to Myvyr, and died instantly, after gasping for breath once or twice.[10]

---

7   [Taliesin ab Iolo], 'Y Maen Chwyf, or Rocking Stone in the Vale of Taff, Glamorganshire', *Saturday Magazine*, no. 164 (1835), 24; Roy Denning, 'Druidism at Pontypridd' in Stewart Williams (ed.), *Glamorgan Historian, Volume I* (Cowbridge, 1963), pp. 139–40.

8   NLW 21278E, Letter no. 885, Gwilym Morganwg to Taliesin ab Iolo, 4 November 1834.

9   The Society's activities are reported in *Seren Gomer*, XXI, no. 269 (1838), 59; XXII, no. 284 (1839), 152; XXIX, no. 369 (1846), 285. See also 'Pontypridd a'r Cylch: Gwlad Beirdd a Derwyddon' in Huw Walters, *Cynnwrf Canrif: Agweddau ar Ddiwylliant Gwerin* (Abertawe, 2004), pp. 190–8.

10 Owen Morgan ('Morien'), 'Death of Archdruid', *Western Mail*, 24 February 1888.

Fig. 31 The celebrated Rocking-stone or Y Maen Chwŷf at Pontypridd, where Iolo Morganwg initiated his son, Taliesin, and Gwilym Morganwg in druidic practices in 1814.

His mother remarried and Myfyr went to live with an uncle at Gwern Tarw. He later moved to Cefn Hirgoed in Coety, where he joined the Congregationalist cause at Bethel, Heol-y-cyw. He began to preach almost immediately and in the late 1840s he assisted the Revd William Jones of Bridgend at his four chapels.[11]

Myfyr had been a frequent participant at eisteddfodau and it was he who established Cymdeithas Cymreigyddion Llanilid (Llanilid Cymreigyddion Society), of which David Evans (Dewi Haran), William Jones (Gwilym Ilid), John Howell (Y Bardd Coch) and his son David Howell (Llawdden) – later Dean Howell – were enthusiastic members.[12] 'Most of the instruction I ever

---

[11]   Isaiah John, 'Hanes Dechreuad a Chynydd Eglwys Gynulleidfaol Bethel, ger Penybont, Morganwg', *Y Diwygiwr*, XXVII, no. 317 (1862), 48–9; Thomas Rees and John Thomas, *Hanes Eglwysi Annibynol Cymru* (5 vols., Liverpool, 1871–5), II, pp. 213–14; Owen Morgan (Morien), 'The Archdruid', *Western Mail*, 15 May 1875. For a collection of his sermons, see Cardiff 1.540.

[12]   See the series of anonymous articles, 'John Howell, Pen-coed, Llangrallo, Morganwg', *Y Cylchgrawn*, XIX, 214 (1880), 229–32; no. 215 (1880), 266–9; no. 216 (1880), 303–6; no. 217

had in the art of Welsh poetry I had from him', Llawdden recalled many years later.[13] He also competed at eisteddfodau held under the auspices of Cymdeithas Cymreigyddion y Fenni (Abergavenny Cymreigyddion Society). He submitted an epic ode on 'Dinistr Jerusalem' (The Destruction of Jerusalem) for the competition at the Powys provincial eisteddfod in 1824 when Ebenezer Thomas (Eben Fardd) was awarded the first prize for his celebrated work. He won two prestigious awards at an eisteddfod at Merthyr Tydfil in 1825: his elegy to William Moses (Gwilym Tew o Lan Taf) was awarded the first prize and his ode on 'Cwymp Goliath' (The Downfall of Goliath) brought him a silver medal.[14] He also attended a Gorsedd held at the Cowbridge eisteddfod on 22 March 1839, during which he delivered an address on 'Coelbren y Beirdd a'r Nod Cyfrin' (the Bardic Alphabet and the Mystic Mark).[15]

Ieuan Myfyr was one of the most vociferous opponents of the temperance movement which had gained ground in many parts of south Wales by the 1840s. A campaigner for moderation, his opposition to total abstinence was challenged by the Revd John Jones (Jones Llangollen), who provoked Myfyr to take part in a public debate at Llantrisant in November 1842. A Congregationalist minister at Rhyd-y-bont near Llanybydder, Jones was a renowned controversialist and debater on theological, moral and ethical issues, and had already taken part in a public debate on baptism through immersion with the Revd Gabriel Jones, Principal of the Baptist College at Haverfordwest, at Rhymni the preceding November. Dadl Ddirwest Llantrisant (The Llantrisant Temperance Debate), as it became known, was held on 18–19 November 1842 and a comprehensive and detailed report of its proceedings was published the following year.[16] Many thousands gathered in Llantrisant to listen to the respective viewpoints and several dramatic reports of their deliberations were published in the columns of the Welsh periodical press.[17]

Scriptural verses from both the Old and New Testament were cited during

(1880), 372–4. Roger L. Brown, *David Howell: A Pool of Spirituality. A Life of David Howell (Llawdden)* (Denbigh, 1998), p. 258.

13 'Canon David Howell B.D. and Myfyr Morganwg', *Western Mail*, 2 March 1888.

14 *Awenyddion Morganwg, neu, Farddoniaeth Cadair Merthyr Tudful, ym Mraint Cadair a Gorsedd Pendefigaeth Morganwg, a Gwent ac Erging, ac Euas, ac Ystrad Yw* (Merthyr Tydfil, 1826), pp. 85–94, 95–126.

15 *Y Gwron*, 1 May 1839; Bowen, *Hanes Gorsedd y Beirdd*, p. 135.

16 *Adroddiad o'r ddadl ar ddirwest a gynnaliwyd yn Llantrisant Tachwedd 18 a 19 1842 rhwng y Parch John Jones, Rhydybont a Mr Evan Davies (Ieuan Myfyr), Llangrallo* (Llanelli, 1843). Myfyr had previously published a pamphlet entitled *Rhesymau E. Davies (Ieuan Myfyr) dros ei ymddygiad yn peidio llaw-arwyddo ardystiad y titotalyddion, cyfran o ba rai a draddododd yn nadl Llantrisant* (Abertawe, 1842).

17 Huw Walters, 'Y Wasg Gyfnodol Gymraeg a'r Mudiad Dirwest', *NLWJ*, XVIII, no. 2 (1993), 166–7.

the course of the debate. Myfyr asserted, on the one hand, that Christ's example in drinking wine and turning water into wine at Cana in Galilee was sufficient proof against the practice of total abstinence. Furthermore, he considered it a slur on the character of a Christian to sign the pledge since he had already promised on oath to lead a sober and temperate life when he first became a church member. John Jones, on the other hand, claimed that alcohol was harmful; basing his argument on verses from the Book of Numbers, Deuteronomy, Proverbs and Ecclesiastes, he quoted literally from the original Hebrew texts.[18] Even though the debate continued for two days, it hardly enhanced the cause of temperance in south Wales in any way. Indeed, two of the movement's historians have claimed that the quarrel hindered the cause of temperance in Glamorgan for many years.[19]

By around 1846 Myfyr had arrived in Pontypridd, where he opened a shop and established his own business as a maker of clocks and watches in Mill Street. He spent the rest of his life as an itinerant clock- and watch-repairer in the rapidly developing coal mining valleys of Glamorgan.[20] He was a skilful craftsman and his notebooks in Cardiff Central Library contain several intricate diagrams of clocks and watches and their complex mechanisms.[21] A gifted mathematician, he was well versed in the movements of the stars and planets. When he was seventeen he compiled an almanac, entitled 'Britannus Mertanus Liberatus, Sef Amgylchiadau Tymorol ac Wybrenol', which was never published.[22] Druidism had fascinated him for many years and he was well acquainted with Iolo Morganwg's theories about the Gorsedd. He also knew Taliesin ab Iolo well and was licensed as a bard by ab Iolo in a Gorsedd ceremony held on the Rocking-stone in 1834. When Taliesin died in 1847, Myfyr composed an elegy in his memory which was published in *Seren Gomer* in July 1848.[23]

---

[18] For lively accounts of the debate, see Owen Morgan (Morien), 'The Archdruid', *Western Mail*, 5 May 1875; idem, 'Myvyr Morganwg and Jones, Llangollen: their debate on Temperance', ibid., 6 March 1888.

[19] John Thomas, *Jubili y Diwygiad Dirwestol yn Nghymru* (Merthyr Tydfil, 1885), pp. 138–9; D. D. Williams, *Hanes Dirwest yng Ngwynedd* (Lerpwl, 1921), p. 41.

[20] Aneurin Jones (Aneurin Fardd) was awarded a prize at an eisteddfod held in Pontypridd on 10 August 1846 for a song welcoming Myfyr to the town. See '[C]roesaw-Gân oreu i Ieuan Myfyr, ar ei ddyfodiad i artrefu yn Mhontypridd', *Seren Gomer*, XXIX, no. 372 (1846), 285.

[21] The only known example of one of his clocks, a late nineteenth-century longcase clock, is now in the Pontypridd Museum. William Linnard, *Cardiff Clocks: Clock and Watchmakers of Cardiff, the Vale of Glamorgan and the Valleys* (Cardiff, 1999), p. 60, plate v. The Museum also possesses a *peithynen* which once belonged to Myfyr and two silver medals which he won at eisteddfodau.

[22] Cardiff 1.207.

[23] 'Llinellau a gyfansoddwyd wrth weled angladd Mr Taliesin Williams (Taliesin ab Iolo) yn myned gyda'r Agerdd-Beiriant drwy Bontypridd, Chwefror 10 1847' ('Lines composed on witnessing the funeral cortege of Mr Taliesin Williams (Taliesin ab Iolo, proceeding through Pontypridd by Train, 10 February 1847'). *Seren Gomer*, XXXI, no. 394 (1848), 212.

Early in 1838, some eight years prior to Myfyr's arrival at Pontypridd, members of Cymdeithas Cymreigyddion y Maen Chwŷf had formed a committee designed to raise the sum of £1,000 to renovate and restore the Rocking-stone and its environs. Dr William Price was appointed its secretary and Philip Thomas of Ynysangharad, manager of the Brown Lenox Chainmakers Company of Pontypridd, its treasurer. Members of the Society were anxious to conserve the site and to protect the Rocking-stone from further damage and ruin following the rapid expansion in the town's population and the influx of outsiders into the area. The Society's main objective was the construction of a tower on the site and William Price duly petitioned the public for contributions to enable the Society to complete the building. A circular appealing for funds was distributed among the Glamorgan gentry in March 1838:

> It was suggested to 'Cymdeithas y Maen Chwyf' that a tower of 100 feet high be built by public subscription near Y Maen Chwyf; the space within the tower to be divided into 8 apartments for a museum and surrounded with a camera obscura. This tower will command a horizon of about ten miles radius. And that a spacious house, some distance from Y Maen Chwyf be built for the bard of the society to reside in and to take care of the temple. This proposition has been unanimously seconded by the society and the whole neighbourhood, as will be seen by the subscribers' names in the order given. The estimated cost of these erections is £1,000. The revenue of the Tower will be about £100 per annum. With the greater part of this sum the society will establish a Free School to be kept by the Bard of the Society for educating the children of the poor. The remainder will go to defray the expenses of the Institution. In this way Y Maen Chwyf will not only be preserved but will continue to operate as a mighty engine of civilisation, the nucleus of a museum, the parent of the Tower that is designed to protect it, and to dispense the blessings of education to the industrious classes of the community.[24]

The names of several subscribers were appended to this appeal; among them were Charles Tanfield Vachell, one of the founder members of the Cardiff Naturalists' Society, Taliesin ab Iolo, Evan Davies, the physician and Unitarian from Dinas in the Rhondda, Lord Dynevor and Francis Crawshay, the industrialist from Trefforest. Unfortunately, this ambitious scheme failed and the site of the Rocking-stone on Coed-pen-maen continued to deteriorate. William Price was incensed by the apathy of the Glamorgan gentry, and gave vent to his feelings in the columns of the *Glamorgan, Monmouth and Brecon Gazette and Merthyr Guardian*.[25] However, as a result of his involvement in the Chartist

---

[24] The circular was reprinted by [Gwilym Rees Hughes], 'Ap Idanfryn', in a series of interviews with William Price published in the *Cardiff Times*, 23 June 1888. A Welsh-language version of this appeal was published in *Seren Gomer*, XXI, no. 277 (1838), 298–300.

[25] *Glamorgan, Monmouth and Brecon Gazette and Merthyr Guardian*, 21 September 1839.

insurrection at Newport in November 1839, Price fled to France and nothing more was heard of the Rocking-stone tower.[26] But his lifelong companion Francis Crawshay, second son of William Crawshay II of Cyfarthfa, and the owner of the Trefforest Tinplate Works, was also interested in druidism. A well-known eccentric, Francis Crawshay constructed a tower on Hirwaun Common in 1849, and in 1878 his son erected a stone circle to his memory on the site now occupied by the University of Glamorgan.[27]

Ieuan Myfyr was also captivated by the Rocking-stone and soon became an enthusiastic advocate of druidism in Pontypridd. He was convinced that the ancient Druids of Glamorgan had held their Gorsedd ceremonies on this site and, as a result, the renovation of the Rocking-stone and its location became one of his main objectives. Probably around 1849 he and his associates planned and designed the renovation of the Rocking-stone with the aim of restoring the site to its former glory. Myfyr's vivid imagination knew no bounds: he erected two stone circles around the Rocking-stone – the inner circle included fourteen standing stones and the outer circle twenty-eight stones. He then designed a meandering avenue of thirty-seven standing stones in the form of a serpent, which led to a smaller circle to the north-west of the Rocking-stone; this small circle formed the head of a serpent equipped with two eyes. Below the eyes he positioned three other stones in the shape of the *Nod Cyfrin* (the mystic druidic mark / | \ ). The right eye bore an inscription in *Coelbren y Beirdd* – the bardic alphabet invented by Iolo Morganwg – within three concentric circles, while the left eye had five concentric circles, but no inscription. The influence of the eighteenth-century antiquary, William Stukeley, can be detected in the whole design. He had claimed that the Druids and the biblical patriarchs were closely related and that they, too, had constructed temples in the form of serpents. Myfyr was familiar with Stukeley's published works and he also possessed copies of *Asiatick Researches* by the Orientalist, Sir William Jones.

The Rocking-stone was transformed as a result of Myfyr's imagination and painstaking industry, and there can be little doubt that the venture cost him a great deal in time, effort and expenditure. However, his vision of restoring the site to what he believed was its former primal splendour was finally realized. He began to perform druidic rituals and ceremonies on the Rocking-stone at quarterly intervals which coincided with the solstices and equinoxes – *Alban Eilir* (the vernal equinox), *Alban Hefin* (the summer solstice), *Alban Elfed* (the

---

[26]   Brian Davies, 'Empire and Identity: The "Case" of Dr William Price' in David Smith (ed.), *A People and a Proletariat: Essays in the History of Wales, 1780–1980* (London, 1980), pp. 72–93; Cyril Bracegirdle, *Dr William Price: Saint or Sinner?* (Llanrwst, 1997), pp. 108–25.

[27]   C. O. Jones-Jenkins, 'Francis Crawshay and Trefforest' in Huw Williams (ed.), *Pontypridd: Essays on the History of an Industrial Community* (Cardiff, 1991), pp. 13–29. See also T. F. and V. A. Holley, 'Francis Crawshay, 1811–1878', *MH*, IV (1989), 163–8.

autumnal equinox), and *Alban Arthan* (the winter solstice) – the Welsh terms of which had been coined by Iolo Morganwg. Members of Cymdeithas Cymreigyddion y Maen Chwŷf played a major part in these rituals, the first of which is alleged to have occurred on 21 June 1849 when Myfyr and his companions gathered on the Rocking-stone to proclaim an eisteddfod to be held at Pontypridd the following year.[28]

Following this proclamation ceremony, Ieuan Myfyr addressed the gathered assembly to thank those who had assisted him in renovating the Rocking-stone and the surrounding area. He then gave a brief outline history of the Gorsedd from the days of Gomer, the grandson of Noah, to the *Cynfeirdd* (the early poets) and the *Gogynfeirdd* (the poets of the princes). He then declared that 'Gorsedd y Maen Chwŷf' in the ancient principality of Siluria was the oldest and most significant of them all, and that it had supreme and absolute authority over all other Gorseddau of the bards of the Isle of Britain. Moreover, he predicted that a new and vibrant age was about to dawn on bardism in Gwent and Glamorgan following the restoration of the Rocking-stone to its original splendour. He also proposed to honour poets, littérateurs and patrons of Welsh literature by conferring upon them one of three bardic orders. Candidates for the order of Ovate were required to be steeped in the arts and the rudiments of science, and he stipulated that all aspirants to the druidic order should be of a respectable character. The degree of Bard was the highest and most important of these orders and candidates were required to know the essentials of Welsh grammar and the rules and conventions of the Welsh bardic tradition.

Three years later, at a Gorsedd held on the Rocking-stone in June 1852, the title 'Arch Dderwydd Ynys Brydain' (the Archdruid of the Isle of Britain) was bestowed upon Ieuan Myfyr. He was invested with the *corwgl gwydrin* (the mundane or mystic egg), which had allegedly been discovered in a druidic burial chamber near Llandaf some 400 years previously.[29] The *corwgl gwydrin* was an oval ball of crystal which, so it was claimed, was commonly worn by the Druids suspended from their necks and, according to Pliny the Elder in the sixteenth book of his *Natural History*, the egg called *anguinem* was formed from the secretion of serpents.[30] It was at this assembly that Ieuan Myfyr claimed to be the true successor of Iolo Morganwg and his son Taliesin. Moreover, he also asserted that he had inherited 'Cyfrinach y Beirdd' (the Secrets of the Bards)

---

[28] 'Cyhoeddiad Eisteddfod', *Seren Gomer*, XXXII, no. 498 (1849), 283.

[29] 'Bardd Cyfrin', 'Yr Archdderwydd a Gorsedd Beirdd Ynys Prydain', *Y Gwladgarwr*, 16 June 1876.

[30] See Edward Davies, *The Mythology and Rites of the British Druids* (London, 1809), pp. 210–11; T. D. Kendrick, *The Druids: A Study in Keltic Prehistory* (London, 1927), pp. 89–90; T. J. Morgan, 'Nodiadau Cymysg: Maen magl – Glain y Nadroedd', *BBCS*, IX, part 1 (1937), 124–5; Lewis Spence, *The History and Origins of Druidism* (London, 1949), pp. 162–3.

following Taliesin's death in 1847. These secrets, Ieuan Myfyr maintained, were the bardic teachings and traditions which had been conveyed uninterrupted from one generation to the next since the times of the Druids in Glamorgan. It was also at this gathering that Ieuan Myfyr announced that henceforth he was to be known by the bardic appellation 'Myfyr Morganwg'. The legendary Dr William Price was incensed by these assertions since he had already claimed the title 'Archdruid' some years previously and, as a result, the relationship between both parties became increasingly antagonistic.

Druidic rituals were held regularly at the Rocking-stone between 1849 and 1878, and the columns of the local and national newspaper press contain detailed and sometimes amusing accounts of Myfyr and his followers, the most prominent of whom were David Evans (Dewi Haran), John Evans (Ieuan Wyn), William John (Mathonwy), John Emlyn Jones (Ioan Emlyn), and Jonathan Reynolds (Nathan Dyfed). Several major Welsh poets of the nineteenth century were invested members of the Rocking-stone Gorsedd from time to time, including Robert Ellis (Cynddelw), Evan James (Ieuan ab Iago), Thomas Essile Davies (Dewi Wyn o Essyllt) and Owen Wynne Jones (Glasynys). It is also known that Ebenezer Thomas (Eben Fardd) was eager to join this illustrious company, though he was publicly censured for his foolishness from the platform of the Morriston eisteddfod in 1854 by no less a celebrity than John Jones (Talhaiarn) himself.[31]

John Williams (Ab Ithel), the credulous cleric of Llanymawddwy, also fell under the influence of Myfyr's teachings. He had for some years co-edited *Archaeologia Cambrensis*, the journal of the Cambrian Archaeological Association, with Harry Longueville Jones, but disagreement between the two editors eventually led to outright mutual hostility.[32] Jones was a scientific scholar, while Williams was an uncritical and gullible romantic who accepted without question the theories and forgeries of Iolo Morganwg. Consequently, Ab Ithel severed all links with the Cambrian Archaeological Association in 1853 and established the Historic Institute of Wales with the aim of promoting Celtic and Welsh literature, the arts and science. The institute published its own quarterly magazine, the *Cambrian Journal*, edited by Williams and subsequently by Thomas James (Llallawg) between 1854 and 1865. This contained articles on linguistics, history, music and literature, but it also published the editor's own implausible speculations on the origins of the Welsh and their language, and his fantastic theories on druidism. By 1853 Ab Ithel had been appointed one of the editors of the Welsh Manuscript Society, which had been originally

---

[31] John Jones, *Gwaith Talhaiarn: The Works of Talhaiarn in Welsh and English* (London, 1855), pp. 414–15.

[32] For an account of this contentious relationship, see John Edward Lloyd, 'Introduction' in V. E. Nash-Williams (ed.), *A Hundred Years of Welsh Archaeology, 1846–1946* (Gloucester, 1946), pp. 11–23. See also Chris Baggs, 'Not Just Another Local Printer and Publisher: Richard Mason of Tenby (1817–81)', *Welsh Book Studies*, 2 (1999), [23]–51.

established by members of the Cymreigyddion Society of Abergavenny in 1836. Among the texts he edited were *Y Gododdin* (1852), *Brut y Tywysogyon* (1860), *Annales Cambriae* (1860) and *Meddygon Myddfai* (1861).[33] The contents of both *Dosparth Edeyrn Davod Aur* (1856) and the two-volume *Barddas* (1862, 1874) were plundered from Iolo's papers at Llanover and clearly show that Ab Ithel had become totally infatuated with Iolo's romantic vision of druidism.[34]

It is not surprising, therefore, that Ab Ithel and Myfyr Morganwg became close associates; as a result, the former was invested as a bard *in absentia* at the Rocking-stone Gorsedd on 21 June 1856.[35] By this stage he had come to the conclusion that the Gorsedd of the Bards was a national institution which possessed ultimate authority in the realm of Welsh culture. His main ambition henceforth was to stage a national eisteddfod held under the supreme authority of the Gorsedd of the Bards, a dream which was finally realized in September 1858 when 'the National Gorsedd of British Bards, and with it the Royal Chair of Powys, accompanied by a Grand Eisteddfod' was held at Llangollen. This eisteddfod had already been formally proclaimed by Myfyr Morganwg and his followers the previous summer at a Gorsedd held on King's Hill near St Bride's Major – a significant fact which clearly shows that the Archdruid of the Isle of Britain himself had officially sanctioned the event.[36] The weird and the wonderful, the bizarre and the eccentric gathered in Llangollen and, according to one commentator, 'all the peculiar beings in the whole of Wales were assembled there' ('Yr oedd pob dyn od yng Nghymru gyfan wedi dyfod yno').[37] Among those who took part in the procession held at ten on the first morning was Dr William Price, dressed in a green trouser suit over which he wore a scarlet mantle, and a head-dress made of foxskin. His daughter, Gweniolen, 'the Countess of Morganwg', mounted upon a horse, was similarly attired, and wrapped in a scarlet robe. 'More picturesque', wrote the correspondent of the *Carnarvon and Denbigh Herald*, 'was the appearance of Mr Jerome Pym ap Ednyfed, who combined a court dress coat and vest with a barrister's robe. On his head was a wreath composed of oak leaves and acorns, and in his hand an oak sprig.'[38] Others, such as the eccentric Revd Richard Williams Morgan (Môr Meirion), the Tractarian curate of Tregynon in

[33] T. L. Bowen, 'Reesiaid y Tonn a Gwasg Llanymddyfri', *JWBS*, X, no. 4 (1971), 269–76.

[34] G. J. Williams, 'Ab Ithel' in Aneirin Lewis (ed.), *Agweddau ar Hanes Dysg Gymraeg: Detholiad o Ddarlithiau G. J. Williams* (Caerdydd, 1969), pp. 253–77.

[35] See 'Congress of Bards, Pontypridd', *Cambrian Journal*, III (1856), 201–4. Myfyr composed several *englynion* in Ab Ithel's memory in 1862 which were published in *Y Gwladgarwr*, 20 September 1862.

[36] A report of the proceedings at St Bride's Major was published in 'Gorsedd Beirdd Ynys Prydain', *Cambrian Journal*, IV (1857), 310–12.

[37] Isaac Foulkes ('Llyfrbryf'), *John Ceiriog Hughes: Ei Fywyd, ei Athrylith, a'i Waith* (Lerpwl, 1887), p. 45.

[38] 'Llangollen Grand National Eisteddfod', *Carnarvon and Denbigh Herald*, 25 September 1858; G. J. Williams, 'Eisteddfod Llangollen, 1858', *TDHS*, 7 (1958), 139–61.

Montgomeryshire who took a prominent part in the festival's proceedings, wore multicoloured waistcoats upon which were inscribed a hotchpotch of mottos drawn from *Coelbren y Beirdd*.[39] In addition, Ab Ithel had insisted that the Druids, Bards and Ovates wore white, blue and green robes.

It was at Llangollen, too, that Myfyr Morganwg was seen parading in a grandiose manner on the eisteddfod platform with the *corwgl gwydrin* or mystic egg fastened to a piece of ribbon around his neck and clearly displayed for the benefit and titillation of all. The entire scene was lampooned by Ellis Owen Ellis (Ellis Bryncoch) in a well-known caricature published in the pages of *Y Punch Cymraeg* in March 1859. Myfyr was depicted as a hen sitting on a nest containing the mystic egg, from which emerged the most weird collection of creatures ever seen. The mystic sign / | \ was suspended above the scene, upon which crawled a snail; below, a spider dangled from its web, and a bat flitted around. Ab Ithel, attired in clerical garb, stood next to Myfyr with a parchment written in the bardic alphabet in his left hand.[40]

The Llangollen eisteddfod of 1858 is generally regarded as a significant milestone in the history of the eisteddfod movement in nineteenth-century Wales. It was attended by the foremost members of the Welsh literati and its colourful, if bizarre, ceremonies drew the crowds in their thousands. More significantly, however, was the extent to which it united the Gorsedd of Bards with the modern eisteddfod, and the exposure and publicity it received in the periodical and newspaper press unquestionably contributed to its huge success. Nonetheless, the event also had its critics. Many of those who attended objected vehemently to the teachings of Myfyr and Ab Ithel on bardism and complained that the mystic mark was accorded far too much prominence on the eisteddfod platform. As a result, a special meeting, chaired by the Revd Richard Parry (Gwalchmai), of some sixty major poets and littérateurs of the day was convened on the first evening of the festival. Among them were the Nonconformist ministers William Roberts (Nefydd), Hugh Hughes (Tegai) and John Jones (Mathetes), together with John Pryse (Gweirydd ap Rhys) and Thomas Stephens, the scholar-chemist of Merthyr Tydfil. Myfyr Morganwg was also summoned to this meeting, during which he was rigorously questioned on the subject of the bardic mysteries. During this taxing interrogation it became apparent that some of the doctrines promulgated by Myfyr were not entirely in harmony with Christianity. Several ministers publicly opposed his views, but Myfyr refused to continue with the debate, as a result

---

[39]   On the colourful Richard Williams Morgan, see Peter Freeman, 'The Revd Richard Williams Morgan of Tregynon and his Writings', *MC*, 88 (2000), 87–93; Roger L. Brown, *Parochial Lives: A Study in the 19th Century Welsh Church* (Llanrwst, 2002), pp. 131–64.

[40]   'Yr Arddangosfa Farddonol', *Y Punch Cymraeg*, no. 2 (1859), 6. A copy of the caricature is preserved among the papers of Robert Parry (Robyn Ddu Eryri). See NLW 8570A.

of which 'in consequence of the want of confidence expressed by Myfyr, the resolution that the discussion should cease was finally adopted'.[41]

Myfyr Morganwg had by this stage abandoned Christianity altogether and had ceased to preach, though he remained a member of Sardis Congregational chapel in Pontypridd for several years. According to one tradition, he was affronted by the diaconate of Sardis because he had not been invited to officiate at the chapel when the Revd Griffith Jones left to minister to the Congregationalist cause at Cefncribwr in 1850. Yet, he was held in high esteem by many of his contemporaries. 'I have a host of most pleasing recollections of him', wrote Canon David Howell (Llawdden):

> I have a vivid recollection of the last sermon I heard him preach, from the text 'Na fydd gyfranog o bechodau rhai ereill' ('Do not share in the sins of others'). He was a dry preacher, but analytical, sententious, and intensely practical. Diametrically opposed to his religious views, as I had been for many years past, I never questioned his sincerity or the intense earnestness of his convictions.[42]

Myfyr spent the rest of his life investigating the bardic mysteries and researching the Eastern religions and their supposed links with the beginnings of Christianity and druidism. He was denounced from the pulpit and condemned by the press on several occasions; some regarded him as a simpleton or an idiot, but all his true acquaintances and friends referred to him as a naive, innocent and sincere man. 'The old man is a harmless old enthusiast, of blameless life and simple tastes and habits', declared Llywarch Reynolds, a scholar from Merthyr Tydfil, while the folklorist Tom Jones of Trealaw regarded him as a 'very kind man and a fervent Welshman' ('gŵr ffein iawn a Chymro aiddgar').[43] To James Bonwick, he was '[the] simple-minded but learned Archdruid, a poet and a scholar', and no less a critic than G. J. Williams described him as a 'remarkable and able man, and not quite the fool he was generally assumed to be' ('gŵr hynod a galluog, a heb fod yn llawn cymaint o ffŵl ag a dybir yn gyffredin').[44]

Subsequently, Myfyr sought to convince the public of the authenticity of his assertions in the pages of the periodical press and in the columns of Welsh newspapers. He was infuriated by a series of articles published by Thomas Stephens in Yr Ymofynydd in 1852–3, in which the author had clearly shown

---

[41] Meeting of Bards', *Carnarvon and Denbigh Herald*, 25 September 1858; 'Llangollen Eisteddfod', *Cambrian Journal*, V (1858), 292; 'Eisteddfod Llangollen a Chyfrinion Barddas', *Yr Amserau*, 20 October 1858.

[42] 'Canon David Howell B.D. and Myfyr Morganwg', *Western Mail*, 2 March 1888.

[43] See the letter from Llywarch Reynolds filed in the copy of *Hynafiaeth Aruthrol y Trwn*, which he presented to Henri Gaidoz on Good Friday 1880: NLW 11726C; Tom Jones, 'Rhondda 'Slawer Dydd', *Y Darian*, 1 June 1933.

[44] James Bonwick, *Irish Druids and Old Irish Religions* (London, 1894), p. 3; Williams, 'Eisteddfod Llangollen 1858', 151.

that the mystic mark /|\ was Iolo Morganwg's own creation and had no validity whatsoever. In one article Stephens had also mockingly referred to the 'Rocking-stone barefoots' ('troednoethiaid y Maen Chwŷf') and maintained that Myfyr's teachings were nothing less than 'the remnants of deceit and ignorance of the ages of darkness and superstition' ('gweddillion twyll ac anwybodaeth oesoedd o dywyllwch a choelgrefydd').[45] An avid letter-writer to various newspapers, Myfyr crossed swords with several of his critics in correspondence published over the years in newspapers such as the two Aberdare weeklies, *Y Gwladgarwr* and *Tarian y Gweithiwr*.[46] When these disagreements finally found their way into the columns of the *Western Mail*, the Cardiff daily, in 1874, William Thomas (Islwyn), the poet-preacher and editor of *Y Gwladgarwr*, was enraged: 'We regret that this nonsense is published in the *Mail* since the English will now believe that he is a representative man, which we totally deny' ('Mae yn ddrwg gennym bod y ffwlbri hwn yn ymddangos yn y *Mail*, oblegid fe all Saeson feddwl fod hwn yn *representative man*, yr hyn yr ydym ni yn ei wadu'n llwyr').[47]

Myfyr also wrote several substantial volumes published at his own expense, including *Hynafiaeth y Delyn Mewn Cysylltiad â Gorsedd Hu neu Drwn y Beirdd* (1860), *Gogoniant Hynafol y Cymmry: sef Arddangosiad o Gyfrin-ddysg Hynaf y Byd allan o gyfrinion Gorsedd Beirdd Ynys Brydain* (1865) and *Hynafiaeth Aruthrol y Trwn neu Orsedd Beirdd Ynys Brydain a'i Barddas Gyfrin* (1875). He left instructions that copies of these works were to be placed in his coffin and buried with him when he died, a wish which was fulfilled several years later. His *Ecce Diabolus: Some Observations upon that Horrible and Cruel Ordinance in Devil Worship, Bloody Sacrifices and Burnt Offerings*, edited by Owen Morgan (Morien), was published by The Truth Seeker Company of New York. Although undated, it was probably published in the 1890s and it is worth noting that its author was referred to as 'The Very Rev Evan Davies (Myfyr Morganwg)' on its title-page – an appellation which would doubtless have offended him deeply.

Myfyr had originally intended writing a sequel to *Hynafiaeth Aruthrol y Trwn* and a summary of the contents of that work is provided in the preface to the

---

[45] Thomas Stephens, 'Iolo Morganwg', *Yr Ymofynydd*, V, no. 56 (1852), 77–82; no. 58 (1852), 149–53; no. 60 (1852), 182–7; no. 61 (1852), 197–203; no. 62 (1852), 221–6; no. 63 (1852), 221–50; no. 64 (1852), 269–75. Myfyr Morganwg responded to these articles in a series of letters published in *Seren Gomer* in 1853–4; these were reprinted in a pamphlet entitled *Amddiffyniad y Bardd Cyfrin i hynafiaeth y Nod Uchod /|\ yn ngwyneb haeriadau T. Stephens (Gwyddon) o Ferthyr* (Caerfyrddin, 1855).

[46] Myfyr and his beliefs were vehemently attacked by an anonymous correspondent who wrote under the pseudonym 'Guilelimus' in a series of articles entitled 'Yr Archdderwydd a'i Honiadau' ('The Archdruid and his Assertions') in *Y Gwladgarwr* between 30 July 1875 and 31 March 1876. Myfyr replied in another series of twenty-three lengthy articles in ibid., between 8 October 1875 and 14 April 1876, when the editor finally brought the correspondence to a close.

[47] 'Yr Archdderwydd a'i Farddas', ibid., 5 September 1874.

first volume. He planned to delineate the chronology of the Brahmins 'as in a nutshell' ('megis mewn *nutshell*'), and to depict the ancient traditions of the Gorsedd of the Bards of the Isle of Britain which had prospered in Greece before the Roman conquest. He also proposed to describe his visit to Avebury and Stonehenge in the company of Daniel Owen of Cowbridge, the proprietor of the *Western Mail*. Having described these monuments, he then proposed to write on Arthur and the Round Table, the Welsh bards of the earliest period from the sixth to the eleventh centuries, and the poets of Tir Iarll in Glamorgan and their eisteddfodau through the ages to the days of Iolo Morganwg. He also planned to compile a history of the Gorseddau held on the Rocking-stone in conjunction with the various eisteddfodau of Pontypridd between 1814 and 1875. This again was an ambitious project which never came to fruition.

The volumes produced by Myfyr Morganwg are remarkably rare and are hardly ever listed in the catalogues of second-hand booksellers. It has been suggested that their scarcity is attributable to the fact that many Nonconformist ministers in Glamorgan encouraged their congregations to buy and then destroy them. According to one commentator: 'From what I heard through my father, after my grandfather, persons who had purchased copies of this book were persuaded to bring together each and every one, and they were consigned to the flames' ('Yn ôl a gl'was i gen y nhâd, ar ôl y nhâdcu, darbwyllwd y rhai brynws hwn i ddod â'r cwbwl i mewn, a gwnawd tân o honi nhw').[48] The three volumes *Hynafiaeth y Delyn*, *Gogoniant Hynafol y Cymmry* and *Hynafiaeth Aruthrol y Trwn* undoubtedly taxed the patience of compositors in the offices of Francis Evans and David J. Hopkin of Pontypridd, where they were printed in 1860, 1865 and 1875 respectively. The first volume contains 30 pages, the second 120 pages and the third 264 pages. The font size of each volume is minute and the three works contain words and phrases printed in the Greek alphabet as well as several diagrams, figures and symbols such as / | \ Δ ∅ Θ Ψ Φ Ω .

As we have seen, Myfyr was familiar with *The Asiatick Researches* of Sir William Jones, but he also owned copies of the standard six-volume work of the linguist Friedrich Max-Müller, *Rig-Veda with Commentary* (1849–73), as well as the works of the Assyriologist, Sir Henry Creswicke Rawlinson, and the Egyptologist, John Gardner Wilkinson, to whom he referred more than once. But any attempt to appraise Myfyr's published writings is not only a daunting and disheartening task but also a frustrating and fruitless endeavour. Having discovered and read *The Institutes of Hindu Law: or, the Ordinances of Menu*,

---

[48] A manuscript note by William Jones (Wiliam Siôn 1874–1947) of Cefncribwr in the author's copy of *Hynafiaeth Aruthrol y Trwn neu Orsedd Beirdd Ynys Brydain*. For William Jones, see Gomer M. Roberts, 'Llawysgrif Wiliam Siôn o Gefn Cribwr', *Y Genhinen*, XVI, no. 1 (1965–6), 20–9.

according to the gloss of Cullúca, which was translated into English from the original Sanskrit by Sir William Jones and published in Calcutta in 1796, Myfyr's imagination ran amok. Convinced that the Menu of Hinduism was one and the same as Menw ap Teirgwaedd, the mythological character of the Welsh legend Culhwch and Olwen, he fabricated around him the most extraordinary fantasies.[49] Pursuing Myfyr's chaotic references and allusions to the Celtic gods and their hypothetical relationship with Hindu deities, patriarchs such as Noah, Japheth and Gomer, and mythological characters like Menw ap Teirgwaedd, Gwron ap Cynfarch, Hu Gadarn, Ceridwen, Alawn and Plenydd – let alone the Druids – reminds us that his ideas had their antecedents in the work of earlier authors stretching back to the days of the Renaissance.

Much to the consternation of many Nonconformist ministers in the Taf and Rhondda valleys, Myfyr Morganwg and his followers continued to hold quarterly druidic rituals on the Rocking-stone for nearly thirty years. Some of them condemned the ceremonies in the local press and threatened fire and brimstone upon the town of Pontypridd. In a letter to *Y Gwladgarwr* in the summer of 1875, D. M. Williams of Coed-pen-maen mercilessly denounced devotees of the Rocking-stone and demanded that a meeting be convened of the town's ministers to consider what should be done with those who were 'sowing the seeds of atheism, and planting unbiblical principles in the minds of the feeble and the young' ('hau hadau anffyddiaeth, a phlanu egwyddorion gwrthfeiblaidd yn meddyliau rhai gweiniaid ac ieuainc').[50] One local historian suggested in 1910 that 'the wave of modern Welsh druidism [which] swept over the locality' between 1866 and 1876 had resulted in a sharp decline in church membership, while another Nonconformist minister, the Revd Benjamin Davies, in discussing the ministry of the Revd Dr Edward Roberts at Tabernacle, Pontypridd, confirmed that 'several prominent members of the nonconformists were deluded by these false interpreters of ancient lore' and had 'contributed, though indirectly, to increase the difficulties to a prosperous ministry'.[51]

Yet, Owen Morgan (Morien), a talented journalist who had joined the staff of the *Western Mail* in 1870, came to Myfyr's defence on more than one occasion.[52] He successfully appealed to the marquess of Bute and Sir William

---

[49] See esp. *Hynafiaeth Aruthrol y Trwn*, pp. 100–55.

[50] D. M. Williams, 'Cyfarchiad at weinidogion Pontypridd a'r cylchoedd', *Y Gwladgarwr*, 2 July 1875.

[51] B. D. Johns (Periander), *Early History of the Rhondda Valley: Baptist Centenary, Pontypridd, 1810–1910* (Pontypridd, 1910), p. 67; Benjamin Davies, *The Rise and Progress of Nonconformity in Pontypridd and District* (Pontypridd, 1897), p. 11. I am indebted to Mr Brian Davies of the Pontypridd Museum for these references.

[52] Accounts of his career were published in the *Western Mail*, 17 December 1921 and the *Rhondda Leader*, 22 December 1921. See also the tributes by John Griffith and J. Llewelyn

Thomas Lewis (later Baron Merthyr of Senghennydd) for financial assistance to sustain Myfyr in his infirmity and old age. Supporters of the Rocking-stone Gorsedd also appealed for subscriptions towards a testimonial for Myfyr and a cheque to the value of £140 12s. was presented to him at a special gathering held at the Butchers Arms, Pontypridd, in December 1875.[53] Three years later, the American University of Philadelphia and Eclectic Medical College of Pennsylvania awarded him the degree of Doctor of Civil Laws 'as evidence of the college's esteem of his genius and learning' ('fel tystiolaeth o edmygedd yr holl athrofa o'i athrylith a'i ddysg').[54] However, it became apparent a few weeks later that Myfyr's DCL was a spurious degree and that the American University of Philadelphia and Eclectic Medical College of Pennsylvania was in fact located in a private office in Pine Street, Philadelphia. Furthermore, Dr John Buchanan, the head of that institution, was a well-known character in the District Court House and had been selling academic degrees to customers for several years.[55] The trade in degrees was a profitable and lucrative industry in America during the last quarter of the nineteenth century, and several ministers in Wales were 'honoured' with all kinds of doctorates from sham colleges and universities.[56] Dr John Buchanan specialized in medical degrees and, as a result, many bona fide and licensed medical practitioners became concerned that a significant number of quacks were practising medicine. As a result, Dr Ludwig Bruck of Australia was induced to publish *The Australian Medical Directory and Hand Book, with an Appendix comprising the names of all known unregistered medical practitioners throughout the Colonies, and also a Complete List of American Medical Colleges, extinct and existing, not recognised* (1886). The American University of Philadelphia and Eclectic Medical College of Pennsylvania, which awarded Myfyr Morganwg his DCL, was listed in this volume.[57] It is known that Morien, gullible as he was, purchased the degree for $30 and in all probability he had no intention of acting dishonestly. Myfyr never used the title and Morien made no mention of the 'honour' in his biography of the archdruid in his *History of Pontypridd and Rhondda Valleys* in 1906.

The Rocking-stone Gorsedd rituals had ceased by the end of the 1870s and the last of those in which Myfyr Morganwg participated was held in 1878.

Thomas in *Y Genhinen*, XL, no. 2 (1922), 100–3; Brian Davies, 'Welsh Identity without Illusion' in T. Graham Williams (ed.), *Hunaniaeth Gymreig = Welsh Identity* (Rhiwfawr, 2004), pp. 56–9.

[53] 'Tysteb Myfyr Morganwg', *Y Gwladgarwr*, 31 December 1875.

[54] 'Myfyr Morganwg D.C.L.', ibid., 28 December 1877.

[55] 'Masnach y Ffugdeitlau', ibid., 3 May 1878.

[56] See Roger L. Brown, 'The Tale of the D.D.', *JWRH*, new series, 3 (2003), 69–77.

[57] For further information, see Philippa Martyr, 'When Doctors Fail: Ludwig Bruck's List of Unregistered Practitioners (1886)', *The Electronic Journal of Australian and New Zealand History*: <http://www.jcu.edu.au/aff/history/articles/bruck.htm>. Viewed 15 March 2004.

Myfyr withdrew from public life and died at his daughter-in-law's home in Pontypridd on 23 February 1888. Seven of his eight children had predeceased him and a few insensitive individuals frequently taunted the old man in the press by insisting that his tribulations were God's judgement upon him for his profane writings and pagan beliefs. Yet, his funeral at Pontypridd was one of the largest ever seen in the town. He was given a Christian burial in Glyn Taff cemetery, where the Revd Rowland Jones read the funeral service from the Book of Common Prayer. Morien published details of Myfyr's will, which he had signed three days before his death, in the *Western Mail* a few days later:

> After disposing of his library and articles of furniture, the will contains the following: 'I bequeath to Morien all my writings and papers, knowing as I do that he is the best qualified to deal with them properly, and to make the Druidic philosophy of our Cambrian ancestors known to the world. I bequeath also to him my large oak chair, known as the Chair of Gwent and Morganwg (Cadair Gwent a Morganwg), together with the Druidic Mundane Egg (Corwgl Gwydrin), a genuine treasure, and worn in remote times by each of the succession of Druidic High Priests of the Druidic hierarchy in the Isle of Britain. I leave also to him two of my framed pictures. One, a printed satire on my Druidic researches and discoveries, which was composed by the late Mr Thomas Stephens, Merthyr (author of *The Literature of the Kymry*), and others. The other picture represents me as the hen Ceridwen sitting on the said Mundane Egg.' The will further states that the Mundane Egg came strangely into his possession many years ago. It seems that the Druidic Egg was at the time it was heard of for the first time by the Welsh literati the theme of endless jokes which annoyed him terribly.[58]

Although a correspondent in *Tarian y Gweithiwr* claimed that Dr William Price was Myfyr's successor as 'Archdruid of the Bards of the Isle of Britain', the *Western Mail* announced in February 1888 that Morien had already claimed that title for himself.[59] This pronouncement caused considerable anxiety to members of the Gorsedd Association of the National Eisteddfod, which probably explains why Morien was invited to address Gorsedd of the Bards

---

[58] Morien, 'More About Myfyr Morganwg', *Western Mail*, 25 February 1888. It is not known what became of the Chair of Gwent and Morganwg or the mystic egg after Morien's day. However, a letter published in the columns of the *Glamorgan County Times* on 20 January 1934 stated that an eisteddfod chair, which once belonged to Myfyr, was in the possession of Charles George Faull of Graig-wen, Pontypridd, a great-grandson of the archdruid: 'The chair, which is in a very good state of preservation, is regarded as a family heirloom and has passed from one member of the family to the other.' A typescript copy of the satire by Thomas Stephens (mentioned in the will), *Gorsedd Beirdd Ynys Prydain a'i Heisteddfod ar y Maen Chwŷf wrth Lan Taf, Mehefin y 23ain 1850*, originally printed by Rees Lewis of Merthyr Tydfil, figures among the papers of W. M. Jones, Cilfynydd, at Cardiff Central Library. The other picture referred to in the will is probably a copy of the caricature by Ellis Owen Ellis (Ellis Bryn Coch).

[59] 'Marwolaeth Myfyr Morganwg', *Tarian y Gweithiwr*, 1 March 1888; 'Morien Appointed Archdruid', *Western Mail*, 27 February 1888.

assemblies at the National Eisteddfodau held in Liverpool in 1884 and Caernarfon in 1886. He was finally admitted to the druidic order at the Wrexham festival in 1888, at which he was invested with the title 'Gwyddon Tir Iarll' in the vain hope that he would relinquish the title 'Archdruid'.[60] Morien, however, remained loyal to the Rocking-stone Gorsedd, though he also played a prominent part in the proceedings of the Gorsedd Association of the National Eisteddfod when the festival visited the town in 1893.[61] He also upheld the druidic tradition in Pontypridd and spent the rest of his life perpetuating the teachings of Myfyr Morganwg on bardism. He recounted his visit to Stonehenge and Avebury in *Y Gwladgarwr* in 1876 and described what he saw there in a lengthy series of articles. He also published several volumes on druidism and a history of Pontypridd.[62] His views were challenged by John Morris-Jones, who published a series of vitriolic articles on the Gorsedd of the Bards in the periodical *Cymru* in 1896, in which he revealed that he had failed to locate any references to its existence or its rituals before the days of Iolo Morganwg.[63] But the druidic tradition in Pontypridd, which had persisted for nearly 120 years, came to an end with Morien's death in December 1921.[64]

Throughout much of the Victorian period the druidic myth, essentially created by Iolo Morganwg, had found a firm foothold in Pontypridd and gave rise to a tradition which manifested itself in the writings and activities of Gwilym Morganwg, Taliesin ab Iolo, Dr William Price and Myfyr Morganwg. However, in contrast to Iolo of 'the soiled hands', as John Morris-Jones referred to him, these were all individuals who were convinced of the antiquity of the Gorsedd of the Bards and its rituals. 'He knew very well what he

---

[60] Geraint Bowen, 'Archdderwydd, y Teitl a'r Swydd', *NLWJ*, XXIV, no. 3 (1986), 379. Morien continued to use the title, however, as can be seen from the title-page of *Pabell Dofydd* (Cardiff, 1889), where he is referred to as 'Archdderwydd yn ôl Braint a Defod' ('Archdruid according to Privilege and Custom').

[61] 'The National Eisteddfod', *Western Mail*, 4 August 1893; 'Eisteddfod Genedlaethol Pontypridd', *Y Geninen*, XI, no. 4 (1893), 257.

[62] 'Morien yn Nghôr Gawr a Chaer Ambawr', *Y Gwladgarwr*, 28 July, 4, 11, 18 August, 1, 8 September 1876. His published works include *Sketches about Wales* (Cardiff, 1875); *Pabell Dofydd: Sef Eglurhad ar Anianyddiaeth Grefyddol yr Hen Dderwyddon Cymreig* (Caerdydd, 1889); *The Royal Winged Son of Stonehenge and Avebury* (Pontypridd, n.d.); *The Light of Britannia: The Mysteries of Ancient British Druidism* (Cardiff, 1893); *Guide to the Gorsedd or Round Table and the Order of the Garter* (Cardiff, c.1899); *History of Pontypridd and Rhondda Valleys* (Pontypridd, 1903).

[63] John Morris-Jones, 'Gorsedd Beirdd Ynys Prydain', *Cymru*, X, no. 54 (1896), 21–9; no. 55 (1896), 133–40; no. 56 (1896), 153–60; no. 57 (1896), 197–204; no. 59 (1896), 293–9. Morien replied to this series in 'Hynafiaeth Aruthrol Gorsedd Beirdd Ynys Prydain', ibid., XI, no. 59 (1896), 331–3; XI, no. 60 (1896), 42–5; no. 61 (1896), 93–6; no. 62 (1896), 114–16; no. 63 (1896), 184–6; no. 64 (1896), 238–42; XII, no. 67 (1897), 143–6.

[64] Nevertheless, a thriving interest in druidism persists. A facsimile reprint edition of Morien's *The Royal Winged Son of Stonehenge and Avebury*, entitled *The Mabin of the Mabinogion*, was published by Whittaker in 1990, while the Ancient Mysteries Archive, which is mainly concerned with druidism, is a popular internet website maintained by the 'Morien Institute'.

believed, and he was emphatic in his opinion as to the history of the Gorsedd and its antiquity', said G. J. Williams of Myfyr ('Gwyddai ef yn iawn pa beth a gredai, ac yr oedd ganddo farn bendant am hanes a hynafiaeth yr Orsedd').[65] Although he was obsessed by the traditions of druidism, to dismiss him as a fool would be both unfair and irrational. His enthusiasm for the myths of bardism belonged to a movement which sought to prove, as Prys Morgan has shown, that the Welsh cultural tradition was older than any other in western Europe.[66] He stressed in his writings, time and time again, the antiquity of the Welsh language and its traditions. In the closing sentences of his preface to *Hynafiaeth Aruthrol y Trwn*, for instance, he wrote: 'Preserve your language . . . and above all, take care to safeguard her entire Gorsedd; that is her crown and splendour, and your own great witness as Welshmen that you are, from the beginning, the First among the Nations' ('Parhewch yn mlaen eich iaith . . . ac yn benaf pobpeth, gofalwch ddwyn yn mlaen ei Gorsedd gron; dyna ei choron a'i gogoniant, a'ch tyst mawr chwithau fel Cymmry eich bod erioed y *First among the Nations*').[67] Similar motives can be discerned in other areas of nineteenth-century Welsh life, not least in the response of the Welsh to the reports of the commission appointed to investigate the state of education in Wales in 1846–7 and the subsequent obsession of Welshmen with their image in the wider world. The druidic myth is a theme which helps us to understand Victorian Wales, and Iolo's shadow lies inescapably over its bizarre manifestations.

[65] G. J. Williams, in a review of Beriah Gwynfe Evans, *The Bardic Gorsedd*, in *Y Llenor*, III, no. 4 (1924), 259.

[66] Prys Morgan, 'From a Death to a View: The Hunt for the Welsh Past in the Romantic Period' in Eric Hobsbawm and Terence Ranger (eds.), *The Invention of Tradition* (Cambridge, 1983), p. 66.

[67] *Hynafiaeth Aruthrol y Trwn*, p. xiii. For similar statements, see ibid., pp. v, vii, x, 240, 245.

Index